AF574997

Olympiad Champs

LOGICAL REASONING

Class 6

with **Chapter-wise Previous**
5 Year (2018 - 2022) Questions

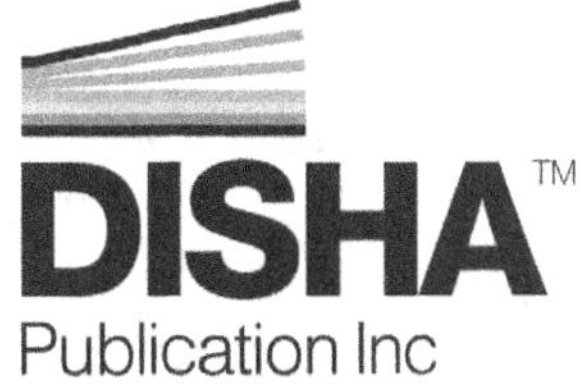

DISHA™
Publication Inc

DISHA Publication Inc.

45, 2nd Floor, Maharishi Dayanand Marg,
Corner Market, Malviya Nagar, new Delhi -110017
Tel: 49842349/ 49842350

Typeset By

DISHA DTP Team

Write To Us At

feedback_disha@aiets.co.in

Preface

We are pleased to launch the 2nd edition of **Olympiad Champs Logical Reasoning Class 6** which is the first of its kind book on Olympiad in many ways.

The Unique Selling Proposition of this new edition is the inclusion of past year questions till 2022 of different Olympiad exams held in schools.

The book is aimed at achieving not only success but deep rooted learning in children. It is prepared on content based on National Curriculum Framework prescribed by NCERT. All the text books, syllabi and teaching practices within the education programme in India must follow NCF. Hence, Olympiad Champs become an ideal book not only for the Olympiad Exams but also for strengthening the concepts for Class 6.

There is an exhaustive range of thought provoking questions in MCQ format to test the student's knowledge thoroughly. The questions are designed so as to test the knowledge, comprehension, evaluation, analytical and application skills. Solutions and explanations are provided for all questions. The questions are divided into two levels - Level 1 and Level 2. The first level, Level 1, is the beginner's level which comprises of questions like fillers, analogy and odd one out. When the child covers Level 1, it means his basic knowledge about the subject is clear and now it is ready for Level 2. The second level is the advanced level. Level 2 comprises of techniques like matching, chronological sequencing, picture, passage and feature based, statement correct/ incorrect, integer based, puzzle, grid based, crossword, venn diagram, table/ chart based and much more.

The first concern which each parent faces is how to make their children read a book especially when it is based on academics. Keeping this in mind interesting facts, real life examples, historical preview, short cut to problem solving, charts, diagrams, illustrations and poems are added. In addition to this, we have introduced comic strip which increases the readability quotient and make the reading experience for the children more exciting.

With the vision to remove all the misconception a child may have pertaining to the subject, to relate his knowledge to the real world and to develop a deeper understanding of the subject this book will cater all the requirements of the students who are going to appear in Olympiads.

While preparing this book, some errors might have crept in. We request our readers to identify those errors and send it across on **feedback_disha@aiets.co.in.**

We wish you all the best for your Olympiads and happy reading.......

Team Disha

For feedback : feedback_disha@aiets.co.in.

CONTENTS

16. Dot Situation 200-206

10 Principles to CRACK ANY EXAM

1. Chase consistency, not intensity.

Doing intensive study makes your day. But it also exhausts you in the long run, leading to lesser output and added pressure. Toppers always focus on doing consistent work daily, for consistency is far more valuable than intensity. Remember consistent study of 4 hours every day is more important and powerful than studying 12 hours a day and then not studying at all for next 2 days.

2. Go beyond the surface.

Most students only see a few reasons (teacher, coaching, books, etc) behind Toppers' success, which is only the tip of the iceberg. What they donot see is Toppers Mindset, self belief, habits and discipline and that is where the real problem is.

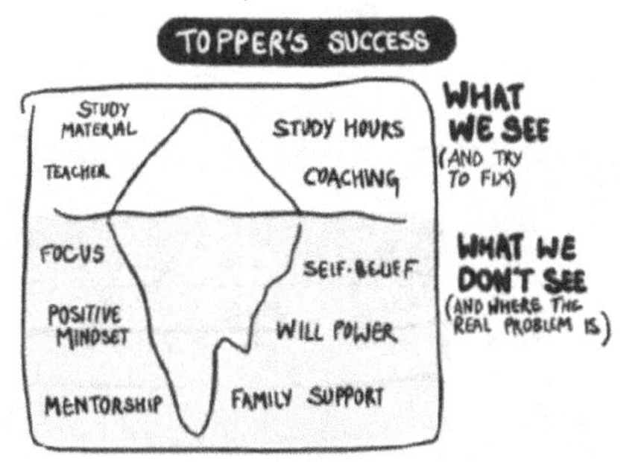

3. Focus on giving your best, not chasing the best.

We want the best coaching, the best teacher, best batch and the best books but we are not ready to give our BEST. Success comes only when we are ready to give our best. We must focus on giving our best than chasing excuses to cover up our failures.

4. Clarity of concept is the key

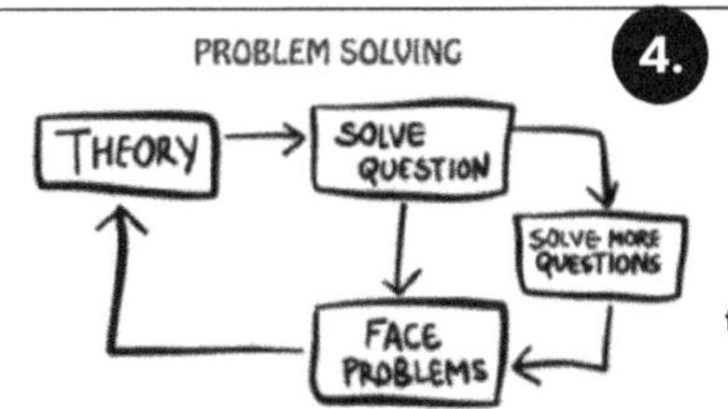

Concept clarity is critical. If you cannot solve a question, you must go back to the theory and thoroughly examine the concept instead of referring to the solutions. Remember question is one of the chehra(face) of the concept. When toppers get stuck in a problem, they go back and refer the theory(read the concept again and again on which the question is based)

5. Every failure should be a lesson learned.

Most students do not learn from their failures and repeat their mistakes. Toppers also face failures, but they learn from mistakes and elevate themselves. Making mistakes and learning from them is the key to success.

6 Choosing the quality of resources is more important than quantity.

More than 90% of the questions in most books are the same as their substitutes. Instead of practicing from four books and failing to complete them, it is best to prepare from two books and complete them with thorough revisions.

7 Difficult things become easy by taking it one day at a time.

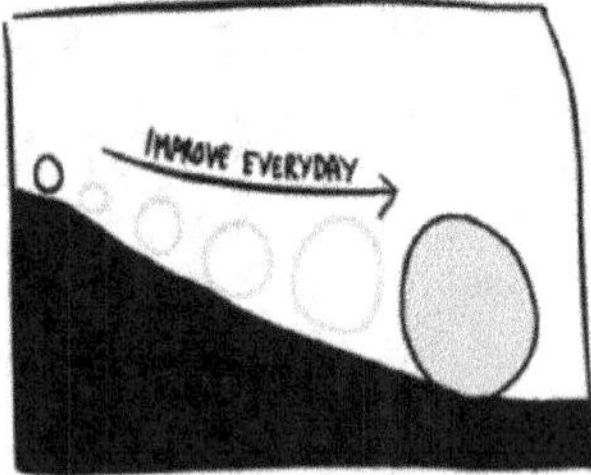

The best way to take any preparation forward is by taking it one day at a time. It makes the impossible possible by taking small steps every day.

Starting a difficult subject. No worries. Keep on working session by session, day by day and week by week and one day you will become unstoppable force.

8. Everything is easy

Before starting everything looks difficult. Once you take a first step, it slowly starts looking easy and over a period of time you become master in the activity. This is toppers secret to become master in any subject.

9. Nobody is gifted

We think toppers are god gifted. We think toppers have high IQ. We think toppers are special/lucky. But the truth is every topper was once an average student(no body is born topper). What makes them different is their consistent and focused efforts

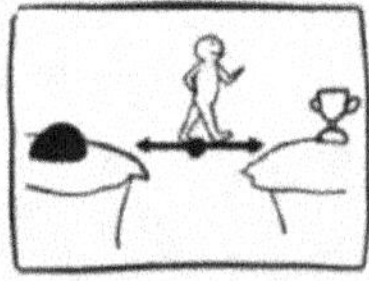

10. Believe in your journey and success will come to you.

There is never a straight path to success; hard work & patience is required for the results to show up. Keep on working hard without thinking too much about the results and success will come to you eventually.

CHAPTER 1

Series Completion and Inserting

NUMBER SERIES

In this type of series, the set of given numbers in a series are related to one another in a particular pattern or manner. The relationship between the numbers may be

(i) consecutive odd/even numbers,

(ii) Consecutive prime numbers,

(iii) Squares/cubes of some numbers with/without variation of addition or subtraction of some number,

(iv) Sum/product/difference of preceding number(s),

(v) Addition/subtraction/multiplication/division by some number, and

(vi) Many more combinations of the relationships given above.

ILLUSTRATION 1 :

Find the missing term in the following sequence.

5, 11, 24, 51, 106, ...

(a) 216 (b) 217

(c) 215 (d) 212

Sol. (b) Double the number and then add to it 1, 2, 3, 4 etc.

Thus the next term is $2 \times 106 + 5 = 217$.

ILLUSTRATION 2 :

Complete the series 4, 9, 16, 25, ...

(a) 32 (b) 42

(c) 55 (d) 36

Sol. **(d)** Each number is a whole square.

ILLUSTRATION 3:

Find the wrong term in the series

3, 8, 15, 24, 34, 48, 63.

(a) 15 (b) 12

(c) 34 (d) 63

Sol. **(c)** $8 - 3 = 5$

$15 - 8 = 7$

$24 - 15 = 9$

$34 - 24 = 10$

$48 - 34 = 14$

$63 - 48 = 15$

Obviously difference should be 11 & 13 instead of 10 & 14.

Therefore, 34 is the wrong term.

ALPHABET SERIES

In this type of question, a series of single, pairs or groups of letters or combinations of letters and numbers is given. The terms of the series form a certain pattern as regards the position of the letters in the English alphabet.

In the following questions, various terms of a letter series are given with one term missing as shown. Choose the missing term out of the options.

ILLUSTRATION 4 :

AZ, GT, MN, ..., YB

(a) KF (b) RX

(c) SH (d) TS

Sol. **(c)** The logic is +6 and –6.

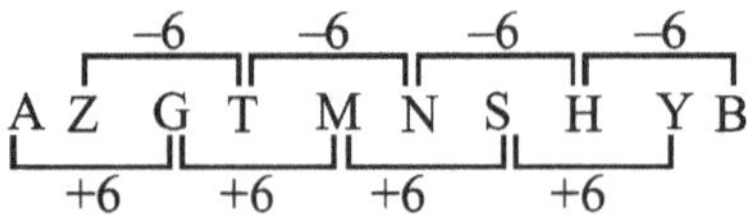

DIRECTIONS (ILLUSTRATION 5) : In the following question, various terms of an alphabet series are given with one or more terms missing as shown by '?'. Choose the missing terms out of the given alternatives.

ILLUSTRATION 5 :

UPI, ?, ODP, MBQ, IAW

(a) RHJ (b) SHJ

(c) SIJ (d) THK

Sol. **(b)**

1st letter : U $\xrightarrow{-2}$ (S) $\xrightarrow{-4}$ O $\xrightarrow{-2}$ M $\xrightarrow{-4}$ I

2nd letter : P $\xrightarrow{-8}$ (H) $\xrightarrow{-4}$ D $\xrightarrow{-2}$ B $\xrightarrow{-1}$ A

3rd letter : I $\xrightarrow{+1}$ (J) $\xrightarrow{+6}$ P $\xrightarrow{+1}$ Q $\xrightarrow{+6}$ W

CONTINUOUS PATTERN SERIES

This type of question usually consists of a series of small letters which follow a certain pattern. However, some letters are missing from the series. These missing letters are then given in a proper sequence as one of the alternatives.

DIRECTIONS (ILLUSTRATION 6) : In the following letters series, some of the letters are missing which are given in that order as one of the alternatives below it. Choose the correct alternative.

ILLUSTRATION 6 :

.... bcc .... ac .... aabb .... ab cc

(a) aabca (b) abaca

(c) bacab (d) bcaca

Sol. **(c)** The series is $\underline{b}$ b c c $\underline{a}$ a / c $\underline{c}$ a a b b / $\underline{a}$ a b $\underline{b}$ c c.

The letter pairs move in a cyclic order.

ALPHA - NUMERIC SERIES

A series in which both alphabets and numbers are used is called Alpha numeric.

DIRECTIONS (ILLUSTRATION 7) : In the following question, a letter number series is given with one or more terms missing as shown by (?). Choose the missing term out of the given alternatives.

ILLUSTRATION 7 :

D-4, F-6, H-8, J-10, ? ?

(a) K-12, M-13 (b) L-12, M-14

(c) L-12, N-14 (d) K-12, M-14

Sol. **(c)** The letters in the series are alternate and the numbers indicate their position in the English alphabet from the beginning.

MISSING CHARACTER

In such type of questions, a figure, a set of figures, an arrangement or a matrix is given, each of which bears certain characteristics, be it numbers, letters or a group/ combination of letters/ numbers, following a certain pattern.

The candidate has to find a missing character in the figure out of the given options.

Let us develop the ability to identify missing character with the help of following examples.

ILLUSTRATION 8 :

11	3	49
5	19	?
7	13	100

(a) 96 (b) 120

(c) 144 (d) 100

Sol. **(c)** In a row the third term is the square of the average of the first two numbers.

$\therefore \left(\frac{5+19}{2}\right)^2 ? = = 12^2 = 144.$

ILLUSTRATION 9 :

1	4	9	?
1	2	3	4
2	4	6	?

(a) 16, 8

(b) 49, 7

(c) 36, 4

(d) 25, 5

Sol. **(a)** I st row : $1^2, 2^2, 3^2, 4^2$,

Third row : 2, 4, 6, 8

$\therefore$ The missing numbers = 16, 8

ILLUSTRATION 10 :

3C	24D	8E
7I	21 K	3M
4D	?	7J

(a) 11 E (b) 28 G

(c) 351 (d) 48 F

Sol. **(b)** In the first row, letters are consecutive CDE.In the 2nd row, letters are one step forward I-K-M

In the third row, the letters are + 2 forward i.e

D – – G – – J.

Number is the product of the two numbers.

Hence, 4 × 7 = 28

ILLUSTRATION 11 :

9 15

4 | 58 | 8   9 | ? | 8

10 10

(a) 117 (b) 100

(c) 78 (d) 63

Sol. **(c)** In the first figure 9 × 10 – 4 × 8 = 58

$\therefore$ The missing figure = 15 × 10 – 9 × 8 = 78

ILLUSTRATION 12 :

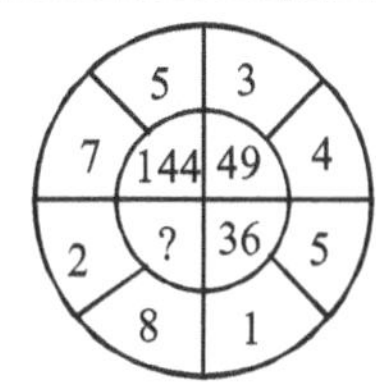

(a) 82 (b) 100

(c) 68 (d) 64

Sol. **(b)** Required number = $(2 + 8)^2 = 100$.

ILLUSTRATION 13 :

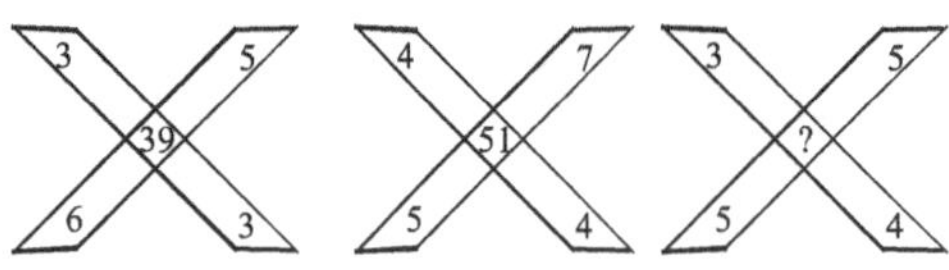

(a) 47 (b) 45

(c) 37 (d) 35

Sol. **(c)** Fig 1 : $3 \times 3 + 6 \times 5 = 39$

Fig 2 : $4 \times 4 + 5 \times 7 = 51$

$\therefore$ So $? = 3 \times 4 + 5 \times 5 = 37$

ILLUSTRATION 14 :

Find the number in place of question mark (?) in the following matrix

3	5	7	9	11	13
8	26	48	82	?	170

(a) 121 (b) 120

(c) 119 (d) 111

Sol. **(b)** The numbers are according to the rule $n^2 \pm 1$.

i.e, $3^2 - 1$, $5^2 + 1$, $7^2 - 1$, $9^2 + 1$. $11^2 - 1$ and $13^2 + 1$.

$\therefore$ the missing number is 120.

ILLUSTRATION 15 :

Find the missing number

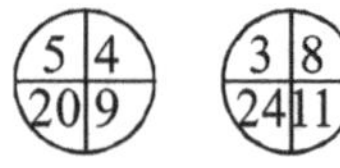

(a) 52 (b) 36

(c) 117 (d) 81

Sol. **(b)** The rule is : In the figure : $5 \times 4 = 20$, $5 + 4 = 9$

In the second figure : $3 \times 8 = 24$ and $3 + 8 = 11$

$\therefore$ In the third figure $9 \times 4 = 36$.

NON VERBAL SERIES.

The word "series" is defined as anything that follows or forms a specific pattern or is in continuation of a given pattern or sequence.

In this type of nonverbal test, two sets of figures pose the problem. The sets are called problem Figures and Answer Figures. Each problem figure changes in design from the preceding one. The answer figure set contains 4 figures marked 1, 2, 3, 4. You are required to choose the correct answer figure which would best continue the series.

TYPE I.

A definite relationship between elements in given figures.

ILLUSTRATION 16 :

Study the problem figures marked (A), (B) and (C) carefully and try to establish the relationship between them. From the answer figures marked a, b, c and d, pick out the figure which most appropriately completes the series.

Problem Figures

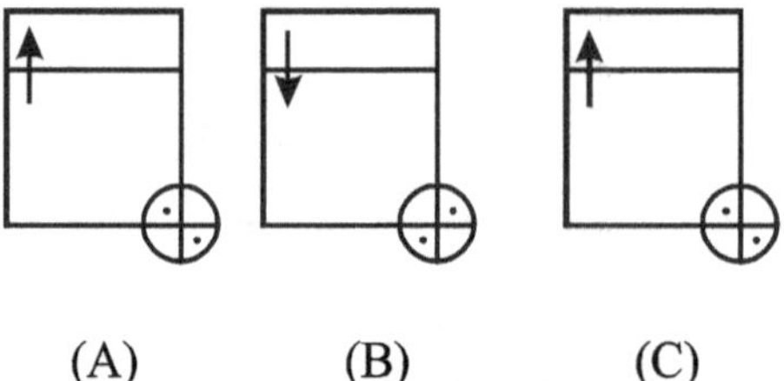

(A) (B) (C)

Answer Figures

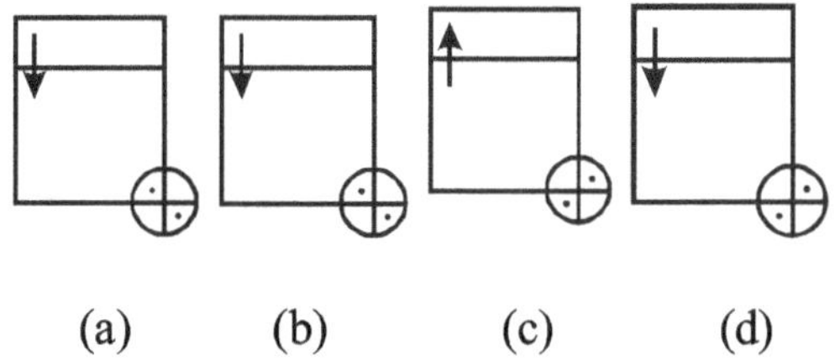

(a) (b) (c) (d)

***Sol.* (d)** Note the direction of arrow which changes alternately. The dots are also changing alternately. Hence, we are looking for a figure in which the arrow points down and the dots and positioned as in figure (B).

TYPE II.

Addition of Elements : In these type of questions, each figure is obtained by either sustaining the element of preceding figure as it is or adding a part of element or one element or more than one element of the preceding figure in a systematic way.

ILLUSTRATION 17 :

Problem Figure

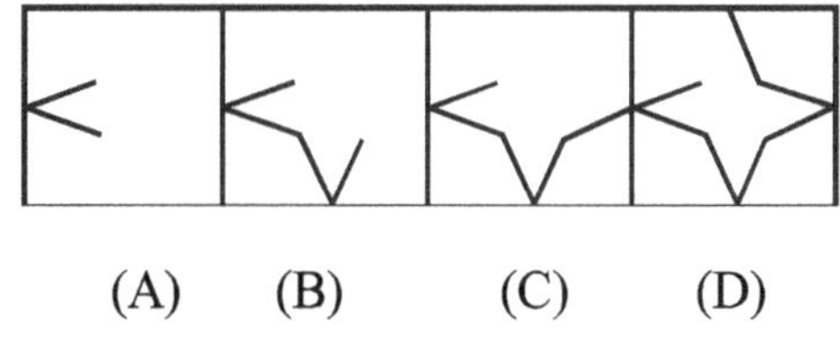

(A) (B) (C) (D)

Answer Figure

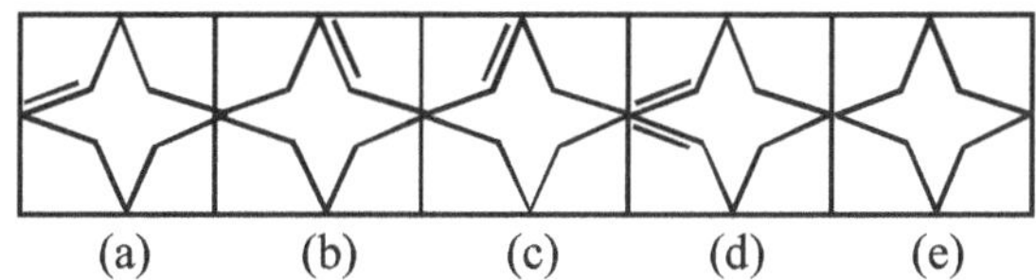

(a) (b) (c) (d) (e)

***Sol.* (e)** Two line segments are added in P1 to obtain P2 and one line segment is added in P2 to obtain P3. This process is repeated again to obtain P4. Hence, answer figure 5 continues the series.

TYPE III.

In these questions the items in the diagrams either increase or decrease in number.

ILLUSTRATION 18 :

Problem Figures

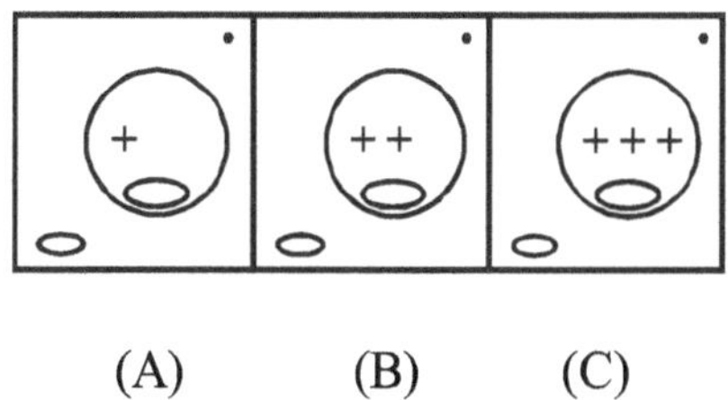

(A) (B) (C)

Answer Figures

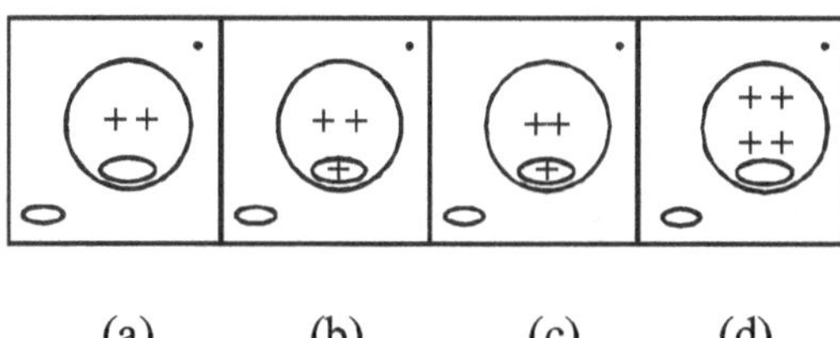

(a) (b) (c) (d)

***Sol.* (d)** Signs of Plus are adding one by one. Figure (1) has one plus sign, Figure (2) has two signs, figures (3) has three signs, the next figure should have 4 signs to keep the same pattern.

TYPE IV

Deletion of Elements : In these type of questions, each figure is obtained by either sustaining the element of preceding figure as it is or deleting a part of an element or one element or more than one element of the preceding figure in a systematic way.

ILLUSTRATION 19 :

Problem Figure

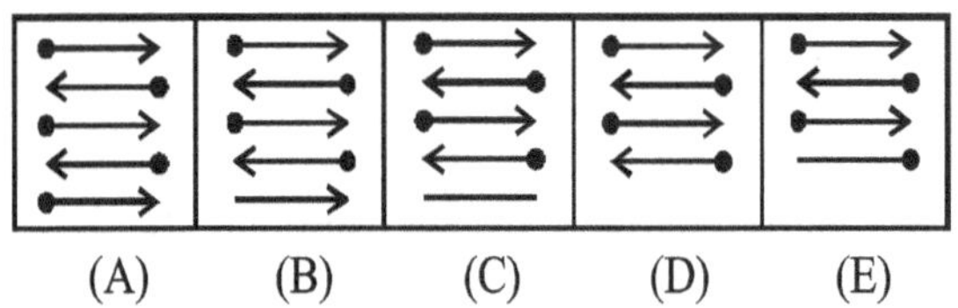

(A) (B) (C) (D) (E)

Answer Figure

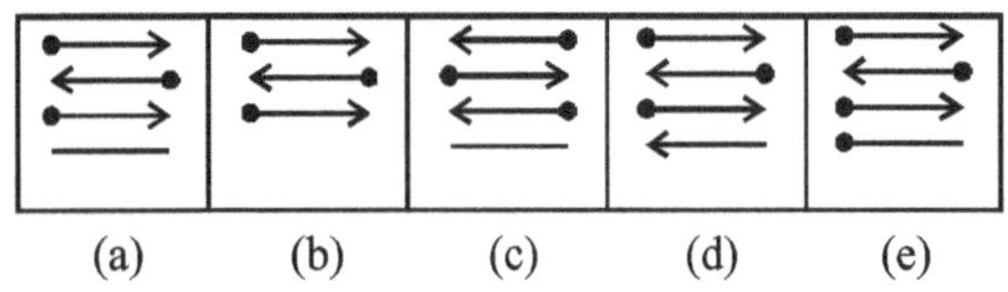

(a) (b) (c) (d) (e)

Sol. **(a)**

TYPE V

The qualitative characteristic of various elements in the diagrams change to complete the series.

Rotation Type : The various elements in the diagrams move in a specific manner. They may rotate in clockwise or anti-clockwise direction.

ILLUSTRATION 20 :

Problem Figures

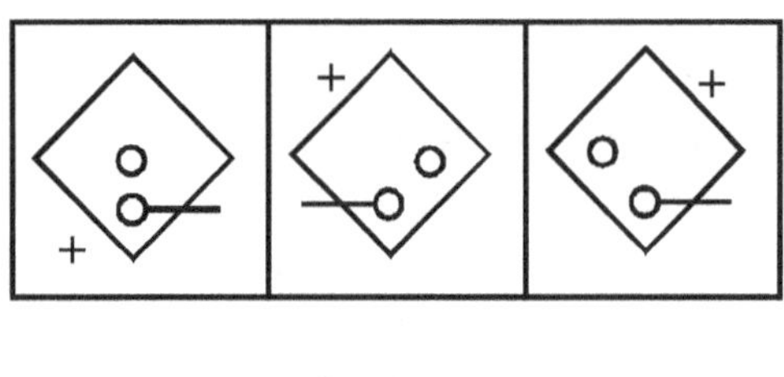

(A) (B) (C)

Answer Figures

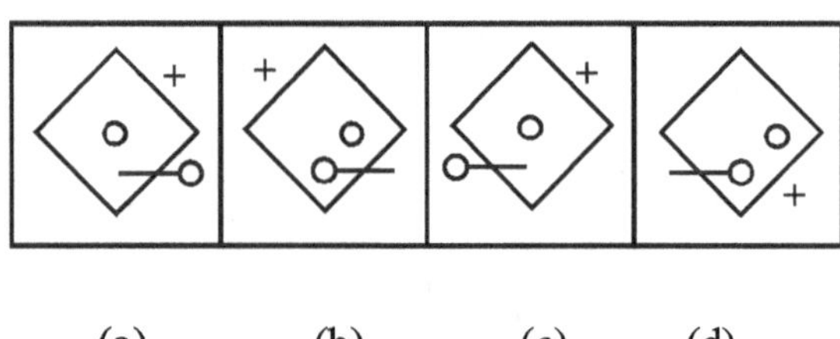

(a) (b) (c) (d)

Sol. **(d).** The sign of plus is rotating clockwise. The pin changes direction alternately.

TYPE VI.

Replacement of Elements : In these type of questions, each figure is obtained by either sustaining the element of preceding figure as it is or replacing a part of element or one element or more than one element by a new element of the preceding figure in a systematic way.

ILLUSTRATION 21:

Problem Figure

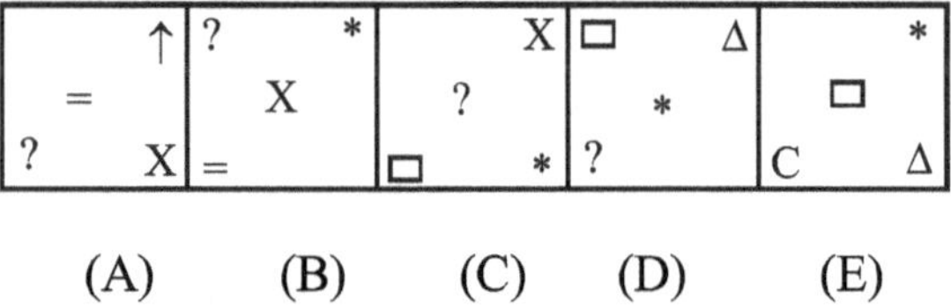

(A) (B) (C) (D) (E)

Answer figure

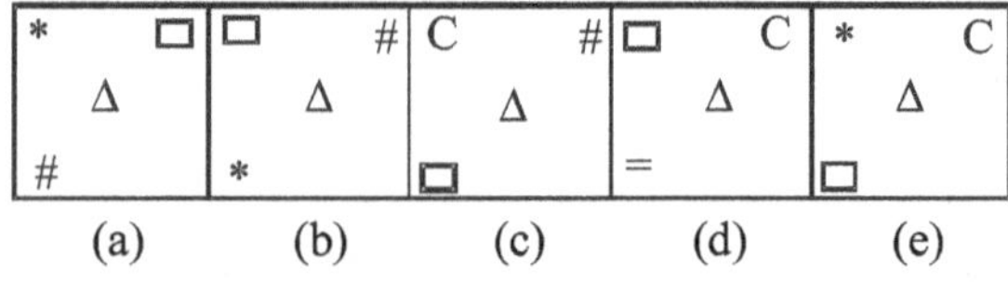

(a) (b) (c) (d) (e)

Sol. **(c)** The elements positioned at north-east (NE) corners disappear from the odd-numbered figures. The elements positioned at the south-west (SW) corners disappear from the even-numbered figures. Therefore * should not appear in the answer figure. Hence 1, 2 and 5 cannot be the answers. Also new elements are introduced at the NE corners in even-numbered figures. Hence, answer 4 is ruled out. Therefore answer figure 3 continues the given series.

TYPE VII

Multi-Relation Series :

These are mixed series in which various elements in diagrams increase/decrease in number, change/positions in a set pattern.

ILLUSTRATION 22:

Problem Figures

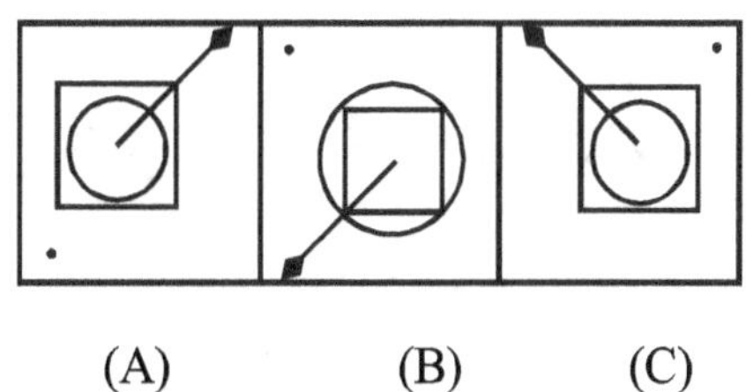

(A) (B) (C)

Answer Figures

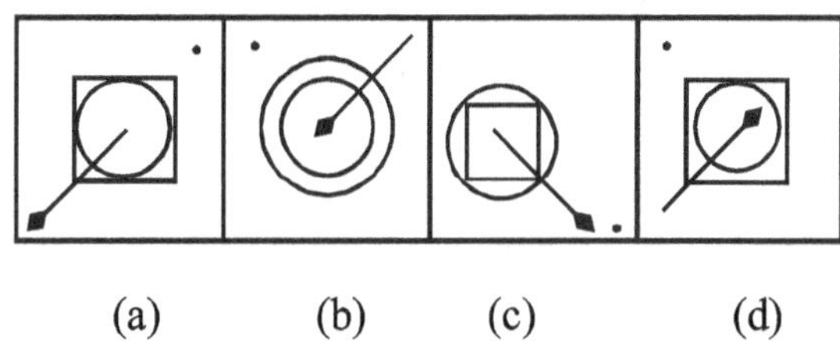

(a) (b) (c) (d)

***Sol.* (c)** Note movement of dot which is clockwise and the arrow moves in and out in opposite direction alternately. The circle and square interchange.

LEVEL 1

DIRECTIONS (Qs. 1-12) : Complete the series.

1. 13, 24, 46, 90, 178, ...
   (a) 354 (b) 266
   (c) 364 (d) 344
2. AZ, CX, FU, ...
   (a) IR (b) IV
   (c) JQ (d) KP
3. 3F, 6G, 11I, 18L, ...
   (a) 21O (b) 25N
   (c) 27P (d) 27Q
4. B Y C X D W E ?
   (a) S (c) T
   (b) U (d) V
5. B D G K ? V
   (a) N (b) P
   (c) Q (d) M
6. B C D B D D B E D B F D B G ?
   (a) B D (b) B F
   (c) H B (d) D B
7. A D E H I L M P Q T U ?
   (a) X Y (b) Y Z
   (c) U V (d) V W
8. 3, 6, 18, 72, 360, ...
   (a) 1296 (b) 2160
   (c) 2254 (d) 4329
9. BA.......B.......AABB.......A.........
   ....A........BB
   (a) ABAAABB (b) BBAABB
   (c) ABABBA (d) BAAABB
10. 24, 46, 68, ?
    (a) 80 (b) 89
    (c) 88 (d) 90
11. 5, 8, 14, 26, ?, 98
    (a) 62 (b) 50
    (c) 40 (d) 35
12. 1, 3, 6, 10, 15, ?, 28
    (a) 20 (b) 21
    (c) 22 (d) 24

DIRECTIONS (Qs. 13-14): *In each of the following number series, a wrong number is given. Find out that number.*

13. 10 15 24 35 54 75 100
    (a) 35 (b) 75
    (c) 24 (d) 15
14. 5 10 17 27 37 50 65
    (a) 10 (b) 17
    (c) 27 (d) 37

DIRECTION (Qs. 15) : *Question is based on number/figure series. In the series missing term is mentioned by question mark (?). Find out the missing term in given alternatives.*

15. 63, 58, 51, 40, 27, ?
    (a) 8 (b) 12
    (c) 10 (d) 14

DIRECTIONS (Qs. 16-22): *What number/ character/letter should replace the question mark?*

16.

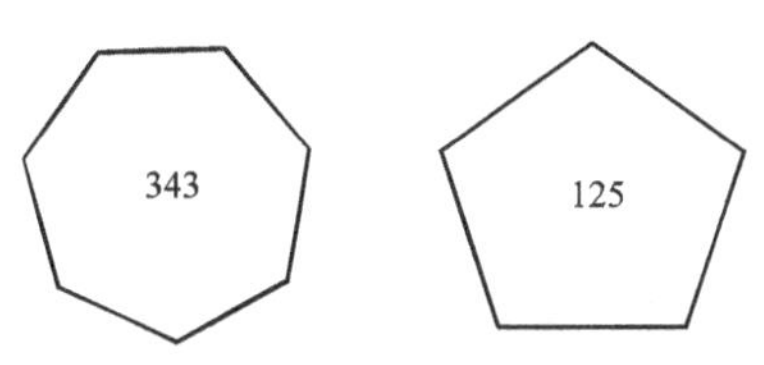

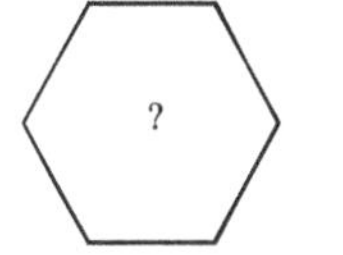

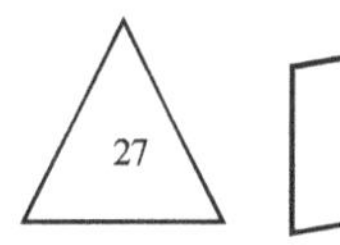

64

(a) 216 (b) 316
(c) 117 (d) 215

17.

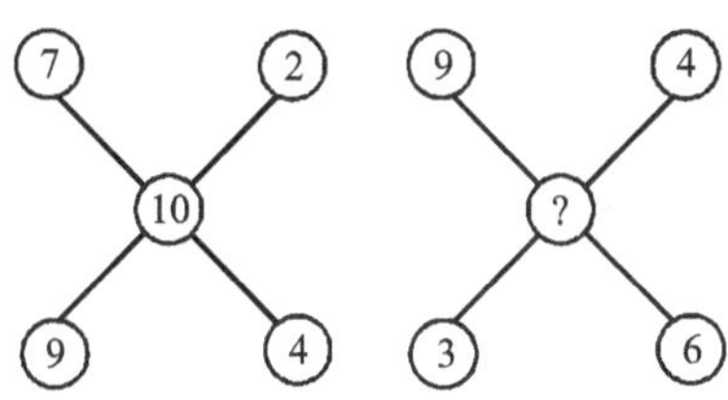

(a) 2 (b) 9
(c) 12 (d) 19

18.

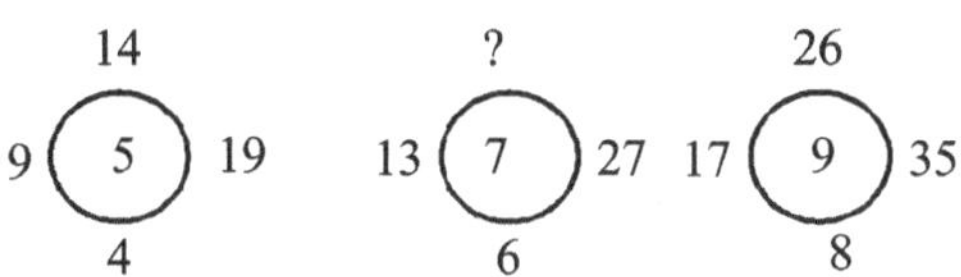

(a) 18 (b) 20
(c) 22 (d) 24

19.

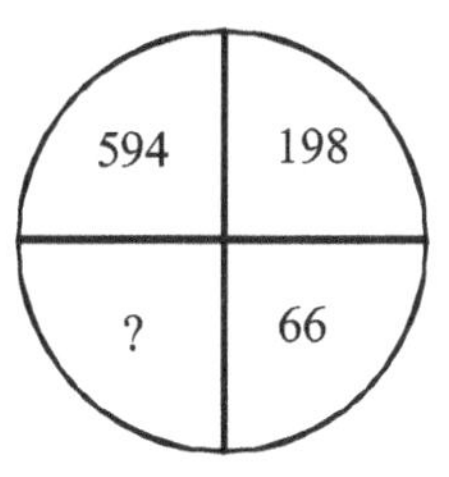

(a) 11 (b) 12
(c) 22 (d) 33

20.

6	6	8
5	7	5
4	3	?
120	126	320

(a) 4 (b) 8
(c) 12 (d) 16

21.

3	6	8
5	8	4
4	7	?

(a) 6 (b) 7
(c) 8 (d) 9

22.

6	9	15
8	12	20
4	6	?

(a) 5 (b) 10
(c) 15 (d) 21

DIRECTIONS (Qs. 23-26) : *In each of the following questions, a figure series is given out of which the last figure is missing, Find which one would complete the series.*

23.

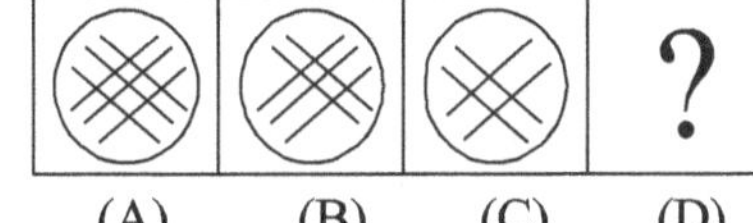

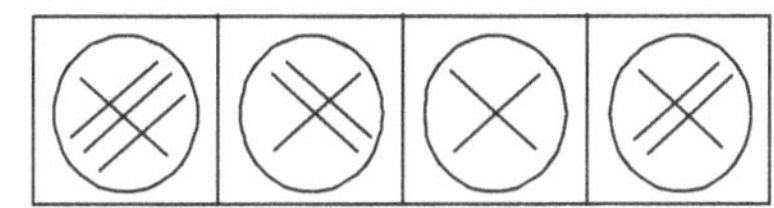

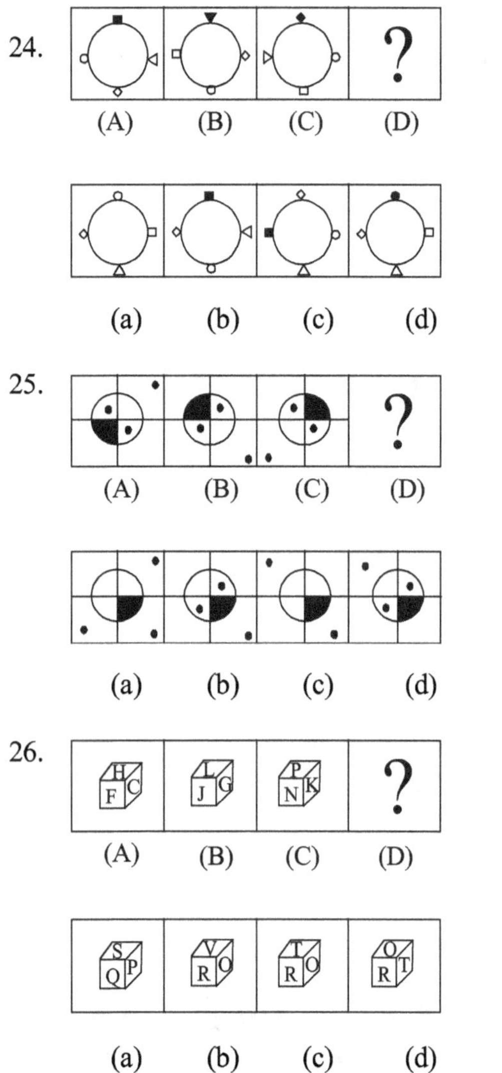

DIRECTIONS (Qs.27-32) : *In the Problem Figures, one figure marked by ? is missing. There is a set of answer figures also in which five alternatives are given. You have to find out the one right answer from answer figures.*

27. **Problem Figures**

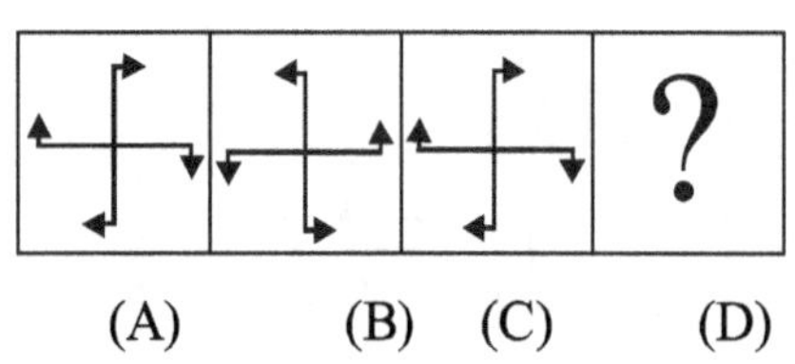

(A) (B) (C) (D)

Answer Figures

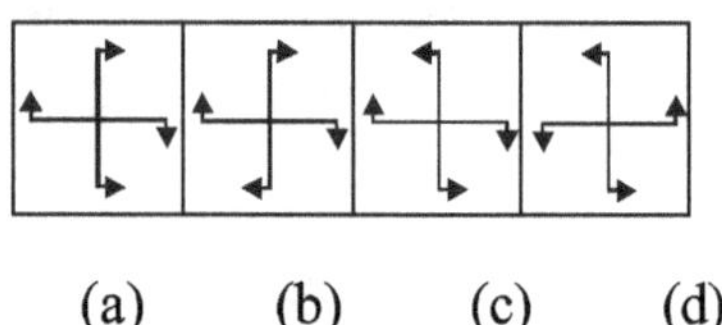

(a) (b) (c) (d)

28. **Problem Figures**

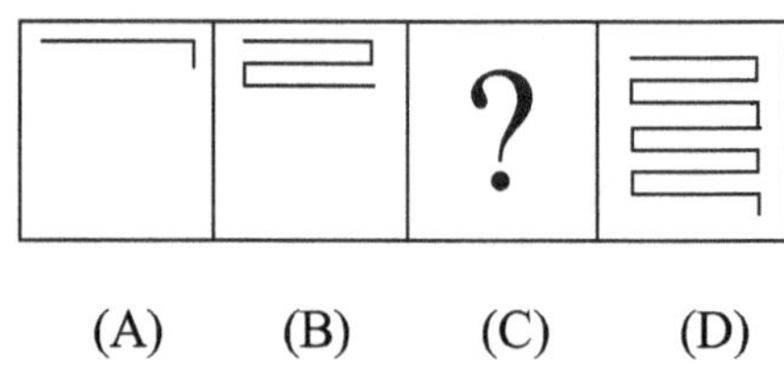

(A) (B) (C) (D)

Answer Figures

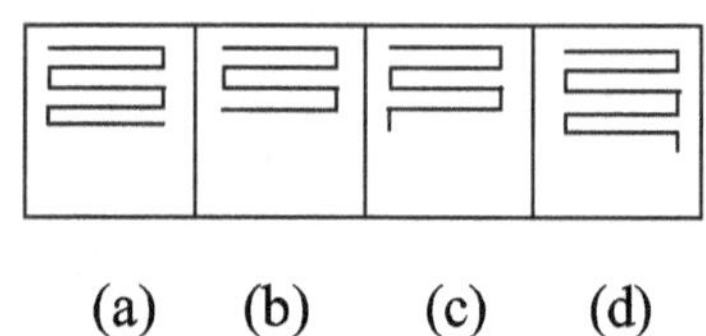

(a) (b) (c) (d)

29. **Problem Figures**

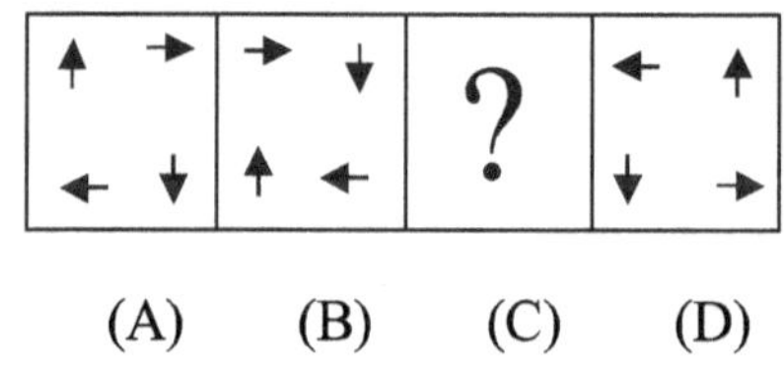

(A) (B) (C) (D)

Answer Figures

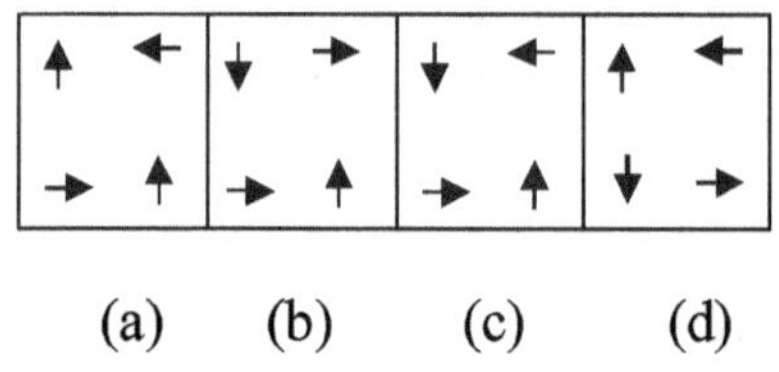

(a) (b) (c) (d)

30. **Problem Figures**

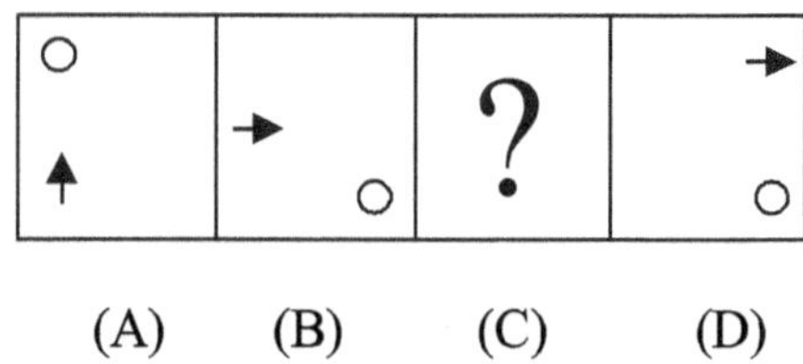

(A) (B) (C) (D)

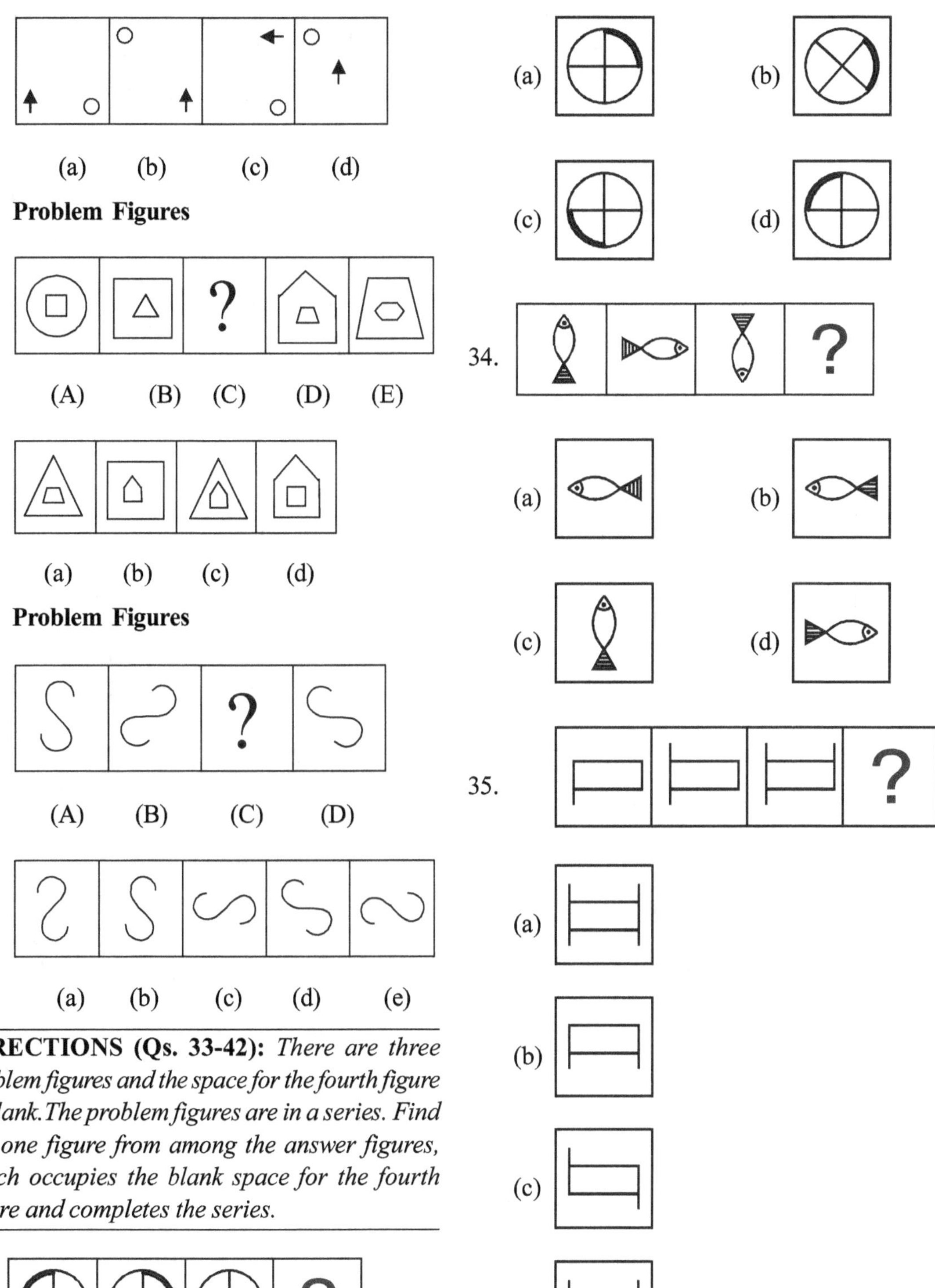

DIRECTIONS (Qs. 33-42): *There are three problem figures and the space for the fourth figure is blank. The problem figures are in a series. Find out one figure from among the answer figures, which occupies the blank space for the fourth figure and completes the series.*

36. 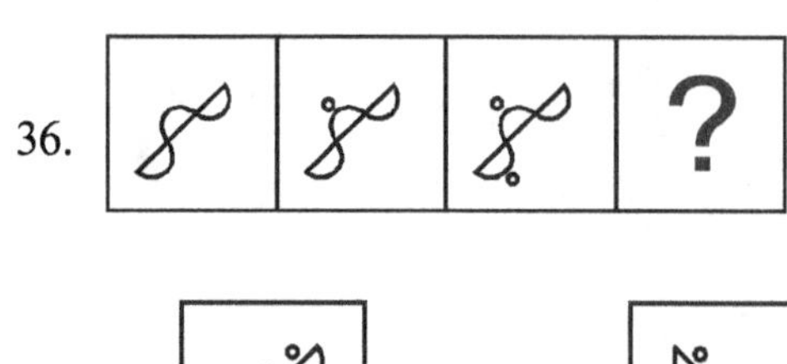

(a) 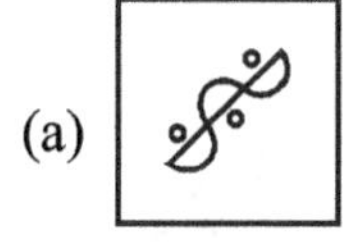 (b)

(c) (d)

39. 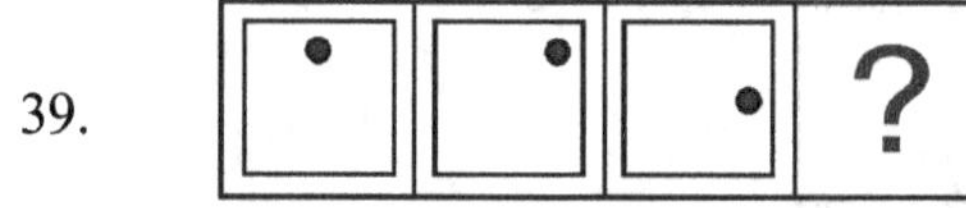

(a) 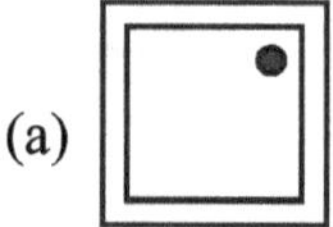 (b)

(c) (d)

37. ?

(a) (b)

(c) (d)

40. 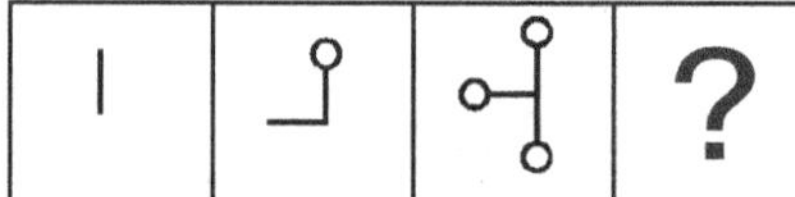

(a) 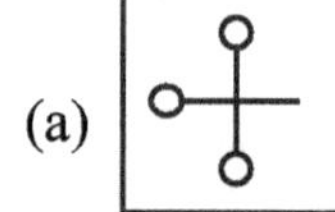 (b) 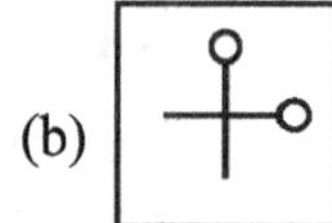

(c) (d)

38. 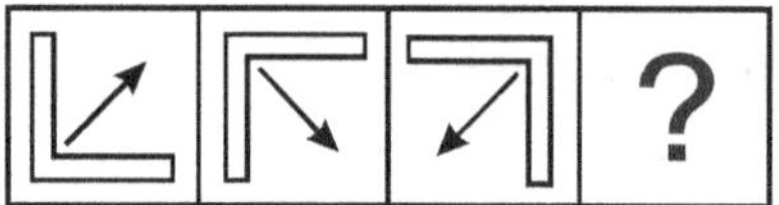

(a) 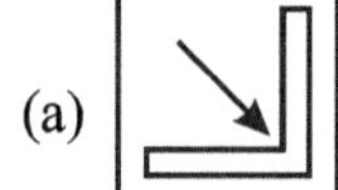 (b) 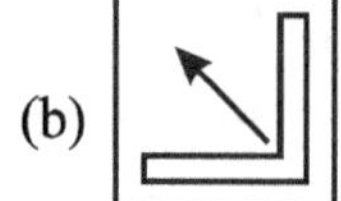

(c) (d)

41. 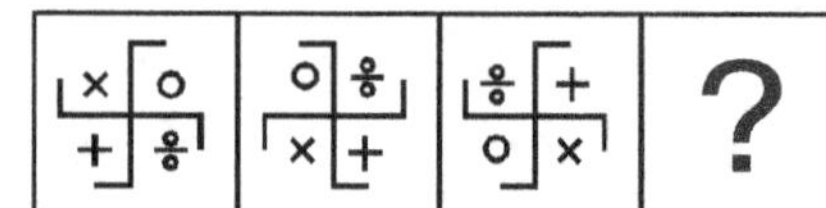

(a) 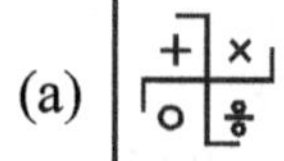 (b) 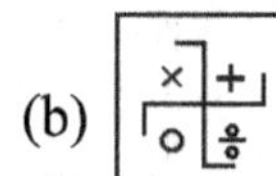

(c) (d)

42.

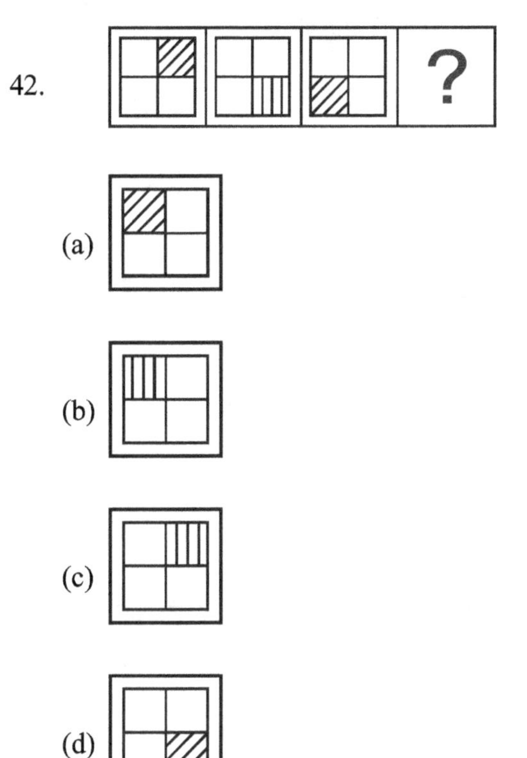

DIRECTIONS (Qs. 43-47): *Three complete and fourth blank space is given, choose the set of figures which follows the rule and would replace the blank space given in question figure from the four alternatives given.*

43. **Question Figure**

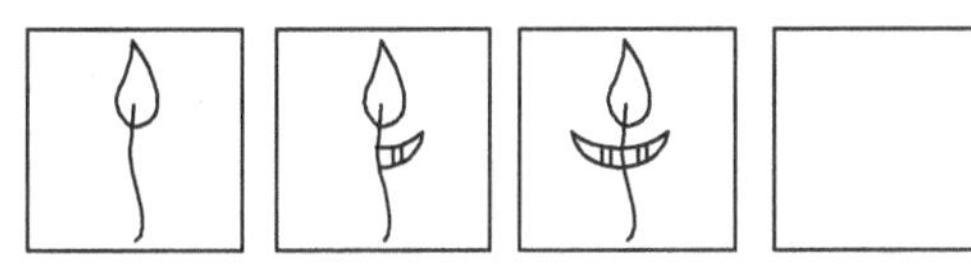

Answer Figures

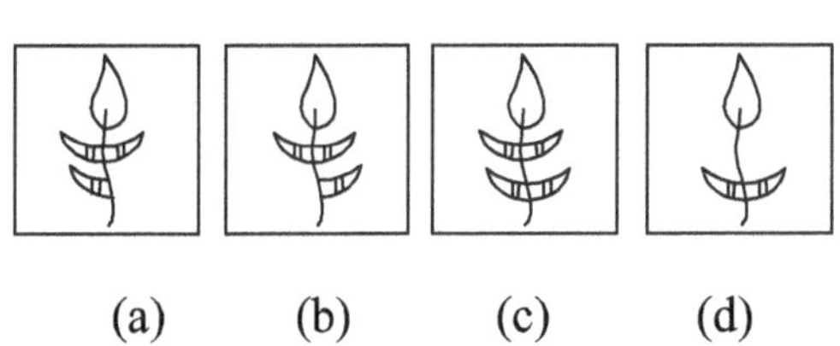

(a) (b) (c) (d)

44. **Question Figure**

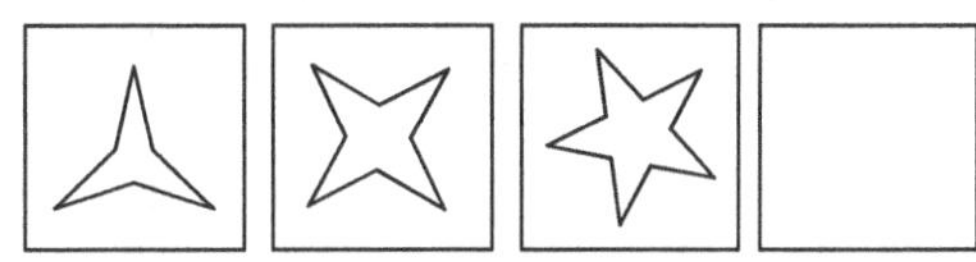

Answer Figures

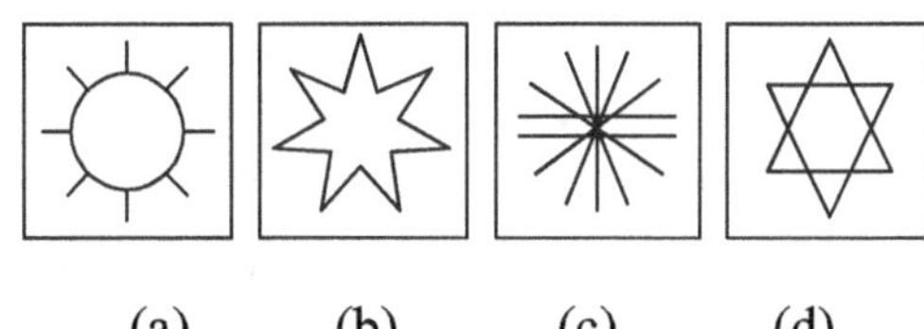

(a) (b) (c) (d)

45. **Question Figure**

Answer Figures

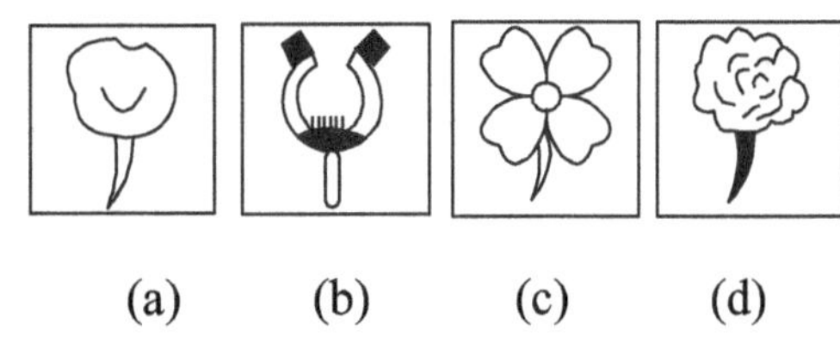

(a) (b) (c) (d)

46. **Question Figure**

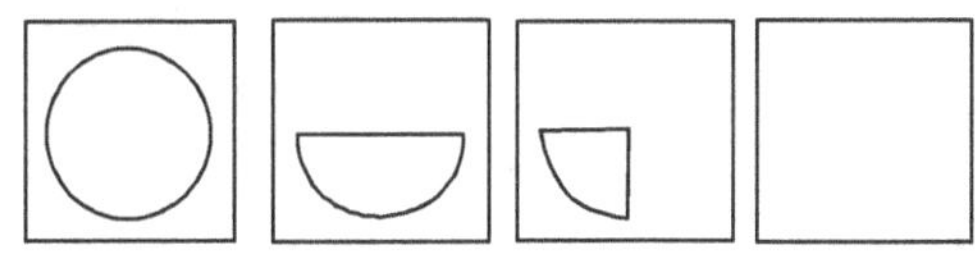

Answer Figures

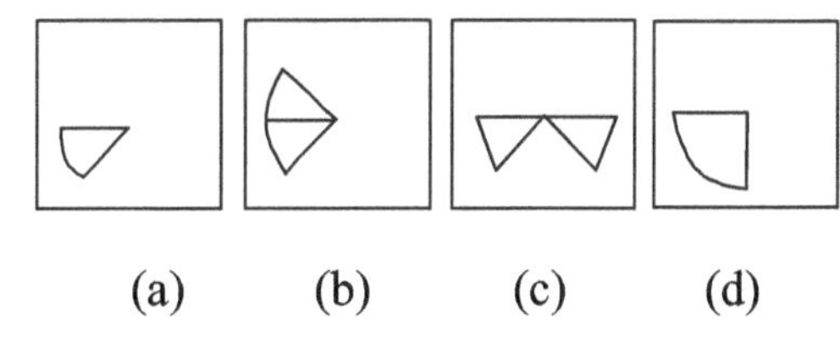

(a) (b) (c) (d)

47. **Question Figure**

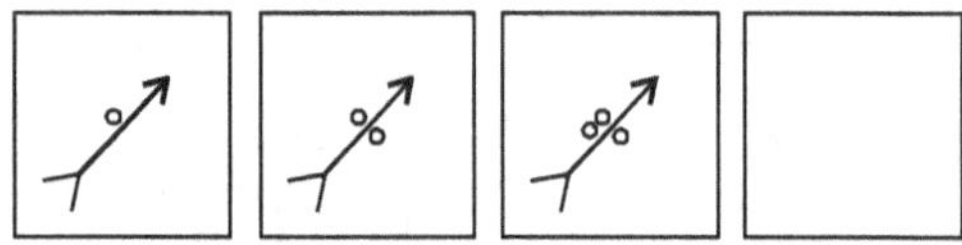

Answer Figures

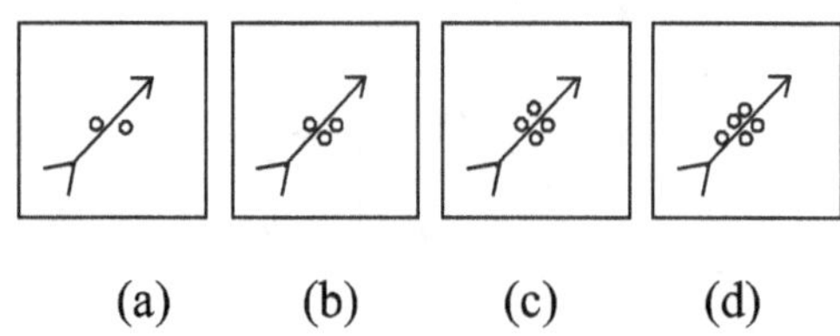

(a) (b) (c) (d)

DIRECTIONS (Qs. 48-52): *Three complete and fourth blank space is given, choose the set of figures which follows the rule and would replace the blank space given in question figure from the four alternatives given.*

48. **Question Figure**

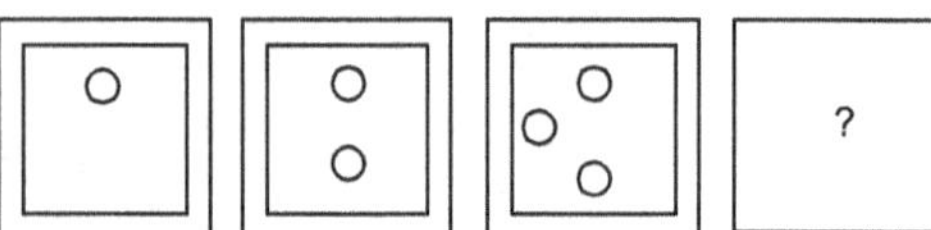

Answer Figures

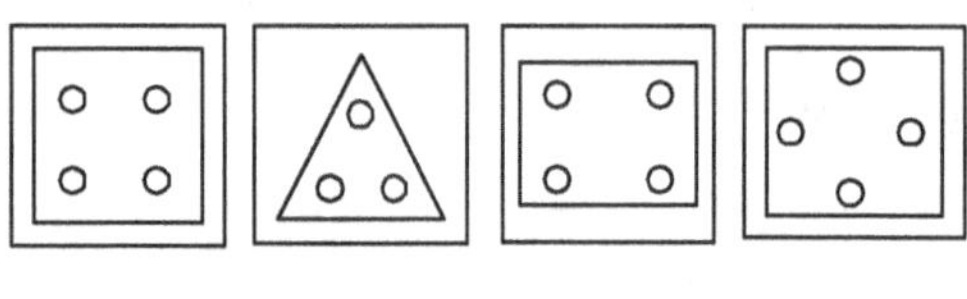

(a) (b) (c) (d)

49. **Question Figure**

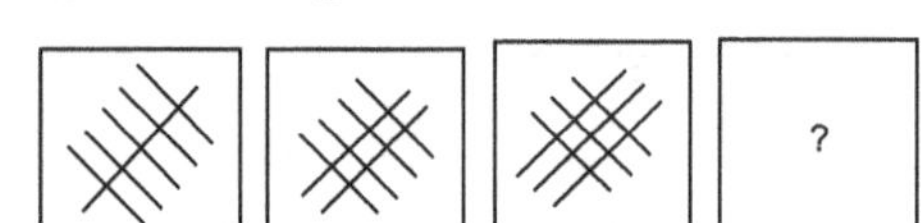

Answer Figures

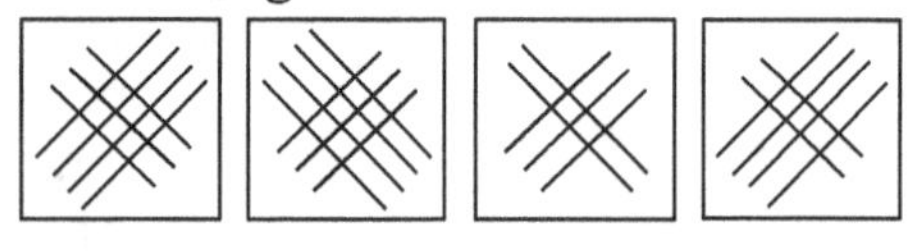

(a) (b) (c) (d)

50. **Question Figure**

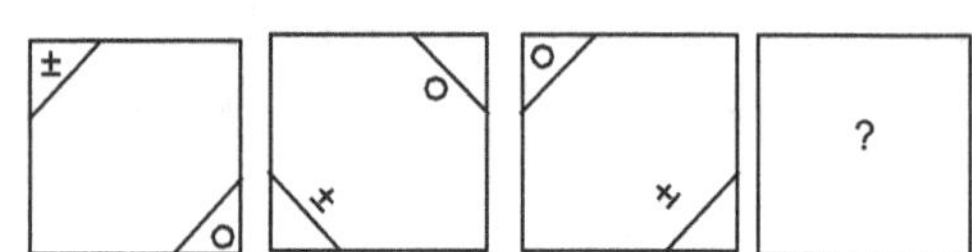

Answer Figures

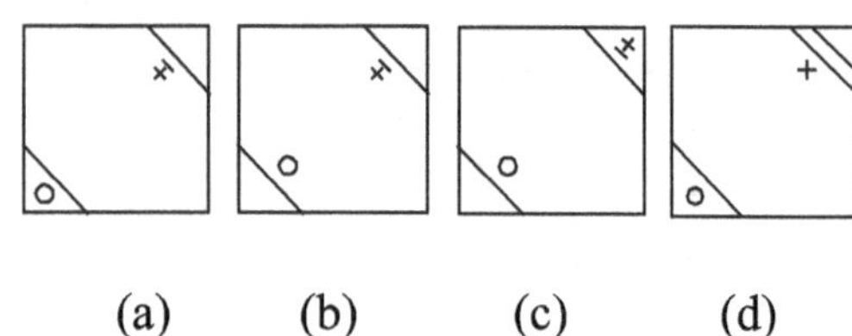

(a) (b) (c) (d)

51. **Question Figure**

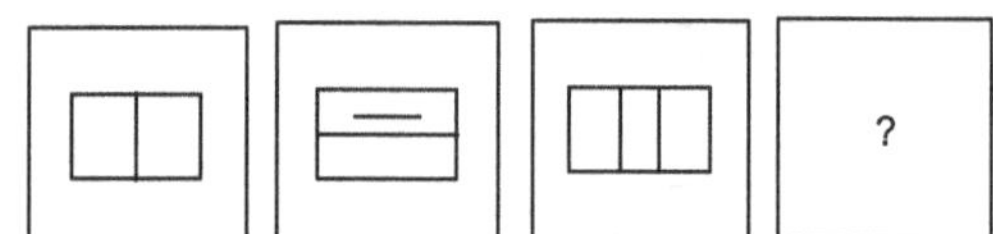

Answer Figures

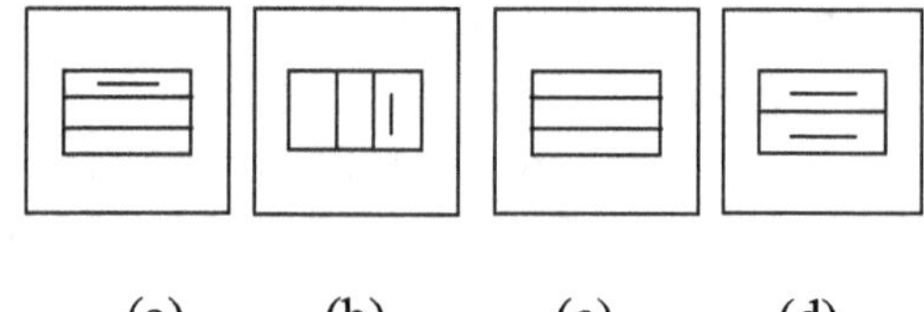

(a) (b) (c) (d)

52. **Question Figure**

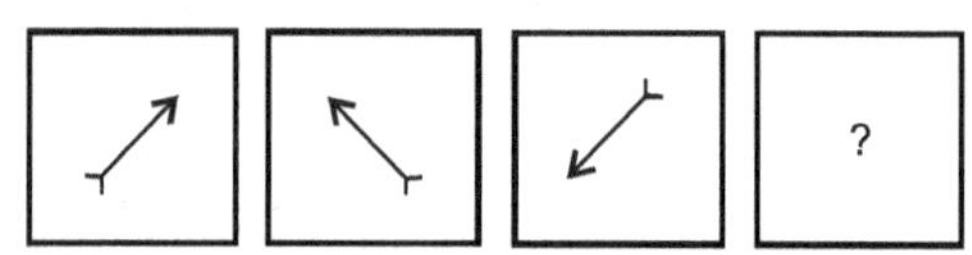

Answer Figures

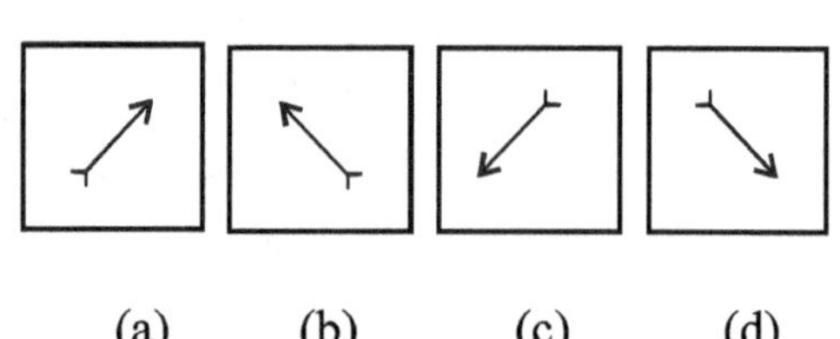

(a) (b) (c) (d)

DIRECTIONS: (Qs. 53-56): *There are three question figure and the space for the fourth figure is left blank. The question figures are in a series. Find out one figure from among the answer figures given which occupies the blank space for the fourth figure and completes the series.*

53. **Question Figures**

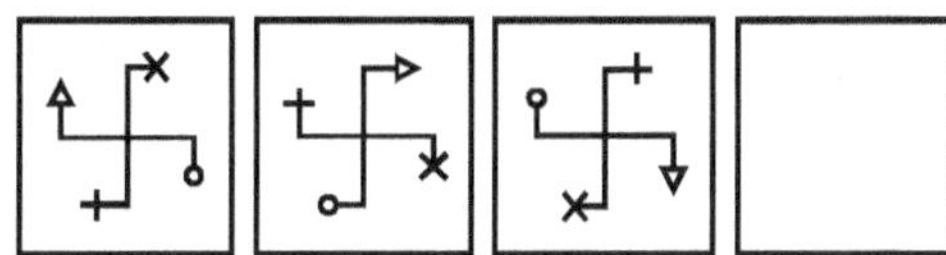

Answer Figures

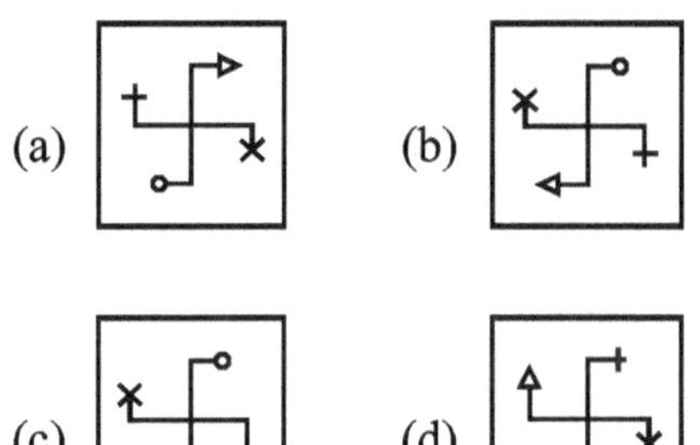

54. **Question Figures**

Answer Figures

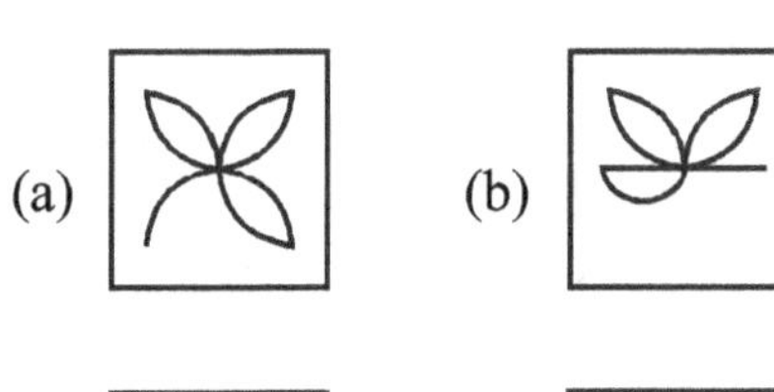

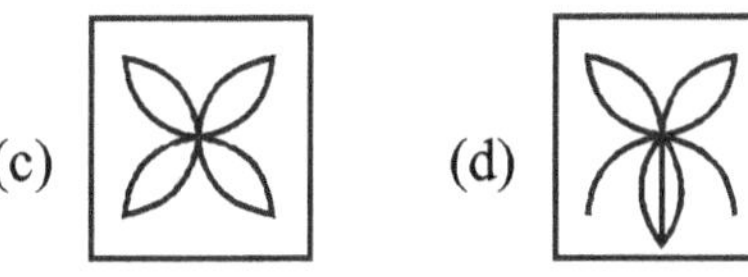

55. **Question Figures**

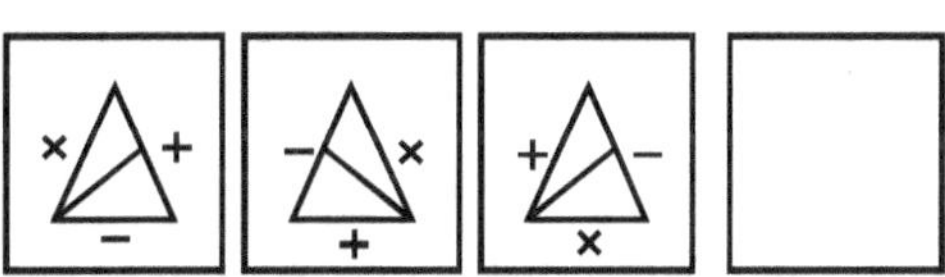

Answer Figures

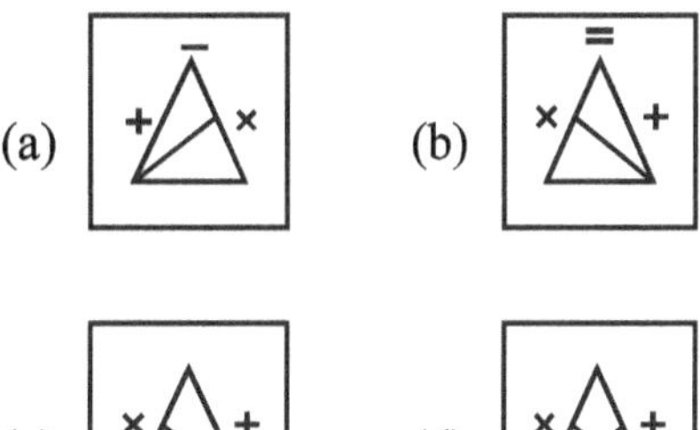

56. **Question Figures**

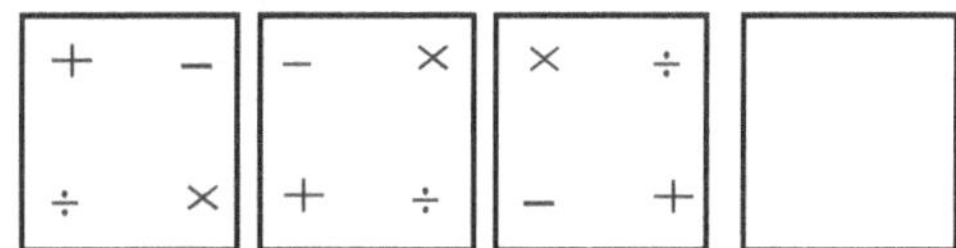

Answer Figures

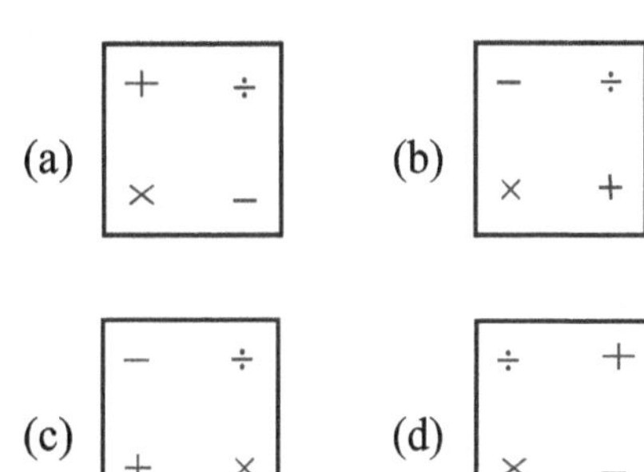

DIRECTIONS (Qs. 57 to 58) : *On there are three question figures and the space for the fourth figure is left blank. The question figures are in a series. Find out one figure from among the answer figures which occupies the blank space for the fourth figure and complete the series.*

57. **Questions Figure**

Answer Figures

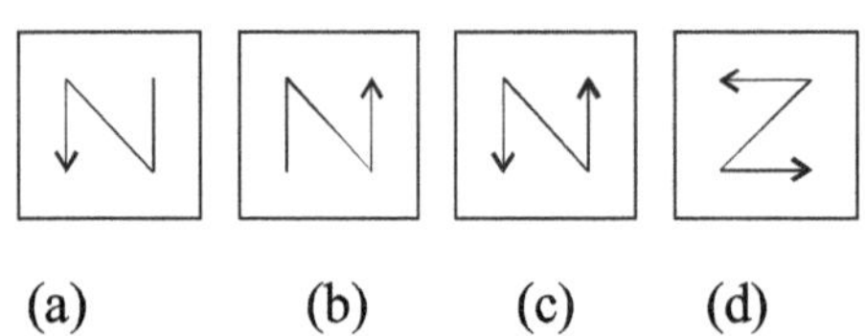

(a) (b) (c) (d)

58. **Questions Figure**

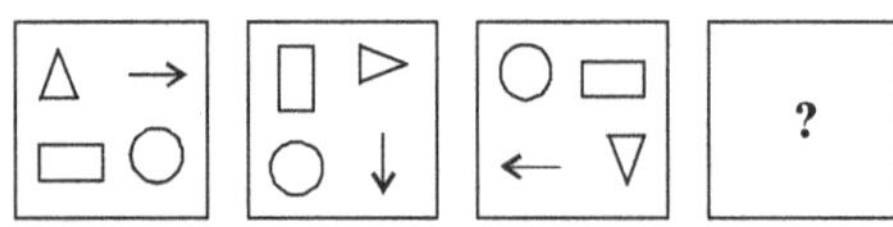

Answer Figures

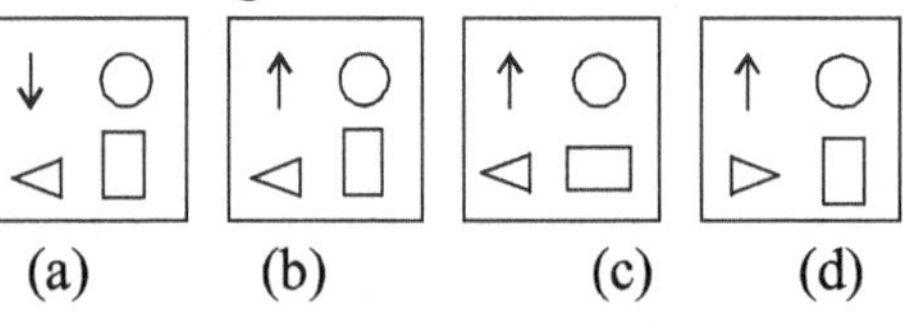

(a) (b) (c) (d)

Directions (Qs. 59-62): There are three question figure on the left side space for the fourth figure is left blank. The question figures are in a series. Find out one figure from among the answer figures which occupies the blank space for the fourth figure and complete the series.

59. **Question Figures**

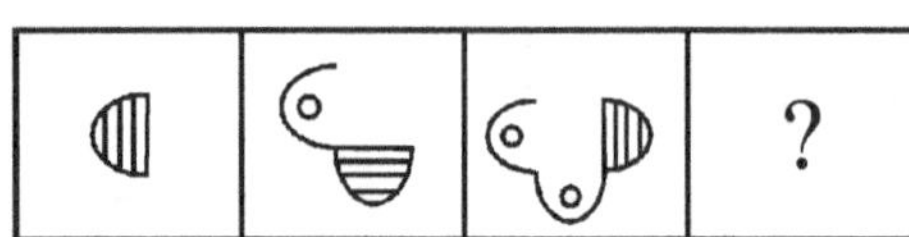

Answer Figures

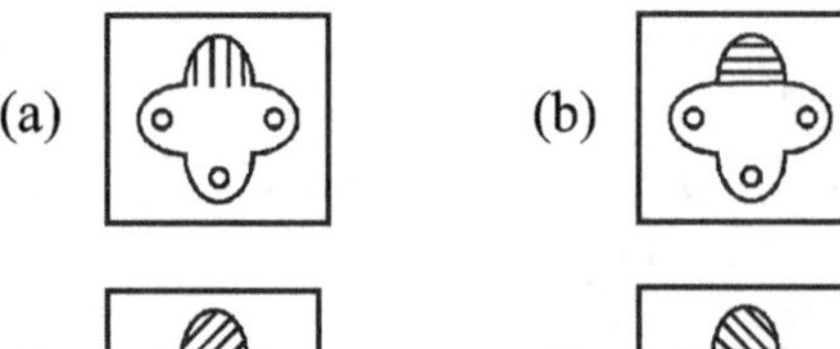

(a) (b) (c) (d)

60. **Question Figures**

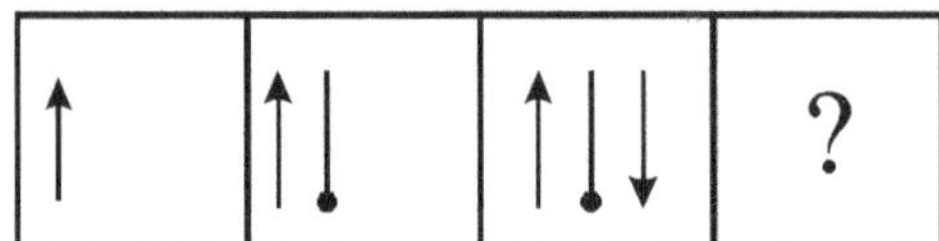

Answer Figures

(a) 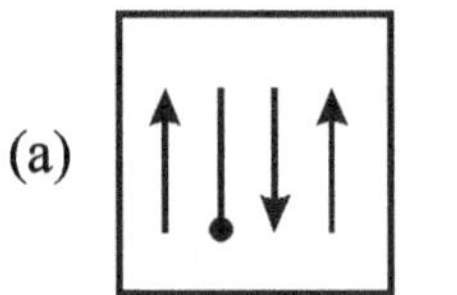

(b) 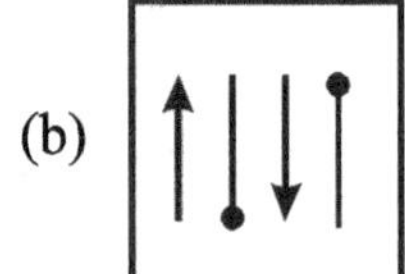

(c) 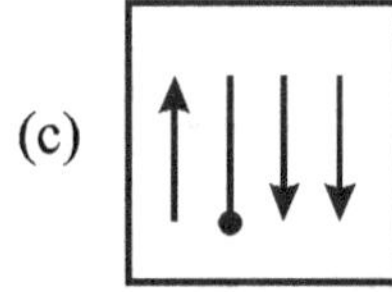

(d) 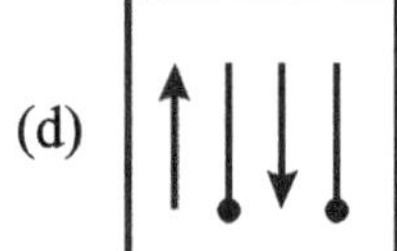

61. **Question Figures**

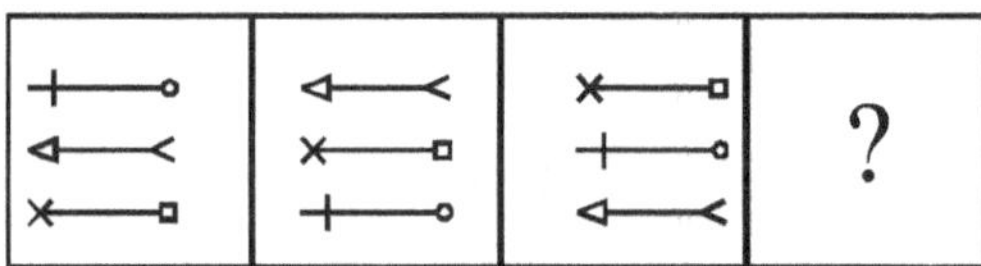

Answer Figures

(a) 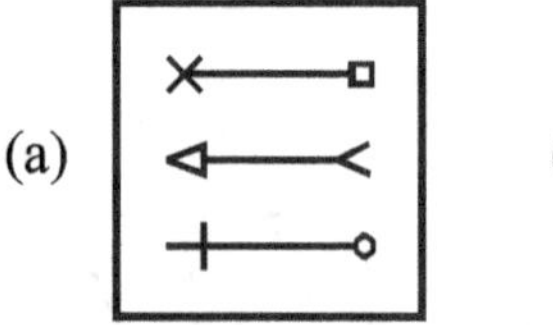

(b) 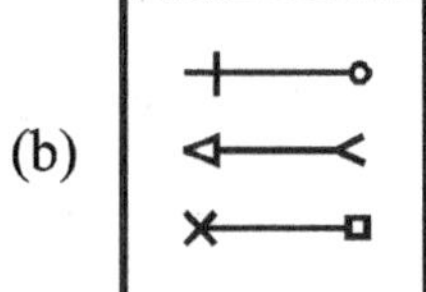

(c) 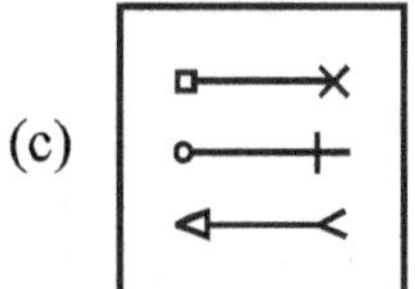

(d) 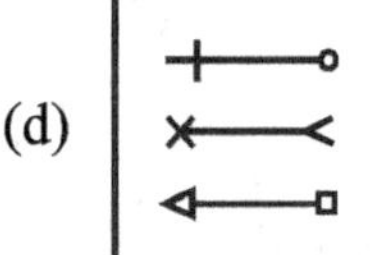

62. **Question Figure**

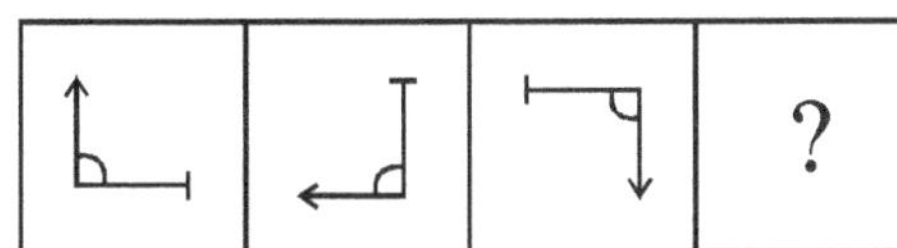

Answer Figures

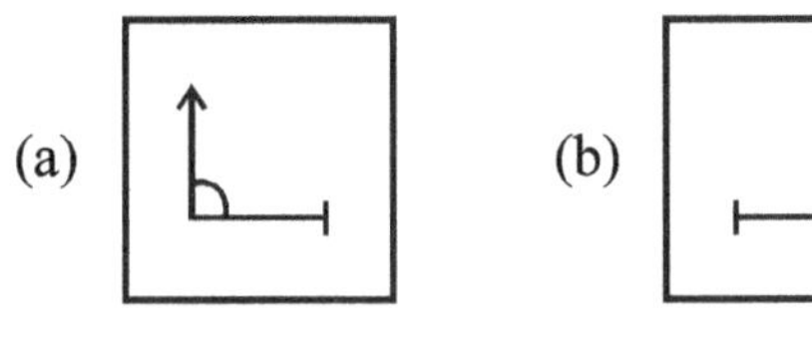

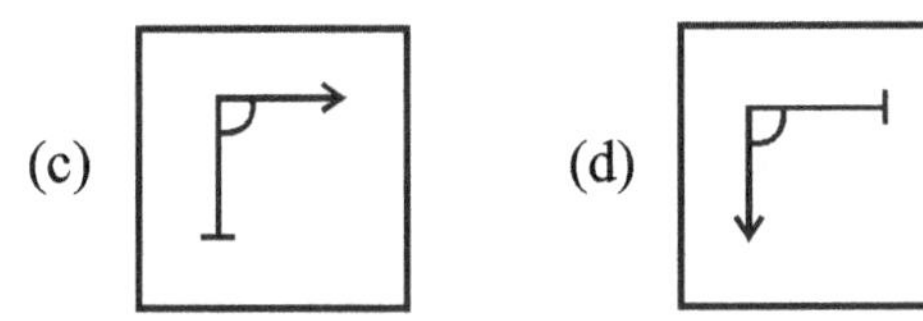

63. Which of the following numbers will replace the (?) **[2018]**

So as to complete the given number pattern?

(a) 216 (b) 225
(c) 144 (d) 196

64. Select a figure from the options which will continue the given series. **[2018]**

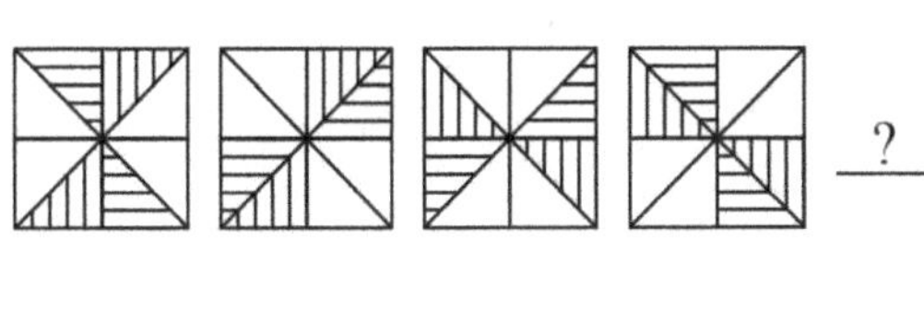

(a) 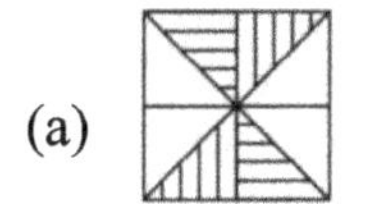 (b) 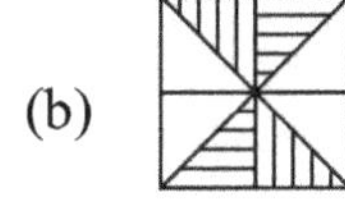

(c) 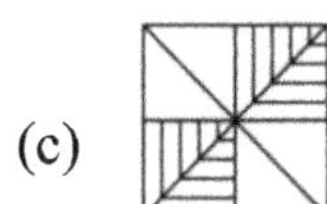 (d) 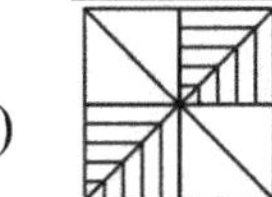

65. Find the missing number which will complete the given series. **[2020]**

8, 14, 26, ?, 68, 98

(a) 32
(b) 44
(c) 52
(d) 48

66. Find the missing number to continue the given number pattern. **[2021]**

3, 8, 15, 24, 35, 48, ?

(a) 53
(b) 54
(c) 63
(d) 62

67. Find the missing number to continue the given number pattern. **[2022]**

21, 25, 33, 49, 81, ?

(a) 144
(b) 133
(c) 154
(d) 145

68. A series is given with one term missing. Choose the correct alternative from the given options that will complete the series.

[2022]

AZ, GT, MN, ? , YB

(a) SK (b) JH
(c) SH (d) TS

LEVEL 2

1. AD, EH, IL ?
   (a) M+P (b) MN
   (c) MO (d) MS
2. 8, 1, 64, 27, ?, 125
   (a) 216 (b) 196
   (c) 169 (d) 81
3. 78, 79, 81, ?, 92, 103, 119
   (a) 88 (b) 85
   (c) 84 (d) 83
4. b – a – bab – ab – a
   (a) a b a b (b) b a b a
   (c) b a bb (d) a bb a
5. a – baa – baa – ba
   (a) aab (b) bab
   (c) bba (d) bbb
6. – b aa – bbb – ab –
   (a) a b a b (b) a a b b
   (c) b a a b (d) b b a b
7. m n o n o p q o p q r s — — — — —
   (a) mnopq (b) oqrst
   (c) pqrst (d) qrstu
8. 2, 3, 6, 7, 10, ...
   (a) 11 (b) 13
   (c) 14 (d) 14
9. 0, 3, 4, 7, 8, ...
   (a) 13 (b) 11
   (c) 14 (d) 15
10. 0, 8, 24, 48, 80, ?
    (a) 110 (b) 96
    (c) 120 (d) 140
11. A letter number series is given with one or more terms missing as shown below. Choose the alternative next in the sequence.
    A4X, D9U, G16R, ___________
    (a) K25P (b) J25P
    (c) J25O (d) J25C
12. Which of the following alternatives will fit in the place of '?' ?
    AZ, GT, MN, ? , YB
    (a) KF
    (b) RX
    (c) SH
    (d) TS
13. Look at this series :
    J14, L16, ____, P20, R22
    Which of the following alternatives will fit in the blank space ?
    (a) N18 (b) S24
    (c) M18 (d) T24

DIRECTIONS (Qs. 14-18): Each of following questions consists of four problem figures marked A, B, C and D and five answer Figures marked a, b, c, and d. Select a figure from amongst the answer Figures which will continue the series established by the four Problem Figures.

14. **Problem Figures**

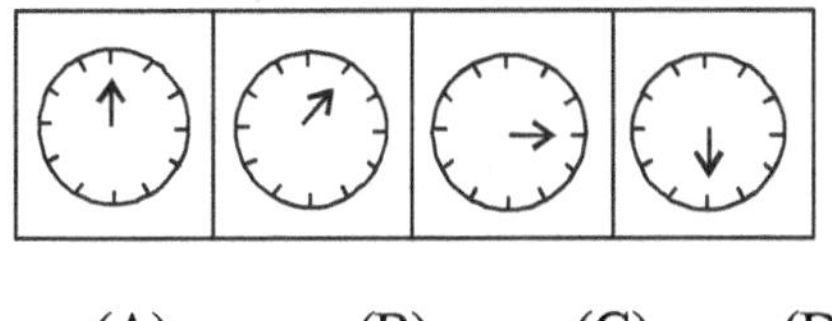

(A) (B) (C) (D)

Answer Figures

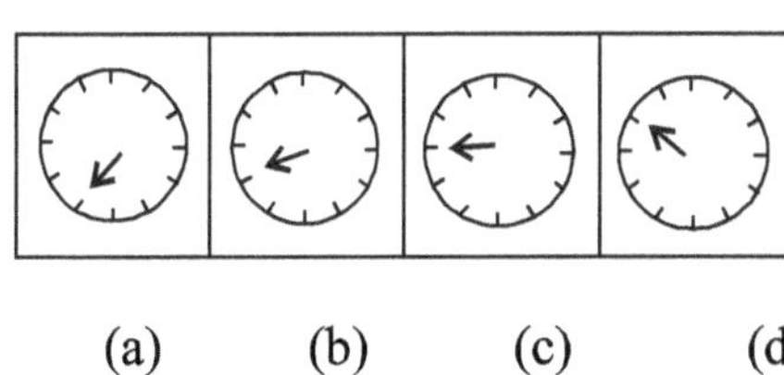

(a) (b) (c) (d)

15. **Problem Figures**

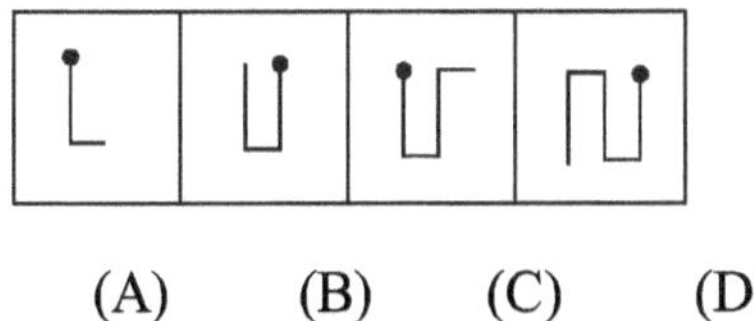

(A) (B) (C) (D)

Answer Figures

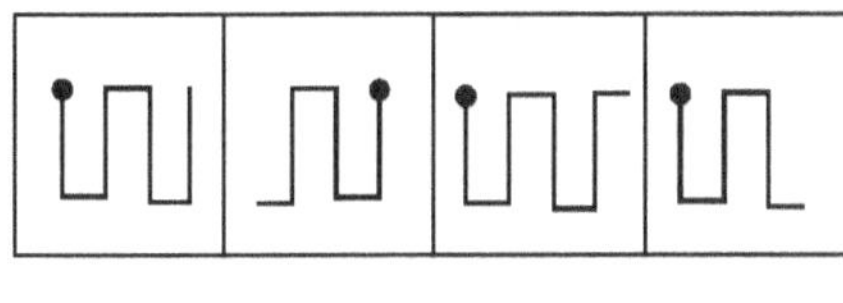

(a) (b) (c) (d)

16. **Problem Figures**

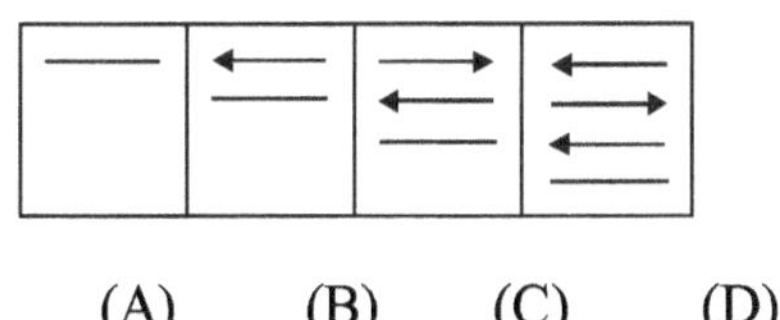

(A) (B) (C) (D)

Answer Figures

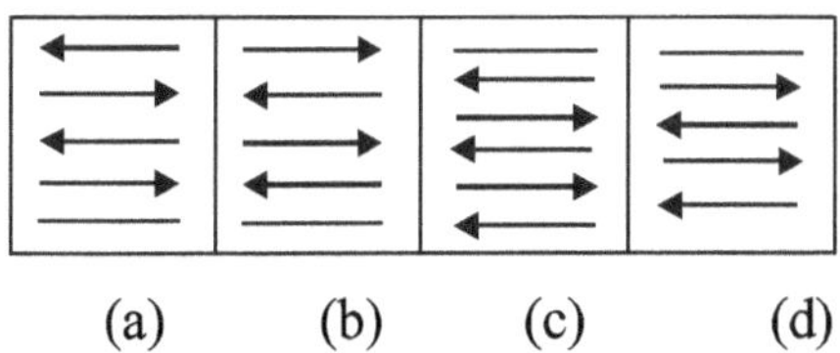

(a) (b) (c) (d)

17. **Problem Figures**

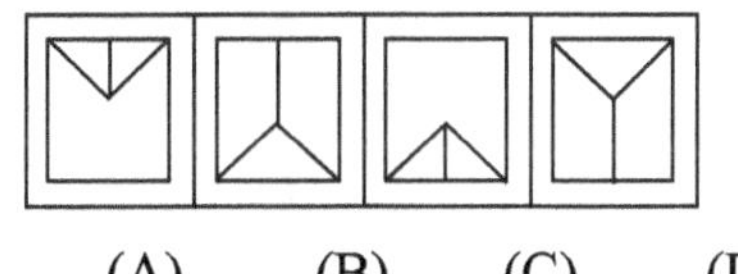

(A) (B) (C) (D)

Answer Figures

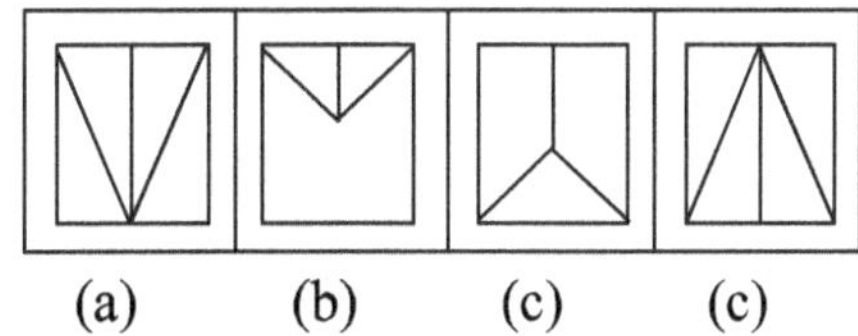

(a) (b) (c) (c)

18. **Problem Figures**

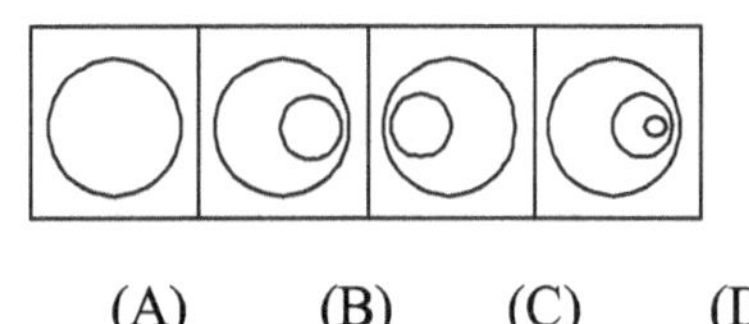

(A) (B) (C) (D)

Answer Figures

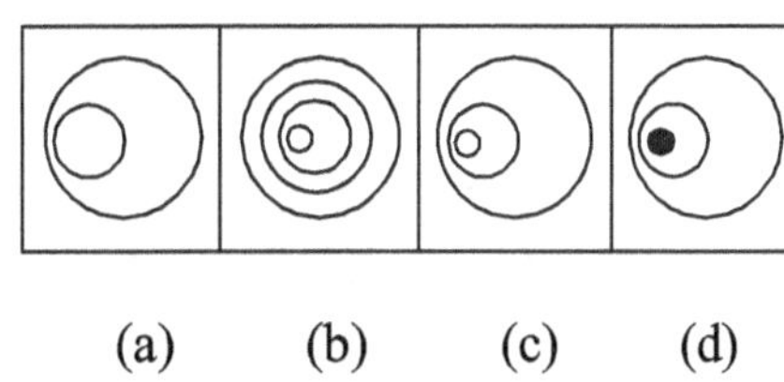

(a) (b) (c) (d)

DIRECTIONS (Qs. 19-20) : In the following questions, which one of the answer figure would occupy the next position in the problem figure. If they continue in the same order.

19. **Problem Figures:**

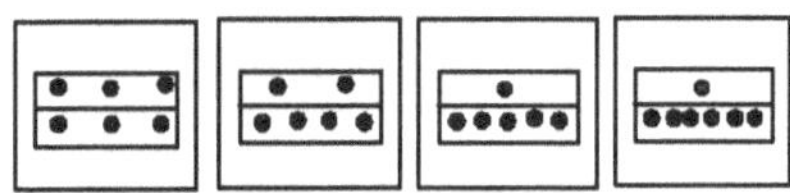

Answer Figures:

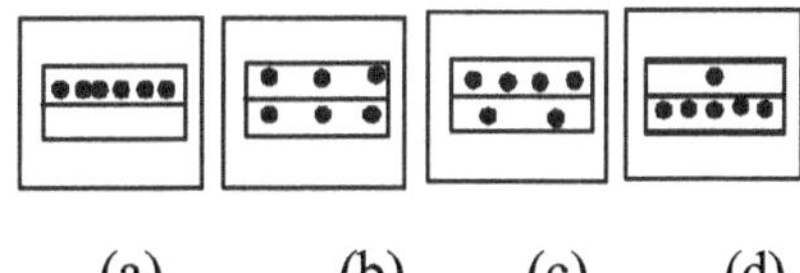

(a) (b) (c) (d)

20. **Problem Figures:**

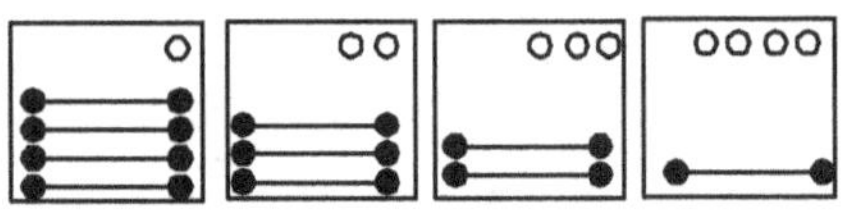

Answer Figures:

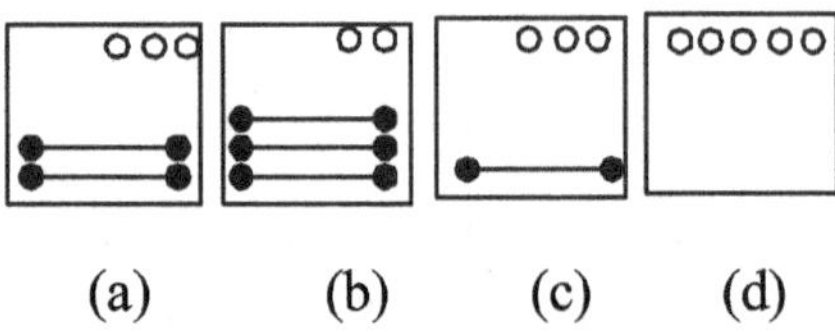

(a) (b) (c) (d)

DIRECTIONS (Qs. 21-24): *In each question, out of the four figures marked (a), (b), (c) and (d), three are similar in a certain manner. Howerer one figure is not like the other three. Choose the figure wchic is diffence from the rest.*

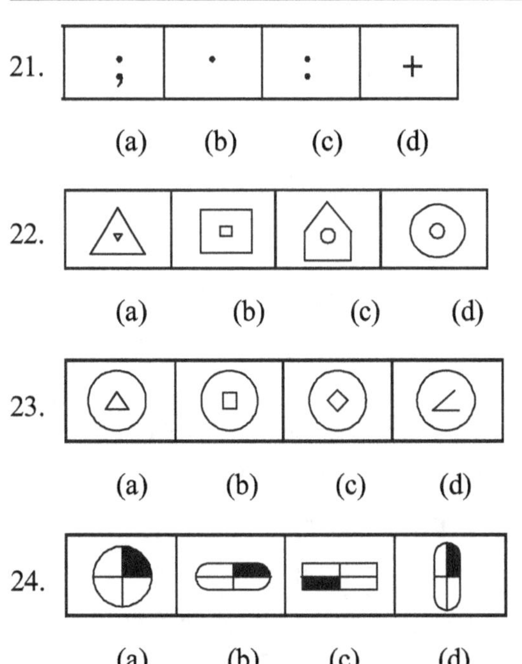

25. Find the missing number, if same rule is followed in all the three figures. **[2018]**

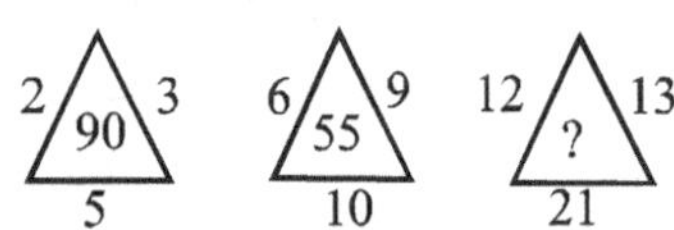

(a) 5336 (b) 1728

(c) 4339 (d) 3239

26. Select a figure from the options which will continue the same series as established by the Problem Figures. **[2018]**

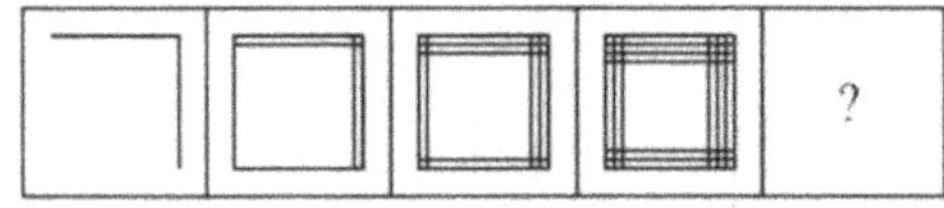

(a) 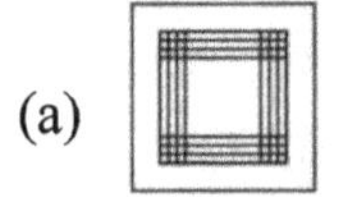 (b) 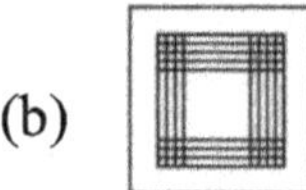

(c) 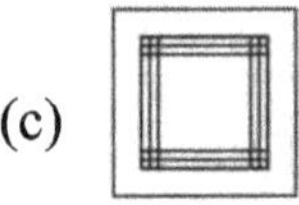 (d) 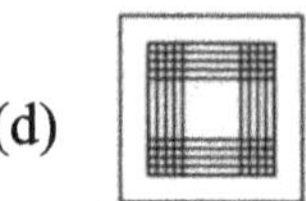

27. Select a figure from the options which will replace the (?) in the series as established by the Problem Figures. **[2018]**

ProblemFigures

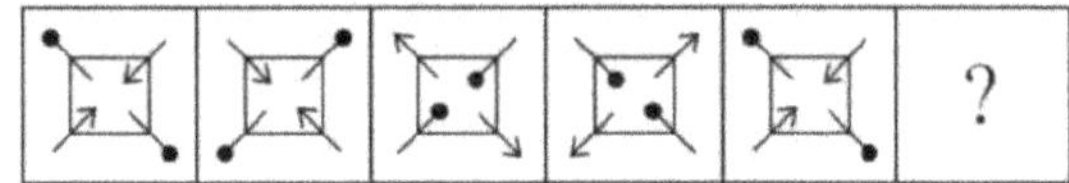

(a) 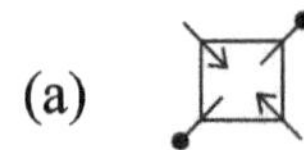 (b) 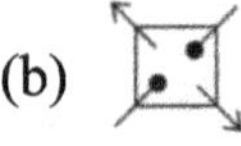

(c) 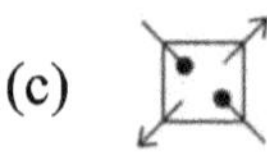 (d) 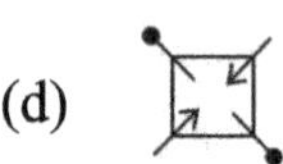

28. Find the missing number, if same rule is followed in all the three figures. **[2018]**

3	5	4
	7	

7	3	8
	53	

4	5	5
	?	

(a) 5 (b) 10

(c) 15 (d) 20

29. Find the missing number, if same rule is followed in all the three figures. **[2018]**

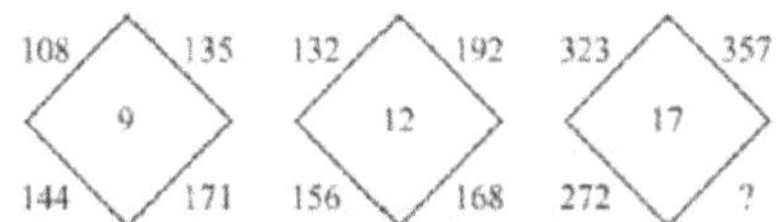

(a) 392 (b) 382
(c) 374 (d) 375

30. Find the missing character, if same rule is followed in all the three figures. **[2019]**

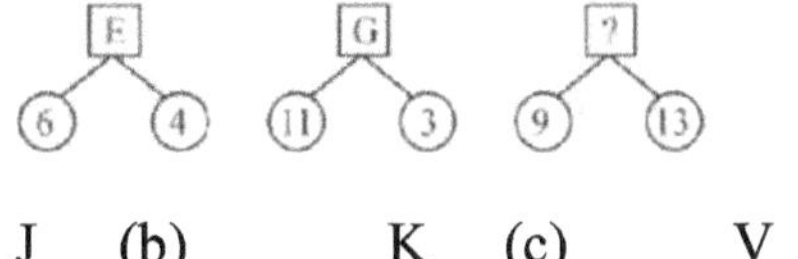

(a) J (b) K (c) V
(d) M

31. Find the missing number. **[2019]**

(a) 190 (b) 221
(c) 136 (d) 131

32. Find the missing character, if a certain rule is followed either row-wise or column-wise. **[2019]**

B	G	N
D	J	R
H	P	?

(a) Z (b) V
(c) W (d) X

33. Find the missing number, if a certain rule is followed either row-wise or column-wise. **[2020]**

42	28	38
28	35	23
39	?	37

(a) 7 (b) 21
(c) 14 (d) 18

34. Which of the following figures will continue the same series as established by the Problem Figures? **[2020]**

Problem Figures

C + / И ↑	И C / ↑ +	+ ↑ / C И	C + / И ↑	↑ И / + C

(a) И ↓ / C + (b) И C / ↑ +
(c) C + / И ↑ (d) + ↑ / C И

35. Find the missing number, if same rule is followed in all the three figures. **[2021]**

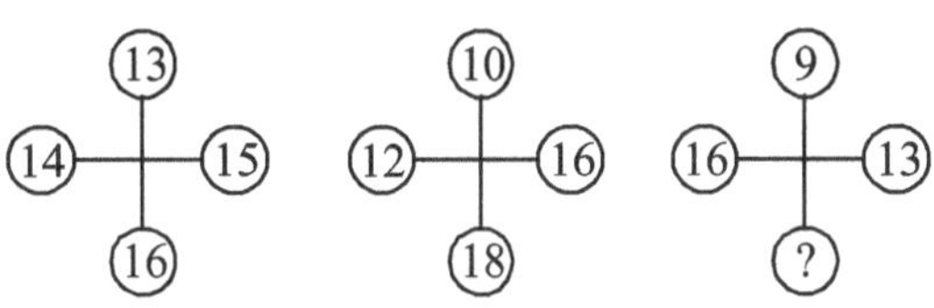

(a) 20
(b) 21
(c) 22
(d) 24

36. Select a letter-number pair from the given options to replace the question marks and complete the series. **[2021]**

1	D	?	P
A	4	?	16

(a) $\frac{J}{10}$ (b) $\frac{9}{I}$

(c) $\frac{M}{16}$ (d) $\frac{P}{11}$

37. Find the missing character, if same rule is followed in all the three figures. **[2021]**

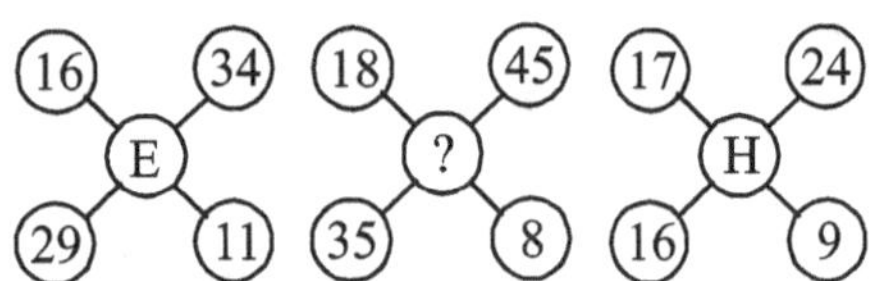

(a) J (b) F

(c) G (d) H

38. Find the missing number, if same rule is followed in all the three figures. **[2022]**

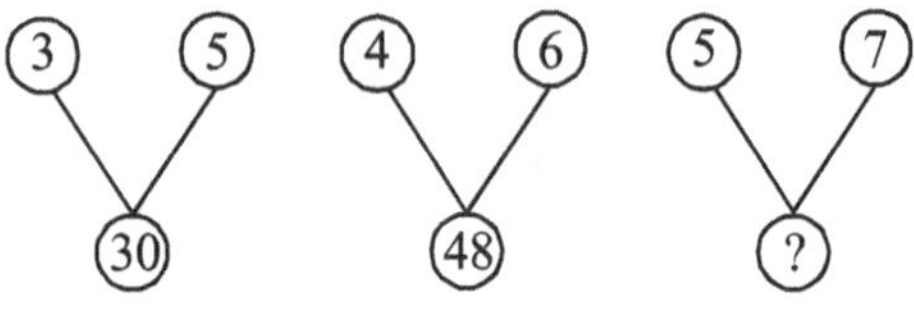

(a) 60 (b) 70

(c) 80 (d) 35

39. Which one of the following terms will replace the question mark(?) in the pattern given below?

?, W40M, U38P, S36S, Q34V, O32Y **[2022]**

(a) X39K (b) Y42J

(c) J42Y (d) Y44K

40. A series is given with one term missing. Choose the correct alternative from the given ones that will complete the series. **[2022]**

1, 9, 17, 33, 49, 73, ____?

(a) 100 (b) 99

(c) 97 (d) 89

41. Which one of the following terms will replace the question mark(?) in the pattern given below? **[2022]**

?	C13P	F17K	H19G	K23D	M25B

(a) A9V

(b) B12U

(c) A11V

(d) A12X

42. Find the missing number. **[2022]**

12	8	24
16	9	36
24	11	?

(a) 66

(b) 44

(c) 36

(d) 28

43. Which one of the following numbers will replace the question mark(?) in the number pattern given below?

[2022]

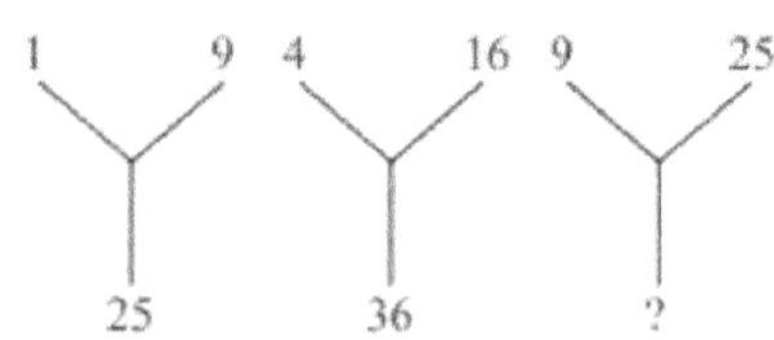

(a) 57 (b) 50

(c) 49 (d) 47

ANSWER KEY																			
LEVEL-1																			
1	(a)	**8**	(b)	**15**	(c)	**22**	(b)	**29**	(c)	**36**	(c)	**43**	(b)	**50**	(b)	**57**	(b)	**64**	(b)
2	(c)	**9**	(c)	**16**	(a)	**23**	(d)	**30**	(d)	**37**	(a)	**44**	(d)	**51**	(a)	**58**	(b)	**65**	(b)
3	(c)	**10**	(d)	**17**	(a)	**24**	(d)	**31**	(c)	**38**	(b)	**45**	(b)	**52**	(d)	**59**	(b)	**66**	(c)
4	(d)	**11**	(b)	**18**	(b)	**25**	(d)	**32**	(c)	**39**	(b)	**46**	(a)	**53**	(b)	**60**	(b)	**67**	(d)
5	(b)	**12**	(b)	**19**	(c)	**26**	(c)	**33**	(c)	**40**	(a)	**47**	(c)	**54**	(a)	**61**	(b)	**68**	(c)
6	(d)	**13**	(a)	**20**	(b)	**27**	(d)	**34**	(a)	**41**	(c)	**48**	(d)	**55**	(c)	**62**	(c)		
7	(a)	**14**	(c)	**21**	(a)	**28**	(a)	**35**	(a)	**42**	(b)	**49**	(d)	**56**	(d)	**63**	(a)		
LEVEL-2																			
1	(a)	**6**	(d)	**11**	(c)	**16**	(b)	**21**	(d)	**26**	(b)	**31**	(d)	**36**	(a)	**41**	(c)		
2	(a)	**7**	(c)	**12**	(c)	**17**	(b)	**22**	(c)	**27**	(d)	**32**	(a)	**37**	(a)	**42**	(a)		
3	(b)	**8**	(a)	**13**	(a)	**18**	(c)	**23**	(d)	**28**	(c)	**33**	(c)	**38**	(b)	**43**	(c)		
4	(a)	**9**	(b)	**14**	(d)	**19**	(b)	**24**	(c)	**29**	(c)	**34**	(d)	**39**	(b)				
5	(d)	**10**	(c)	**15**	(d)	**20**	(d)	**25**	(a)	**30**	(b)	**35**	(a)	**40**	(c)				

CHAPTER 2

Analogy and Classification

CLASSIFICATION

Classification means 'to sort the items of a given group on the basis of a certain common quality they possess and then spot the stranger or odd one out'.

ODD ONE OUT WORDS CONCEPTS :

In this type of classification, four words are given, out of which three are almost same in matter or meaning and one word is different from the other three. One has to find out the word which is different from the rest.

DIRECTIONS (ILLUSTRATION 1-10) : Choose the option which is least like the others in the group.

ILLUSTRATION 1:

(a) Copper (b) Zinc

(c) Brass (d) Aluminium

Sol. Here, all except Brass are metals, while Brass is an alloy. Hence, the answer is (c).

ILLUSTRATION 2:

(a) Volume : Litre

(b) Time : Seconds

(c) Length : Metre

(d) Pressure : Barometer

Sol. In all other pairs, except (d), the second word is the unit to measure the first. On the other hand, barometer is an instrument.

ILLUSTRATION 3:

(a) Painter : Gallery (b) Actor : Stage

(c) Mason : Wall (d) Farmer : Field

Sol. Clearly, the answer is (c). In all other pairs, second is the working place of the first.

ILLUSTRATION 4:

(a) Lion : Roar (b) Snake : Hiss

(c) Frog : Bleat (d) Bees : Hum

Sol. Clearly, the answer is (c). In all other pairs, second is the noise produced by the first.

ODD ONE OUT LETTER COMPARISON:

In this classification of letters, four groups of letters or a series of letters are given as options. One has to select the option as answer which does not share the commonness of the others.

ILLUSTRATION 5:

(a) ABC : CBA (b) JKL : KLJ

(c) XYZ : ZYX (d) MNO : ONM

Sol. Clearly, the answer is (b). In all other pairs of groups, the letters in the second group are the letters of the first group written backwards.

GROUP OF NUMBERS :

The group of numbers can be consecutive numbers in natural or reverse series, multiplication, subtraction and mathematical rules can also be used to frame the groups.

ILLUSTRATION 6:

(a) 14, 28 (b) 40, 80

(c) 16, 32 (d) 15, 35

Sol. In each pair the second number is double the first number. In option (d), the number 35 should have been 30, the very reason as to why it is the odd one out.

ILLUSTRATION 7:

(a) 70 : 80 (b) 54 : 62

(c) 28 : 32 (d) 21 : 24

Sol. In each of the pairs except (b), the ratio of the two numbers is 7 : 8.

ILLUSTRATION 8:

(a) 16 : 64 (b) 9 : 36

(c) 36 : 216 (d) 49 : 343

Sol. Clearly, the answer is (b). In all other pairs contain square and cube of the same number e.g. $36 = 6^2$ and $216 = 6^3$.

CHOOSING THE ODD NUMERAL :

In this type of question, certain numbers are given, out of which all except one have some common property and hence are alike, while one is different and this number is to be chosen as the answer.

ILLUSTRATION 9:

(a) 8 (b) 64

(c) 125 (d) 28

Sol. **(d).** All except 28 are perfect cubes of some number.

ILLUSTRATION 10:

(a) 131 (b) 151

(c) 161 (d) 171

Sol. **(c)** The sum of the digits of each of the numbers except 161, is an odd number.

ANALOGY

In questions based on analogy, a particular relationship is given and another similar relationship has to be identified from the alternatives provided.

For example :

1. Action Object Relationship

ILLUSTRATION 1:

Shoot is to Gun as Eat is to ....

(a) Hunger (b) Thirst

(c) Dinner (d) Fruit

Sol. **(d)** The relationship between the given words is that 'shoot' is the action and 'Gun' is the specified object of action . Similarly 'eat' is the action and 'fruit' is the specified object.

2. Antonym Relationship

ILLUSTRATION 2:

INTROVERT :EXTROVERT

(a) ANGLE : TANGENT

(b) EXTREME : INTERIM

(c) AGAINST : FAVOUR

(d) ACTION : LAW

Sol. **(c)** The related words are opposite in meaning.

3. Grammatical Relationship

ILLUSTRATION 3:

Clever is to Beautiful as Sour is to.........

(a) Lemon (b) Cunning

(c) Loathing (d) Taste

***Sol.* (b)** The related words are Adjectives.

4. Part Whole Relationship

ILLUSTRATION 4:

MAN : MAMMAL

(a) HALL : SNOW

(b) NATIVE : INHABITANT

(c) OFFSPRING : FAMILY

(d) LIBERTY : URBANISM

***Sol.* (c)** Man is a part of the whole species of mammal, so is an offspring of the whole family.

5. Sequence Relationship

ILLUSTRATION 5:

.........is to Dusk as Summer is to Monsoon.

(a) Evening

(b) Dawn

(c) Night

(d) Noon

***Sol.* (a)** Summer season is immediately followed by monsoon (rainy season) and evening is immediately followed by dusk.

6. Volume Relationship

ILLUSTRATION 6:

GALLONS : SWIMMING POOL

(a) SPECTATORS : AUDITORIUM

(b) CURRENCY : SHARES

(c) DUST : MOUNTAIN

(d) BOOKS : CATALOGUE

***Sol.* (a)** Gallons of water is needed to fill a swimming pool and large number of spectators can be admitted into an auditorium.

COMMON RELATIONSHIPS

1. Country and currency :

India : Rupee

Argentina : Peso

China : Yaun,

Iraq : Dinar

Kuwait : Dinar

Thailand : Baht

Bangladesh : Taka

Greece : Drachma

Japan : Yen

UK : Pound

UAE : Dirham

Burma : Kyat

Iran : Rial,

Korea : Won

USA : Dollar

Turkey : Lira

2. Quantity and Unit :

Length: Metre

Metre is the unit of measuring length.

Mass : Kilogram

Time : Seconds

Energy: Joule

Resistance: Ohm

Angle : Radians

Power: Watt

Work: Joule

Current: Ampere

Area: Hectare

Temperature: Degrees

Luminosity: Candela

Magnetic field: Oersted

Force: Newton

Volume : Litre

Potential : Volt

Pressure : Pascal

Conductivity: Mho

3. Animal and Young One :

Cow: Calf

Calf is the young one of cow.

Bear : Cub

Hen: Chick

Horse : Colt/Filly/Foal Lion/tiger : Cub

Duck: Duckling

Sheep : Lamb

Butterfly : Caterpillar

Stag: Fawn

Dog: Puppy

Deer: Fawn

Cockroach: Nymph

Cat : Kitten

Man : Child

Insect: Larva

Frog: Tadpole

Swan: Cygnet

4. Animal and Movement:

Duck: Waddle

Waddling is the name given to the movement of the duck.

Bird: Fly

Cock: Strut

Owl : Flit

Bear: Lumber

Elephant: Amble

Horse : Gallop

Lion: Prowl

Mouse: Scamper

Eagle : Swoop

Donkey: Trot

Lamb : Frisk

Rabbit : Leap

5. Animal/Thing and Sound:

Lion: Roar

Roar is the sound produced by a lion.

Donkey: Bray

Frog: Croak

Horse: Neigh

Snake : Hiss

Mice : Squeak

Cat: Mew

Camel : Grunt

Elephant : Trumpet

Cock: Crow

Owl : Hoot .

Crow: Caw

Duck: Quack

Bells : Chime

Drum : Beat

Thunder: Roar

Leaves : Rustle

Goat : Bleat

Jackal: Howl

Cattle : Low

Monkey: Gibber

Sparrow: Chirp

Hen: Cackle

Coins : Jingle

Rain : Patter

6. **Individual/Thing and Class :**

Lizard: Reptile

Lizard belongs to the class of Reptiles.

Man: Mammal Butterfly : Insect

Ostrich: Bird Snake : Reptile

Frog: Amphibian Pen: Stationery

Chair: Furniture Cup: Crockery

Whale: Mammal Rat : Rodent

Curtain: Drapery Shirt: Garment

7. **Animals/Things and Keeping Place:**

Car : Garage

A car is kept in a garage.

Aeroplane : Hangar Bees : Apiary

Animals : Zoo Clothes : Wardrobe

Grains: Granary Guns: Armory

Medicine: Dispensary Patient: Hospital

Birds: Aviary Fish: Aquarium

Curios : Museum Wine : Cellar

8. **Games and Place of Playing:**

Badminton : Court

Badminton is played on a court

Boxing: Ring Athletics : Stadium

Hockey: Ground Skating: Rink

Race: Track Tennis: Court

Exercise: Gymnasium Cricket: Pitch

Wrestling: Arena

9. **Worker and Tool:**

Blacksmith : Anvil

Anvil is the tool used by a blacksmith.

Carpenter : Saw Chef: Knife

Author: Pen Soldier: Gun

Doctor : Stethoscope Farmer: Plough

Gardener: Harrow Mason: Plumbline

Labourer: Spade Tailor: Needle

Woodcutter: Axe Warrior: Sword

Surgeon: Scalpel Sculptor : Chisel

10. **Worker and Working Place:**

Chef: Kitchen .

A chef works in a kitchen.

Farmer: Field Teacher: School

Sailor : Ship Engineer: Site

Doctor: Hospital Servant: House

Painter: Gallery Waiter: Restaurant

Umpire: Pitch Gambler: Casino

Artist: Theatre Actor : Stage

Lawyer: Court Scientist : Laboratory

Clerk: Office Warrior : Battlefield

Grocer: Shop Worker: Factory

Beautician : Parlour Mechanic: Garage

Astronomer:Observatory

11. **Worker and Product:**

Mason: Wall

A mason builds a wall.

Choreographer: Ballet Dramatist : Play

Editor: Newspaper

Producer: Film

Architect: Design

Tailor: Clothes

Farmer: Crop

Author: Book

Carpenter: Furniture

Butcher: Meat

Cobbler : Shoes

Chef: Food

Poet : Poem

Goldsmith: Ornaments

Teacher: Education

12. Word and Synonym :

Abode: Dwelling

Abode means almost the same as Dwelling. Thus, Dwelling is the synonym of Abode.

Blend: Mix	Solicit : Request
Presage: Predict	Assign : Allot
Flaw: Defect	Fierce: Violent
Substitute: Replace	Mend: Repair
Presume: Assume	Brim : Edge
Sedate : Calm	Dissipate : Squander
Abduct: Kidnap	Vacant: Empty

13. Study and Topic:

Ornithology: Birds

Ornithology is the study of birds.

Seismology : Earthquakes

Entomology: Insects

Anthropology: Man

Cardiology: Heart

Pathology : Diseases

Physiology: Body

Phycology : Algae

Pedology: Soil

Palaeontology : FossilsIchthyology: Fishes

Taxonomy : Classification

Selenography : Moon

Botany : Plants

Mycology: Fungi

Haematology: Blood

Nephrology: Kidney

Herpetology: Amphibians

Eccrinology: Secretions

14. Word and Intensity :

Anger: Rage

Rage is of higher intensity than Anger.

Some more examples are given below :

Wish: Desire	Touch: Push
Sink: Drown	Quarrel: War
Famous: Renowned	Unhappy: Sad
crime : Sin	Moisten: Drench
Kindle: Burn	Error: Blunder
Refuse: Deny	Speak: Shout

15. Product and Raw Material :

Prism : Glass

Prism is made of glass.

Butter: Milk

Cloth : Fibre

Wine : Grapes

Fabric: Yarn

Road : Asphalt

Furniture: Wood

Shoes : Leather

Pullover: Wool

Omelette: Egg

Metal : Ore

Rubber: Latex

Linen: Flax

Oil : Seed

Paper: Pulp

Wall : Brick

Book: Paper

Sack : Jute

Jewellery: Gold

Jaggery : Sugarcane

RELATION ANALOGY

DIRECTIONS (ILLUSTRATION 7-8) : *There is a certain relation between two given words on one side of : : and one word is given on another side of : : while another word is to be found from the given alternatives, having the same relation with this word as the given pair has. Select the best alternative.*

ILLUSTRATION 7 :

Pigeon : Peace : : White flag : ?

(a) Enmity

(b) Victory

(c) Surrender

(d) War

***Sol.* (c)** Pigeon is a symbol of peace and white flag is a symbol of surrender.

ILLUSTRATION 8 :

Mature : Regressed : : Varied : ?

(a) Rhythmic

(b) Monotonous

(c) Decorous

(d) Obsolete

***Sol.* (b)** The words in each pair are opposites of each other.

SIMPLE ANALOGY

DIRECTIONS (EXAMPLE 9-10) : *For the following questions, choose the best option.*

ILLUSTRATION 9:

Cyclone is related to Anticyclone in the same way as Flood is related to .... ? ....

(a) Devastation (b) Havoc

(c) River (d) Drought

***Sol.* (d)** Both words are opposite to each other.

ILLUSTRATION 10 :

Accident is related to Carefulness in the same way as Disease is related to .... ?

(a) Sanitation (b) Treatment

(c) Medicine (d) Doctor

***Sol.* (a)** Lack of second results in the first.

CHOOSING A SIMILAR WORD

DIRECTIONS (ILLUSTRATION 11-12) : *In each of the following questions, a group of three interrelated words is given. Choose a word from the given alternatives that belongs to the same group.*

ILLUSTRATION 11 :

Potato : Carrot : Raddish

(a) Tomato (b) Spinach

(c) Sesame (d) Groundnut

***Sol.* (d)** All grow underground.

ILLUSTRATION 12 :

Patna : Mumbai : Dispur

(a) Cochin (b) Trombay

(c) Udaipur (d) Chennai

***Sol.* (d)** All are Capitals of states

DETECTING ANALOGIES

DIRECTIONS (ILLUSTRATION 13-14) : *In each question three words in bold letters are given which have something in common among themselves. Out of the four given alternatives, choose the most appropriate description about these three words.*

ILLUSTRATION 13 :

Mars : Mercury : Venus :

(a) They have no opposite motion

(b) They are evil planets

(c) They are the planets nearest to the earth

(d) They have no corresponding lucky stone.

***Sol.* (c)**

ILLUSTRATION 14 :

Canoe : Yacht : Dinghy

(a) These are tribal people

(b) These are famous clubs

(c) These are names of boats

(d) These are rest houses

***Sol.* (c)**

THREE WORD ANALOGY

DIRECTIONS (ILLUSTRATION 15-16) : *In each of the following questions, some words are given which are related in some way. The same relationship is obtained among the words in one of the four alternatives given under it. Find the correct alternative.*

ILLUSTRATION 15:

Evaporation : Cloud : Rain

(a) Sneezing : Cough : Cold

(b) Accident : Injury : Pain

(c) Tanning : Leather : Purse

(d) Bud : Flower : Fragrance

***Sol.* (b)** First causes the second and second leads to the third.

ILLUSTRATION 16:

Lizard : Reptile : Insects

(a) Fox : Wolf : Forest

(b) Fly : Insect : Bee

(c) Man : Mammals : Meat

(d) Tiger : Mammal : Deer

***Sol.* (c)** Second denotes the class to which the first belongs. Also, first feeds on the third.

NUMBER ANALOGY

DIRECTIONS (ILLUSTRATION 17-18) : *In the following question, there is a certain relation between two given numbers on one side of : : and one number is given on another side of : : while another number is to be found from the given alternatives, having the same relation with this number as the numbers of the given pair. Choose the best alternative:*

ILLUSTRATION 17 :

583 : 293 : : 488 : ?

(a) 777 (b) 945

(c) 1155 (d) 324

***Sol.* (b)** Sum of digits of the first number is 2 more than the sum of digits of the second number.

ILLUSTRATION 18 :

5 : 35 : : ?

(a) 7 : 77 (b) 9 : 45

(c) 11 : 55 (d) 3 : 24

***Sol.* (a)** The first number is multiplied by the next prime number to obtain the second number.

ALPHABET ANALOGY

DIRECTIONS (ILLUSTRATION 19-20) : *In each of the following questions, there is some relationship between the two terms to the left of : : and the same relationship holds between the two terms to its right. Also, in each question, one term either to the right of : : or to the left of it is missing. This term is given as one of the alternatives below each question. Find out this term.*

ILLUSTRATION 19 :

ACE : FHJ: : OQS : ?

(a) PRT (b) RTU

(c) TVX (d) UWY

***Sol.* (c)** Each letter of the first group is moved five steps forward to obtain the corresponding letter of the second group.

ILLUSTRATION 20:

BUCKET : ACTVBDJLDFSU : : BONUS : ?

(a) ACMNMOTVRT

(b) SUNOB

(c) ACNPMOTVRT

(d) ACMNMOTURT

***Sol.* (c)** Each letter of the first group is replaced by two letters - one that comes after it and one that comes before it, in the second group.

PYRAMIDS :

Brief review of concepts : The questions in this unit are based on the pyramid of numbers from 1 to 100, as given below.

1
2 3 4
9 8 7 6 5
10 11 12 13 14 15 16
25 24 23 22 21 20 19 18 17
26 27 28 29 30 31 32 33 34 35 36
49 48 47 46 45 44 43 42 41 40 39 38 37
50 51 52 53 54 55 56 57 58 59 60 61 62 63 64
81 80 79 78 77 76 75 74 73 72 71 70 69 68 67 66 65
82 83 84 85 86 87 88 89 90 91 92 93 94 95 96 97 98 99 100

Many types of questions are possible based on the above pattern. For instance, formation of parallel lines, perpendicular lines, triangles, squares etc. by taking numbers in order.

ILLUSTRATION 21 :

Fill the blanks from the choice given below.

129 : 145 : : 3811 : ?

(a) 3713 (b) 328

(c) 346 (d) 3615

***Sol.* (d)** There are two groups of numbers. The numbers on the right hand side must have the same relation as the numbers on the left hand side. 129 and 145, in the above pyramid, from a pattern.

Hence, the number in the blank on the right hand side must form same pattern with 3811. Therefore, the answer is 3615 which forms the pattern.

ILLUSTRATION 22 :

Fill the blank from the choice given below.

2812 : 765 : : 91123: ?

(a) 121110 (b) 121314

(c) 122132 (d) 303132

***Sol.* (b)** The two numbers on the left hand side from perpendicular line in the pyramid . Therefore, the numbers on the right hand side must be of the same pattern .The answer to the above question should be (2) 121314 to satisfy the same relation.

NON VERBAL ANALOGY

In these type of question, four figures (a),(b),(c), and (d) are given. These are treated both as Problem Figures as well as the Answer Figures. Out of these four figures are related to each other by way of having some common three characteristics and so form a group. Out of these four, you have to identify one figure which does not belong to the group.

Hence the problems are of odd-man-out type.

ILLUSTRATION 23 :

Choose the figure which is different from the others.

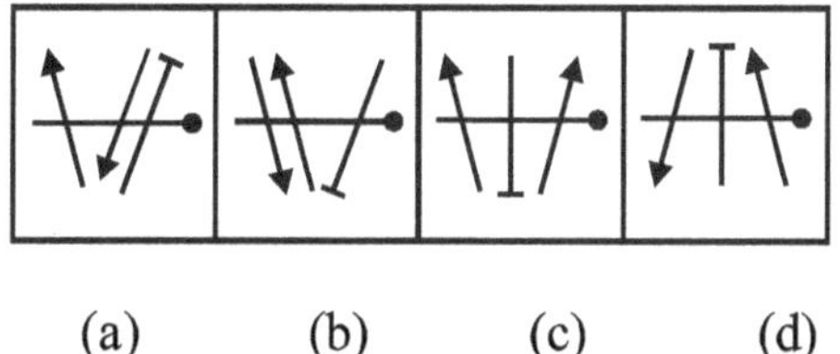

(a) (b) (c) (d)

***Sol.* (c)** Both the arrowheads are in the same direction in figure (c). In all other figures, they are in the opposite direction. Hence, (c) is the answer.

ILLUSTRATION 24 :

Choose the figure which is different from the others.

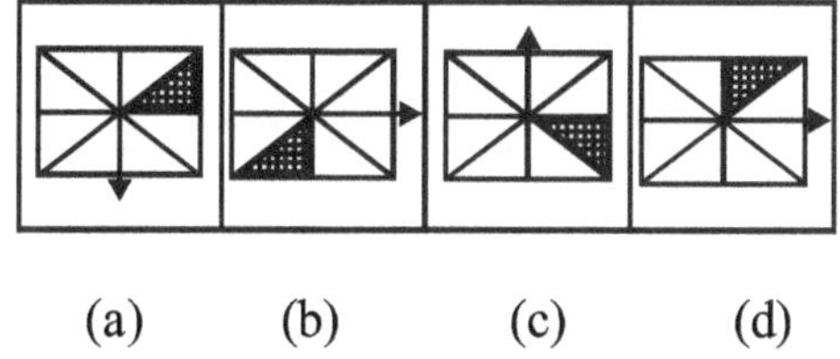

(a) (b) (c) (d)

***Sol.* (d)** Between the shaded portion and the arrow, there are two triangles in figures (a), (b), (c), and (d). Hence (d) is the answer

ILLUSTRATION 25 :

Identify the figure which is different from the remaining.

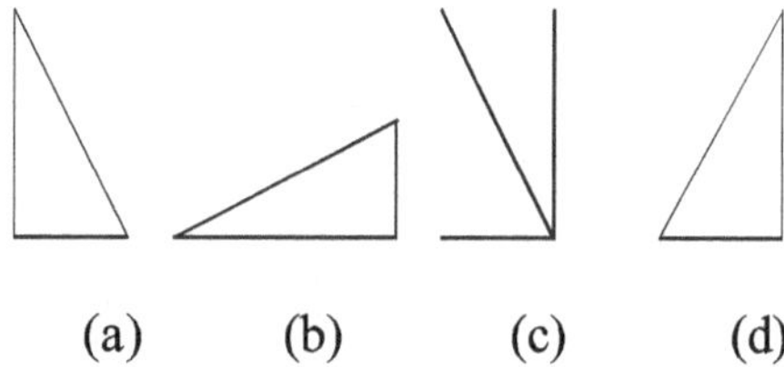

(a) (b) (c) (d)

***Sol.* (d)** Figures (a) to (d) can be obtained from one another by rotating suitably in the clockwise or anticlockwise direction.

Figure no. (d) cannot be obtained by rotation.

ILLUSTRATION 26 :

Choose the figure which is different from the others.

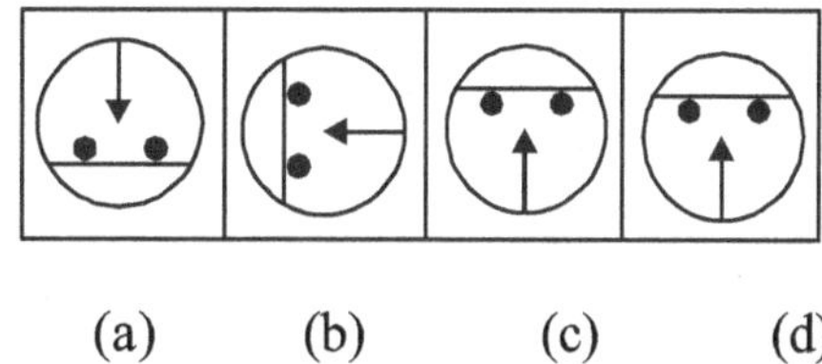

(a) (b) (c) (d)

***Sol.* (d)** The figures form a series. The complete figure rotates 90° CW in each step. Fig. (d) does not fit in the series as it is the same as fig. (c).

Hence fig. (d) is the answer.

ILLUSTRATION 27 :

Choose the figure which is different from the others.

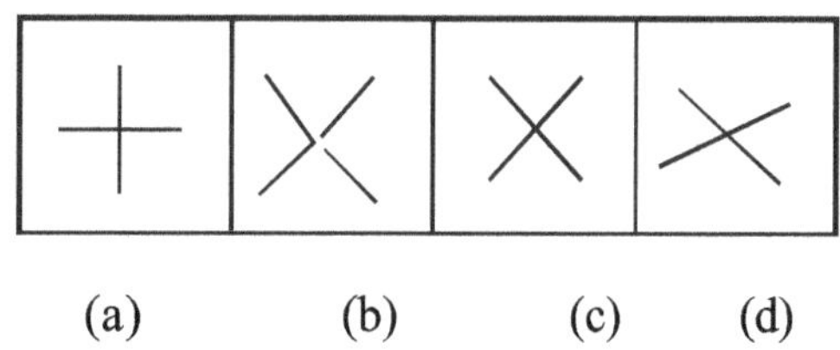

(a) (b) (c) (d)

***Sol.* (d)** The two lines cut at right angles in all the figures except (d).

The dictionary defines 'analogy' as a process of reasoning from parallel cases. These are also called relationship tests. The figures are presented in two sets ; one is called problem figure and the other answer figure. The problem figure consists of two sets. The first set has two units marked A and B. [Sometimes separated by the sign of colon (:)] and the second set (which is sometimes separated by the sign :) also has two units marked C and D. The figures in the first set bear a certain analogy or relationship with each other. The same relationship is reflected in the third figure of the second set. The fourth unit is either blank or contains a question mark (?). You have to choose from the set of answer figures marked A, B, C and D (sometimes E also) one figure bearing the same analogy in the first unit to fill the blank column or to replace the question mark.

DIRECTIONS (ILLUSTRATION 28-31) :

Each of the following examples consists of two sets of figures. Figures a, b, c and d constitute the problem set while figures (a), (b), (c), (d) and (e) constitute the answer set. There is a definite relationship between figures a and b. Establish a similar relationship between figures c and d and choose the one figure from answer set as the correct answer.

ILLUSTRATION 28 :

Problem Figures

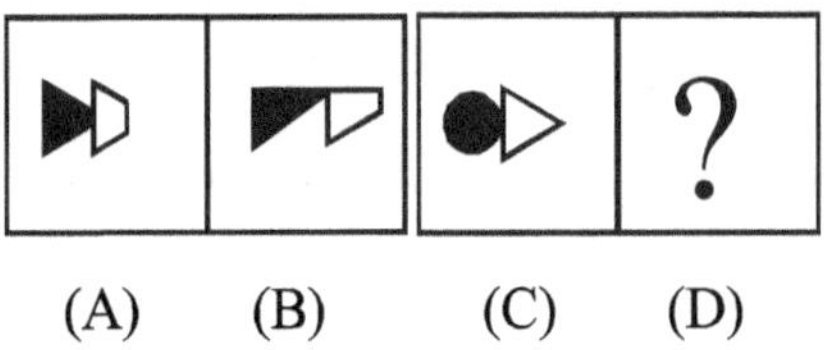

(A) (B) (C) (D)

Answer Figures

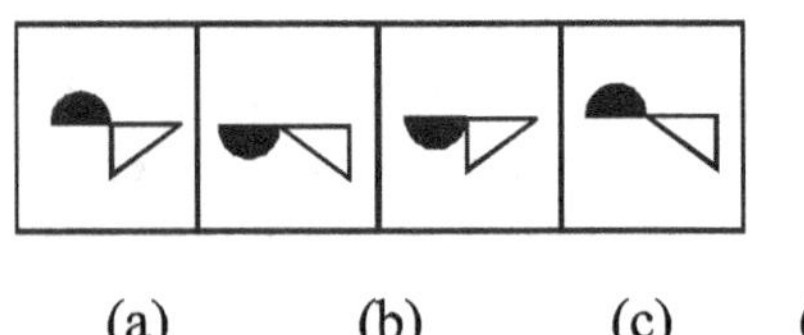

(a) (b) (c) (d)

***Sol.* (c)** (B) contains the lower half of (A). Answer figure (c) replaces the question mark.

ILLUSTRATION 29 :

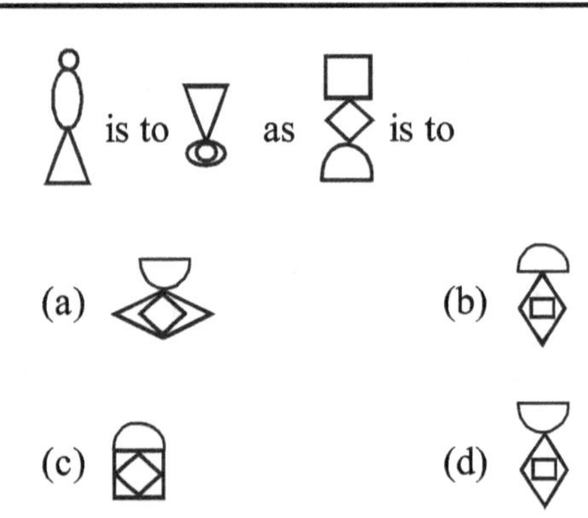

***Sol.* (d)** The diamond rotates 90°. The square goes inside the diamond. The semicircle rotates 180° and moves to the top.

ILLUSTRATION 30 :

Problem Figures

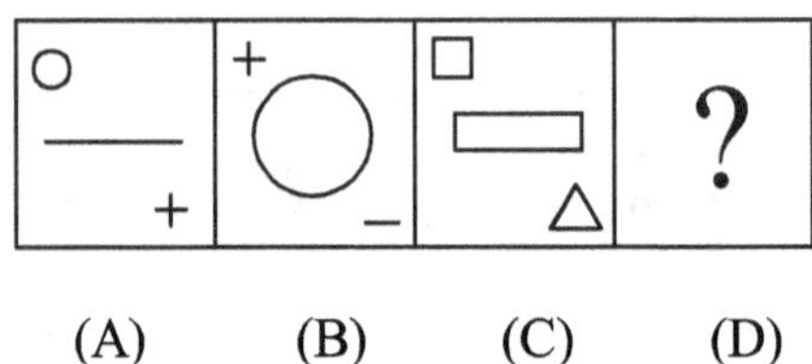

(A) (B) (C) (D)

Answer Figures

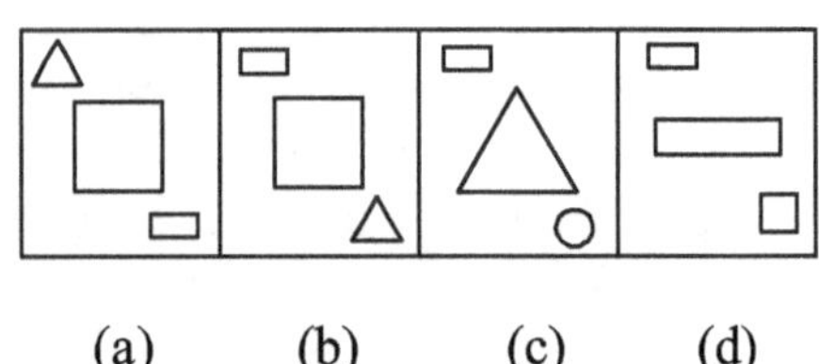

(a) (b) (c) (d)

***Sol.* (a)** The upper element gets enlarged and becomes the central element. The central element reduces in size and becomes the lower element. The lower element becomes the upper element.

ILLUSTRATION 31 :

Problem Figures

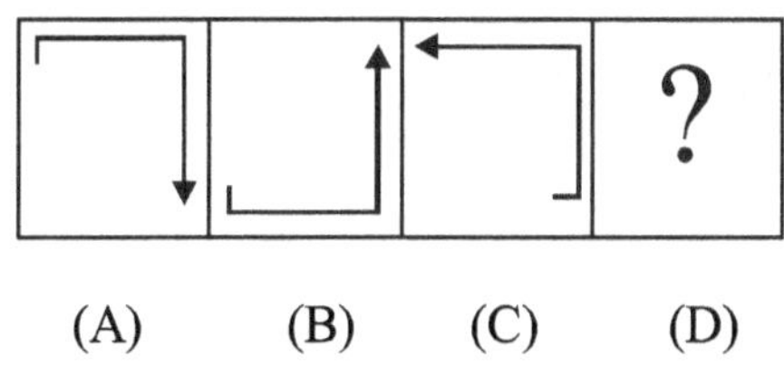

(A) (B) (C) (D)

Answer Figures

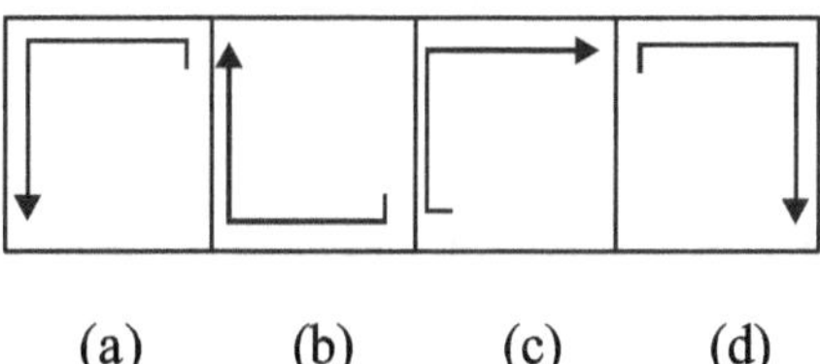

(a) (b) (c) (d)

***Sol.* (c)** The figure gets turned to the other side by rotating about the main line joining the arrow with the small line segment.

LEVEL 1

DIRECTIONS (Qs. 1-34) : *In each of the following questions, four terms/words have been given, out of which three are alike in some manner and one is different. Choose the odd one out.*

1. (a) Venus (b) Saturn (c) Earth (d) Mercury
2. (a) Metre (b) Furlong (c) Acre (d) Mile
3. (a) Raniganj (b) Jharia (c) Baroda (d) Bokaro
4. (a) Faraday (b) Newton (c) Edison (d) Beethoven
5. (a) Bottle : Wine (b) Cup : Tea (c) Pitcher : Water (d) Ball : Bat
6. (a) Atom : Electron (b) Train : Engine (c) House : Room (d) Curd : Milk
7. (a) Crime : Punishment (b) Judgment : Advocacy (c) Enterprise : Success (d) Exercise : Health
8. (a) Broad : Wide (b) Light : Heavy (c) Tiny : Small (d) Big : Large
9. (a) 001011 (b) 1101011 (c) 101101 (d) 100101
10. (a) 3,4, 8 (b) 6, 2, 9 (c) 2, 5, 7 (d) 2, 6, 9
11. (a) 3, 7, 5 (b) 2, 8, 6 (c) 7,9, 5 (d) 3, 8, 2
12. (a) 13, 50, 37 (b) 23, 39, 40 (c) 18, 38, 44 (d) 74, 10, 16
13. (a) 7, 4, 9 (b) 13, 36, 7 (c) 5, 25, 9 (d) 11, 16, 7
14. (a) Pen (b) Calculator (c) Pencil (d) Ink
15. (a) Snake (b) Lizard (c) Turtle (d) Whale
16. (a) Lake (b) Pond (c) Pool (d) Brook
17. (a) Club (b) Brush (c) Crayon (d) Pen
18. (a) Ring (b) Ornament (c) Necklace (d) Bangle
19. (a) Himachal Pradesh (b) Haryana (c) Punjab (d) Chandigarh
20. (a) April (b) May (c) July (d) September
21. (a) Engineer (b) Advocate (c) Doctor (d) Court
22. (a) He-goat (b) He-buffalo (c) Cow (d) Bull
23. (a) Plateau (b) Star (c) Mountain (d) Forest
24. (a) Haryana (b) Gujarat (c) Kerala (d) Tamilnadu

25. (a) DE (b) PQ
(c) TU (d) MO

26. (a) KP (b) MN
(c) HR (d) GT

27. (a) BCD (b) NPR
(c) KLM (d) RST

28. (a) PRT (b) MOQ
(c) GEC (d) TVX

29. (a) VWY (b) QRT
(c) LMO (d) JKL

30. (a) EBA (b) XUT
(c) TQP (d) JFE

31. (a) JOT (b) OUT
(c) FED (d) DIN

32. (a) PUT (b) END
(c) OWL (d) ARM

33. (a) STUA (b) RQPA
(c) MLKA (d) HGFA

34. (a) BDYW (b) CEXZ
(c) DFYW (d) EGXV

DIRECTIONS (Qs. 35-59) : *Out of the four choices given for each question, you have to select one that will maintain the relationship on the two sides of the sign : : the same if it is substituted for the question mark '?'*

35. 12 : 30 : : 20:?
(a) 25 (b) 32
(c) 35 (d) 42

36. 3 : 10 :: 8 : ?
(a) 10 (b) 13
(c) 14 (d) 17

37. 13 : 19 :: ? : 31
(a) 21 (b) 23
(c) 25 (d) 26

38. 48 : 122 : : 168 : ?
(a) 284 (b) 286
(c) 288 (d) 290

39. TSR : FED :: WVU : ?
(a) CAB (b) MLK
(c) PQS (d) GFH

40. ACBD : EFGH : : OQPR : ?
(a) STUV (b) RSTU
(c) UVWX (d) QRST

41. CEG : EGC : : LNP : ?
(a) LPN (b) UWY
(c) NPL (d) MOP

42. E : V : : I : ?
(a) Q (b) R
(c) S (d) T

43. ACE : FGH :: LNP : ?
(a) QRS (b) PQR
(c) QST (d) MOQ

44. Wine : Grapes :: Vodka : ?
(a) Apple (b) Potatoes
(c) Oranges (d) Flour

45. UVST : WtUr :: ? : RiLo
(a) P K J Q (b) T S U V
(c) U V T S (d) T S V U

46. Race : Fatigue : : Fast : ?
(a) Food (b) Appetite
(c) Hunger (d) Weakness

47. Moon : Satellite : : Earth : ?
(a) Sun (b) Planet
(c) Solar system (d) Asteroid

48. Ocean : Water : : Glacier : ?
(a) Refrigerator (b) Ice
(c) Mountain (d) Cave

49. Bank : River : : Coast : ?
(a) Flood (b) Waves
(c) Sea (d) Beach

50. Knife : Chopper : : ? : ?
(a) Walking : Fitness
(b) Swim : Float
(c) Scissors : Cloth
(d) Quilt : Blanket

51. Fury : Ire :: ? : ?
(a) Amusement : Happiness
(b) Joke : Laugh
(c) Cry : Hurl
(d) Convulsion : Spasm

52. Food : Hungry :: ? : ?
(a) Thought : Politics
(b) Water : River
(c) Rest : Weary
(d) Wine : Intoxication

53. Jute : Cotton : Wool : ?
(a) Terylene (b) Silk
(c) Rayon (d) Nylon

54. Basic : Pascal : Fortran : ?
(a) Cyclotrone (b) Computer
(c) Cobol (d) Bhopal

55. Man : Walk :: Fish : ?
(a) Swim (b) Eat
(c) Live (d) Sleep

56. Medicine : Sickness :: Book : ?
(a) Ignorance
(b) Knowledge
(c) Author
(d) Teacher

57. Supervisor : Worker ::
(a) Junior : Senior
(b) Elder : Younger
(c) Debtor : Creditor
(d) Officer : Clerk

58. NUMBER : UNBMER : : GHOST : ?
(a) HOGST (b) HOGTS
(c) HGOST (d) HGSOT

59. Ocean : Pacific :: Island : ?
(a) Greenland (b) Ireland
(c) Netherland (d) Borneo

60. Neck is related to Tie in the same way as Waist is related to–
(a) Watch (b) Belt
(c) Ribbon (d) Shirt

61. ACFJ is related to ZXUQ in the same way as EGJN is related to –
(a) DBYU (b) VTQM
(c) VTRP (d) VUSQ

62. 'Chapter' is related to 'Book' in the same way as 'brick' is related to
(a) heap (b) building
(c) clay (d) mason

63. *Chef* is related to *Restaurant* in the same way as *Druggist* is related to .....?

(a) Medicine (b) Pharmacy

(c) Store (d) Chemist

64. *Kilogram* is related to *Quintal* in the same way as *Paisa* is related to ......?

(a) Rupee (b) Coin

(c) Wealth (d) Money

65. Which of the following has the same relationship as that of 'PS' : 'TW'?

(a) JM : RQ (b) AD : DI

(c) AD : EH (d) FC : ZE

DIRECTIONS (Qs 66) : *In the following questions there is a specific relationship between the first and. second term. The same relationship exists between the third and fourth term which will replace the question mark (?). Select the correct term from the alternatives given :*

66. ACG : ZXT : : HJN : ?

(a) SQM (b) TRN

(c) SQN (d) SOM

DIRECTIONS (Qs. 67-82): *Choose the figure which is different from the others.*

67. **Problem figures**

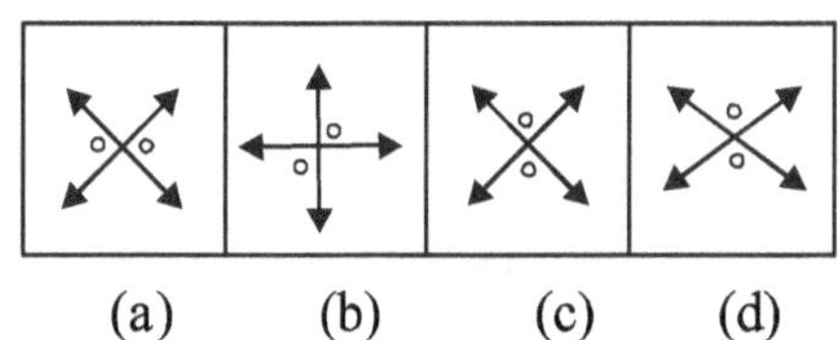

(a) (b) (c) (d)

68. **Problem figures**

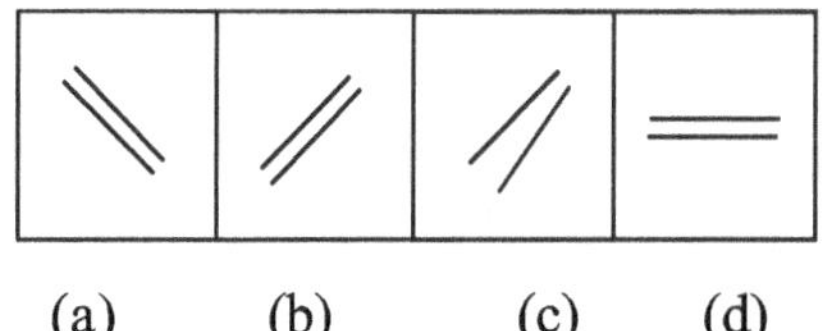

(a) (b) (c) (d)

69. **Problem figures**

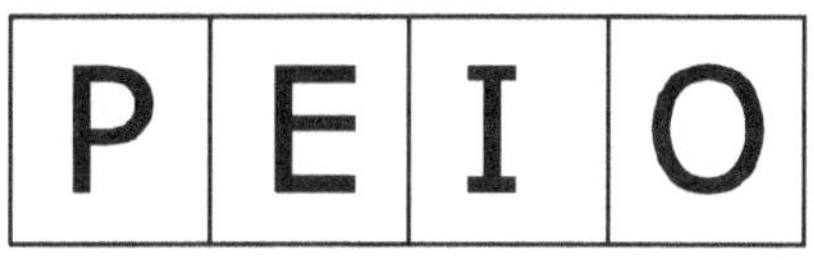

(a) (b) (c) (d)

70. **Problem figures**

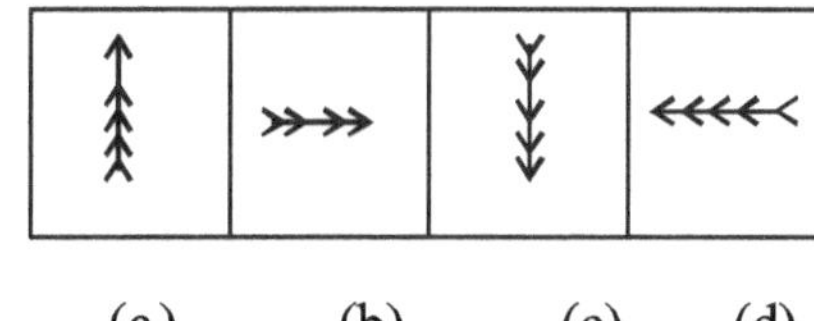

(a) (b) (c) (d)

71. **Problem figures**

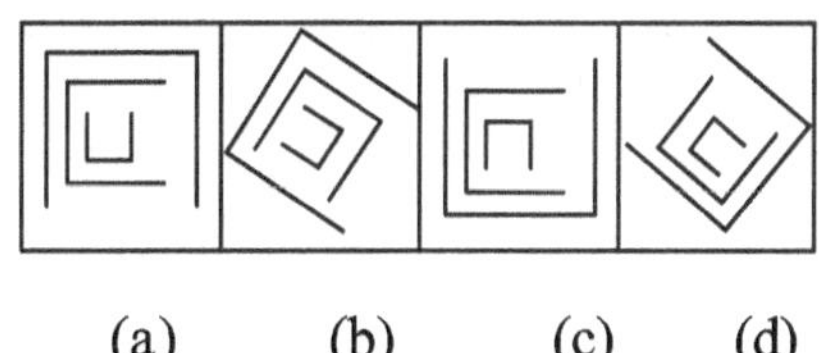

(a) (b) (c) (d)

72. **Problem figures**

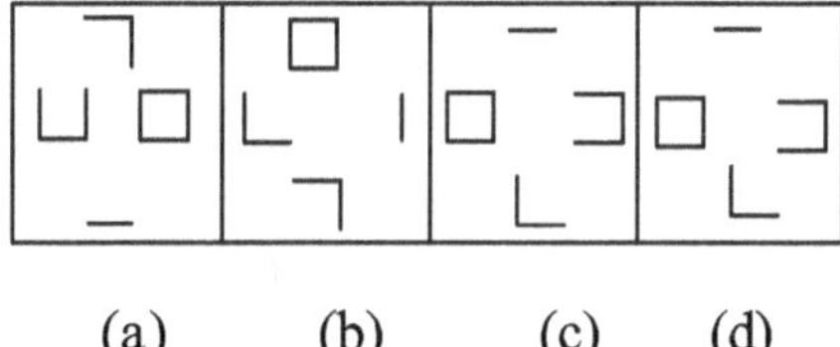

(a) (b) (c) (d)

73. **Problem figures**

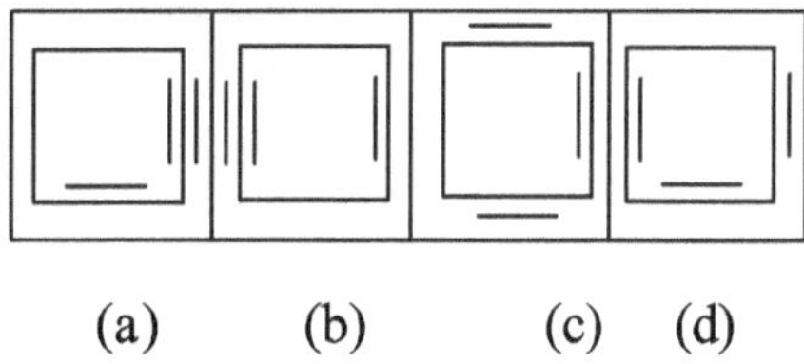

(a) (b) (c) (d)

74. **Problem figures**

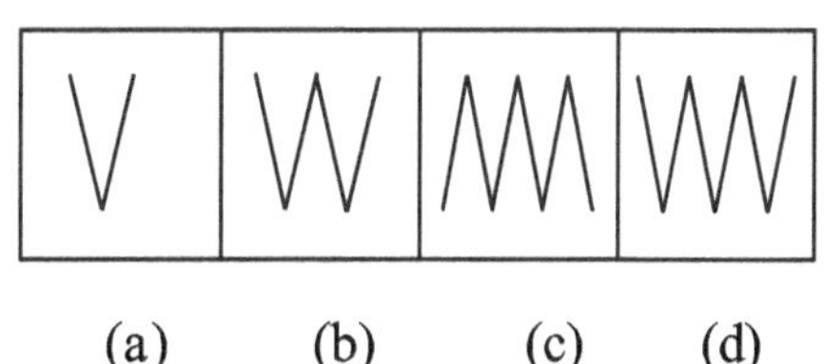

(a) (b) (c) (d)

75. **Problem figures**

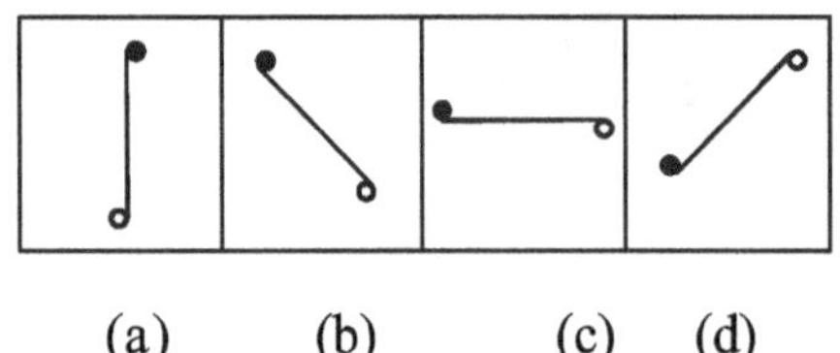

(a) (b) (c) (d)

76. **Problem figures**

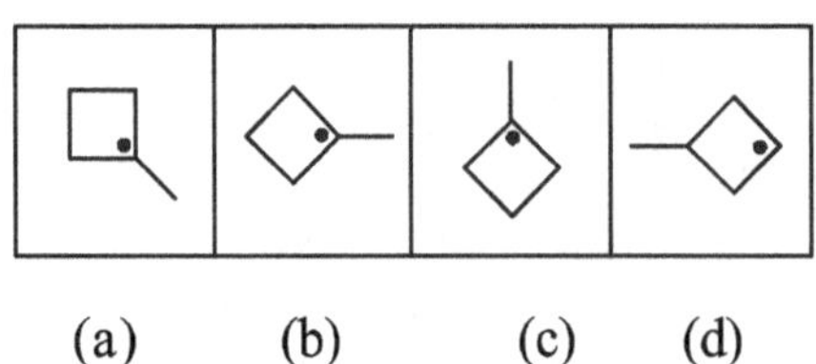

(a) (b) (c) (d)

77. **Problem figures**

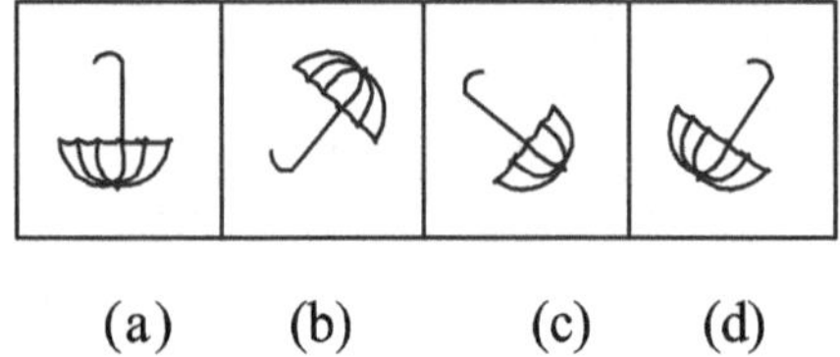

(a) (b) (c) (d)

78. **Problem figures**

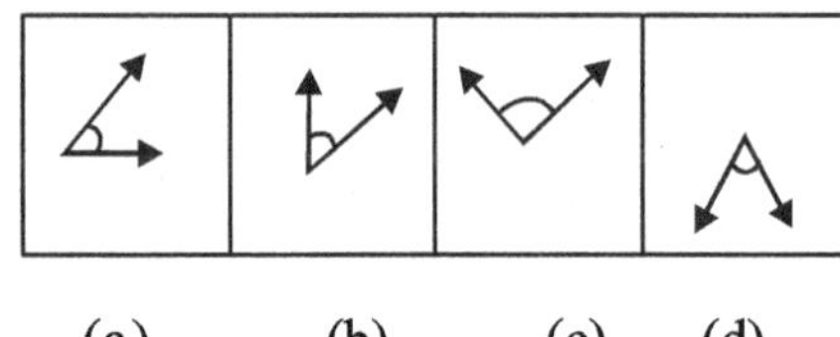

(a) (b) (c) (d)

79. **Problem figures**

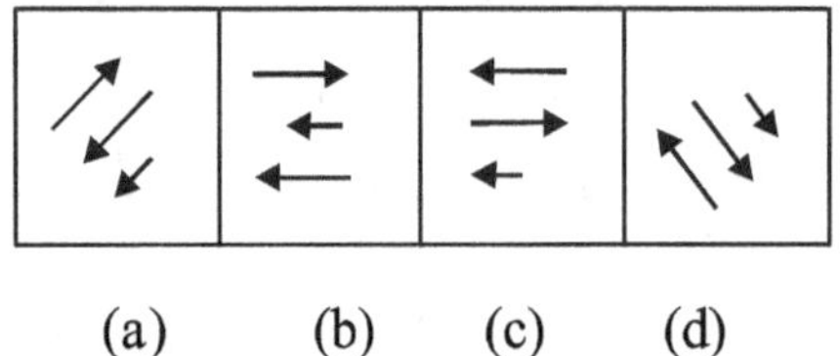

(a) (b) (c) (d)

80. **Problem figures**

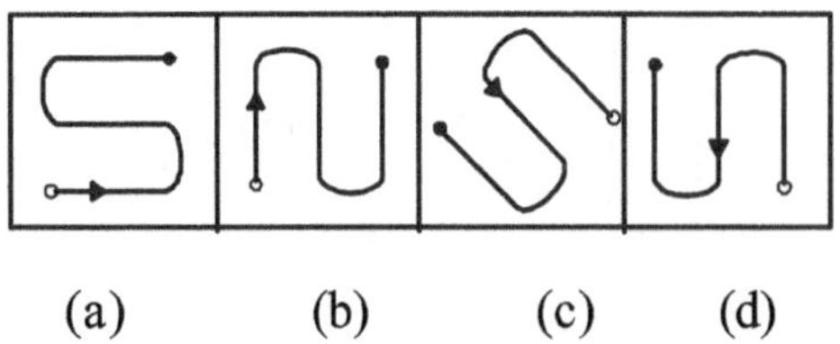

(a) (b) (c) (d)

81. **Problem figures**

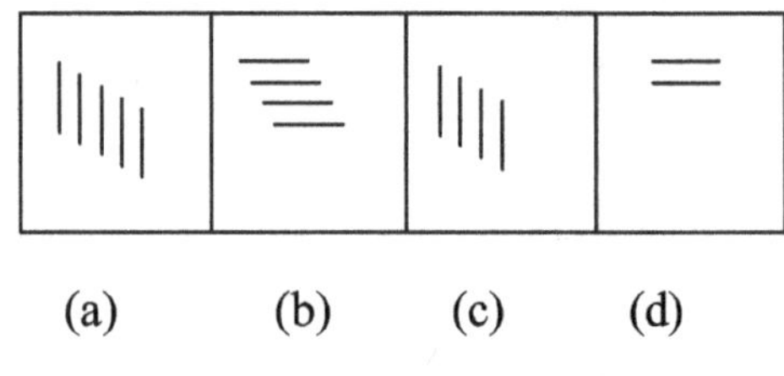

(a) (b) (c) (d)

82.

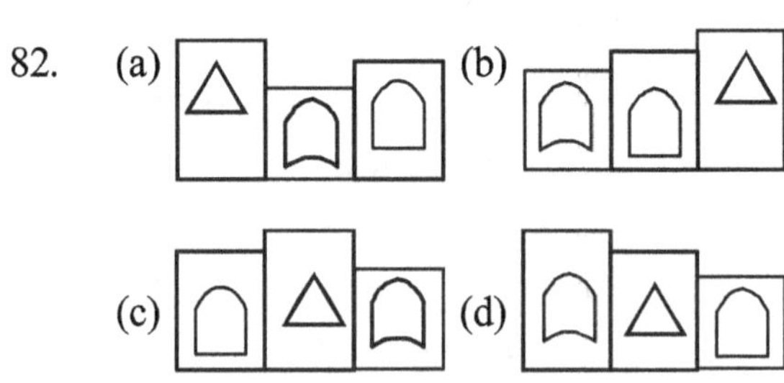

DIRECTIONS (Qs. 83-84) : *In each of the following questions, four pairs of figures are given in three of them; the first figure is related to the second figure in the same manner. Find the odd pair out which is different from others.*

83.

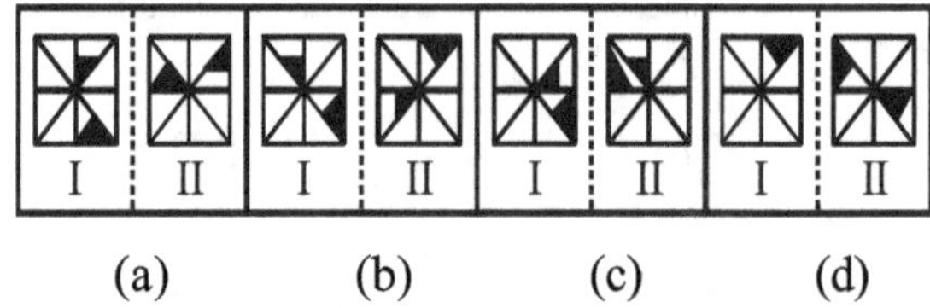

(a) (b) (c) (d)

84.

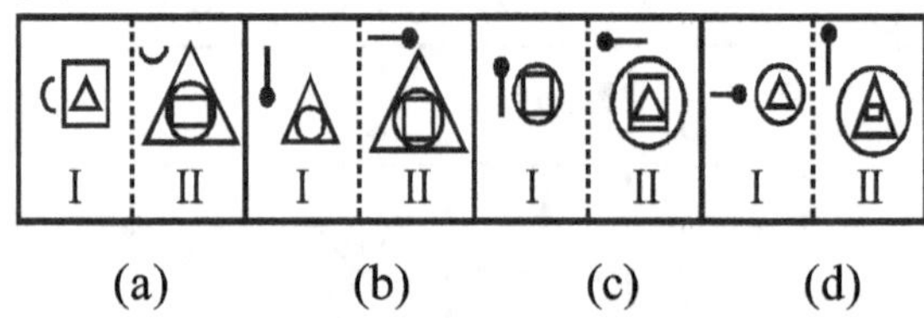

(a) (b) (c) (d)

DIRECTIONS (Q. 85) : *From the question has four terms. Three terms are alike in some way one term is different from three others. Find out the correct term which is different from three others and write its alternative number on your answer sheet against the proper question number.*

85.

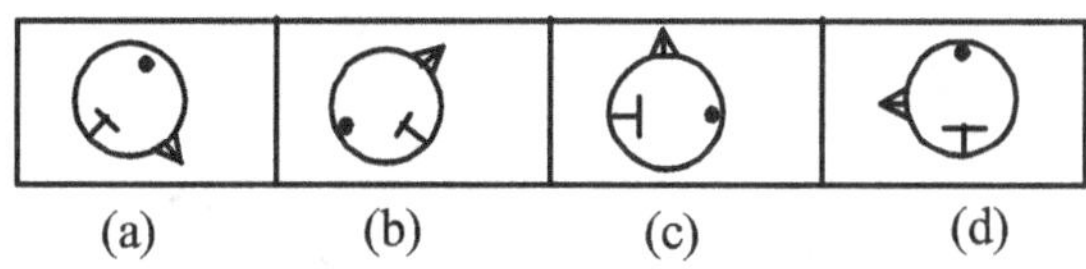

(a) (b) (c) (d)

DIRECTIONS (Qs. 86-97) : *Each of the following questions consists of two sets of figures. Figures A, B, C and D constitute the problem set while figures 1, 2, 3 and 4 constitute the answer set. There is a definite relationship between figures A and B. Establish a similar relationship between figures C and D and choose the one figure from answer set as alternative letter.*

86. **Problem Figures**

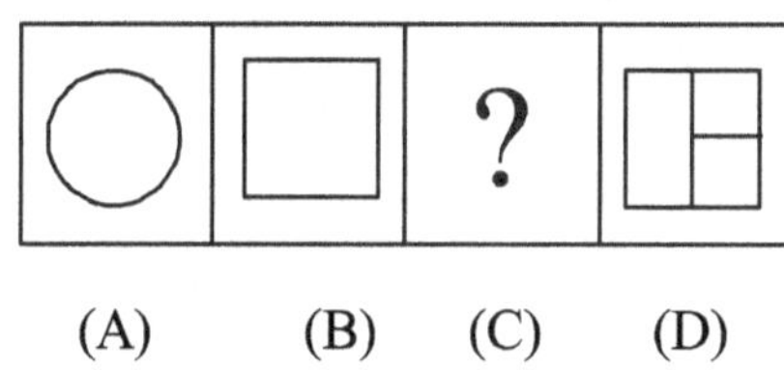

(A) (B) (C) (D)

Answer Figures

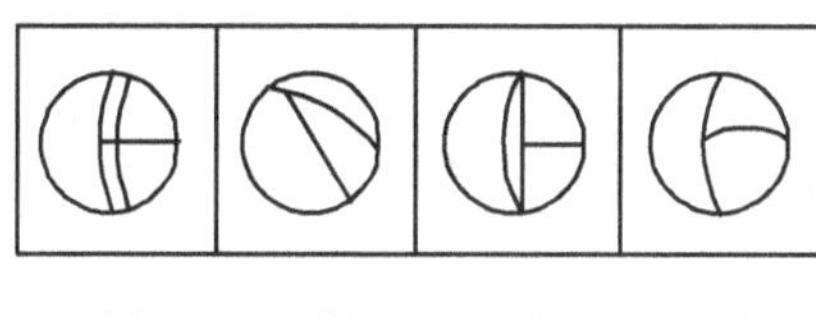

(a) (b) (c) (d)

87. **Problem Figures**

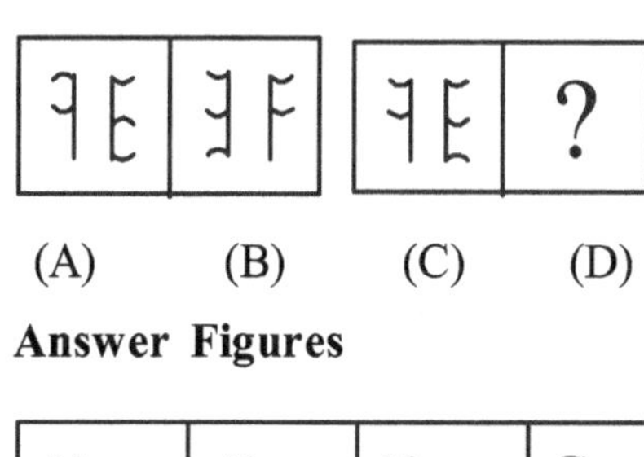

(A) (B) (C) (D)

Answer Figures

(a) (b) (c) (d)

88. **Problem Figures**

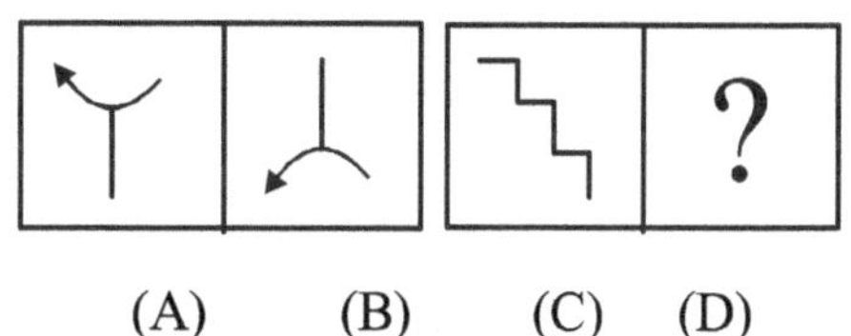

(A) (B) (C) (D)

Answer Figures

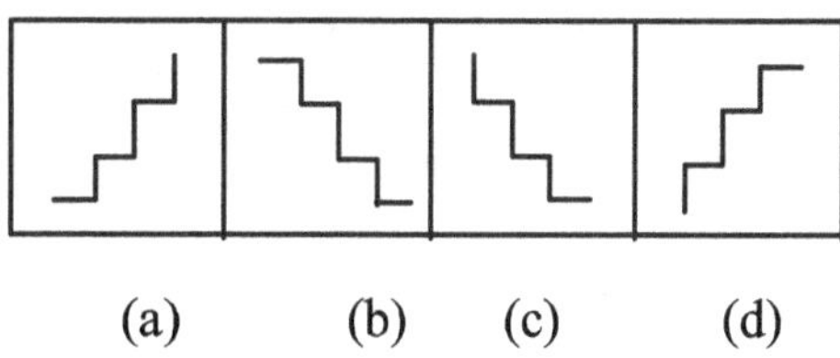

(a) (b) (c) (d)

89. **Problem Figures**

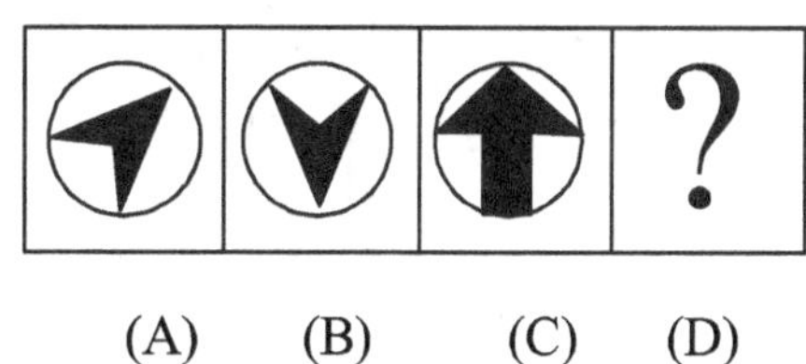

(A) (B) (C) (D)

Answer Figures

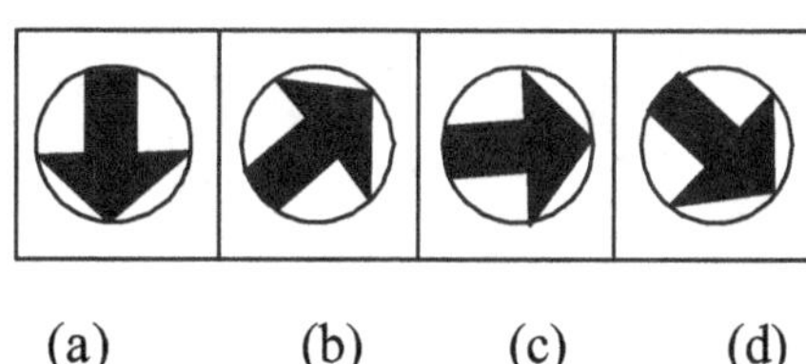

(a) (b) (c) (d)

90. **Problem Figures**

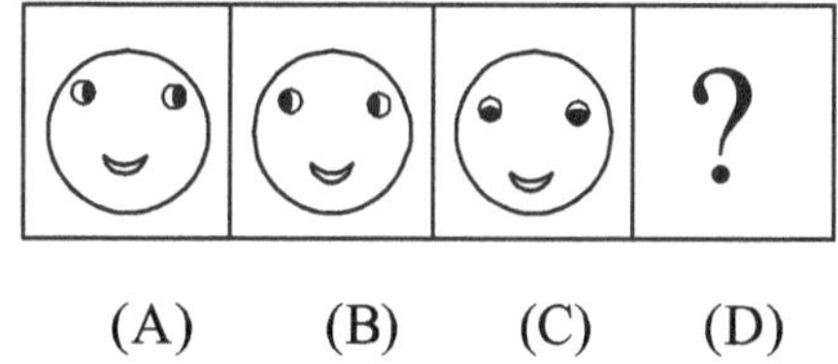

(A) (B) (C) (D)

Answer Figures

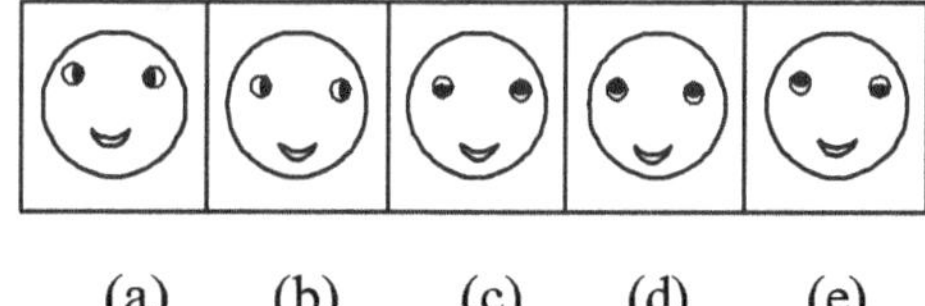

(a) (b) (c) (d) (e)

91. **Problem Figures**

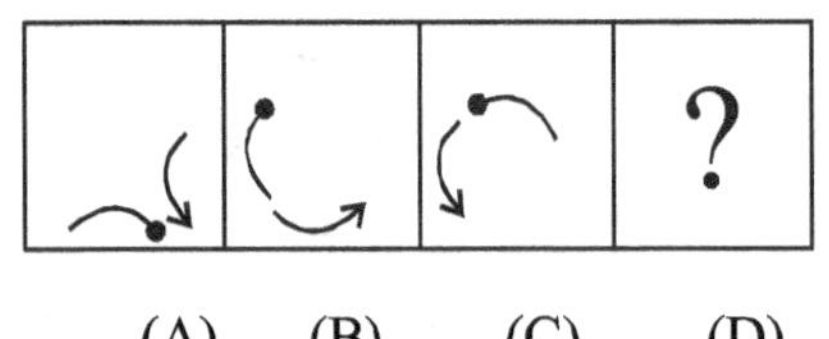

(A) (B) (C) (D)

Answer Figures

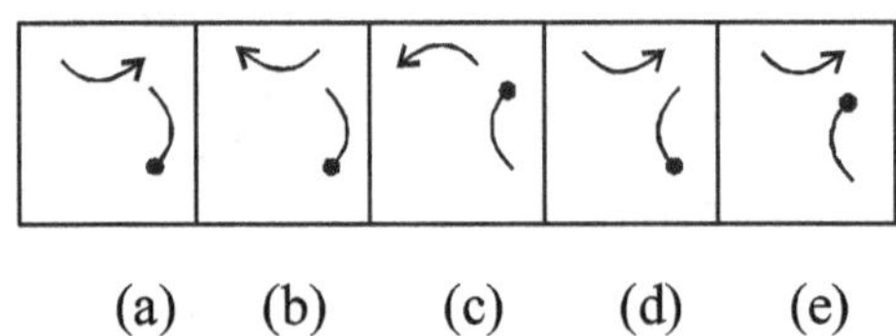

(a) (b) (c) (d) (e)

92. **Problem Figures**

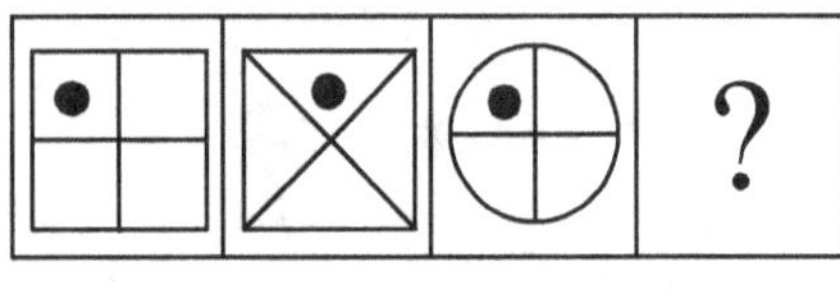

(A) (B) (C) (D)

Answer Figures

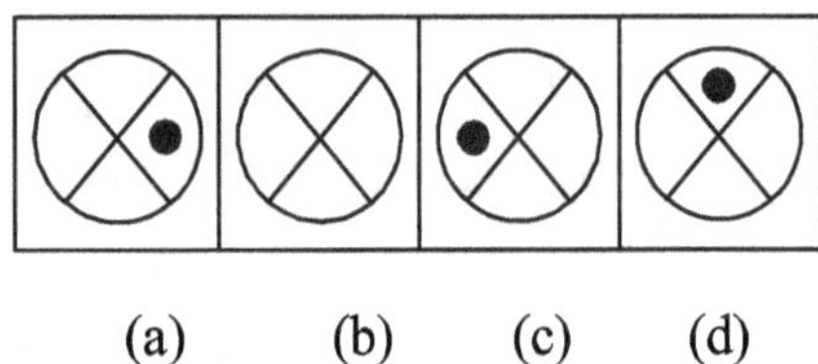

(a) (b) (c) (d)

93. **Problem Figures**

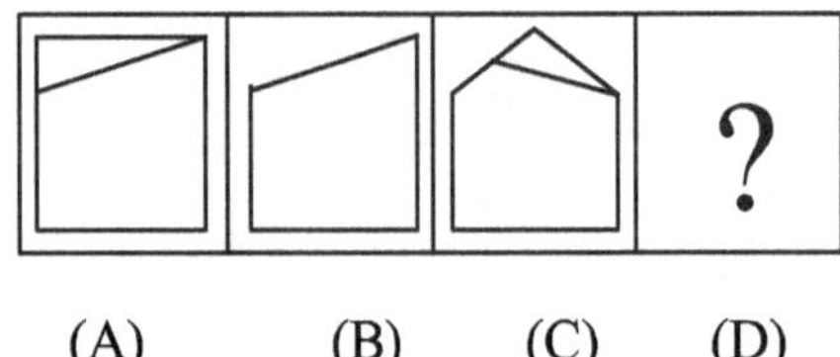

(A) (B) (C) (D)

Answer Figures

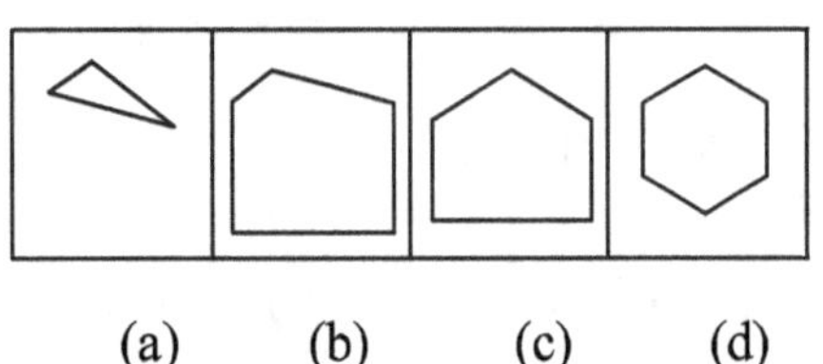

(a) (b) (c) (d)

94. **Problem Figures**

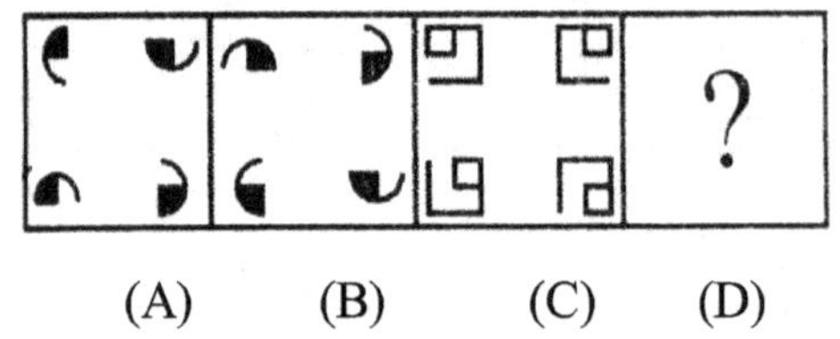

(A) (B) (C) (D)

Answer Figures

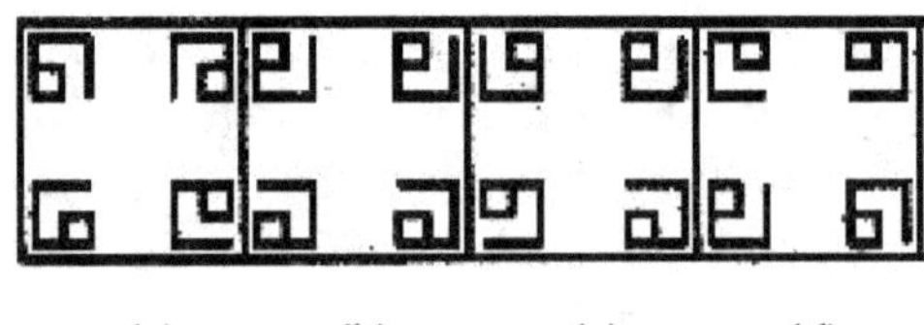

(a) (b) (c) (d)

95. **Problem Figures**

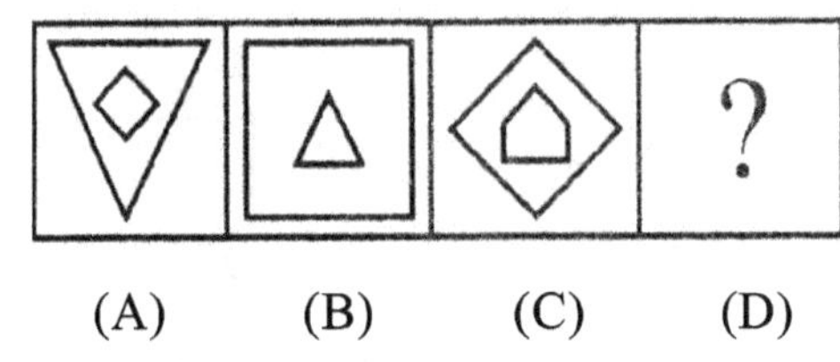

(A) (B) (C) (D)

Answer Figures

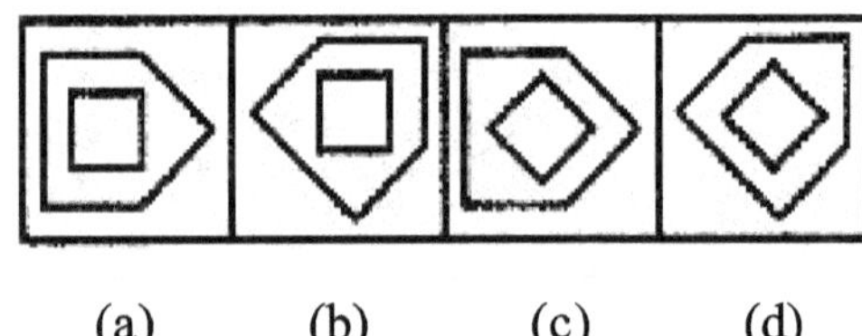

(a) (b) (c) (d)

96. **Problem Figures**

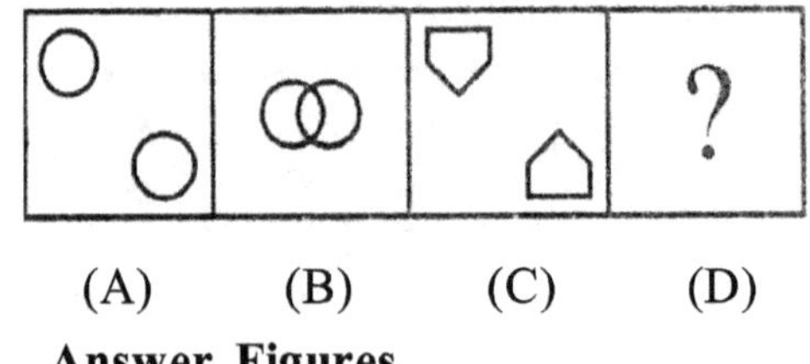

(A) (B) (C) (D)

Answer Figures

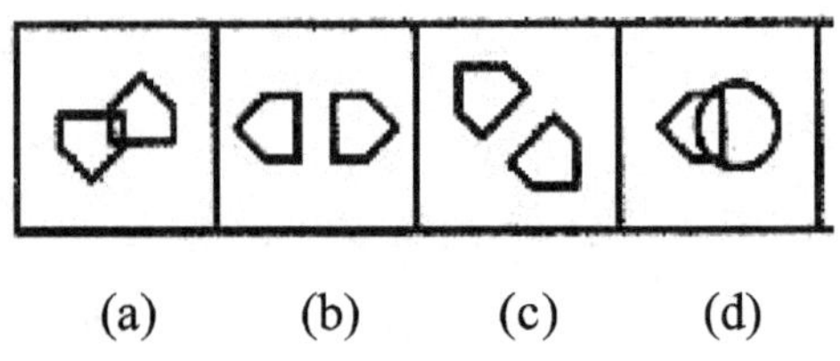

(a) (b) (c) (d)

97. **Problem Figures**

(A) (B) (C) (D)

Answer Figures

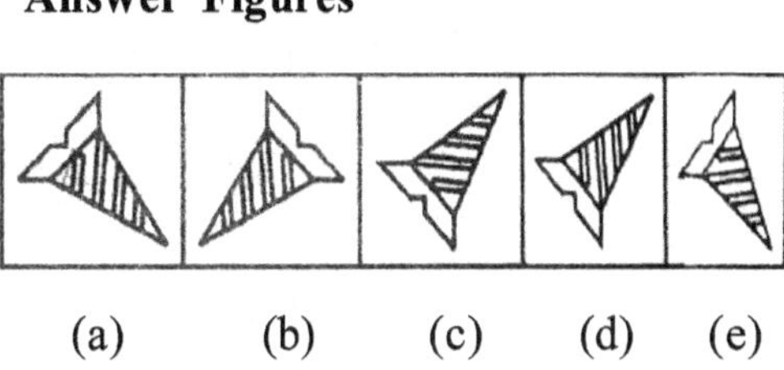

(a) (b) (c) (d) (e)

DIRECTIONS: *In questions 98 to 107, four figures (a), (b), (c), (d) have been given in each question. Of these four figures three figures are similar in some way and one figure is different. Select the figure which is different.*

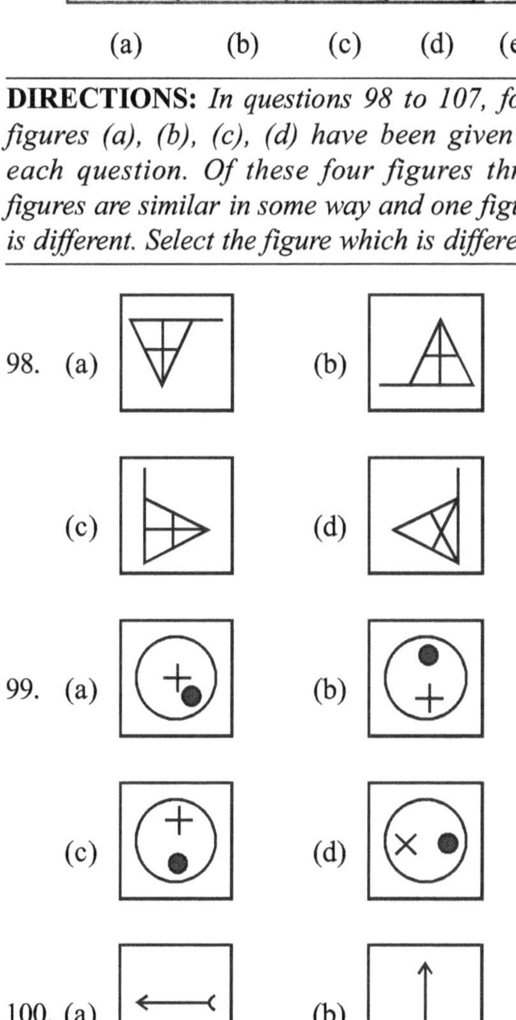

98. (a) (b) (c) (d)

99. (a) (b) (c) (d)

100. (a) 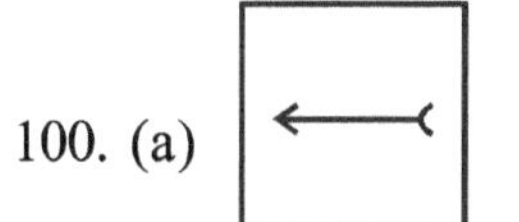 (b) 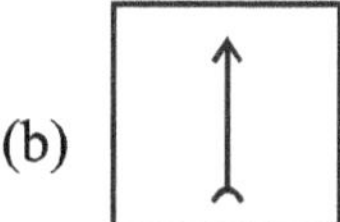

(c) 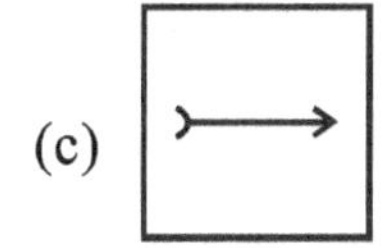 (d)

101. (a)  (b) 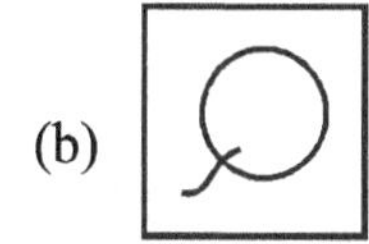

(c) 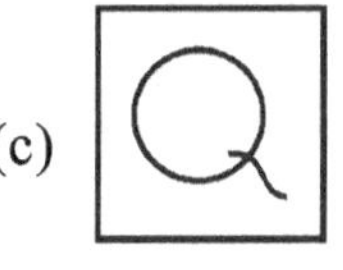 (d) 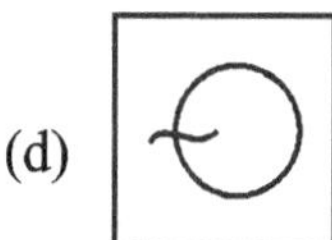

102. (a) 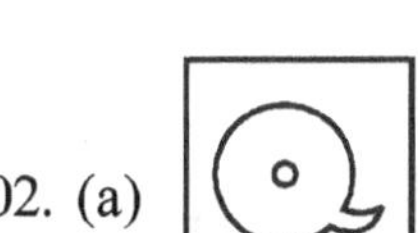  (b) 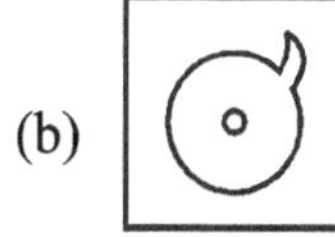

(c) 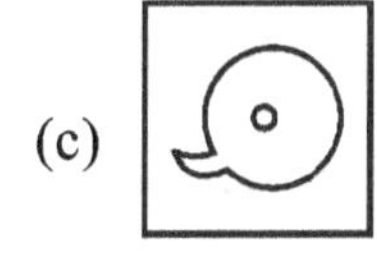 (d) 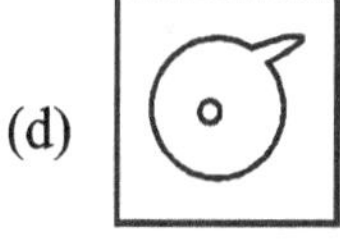

103. (a) 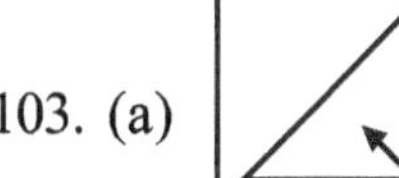 (b) 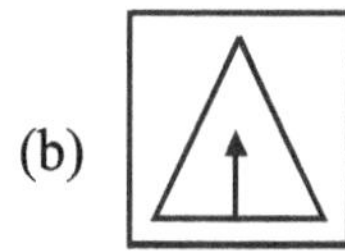

(c) 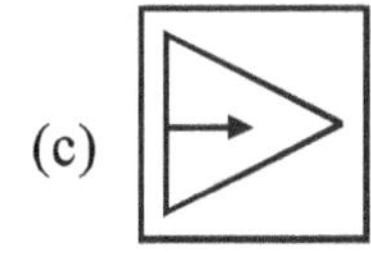 (d) 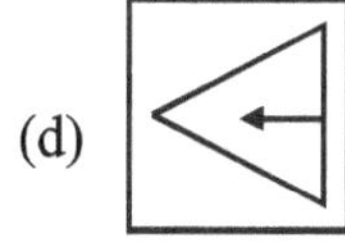

104. (a) 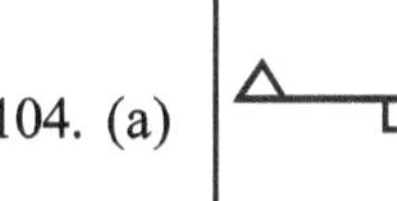 (b) 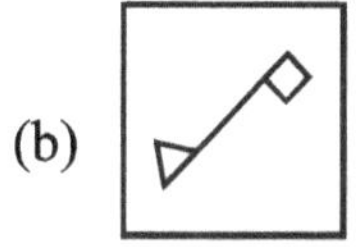

(c) 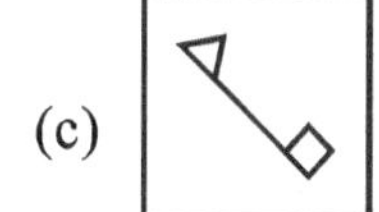 (d) 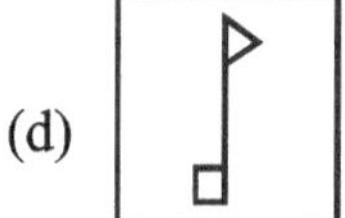

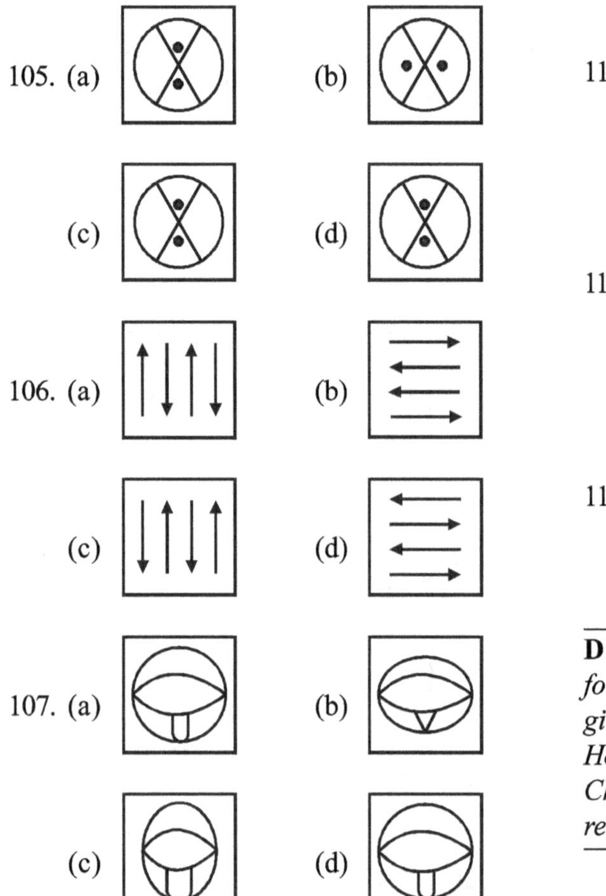

DIRECTIONS (Qs. 108-112): *In the following four figures (a), (b), (c) and (d) are given, three are similar in a certain manner. However, one figure is not like the other three. Choose the figure which is different from the rest.*

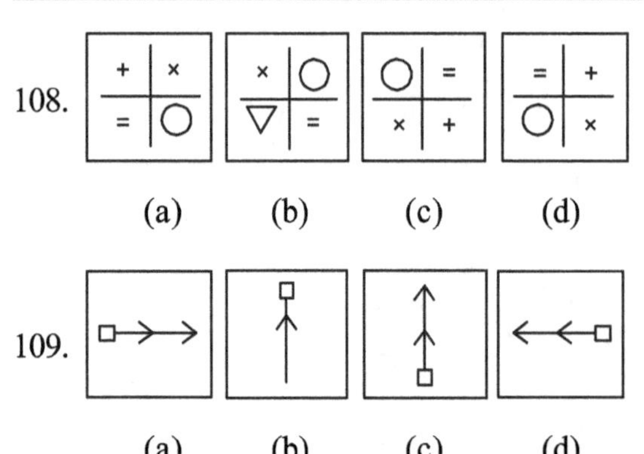

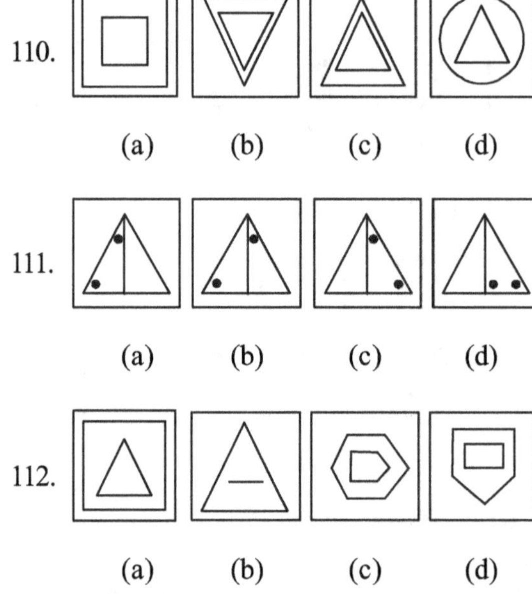

DIRECTIONS (Qs. 113-117): *In the following four figures (a), (b), (c) and (d) are given, three are similar in a certain manner. However, one figure is not like the other three. Choose the figure which is different from the rest.*

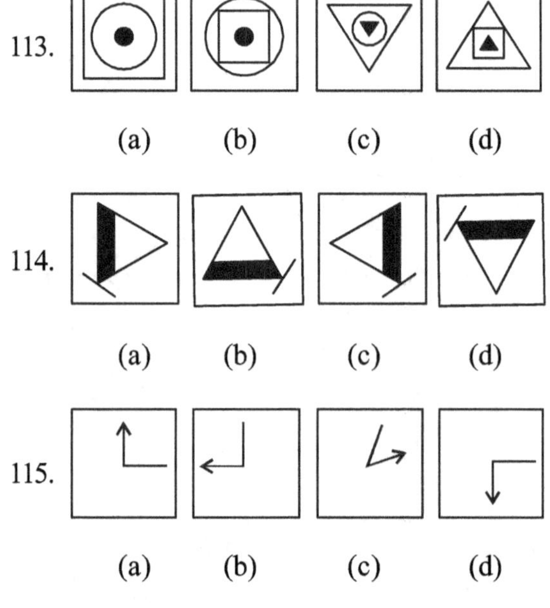

116. 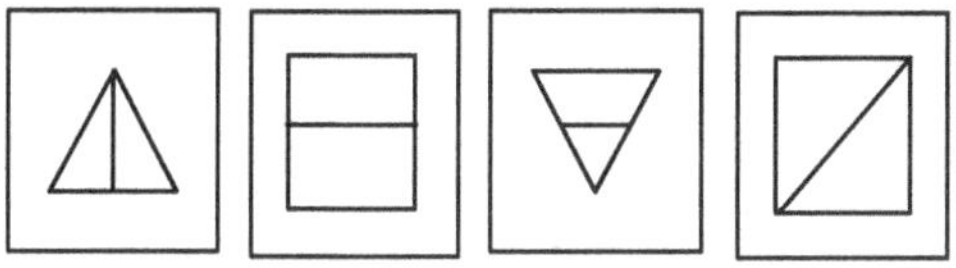 (a) (b) (c) (d)

117.  (a) (b) (c) (d)

DIRECTIONS (QS. 118-121): *Four figures (a), (b), (c) and (d) have been given in each question. Of these four figures, three figures are similar in some way and one figure is different. Select the figure which is different.*

118. (a)

(b)

(c)

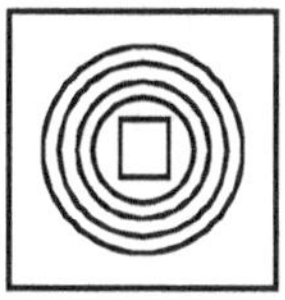

(d)

119. (a) RUN (b) UNR

(c) NKU (d) RNU

120. (a)  (b)

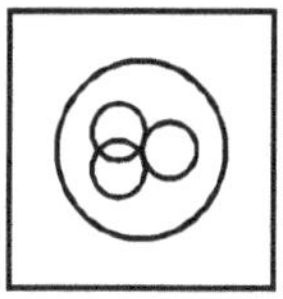

(c) 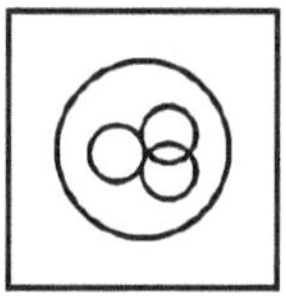 (d)

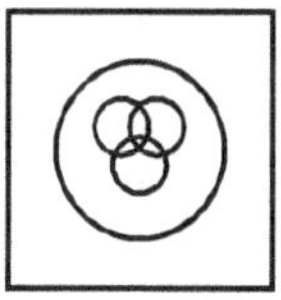

121. (a) 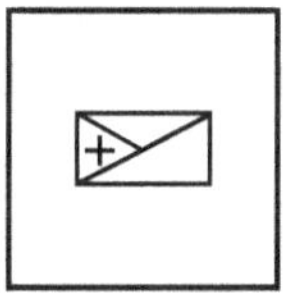 (b)

(c) 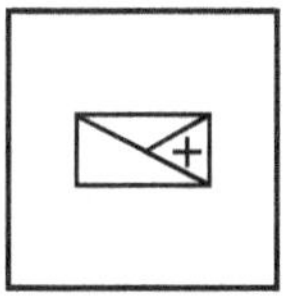 (d)

DIRECTIONS (Qs. 122 to 123) : *Four figures (a), (b), (c) and (d) have been given in each question. Of these four figures, three figures are similar in some way and one figure is different. Select the figure which is different.*

122.

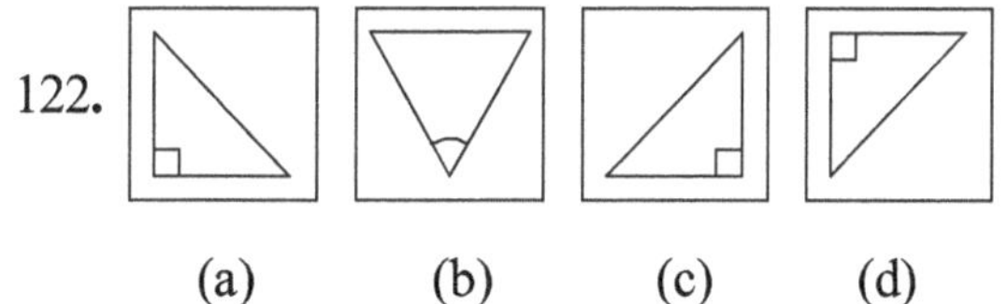

(a) (b) (c) (d)

123. 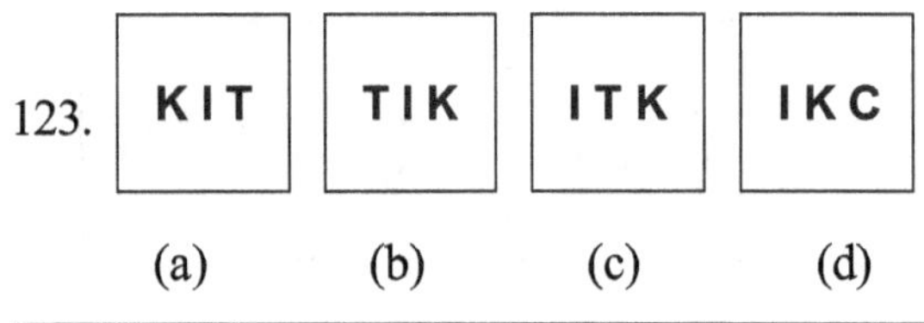

DIRECTIONS (Qs 124-127) : Four figures (a), (b), (c) and (d) have been given in each question. Of these four figures, three figures are similar in some way and one figure is different. Select the figure which is different.

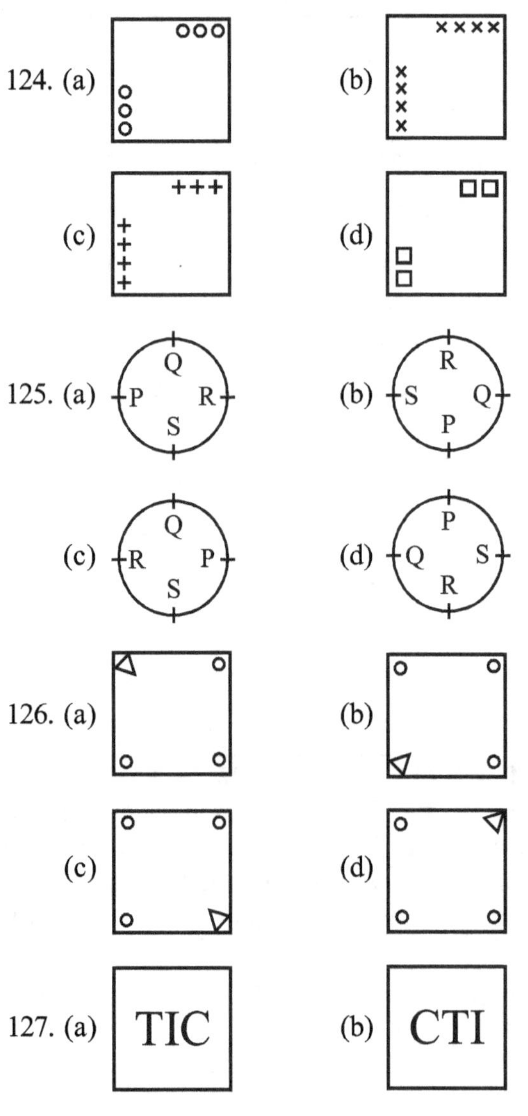

(c) 

(d) 

128. In a certain way 'Diploma' is related to 'Education'. Which of the following is related to 'Trophy' in a similar way?
    (a) Sports (b) Athlete
    (c) Winning (d) Prize
129. 'Necklace' is related to 'Jewellery' in the same way as 'Shirt' is related to
    (a) Cloth (b) Cotton
    (c) Apparel (d) Thread
130. 'Hospital' is related to 'Nurse' in the same way as 'Court' is related to
    (a) Justice (b) Lawyer
    (c) Judgement (d) Trial

DIRECTIONS (Qs. 131-133) : *Choose the right answer and write the answer in the answer box.*

131. Uncle is to Aunt as Cook is to ....
    (a) Fowl (b) Hen
    (c) Chicken (d) Duck
132. Wood is to table as .... is to coat
    (a) Shirt (b) Wear
    (c) Trouser (d) Cloth
133. Boy is to Girl as nephew is to ....
    (a) Uncle (b) Niece
    (c) Brother in law (d) Aunt

DIRECTIONS (Qs. 134-135) : *In the questions given below one term is missing. Based on the relationship of the two given words/ numbers find the missing term from the given options.*

134. Physicist : Physics : : ? : Anatomy
    (a) Botany (b) Botanist
    (c) Body (d) Biologist

135. Frequently : Always : : Selden : ?

(a) Often (b) Rarely
(c) Occasionally (d) Never

DIRECTIONS (Qs. 136-137) : *In the questions given below one term is missing. Based on the relationship of the two given words/ letters/ numbers find the missing term from the given options.*

136. ACE : FGH : : LNP : ?

(a) QRS (b) PQR
(c) QST (d) MOQ

137. EIGHTY : GIEYTH : : OUTPUT : ?

(a) UTOPTU (b) UOTUPT
(c) TUOUTP (d) TUOTUP

138. Find the missing numbevr that has same relation to 289 as 13 has to 169.

169 : 13 : : 289 : ?

(a) 19 (b) 17 (c) 27 (d) 23

139. Choose the word which is least like the other words in the group?

(a) Ladder (b) Staircase
(c) Bridge (d) Escalator

140. Choose the alternative that has the same relationship to 16 has 12 as with 168.

12 : 168 :: 16 : ?

(a) 232 (b) 256 (c) 224 (d) 208

Directions (Qs. 141-142) : *In each of the following sets of figures, select the one that is different from the rest.*

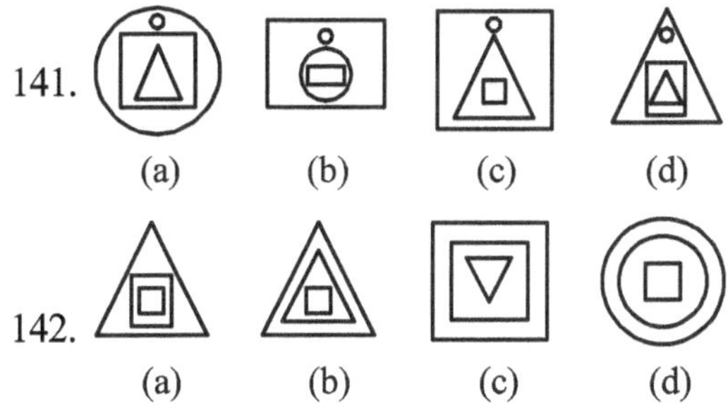

Directions (Qs. 143-145) : *The second figure in the first unit of the Problem Figures bears a certain relationship to the first figure. Similarly, one of the figures in the Answer Figures bears the same relationship to the first figure in the second unit of the Problem Figures. Locate the figure which would fit the question mark.*

143. **Problem Figures**

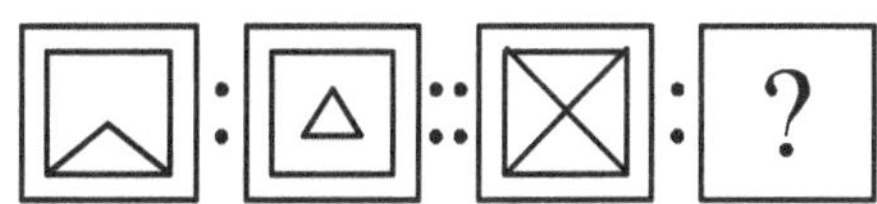

Answer Figures

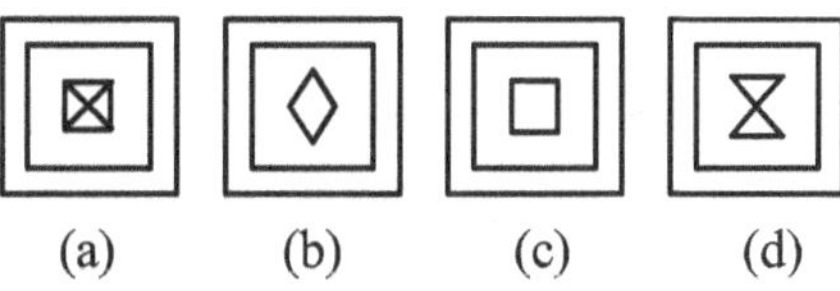

144. **Problem Figures**

Answer Figures

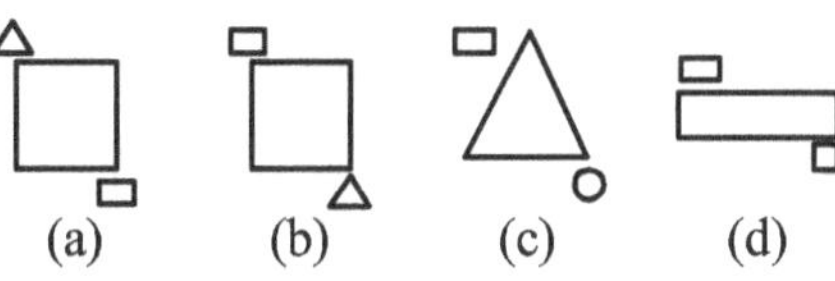

145. **Question Figures**

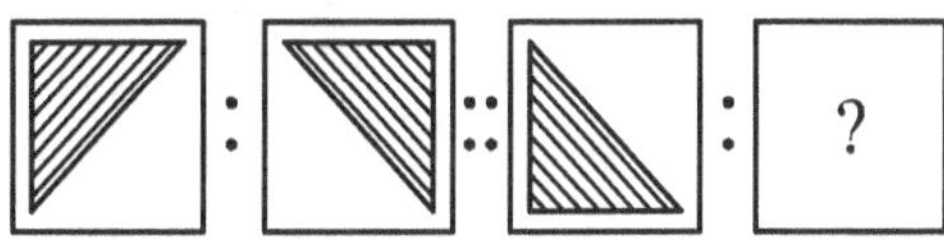

Answer Figures

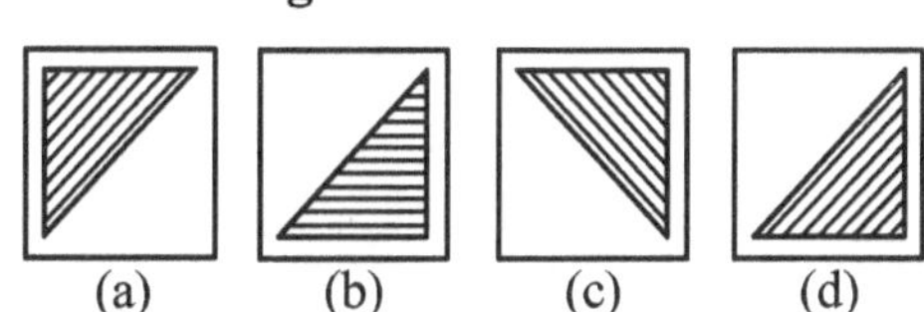

146. Sword, arrow, dagger, trident

(a) sword (b) arrow
(c) dagger (d) trident

147. Man, drone, bison, bull
(a) man (b) drone
(c) bison (d) bull

148. Army, corps, brigade, division, company
(a) army (b) corps
(c) brigade (d) company

149. Dermatologist, neurologist, obstetrician, dentist, oculist
(a) oculist (b) neurologist
(c) obstetrician (d) dermatologist

150. Viable, feasible, ample, dirigible
(a) viable (b) feasible
(c) ample (d) dirigible

151. Select the odd one out. **[2018]**

(a) 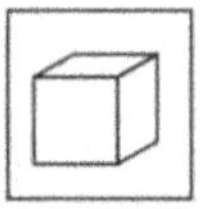 (b)

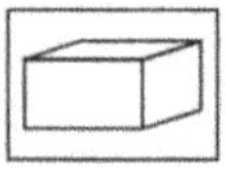

(c)  (d)

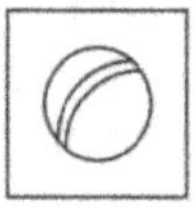

152. There is a certain relationship between figures (i) and (ii). Establish a similar relationship between figures (iii) and (iv) by selecting a suitable figure from the given options which will replace the (?) in figure (iv). **[2019]**

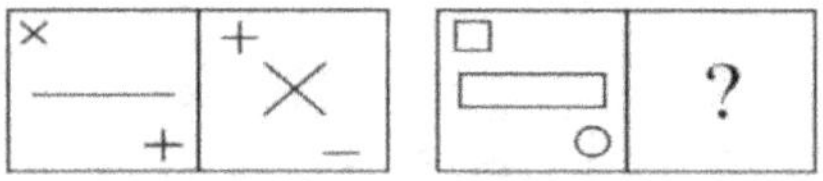

?

(i) (ii) (iii) (iv)

(a) 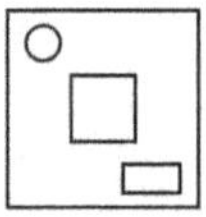 (b)

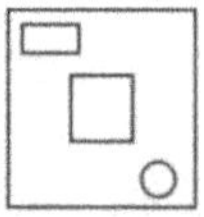

(c) 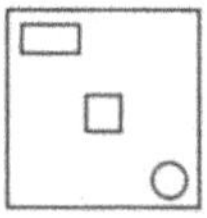 (d)

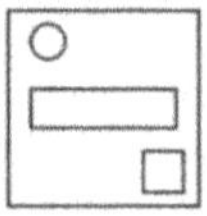

153. Find the odd one out. **[2020]**

(a)  (b)

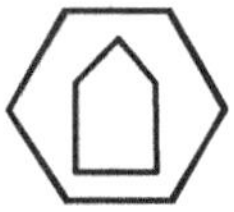

(c)  (d)

154. Select the odd one out. **[2021]**
(a) 415 (b) 165 (c) 325 (d) 247

155. There is a certain relationship between the numbers on the left pair. Establish the same relationship in the right pair and find the missing number. **[2021]**

14 : 72 : : ? : 82

(a) 12 (b) 14 (c) 16 (d) 18

156. Select the odd one out. **[2022]**
(a) RTW (b) KMP
(c) ACE (d) QSV

157. If 346 is related to 8 in some way, then in the same way 592 is related to ?. **[2022]**
(a) 4 (b) 7 (c) 10 (d) 6

158. There is a certain relationship between the terms on the either side of : :. Identify the relationship on the left pair and find the missing term.

LNQ : MOP : : TVY : ? **[2022]**

(a) UVX (b) SVX
(c) UWX (d) UWZ

LEVEL 2

DIRECTIONS (Qs. 1-5): In each of the following questions, a pair of words is given, followed by four pairs of words as alternatives. Choose the correct word pair in which the words bears the same relationship to each other as the words of the given pair bear.

1. Teeth : Chew : ..? .... : ......?.....
   (a) Mind : Think (b) Sweater : Heat
   (c) Food : Taste (d) Eyes : Flicker
2. Eyes : Tears:: ..? .... : ......?.....
   (a) Sea : Water (b) Volcano : Lava
   (c) Heart : Artery (d) Hunger : Bread
3. Lawn : Grass :: ..? .... : ......?.....
   (a) Wool : Sheep (b) Skin : Goat
   (c) Pelt : Fur (d) Rice : Farm
4. Telephone : Ring : : .... : ....
   (a) Door : knock (b) Gate : open
   (c) Door : wood (d) Lock : key
5. Always : Never :: ..? .... : ......?.....
   (a) Often : Rarely
   (b) Frequently : Normally
   (c) Constantly : Frequently
   (d) Intermittently : Casually

DIRECTIONS (6-10): *In questions 6 to 10, there are two sets of two problem figures each. The second set has a mark of interrogation (?). There exists a relationship between the first two problem figures. Similar relationship should exist between the third and fourth problem figure. Select one of the answer figure which replaces the mark of interrogation.*

6. 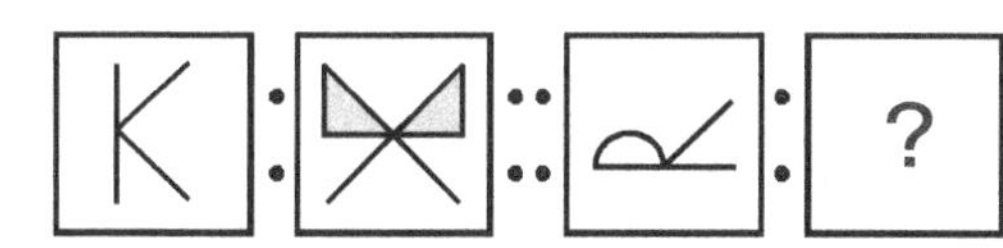

(a) 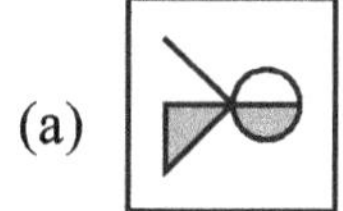 (b) 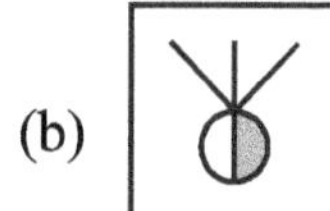

(c) 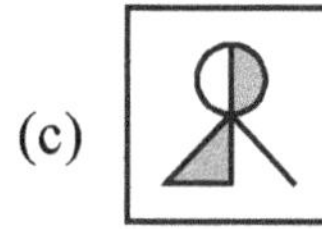 (d) 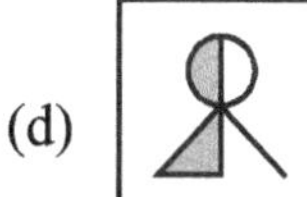

7. 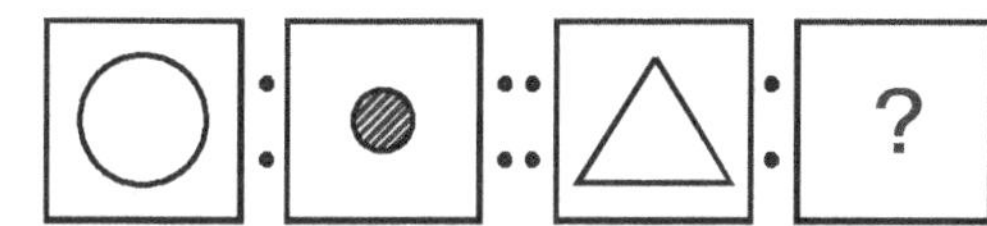

(a) 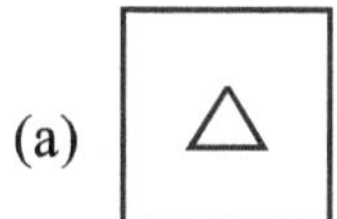 (b) 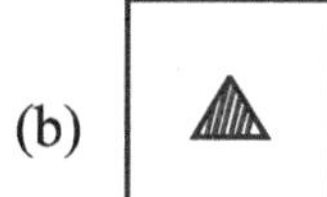

(c) 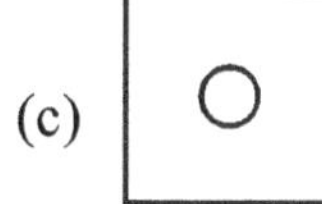 (d) 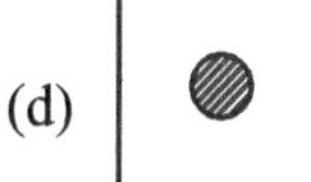

8. 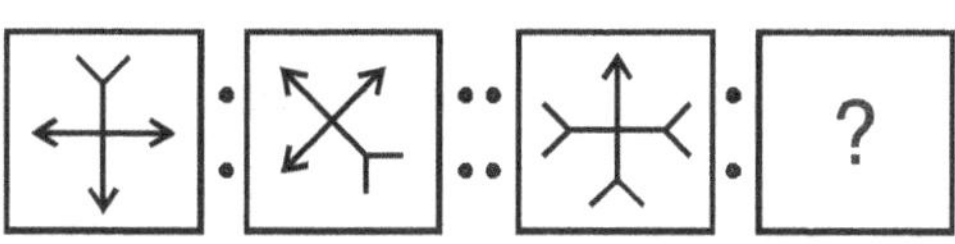

(a) 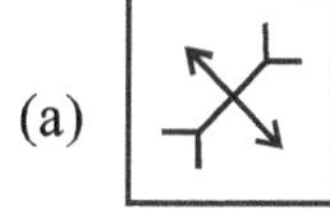 (b) 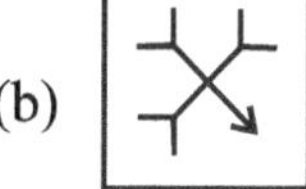

(c) 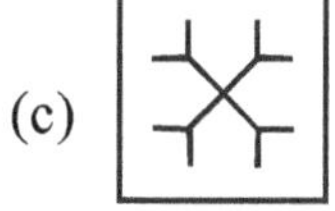 (d) 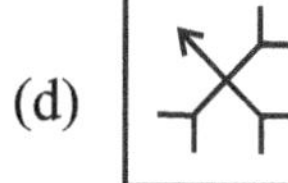

9.

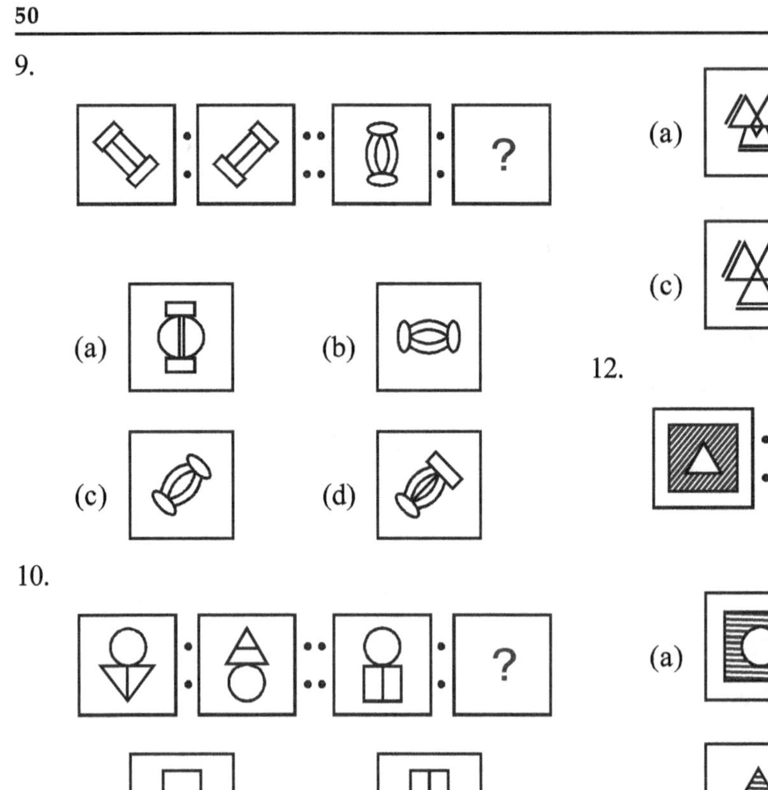

10.

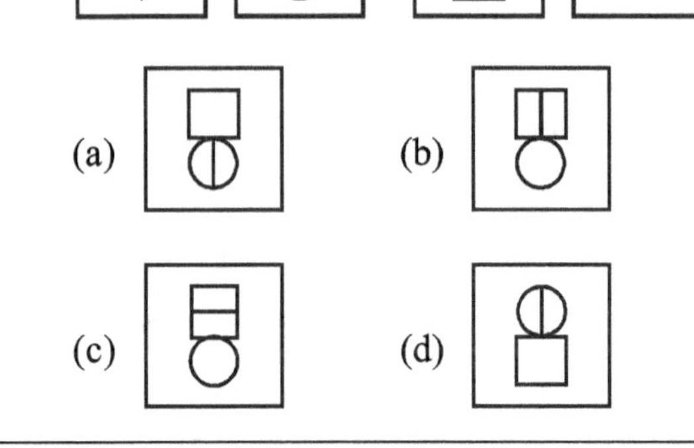

DIRECTIONS: *In questions 11 to 15, there are two sets of two problem figures each. The second set has a mark of interrogation (?). There exists a relationship between the first two problem figures. Similar relationship should exist between the third and fourth problem figure. Select one of the answer figure which replaces the mark of interrogation.*

11.

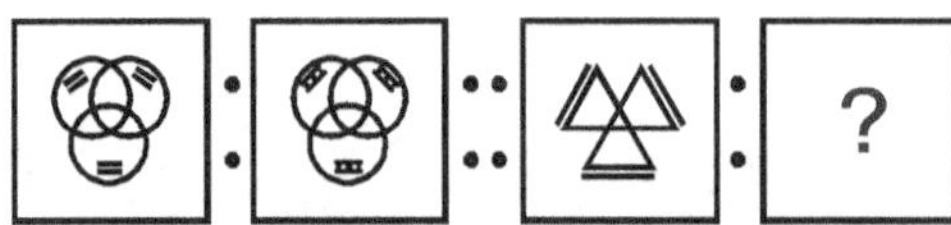

(c) 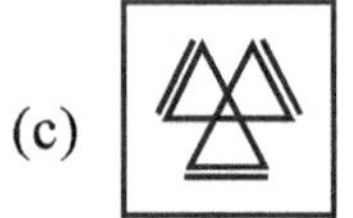

(d) 

12.

(a) 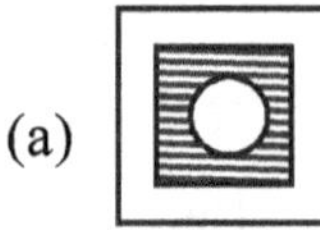

(b) 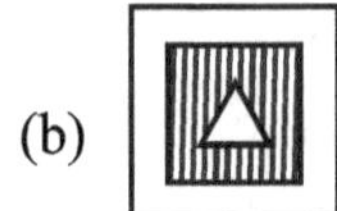

(c) 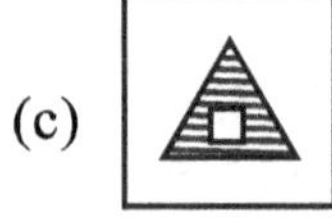

(d) 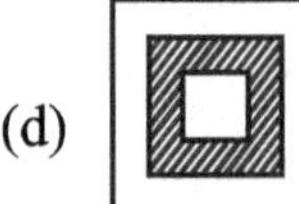

13.

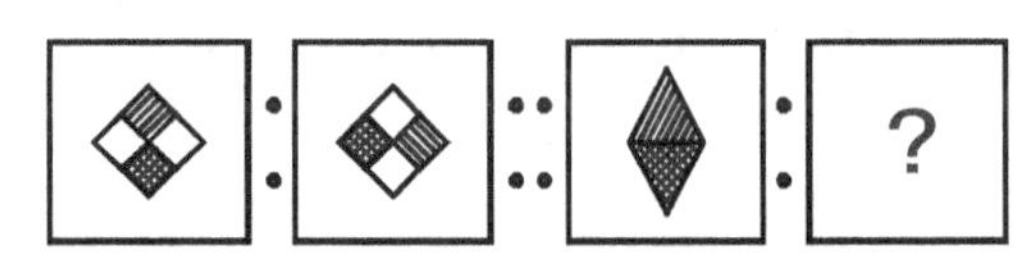

(a) 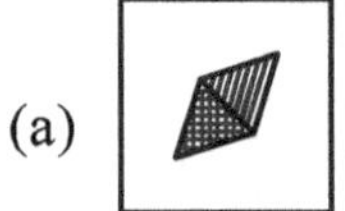

(b) 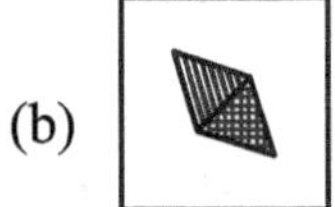

(c) 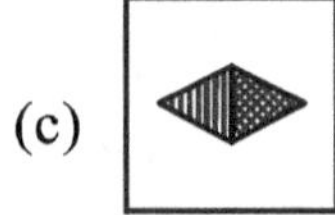

(d) 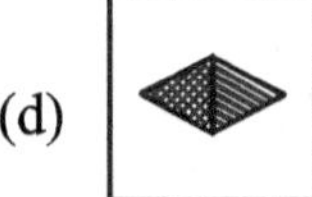

14.

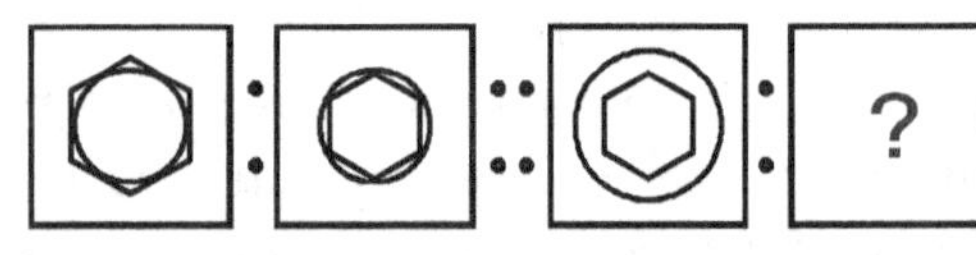

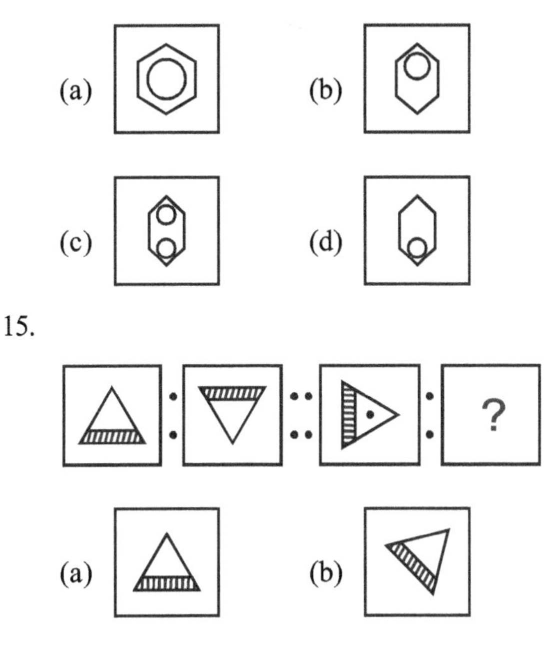

15.

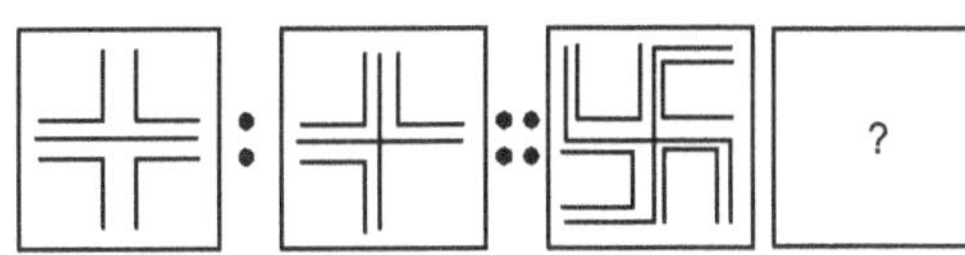

DIRECTIONS (Qs. 16-20): *There are two sets of figure given. There is a definite relationship between first two. Establish a similar relationship between third and fourth by selecting a suitable figure from answer that would replace the question mark.*

16. **Question Figures**

Answer Figures

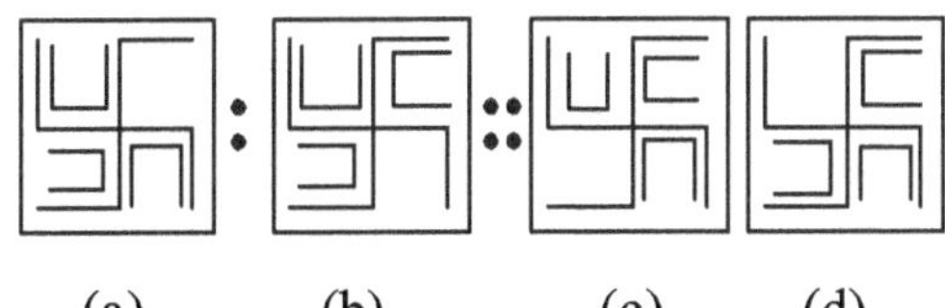

(a) (b) (c) (d)

17. **Question Figure**

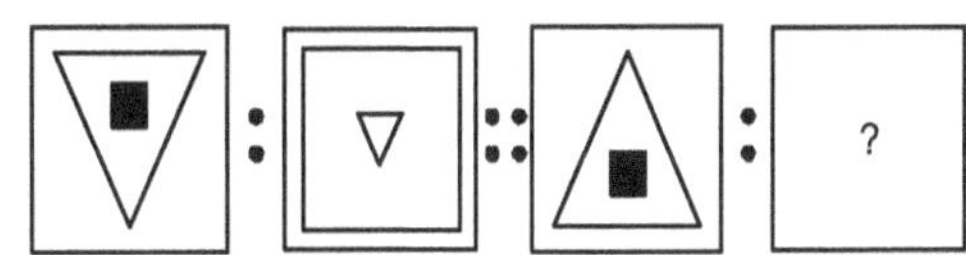

Answer Figures

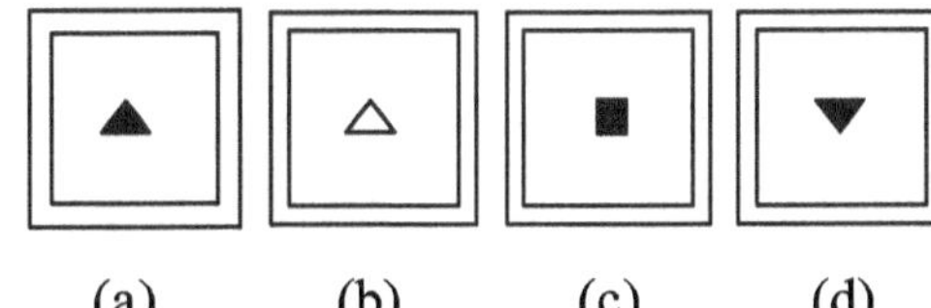

18. **Question Figures**

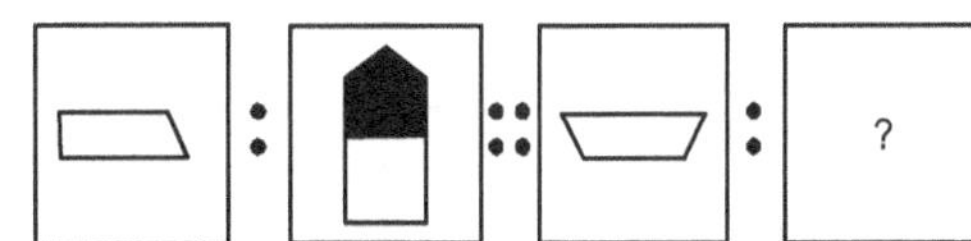

Answer Figures

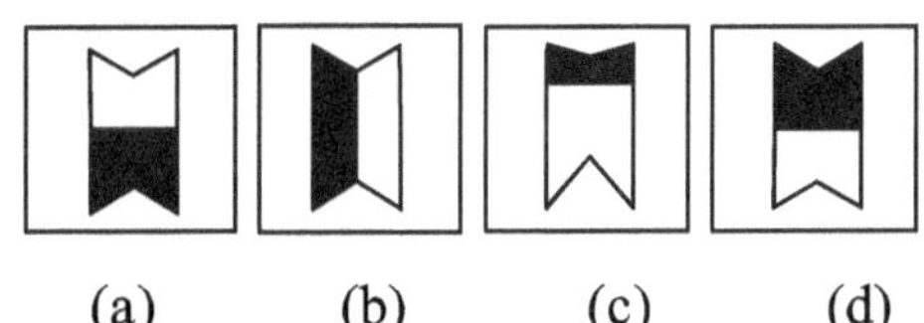

19. **Question Figures**

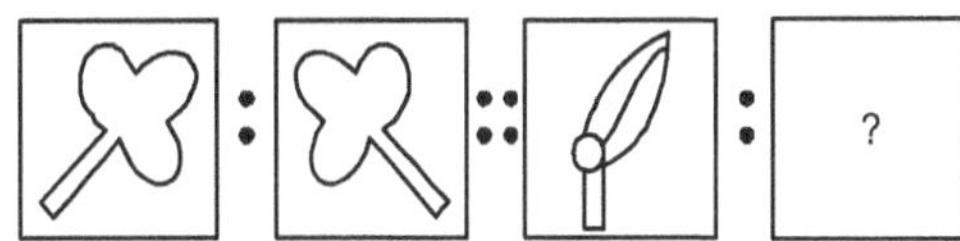

Answer Figures

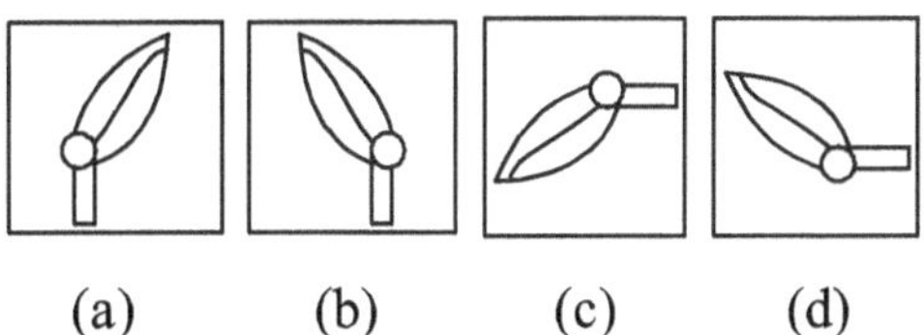

20. **Question Figures**

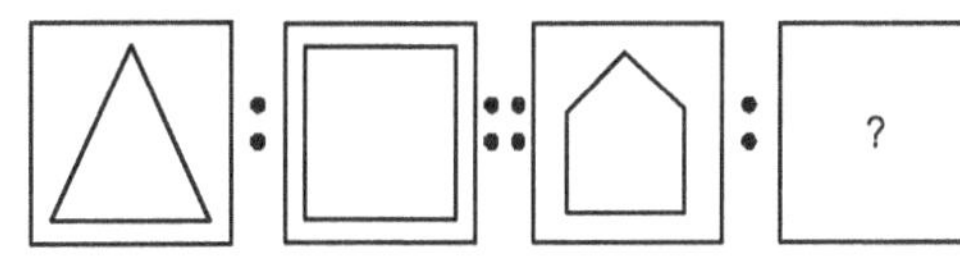

Answer Figures

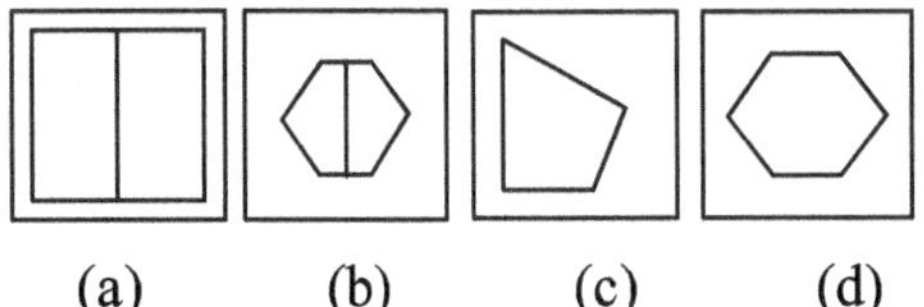

(a) (b) (c) (d)

DIRECTIONS (Qs. 21-25): *There are two sets of figure given. There is a definite relationship between first two. Establish a similar relationship between third and fourth by selecting a suitable figure from answer that would replace the question mark.*

21. **Question Figure**

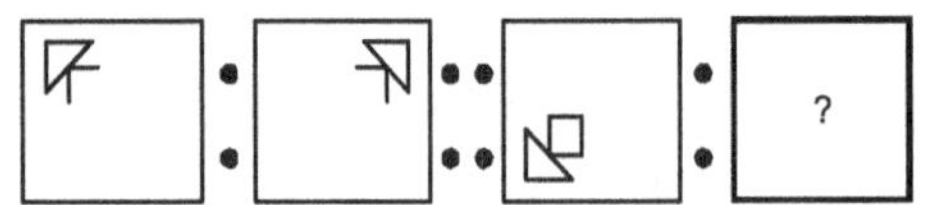

Answer Figures

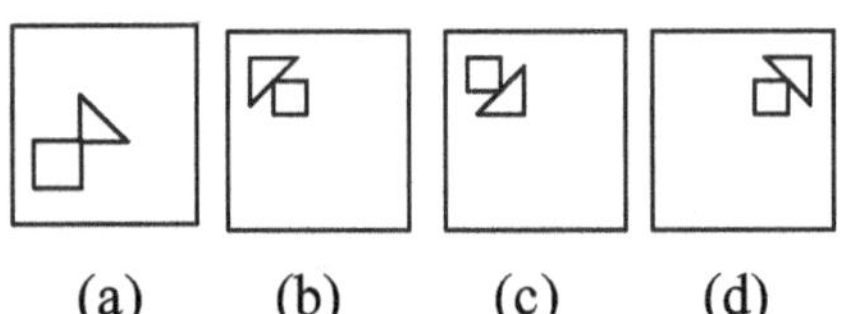

(a) (b) (c) (d)

22. **Question Figures**

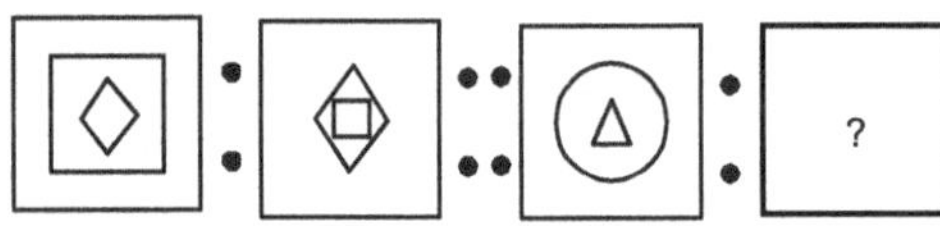

Answer Figures

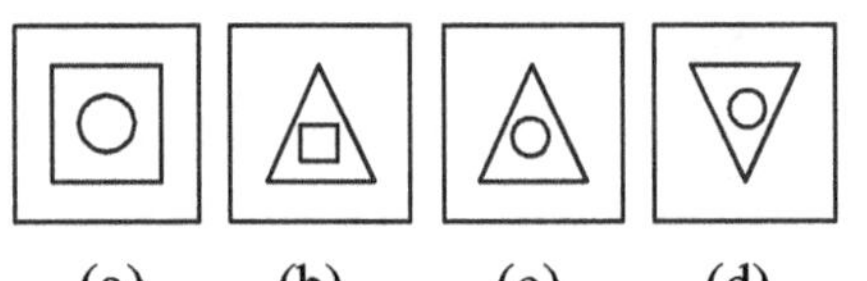

(a) (b) (c) (d)

23. **Question Figures**

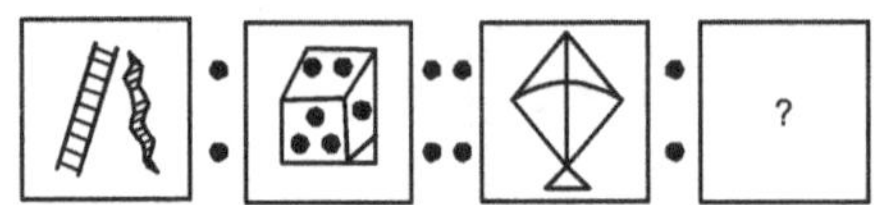

Answer Figures

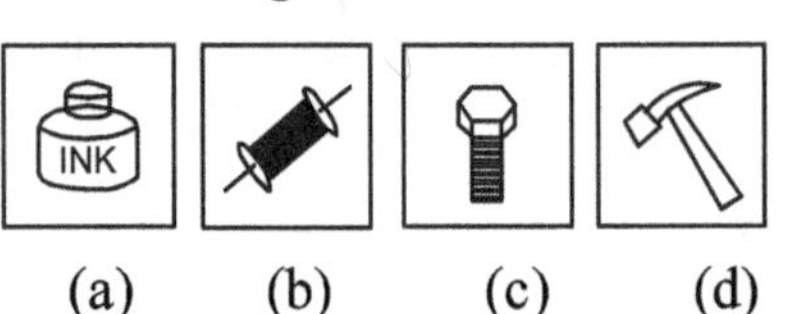

(a) (b) (c) (d)

24. **Question Figures**

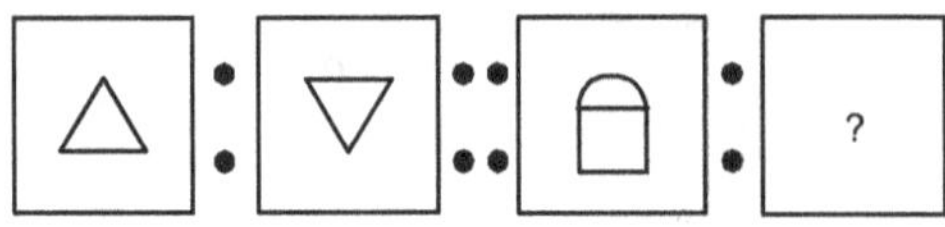

Answer Figures

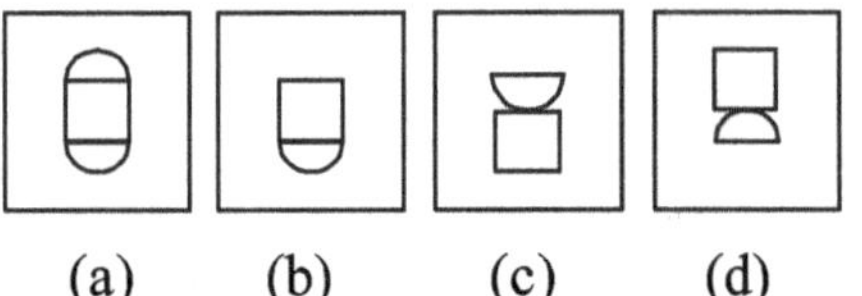

(a) (b) (c) (d)

25. **Question Figures**

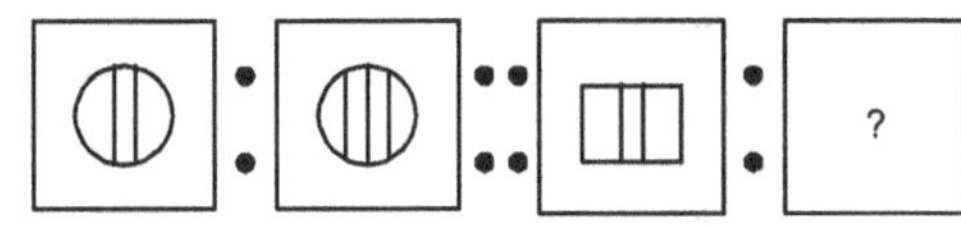

Answer Figures

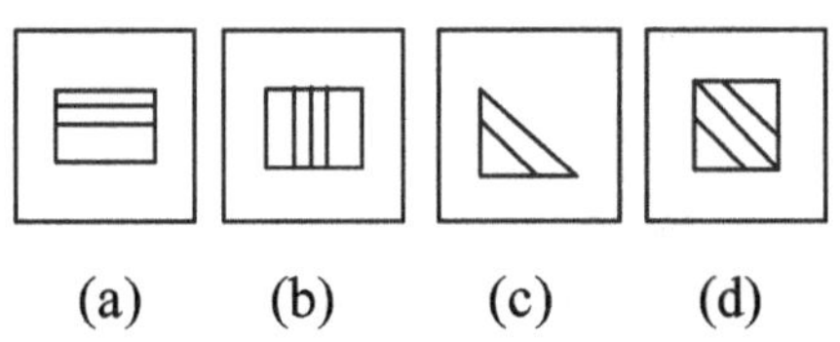

(a) (b) (c) (d)

DIRECTIONS: *In Question Nos. 26 to 29, there are two sets of two question figures each. The second set has an interrogation mark (?). There exists a relationship between the first two question figure. Similar relationship should exist between the third and fourth question figure. Select one of the answer figures which replaces the mark of interrogation.*

26. **Question Figures**

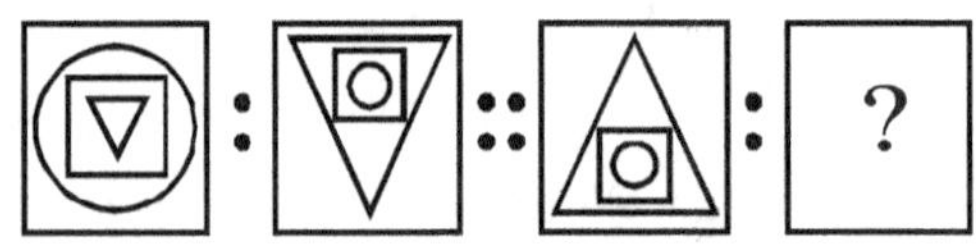

Answer Figures

(a) 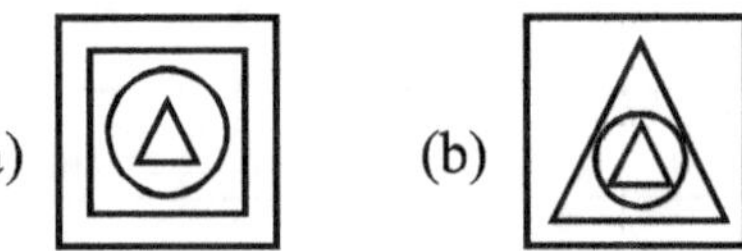 (b)

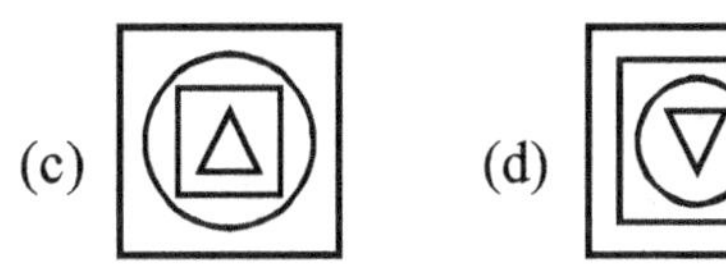

27. **Question Figures**

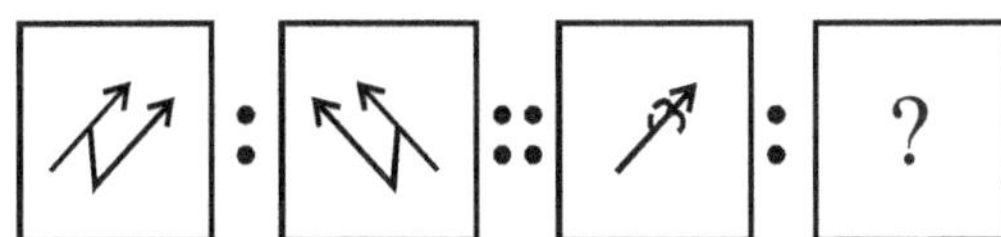

Answer Figures

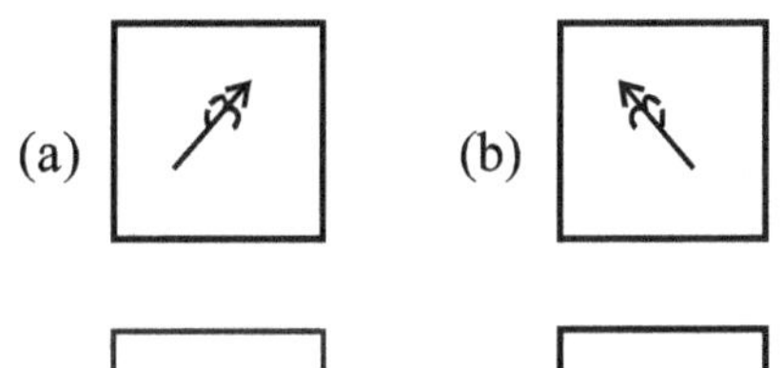

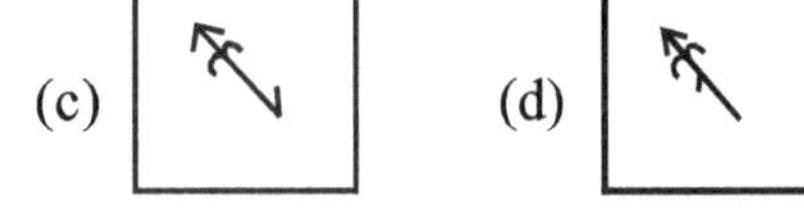

28. **Question Figures**

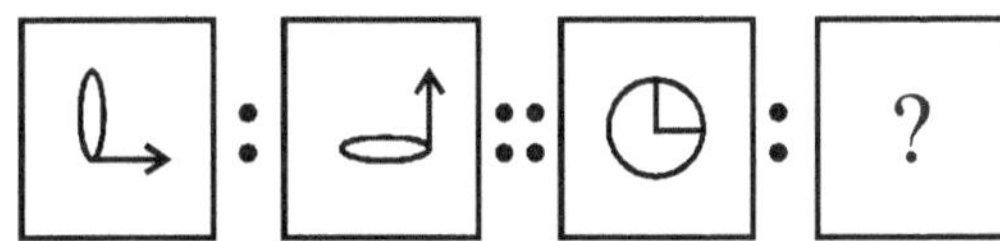

Answer Figures

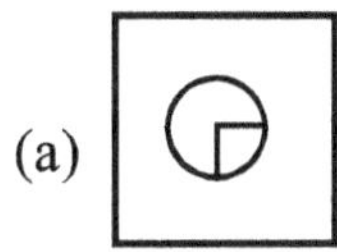

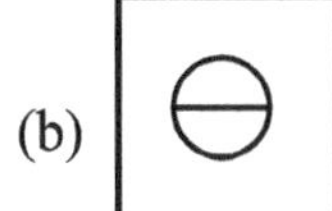

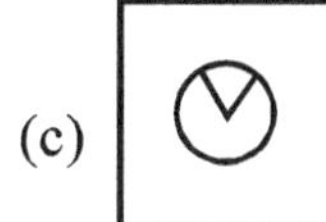

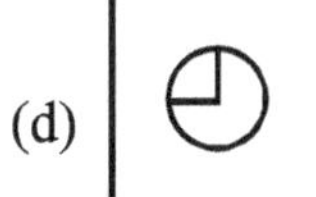

29. **Question Figures**

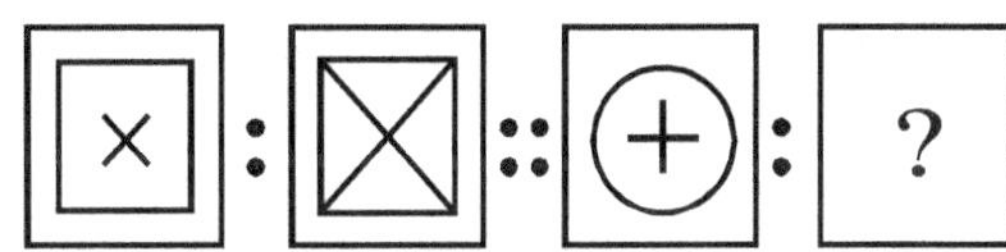

Answer Figures

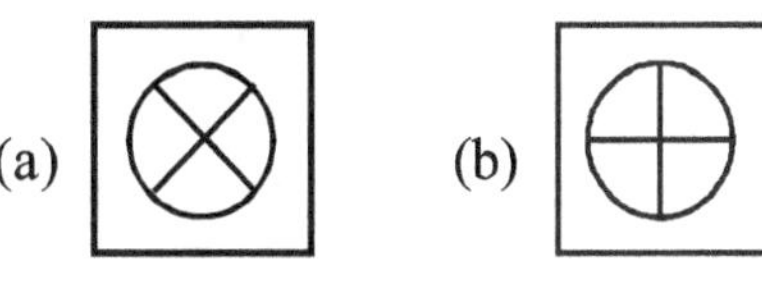

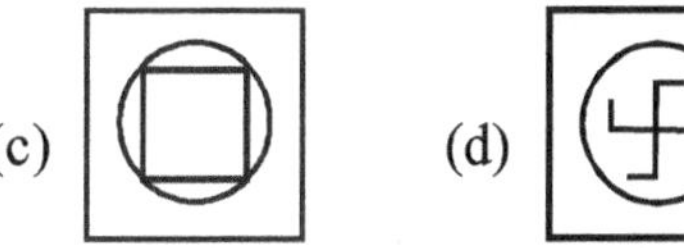

DIRECTIONS (Qs. 30 to 31) : *There are two sets of two question figures each. The second set has an interrogation mark (?). There exists a relationship between the first two question figures. Similar relationship should exist between the third and fourth question figure. Select one of the answer figures which replaces the mark of interrogation.*

30. **Questions Figure**

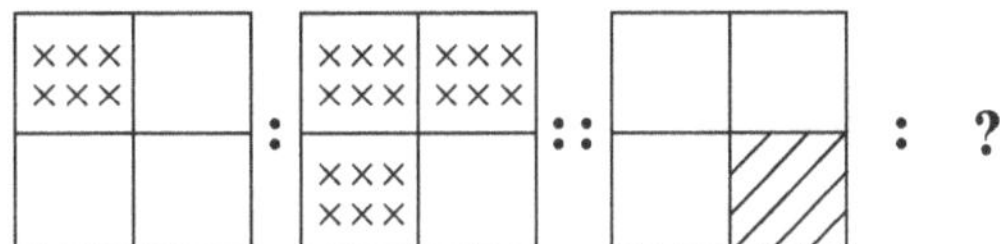

Answer Figures

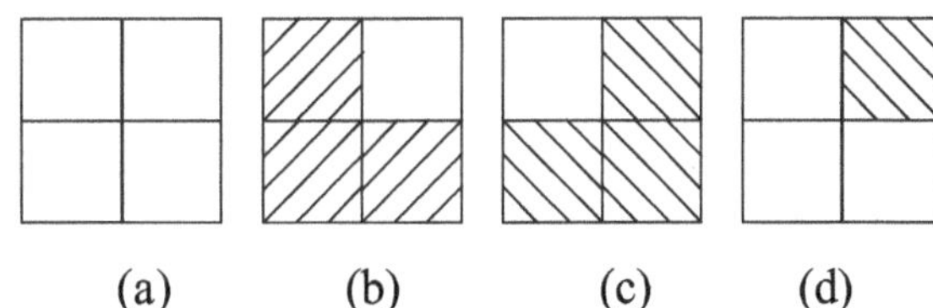

31. **Questions Figure**

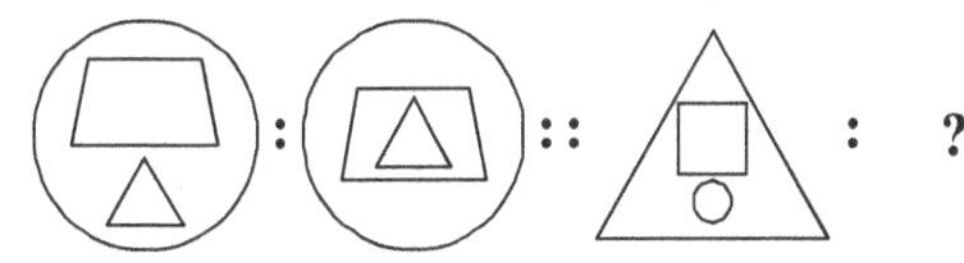

Answer Figures

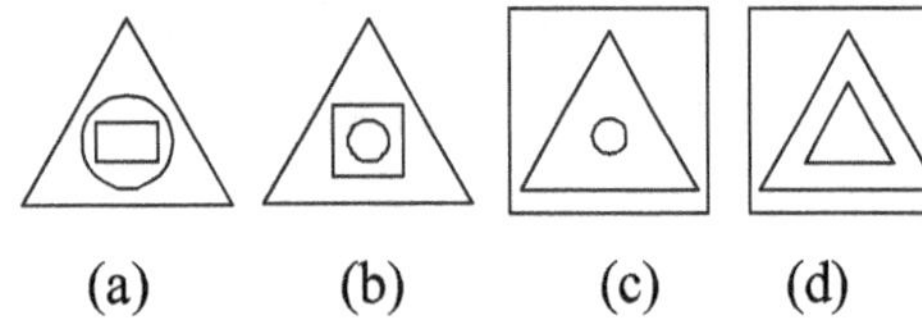

DIRECTIONS (Qs. 32-35): *There are two sets of two question figures each. The second set has an interrogation mark (?). There exist a relationship between the first two question figures. Similar relationship should exist between the third and the fourth question figure. Select one of the answer figures which replace the mark of interrogation.*

32. **Question Figure**

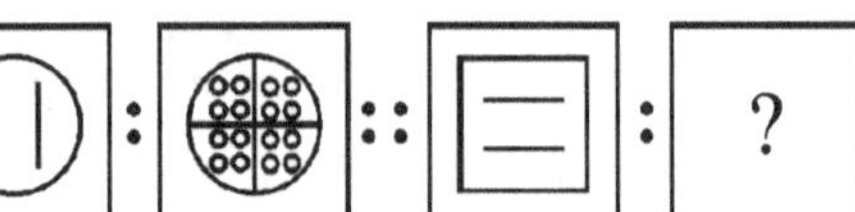

Answer Figures

(a) 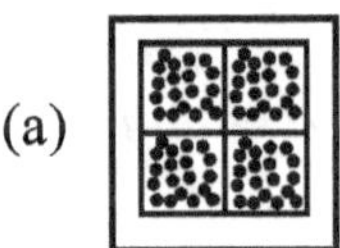 (b) 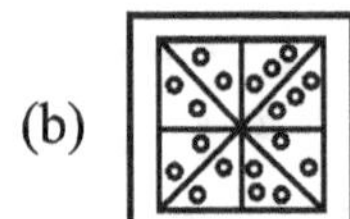

(c) 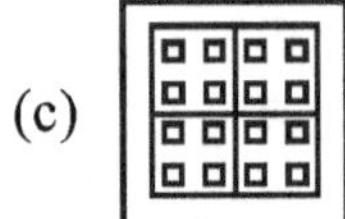 (d) 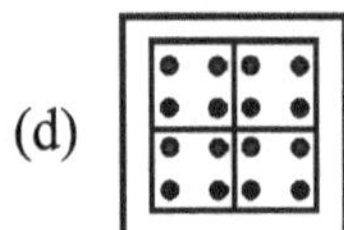

33. **Question Figures**

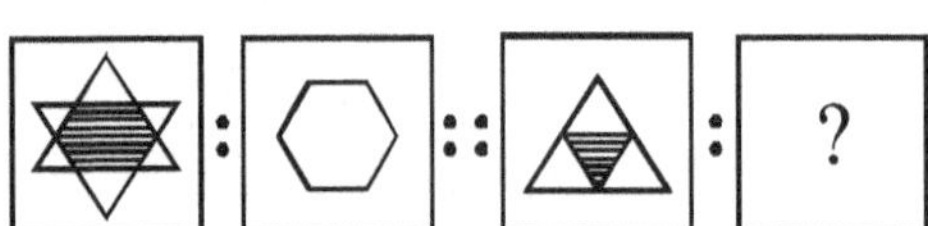

Answer Figures

(a) 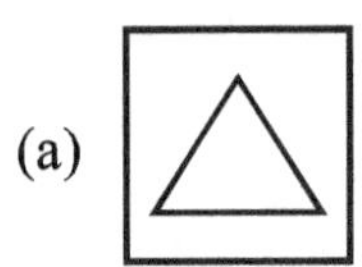

(b) 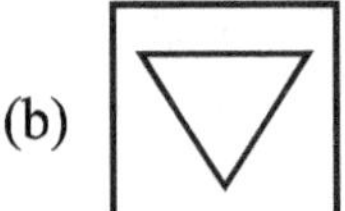

(c) 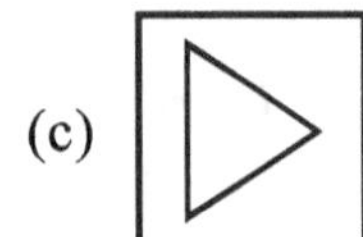 (d) 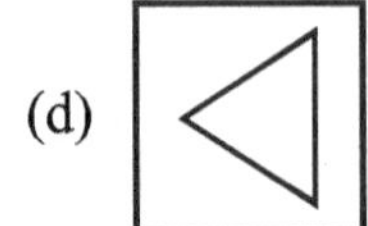

34. **Question Figures**

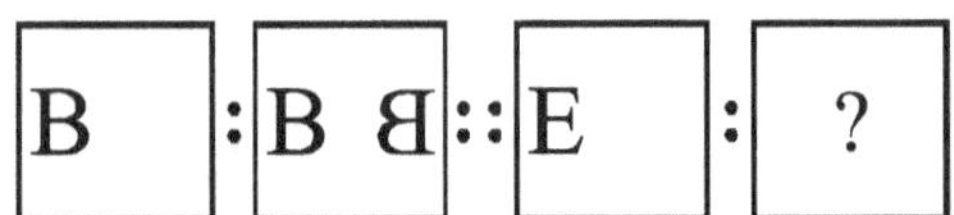

Answer Figures

(a) 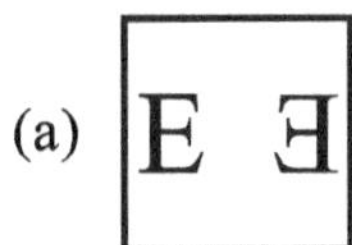

(b) 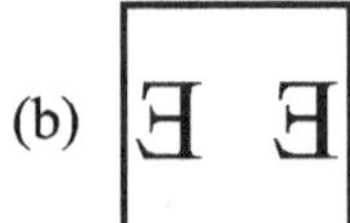

(c) 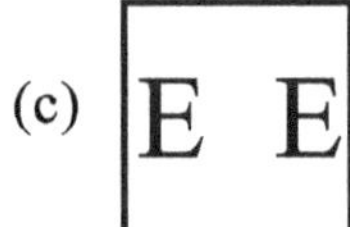

(d) 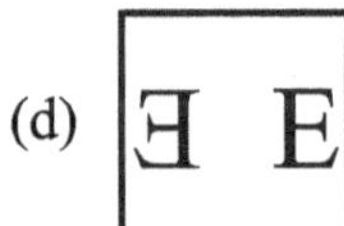

35. **Question Figures**

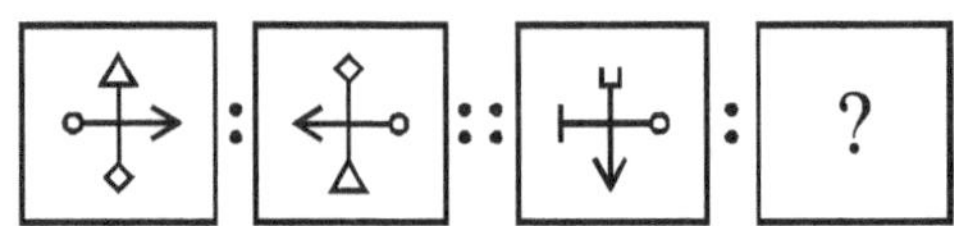

Answer Figures

(a) 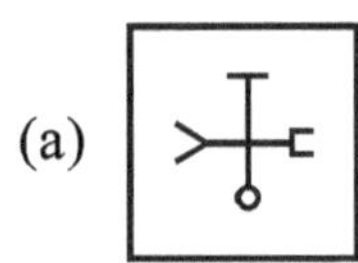 (b) 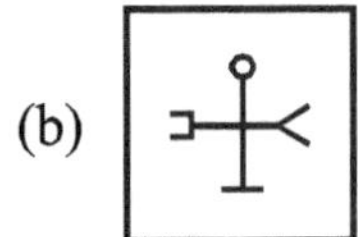

(c) 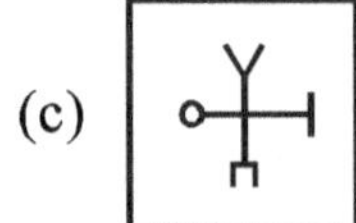 (d) 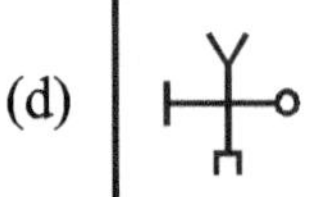

DIRECTIONS (Qs. 36-43): *In each question, out of the four figures marked (a), (b), (c) and (d), three are similar in a certain manner. Howerer one figure is not like the other three. Choose the figure wchic is diffence from the rest.*

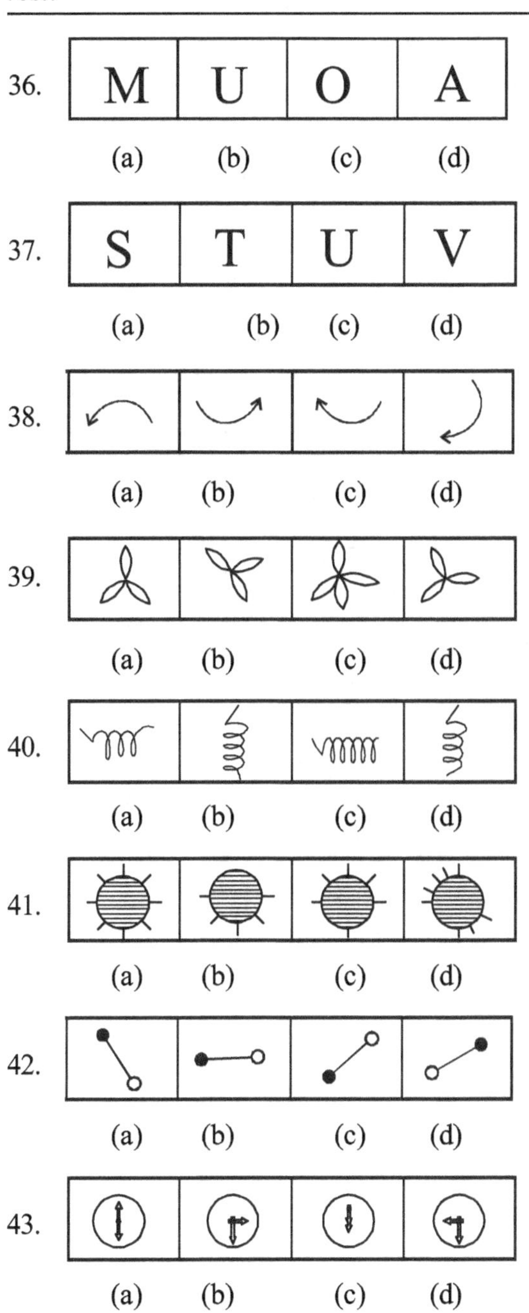

44. There is a certain relationship between figures (1) and (2). Establish a similar relationship between figures (3) and (4) by selecting a suitable figure from the given options which would replace the (?) in Fig. (4). **[2019]**

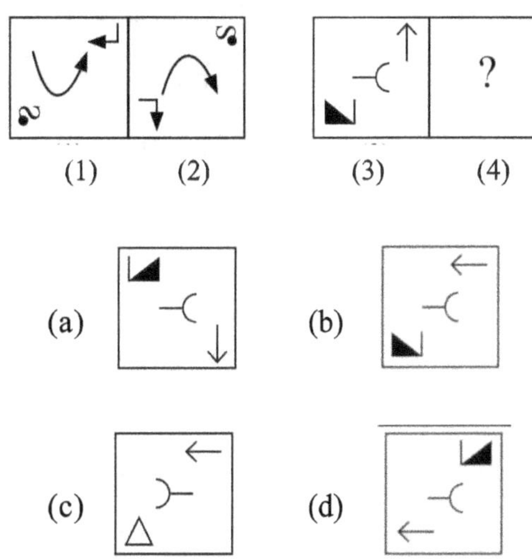

45. There is a certain relationship between figures (i) and (ii). Establish a similar relationship between figures (iii) and (iv) by selecting a suitable figure from the options that will replace the (?) in fig. (iv). **[2021]**

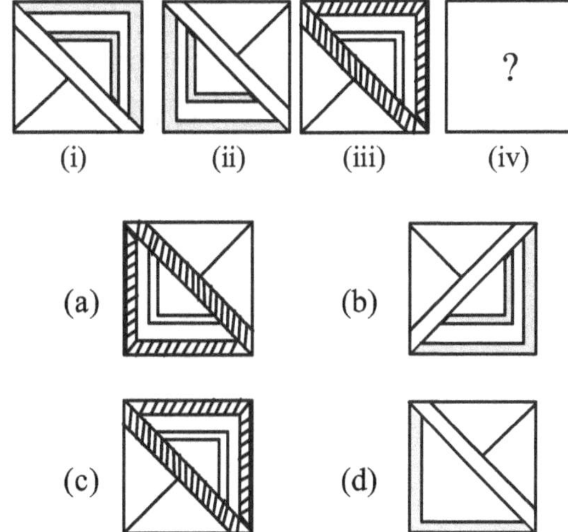

46. Select the option that is related to the third word in the same way as the second word is related to the first word. **[2022]**
Thermometer : Temperature :: Hygrometer : ?
(a) Pressure (b) Density
(c) Stress (d) Humidity

47. Find the odd one out. **[2022]**
(a) 68 – 43 (b) 74 – 40
(c) 85 – 60 (d) 103 – 78

ANSWER KEY																			
LEVEL-1																			
1	(c)	**17**	(a)	**33**	(a)	**49**	(c)	**65**	(c)	**81**	(a)	**97**	(e)	**113**	(a)	**129**	(c)	**145**	(d)
2	(c)	**18**	(b)	**34**	(b)	**50**	(d)	**66**	(a)	**82**	(d)	**98**	(d)	**114**	(c)	**130**	(b)	**146**	(b)
3	(c)	**19**	(d)	**35**	(d)	**51**	(d)	**67**	(d)	**83**	(c)	**99**	(d)	**115**	(c)	**131**	(b)	**147**	(c)
4	(d)	**20**	(a)	**36**	(d)	**52**	(c)	**68**	(c)	**84**	(a)	**100**	(d)	**116**	(c)	**132**	(d)	**148**	(a)
5	(d)	**21**	(d)	**37**	(b)	**53**	(b)	**69**	(a)	**85**	(b)	**101**	(d)	**117**	(c)	**133**	(b)	**149**	(a)
6	(d)	**22**	(c)	**38**	(d)	**54**	(c)	**70**	(b)	**86**	(d).	**102**	(d)	**118**	(b)	**134**	(d)	**150**	(d)
7	(b)	**23**	(b)	**39**	(b)	**55**	(a)	**71**	(a)	**87**	(c)	**103**	(a)	**119**	(c)	**135**	(c)	**151**	(d)
8	(b)	**24**	(a)	**40**	(a)	**56**	(a)	**72**	(b)	**88**	(a)	**104**	(c)	**120**	(d)	**136**	(a)	**152**	(a)
9	(b)	**25**	(d)	**41**	(c)	**57**	(d)	**73**	(c)	**89**	(d)	**105**	(b)	**121**	(b)	**137**	(d)	**153**	(d)
10	(c)	**26**	(c)	**42**	(b)	**58**	(d)	**74**	(c)	**90**	(d)	**106**	(b)	**122**	(b)	**138**	(b)	**154**	(d)
11	(d)	**27**	(b)	**43**	(a)	**59**	(a)	**75**	(c)	**91**	(d)	**107**	(b)	**123**	(d)	**139**	(c)	**155**	(c)
12	(b)	**28**	(c)	**44**	(b)	**60**	(b)	**76**	(d)	**92**	(d)	**108**	(b)	**124**	(c)	**140**	(c)	**156**	(c)
13	(c)	**29**	(d)	**45**	(a)	**61**	(b)	**77**	(d)	**93**	(b)	**109**	(b)	**125**	(a)	**141**	(a)	**157**	(c)
14	(c)	**30**	(d)	**46**	(c)	**62**	(b)	**78**	(c)	**94**	(c)	**110**	(d)	**126**	(d)	**142**	(a)	**158**	(c)
15	(d)	**31**	(b)	**47**	(b)	**63**	(b)	**79**	(c)	**95**	(d)	**111**	(b)	**127**	(c)	**143**	(d)		
16	(d)	**32**	(a)	**48**	(b)	**64**	(a)	**80**	(b)	**96**	(a)	**112**	(b)	**128**	(a)	**144**	(a)		
LEVEL-2																			
1	(a)	**6**	(d)	**11**	(c)	**16**	(b)	**21**	(b)	**26**	(c)	**31**	(b)	**36**	(a)	**41**	(b)	**46**	(d)
2	(b)	**7**	(b)	**12**	(a)	**17**	(b)	**22**	(c)	**27**	(b)	**32**	(c)	**37**	(c)	**42**	(d)	**47**	(b)
3	(c)	**8**	(b)	**13**	(d)	**18**	(d)	**23**	(b)	**28**	(d)	**33**	(b)	**38**	(d)	**43**	(d)		
4	(a)	**9**	(b)	**14**	(a)	**19**	(b)	**24**	(b)	**29**	(b)	**34**	(a)	**39**	(c)	**44**	(d)		
5	(a)	**10**	(c)	**15**	(c)	**20**	(d)	**25**	(b)	**30**	(c)	**35**	(c)	**40**	(d)	**45**	(a)		

CHAPTER

Coding-Decoding

CODING

The word 'coding' stands for converting a **word from English language** into a certain pattern or expression.

Therefore, **code** is a sequence of letters/numbers, which is used in place of the original **word/series of numbers** that is coded.

Coding can be done for a group of letters (a word), a series of numbers or an **alphanumeric series** (*i.e.,* a series having both alphabets as well as numerals).

There are 7 types of coding methods :

1. **Simple Arrangement.**
2. **Direct Coding**
3. **Letter coding**
4. **Alphanumeric Coding.**
5. **Substitution Coding**
6. **Decephering message word/Number/ Symbol Coding.**
7. **Jumbled Coding.**

I. Simple Arrangement Method : This is the most common & the simplest kind of coding. These codes are generally obtained by simply re-aligning the given alphabets in a word.

ILLUSTRATION 1 :

In a code language, if TRAINS is coded as RTIASN, how will FLOWER be coded in the same language ?

(a) LFOWER (b) LFWORE
(c) WORELF (d) ERFLOW

Sol. (b) TRAINS $\longrightarrow$ RTIASN

In the above code, we can clearly observe that the code is obtained simply by interchanging the positions of 2 **consecutive alphabets** *i.e.,* TR becomes RT, AI becomes IA and NS becomes SN similarly,

FLOWER will be coded as (FL becomes LF, OW becomes WO and ER becomes RE) LFWORE.

FLOWER $\longrightarrow$ LFWORE

Therefore, correct answer is option (b).

ILLUSTRATION 2 :

In a certain code language, the word 'PARTNER' is coded as 'TRAPREN', how will 'FOUNDER' be coded in the same language.

(a) NUOFDER (b) NUOFRED
(c) FOUNRED (d) OFNUEDR

Sol. (b) When we divide letters of the word 'PARTNER' in two group.

First group of first 4 letters and second group of last 3 letters, *i.e.,* PART and NER and then reverse the order of the letters in these two groups.

PART ⟶ TRAP
NER ⟶ REN
⇒ TRAPREN

Similarly, we divide the letters of the word 'FOUNDER' in two group.

First group with first 4 letters (FOUN) and second group with last 3 letters (DER) & then reverse the order of the letters in the 2 groups.

FOUN ⟶ NUOF DER ⟶ RED

∴ the code for FOUNDER is NUOFRED

Therefore, correct answer is option (b).

Quick Tips

Notes for simple arrangement :

(i) Number of characters (letters / numbers / symbols) in the code should be same as that of the original word, otherwise coding is not possible.

(ii) Pay attention to the alignment of the word, *i.e,* if the letter/ number has changed its position from first to last & vice versa, a swap coding is possible.

For e.g. : in ***e.g.* 3**, first group had 4 letters — 'FOUN' & there was a swap between letters at first & last position.

Swap coding

II. Direct Coding : When the characters, *i.e.,* letters of a word or numerals of a series are substituted by a coded character, *i.e.,* an alphabet, a numeral or a symbol & are placed in the coded word at similar positions as in the given / original word, it is known as direct substitution method.

These codes (substitutions) may either be in a direct fashion or in a jumbled fashion in order to make the questions tricky.

ILLUSTRATION 3 :

In a code language, if SUGAR is coded as ZNMDB and TEA is coded as FLD, how would you code GRATE in the same code language.

(a) BNDFL (b) MBDFL
(c) LDZMN (d) FLDZB

Sol. (b)

Original word :
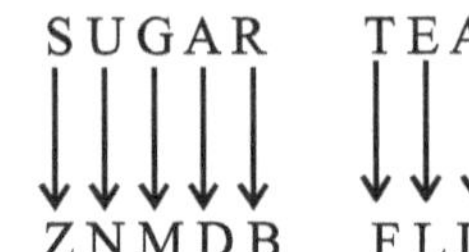

Coded word :

First we write the original words SUGAR & TEA and is corresponding alignment to these, we write down their codes respectively.

Therefore, we see that Z is coded for S, N for U, M for G, D for A and B for R, in the word SUGAR. While in the word TEA, F is substituted for T, L for E & D for A.

This implies that this code is in direct fashion as in both the words 'D' is coded for A.

Therefore, code for GRATE will be MBDFL.

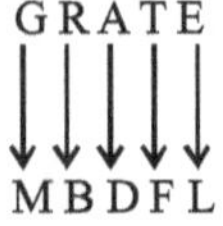

So, correct answer option is (b).

ILLUSTRATION 4 :

If in a certain code language, TWENTY is coded as 863985 and ELEVEN is coded as 323039, how will TWELVE be coded?

(a) 863903 (b) 863650

(c) 863203 (d) 683583

Sol. (c)

Therefore, in the word TWELVE, 8 will be the code for T, 6 will be the code for W, 3 for E, 2 for L, and 0 for V.

So,

Hence, answer option (c) is the correct answer.

Quick Tips

Notes for direct substitution :

(i) If there are 2 words in the question for which codes are given and these 2 words have 1 or more same alphabets, then the codes for these alphabets will be the same as well.

(ii) In case of confusion, note (a), *i.e.*, same codes in both the words for same alphabet, will help us identify that the question belongs to the category of **direct substitution.**

III. Letter Coding : This method involves the use of the alphabet series (A B C D E F ....X Y Z).

A certain word will be coded as certain other letters from the alphabet series following a certain pattern. It is further explained by examples.

ILLUSTRATION 5 :

In a certain code language, the word 'RECTANGLE' is coded as TGEVCPING, then how is the word 'RHOMBUS' coded ?

(a) TJOQDWV (b) UVWTJQN

(c) TJQODWU (d) JTQOEWN

Sol. (c) Each letter of the word RECTANGLE is moved two steps forward to obtain the corresponding letters of the code, *i.e.*,

R E C T A N G L E

+2 +2 +2 +2 +2 +2 +2 +2 +2

T G E V C P I N G

Similarly, we have :

R H O M B U S

+2 +2 +2 +2 +2 +2 +2

T J Q O D W U

So, the desired code is 'TJQODWU'. So, option (3) is the correct answer.

IV. Alpha-Numeric Series Coding : Out of the entire alphabet series numbered 1 to 26, *i.e.*,

A	B	C	D	E	F	G	H	I	J	K
1	2	3	4	5	6	7	8	9	10	11
L	M	N	O	P	Q	R	S	T	U	
12	13	14	15	16	17	18	19	20	21	
V	W	X	Y	Z						
22	23	24	25	26						

it is difficult to remember each and every alphabets' numeric value, therefore, we just have to remember.

E = 5, J = 10, O = 15, T = 20 and Y = 25 which are multiples of 5.

In alphanumeric coding, the alphabets of the word are given and we code them in terms of their numeric value or some pattern according to their numeric values.

ILLUSTRATION 6 :

If in a certain code language, 'MIRROR' is coded as '13918181518', how will 'APPLE' be coded in the same language ?

(a) 11616125 (b) 3984145
(c) 1162254 (d) 11213147

Sol. (a) As we can see from the alphabet series, numeric values for the alphabets M is 13, I is 9, R is 18 and O is 15.
Similarly, for the word APPLE, A = 1, P = 16, P = 16, L = 12 & E = 5. So, the code is 11616125. Therefore, option (a) is the correct answer.

V. Substitution Coding: In this type of questions, some particular words are assigned certain substituted names. Then a question is asked that is to be answered in the substituted code language.

ILLUSTRATION 7:

If white is called blue, blue is called red, red is called yellow, yellow is called green, green is called black, black is called violet and violet is called orange, what would be the colour of human blood?

(a) Red (b) Green
(c) Yellow (d) Violet

Sol. (c) Yellow
The colour of the human blood is 'red' ans as given, 'red' is called 'yellow.'
So, the colour of human blood is 'yellow.'

VI. Deciphering Message Word Codes: In this type of questions, some messages are given in the coded language and the code for a particular word or message is asked. To analyse such codes, any two messages bearing a common word are picked up. The common code-word will thus represent that word. Proceeding similarly by picking up all possible combinations of two, the entire message can be decoded and the codes for individual words found.

ILLUSTRATION 8:

In a certain code, 'bi nie pie' means 'some good jokes': 'nie bat lik' means 'some real stories'; and 'pie lik tol' means 'many good stories.' Which word in that code means 'jokes'?

(a) bi (b) nie
(c) pie (d) Can't be determined

Sol. (a) bi In the first and second statements, the common code word is 'nie' and the common word is 'some'.
So, 'nie' means 'some'.
In the first and third statements, the common code word is 'pie' and the common word is 'good'.
So, 'pie' means 'good'.

VII. Deciphering Number and Symbol Codes for Messages

In this type of questions, a few groups of numbers/symbols, each coding a certain message, are given. Through a comparison of the given coded messages, taking two at a time, the candidate is required to find the number/symbol code for each word and them formulate the code for the given message.

ILLUSTRATION 9:

In a certain code language, '743' means 'mangoes are good', '657' means 'eat good food and '934' means 'mangoes are ripe.' Which digit means 'ripe' in the that language?

(a) 9 (b) 4
(c) 5 (d) 7

Sol. (a) 9 In the first and third statements, the common code digits are '4' and '3' and the common words are 'mangoes' and 'are'.
So, '4' and '3' are the codes for 'mangoes' and 'are'.
Thus, in the third statements, '9' means 'ripe'.

VIII. Jumbled Coding: In this type of questions, certain sample words are given along with their codes. The candidate is required to decipher individual codes for different letters by comparing, taking two words at a time, and then answer the given questions accordingly.

DECODING

The word decoding stands for converting a certain pattern or expressions, *i.e.,* the code, to a word from English language or a certain series of numbers.

In other words, decoding refers to the process of converting the code back to the original word.

Similar to coding, there are 4 types of Decoding Methods :

I. Simple Arrangement

II. Direct Decoding

III. Letter Decoding

IV. Alphanumeric Decoding

We would first like you to go back and revise the four types of CODING methods before we move on.

I. Simple Arrangement Method : Under this, the code will be obtained simply by re-arrangement of the alphabets of the word. The questions will test you on decoding these codes.

ILLUSTRATION 1 :

In a certain language, 'SIMPLE' is written as 'ISPMEL' and 'CHAPTER' is written as 'HCPARET'. Then 'LFWORE' stands for which word ?

(a) LOWFER (b) FLOREW
(c) FLOWER (d) WORFEL

Sol. (c) SIMPLE ⟶ ISPMEL

The word 'SIMPLE' is of 6 letters and so is the code given in the question. Therefore, we have to follow the pattern of the word 'SIMPLE'.

In the above code, we can clearly observe that the code is obtained simply by inter changing the positions of consecutive alphabets, *i.e.,*

Similarly,

Hence, option (c) is the correct answer. 'FLOWER' is the word for which the code is given.

ILLUSTRATION 2 :

In a certain language, if 'CARROM' is written as 'MORRAC', then what is the word coded as 'TIBBAR'.

(a) RIBBAT (b) RABBIT
(c) BARTIB (d) BITRAB

Sol. (b) The code for the word 'CARROM', is obtained by reversing the order of the alphabets of the word *i.e.,*

CARROM

⟵ reverse the order

MORRAC

Similarly, the word for code 'TIBBAR' will be an outcome of the same pattern as followed for the word 'CARROM', *i.e.,* the code TIBBAR will also be written in reverse order.

TIBBAR

RABBIT

Hence, 'RABBIT' is the word, making option (2) the correct answer.

Note for Decoding : Solve by options, *i.e.*, by taking one option at a time into consideration.

II. Direct Decoding : In these kind of questions, there will be one or more words given in the question for which codes will be given either in direct fashion or in jumbled up fashion. We'll discuss both.

We will be asked to find out the original word (s) for the given code(s).

Command data for Illustration 3 & 4 :

In a certain code language, if P O U R I N G is written as x f n p l o m, S A M P L E is written as z e h x c j and W H I T E N E R is written as a t l k j o j p.

ILLUSTRATION 3 :

Then which word is written as 'hjecz' ?

(a) LEAMS (b) SMEAL

(c) MEALS (d) MALES

Sol. **(c)** The codes for the three words are direct substitution of the small alphabets for the capital ones, because 'N' & 'I' are codes as 'o' & 'l' respectively in both POURING as well as WHITENER, while 'E' is written as 'j' both the times in the word WHITENER and also in the word SAMPLE.

Words	P	O	U	R	I	N	G	S	A	M	P	L	E	W	H	I	T	E	N	E	R
Codes	x	f	n	p	l	o	m	z	e	h	x	c	j	a	t	l	k	j	o	j	p

Letter	P	O	U	R	I	N	G	S	A	M	L	E	W	H	T
Codes :	x	f	n	p	l	o	m	z	e	h	c	j	a	t	k

Therefore, the code 'h j e c z' stands for MEALS.

deriving the word from the code (see arrows)

Hence, option (3) is the correct answer.

ILLUSTRATION 4 :

Which word is coded as 'ajlmtk' ?

(a) WAISTE (b) WEIGHT

(c) WASTES (d) HEIGHT

Sol. (b) Following the same concept as in example 5, the code 'ajlmtk' represents

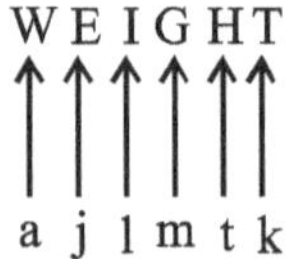

deriving the word from the code.

Hence, option (b) 'WEIGHT' is the correct answer.

Quick Tips

(i) Spot out the common letters in the words and try to find the code for the common letters first.

(ii) As soon as you find the codes for some letters, tick those letters as well as codes so you don't keep checking them again & again. This will save your time & save you from any kind of confusion while solving the questions.

III. Letter Decoding

Under this method, a code will be given to you, you will have to recognize the pattern the code is following.

The pattern may be moving a few alphabets forward, a few alphabets backward or alternate forward & backward.

ILLUSTRATION 5 :

If, in a certain language, POWERFUL is coded as QQZIWLBT, then which word is coded as ECQGJXZ ?

(a) DANCERS (b) HARMLESS

(c) PRACTISE (d) DANGERS

Sol. **(a)** The pattern followed by the code is moving up in an increasing order.

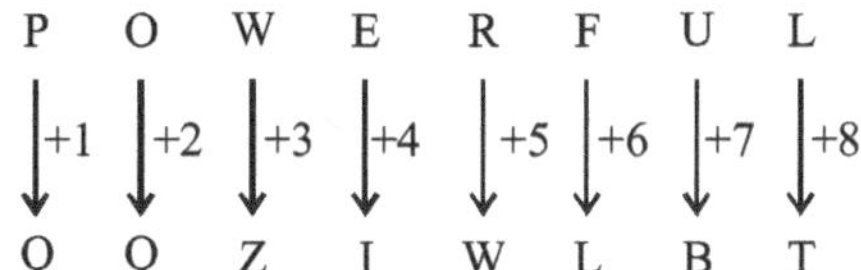

First method : similarly, the code given will also follow the same pattern. Therefore, we subtract or move the alphabets of the code backwards to form the word.

E C Q G J X Z

–1 –2 –3 – 4 –5 –6 –7

D A N C E R S

Second method : We can also go by the options, *i.e.,* check each option one by one and see if it forms the code given in the questions using the same pattern as coded in the word 'POWERFUL'.

IV. Alpha-Numeric Decoding

This is similar to alpha-numeric coding, with the only difference that we have to derive the code from a given word in case of alpha-numeric coding. While in decoding, we have to derive the word from the code following the alphabet series (ABCDEFG. .... PQRSTUVWXYZ).

ILLUSTRATION 6 :

If the code in a certain language, for PAPER = 56 and SHEET = 57, then for which of the following words is the code 88 ?

(a) IRON (b) PUPPET

(c) HELMETS (d) PARROT

Sol. (d) As we know the values of each alphabet in the alphabet series, so we can unlock the codes.

PAPER $\longrightarrow$ P = 16, A = 1, P = 16, E = 5, R = 18

$16+1+16+5+18=56$

SHEET $\longrightarrow$ S = 19, H = 8, E = 5, E = 5, T = 20

$19+8+5+5+20=57$

Now, to find the word for the code 88, we have to check all the options.

Option (a)

IRON $\longrightarrow$ I = 9, R = 18, O = 15, N = 14

$9+18+15+14=56$

Option (b)

PUPPET $\rightarrow$ P = 16, U = 21, P = 16, P = 16, E = 5, T = 20,

$16+21+16+16+5+20=94$

Option (c)

HELMETS $\rightarrow$ H = 8, E = 5, L = 12, M = 13, E = 5, T = 20, S = 19

$8+5+12+13+5+20+19=82$

Option (d)

PARROT $\rightarrow$ P = 16, A = 1, R = 18, R = 18, O = 15, T = 20

$16+1+18+18+15+20=88$

The required word.

Therefore, option (d) PARROT is the answer.

LEVEL 1

1. If in a certain code, HAT is 782, RABBIT is 681192. Then how will HABIT be coded as ?
   (a) 78139 (b) 78192
   (c) 68192 (d) 78129

2. If CAT is 48, Z is 52. Then what is TEA equal to?
   (a) 48 (b) 52
   (c) 60 (d) 50

3. If HELMET is written as IFMNFU. Then how will CHOCOLATE be written as ?
   (a) DIDPMPBUF
   (b) EIDPMPBUF
   (c) DIPDPMBFU
   (d) DIPDPMBUF

4. If FAIR is written as IENX. Then TAPE will be written as ?
   (a) WEVL (b) WEUK
   (c) WFUK (d) XEUK

5. If DELHI is coded as 73541 and CALCUTTA coded as 82589662, how can CALICUT be written?
   (a) 5279431 (b) 5978213
   (c) 5473628 (d) 8251896

6. In a certain code, 3456 is coded as ROPE, 15526 is coded as APPLE. Then how is 54613 coded as?
   (a) POEAR (b) PROEA
   (c) PEORA (d) RPOEA

7. In a certain code if FRIEND is written as DNEIRF. Then, what will be the code for DESERT ?
   (a) TRESED (b) DSERET
   (c) TRSEED (d) TESERD

8. In a certain code, if AFFAIR is FAAFRI, then FERRARIS is coded as ?
   (a) EFRRARIS (b) EFRRRASI
   (c) EFRRRAIS (d) EFRRARSI

9. In a certain code, if BLACK is KCALB then THEFT is ?
   (a) TFEHT (b) FHETT
   (c) TEHFT (d) TFHET

10. If in a certain language, POPULAR is coded as QPQVMBS, which word would be coded as GBNPVT ?
    (a) FARMER (b) FAMOUS
    (c) FRAMES (d) FAMOTH

11. If SIMPLE is coded as TJNQMF, then SJQQMF can be written as ________.
    (a) PIPPLE (b) TKRRNG
    (c) DIMPLE (d) PIMPLE

DIRECTIONS (Qs. 12-13) : In a certain code language, '782' means 'Flowers are beautiful', '692' means 'Roses are red', '628' means 'Roses are beautiful'..

12. Which number denotes 'Flowers' ?
    (a) 8 (b) 7 (c) 2 (d) 6

13. What does number '9' denote ?

(a) Roses (b) Flowers

(c) Red (d) are

DIRECTIONS (Qs. 14 – 15) : *If MISTAKE is coded as 9765412 and NAKED is coded as 84123, how the words will be coded in the following questions:*

14. DISTANT:

(a) 3765485 (b) 4798165

(c) 3697185 (d) 4768296

15. STAIN:

(a) 98175 (b) 89483

(c) 68194 (d) 65478

16. If REASON is coded as 5, BELIEVED as 7, what is the code number of GOVERNMENT?

(a) 6 (b) 8

(c) 9 (d) 10

17. In a certain code language, if 'M U M B A I' is written as 'NWPFFO', then in the same language, 'CARPET' will be written as___________. **[2019]**

(a) DCTTJY (b) DCUTJY

(c) DDUTJZ (d) DCUTJZ

18. In a certain code language, PROTEIN is coded as OTNVDKM. How will MINERAL be coded in the same language? **[2021]**

(a) NJOFSBNM (b) LHMDQBM

(c) OKPGTCN (d) LKMGQCK

19. In a certain code language, if NOISE is written as PQKUG, then how will PEACE be written in the same code language? **[2022]**

(a) FDBFQ (b) ODZBD

(c) RGCEG (d) QFBDF

20. In a certain code language, if 'BALL' is coded as '54' and 'BAT' is coded as '46', then what is the code for 'STUMP' in that language? **[2022]**

(a) 89 (b) 98

(c) 178 (d) 196

LEVEL 2

DIRECTIONS (Qs. 1-6) : *Read the following information and answer the question that follows:*

Code :	Z	A	X	B	Y	O	T	W	C	M	I
Original alphabet	B	U	E	T	F	A	I	R	V	L	D

1. BEAUTIFUL.
   (a) ZXOABTYAM
   (b) ZXOBATYAM
   (c) ZXOBYAMAT
   (d) XOBYATAM
2. FLAIR
   (a) YMOTW
   (b) YMUTW
   (c) YMIOW
   (d) YMOIW
3. BUILT
   (a) ZABMT
   (b) ZATMB
   (c) ZATBM
   (d) ZTABM
4. VALID
   (a) CITMO
   (b) CIMTO
   (c) COMTI
   (d) COMIT
5. AFRAID
   (a) OYTWOI
   (b) OYWTOI
   (c) OWYOTI
   (d) OYWOTI
6. BULLET
   (a) BAMMXZ
   (b) ZAMMXI
   (c) OWYOTI
   (d) OYWOTI
7. Here are some words translated from an artificial language

   mie pie is blue light

   mie tie is blue berry

   aie tie is rasp berry

   Which words could possibly mean "light fly"?
   (a) pie zie
   (b) pie mie
   (c) aie zie
   (d) aie mie
8. If REASON is coded as PGYUMP, then DIRECT will be coded as?
   (a) BKPGAV (b) FKTGEV
   (c) FGTCER (d) BGPCAR
9. If in a certain code language, 'PHONE' is written as 'OGNMD', then will be written as 'MZSHNMZK' in the same language. **[2018]**
   (a) SURPRISE
   (b) NATIONAL
   (c) BUSINESS
   (d) FEBRUARY
10. If in a certain code language. 'AEIOU' is written as 'CGKQW', then in the same language 'KMTSR' is the code for _____. **[2018]**

(a) MOVUT
(b) LNUTS
(c) IKRQP
(d) STUNL

11. In a certain code language, if ‘nice big home’ is coded as ‘emoh gib ecin’ and ‘nice small family’ is coded as ‘ylimaf llams ecin’, then in the same code language, ‘all the best’ is coded as ______________. **[2018]**

(a) tseb eht lla
(b) tesb the lla
(c) tseb eht all
(d) tseb the lal

12. Some letters are coded as follows :

Y	C	L	S	I	O	U	M	D	T	P	H	E
×	÷	*	£	–	$	?	+	α	β	γ	#	•

The word which is coded as $ * × + ³ “‘ £ is _______. **[2018]**

(a) OLYMPIAD (b) OLYNTHUS (c) OLYMPICS (d) OLYMPUS

13. If in a certain code language, ‘BRIGHT’ is written as ‘ZTGIFV’, then how will ‘AROUND’ be written in that code language? **[2019]**

(a) YSNVLF (b) ZTMUMF
(c) YTMWLF (d) XUMWMF

14. In a certain code language, GYPSUM is written as GMPSUY. How will GARDEN be written in that language? **[2019]**

(a) ADENGR (b) ADEGRN
(c) ADEGNR (d) GEDANR

15. In a certain code language, MIRACLE is coded as ACEILMR. How will BUILDER be coded in the same language? **[2020]**

(a) BEDRILU (b) BDEILRU
(c) BDEJLRT (d) CDEIJRT

16. In a certain code language, OPERATION is written as PQKVCTGRQ. How will INVISIBLE be written in the same language? **[2020]**

(a) KPXKUKDNG
(b) KPXKVKENH
(c) GNDKUKXPK
(d) GNDKVJXPK

17. In a certain code language, if CREATE is written as ACEERT, then how will BRIGHT be written in that language? **[2021]**

(a) BHGRIT (b) GHBITR
(c) BGHIRT (d) CSJHIU

18. In a certain code language, PLAYER is written as SODBHU, then how will SINGER be written in the same language? **[2021]**

(a) QMBZFS (b) UKPIGT
(c) TJOHFS (d) VLQJHU

19. In a certain code language, if RANDOM is written as OBSLNC, then what will be the code of ABROAD in the same code language? **[2022]**

(a) BCSNZC
(b) SCBEBP
(c) BCSCZN
(d) SCBCZN

20. In a certain code language, 'SATURN' is written as 'JVQXWW' and 'URANUS' is written as 'OYJENY'. How is 'PAPERS' written in that code language? **[2022]**

(a) OVATWT (b) OVBTWT

(c) OVATXY (d) None of these

21. If Z = 26, NET = 39 and MEO = 33, then NUT = ? **[2022]**

(a) 56 (b) 55

(c) 53 (d) None of these

ANSWER KEY																			
LEVEL-1																			
1	(b)	**3**	(d)	**5**	(d)	**7**	(a)	**9**	(a)	**11**	(b)	**13**	(c)	**15**	(d)	**17**	(d)	**19**	(c)
2	(b)	**4**	(b)	**6**	(a)	**8**	(b)	**10**	(b)	**12**	(b)	**14**	(a)	**16**	(c)	**18**	(d)	**20**	(c)
LEVEL-2																			
1	(a)	**4**	(c)	**7**	(a)	**10**	(c)	**13**	(c)	**16**	(c)	**19**	(d)						
2	(a)	**5**	(d)	**8**	(a)	**11**	(a)	**14**	(c)	**17**	(a)	**20**	(a)						
3	(b)	**6**	(b)	**9**	(b)	**12**	(d)	**15**	(b)	**18**	(d)	**21**	(b)						

CHAPTER

Blood Relations

While attempting questions on blood relations, one should be clear of all the relation patterns that can exist between any two individuals.

These type of questions are given mainly to test one's relationship ability.

Mother's or father's son	Brother
Mother's or father's daughter	Sister
Mother's or father's brother	Uncle
Mother's or father's sister	Aunt
Mother's or father's father	Grandfather
Mother's or father's mother	Grandmother
Son's wife	Daughter-in-law
Daughter's husband	Son-in-law
Husband's or wife's sister	Sister-in-law
Husband's or wife's brother	Brother-in-law
Brother's son	Nephew
Brother's daughter	Niece
Uncle or aunt's son or daughter	Cousin
Sister's husband	Brother-in-law
Brother's wife	Sister-in-law
Grandson's or Grand daughter's daughter	Great granddaughter

A relation on the mother's side is called maternal while that on the father's side is called paternal.

Thus, mother's brother is maternal uncle while father's brother is paternal uncle.

To solve problems on relationship you can construct family tree.

To build a family tree, certain standard notations are used to indicate a relationship between the members of the family. It is not necessary to follow them implicity; you can formulate your own notations to draw the family tree quickly and accurately

1. A is male [A]
2. A is a female 
3. Sex of A not known A
4. A and B are married to each other A = B
5. A and B are siblings A $\leftrightarrow$ B
6. A and C are B's children — B with arrows down to A and C
7. A is the uncle/ aunt of B 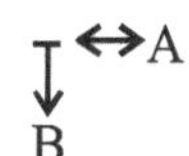
8. A is the only child of B  $\downarrow$ A

To make a family tree from the given data, we will first identify the males and the females in the family and then try to put each member in their respective position in the tree. For example A, B, C, D, E and F are related to each other as given here, B is F' s daughter-in-law. D is A's only grand child. C is D's only uncle. A has only 2 children F and C, one male and one female (not necessarily in the same order). E is the father of C.

(i) Who is the grandmother of D ?

(ii) Who is the mother-in-law of B?

(iii) When a girl G is married into the family, what is the relationship between G and D?

Step I : Identify the elements A, B, C, D, E and F,

From the given conditions we can determine who are the males/ females in the above group.

(1) B is F's daughter-in-law (B)

(2) C is D's only uncle 

(3) A has 2 children F and C, one male (F) and one female, Since C is male, F is Female.

Step II : Try to identify the positions of the members in the family tree. For this , determine the number of generations involved from the statements. D is A's only grand child. Thus, we know that there are three generations.

Step III : Use the conditions to arrange A , B , C, D, E and F in these three generations.

(a) B is F 's daughter-in-law,

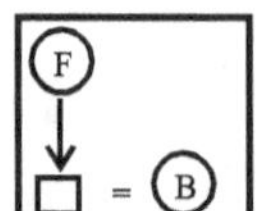

(b) D is A 's only grandchild

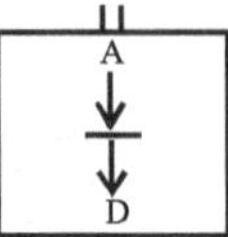

(c) C is D's uncle.

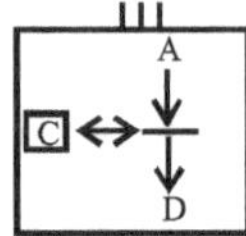

(d) A has only two children F and C, one male and one female.

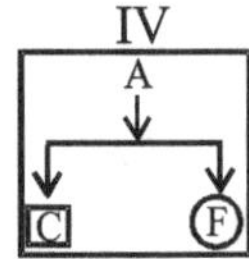

(e) E is C's father.

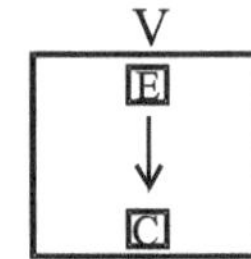

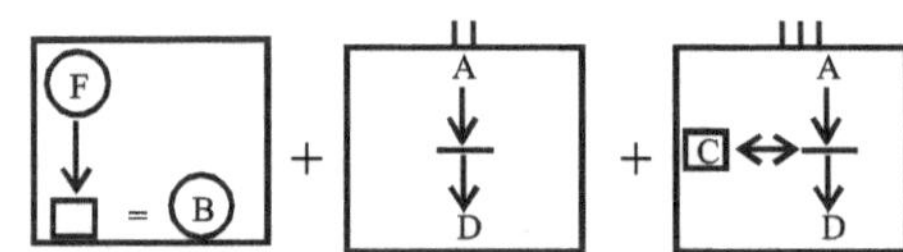

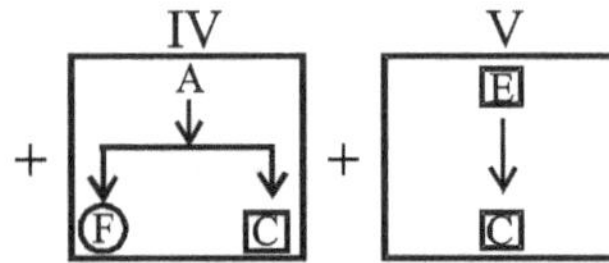

Level- I

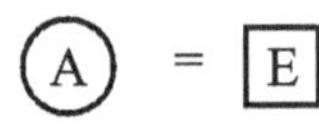

Level - II

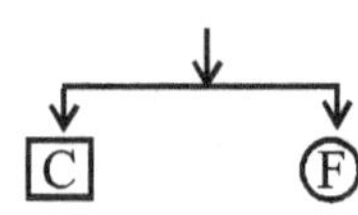

Level- III

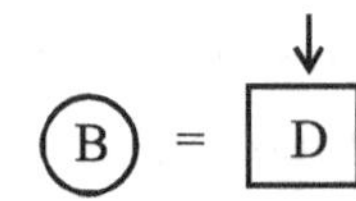

Question (i) and (ii) can be answered easily by looking at the family tree. A is the grandmother of D and F is the mother-in - law of B. For question (iii), C is the only male in the family who is unmarried. G will be married to C and hence she will be D's aunt.

DIRECTIONS (ILLUSTRATION 1-3) : Abra is Rambo's daughter. Shintu is Rambo's sister. Shintu's daughter is called Cabra and son is called Dabra. Limba is Cabra's maternal Aunt.

ILLUSTRATION 1 :

Abra is Limba's

(a) Aunt (b) Nephew
(c) Uncle (d) None of these

Sol. **(d)** Abra can be Limba's niece or daughter.

ILLUSTRATION 2 :

Cabra is Rambo's;

(a) Nephew (b) Niece
(c) Uncle (d) Cannot say

Sol. **(b)** Cabra is Rambo's niece.

ILLUSTRATION 3 :

Dabra is Limba's

(1) Niece (b) Aunt
(c) Nephew (d) None of these

Sol. **(c)** Dabra is Limba's nephew.

For answers to examples 1 to 3 :

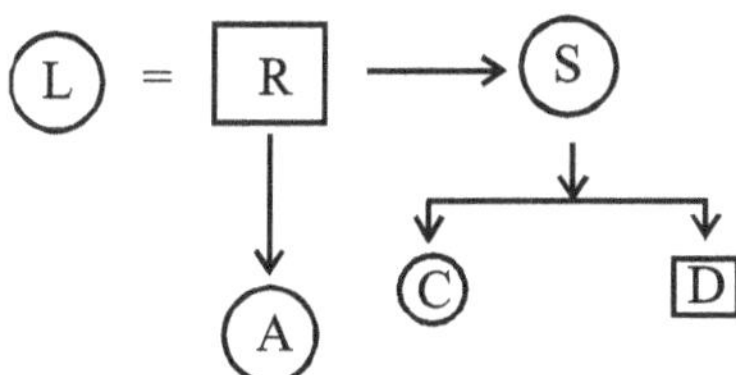

or

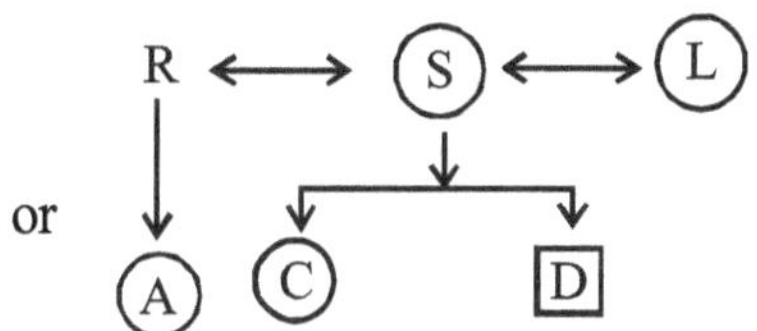

PROBLEMS IN DECIDING RELATIONSHIP

TYPE 1 :

In this type of question, a roundabout description is given in the form of certain small relationships and you are required to analyse the whole chain of relations and decipher the direct relationship between the persons concerned.

ILLUSTRATION 4:

Anil introduces Rohit as the son of the only brother of his father's wife. How is Rohit related to Anil ?

(a) Cousin (b) Son
(c) Uncle (d) Son-in-law

Sol. **(a)** The relations may be analysed as follows.

Father's wife– mother, Mother's brother — Uncle; Uncle's son— Cousin.

So, Rohit is Anil's cousin. Hence, the answer is (a)

TYPE 2 :

In this type of question, mutual blood relations of more than two persons are mentioned. The candidate is required to analyse the given information, work out a family chart and then answer the given questions.

DIRECTIONS (ILLUSTRATION 5-8) : Read the following information carefully and answer the questions given below.

There are six children playing football, namely A,B,C,D, E and F. A and E are brothers. F is the sister of E. C is the only son of A's uncle. B and D are the daughter of the brother of C's father.

ILLUSTRATION 5 :

How is C related to F ?

(a) Cousin (b) Brother son

(c) Son (d) Uncle

Sol. **(a)** F is E's and hence A's sister. So, C is also the son of F's uncle and is, therefore, F's Cousin.

ILLUSTRATION 6 :

How many male players are there ?

(a) One

(b) Three

(c) Four

(d) Five

Sol. **(b)** As given, A and E are brothers. Hence both are males. F is the sister of E and hence female. C is the son and hence male. B and D are daughters and hence female. Thus, there are three males. So, the answer is (b)

ILLUSTRATION 7 :

How many female players are there ?

(a) One (b) Two

(c) Three (d) Four

Sol. **(c)** Clearly, from the solution of 2, we find that there are three females. So, the answer is (c).

ILLUSTRATION 8 :

How is D related to A?

(a) Uncle (b) Sister

(c) Niece (d) Cousin

Sol. **(d)** Clearly, D's father is the brother of C's father and C's father is A's uncle. So D is A's sister. Hence the answer is (d).

TYPE 3 :

Coded Relations

In such questions, the relationships are represented by certain specific codes or symbols. The candidate is then required to analyse some given codes to determine the relationship between a set of persons, or to express a given relationship in the coded form.

DIRECTIONS (ILLUSTRATION 9-12) : Study the information given below and answer the questions that follow :

A + B ' means 'A is the daughter of B; A – B ' means ' A is the husband of B'. A × B means A is the brother of B.

ILLUSTRATION 9 :

If P + Q – R, which of the following is true ?

(a) R is the mother of P.

(b) R is the sister in -law of P.

(c) R is the aunt of P.

(d) R is the mother in- law of P.

Sol. **(a)** P + Q – R means P is the daughter of Q who is the husband of R i.e, R is the mother of P.

ILLUSTRATION 10 :

If P × Q + R, which of the following is true ?

(a) P is the brother of R.

(b) P is the uncle of R.

(c) P is the son of R.

(d) P is the father of R.

Sol. **(c)** P × Q + R means P is the brother of Q, who is the daughter of R i.e, P is the son of R.

ILLUSTRATION 11 :

If P + Q × R which of the following is true ?

(a) P is the niece of R.

(b) P is the daughter of R.

(c) P is the cousin of R.

(d) P is the daughter-in law of R.

Sol. **(a)** P + Q × R means P the daughter of Q, who is the brother of R i.e, P is the niece of R.

ILLUSTRATION 12 :

If P + Q means P is the son of Q and

P = Q means P is the sister of Q.

Then what does P = R + Q means ?

Sol. P = R + Q ⇒ P = R which mean P is the sister of R.

R + Q means R is the son of Q.

∴ P is the daughter of Q.

Useful Tips

1. The only son of your father — Yourself
2. Wife of the father —Mother
3. The only son of grand father or grand mother – father
4. The only daughter-in-law of grand father or grand mother – Mother
5. Mother-in-law of mother –Grand mother
6. Father-in-law of mother – Grand father
7. The only daughter of the father –Sister
8. Son of the father of the sister – Brother
9. Son of the only son of the father –son
10. Son of the only son of grand father – Brother
11. Daughter of the only son of Grand father – Sister

LEVEL 1

1. Given that

   1. A is the mother of B
   2. C is the son of A
   3. D is the brother of E
   4. E is the daughter of B.

   The grandmother of D is

   (a) A (b) B
   (c) C (d) E

2. Deepak said to Nitin, " That boy playing football is the younger of the two brothers of the daughter of my father's wife " How is the boy playing football related to Deepak ?

   (a) Son (b) Brother
   (c) Cousin (d) Niece

3. A and B are brothers. C and D are sisters A's son is D's brother. How is B related to C

   (a) Father (b) Brother
   (c) Grand father (d) Uncle

4. 'X' is the wife of 'Y' and 'Y' is the brother of 'Z' , 'Z' is the son of 'P' . How is 'P' related to 'X'

   (a) Sister (b) Aunt
   (c) Brother (d) Father-in-law

5. Ajay is the brother of Vijay. Mili is the sister of Ajay. Sanjay is the brother of Rahul and Mehul is the daughter of Vijay. Who is Sanjay's Uncle ?

   (a) Rahul (b) Ajay
   (c) Mehul (d) Data inadequate

6. A man pointing to a photograph says. " The lady in the photograph is my nephew's maternal grandmother" How is the lady in the photograph related to the man's sister who has no other sister.

   (a) Cousin (b) Sister-in-law
   (c) Mother (d) Mother-in-law

7. A is the uncle of B, who is the daughter of C and C is the daughter-in-law of P. How is A related to P?

   (a) Brother
   (b) Son
   (c) Son-in-law
   (d) Data inadequate

8. E is the son of A. D is the son of B. E is married to C. C is B's daughter. How is D related to E?

   (a) Brother
   (b) Uncle
   (c) Father-in-law
   (d) Brother-in-law

9. A is the brother of B, C is the brother of A . To establish a relationship between B & C, which of the following information is required.

   I Sex of C
   II. Sex of B

   (a) Only I is required
   (b) Only II is required
   (c) Both I and II are required
   (d) Neither required

10. Pointing towards a man in the photograph, Arachana said, " He is the son of only son of may grandmother". "How is man related to Archana ?
    (a) Cousin (b) Nephew
    (c) Brother (d) Son

DIRECTION (Q. 11): *Read the following information carefully and answer the question given below :–*

A + B means A is the daughter of B;

A – B means A is the husband of B;

A × B means A is the brother of B.

11. If P + Q – R, which one of the following is true ?
    (a) R is the mother of P
    (b) R is the sister-in-law of P
    (c) R is the aunt of P
    (d) R is the mother-in-law of P

DIRECTIONS (Qs. 12-15) : *To answer the questions, read the information carefully :*

The six members of a family A, B, C, D, E and F are travelling together. B is the son of C but C is not the mother of B. A and C are married coupple. E is the brother of C. D is the daughter of A. F is the brother of B.

12. How many male members are there in family ?
    (a) 1 (b) 2
    (c) 3 (d) 4
13. Who is the mother of B ?
    (a) D
    (b) F
    (c) E
    (d) A
14. How many children does A have ?
    (a) One (b) Two
    (c) Three (d) Four
15. Which of the following is a pair of females ?
    (a) AE (b) BD
    (c) DF (d) AD
16. Amit said, this girl is the wife of the grandson of my mother. How is Amit related to the girl?
    (a) Father (b) Grand Father
    (c) Husband (d) Father-in-law
17. Pointing to a photograph, Kabeer said "He is the son of the only daughter of the father of my brother." How is Kabeer related to the man in the photograph? **[2018]**
    (a) Nephew (b) Brother
    (c) Father (d) Maternal uncle
18. Pointing to a man, Deepak said, "His only brother is the father of my daughter's father". How is the man related to Deepak? **[2018]**
    (a) Grandfather (b) Father
    (c) Uncle (d) Grandson
19. Pointing to a man in a photograph, Kunal said, "He is the father of my son's wife's son". How is the man related to Kunal's wife? **[2019]**
    (a) Son (b) Father-in-law
    (c) Grandson (d) Cousin
20. Ram is the husband of Reenu. Reena is the sister of Raju and Raju is the a son of Hemant. How is Ram related to Hemant? **[2022]**
    (a) Father (b) Brother-in-law
    (c) Father-in-law (d) Son-in-law

LEVEL 2

DIRECTIONS (Qs. 1-2) : *Study the following information and answer the question given below. S and R are brothers. T is daughter of S. U is the spouse of R and mother of Q. P is the daughter of V, who is the spouse of T.*

1. Who is the grand father of P ?
   (a) U (b) S
   (c) R (d) V
2. Who is the cousin of Q ?
   (a) T (b) V
   (c) R (d) P
3. A is B's sister. C is B's mother. D is C's father. E is D's mother. Then, how is A related to D?
   (a) Grandmother
   (b) Grandfather
   (c) Daughter
   (d) Granddaughter
4. If C is husband of B, B is daughter of A, A is mother of D and D is a boy, then how D is related to B?
   (a) Husband
   (b) Brother
   (c) Son
   (d) Father
5. If C is brother of B, B is son of A, D is father of C and A is a female, then how A is related to D?
   (a) Mother (b) Father
   (c) Sister (d) Wife
6. In a joint family, there are father, mother, 4 married sons, 2 unmarried sons and three unmarried daughters. Out of the married sons, two have 2 sons each and two have a son and a daughter each. How many male members are there in the family? **[2019]**
   (a) 13 (b) 12
   (c) 14 (d) 11
7. Shivam points to a photograph and says, "The woman is my niece's maternal grandmother". How is the woman in the photograph related to Shivam's brother who has no other sibling? **[2019]**
   (a) Sister-in-law
   (b) Mother
   (c) Mother-in-law
   (d) Can't be determined
8. Pointing to a person, Arjun said, "His only brother is the father of my daughter's father". How is the person related to Arjun?
   (a) Father (b) Uncle **[2020]**
   (c) Grand father (d) Brother-in-law
9. Five members D, E, F, G and H are living in a family. D is the father-in-law of F. H is the son of E. G is the sister of H. F is married to E. Then, how is H related to D?
   (a) Son **[2021]**
   (b) Daughter
   (c) Grandson
   (d) Grand daughter

10. Pointing to a girl in the picture, Sahil said, "She is the daughter of my mother's only daughter". How is Sahil related to the girl in the picture? **[2021]**
    (a) Father
    (b) Brother
    (c) Maternal uncle
    (d) Paternal uncle
11. Pointing to a girl in the picture, Vansh said, "She is the daughter of my father's brother". How is that girl related to Vansh? **[2021]**
    (a) Sister (b) Mother
    (c) Cousin (d) Aunt
12. If P is the father of Q, Q is the sister of R and R is the daughter of S, then how is S related to P? **[2022]**
    (a) Daughter
    (b) Sister
    (c) Wife
    (d) Aunt
13. Pointing to an old man, Rahul said, "His son is my son's uncle". How is the old man related to Rahul? **[2022]**
    (a) Grandfather
    (b) Father
    (a) Uncle
    (d) Brother
14. Pointing to a girl, Rahul said, "She is the daughter of my grandfather's only son". How is the girl related to Rahul? **[2022]**
    (a) Father (b) Brother
    (c) Sister (d) Mother

ANSWER KEY																			
LEVEL-1																			
1	(a)	**3**	(d)	**5**	(d)	**7**	(b)	**9**	(b)	**11**	(a)	**13**	(d)	**15**	(d)	**17**	(d)	**19**	(a)
2	(b)	**4**	(d)	**6**	(c)	**8**	(d)	**10**	(c)	**12**	(d)	**14**	(c)	**16**	(d)	**18**	(c)	**20**	(d)
LEVEL-2																			
1	(b)	**3**	(b)	**5**	(d)	**7**	(c)	**9**	(c)	**11**	(a)	**13**	(b)						
2	(a)	**4**	(b)	**6**	(c)	**8**	(b)	**10**	(c)	**12**	(c)	**14**	(c)						

CHAPTER

Direction Sense Test

DIRECTION SENSE TEST :

There are four directions North, South, East and West. The word NEWS came from North, East, West and South. There are four regions :

North-East (I); South-East (IV); North-West (II); South-West (III). The directions OP, OS, OQ and OR are North East direction; North-West direction; South-West and South-East direction.

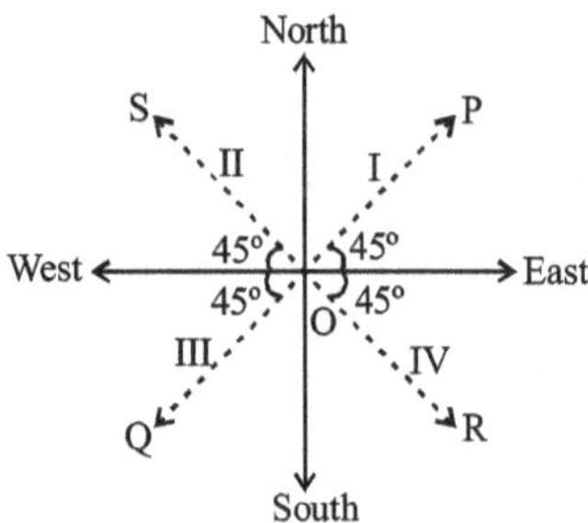

The candidate must distinguish between the regions and directions i.e. between North-East region and North-East direction.

If you move with your face east-wards, your left hand is towards north and your right hand is towards south. Similarly the positions of the directions of the hands can be fixed when you move in any of the other three directions.

To solve the question, first draw the direction figure

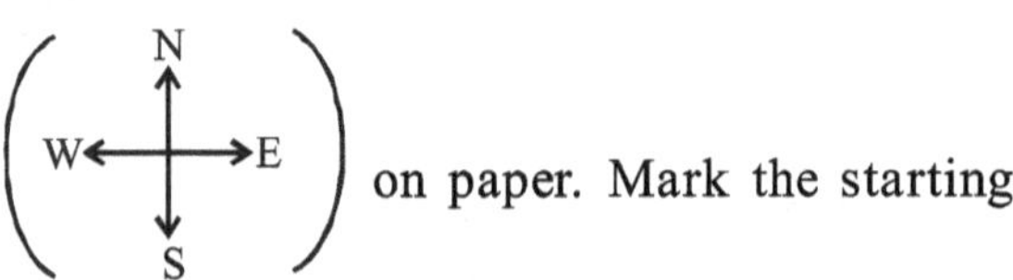

on paper. Mark the starting point. After that move carefully according to the directions given in the question.

DIRECTIONS (ILLUSTRATION 1-3) : Read the information given below to answer these questions.

a, b, c, d, e, f, g, h and i are nine houses. c is 2 km east of b. a is 1 km north of b and h is 2 km south of a, g is 1 km west of h while d is 3 km east of g and f is 2 km north of g. i is situated just in the middle of b and c while e is just in middle of h and d.

ILLUSTRATION 1:

Distance between e and g is :

(a) 2 km (b) 1 km
(c) 5 km (d) 1.5 km

ILLUSTRATION 2:

Distance between a and f is :

(a) 1.41 km
(b) 3 km
(c) 2 km
(d) 1 km

ILLUSTRATION 3:

Distance between e and i is :

(a) 4 km (b) 2 km

(c) 1 km (d) 3 km

***Sol.* (1-3) :**

From the information given, positions of houses are as follows :

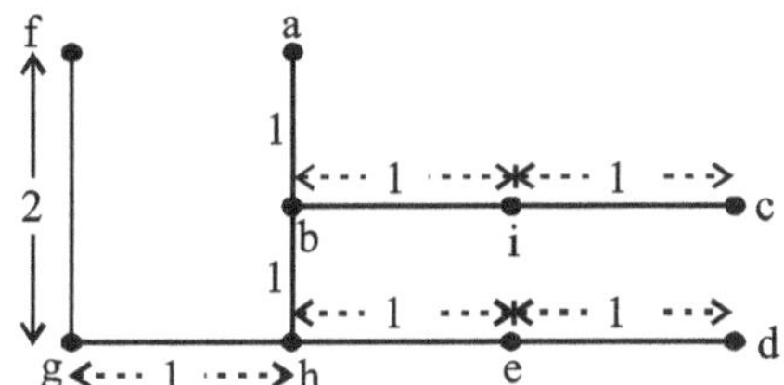

***Sol.* 1 : (a)** Clearly, the distance between e and g is 2 km.

***Sol.* 2 : (d)** From the above diagram, the distance between a and f is 1 km.

***Sol.* 3 : (c)** Clearly, the distance between e and i is 1 km.

ILLUSTRATION 4:

In the given figure, P is 300 km eastward of O and Q is 400 kms North of O, R is exactly in the middle of Q and P. The distance between Q and R is :

(a) 250 kms

(b) $250\sqrt{2}$ kms

(c) 300 kms

(d) 350 kms

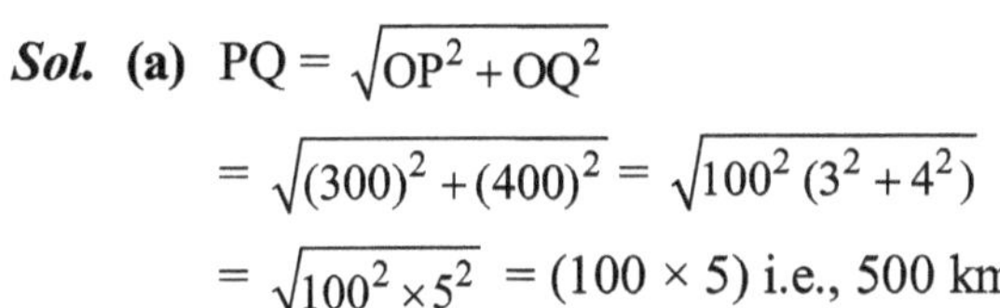

***Sol.* (a)** $PQ = \sqrt{OP^2 + OQ^2}$

$= \sqrt{(300)^2 + (400)^2} = \sqrt{100^2 (3^2 + 4^2)}$

$= \sqrt{100^2 \times 5^2} = (100 \times 5)$ i.e., 500 km.

R being in the midway of PQ, so QR = 250 kms.

ILLUSTRATION 5:

Four persons stationed at the four corners of a square piece as shown in the diagram. P starts crossing the field diagonally. After walking half the distance, he turns right, walks some distance and turns left.

Which direction is P facing now ?

(a) North-east

(b) North-west

(c) North

(d) South-east

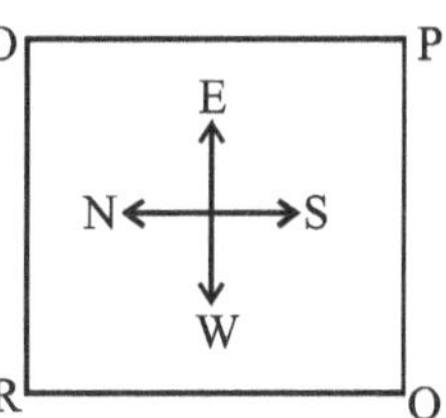

***Sol.* (b)** The route of P is shown in the diagram.

Clearly the direction of P is North-west.

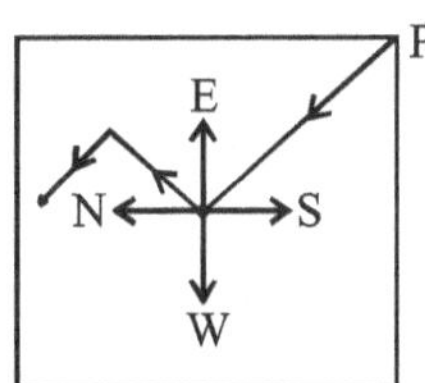

ROTATION OF ANGLES

To solve angle movement questions. It is necessary to know about the rotations of angles which are given below.

i) For right direction movement (Clockwise)

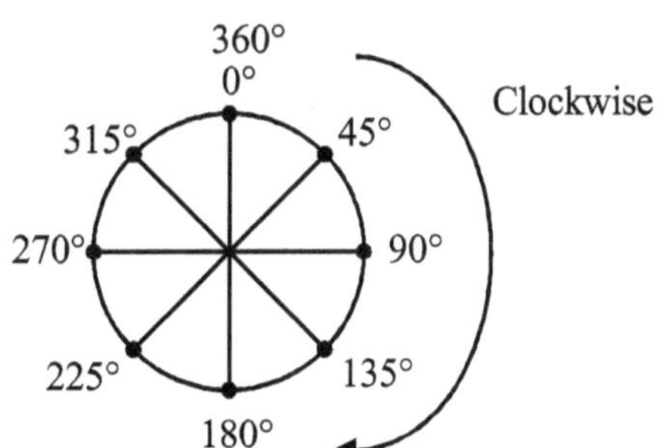

ii) For left direction movement (Anti-clock-wise)

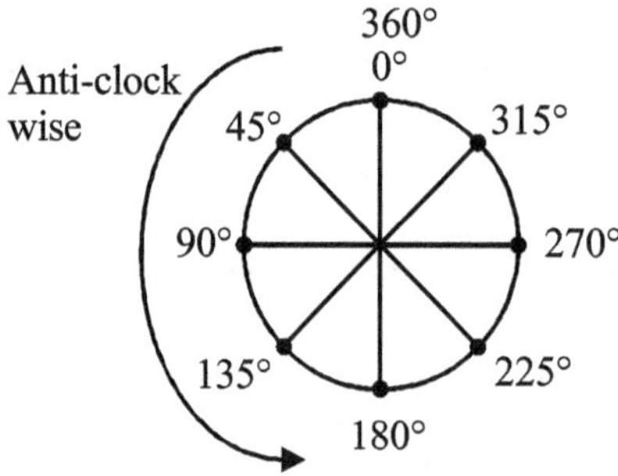

Left turn Anti-clockwise direction

Right turn Clockwise direction

The Change in Direction when a Person or Vehicle Takes A Right or a Left Turn

Direction before taking	**Direction in which the person or vehicle will be moving after taking**	
the turn	**the turn**	
	Right	**Left**
North	East	West
South	West	East
East	South	North
West	North	South

Pythogoras Theorem

While solving the distance related question, one must be through with the Pythagorean Theorem to be able to solve most of the questions, The Pythagorean Theorem is used calculate the shortest path traveled, the minimum distance between two points, etc.

It states that, in **a right angled triangle** the length of the **hypotenuse** is equal to the **square root of the sum of squares of the other two sides.**

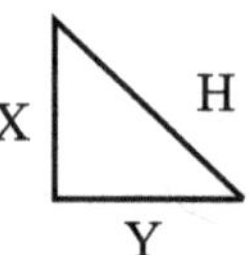

Where, H = Hypotenuse

X = Height

Y = Base

Therefore, according to the theorem $H^2 = X^2 + Y^2$

i.e., $H = \sqrt{(X^2 + Y^2)}$

Shadow Case

In morning/Sunrise time

a) If a person facing towards Sun, the shadow will be towards his back or in west.

b) If a person facing towards South, the shodow will be towards his right.

c) If a person facing towards West, the shadow will be towards his front.

d) If a person facing towards North, the shadow will be towards his left.

In evening/Sunset time

a) If a person facing towards Sun, the shadow will be towards his back or in East

b) If a person facing towards North, the shadow will be towards his right.

c) If a person facing towards East, the shadow will be towards his front.

d) If a person facing towards South, the shadow will be towards his left.

LEVEL 1

1. If A to the south of B and C is to the east of B, in what direction is A with respect to C ?
   (a) North-east (b) North-west
   (c) South-east (d) South-west

2. Divya journeys 10 km to east then 10 km to south-west. He turns again and journeys 10 km to North-West. Whic h direction is he in from the starting point ?
   (a) South (b) North
   (c) West (d) East

3. Sobha was facing East. She walked 20 metres. Turning left she moved 15 metres and then turning right moved 25 metres. Finally, she turned right and moved 15 metres more. How far is she from her starting point?
   (a) 25 metres
   (b) 35 metres
   (c) 50 metres
   (d) 45 metres

4. Jatin leaves his house and walks 12 km towards North. He turns right and walks another 12 km. He turns right again, walks 12 km more and turns left to walk 5 km. How far is he from his home and in which direction ?
   (a) 7 km East
   (b) 10 km East
   (c) 17 km East
   (d) 24 km East

5. Ramakant walks northwards. After a while, he turns to his right and a little further to his left. Finally, after walking a distance of one kilometre, he turns to his left again. In which direction is he moving now ?
   (a) North (b) South
   (c) East (d) West

6. P, Q, R, S, T, U, V and W are sitting around a round table in the same order, for group discussion at equal distance. Their positions are clockwise. If V sits in the north, then what will be the position of S?
   (a) East (b) South-east
   (c) South (d) South-west

7. If all the directions are rotated, i.e., if North is changed to West and East to North and so on, then what will come in place of North-West ?
   (a) South-West (b) North-East
   (c) East-North (d) East-West

8. If a person is walking towards North, what direction should he follow so that he is walking towards West ?
   (a) right, right, left (b) left, left, right
   (c) left, right, left (d) left, left, left

9. From his house, Lokesh went 15 km to the North. Then he turned West and covered 10 km. Then, he turned South and covered 5 km. Finally , turning to East, he covered 10 km. In which direction is he from his house?
   (a) East (b) West
   (c) North (d) South

10. Deepa moved a distance of 75 metres towards the north. She then turned to the left and walking for about 25 meters, turned left again and walked 80 meters. Finally, she turned to the right at an angle of 45°. In which direction was she moving finally ?

(a) North-east (b) North-west
(c) South (d) South-west

11. Johnson left for his office in his car. He drove 15 km towards north and then 10 km towards west. He then turned to the south and covered 5 km. Further, he turned to the east and moved 8 km. Finally, he turned right and drove 10 km. How far and in which direction is he from his starting point?

(a) 2 km west (b) 5 km East
(c) 3 km north (d) 6 Km south

12. You go North, turn right, then right again and then go to the left. In which direction are you now?

(a) North (b) South
(c) East (d) West

13. If A is to the South of B and C is to the East of B, in what direction is A with respect to?

(a) North-East (b) North-West
(c) South-East (d) South-West

14. A farmer travels 20 m north from his house. He then turns east and walks 6 m, from there he again turns south and walks 12 m. How far is he from his original position?

(a) 6 meter (b) 8 meter
(c) 10 meter (d) 14 meter

15. Two person are sitting back to back. If the first person face is towards north. In which direction will be right hand of the second person.

(a) South (b) East
(c) West (d) North

16. If North-West becomes East, then what will West become? **[2018]**

(a) South-West (b) North-East
(c) West (d) North

17. Komal goes 3 m towards South, then she takes a left turn and goes 5 m. Again she turns left and goes 3 m. How far is she now from her starting point? **[2021]**

(a) 3 m (b) 4 m
(c) 5 m (d) 8 m

LEVEL 2

1. I am facing south. I turn right and walk 20 m. Then I turn right again and walk 10 m. Then I turn left and walk 10 m and then turning right walk 20 m. Then I turn right again and walk 60 m. In which direction am I from the starting point
   (a) North (b) North-west
   (c) East (d) North-east

2. Going 50 m to the south of her house, Radhika turns left and goes another 20 m. Then turning to the North, she goes 30 m and then starts walking to her house. In which direction is she walking now ?
   (a) North-west (b) North
   (c) South east (d) East

3. One day, Ravi left home and cycled 10 km southwards, turned right and cycled 5 km and turned right and cycled 10 km and turned left and cycled 10 km. How many kilometres will he have to cycle to reach his home straight?
   (a) 10 km (b) 15 km
   (c) 20 km (d) 25 km

4. A is East of B and West of C, D is South-West of C, and B is South-East of E. When seen from West to East, which of the following sequences are possible?
   I. EBDAC
   II. DEBAC
   III. EBADC
   IV. EDBAC
   (a) I and II
   (b) I, III and IV
   (c) I, II and III
   (d) All I, II, III and IV

5. If South-East becomes North; and North-East becomes West; then West becomes
   (a) North East
   (b) South East
   (c) North West
   (d) South West

6. A watch reads 9: 25. If the minute hand is in the North direction, then hour hand will be in __________direction. **[2018]**
   (a) North-West
   (b) South-East
   (c) North-East
   (d) South-West

7. Tarun is facing South-West. He turns 135° anti-clockwise and then again turns 225° clockwise. Finally he turns 270° anti-clockwise. In which direction is he facing now? **[2019]**
   (a) North-East (b) North-West
   (c) South-East (d) South-West

8. Shanaya left for her office in her car. She drove 6 km towards North and then 12 km towards West. She then turned to the South and covered 1 km. Further, she turned to the East and moved 8 km. Finally, she turned right and drove 5 km. How far and in which direction is she now from her starting point? **[2019]**
   (a) 2 km, West (b) 4 km, East
   (c) 4 km, West (d) 2 km, North

9. Ashwini is facing towards South-West. He turns 180° clockwise and then turns 90° anti-clockwise. Finally he turns 315° clockwise. In which direction is he facing now? **[2019]**
   (a) North (b) North-West
   (c) West (d) South-East

10. Vinita walked 20 m towards North. Then, she turned right and walks 30 m. Then, she turns right and walks 35 m. Then, she turns left and walks 15 m. Finally, she turns left and walks 15 m. How far and in which direction is she now with respect to her starting point? **[2020]**
   (a) 45 m, East (b) 45 m, West
   (c) 35 m, West (d) 35 m, East

11. A girl is facing towards East. She turns 225° in the anticlockwise direction and then 90° in the clockwise direction. Which direction is she facing now? **[2021]**
   (a) North (b) South
   (c) North-West (d) South-East

12. Shreya is facing South-West. She wants to go to her friend's house, so she turns through 135° in clockwise direction. In which direction is she facing now? **[2021]**
   (a) North-West (b) South-East
   (c) North (d) South

13. Ali starts walking towards North. He walked a distance of 20 m and then took a right turn and walked a distance of 30 m. Then he took a right turn again and walked a distance of 20 m. How far and in which direction is Ali now from the starting point?
   (a) 30 m, East **[2022]**
   (b) 20 m, North
   (c) 30 m, South-East
   (d) 10 m, North-West

14. Meena walks 3 km North, then turns West and walks 4 km, then turns South and walks 7 km, then turns to her left and walks 4 km. Where is she now from her starting position? **[2022]**
   (a) 10 km North (b) 4 km South
   (c) 10 km South (d) 4 km North

15. Raj walked 55 m towards South, then he took a left turn and walked 38 m. After that, he turned 270° clockwise and walked 55 m. How far is Raj from the starting point? **[2022]**
   (a) 55 m (b) 93 m
   (c) 17 m (d) None of these

ANSWER KEY																			
LEVEL-1																			
1	(d)	**3**	(d)	**5**	(d)	**7**	(a)	**9**	(c)	**11**	(a)	**13**	(d)	**15**	(c)	**17**	(c)		
2	(c)	**4**	(c)	**6**	(d)	**8**	(c)	**10**	(d)	**12**	(c)	**14**	(c)	**16**	(b)				
LEVEL-2																			
1	(d)	**3**	(b)	**5**	(b)	**7**	(a)	**9**	(c)	**11**	(c)	**13**	(a)	**15**	(d)				
2	(a)	**4**	(d)	**6**	(b)	**8**	(c)	**10**	(a)	**12**	(c)	**14**	(b)						

Logical Venn Diagrams

The best method of solving the problems based on inference or deduction is Venn diagram.

Venn diagram is a way representing sets pictorially.

Various cases of Venn diagram

Case I :

An object is called a subset of another object, if the former is a part of the latter and such relation is shown by two concentric circles.

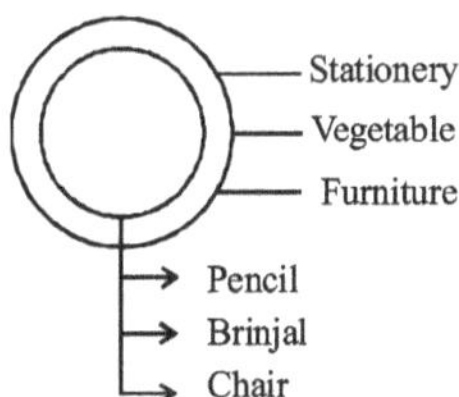

(i) Pencil, Stationery

(ii) Brinjal, Vegetable

(iii) Chair, Furniture It is very clear from the above relationship that one object is a part of the other, and hence all such relationships can be represented by the figure shown.

Case II :

An object is said to have an intersection with another object that share some things in common.

(i) Surgeon, Males

(ii) Politicians, Indian

(iii) Educated, Unemployed

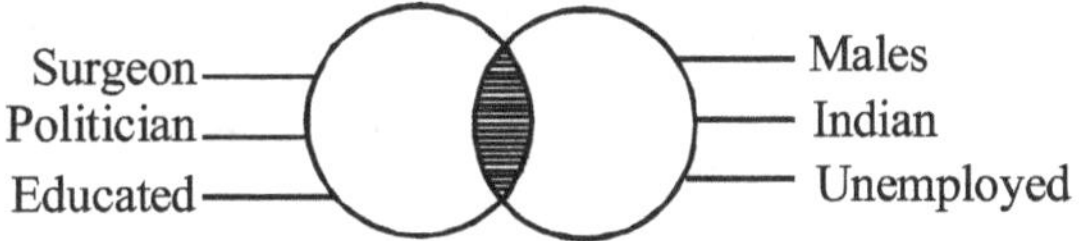

All the three relationships given above have something in common as some surgeons can be male and some female, some politicians may be Indian and some may belong to other countries, educated may be employed and unemployed as well and all the three relationships can be represented by the figure shown.

Case III :

Two objects are said to be disjoint when neither one is subset of another and nor do they share anything in common. In other words, totally unrelated objects fall under this type of relationship.

(i) Furniture, Car (ii) Copy, Cloth

(iii) Tool, Shirt

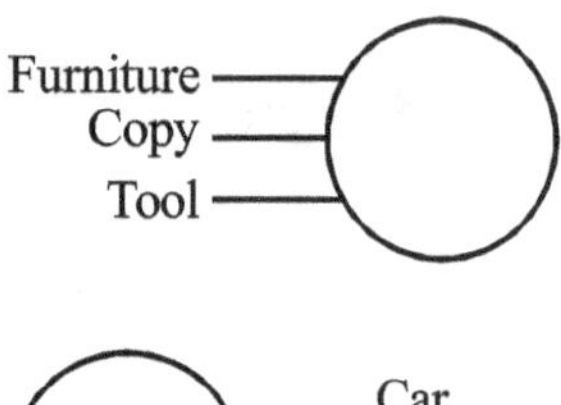

It is clear from the above relationships that both the objects are unrelated to each other, and hence can be represented diagrammatically as shown in figure above.

From the above discussion we observe that representation of the relationship between two objects is not typical if students follow the above points. But representation of three objects diagrammatically pose slight problems before the students.

ANALYTICAL METHOD :

Try to understand these type of questions using analytical method.

A statement always has a subject and a predicate:

All politicians are liars.

(subject) (predicate)

Basically, there are four types of sentences.

A - type ⇒ All politicians are liars.

I-type ⇒ Some politicians are liars

O-type ⇒ Some politicians are not liars

E-type ⇒ No politicians are liars

Conclusions can be drawn by taking two of the above statements together. The rules of conclusion are :

A + A = A A + E = E I + A = I

I + E = O E + A = O* E + I = O*

Conclusion can only be drawn from the two statements if the predicate of the first statement is the subject of the second statement. The common term disappears in the conclusion and it consists of subject of the first statement and predicate of the second statement. For examples

A + A = A

(i) All boys are girls. (ii) All girls are healthy

Conclusion : All boys are healthy.

A + E = E

(i) All boys are girls. (ii)No girls are healthy

Conclusion : No boys are healthy.

I + A = I

(i) Some boys are girls. (ii) All girls are healthy

Conclusion : Some boys are healthy.

I + E = O

(i) Some boys are girls. (ii) No girls are healthy

Conclusion : Some boys are not healthy.

E + A = O*

(i) No boys are girls. (ii)All girls are healthy

Conclusion : Some healthy are not boys.

I + I = O*

(i) No boys are girls. (ii)Some girls are healthy

Conclusion : Some healthy are not boys.

LEVEL 1

1. Which of the following diagrams correctly represents the relationship among Tennis fans, Cricket players and students.

(a) 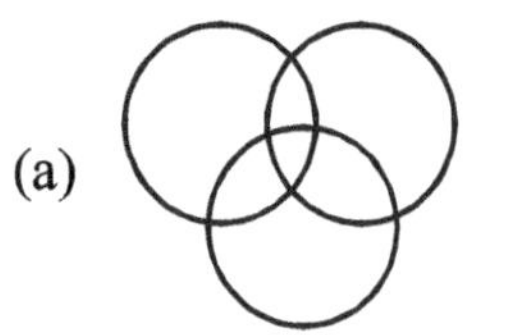 (b) 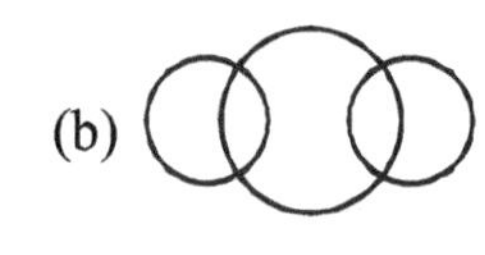

(c) 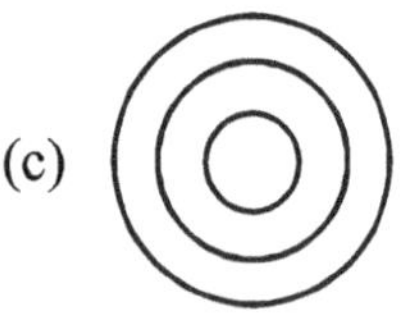 (d) 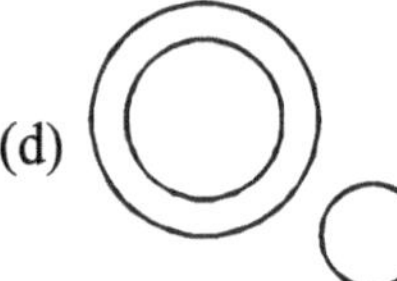

2. Which of the following diagrams correctly represents the relationship among smokers, bidi smokers, cancer patients.

(a)  (b) 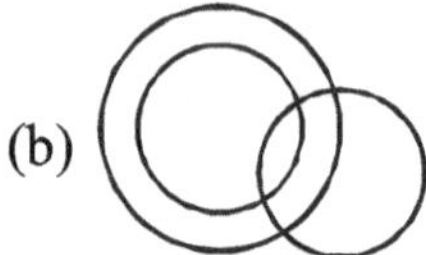

(c) 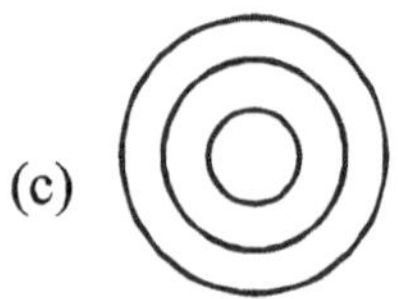 (d) 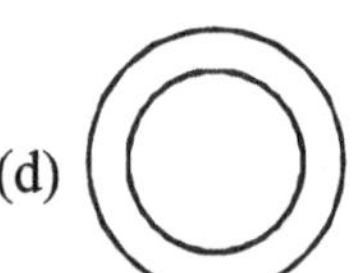

DIRECTIONS (Qs. 3-7) : *Choose the Venn diagram which best illustrates the three given classes in each questions:*

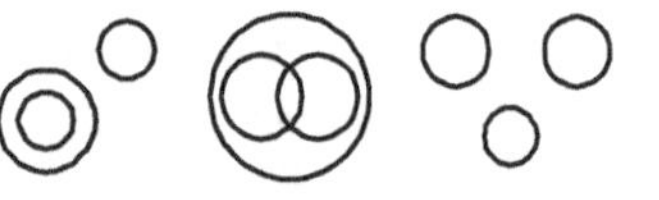  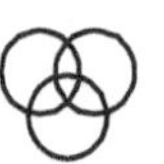 

(a) (b) (c) (d) (e)

3. Citizens, Educated, Men
4. Sun, Moon, Stars
5. Mercury, Mars, Planets
6. Water, Atmosphere, Hydrogen
7. Doctors, Lawyers, Professionals

DIRECTIONS (Qs. 8-11) : *Read the statements and choose the letter of the region which correctly represents the statement.*

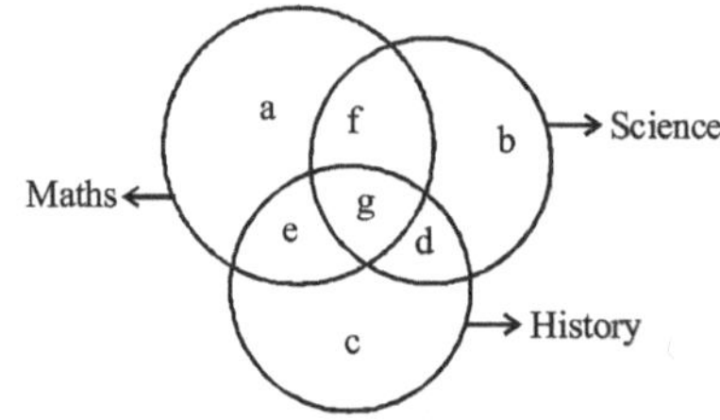

8. Students who took science but opted neither maths nor history:
   (a) b (b) e
   (c) d (d) g
9. Students who took maths and history both:
   (a) c (b) a
   (c) e (d) g
10. Students who took all three subjects i.e. maths, history and science:
    (a) f (b) g
    (c) e (d) d
11. Students who took science and history both:
    (a) g (b) e
    (c) f (d) d

DIRECTIONS (Qs. 12-13) : *In the following Venn Diagram the number of students who likes Science, Mathematics and Language is given. Observe the figure and answer the following questions:*

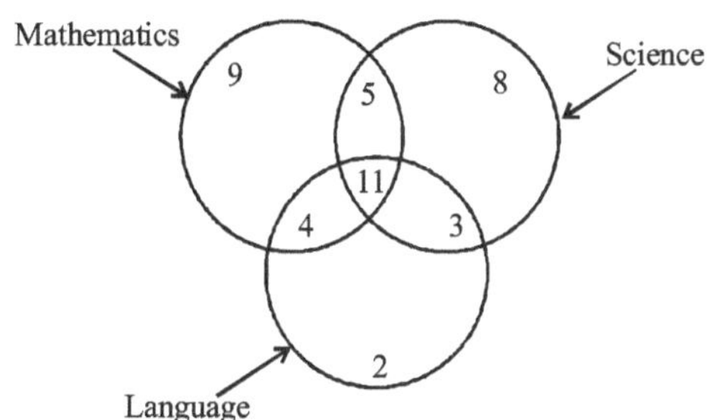

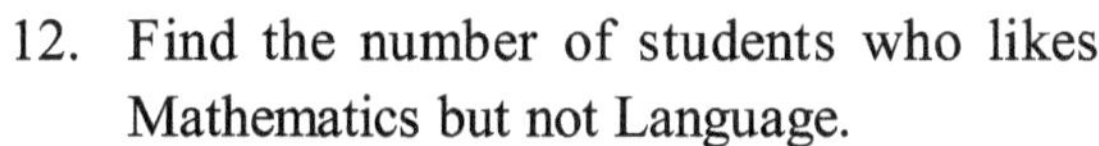

12. Find the number of students who likes Mathematics but not Language.
    (a) 15 (b) 14
    (c) 11 (d) 10
13. How many students, who like Science and Mathematics do not like Language?
    (a) 4 (b) 8
    (c) 11 (d) 5
14. Which of the following Venn diagrams best represents the relationship amongst, "Polygons, Quadrilaterals and Triangles"? **[2018]**

(a) (b)
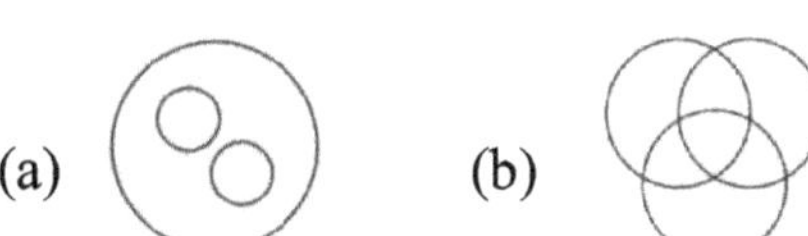

(c) (d)
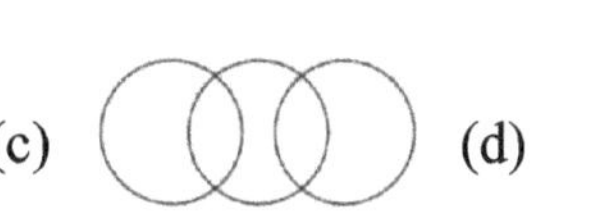

15. Which of the following Venn diagrams best depicts the relationship amongst, 'India, Asia and Australia'? **[2018]**

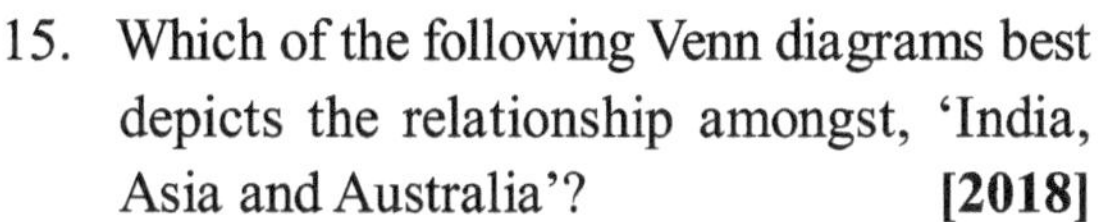

(a) (b)
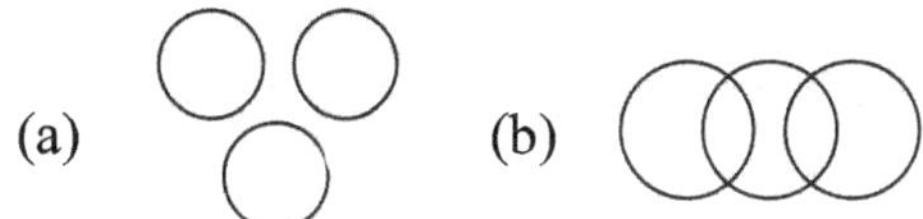

(c) (d)
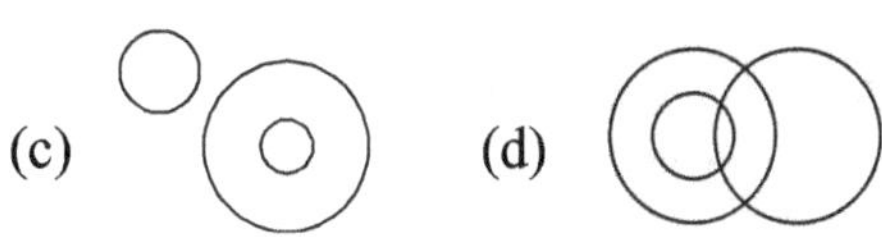

16. Which of the following Venn diagrams best represents the relationship amongst, "Teachers, Youths and Females"? **[2019]**

(a) (b)

(c) (d)
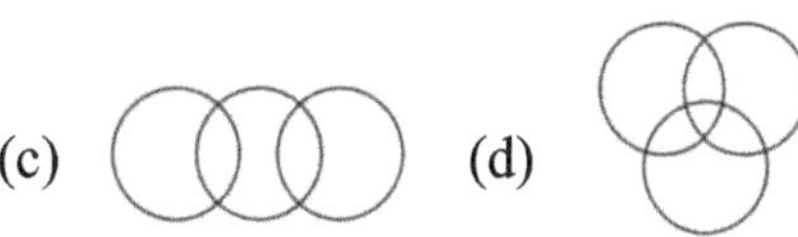

17. Which of the following Venn diagrams best represents the relationship amongst, "Mobile phones, Washing machines and Electronic devices"? **[2021]**

(a) (b)
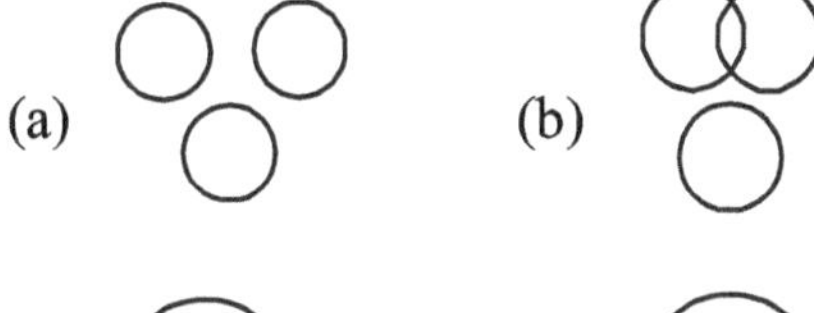

(c) (d)

18. Which of the following Venn diagrams best represents the relationship amongst, "Liquid, Sand and Water"? **[2022]**

(a) (b)
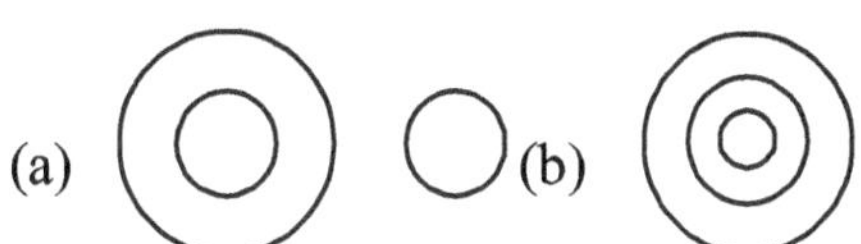

(c) (d)
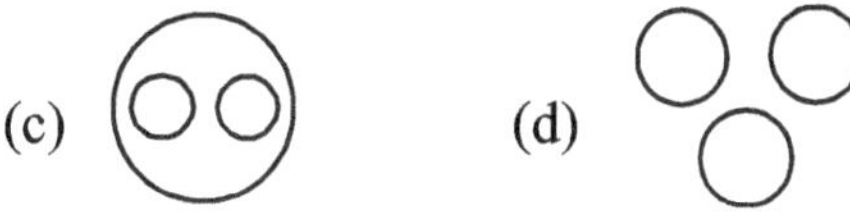

LEVEL 2

DIRECTIONS (Qs. 1-2) : *There are three circles in the following diagram. A total number of 100 persons were surveyed and the number in the diagram indicates the number of tourists who visited different states. 46 tourists visited Sikkim and 42 tourists visited Karnataka.*

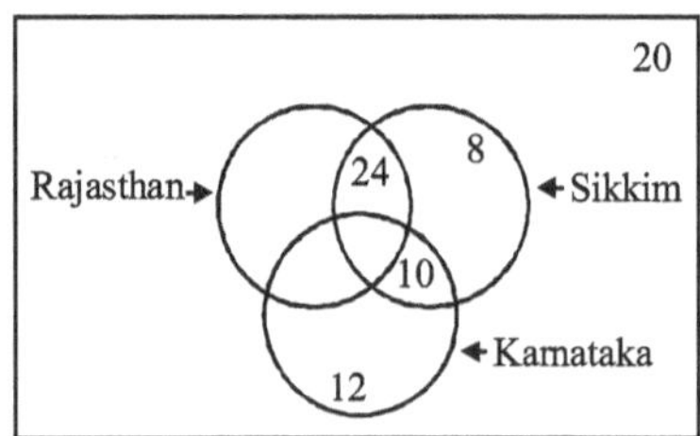

1. How many tourists have visited at least two states?
   (a) 46 (b) 50
   (c) 54 (d) 58
2. How many tourists have visited only two states
   (a) 46 (b) 50
   (c) 54 (d) 96
3. Which of the following diagrams indicates the best relation among men, fathers and teachers ?

   (a) 

   (b) 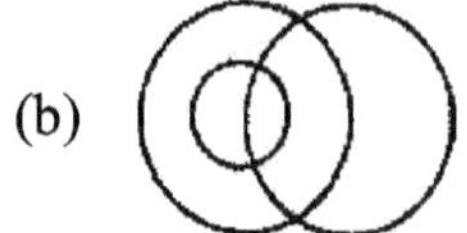

   (c) 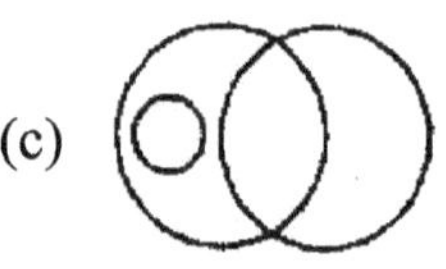

   (d) 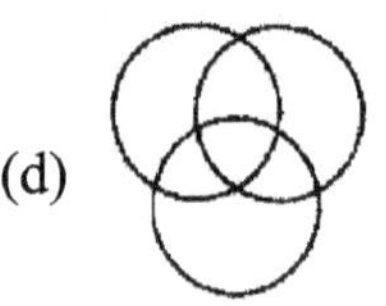

4. Which of the following Venn diagrams best represents the relationship amongst "Cylinder, Cuboid and Cone"? **[2018]**

   (a) 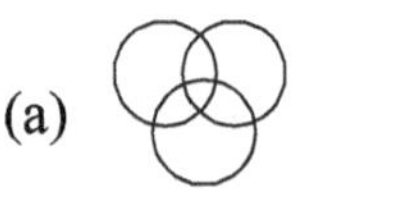 (b) 

   (c) 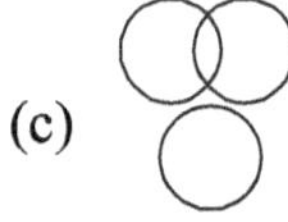 (d) 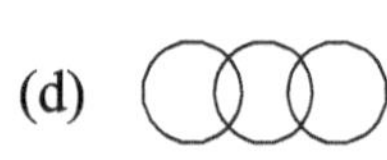

5. Study the given Venn diagram carefully and answer the question that follows. **[2019]**

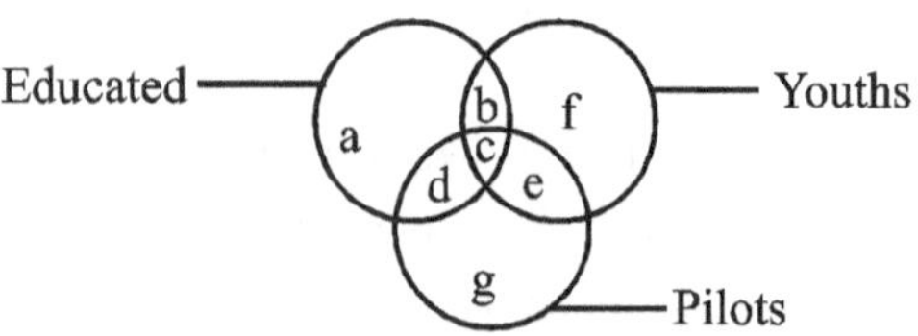

   Which of the following represents the youths who are educated but are not pilots?
   (a) b
   (b) c
   (c) f
   (d) g
6. In the given Venn diagram, square

represents people who like to play badminton, circle represents people who like to play cricket and triangle represents people who like to watch movies. Which of the following numbers represents people who like to play cricket as well as watch movies but do not like to play badminton? **[2019]**

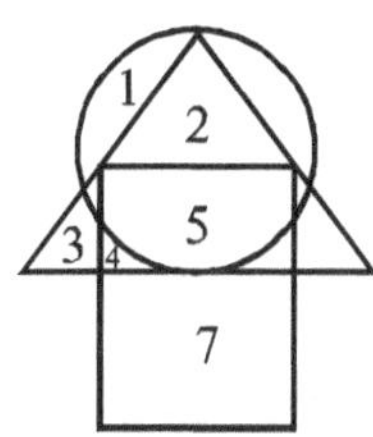

(a) 4 (b) 5
(c) 2 (d) 3

7. Which of the following Venn diagrams correctly represents the relationship amongst, "Wheat, Maize and Grains"? **[2020]**

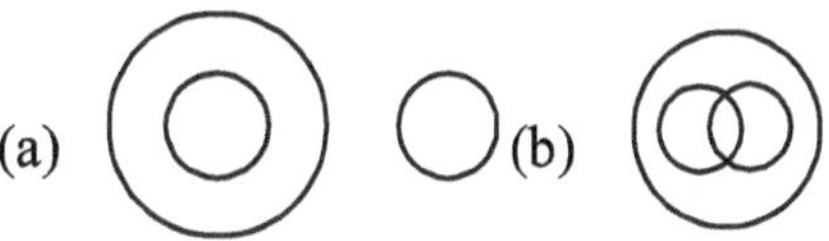

(c) (d)

8. Which of the following Venn diagrams best represents the relationship amongst, "Papers, Pens and Books"? **[2021]**

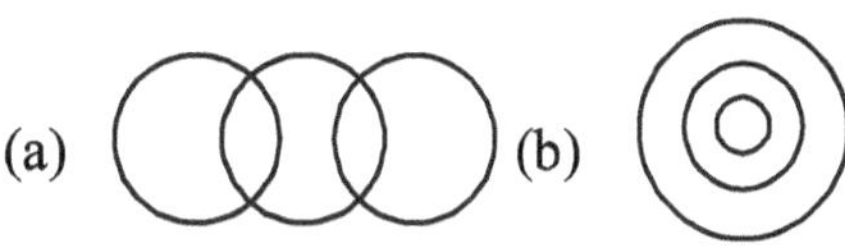

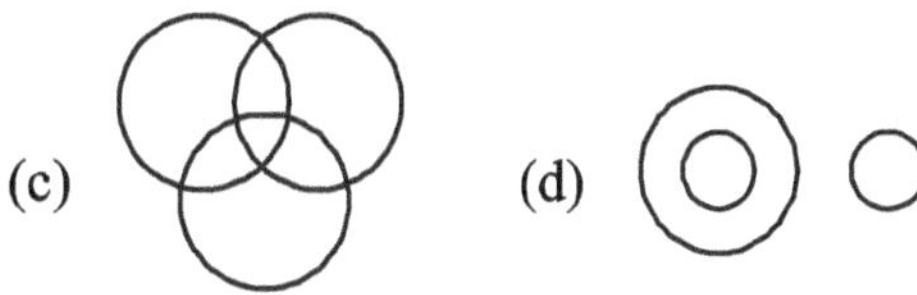

ANSWER KEY																			
LEVEL-1																			
1	(a)	**3**	(b)	**5**	(e)	**7**	(e)	**9**	(c)	**11**	(d)	**13**	(d)	**15**	(c)	**17**	(d)		
2	(b)	**4**	(a)	**6**	(d)	**8**	(a)	**10**	(b)	**12**	(b)	**14**	(a)	**16**	(d)	**18**	(a)		
LEVEL-2																			
1	(c)	**2**	(b)	**3**	(b)	**4**	(b)	**5**	(a)	**6**	(c)	**7**	(d)	**8**	(d)				

CHAPTER 7

Alpha-Numeric Sequence

TYPE I : WORD-FORMATION

In these types of questions, certain words are given. The candidate is required to arrange them in the order in which they are asked.

ILLUSTRATION 1 :

If it is possible to make a meaningful word with the 3rd, 4th and 11th letters the of word 'CONTROVERSIAL', write the first letter of the word. Write M if more than one word can be made, otherwise write X.

(a) M (b) T

(c) N (d) X

***Sol.* (b).** The 3rd, 4th and 11th, letters of the word 'CONTROVERSIAL' are N, T and I respectively. With these three letters, the following word can be formed : TIN. Therefore, Answer is T.

TYPE II : LETTER WORD PROBLEM

In these type of questions, a word is given and candidates are required to find out the Number of pairs of letters that matches the same sequence as in the English Alphabets.

ILLUSTRATION 2 :

How many letters are there in the word BACKLASH, each of which is as far away from the beginning of the word as it is from the beginning of the English alphabet ?

(a) None (b) One

(c) Two (d) Three

***Sol.* (c)** Clearly, C and H are respectively the third and eighth letters in the word BACKLASH as well as in the English alphabet. Thus, there are two such letters.

TYPE III : ALPHABETICAL QUIBBLE

In this type of question, generally a letter series is given, be it the English alphabets from A to Z or a randomised sequence of letters. The candidate is required to trace the letters satisfying certain given conditions as regards their position in the given sequence or the sequence obtained by performing certain given operations on the given sequence.

DIRECTIONS (ILLUSTRATION 3-4) : Each of the following questions is based on the following alphabet series : A B C D E F G H I J K L M N O P Q R S T U V W X Y Z

ILLUSTRATION 3 :

Which letter will be the eighth to the right of the third letter of the second half of the English alphabet ?

(a) V (b) W

(c) X (d) Y

***Sol.* (c)** Clearly, the first half of English alphabet has letters from A to M, and the second half has letters from N to Z.

The third letter of the second half is P, and the eighth letter to the right of P is X.

ILLUSTRATION 4 :

If only the last ten letters of the alphabet are written in the reverse order, which of the following will be the sixth to the right of the thirteenth letter from the left end ?

(a) U (b) V

(c) W (d) X

***Sol.* (d)** The new alphabet series is :

A B C D E F G H I J K L M N O P Z Y X W V U T S R Q

The thirteenth letter from the left is M. The sixth letter to the right of M is X.

ILLUSTRATION 5 :

If every alternative letter of English alphabet from B onwards (including B) is written in lower case (small letters) and the remaining letters are capitalized, then how will the first month of the second half of the year be written ?

(a) JuLy (b) AuGuSt
(c) jUlY (d) AugUSt

Sol. (c) The new letter series becomes :
A b C d E f G h I j K l M n O p Q r S t U v W x Y z
The first month of the second half of the year is July, which shall be written as jUlY.

TYPE IV : ALPHABETICAL ORDER

Arranging words in alphabetical order implies 'to arrange them in the order as they appear in a dictionary', i.e., as per the order in which the beginning letters of these words appear in the English alphabet. First consider the first letter of each word. Arrange the words in the order in which these letters appear in the English alphabet.

In some cases, two or more words begin with the same letter. Such words should be arranged in the order of second letters in the alphabet.

DIRECTIONS (ILLUSTRATION 6-8): In each of the following questions, four words are given. Which of them will be the last if all of them are arranged alphabetically as in a dictionary?

ILLUSTRATION 6 :

(a) Praise (b) Practical
(c) Prank (d) Prayer

Sol. **(d)** Practical, Praise, Prank, Prayer.

ILLUSTRATION 7 :

(a) Nature (b) Native
(c) Narrate (d) Nascent

Sol. **(a)** Narrate, Nascent, Native, Nature.

ILLUSTRATION 8 :

(a) Relieve (b) Ringlet
(c) Rightful (d) Rigour

Sol. **(b)** Relieve, Rightful, Rigour, Ringlet

LEVEL 1

1. Arrange the given words in alphabetical order and choose the one that comes in the 2nd position.
   (a) Restrict (b) Rocket
   (c) Robber (d) Random

DIRECTIONS (Qs. 2-3) : *Arrange the given words in the sequence in which they occur in the dictionary and then choose the correct sequence.*

2. 1. Page 2. Pagan
   3. Palisade 4. Pageant
   5. Palate
   (a) 1, 4, 2, 3, 5 (b) 2, 4, 1, 3, 5
   (c) 2, 1, 4, 5, 3 (d) 1, 4, 2, 5, 3
3. 1. Brook 2. Bandit
   3. Boisterous 4. Baffle
   5. Bright
   (a) 4, 2, 3, 5, 1 (b) 2, 4, 3, 1, 5
   (c) 2, 4, 3, 5, 1 (d) 4, 2, 3, 1, 5

DIRECTIONS (Qs. 4-6) : *Find which one word cannot be made from the letters of the given word.*

4. UNCONSCIOUS
   (a) SON (b) COIN
   (c) SUN (d) NOSE
5. CREDENTIAL
   (a) DENTAL (b) CREATE
   (c) TRAIN (d) CREAM
6. TEACHERS
   (a) REACH (b) CHAIR
   (c) CHEER (d) SEARCH

DIRECTIONS (Qs. 7-8) : *Find the words which can be formed from the given word.*

7. CHOCOLATE
   (a) TELL (b) HEALTH
   (c) LATE (d) COOLER
8. MEASUREMENT
   (a) MASTER (b) MANTLE
   (c) SUMMIT (d) ASSURE
9. Alphabet series
   X c w m vc x w m w m x c x w m x m
   In the given alphabet series how many times m is succeeded by w and preceded by w?
   (a) 1 (b) 0
   (c) 2 (d) 3
10. If the first half of the English alphabet is reversed and so is the 2nd half, then which letter is 7th to the right of the 12th letter from the left side?
    (a) S (b) U
    (c) R (d) T
11. How many such odd numbers are there each of which is followed by a multiple of 2 in the given series? 6 4 3 2 4 8 3 1 5 4 2 3 2 4 6 4 8 1 3 2 4 2 6 4 5 **[2018]**
    (a) 4 (b) 3
    (c) 2 (d) 5

12. If every alternate letter starting from C is deleted from the given series, then which of the following will be the eighth letter from the left end in the new series formed?

A C B E D G F I H K J M L O N Q P S R U T W V Y X Z **[2018]**

(a) L (b) J
(c) N (d) P

13. If second Saturday and all Sundays are holidays in a 30 days month beginning with Saturday, then how many days are working in that month? **[2018]**

(a) 20 (b) 24
(c) 22 (d) 23

14. In the word TECHNOLOGY, if the first and the second letters, the third and the fourth letters, the fifth and the sixth letters and so on were interchanged, then which of the following would be the fifth letter from the right end? **[2019]**

(a) O (b) H
(c) N (d) L

15. If the digits of the following numbers are reversed and then the numbers are arranged in descending order, then what will be the middle digit of the second number? **[2019]**

221 325 431 749 915

(a) 4 (b) 2
(c) 1 (d) 3

16. How many such odd numbers are there in the given arrangement each of which is not immediately followed by a multiple of 2 ? **[2019]**

8 4 3 2 4 6 3 1 5 4 2 3 2 4 6 4 8 1 3 2 4 2 6 4 8

(a) 4 (b) 3
(c) 2 (d) None of these

17. If two is subtracted from each of the following numbers, then which of the following is the sum of the second digit of the second highest number and the second digit of the highest number? **[2019]**

486 441 634 932 873

(a) 8 (b) 3
(c) 7 (d) 10

18. How many consonants are there in the given series which is immediately preceded by a vowel? **[2021]**

V E T R V T E S B A W R I P V O T

(a) Two (b) Three
(c) Four (d) Five

19. Arrange the following words in a meaningful sequence and select the correct option. **[2022]**

1. Word 2. Chapter
3. Book 4. Sentence
5. Paragraph

(a) 2, 3, 4, 1, 5 (b) 3, 2, 5, 4, 1
(c) 3, 5, 2, 1, 4 (d) 2, 4, 3, 5, 1

20. Rahul ranks eleventh from the top in a class of 40 students. What will be his rank from the bottom? **[2022]**

(a) 29th (b) 30th
(c) 31st (d) 32nd

LEVEL 2

DIRECTION (Q. 1) : *The following question is based on the following alphabet series.*

A B C D E F G H I J K L M N O P Q R S T U V W X Y Z

1. If the alphabet is written in the reverse order and every alternate letter starting with Y is dropped, which letter will be exactly in the middle of the remaining letters of the alphabet.

   (a) M (b) N
   (c) O (d) M or O

DIRECTIONS (Qs. 2-7) : *Each of the following questions is based on the following alphabet series.*

A B C D E F G H I J K L M N O P Q R S T U V W X Y Z

2. Which letter is eighth to the left on sixteenth letter from the right end?

   (a) B (b) S
   (c) C (d) H

3. Which letter is exactly midway between H and S in the given alphabet?

   (a) No such letter (b) L
   (c) M (d) O

4. If the english alphabet are divided into two equal halves – from A to M and N to Z, which letter in the later half would be corresponding to letter J?

   (a) Q (b) V
   (c) X (d) W

5. Which letter is midway between 22nd letter from the left and 21st letter from the right?

   (a) L (b) M
   (c) O (d) N

6. Which letter should be ninth letter to the left of ninth letter from the right, if the first half of the given alphabet is reversed?

   (a) D (b) E
   (c) F (d) I

7. If the first and the second letters interchange their positions and similarly the third and the fourth letters, the fifth and the sixth letters and so on, which letter will be the seventeenth from your right?

   (a) F (b) H
   (c) I (d) J

8. How many pairs of letters are there in the word 'BUCKET' which have as many letters between them in the word as in the alphabet?

   (a) One (b) Two
   (c) Three (d) Four

9. If the letters of RUTHLESS are arranged alphabetically then which letter would be the last letter

   (a) T (b) E
   (c) H (d) U

10. If the English letters A to Z are written in a reverse order then what is the fourth letter to the right of 12th letter from the left ?

(a) K (b) J

(c) R (d) L

11. If the given alphabets are written in the reverse order, then what will be the sixth letter to the right of the fourteenth letter from the left end?

B A D C F E H G J I L K N M P O R Q T S V U X W Z Y **[2018]**

(a) H (b) G

(c) O (d) P

12. How many 5's are there in the following sequence, each of which is immediately preceded by 4 but not immediately followed by 9? **[2020]**

3 5 9 5 4 5 5 3 5 8 4 5 6 7 3 5 7 5 5 4 5 2 4 5 9 0

(a) 2 (b) 3

(c) 4 (d) 5

13. If a meaningful English word is formed from the first, the fourth, the seventh and the eleventh letters of the word EXPLORATION, then what is the third letter of the word formed? If more than one such words are formed, then give 'Y' as the answer and if no such word is formed, then give 'Z' as the answer. **[2020]**

(a) N (b) Y

(c) A (d) Z

14. How many symbols are there in the given arrangement each of which is immediately followed by an even digit? **[2021]**

1 % 6 K ★ L # 2 T R @ 4 J A ? 2 M % 8 * 6 B 5 $ 8 % @ 2

(a) 4 (b) 5

(c) 6 (d) More than 6

15. Some letters are given which are numbered as 1, 2, 3, 4, 5 and 6. Select the combination of numbers so that the letters are arranged accordingly to form a meaningful English word.

T H Y M R H **[2022]**

1 2 3 4 5 6

(a) 6, 4, 3, 2, 1, 5

(b) 5, 6, 3, 1, 2, 4

(c) 6, 3, 4, 1, 2, 5

(d) 5, 1, 3, 4, 6, 2

16. How many 7's are there in the given series each of which is immediately preceded by 3 and immediately followed by 8? **[2022]**

8 6 2 1 4 3 7 9 6 3 7 8 7 8 4 3 7 8 9 3 5

(a) 1 (b) 2

(c) 3 (d) 4

17. Renu remembers that her brother Ram's birthday was after 15th but before 21st March, while her mother remembers that Ram's birthday was after 17th but before 19th March. On which date in March was Ram's birthday? **[2022]**

(a) 16th March (b) 17th March

(c) 19th March (d) 18th March

ANSWER KEY

LEVEL-1

1	(a)	**3**	(a)	**5**	(d)	**7**	(c)	**9**	(a)	**11**	(c)	**13**	(b)	**15**	(b)	**17**	(d)	**19**	(b)
2	(c)	**4**	(d)	**6**	(b)	**8**	(a)	**10**	(b)	**12**	(c)	**14**	(c)	**16**	(b)	**18**	(d)	**20**	(b)

LEVEL-2

1	(b)	**3**	(a)	**5**	(d)	**7**	(c)	**9**	(d)	**11**	(a)	**13**	(b)	**15**	(b)	**17**	(d)		
2	(c)	**4**	(d)	**6**	(b)	**8**	(a)	**10**	(a)	**12**	(d)	**14**	(d)	**16**	(b)				

CHAPTER 8

Mathematical Operations

MATHEMATICAL OPERATIONS

This section deals with questions on simple mathematical operations. There are four fundamental operations, namely :

Additions i.e, + ; Subtraction i.e, – ;

Multiplication i.e, × ; and Division i.e. , ÷

There are also statements such as Less than i.e. <, greater than i.e. >, and equal to i.e =, not equal to i.e ≠ , etc.

Such operations are represented by symbols different from the usual ones. The questions involving these operations are coded using artificial symbols. The candidate has to make a substitution of the real signs and solve the equation accordingly.

We always, while solving a mathematical expression, proceed according to the rule B O D M A S.

i.e, B for Brackets ; O for ' of (literally multiplication),

D for division ; M for multiplication , A for additions and S for subtraction in sequence.

DIFFERENT TYPES OF PROBLEMS

TYPE 1 : Problem-solving By Substitution

In this type, you are provided with substitutes for various mathematical symbols or numbers. Followed by a question involving calculation of an expression or choosing the correct/ incorrect equations. The candidate is required to put in the real signs or numerals in the given equation and then solve the questions as required.

ILLUSTRATION 1:

If L stands for +, M stands for –, N stands for ×, P stands for ÷, then 14 N 10 L 42 P 2 M 8 = ?

(a) 153 (b) 216

(c) 248 (d) 251

Sol. **(a)** Using the proper signs, we get

Given expression

$= 14 \times 10 + 42 \div 2 - 8 = 14 \times 10 + 21 - 8$

$= 140 + 21 - 8 = 161 - 8 = 153.$

DIRECTIONS (ILLUSTRATION 2) : In each of the following examples which one of the four interchanges in signs and numbers would make the given equation correct ?

ILLUSTRATION 2:

$6 \times 4 + 2 = 16$

(a) + and ×, 2 and 4 (b) + and ×, 2 and 6

(c) + and ×, 4 and 6 (d) None of these

***Sol.* (c)** On interchanging + & × and 4 and 6, we get the equation as

$4 + 6 \times 2 = 16$ or $4 + 12 = 16$ or $16 = 16$, which is true

MATHEMATICAL LOGIC

Consider the statement "5 is greater than 3".

Now consider which of the following statements are true and which are false.

" 5 is not greater than 3 " (False)

" 5 is equal to 3 " (False)

" 5 is less than 3 " (False)

" 5 is not equal to 3" (True)

" 5 is not less than 3 " (True)

In general, between any two numbers a and b, only one of the following relations can exist at a time

$a > b$ or $a < b$

or $a = b$

If $a > b$, then $a \nless b$ and $a \neq b$

If $a < b$, then $a \ngtr b$ and $a \neq b$

If $a = b$, then $a \ngtr b$ and $a \nless b$

DIRECTIONS (ILLUSTRATION 3-4): *Let the following symbols denote some relationships between numbers.*

O = greater than ϕ = not greater than

+ = equal to Δ = not equal to

÷ = less than x = not less than

In the examples below, find the correct answer.

ILLUSTRATION 3:

If p ÷ q O r, it is possible that

(a) p ϕ q ÷ r (b) p ϕ q × r

(c) p + q × r (d) p Δ q ϕ r

Sol. (b) ÷ (less than ⇒ Δ (Not equal to or ϕ (not greater than)

O (greater than) ⇒ Δ (Not equal to) or × (not less than)

For p, and q, option (a), (b), (d) are possible.

For q and r, options (b), (c) are possible.

Hence the answer is (b)

ILLUSTRATION 4:

If p Δ q O r, it is possible that

(a) p × q × r (b) p × q ÷ r

(c) P ÷ q ϕ r (d) p ϕ q ϕ r

***Sol.* (a)** Δ = not equal to

Hence, Δ ⇒ O (greater than)

or Δ ⇒ ÷ (Less than)

Δ ⇒ ϕ (not greater than)

or Δ ⇒ × (not less than)

Similarly, O ⇒ Δ and O ⇒ ×

hence P Δ q ⇒ p O q or p ÷ q or p ϕ q or p × q

and q O r ⇒ q Δ r or q × r

All four options are possible so far as p and q are concerned.

Between q and r, only the first is correct.

TYPE II

DIRECTIONS (ILLUSTRATION 5-6) : *In each of the following questions, an equation becomes incorrect due to the interchange of* *two signs. One of the four alternatives, specifies the interchange of sign in the equations, which when made, will make the equation correct. Find the correct alternative.*

ILLUSTRATION 5:

$16 - 8 \div 4 + 5 \times 2 = 8$

(a) $\div$ and $\times$ (b) $-$ and $\div$

(c) $\div$ and $+$ (d) $-$ and $+$

***Sol.* (b)** On interchanging – and ÷ we get :

Given expression $= 16 \div 8 - 4 + 5 \times 2$
$= 2 - 4 + 10 = 8$

ILLUSTRATION 6:

$121 \div 11 - 3 \times 13 + 2 = 22$

(a) $-$ and $\times$ (b) $-$ and $\div$

(c) $\div$ and $-$ (d) $+$ and $-$

***Sol.* (a)** On interchanging – and × we get

Given expression $= 121 \div 11 \times 3 - 13 + 2$

$= \frac{121}{11} \times 3 - 13 + 2 = 11 \times 3 - 13 + 2 = 22$

TYPE III

DIRECTION (ILLUSTRATION 7) : *In the following question, three statements of numbers following same rules are given. Find the rule and accordingly find the value of the number ?*

ILLUSTRATION 7:

If $32 \times 41 = 15$; $51 \times 34 = 47$; $41 \times 52 = 37$, then $87 \times 53 = ?$

(a) 68 (b) 64

(c) 85 (d) 18

Sol. (d) The logic is $32 \times 41 = (3 - 2)(4 + 1) = 15$;

$51 \times 34 = (5 - 1)(3 + 4) = 47$ etc.

$\therefore 87 \times 53 = (8 - 7)(5 + 3) = 18$

DIRECTIONS (ILLUSTRATION 8) : *In each of the following questions, three statements of numbers following same rules are given. Find the rule and accordingly find the value of the number.*

ILLUSTRATION 8:

If $2 \times 1 = 81$; $3 \times 2 = 278$; $2 \times 5 = 8125$, then $1 \times 3 =$

(a) 127 (b) 271

(c) 126 (d) 129

Sol. (a) The rule is $a \times b = a^3\ b^3$

$2 \times 1 = 2^3\ 1^3 = 81$ etc. So, $1 \times 3 = 1^3\ 3^3 = 127$

LEVEL 1

1. In the following questions which one of the four interchanges in signs and numbers would make the given equation correct ?

   $(3 \div 4) + 2 = 2$

   (a) + and ÷, 2 and 3
   (b) + and ÷, 2 and 4
   (c) + and ÷, 3 and 4
   (d) No interchanges, 3 and 4

2. If A stands for +, B stands for –, C stands for ×, then what is the value of (10 C4) + (4 C 4) B 6 = ?

   (a) 60 (b) 56
   (c) 50 (d) 20

3. If P denotes ÷, Q denotes ×, R denotes + and S denotes –, then the value of 18 Q 12 P 4 R 5 S 6 when simplified gives

   (a) 36 (b) 53
   (c) 59 (d) 65

4. If + means ÷, – means ×, ÷ means + and × means –, then $36 \times 8 + 4 \div 6 + 2 - 3 = ?$

   (a) 2 (b) 18
   (c) 43 (d) $6\frac{1}{2}$

5. If L denotes ×, M denotes ÷ , P denotes + and Q denotes –,

   than 8 P 36 M 6 Q 6 M 2 L 3 = ?

   (a) $\frac{13}{6}$ (b) $-\frac{1}{6}$
   (c) $14\frac{1}{2}$ (d) 5

6. If + means × , × means –, ÷ means + and – means ÷, then which of the following gives the result of

   $175 - 25 \div 5 \div 20 \times 3 + 10$?

   (a) 2 (b) 6
   (c) 4 (d) 12

7. If ' + ' means ' divided by', '–' means ' added to', '×' means ' subtracted from' and ÷ means ' multiplied by', then what is the value of $24 \div 12 - 18 + 9$?

   (a) – 25 (b) 0.72
   (c) 15.30 (d) 290

8. If × means ÷, – means × , ÷ means + and + means – then

   $(3 - 15 \div 19) \times 8 + 6 = ?$

   (a) – 1 (b) 2
   (c) 4 (d) 8

9. If P means ' division', T means ' additions', M means ' subtraction and D means multiplication', then what will be the value of the expressions 12 M 12 D 28 P 7 T 15 ?

   (a) – 30 (b) – 15
   (c) 15 (d) –21

10. If $36 \times 92 = 9623$; $25 \times 82 = 8522$; $68 \times 75 = 7856$, then $47 \times 52 = ?$

    (a) 5742 (b) 5274
    (c) 7427 (d) 5724

11. Which one of the four interchanges in signs and numbers would make the given equation correct ? 3 + 5 – 2= 0

(a) + and –, 2 and 3

(b) + and –, 2 and 5

(c) + and – , 3 and 5

(d) None of these

12. If '×' means '–', '+' means '÷', '–' means '×' and '÷' mean '+', then.

15 – 12 ÷ 900 + 90 × 100 = ?

(a) 180 (b) 190

(c) $\frac{3}{1600}$ (d) 90

13. Choose the correct arrangement of mathematical signs at the place of * for equating given equation.

7 * 2 * 3 * 5 * 6

(a) –, +, =, × (b) +, ×, =, +

(c) =, ×, +, – (d) ×, =, +, +

14. If x means –, + means÷, – means × and ÷ means + then 15–2 ÷ 900 + 90 × 100 = ?

(a) 190 (b) 180

(c) 90 (d) – 60

15. If > stands for +

< stands for – ∧ stands for ×

∨ stands for ÷

Then what is the value of 52 < 4 ∧ 5> 8 ∨ 2

(a) 38 (b) 36

(c) 124 (d) 312

16. If + is called ×, ÷ is called + and – is called ÷, then which of the following is divisible by the result of the given expression? **[2018]**

175 – 25 ÷ 5 + 30

(a) 157

(b) 308

(c) 450

(d) 385

17. If ‘P’ is called ‘÷’,‘Q’ is called ‘×’, ‘R’ is called ‘+’ and ‘S’ is called “‘‘, then find the value of 2 Q 40 P 10 R 6 S 8. **[2019]**

(a) 10 (b) 6

(c) 4 (d) 5

18. If M denotes ÷, L denotes –, P denotes × and J denotes +, then find the value of 25 M 5 L 10 P 2 J 15. **[2020]**

(a) 10 (b) 0

(c) 5 (d) 15

19. If 'P' denotes '×', 'Q' denotes '+', 'R' denotes '÷' and 'S' denotes '–', then find the value of 34 P 2 Q 14 R 7 S 8. **[2021]**

(a) 64 (b) 63

(c) 62 (d) 60

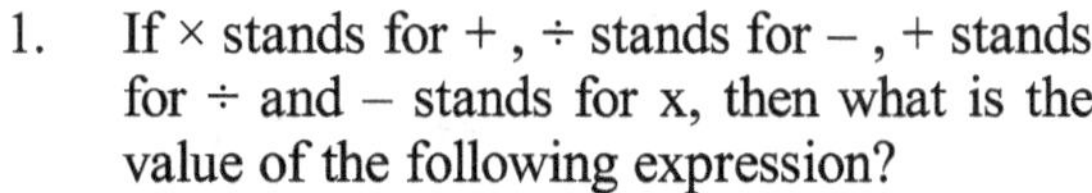

1. If × stands for + , ÷ stands for – , + stands for ÷ and – stands for x, then what is the value of the following expression?

   ÷ 33 × 11 ÷ 9 × 28 + 4 – 5

   (a) 16 (b) 8
   (c) 4 (d) 2

2. If '÷' is '+', '×' is '–', '–' is '÷' and '+' is '×' then what is the value of

   20 ÷ 4 × 12 – 6 + 11

   (a) 2 (b) 5
   (c) 56 (d) 65

3. If Q means 'addition sign', J means multiplication sign'. T means subtraction sign and K means 'division sign' then, 30 K 2 Q 3 J 6 T 5 = ?

   Find the number in place of '?'

   (a) 18 (b) 28
   (c) 31 (d) 103

4. If '+' stands for '×', '×' stands for '–', '–' stands for '÷' and '÷' stands for '+' then (16 ÷ 64 – 8 × 4 + 2) – (2 + 15 ÷ 15 – 3 × 8) = **[2018]**

   (a) $\frac{16}{27}$ (b) $\frac{15}{28}$
   (c) $\frac{18}{35}$ (d) $\frac{16}{29}$

5. If '@' stands for 'multiplication', '©' stands for 'division', '$' stands for 'addition' and '£' stands for subtractions then find the value of 30 © 6 @ 5 $ 4 £ 2. **[2019]**

   (a) 21 (b) 29
   (c) 27 (d) 28

6. If '+' denotes '×', '÷' denotes '–', '×' denotes '÷' and '–' denotes '+', then 120 × 8 – 14 + 4 ÷ 16 = ? **[2021]**

   (a) 35 (b) 45
   (c) 55 (d) 65

7. If '+' denotes '×', '–' denotes '÷', '×' denotes '–' and '÷' denotes '+', then find the value of 5 + 14 – 2 × 3. **[2022]**

   (a) 31 (b) 32
   (c) 33 (d) 34

ANSWER KEY

LEVEL-1

1	(a)	3	(b)	5	(d)	7	(d)	9	(d)	11	(a)	13	(d)	15	(b)	17	(b)	19	(c)
2	(c)	4	(c)	6	(a)	8	(b)	10	(d)	12	(d)	14	(d)	16	(a)	18	(b)		

LEVEL-2

1	(c)	2	(a)	3	(b)	4	(a)	5	(c)	6	(c)	7	(b)						

CHAPTER

9

Seating (Linear) Arrangement & Puzzle

In Linear arrangement problems we are generally given a set of information about positioning of different elements with respect to other elements. From the given set of information we have to use the given information systematically to find the actual arrangement of the elements. The arrangements can be in a straight line, on chair, in rooms in a row. Another type of arrangement is arrangement in two rows parallel to each other.

Left & Right: We can use Left and Right as per Information that generally is given and its interpretation is as follows:

- **Left & Right:** We can use Left and Right as per our convenience. Generally (and in this book) we will use as follow:

Left End									Right End

- **A is 2 places right of B:** Generally students used to get confuse that how many gaps are there between A and B. Here in this case there is only 1 gap between A and B. As it is explained in the diagram below.

Left End	1st Place	2nd Place	3rd Place	Right End
	B		A	

- **A is 3 places left of B:** Here in this case there is only 2 gaps between A and B. As it is explained in the diagram below. If B is at 1st place then A ia at 4th place.

Left End	1st Place	2nd Place	3rd Place	4th place	Right End
	B			A	

- **A stays 2 places away of B:** Here in this case it is not given who is in right and who is in left so we have two different cases:

Left End	1st Place	2nd Place	3rd Place	Right End
	B/A		A/B	

- **A stays 2 places away of B who is 3 place left of C:** In this case, we can assume that B is at 3rd place then C is at 6th place,

Left End	1st Place	2nd Place	3rd Place	4th place	5th place	6th place	Right End
			B			C	

Example 1. Six friends A, B, C, D, E and F are sitting in a row facing towards North. C is sitting between A and E. D is not at the end. B is sitting immediate right to E. F is not at the right end.

1. Who is on the extreme right?

   (a) B (b) E

   (c) F (d) G

2. Who is exactly in between F and A?

   (a) A

   (b) C

   (c) E

   (d) D

Solution: B is to the immediate right of E i.e E, B. C is between A and E i.e A, C, E, B. as, D is not at the ends and f is not inn right end, so sequence in the row becomes:

F D A C E B N

1. So, extreme right is B, option (a)
2. So, exactly in between F & A, is D, option (d).

Example 2. A,B,C,D,E,F and G are sitting on a wall and all of them are facing east. C is on the immediate right of D. B is at an extreme end and has E as his neighbour. G is between E and F. D is sitting third from the south end.

3. Who is sitting to the right of E?

   (a) A (b) C

   (c) D (d) G

4. Which of the following pairs are sitting at the extreme ends?

   (a) AB (b) AE

   (c) CB (d) FB

Solution: The arrangement is :

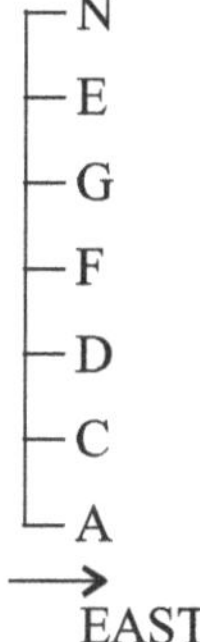

3. Option (d). G is right of E
4. Option (a) AB

PUZZLE TEST :

This chapter comprises questions given in the form of puzzles, involving certain number of items, persons or things. You are required to analyse the given information or clues and answer the questions accordingly.

HINTS FOR HANDLING THE QUESTIONS :

1. Generally, several conditions in the form of information are given with the question. So, do not make hurry to mix all the given information, instead go step by step.
2. To avoid confusion while solving such questions, you should symbolize persons, items by dot, lines etc. If sitting arrangement is a circular one, then draw a circle.

ILLUSTRATION 1 :

On a shelf are placed six volumes side by side labelled A, B, C, D, E and F; B, C, E and F have green covers while others have yellow covers. A, D, B are new volumes while the rest are old volumes. A, C, B, are law reports while the rest are medical extracts. Which two volumes are old medical extracts and have green covers ?

(a) B, C

(b) C, D

(c) C, E

(d) E, F

Sol. **(d)**

	Green cover	Yellow cover	New volume	Old volume	Law reports	Medical extracts
A		√	√		√	
B	√		√		√	
C	√			√	√	
D		√	√			√
E	√			√		√
F	√			√		√

Clearly, E and F are old volumes which have green covers and are medical extracts.

ILLUSTRATION 2 :

Mr. A, Miss. B, Mr. C and Miss. D are sitting around a table and discussing their trades

(A) Mr. A sits opposite to cook

(B) Miss B sits right to the barber

(C) The washerman is on the left of the tailor

(D) Miss D sits opposite Mr. C

What are the trades of A and B?

(a) Tailor and Barber

(b) Tailor and cook

(c) Barber and cook

(d) Washerman and cook

Sol. **(b)** Clearly, C and D sit opposite to each other. So, if A sits opposite to cook, B shall be the cook. Now B is to the right of barber, so, one of the rest, say C will be barber. Clearly, then D on the opposite side shall be washerman or tailor. But washerman is left of tailor and D is to the left of A. So, D is washerman and A is tailor. Thus A and B are tailor and cook.

ILLUSTRATION 3 :

A worker may claim ₹. 15 for each km which he travels by taxi and ₹. 5 for each km when he drives his own car. If in one week he claimed ₹. 500 for travelling 80 kms, how many kms did he travel by taxi ?

(a) 10 (b) 20

(c) 30 (d) 40

Sol. **(a)** The problem can be solved by considering the options one by one.

Option (a) implies 10 km by taxi and 70 km by own car. Total charges

$= ₹\ 10 \times 15 + ₹\ 5 \times 70$

$= ₹\ 500$ which is true.

ILLUSTRATION 4 :

There are five persons P, Q, R, S and T. One is football player, one is chess player and one is hockey player. P and S are unmarried ladies and do not participate in any game. None of the ladies plays chess or football. There is a married couple in which T is the husband. Q is the brother of R and is neither a chess player nor a hockey player.

(i) Who is the football player ?

(a) P (b) Q

(c) R (d) S

(ii) Who is the hockey player ?

(a) P (b) Q

(c) R (d) S

(iii) Who is the chess player ?

(a) P

(b) Q

(c) R

(d) T

(iv) Who is the wife of T ?

(a) P (b) Q

(c) R (d) S

(v) The three ladies are :

(a) P, Q, R

(b) Q, R, S

(c) P, Q, S

(d) P, R, S

Sol. Q is neither a hockey player nor a chess player. So, Q must be a football player and thus cannot be a lady. T is a husband (not a lady) and so must be a chess player. Hence, R must be a hockey player, and therefore she must be a lady and T's wife. So, the information can be summarised as follows :

Person	Sex	Interest in Games	Relationships
P	Female	No	Unmarried
Q	Male	Football	Brother of R
R	Female	Hockey	Wife of T
S	Female	No	Unmarried
T	Male	Chess	Husband of R

(i) (a) Q is the foot ball player.

(ii) (c) R is the hockey player.

(iii) (d) T is the chess player.

(iv) (c) R is the wife of T.

(v) (d) The three ladies are P, R and S.

LEVEL 1

1. In a classroom, there are 5 rows, and 5 children A, B, C, D and E are seated one behind the other in 5 seperate rows as follows :

   A is sitting behind C, but in front of B.

   C is sitting behind E, D is sitting in front of E.

   The order in which they are sitting from the first row to the last is

   (a) DECAB (b) BACED
   (c) ACBDE (d) ABEDC

2. There are five buses M, N, O, P, Q in a row on a road. Bus M is standing at the front and Q is standing at the back end. Bus N stands between M and O. Bus P stands between O and Q. Which bus is in the middle of the five?

   (a) M (b) O
   (c) N (d) Q

3. Five coaches P, L, R, M, O are in a row. R is to the right of M and left of P. L is to the right of P and left of O. Which coach is in the middle?

   (a) P (b) L
   (c) R (d) O

4. Five boys A, B, C, D and E are standing in a row. D is on the right of E. B is on the left of E, but on the right of A. D is on the left of C, who is standing on the extreme right. Who is standing in the middle ?

   (a) D (b) E
   (b) B (d) C

5. Five policemen are standing in a row facing south. Shekhar is to the immediate right of Dhanush. Bala is between Basha and Dhanush. David is at the extreme right end of the row. Who is standing in the middle of the row?

   (a) Bala (b) Basha
   (c) Shekhar (d) Dhanush

6. Seven persons A, B, C, D, E, F and G are standing in a straight line.

   D is to the right of G.

   C is between A and B.

   E is between F and D.

   There are three persons between G and B. Who is on the extreme left?

   (a) A (b) B
   (c) D (d) G

7. Five boys A, B, C, D and E are standing in a line. A is taller than E but shorter than D. B is shorter than E and C is the tallest. Who is in the middle?

   (a) A (b) C
   (c) D (d) E

8. In an automobile showroom, seven two-wheelers of seven different companies, viz. H, M, T, V, Y, B and S are displayed in a row, facing east such that:

   (A) The H vehicle is to the immediate right of the S vehicle.

   (B) The S is fourth to the right of T.

(C) The V is between the M and the B.

(D) The T, which is third to the left of the M, is at one of the ends.

Which vehicle is second to the left of the M?

(a) V (b) S

(c) B (d) T

9. Eight persons A, B, C, D, E, F, G and H are sitting in a straight line facing the north. C is between B and A. D is between B and H. E is third to the left of A. B is second to the right of A. G is between A and F. H is at one of the corners. Who is sitting at the other corner?

(a) E (b) G

(c) B (d) F

DIRECTIONS (Qs. 1-3) : *Study the following information and answer the questions given below it.*

There is a group of five persons K, G, H, R and J.

(i) K, G and H are intelligent.

(ii) K, R and J are hard working.

(iii) R, H and J are honest and

(iv) K, G and J are ambitious

1. Which of the following persons is neither hard working nor ambitious ?

(a) K (b) G

(c) H (d) R

2. Which of the following persons is neither honest nor hard working but is ambitious ?

(a) K (b) G

(c) R (d) H

3. Five persons A, B, C, D and E are sitting in a row facing you such that D is on the left of C and B is on the right of E. A is on the right of C and B is on the left of D. If E occupies a corner position, then who is sitting in the centre ?

(a) A (b) B

(c) C (d) D

DIRECTIONS (Qs. 4-6) : *Read the following information carefully and answer the questions given below.*

Ravi and Kunal are good in Hockey and Volleyball. Sachin and Ravi are good in Hockey and Baseball. Gaurav and Kunal are good in Cricket and Voleyball. Sachin, Gaurav and Micheal are good in Football and Baseball.

4. Who is good in Hockey, Cricket and Volleyball ?

(a) Sachin (b) Kunal

(c) Ravi (d) Gaurav

5. Who is good in Baseball, Cricket, Volleyball and Football ?

(a) Sachin (b) Kunal

(c) Gaurav (d) Ravi

6. Who is good in Baseball, Volleyball and Hockey ?
   (a) Sachin (b) Kunal
   (c) Ravi (d) Gaurav

DIRECTIONS (Qs. 7-9) : *Questions are based on the information given below. Read the information carefully and find out the correct answer from the four alternative and write its alternative number on you answer sheet against the proper question number.*

For being graduate Dinesh opted Sanskrit, Science and Hindi, Ganesh opted English, Mathematics and Hindi, Umesh opted English, Science and Hindi. Nita opted Sanskrit, Science and Hindi. While Gita opted English, Sanskrit and Hindi. Then answer the following question.

7. Which subject opted by the most students.
   (a) Sanskrit (b) Science
   (c) Hindi (d) English
8. Which subject opted by the least student.
   (a) Science
   (b) Mathematics
   (c) English
   (d) Sanskrit
9. How many student opted Sanskrit subject.
   (a) 2 (b) 4
   (c) 5 (d) 3

DIRECTIONS (10-12): *Read the given information carefully to answer the question.*

A, B, C, D, E, F and G are sitting in a row facing North. F is to the immediate right of E. E is 4th to the right of G. C is the neighbour of B and D. Person who is third to the left of D is at one of the ends.

10. Who are to the left of C?
    (a) Only B
    (b) G, B and D
    (c) G and B
    (d) D,E,F and A
11. Who are the neighbours of B?
    (a) C and D (b) C and G
    (c) G and F (d) C and E
12. Which of the following statements is not true?
    (a) E is to the immediate left of D
    (b) A is at one of the ends
    (c) G is to the immediate left of B
    (d) F is second to the right of D
13. P, Q, R, S, T and U are sitting in a row. T and U are in the centre, Q and R are at the ends. S is sitting to the immediate left of Q. Who is to the immediate right of R?
    (a) Q (b) P
    (c) T (d) U

DIRECTIONS (Qs. 14-20): *Read the following information and answer the questions given below it.*

Six students A, B, C, D, E and F are sitting in the field. A and B are from Nehru House while the rest belong to Gandhi House. D and F are tall while the others are short. A, C and D are wearing glasses while the others are not.

14. Which two students, who are not wearing glasses, are short?
    (a) A and F
    (b) C and E
    (c) B and E
    (d) E and F

15. Which short student of Gandhi House is not wearing glasses?
    (a) F (b) E
    (c) B (d) A

16. Which tall student of Gandhi House is not wearing glasses?
    (a) B (b) C
    (c) E (d) F

17. Riya and Kiara are good in Hindi and Sanskrit. Seema and Riya are good in Hindi and Science. Garima and Kiara are good in Maths and Sanskrit. Seema, Garima and Meena are good in English and Science. Who is good in Hindi, Maths and Sanskrit?
    (a) Riya (b) Kiara **[2018]**
    (c) Seema (d) Garima

18. Six persons are sitting in a row facing North. P is third to the left of S, who is to the immediate right of R. U is at the one end and fourth to the right of Q. If T is between S and U, then R is _______________ to the left of T. **[2018]**
    (a) Secord
    (b) Third
    (c) Fourth
    (d) None of these

19. P, Q, R, S and T are to be seated in a row facing East, but R and S cannot be together. Also, Q cannot be at third place. If P and Q are together and R is at the first place, then which of the following cannot be true?
    (a) S is at the second place. **[2018]**
    (b) S is at the third place.
    (c) P is at the third place.
    (d) None of these

20. Five boys are sitting in a circular table, Amit is left side of Shyam and Radhey is sitting between Miraj and Pankaj. Pankaj is sitting left side of Amit. **[2022]**

    Who is sitting left of Miraj?
    (a) Radhey (b) Pankaj
    (c) Amit (d) Shyam

ANSWER KEY

LEVEL-1

1	(a)	2	(b)	3	(a)	4	(b)	5	(d)	6	(d)	7	(a)	8	(c)	9	(a)		

LEVEL-2

1	(c)	3	(d)	5	(c)	7	(c)	9	(d)	11	(b)	13	(b)	15	(b)	18	(a)	17	(b)
2	(b)	4	(b)	6	(c)	8	(b)	10	(c)	12	(a)	14	(c)	16	(d)	19	(a)	20	(d)

CHAPTER 10 Analytical Reasoning (Diagrammatic Puzzle)

FIGURE PARTITION :

The problems on figure partition are based on counting the number of figures generated due to partition lines.

1. If a square is subdivided into n parts on each side, then the total number of squares formed is given by

$$\frac{n(n+1)(2n+1)}{6}$$

2. Total no. of rectangles (including squares) in a rectangular figure of size n × m

$$= \frac{n(n+1)}{6}\frac{m(m+1)}{2}$$

ILLUSTRATION 1 :

What is the number of straight lines in the following figure?

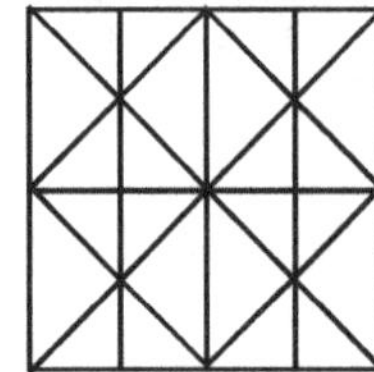

(a) 11 (b) 14
(c) 16 (d) 17

Sol. **(b)** The figure is labelled as shown.

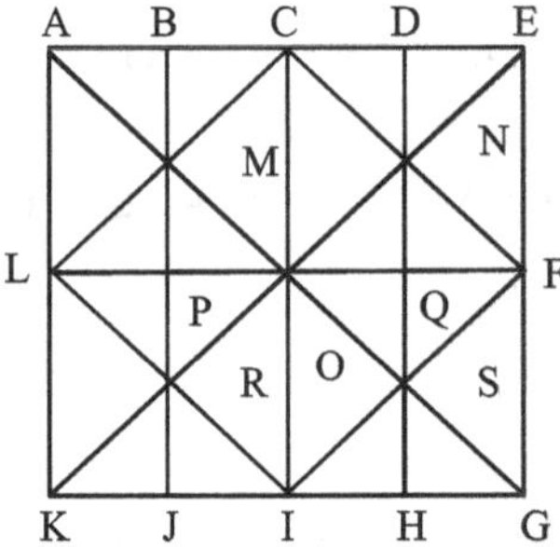

Clearly, there are 3 horizontal lines namely AE, LF and KG.
There are 5 vertical lines : AK, BJ, CI, DH and EG.
There are 6 slanting lines : LC, KE, IF, LI, AG and CF.
Thus, there are 3 + 5 + 6 = 14 straight lines in the figure.

ILLUSTRATION 2 :

How many squares does the figure have ?

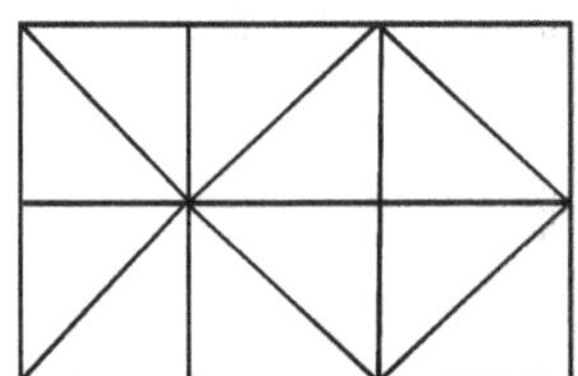

(a) 6 (b) 7
(c) 9 (d) 10

***Sol.* (c)** The figure may be labelled as shown :

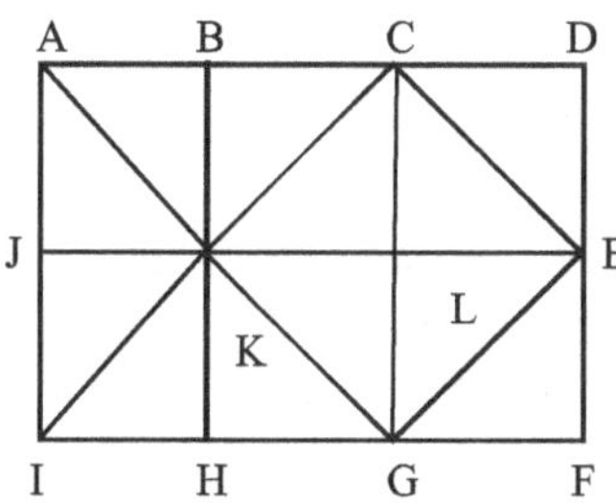

The squares composed to two components each, are ABKJ, BCLK, CDEL, LEFG, KLGH, JKHI. Thus, there are 6 such squares. Only one square, KCEG is composed of four components. Two squares namely, ACGI and BDFH are composed of eight components each. Thus, there are 2 such squares.

∴ There are 6 + 1 + 2 = 9 squares in the figure

ILLUSTRATION 3 :

What is the number of rectangles in the following figure ?

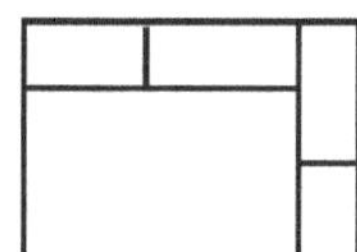

(a) 5 (b) 7

(c) 8 (d) 9

Sol. (d) The figure is labelled as shown :

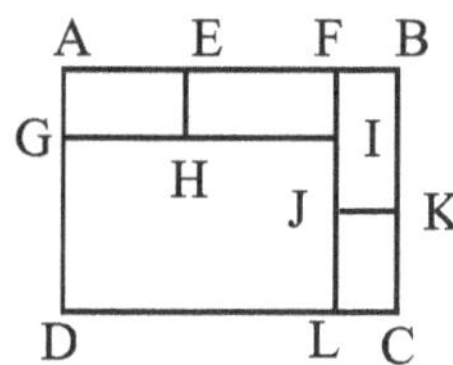

Simplest rectangles are AEHG, EFIH, FBKJ, JKCL and GILD. i.e. there are 5 such rectangles.

The rectangles composed of two components each are AFIG and FBCL. Thus, there are 2 such rectangles. Only one rectangle, namely AFLD is composed of 3 components and only one rectangle, namely ABCD is composed of 5 components.

Thus, there are 5 + 2 + 1 + 1 = 9 rectangles in the figure.

ILLUSTRATION 4 :

Determine the number of pentagons in the following figure:

(a) 5 (b) 6

(c) 8 (d) 10

***Sol.* (d)** The figure is labelled as shown. In this case, six pentagons have been formed by the combination of three triangles and two rhombuses- ADFHJ, CFHJL, EHJLB, GJLBD, ILBDF and KBDFH.

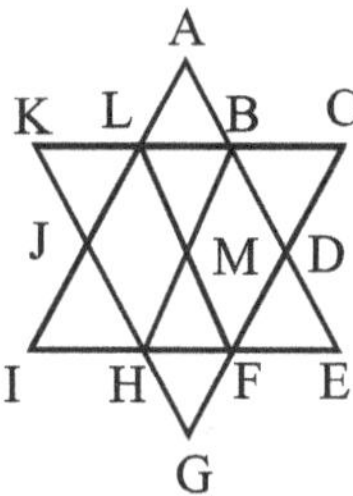

Four other pentagons are formed by the combination of three triangles and one rhombus -LCFHM, LBEHM, BKFHM and BLIFM. Thus, there are 10 pentagons in the figure.

LEVEL 1

1. How many parallelograms are there in the figure?

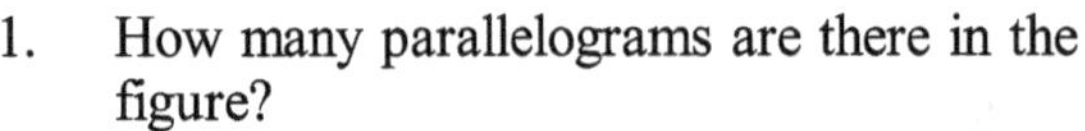

   (a) 14
   (b) 15
   (c) 16
   (d) 18

2. Count the number of triangles in the figure.

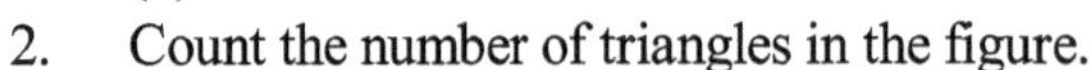

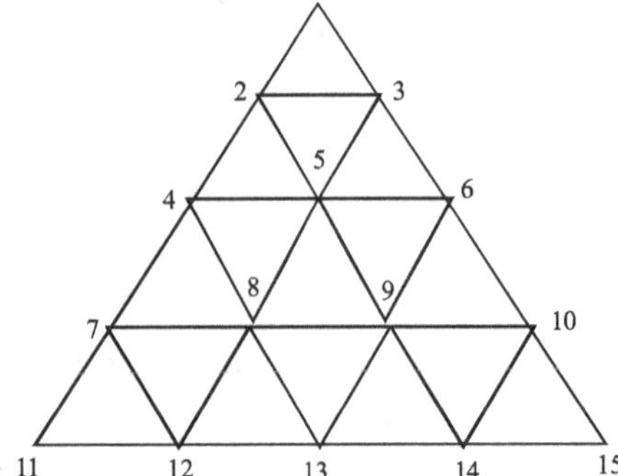

   (a) 40 (b) 48
   (c) 30 (d) 50

3. What is the number of triangles in figure.
   (a) 16
   (b) 28
   (c) 32
   (d) 38

4. What is the number of rectangles (excluding squares) in figure.

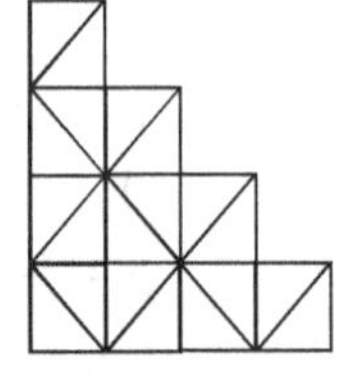

   (a) 10
   (b) 12
   (c)
   (d) 22

5. What is the minimum number of different colours required to colour the given figure such that no two adjacent regions have the same colour? **[2018]**

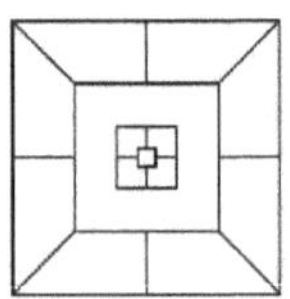

   (a) 3 (b) 2
   (c) 4 (d) 5

6. Count the number of rectangles in the given figure. **[2021]**

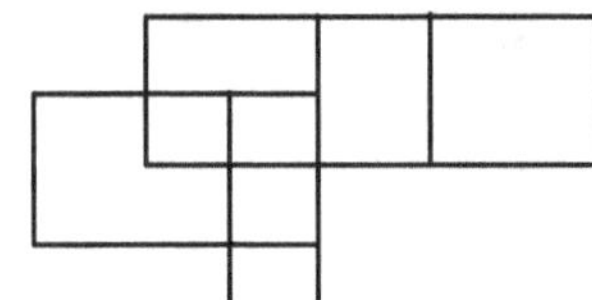

   (a) 15 (b) 16
   (c) 14 (d) More than 16

7. Find the minimum number of straight lines required to draw the given figure. **[2021]**

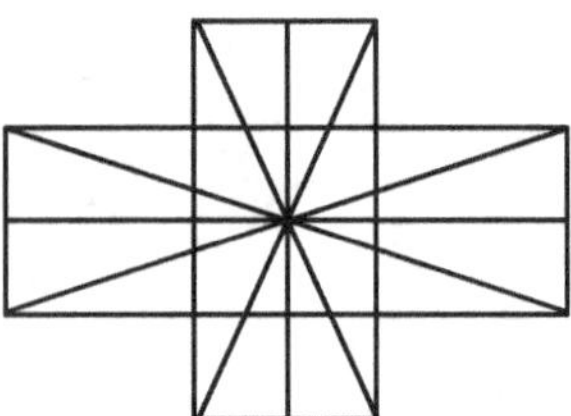

   (a) 12 (b) 15
   (c) 13 (d) 14

LEVEL 2

1. 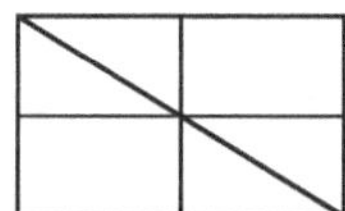

How many triangles and quadrilaterals are there in this figure?

(a) 7 and 6 (b) 6 and 7
(c) 6 and 8 (d) 6 and 9

2. 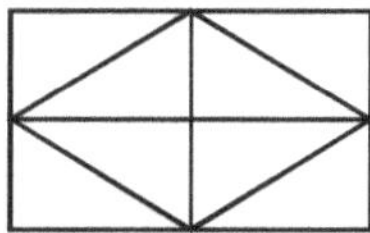

How many quadrilaterals are there in this figure?

(a) 8 (b) 9
(c) 10 (d) 11

DIRECTION (Q. 3-4): Identify the number of specified geometric shapes in the given diagram and mark the correct answer.

3. How many triangles are in the given figure?

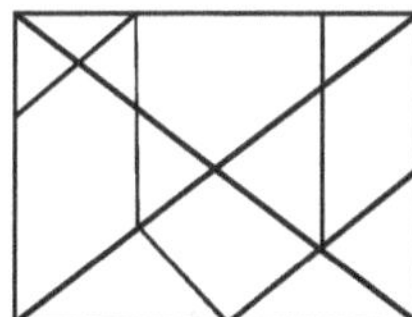

(a) 19 (b) 20
(c) 21 (d) 22

4. Find the number of squares/rectangles in the given figure.

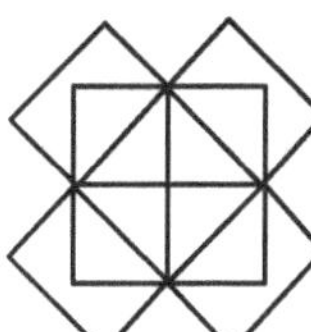

(a) 20 (b) 18
(c) 16 (d) 15

DIRECTION (Q. 5): Find the number of triangles in the given figure.

5. 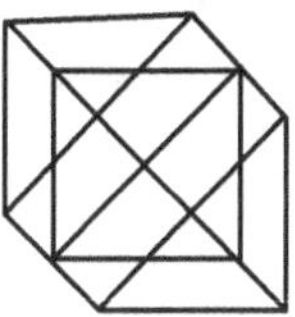

(a) 18 (b) 20
(c) 24 (d) 27

6. What is the minimum number of straight lines required to form the given figure? **[2018]**

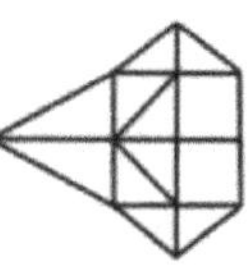

(a) 13 (b) 14
(c) 15 (d) 16

7. Count the number of triangles in the given figure. **[2018]**

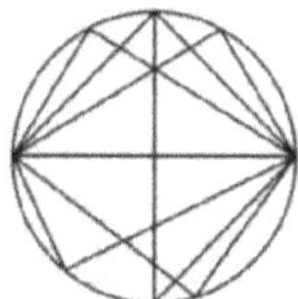

(a) 30 (b) 28
(c) 25 (d) None of these

8. How many minimum number of straight lines are required to form the given figure? **[2018]**

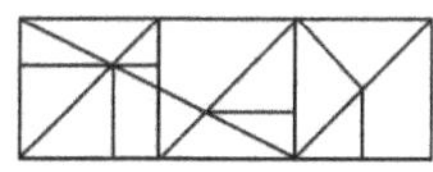

(a) 13 (b) 14
(c) 15 (d) None of these

9. How many triangles are there in the given figure? **[2019]**

(a) 20 (b) 28
(c) 30 (d) None of these

10. Find the minimum number of straight lines required to draw the given figure. **[2019]**

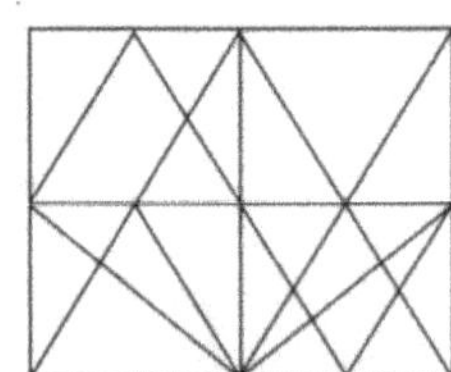

(a) 15 (b) 16
(c) 14 (d) 17

11. Count the number of triangles in the given figure. **[2019]**

(a) 20 (b) 18
(c) 22 (d) None of these

12. How many squares are there in the given figure? **[2020]**

(a) 10 (b) 14
(c) 12 (d) 15

13. How many triangles are there in the given figure? **[2022]**

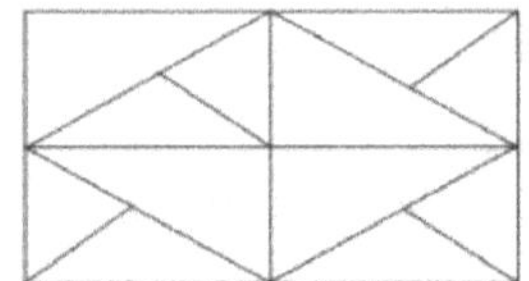

(a) More than 19
(b) Less than 14
(c) Between 16 to 19
(d) 15

ANSWER KEY																			
LEVEL-1																			
1	(c)	**2**	(b)	**3**	(d)	**4**	(d)	**5**	(a)	**6**	(b)	**7**	(d)						
LEVEL-2																			
1	(d)	**3**	(a)	**5**	(c)	**7**	(a)	**9**	(d)	**11**	(d)	**13**	(a)						
2	(c)	**4**	(a)	**6**	(b)	**8**	(c)	**10**	(a)	**12**	(c)								

CHAPTER

Mirror and Water Images

Mirror Images

In this category questions are based on the criteria that a few figures are given and you have to find out which one is the exact image of the given figure in a mirror placed in front of it. This image formation is based on the principle of 'lateral inversion' which implies that size of the image is equal to the size of the object but both sides are interchanged. The left portion of the object is seen on the right side and right portion of the object is seen on the left side. For example, mirror image of ABC = ƆᙠA

Note : There are '11' letters in English Alphabet which have identical mirror images: A, H, I, M, O, T, U, V, W, X, Y.

Characteristics of Reflection by plane mirror

1. Perpendicular distance of object from mirror = Perpendicular distance of image from mirror.
2. The image is laterally inverted.

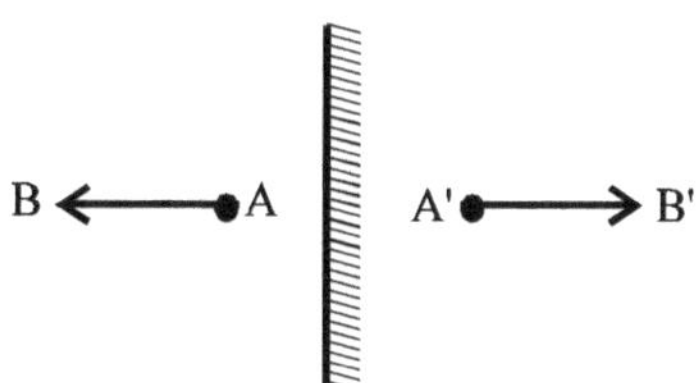

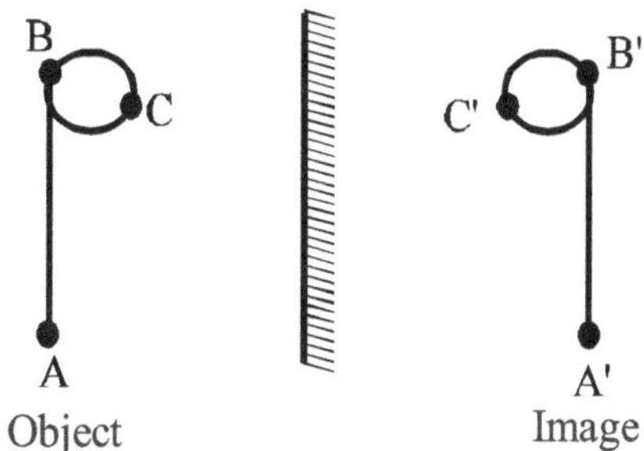

3. The line joining the object point with its image is normal to the reflecting surface.
4. The size of the image is the same as that of the object.

***E.g* -1:** Mirror-images of certain words are given below :

(1) F U N : И U ꟻ

(2) GOLKONDA : AᗡИOꓘ⅃OᎮ

***E.g* -2:** Mirror-image of certain combinations of alphabets and numbers are given below :

(1) BMC49JN2317 : 7132ИႱ94ƆMᙠ

(2) 15bg82XQh : ԃQX28gdƻ1

I. Mirror Images of Capital Letters

A	A
B	ᗺ
C	Ɔ
D	ᗡ
E	Ǝ
F	ꟻ
G	Ә
H	H
I	I
J	Ⴑ
K	ꓘ
L	⅃
M	M

N	И
O	O
P	ꟼ
Q	Ϙ
R	Я
S	Ƨ
T	T
U	U
V	V
W	W
X	X
Y	Y
Z	Ƹ

II Mirror Images of Small Letters

a	ɒ
b	d
c	ɔ
d	b
e	ɘ
f	ʇ
g	ϱ
h	ʜ
i	i
j	ɾ
k	ʞ
l	l
m	m

n	n
o	o
p	q
q	p
r	ɿ
s	ƨ
t	ɟ
u	u
v	v
w	w
x	x
y	γ
z	ƹ

III. Mirror Images of Numbers

0	0
1	I
2	Ƨ
3	Ɛ
4	ᔭ
5	ƽ

6	∂
7	ᒣ
8	8
9	ɘ
10	01

Examples of lateral inversion of few figures and words are given below :

IV. Mirror Images of Various Objects :

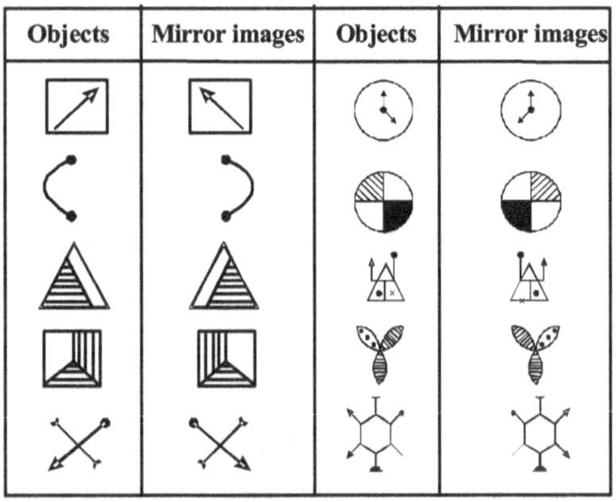

Objects	Mirror images	Objects	Mirror images

V. Mirror Images of Certain Words and Numbers:

Words	Mirror images	Numbers	Mirror images
PREDICTION	ИOITƆIᗡƎЯꟼ	32596	∂ɘƧƧƐ
HOSPITAL	⅃ATIꟼƧOH	8932	ƧƐɘ8
DARPAN	ИAꟼЯAᗡ	868	8∂8
STRIDENT	TИƎᗡIЯTƧ	786	∂8ᒣ
OPULENT	TИƎ⅃UꟼO	10190	0ɘ10I
SARCASM	MƧAƆЯAƧ	5693	Ɛɘ∂ƽ
LIBERAL	⅃AЯƎᗺI⅃	8964	ᔭ∂ɘ8
OFFENCE	ƎƆИƎꟻꟻO	7362	Ƨ∂Ɛᒣ
ADVANCE	ƎƆИAVᗡA	5893	Ɛɘ8ƽ
IMAGES	ƧƎӘAMI	7839	ɘƐ8ᒣ

VI. Mirror Images of Clock:

There are certain questions in which the position of the hour-hand and the minute-hand of a clock as seen in a mirror are given. On the basis of the time indicated by the mirror-image of the clock we have to detect the actual time in the clock. In the solution of such questions we use the fact that if an object A is the mirror-image of another object B then B is the mirror-image of A.

Time of image in plane mirror

(a) Real time = X^H, Image time = $12^H - X^H$ (H = hours)

(b) Real time = X^HY^M, Image time = $11^H60^M - X^HY^M$ (M = minutes)

(c) Real time = $X^HY^MZ^S$, Image time = $11^H59^M60^S - X^HY^MZ^S$ (S = seconds)

(d) if $X^HY^MZ^S > 11^H59^M60^S$, image time $= 23^H59^M60^S - X^HY^MZ^S$

Quick Tip

Whenever you have to solve a mirror image question, imagine a mirror placed in front of the object and then try to find its inverted image. The portion of the object that is near the mirror will now be the portion of the image near to the mirror in the inverted form.

ILLUSTRATION 1 :

By looking in a mirror, it appears that it is 6 : 30 in the clock. What is the real time ?

(a) 6 : 30 (b) 5 : 30
(c) 6 : 00 (d) 4 : 30

Sol. **(b)**

(Fig A) (Fig B)

Clearly, fig (A) shows the time (6 : 30) in the clock as it appears in a mirror. Then its mirror-image i.e. Fig (B) shows the actual time in the clock i.e. 5 : 30. You can solve it quickly if you remember that the sum of actual time and image time is always 12 hours.

DIRECTIONS (ILLUSTRATION 2) :

Find the correct option for the mirror image for the following examples.

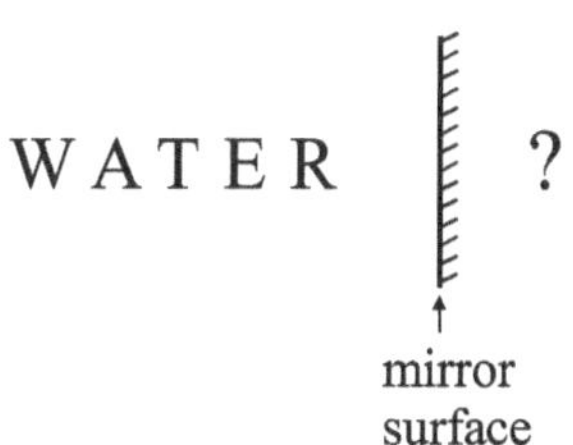

(a) W A T Ǝ Я
(b) Я Ǝ T Ǝ W
(c) W A Я Ǝ T
(d) Я Ǝ T A W

Sol. (d) We have to find the correct mirror image for the word 'WATER' for which we need to find the mirror image for each letter separately and then arrange it, like the mirror image for the letters W is W, A is A, T is T, E is Ǝ and R is Я.

Since, the word ends with R, i.e., where the mirror is placed, therefore the mirror image will start from the mirror images of R, i.e.; Я. Thus the mirror image for water is Я Ǝ T A W

WATER | ЯƎTAW

Thus option (4) is the correct answer.

ILLUSTRATION 3 :

8 6 9 5 2 | ?

(a) 8 ∂ 9 ƨ ς
(b) 8 9 ∂ 5 ς
(c) 8 ∂ ƨ ς ϱ
(d) ς ƨ ϱ ∂ 8

Sol. (d) Mirror image for '8' is '8', '6' is '∂', '9' is 'ϱ', '5' is 'ƨ' and '2' is 'ς'.

8 6 9 5 2 | ς ƨ ϱ ∂ 8

Thus, option (d) is the answer.

ILLUSTRATION 4 :

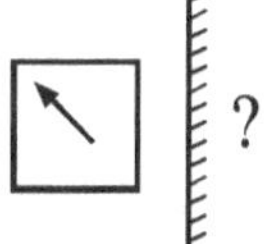

Sol. (a) The mirror image of a square remains a square while the arrow inside it will be changed.

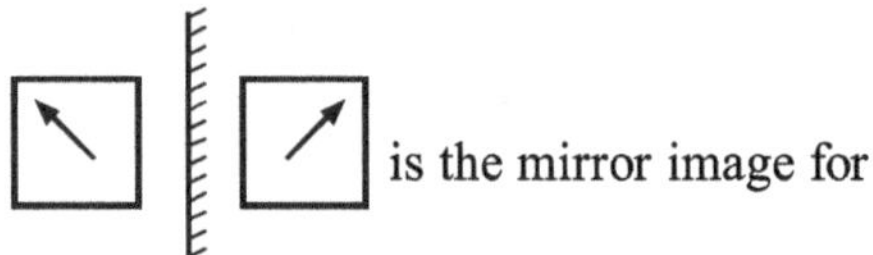

is the mirror image for the given image. Thus opiton (a) is the correct answer.

ILLUSTRATION 5 :

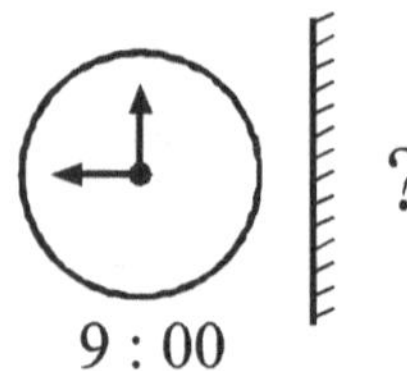

(a) 12 : 00 (b) 5 : 00
(c) 3 : 00 (d) 6 : 00

Sol. (c) The mirror image of circle remains a circle, and the arrow facing north also remains the same but the arrow facing will face East in its mirror image.

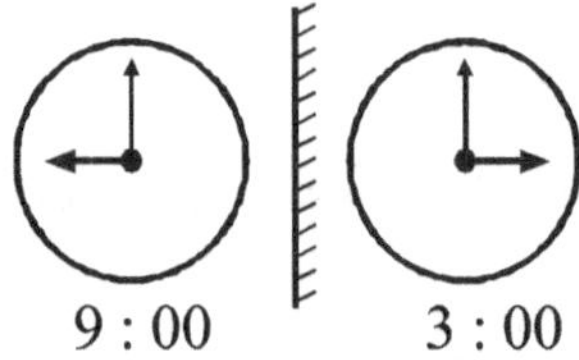

Thus, answer is 3 : 00, i.e., option (c).

Water Image

The reflection of an object as seen in water is called its water image. It is the inverted image obtained by turning the object upside down.

Water-images of capital letters

Letters	A	B	C	D	E	F	G	H	I	J	K	L	M
Water-image	∀	B	C	D	E	Ⅎ	⅁	H	I	ɿ	K	Γ	W
Letters	N	O	P	Q	R	S	T	U	V	W	X	Y	Z
Water-image	И	O	b	Ó	ʁ	ƨ	⊥	∩	Λ	M	X	⅄	Z

Water-images of small letters

Letters	a	b	c	d	e	f	g	h	i	j	k	l	m
Water-image	ɘ	p	c	q	ɕ	ɟ	ƍ	ɥ	!	ʇ	ʞ	l	ɯ
Letters	n	o	p	q	r	s	t	u	v	w	x	y	z
Water-image	u	o	b	d	ɹ	ƨ	ʇ	n	ʌ	ʍ	x	ʎ	z

Water-images of numbers

Letters	0	1	2	3	4	5	6	7	8	9
Water-image	0	I	Ƨ	3	ᔭ	ƨ	ɘ	⅃	8	ƍ

Note :

1. The letters whose water-images are identical to the letter itself are : C, D, E, H, I, K, O, X
2. Certain words which have water-images identical to the word itself are : KICK, KID, CHIDE, HIKE, CODE, CHICK

Quick Tip

Whenever we have to analyze the water image of an object, imagine a mirror or a surface that forms an image just under the given object. The portion of the object that is near the water surface will be inverted but will be near the water surface in the image as well.

DIRECTIONS (ILLUSTRATION 6-8) :
Find the correct option for the water images for the following examples.

ILLUSTRATION 6 :

STORE
////////////// ← water surface
?

(a) S⊥ORE (b) S⊥OᴚE
(c) S⊥OʁE (d) ƨ⊥OʁE

Sol. (d) In case of water image, the water reflection will usually be formed under the object / word.

In this case, the water image of the word will be an outcome of the water images of each of the letters like, the water images of S is Ƨ, T is ⊥, O is O, R is ꓤ and E is E. Thus the water image of the word 'STORE' is 'Ƨ ⊥ O ꓤ E.'

STORE

Ƨ⅃OꓤE

ILLUSTRATION 7 :

1 6 8 9 2

?

(a) 1 ɐ 8 ə Ƨ (b) ⇃ ɐ 8 ə Ƨ

(c) ⇃ ɐ 8 ə 5 (d) ⇃ ɐ 8 6 Ƨ

Sol. (b) The water image of '1' is ⇃, '6' is 'ɐ', '8' is 8, '9' is 'ə' and '2' is 'Ƨ'.

Thus, the water image of 1 6 8 9 2 is ⇃ ɐ 8 ə Ƨ

ILLUSTRATION 8 :

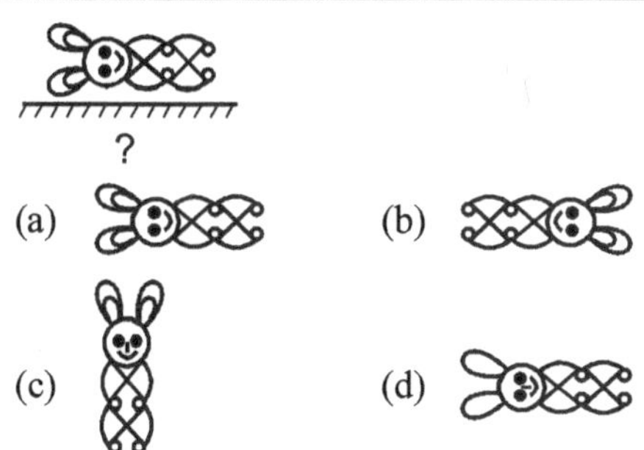

Sol. (a) Since, the teddy bear is facing west, in its water image also it will face west. Therefore, options (b) & (c) are ruled out. Now among options (a) & (d) check the ears and nose of the bear in the actual diagram, it does not have a nose, but the image in option (d) has a nose. Therefore, option (a) is the correct representation.

Quick Tips

(i) While solving a question, try eliminating some options and solving the questions will become easier.

To eliminate options, keep in mind the pattern used in the object (given diagram whose image is to be formed) as well as the position of mirror or water such that the portion of the object near to the mirror / water will produce the same portion near the mirror / water in an inverted form.

(ii) Images are images, be it water or mirror, in both the cases an inverted image of the alphabets / numerals / clocks / any other object are formed by inverting the object. Inverting of the object solely depends upon the position of mirror or water surface w.r.t. the object.

LEVEL 1

DIRECTIONS (Qs. 1–18) : Find the correct option for the mirror images for the following questions.

1. DREAM | ?

(a) MAEЯD (b) ᗡЯƎAM
(c) MAƎЯᗡ (d) MAƎЯD

2. NEWS | ?

(a) ƧWƎИ (b) ИƎWƧ
(c) NƎWƧ (d) SWƎИ

3. jealous | ?

(a) ⅰɘɒlouƨ (b) ⅰɘɒlous
(c) souⅼɒɘj (d) ƨuolɒɘⅰ

4. 312568 | ?

(a) 3ƖZƼ68 (b) 86ƼSƖƐ
(c) 865SƖƐ (d) 86ƼSƖƐ

5. Rotate the mirror image 90° clockwise.

B | ᗺ

(a) ᗺ (b) ᗺ
(c) B (d) ᗺ

6. Rotate the mirror image 90° anticlockwise.

72 | SΓ

(a) 27 (b) SΓ
(c) SΓ (d) 27

7. Rotate the mirror image 90° clockwise.

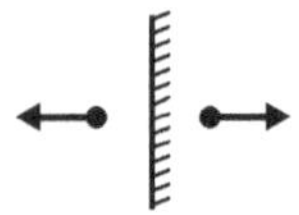

(a) ↑ (b) ←
(c) → (d) ↓

8. Rotate the mirror image of the given clock 90° clockwise and the time will be.

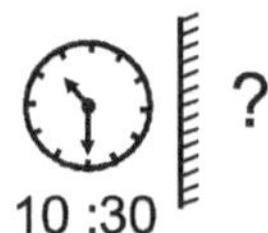

(a) 4 : 45
(b) 5 : 45
(c) 3 : 45
(d) 4 : 30

9. Rotate the mirror image 90° clockwise.

TIME | ?

(a) TIME (b) ƎTIM

(c) TIME (d) TIME

10. 9 :15 ?

(a) 2 : 45 (b) 3 : 15

(c) 9 : 15 (d) 9 : 45

11. ?

(a) (b)

(c) (d)

12. Rotate the mirror image 90° anticlockwise.

? | ?

(a) (b)

(c) (d)

13. Rotate the mirror image 90° anticlockwise.

ANT | TИA

(a) TИA (b) TИA

(c) AИT (d) ANT

14. 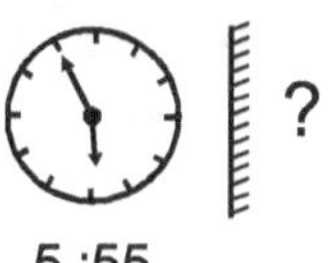

5 :55

(a) 6 : 15

(b) 6 : 05

(c) 5 : 05

(d) 5 : 15

15. 8934 | ?

(a) 8ɘƐ4

(b) 8ɘ34

(c) 8ɘƐ4

(d) 4Ɛɘ8

16. NATIONAL

(a) JAИOIJAИ

(b) JAИOITAИ

(c) JANOITAИ

(d) LAИOITAИ

17. ANS43Q12

(a) AИƧ4ƐQ1Ƨ

(b) Ƨ1QƐ4ƧИA

(c) ƧИAƐ4Q21

(d) 12Q4ƐAИƧ

18. 1965INDOPAK

(a) KAPODNI5961

(b) PAKINDO1965

(c) KAPODNI5691

(d) KAPODNI5961

DIRECTIONS (Qs. 19-21) : *In each of the following questions, choose the correct mirror-image of the Fig. (X) from amongst the four alternatives (a), (b), (c) and (d) given along with it.*

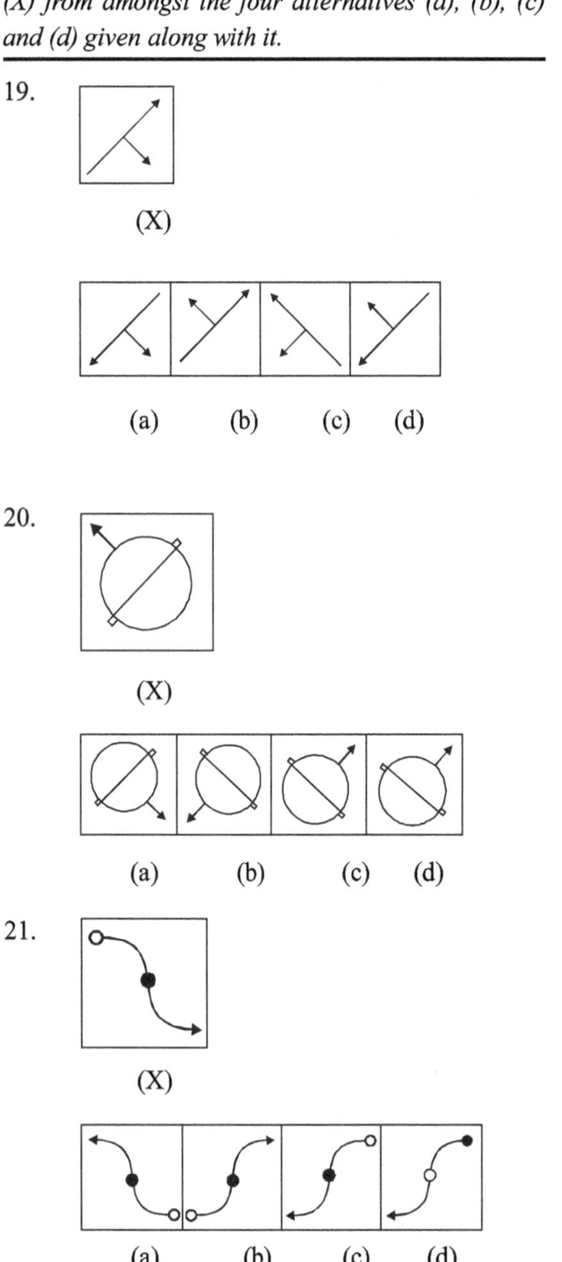

DIRECTIONS: *In questions 22 to 31, there is a problem figure and four answer figures marked (a), (b), (c), (d) are given. Select the answer figure which is exactly the mirror image of the problem figure.*

22. 

(a) 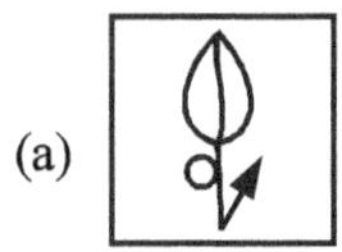 (b) 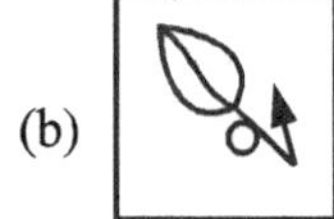

(c) 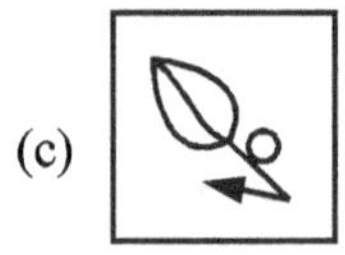 (d) 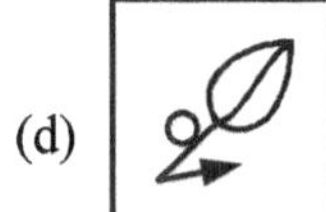

23. 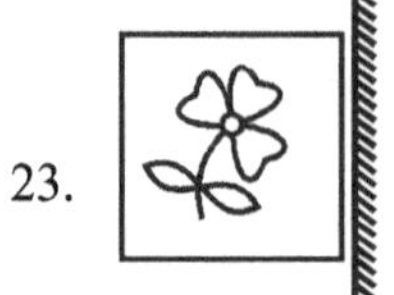

(a) 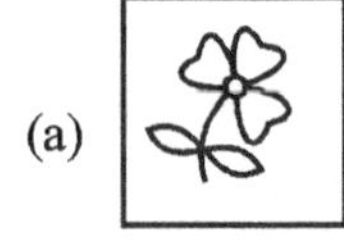 (b) 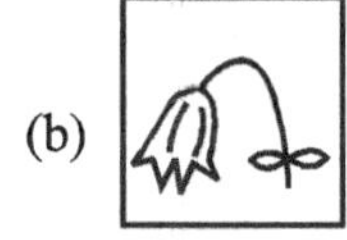

(c) 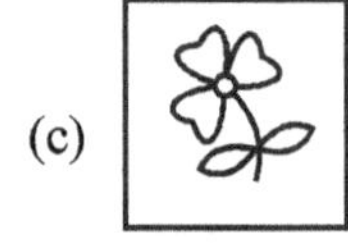 (d) 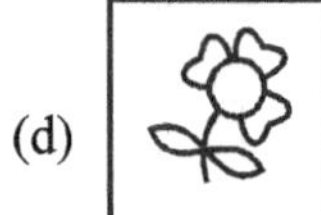

24. 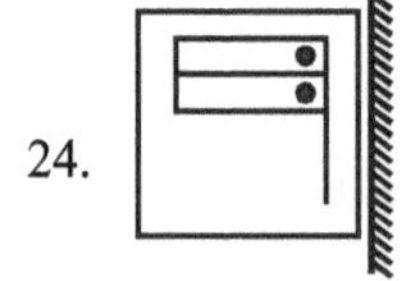

(a) 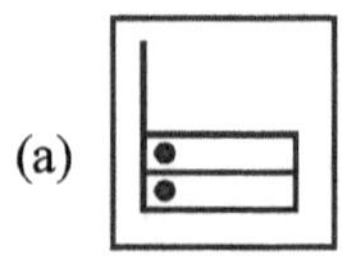 (b) 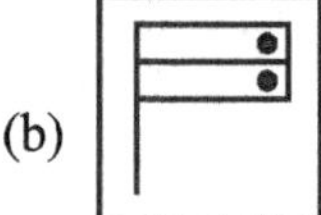

(c) 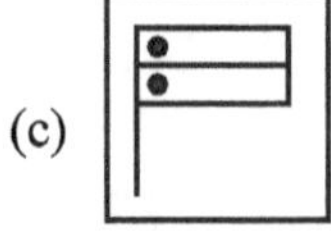 (d) 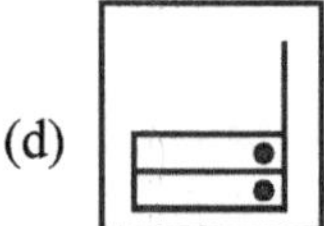

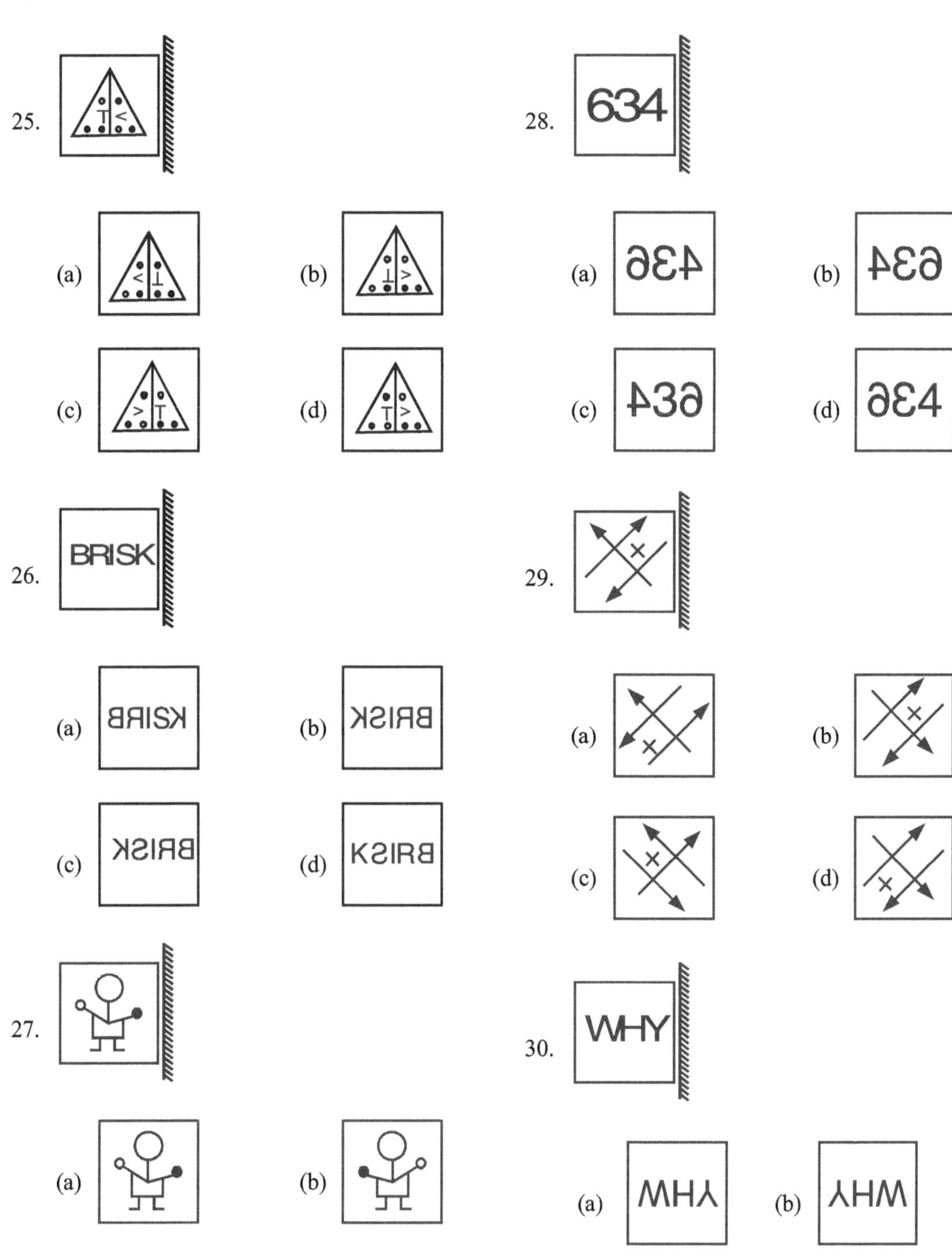
25.
(a)
(b)
(c)
(d)
28.
634
(a)
(b)
(c)
(d)
26.
BRISK
(a)
(b)
(c)
(d)
29.
(a)
(b)
(c)
(d)
27.
(a)
(b)
(c)
(d)
30.
WHY
(a)
(b)
(c)
YHW
(d)

31.

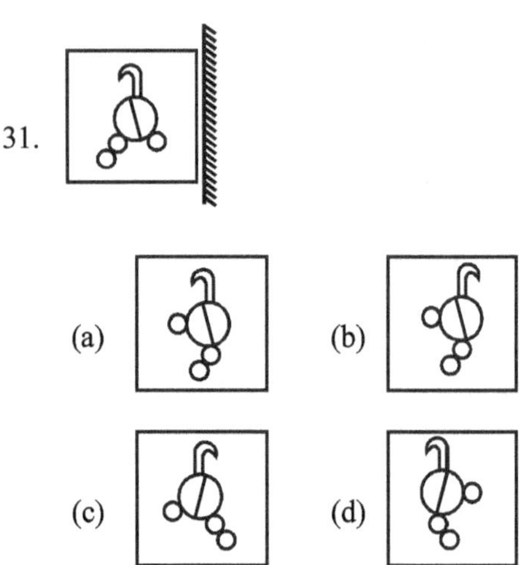

DIRECTIONS (Qs. 32-36): *There are four alternatives (a), (b), (c) and (d) given. You have to choose the correct mirror image of the question figure, when the mirror held on the line XY.*

32. Question Figure

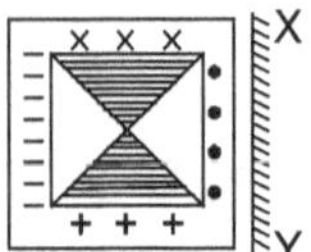

Answer Figures

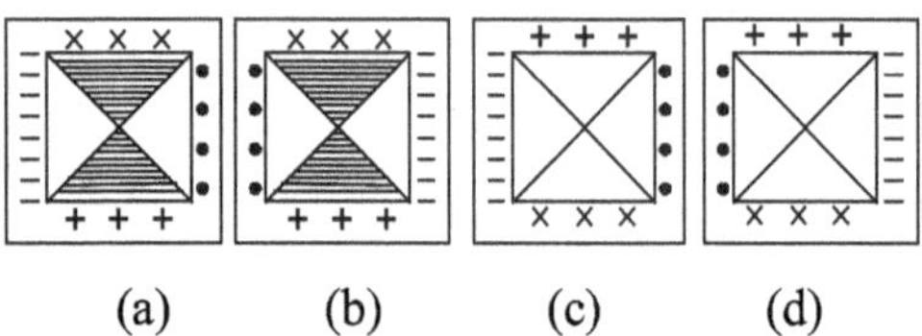

33. **Question Figure**

Answer Figures

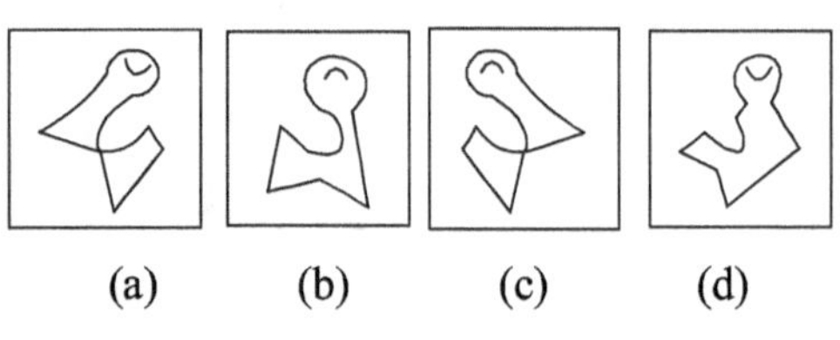

34. **Question Figure**

Answer Figures

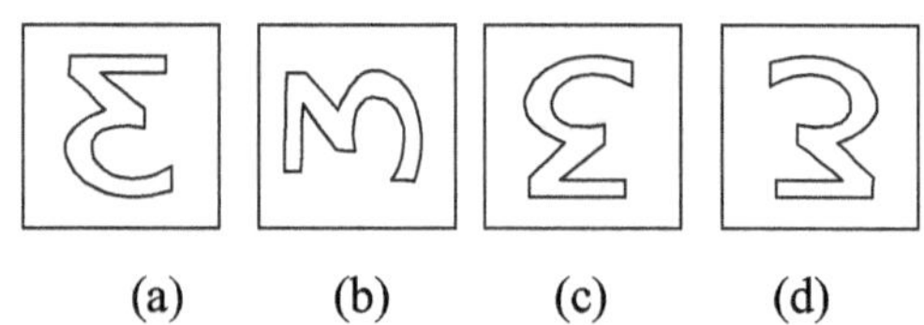

35. **Question Figure**

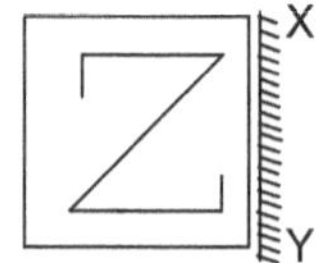

Answer Figures

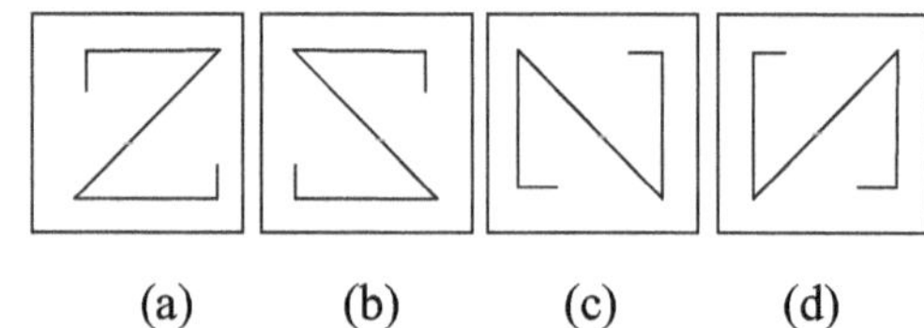

36. **Question Figure**

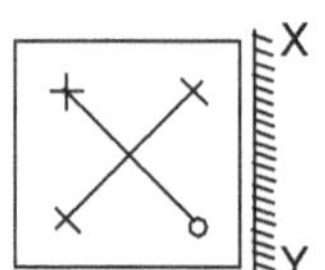

Answer Figures

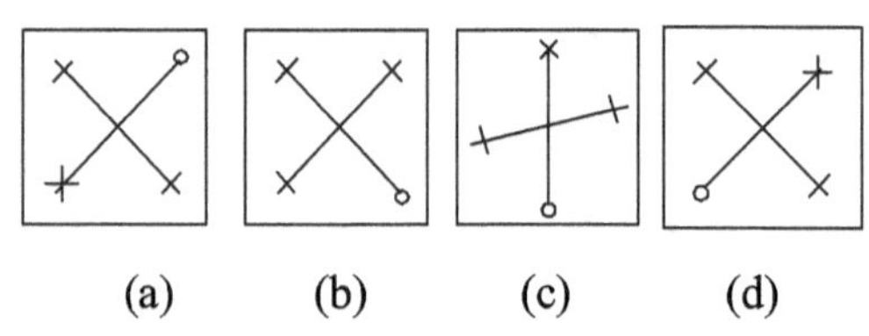

DIRECTIONS (Qs. 37-41): *There are four alternatives (a), (b), (c) and (d) given. You have to choose the correct mirror image of the question figure, when the mirror held on the line XY.*

37. **Question Figure**

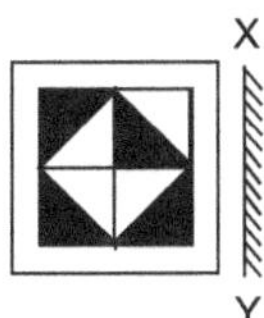

Answer Figures

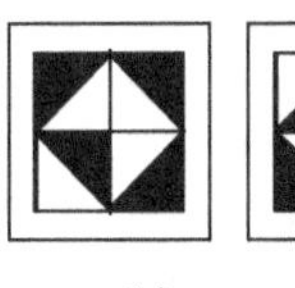
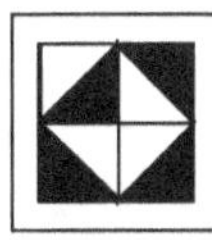
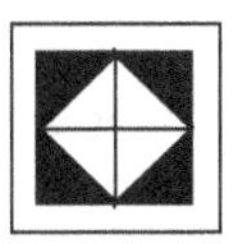
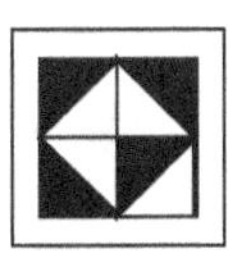

(a) (b) (c) (d)

38. **Question Figure**

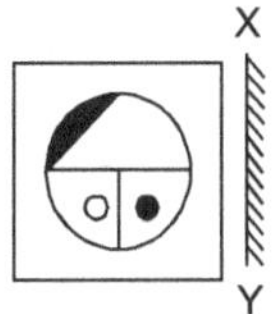

Answer Figures

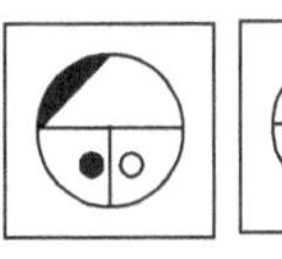

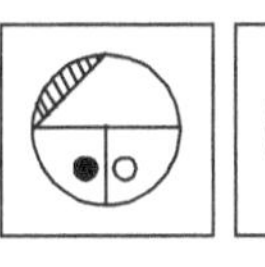
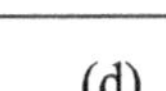

(a) (b) (c) (d)

39. **Question Figure**

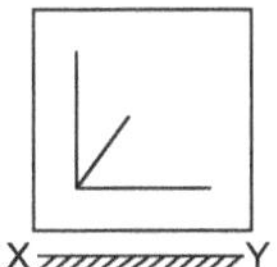

Answer Figures

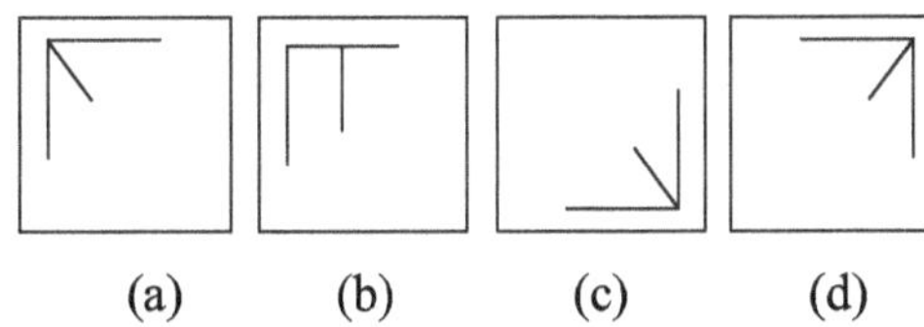

(a) (b) (c) (d)

40. **Question Figure**

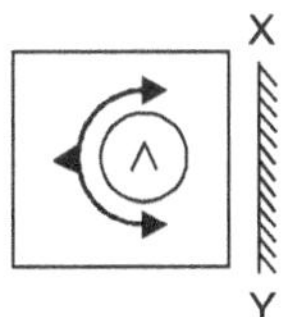

Answer Figures

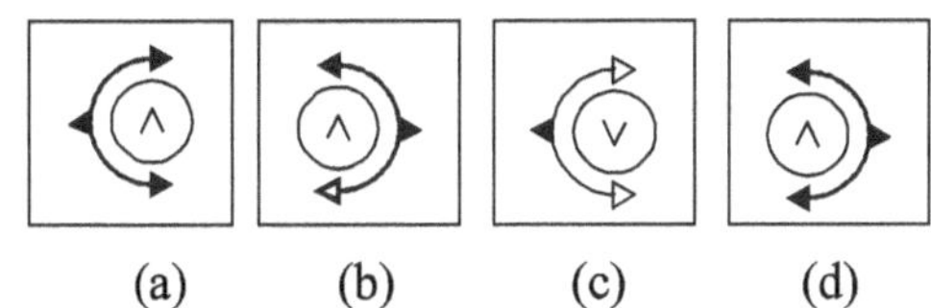

(a) (b) (c) (d)

41. **Question Figure**

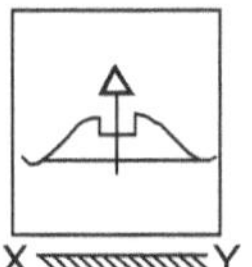

Answer Figures

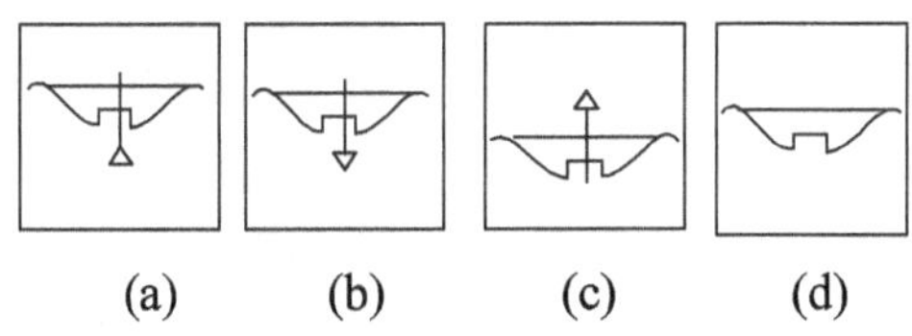

(a) (b) (c) (d)

DIRECTIONS: (Qs. 42-45): *There is a question figure and four answer figures marked (a), (b), (c) and (d) are given. Select the answer figure which is exactly the mirror image of the question figure when the mirror is held at XY.*

42. **Question Figure**

Answer Figures

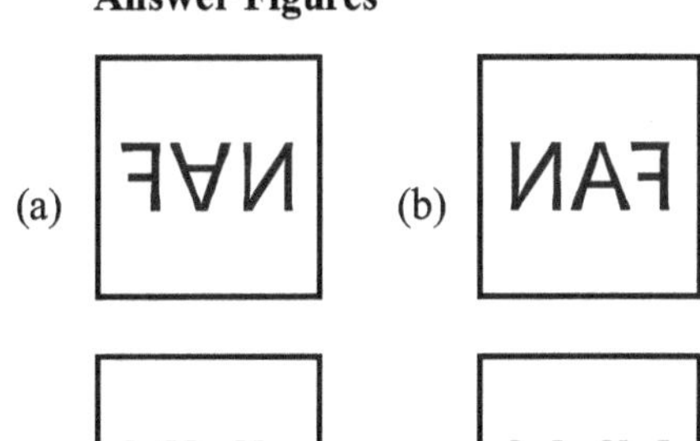

(a) (b)

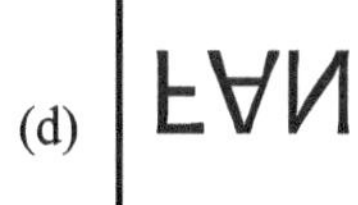

(c) (d)

43. **Question Figure**

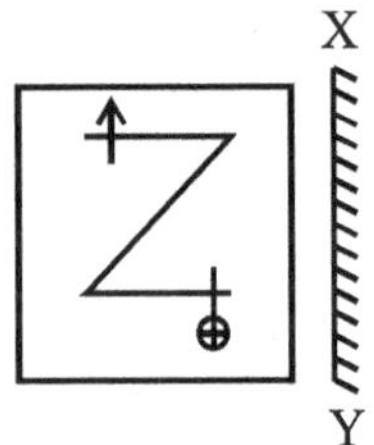

Answer Figures

(a) 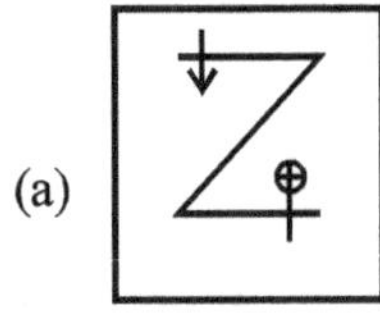 (b) 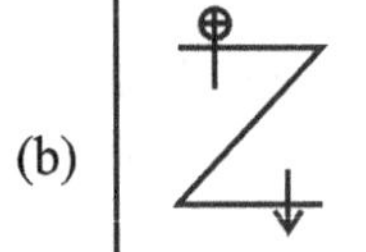

(c) 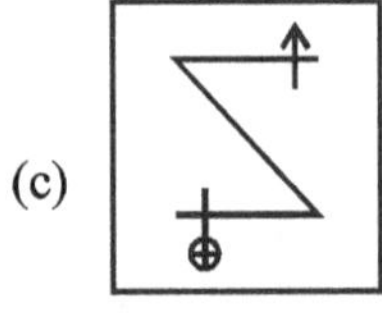 (d) 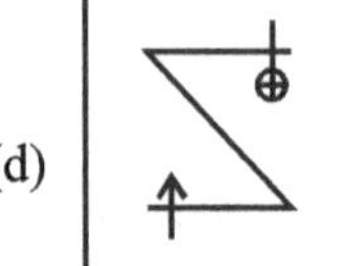

44. **Question Figure**

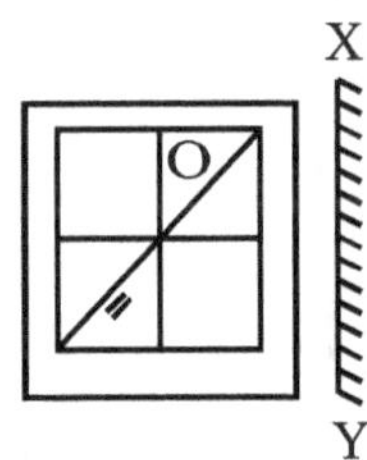

Answer Figures

(a) 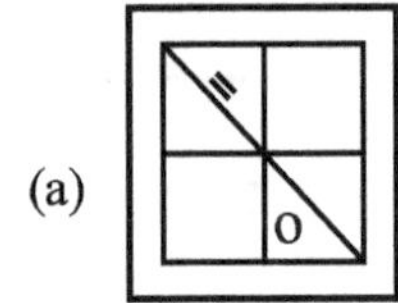 (b) 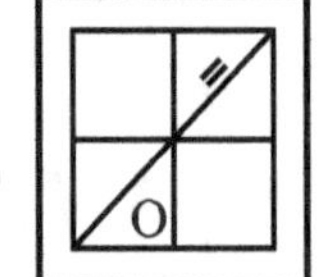

(c) 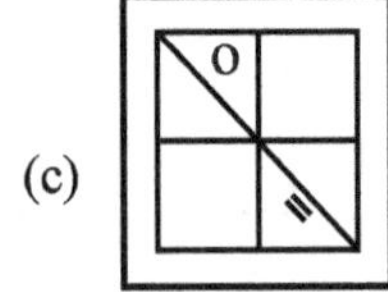 (d) 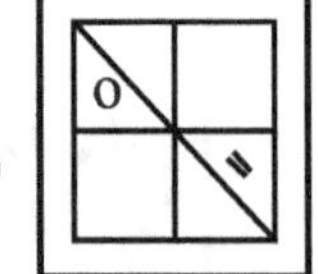

45. **Question Figure**

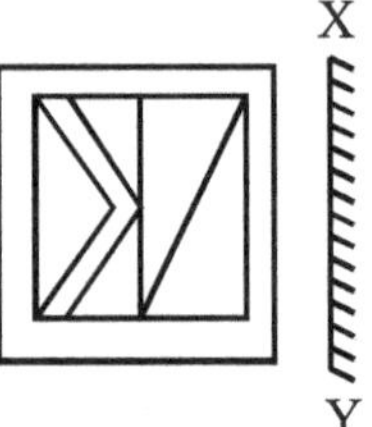

Answer Figures

(a) 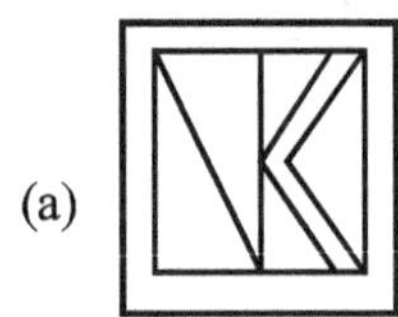 (b) 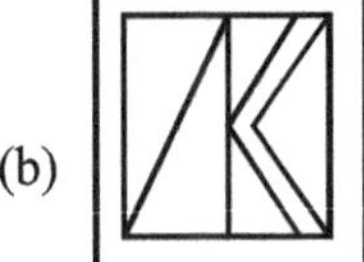

(c) 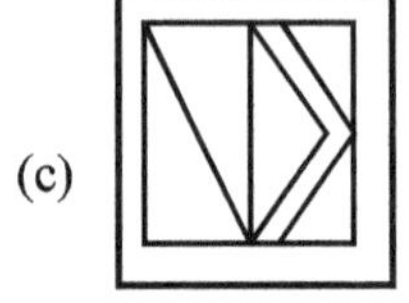 (d) 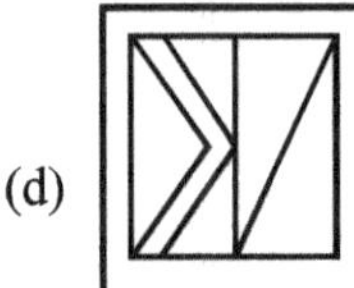

DIRECTIONS (Qs. 46 to 47) : *On there is a question figure and four answer figures (a), (b), (c) and (d) are given. Select the answer figure which is exactly the mirror image of the question figure when the mirror is held at XY.*

46. **Questions Figure**

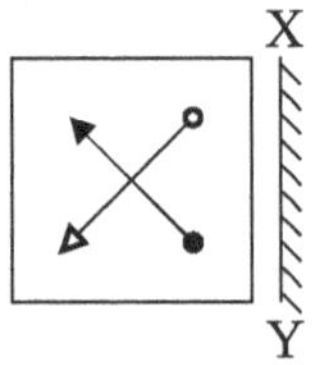

Answer Figures

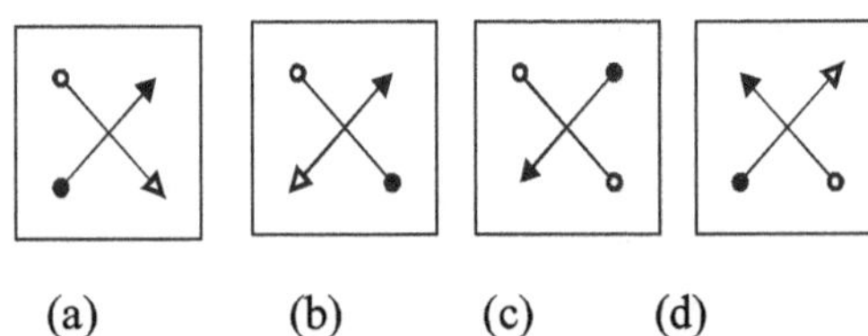

(a) (b) (c) (d)

47. **Questions Figure**

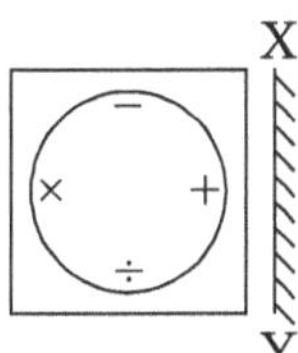

Answer Figures

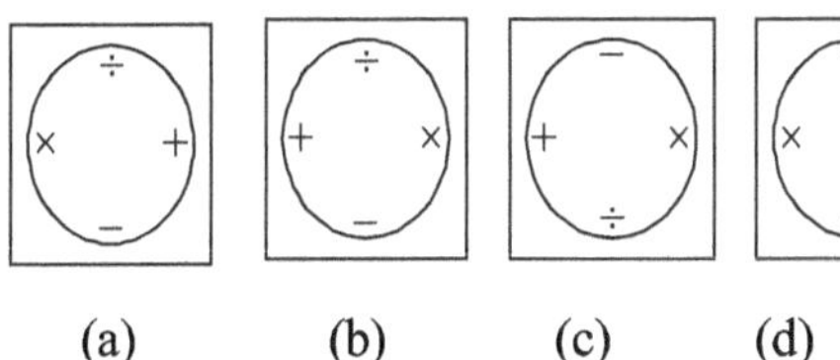

(a) (b) (c) (d)

DIRECTIONS : *In Question Nos.* ***48*** *to* ***51****, there is a question figure on the left side of the mirror and four answer figures marked (a), (b), (c) and (d) are given. Select the answer figure which is exactly the mirror image of the question figure when the mirror is held at XY.*

---

48. **Question Figures**

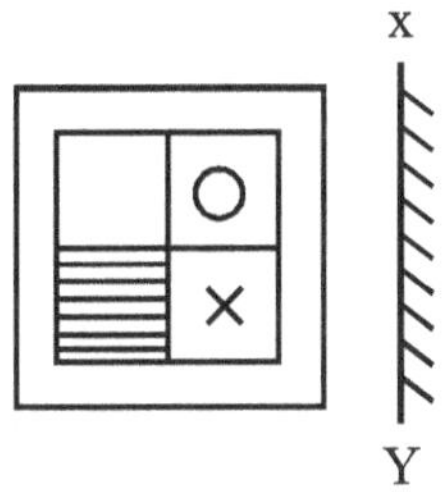

Answer Figures

(a) 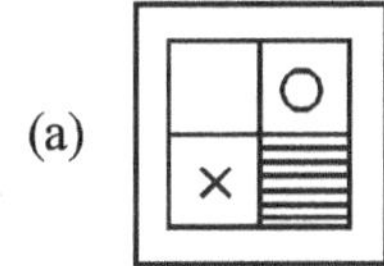 (b)

(c) 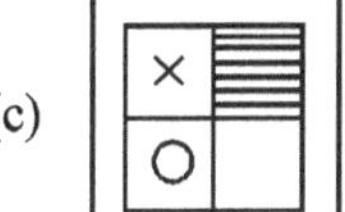 (d) 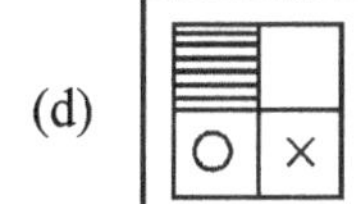

49. **Question Figures**

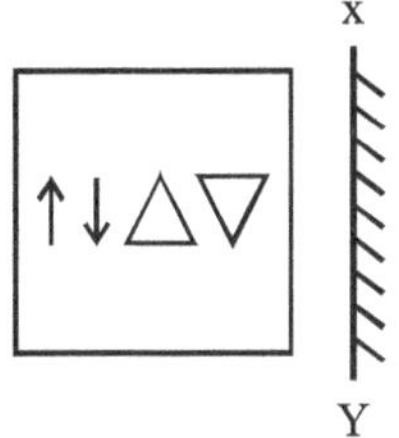

Answer Figures

(a) 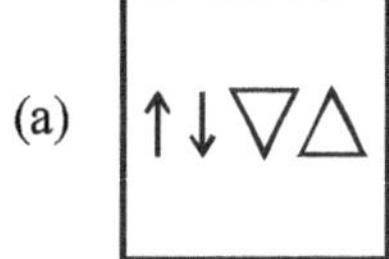 (b) 

(c) 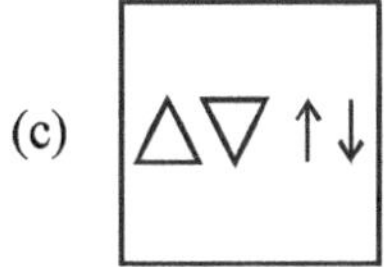 (d) 

50. **Question Figure**

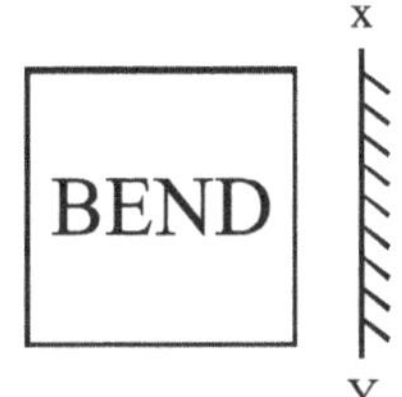

Answer Figures

(a)  (b) 

(c) 

(d) 

51. **Question Figure**

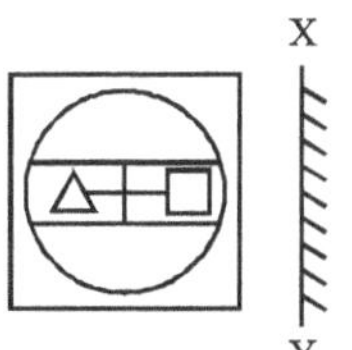
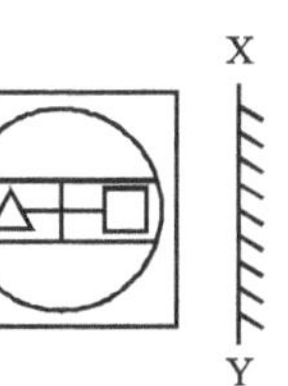

Answer Figures

(a) 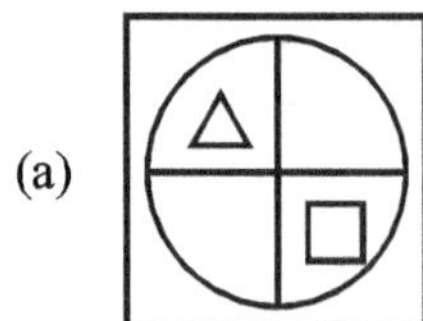

(b) 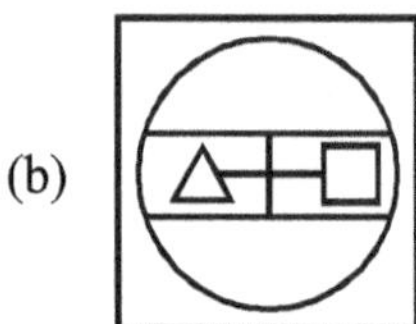

(c) 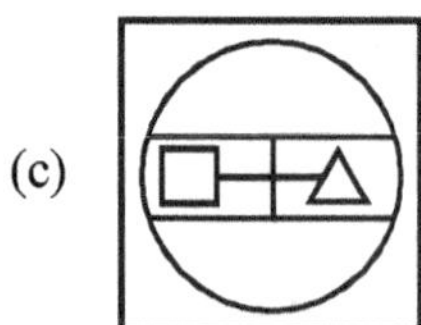

(d) 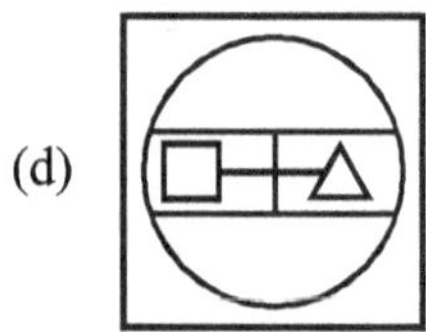

52. Select the correct water image of the given combination of letters. **[2018]**

SWIMMING

(a) ƨ WIM MIN Ә

(b) ƨ ꟽI M MI И G

(c) S ꟽI M MI И G

(d) Ә И I M MI ꟽƨ

53. Select the mirror image of the given figure. **[2018]**

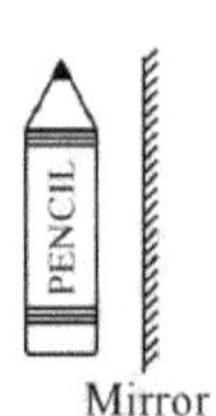

(a) 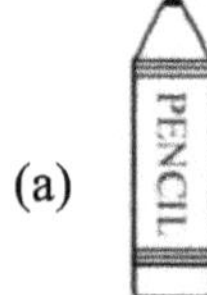

(b) 

(c) 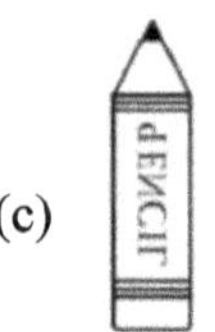

(d) 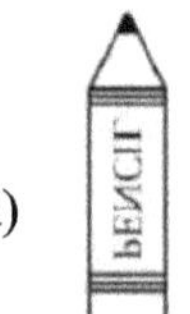

54. Select the correct water image of the given combination of letters. **[2019]**

I N D I A N A I R F O R C E

(a) IИDIVИVIꓤꟻOꓤCE

(b) IИDIVИVIꓤꟻOCꓤE

(c) IDИVIVИIꓤꟻOꓤEC

(d) IDИVIVИIꓤOꟻEꓤC

55. Find the mirror image of the given figure, if the mirror is placed vertically to the left. **[2020]**

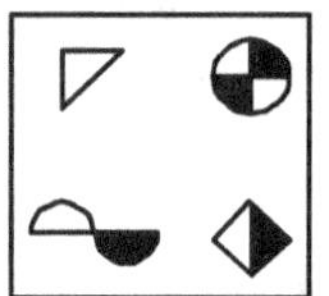

(a) 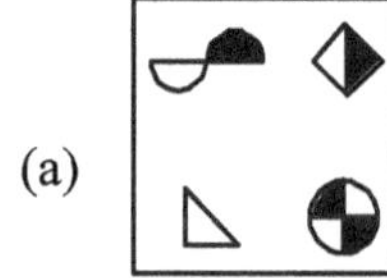

(b) 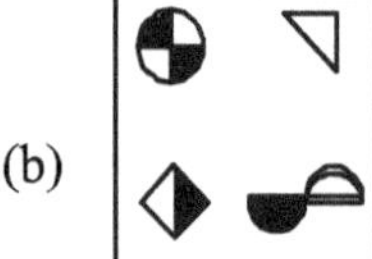

(c) 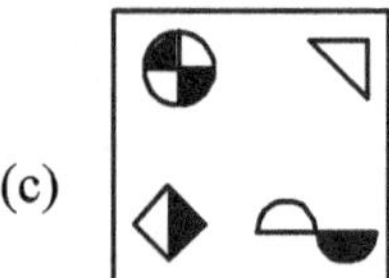

(d) 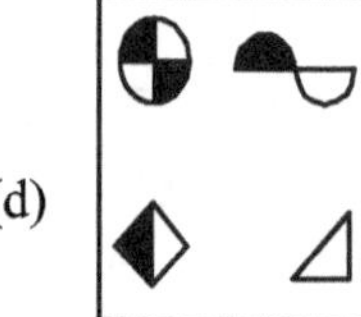

56. Find the correct water image of the given figure. **[2021]**

(a) 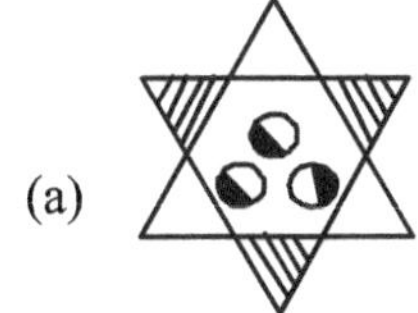 (b) 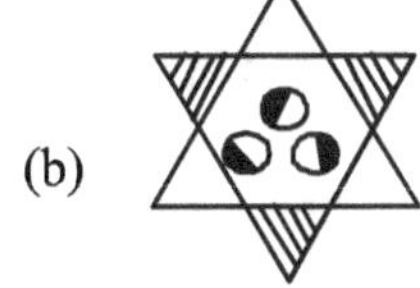

(c) 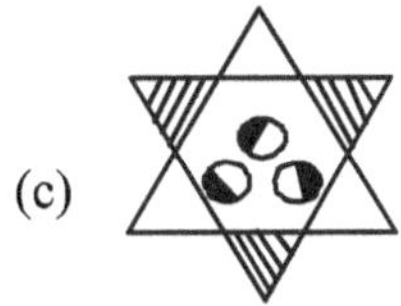 (d) 

57. Select the correct water image of the given figure. **[2021]**

 (b)

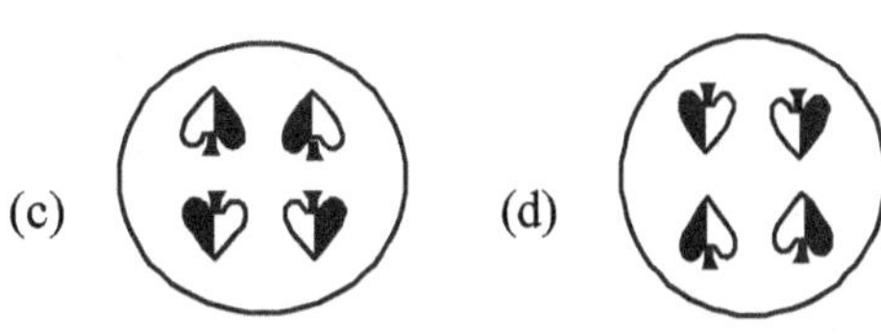

58. Find the mirror image of the given word, if mirror is placed vertically to the left. **[2021]**
PLAY
(a) YA⅃ꟼ
(b) YA⅃P
(c) YAPL
(d) YALꟼ

59. Select the correct mirror image of the given word, if mirror is placed vertically to the right. **[2022]**

HINDI

(a) IᗡNIH
(b) IᗡИIH
(c) IᗡNIH
(d) IᗡИIH

LEVEL 2

DIRECTIONS (Qs. 1-12) *Find the correct option for the water images for the following questions.*

1. PLEDGE
?

(a) PΓ∃DGE
(b) ЬΓ∃DGE
(c) ЬΓEDGE
(d) ЬΓ∃ᗡGE

2. heLP
?

(a) ɥəΓd
(b) ɥɵΓb
(c) ɥɵ˥b
(d) ɥəΓb

3. DOLLAR
?

(a) ᗡOΓΓ∀ʁ
(b) DOΓΓ∀ʁ
(c) DO˥˥∀ʁ
(d) DO˥˥∀ᴚ

4. absence
?

(a) ɘpƨɵuɔɵ
(b) ɘqƨɵuɔɵ
(c) ɘpƨəuɔə
(d) ɘpsɵuɔɵ

5. 918423
?

(a) 6↓8ϯZ3
(b) 6↓8ᔭZ3
(c) 6↾8ᔭZ3
(d) 6↓8ᔭZ3

6. What will be the water image of given diagram?

?

(a) ¿
(b) ¿
(c) ·ɔ
(d) ɔ·

7. gLad
?

(a) ƃΓɐq
(b) ƃ˥ɘq
(c) ƃΓɘq
(d) ƃΓɘp

8. SNOW
?

(a) ƧИOM
(b) SИOM
(c) SИOM
(d) SИOW

9. drain

?

(a) qɹɐ!u (b) qɹɐ!u

(c) qɹɐ!u (d) qɹɐ!u

10. ZEBRA

?

(a) ƩƎBꓤ∀

(b) ƩEBꓤ∀

(c) ƩEBꓤ∀

(d) ƩEBꓤ∀

11. 671

?

(a) 9ㄥ⇂ (b) 6ㄥ⇂

(c) 6ㄥ⇂ (d) 6ㄥ⇂

12. 9283

?

(a) 6ᘔ8Ɛ

(b) 6ᘔ8Ɛ

(c) 6ᘔ83

(d) 6ᘔ83

DIRECTIONS (Qs. 13-20) : *In each of the following questions, choose the correct* ***water image*** *of the figure (X) from amongst the four alternatives (a), (b), (c), (d) given alongwith it.*

13. 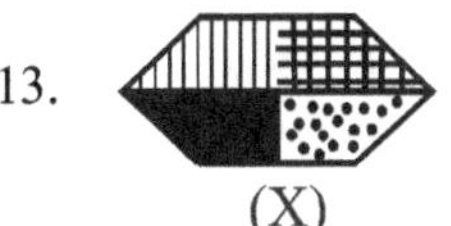

(X)

(a)  (b) 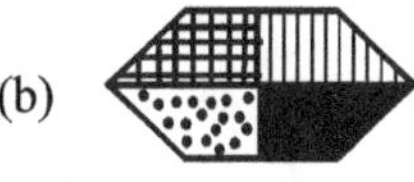

(c)  (d) 

14. 

(X)

(a) 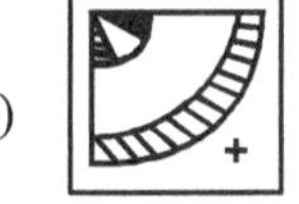 (b) 

(c)  (d) 

15. 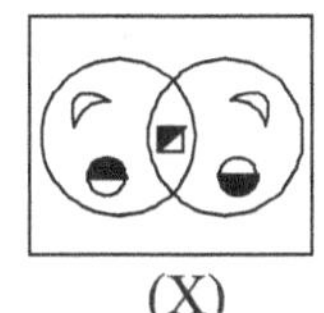

(X)

(a) 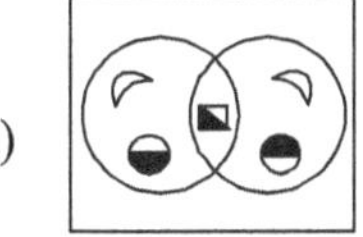 (b) 

(c)  (d) 

16. 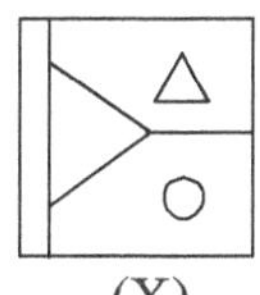

(X)

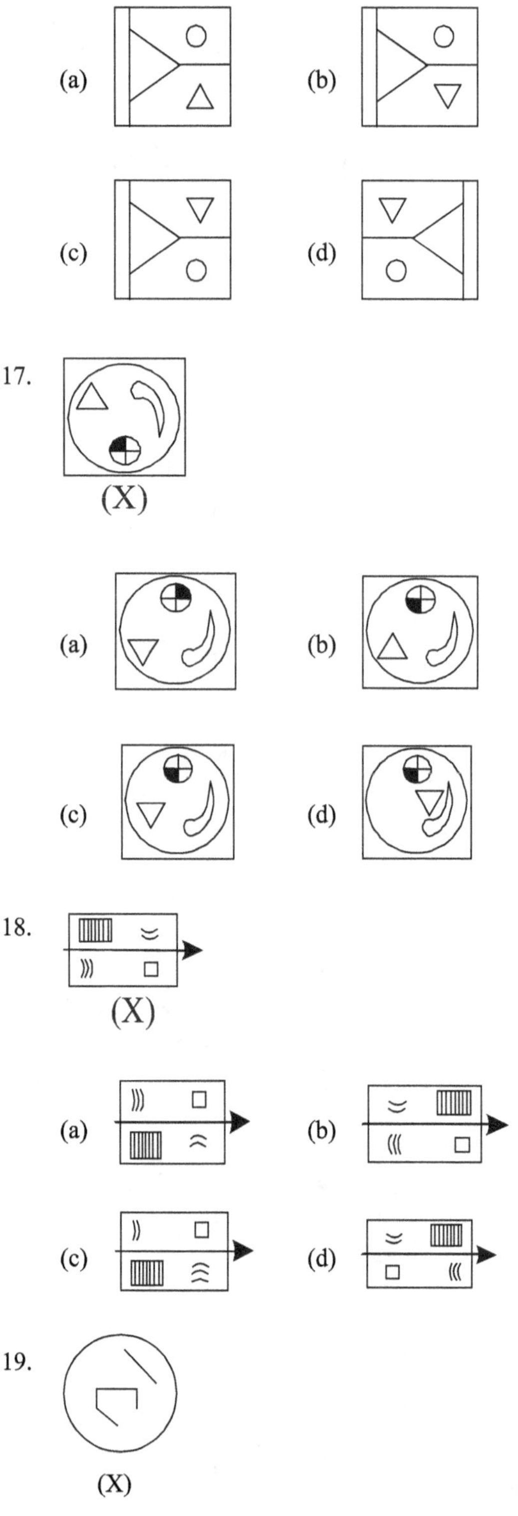

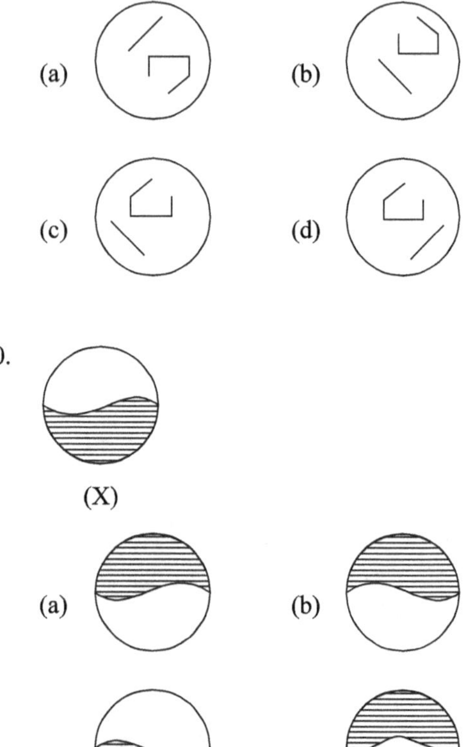

21. Observe the figures below :

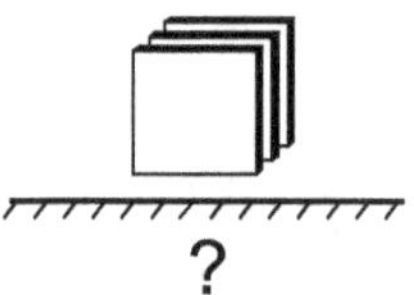

First rotate the figure by 90° in clock-wise direction and find out its water reflection from the given alternatives

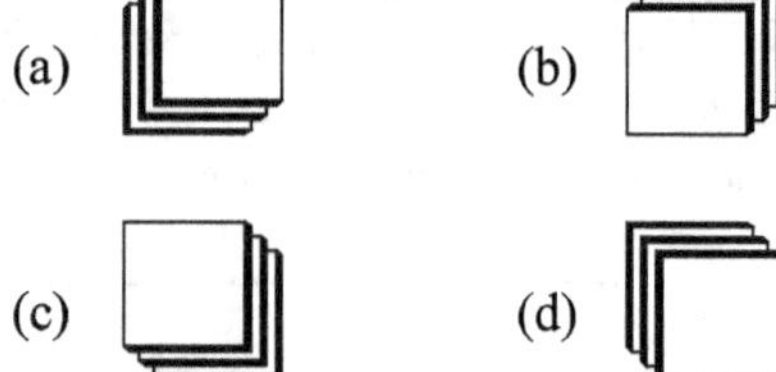

22. Directions - Choose the water image of the 'Question Figure' from the given alternatives.

Question Figure:

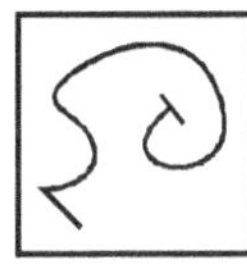

Answer Figures:

(a) 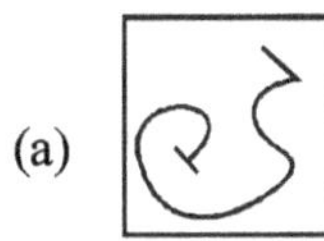 (b) 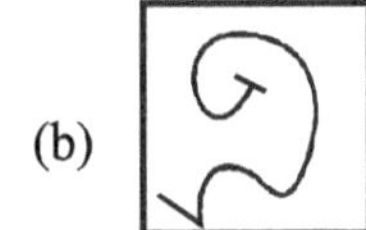

(c) 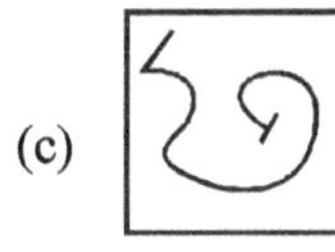 (d) 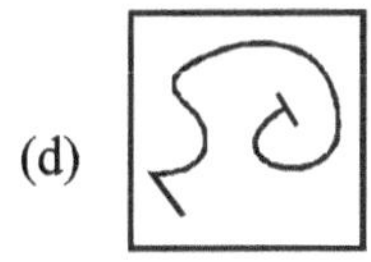

DIRECTIONS (Q. 23): *In this question, out of the four figures marked (a), (b), (c) and (d), three are similar in a certain manner. Howerer one figure is not like the other three. Choose the figure wchic is diffence from the rest.*

23.

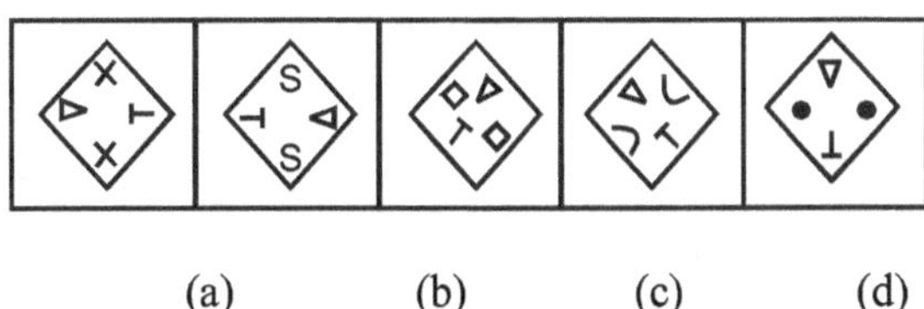

(a) (b) (c) (d)

DIRECTIONS: *In questions 24 to 26, four figures (a), (b), (c), (d) have been given in each question. Of these four figures three figures are similar in some way and one figure is different. Select the figure which is different.*

24. (a) 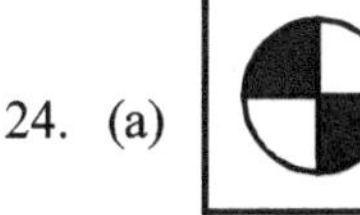 (b) 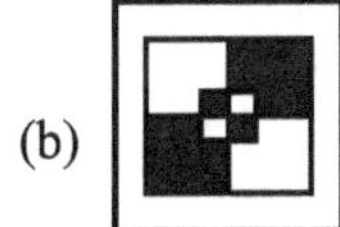

(c) 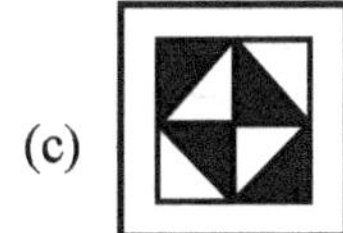 (d) 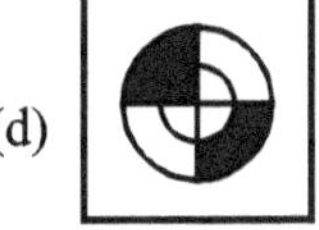

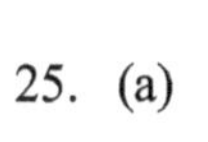

25. (a)  (b) 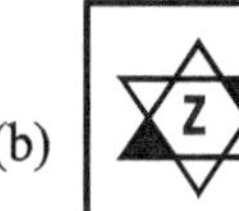

(c) 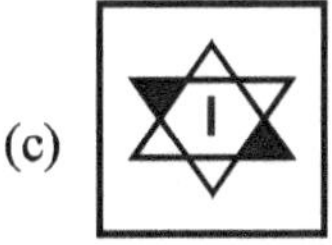 (d) 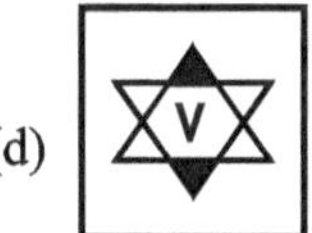

26. (a)  (b) 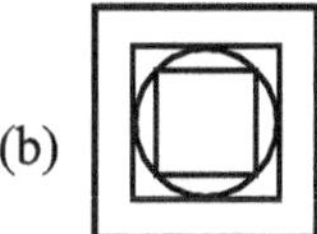

(c) 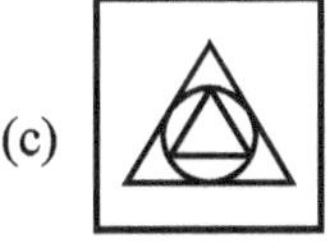 (d) 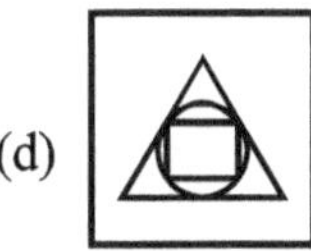

27. Select the correct water image of the given figure. **[2018]**

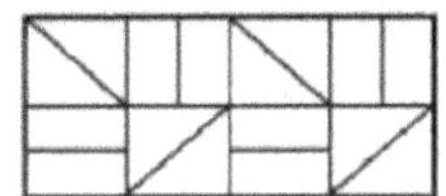

(a) 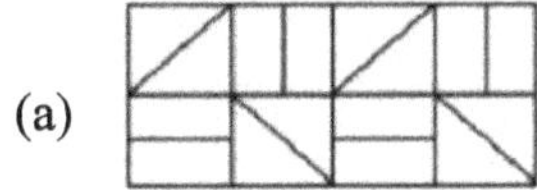

(b) 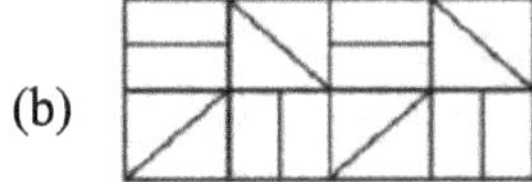

(c) 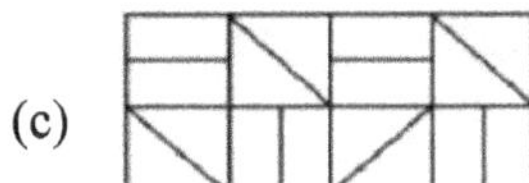

(d) 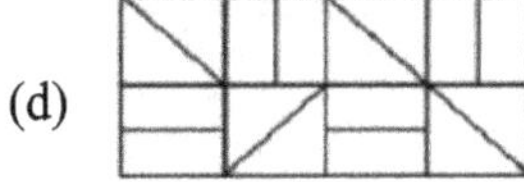

28. Select the correct mirror image of the given figure.

[2018]

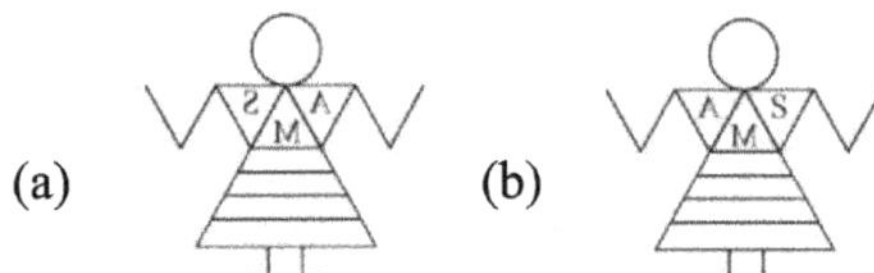

(c) 

(d) 

29. Select the correct mirror image of the given combination, if the mirror is placed vertically to the left. **[2019]**

PoWer ◧ ◨ loGic

(a) ɔiGol ◨ ◧ ЯɘWoꟼ

(b) ɔiGol ◨ ◧ ЯɘWoP

(c) ɔiGol ◨ ◧ ЯɘWoꟼ

(d) ɔiGol ◨ ◧ RɘWoꟼ

30. Identify the correct water image of the given figure. **[2022]**

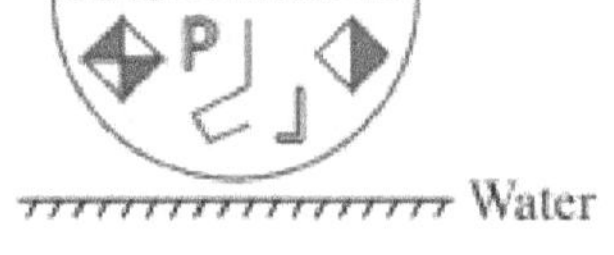

(a) 

(b) 

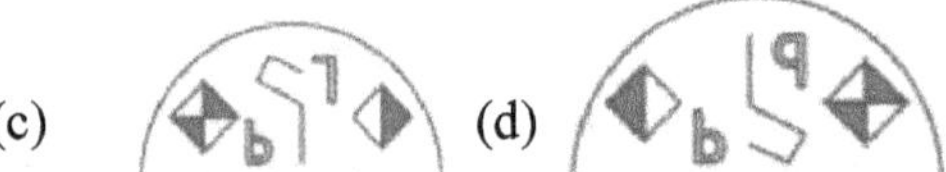

ANSWER KEY																			
LEVEL-1																			
1	(c)	**7**	(d)	**13**	(b)	**19**	(c)	**25**	(c)	**31**	(c)	**37**	(b)	**43**	(c)	**49**	(d)	**55**	(b)
2	(a)	**8**	(a)	**14**	(b)	**20**	(c)	**26**	(b)	**32**	(b)	**38**	(d)	**44**	(c)	**50**	(a)	**56**	(a)
3	(d)	**9**	(c)	**15**	(d)	**21**	(c)	**27**	(b)	**33**	(c)	**39**	(a)	**45**	(a)	**51**	(c)	**57**	(a)
4	(d)	**10**	(a)	**16**	(b)	**22**	(c)	**28**	(b)	**34**	(a)	**40**	(d)	**46**	(a)	**52**	(b)	**58**	(a)
5	(b)	**11**	(b)	**17**	(b)	**23**	(c)	**29**	(c)	**35**	(b)	**41**	(b)	**47**	(c)	**53**	(d)	**59**	(b)
6	(c)	**12**	(a)	**18**	(d)	**24**	(c)	**30**	(c)	**36**	(d)	**42**	(b)	**48**	(a)	**54**	(a)		
LEVEL-2																			
1	(c)	**4**	(a)	**7**	(c)	**10**	(c)	**13**	(a)	**16**	(b)	**19**	(d)	**22**	(b)	**25**	(a)	**28**	(a)
2	(b)	**5**	(d)	**8**	(a)	**11**	(b)	**14**	(d)	**17**	(c)	**20**	(b)	**23**	(d)	**26**	(d)	**29**	(a)
3	(b)	**6**	(b)	**9**	(b)	**12**	(c)	**15**	(d)	**18**	(a)	**21**	(b)	**24**	(d)	**27**	(b)	**30**	(c)

CHAPTER

Paper Folding & Paper Cutting

PAPER FOLDING :

The problems on paper folding involve the process of selecting a figure which would most nearly match the pattern that would be formed when a transparent sheet carrying designs on either side of a dotted line is folded along this line. The figure has to be selected from a set of four alternatives (answer or response figures).

DIRECTION : In each one of the following examples, find from amongst the four response figures, the one which resembles the pattern formed when the transparent sheet, carrying a design, is folded along the dotted line.

ILLUSTRATION 1 :

Transparent Sheet

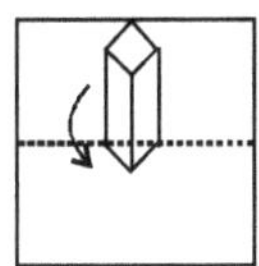

Response Figures

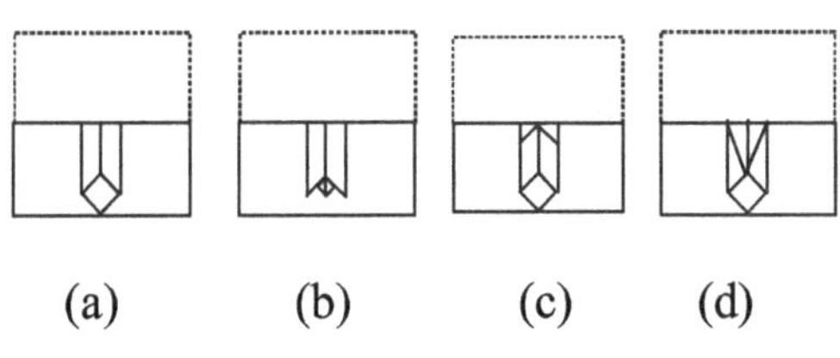

(a) (b) (c) (d)

Sol. **(d)** Clearly, the upper half of the square sheet has been folded over the lower half. The combination of the design in the lower half and the water image of the design in the upper half will appear as the resultant design when the sheet is folded. Visualising this combination we get the design shown in fig. (d). Hence, fig. (d) is the answer.

ILLUSTRATION 2 :

Transparent Sheet

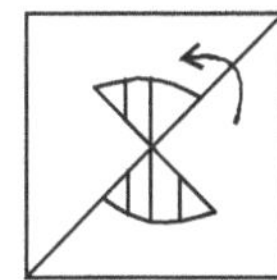

Response Figures

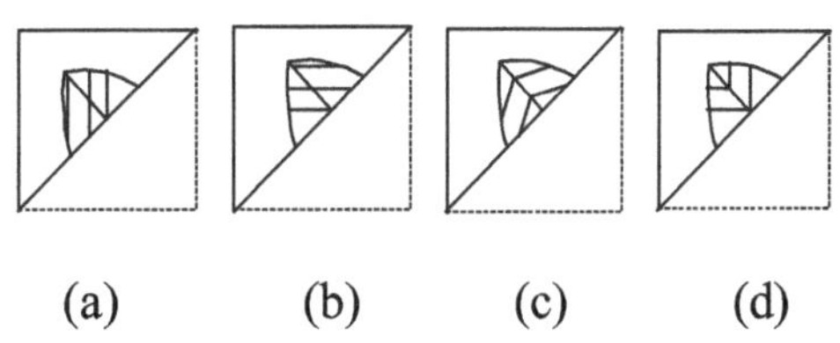

(a) (b) (c) (d)

Sol. **(d)** Here, the sheet has been folded diagonally and design on either side of the dotted line combine to from fig .(d). Hence, fig.(d) is the answer.

PAPER CUTTING :

The problems on paper cutting contain a set of three figures showing the manner in which a piece of paper has been folded. In each of the first two figures, a dotted line together with an arrow on it has been given indicating the line along which the paper is to be folded and the direction of the fold respectively. In the third figure, there are marks showing the position and nature of the cut made in the folded sheet. The candidate has to select one of the figures from the set of four answer figures (1), (2), (3) and (4), that would most nearly match the pattern when the paper is unfolded. It will be interesting to see that the designs of the cut will appear on each fold made in the paper.

ILLUSTRATION 3 :

Consider the three figures, marked X, Y, and Z showing one fold in X, another in Y and cut in Z. From amongst the four alternative figures (a), (b), (c) and (d), select the one showing the unfolded position of Z.

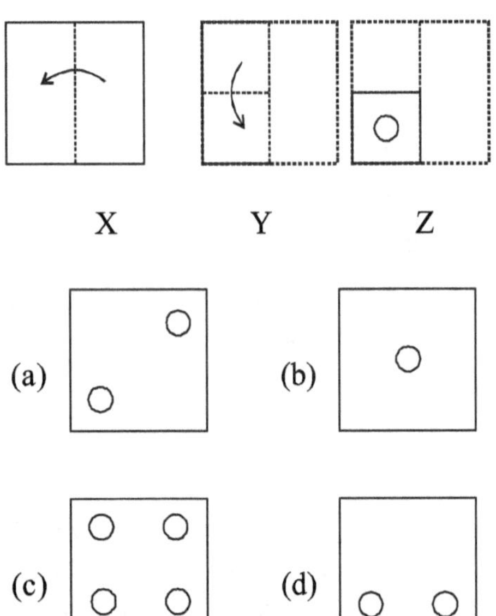

Sol. **(c)** In fig. (X), the square sheet of paper has been folded along the vertical line of symmetry so that the right half of the sheet overlaps the left half.

In fig. (Y), the sheet is folded further to a quarter.

In fig.(Z), a circle has been punched in the folded sheet.

Clearly, the punched circle will be created in each quarter of the paper .

Thus, when the paper is unfolded, four circles will appear symmetrically over it and the paper will then appear as shown in fig. (c). Hence, fig. (c) is the answer.

ILLUSTRATION 4 :

Find from amongst the four response figures, the one that resembles the pattern formed when the transparent sheet, carrying a design is folded along the dotted line.

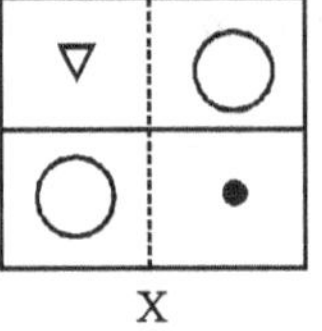

(a) 

(b) 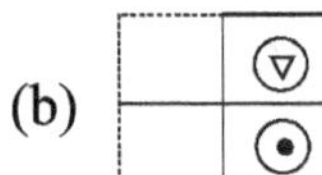

(c) 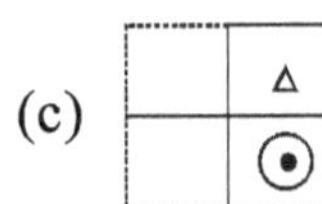

(d) 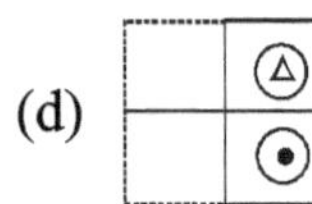

Sol. **(b)** Clearly left half is folded on the right half. Hence triangle is in side the circle and circle is surrounding the dot. The answer is (b).

ILLUSTRATION 5 :

Consider the figures X and Y showing a rectangular sheet of paper folded in fig. (X) and punched in fig. (Y). From amongst the answer figures (a), (b), (c), (d), select the figure which will most closely resemble the unfolded position of figure (Y).

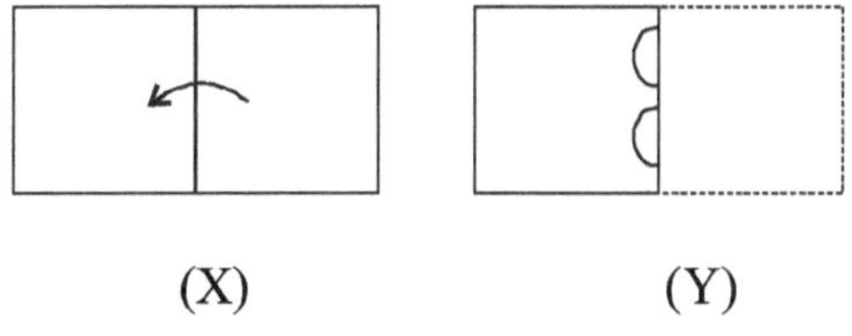

(X) (Y)

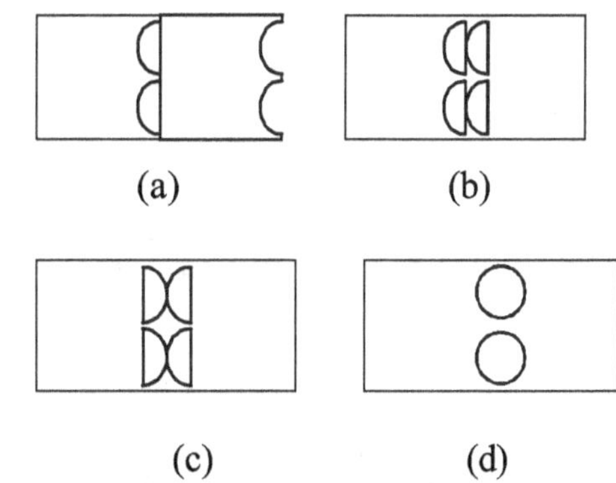

(a) (b)

(c) (d)

***Sol.* (d)** In fig. (X), the rectangular sheet of paper has been folded along a line that divides the sheet into two equal halves. In figure (Y), two semicircular holes are punched close at the centre of the sheet as shown figure (d).

LEVEL 1

DIRECTIONS (Qs.1-5): *In each one of the following questions, find from amongst the four response figures, the one which resembles the pattern formed when the transparent sheet, carrying a design, is folded along the dotted line.*

1. **Transparent Sheet**

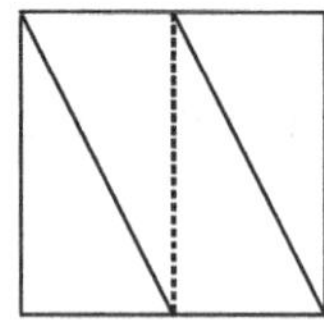

Response Figures

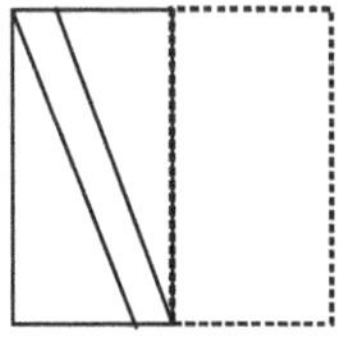

(a)

(b)

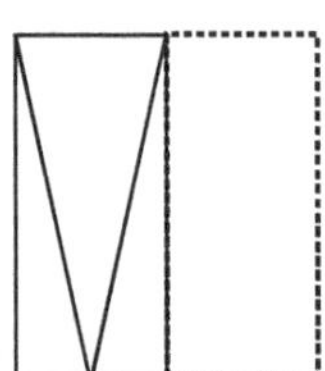

(c)

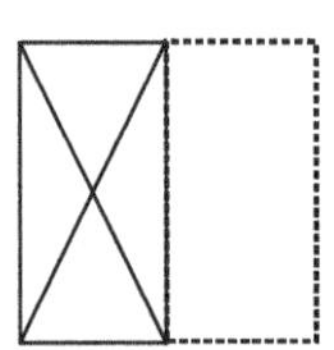

(d)

2. **Transparent Sheet**

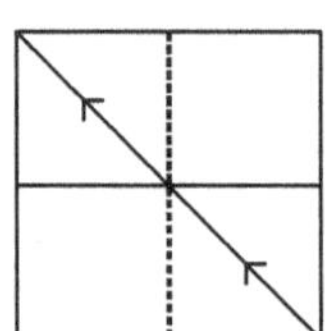

Response Figures

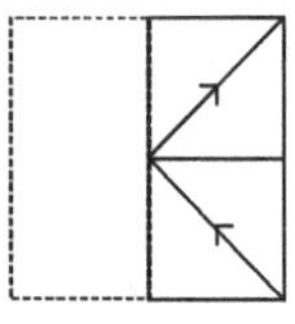

(a)

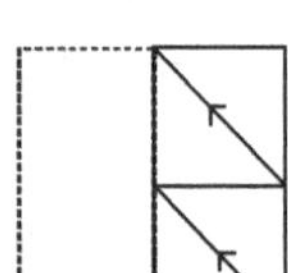

(b)

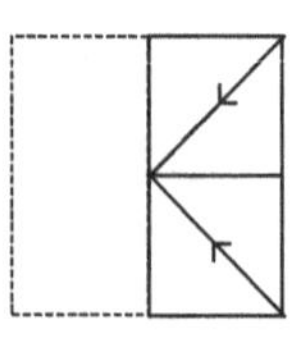

(c)

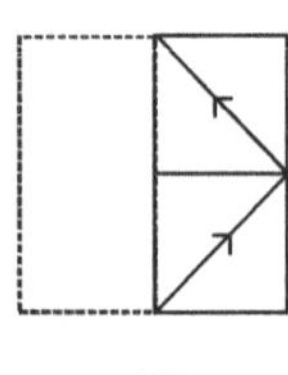

(d)

3. **Transparent Sheet**

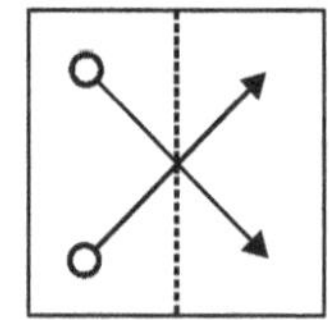

Response Figures

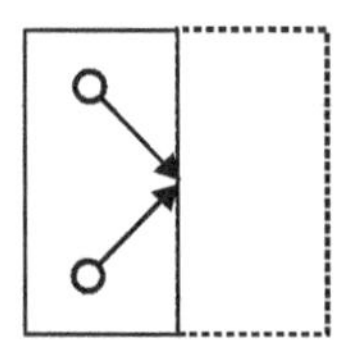

(a)

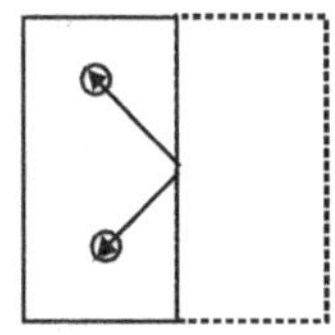

(b)

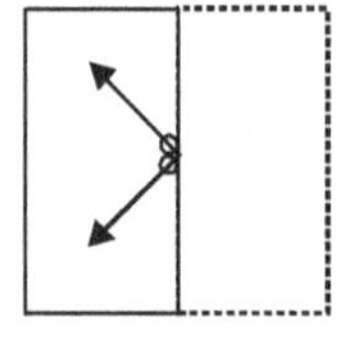

(c)

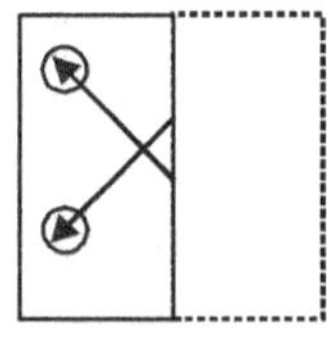

(d)

4. **Transparent Sheet**

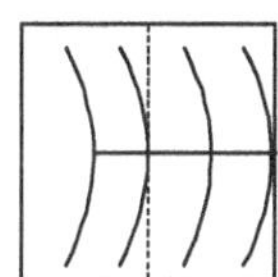

Response Figures

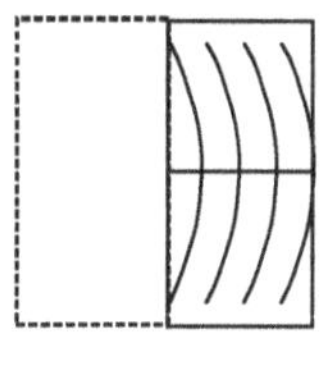

(a)

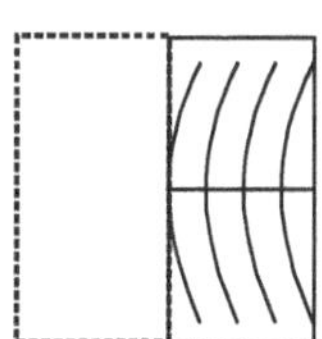

(b)

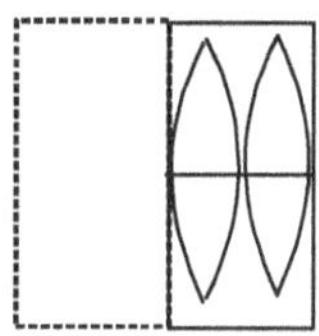

(c)

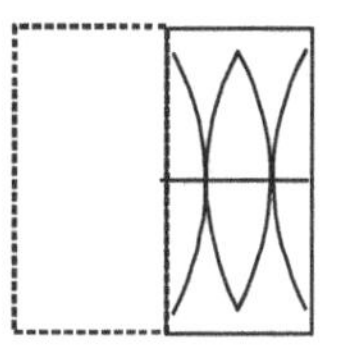

(d)

5. **Transparent Sheet**

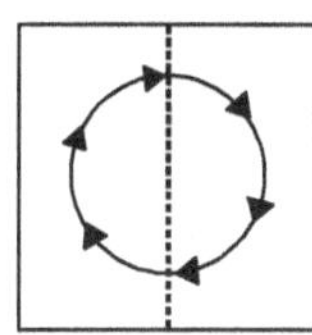

Response Figures

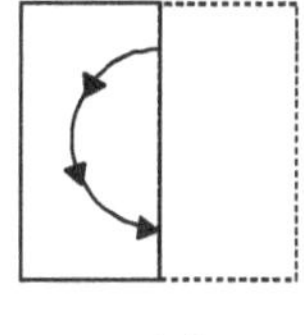

(a)

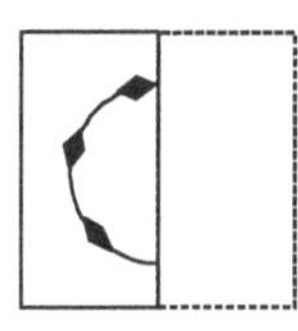

(b)

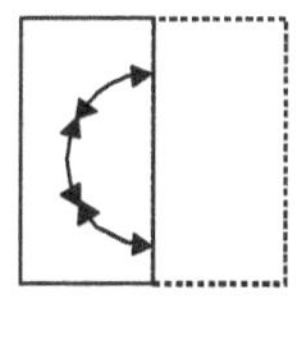

(c)

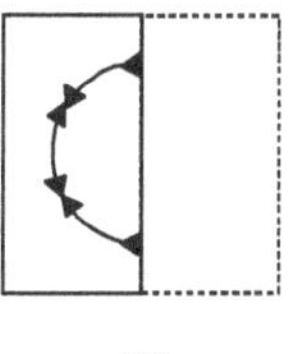

(d)

DIRECTIONS: *In questions 6 to 15 a piece of paper is folded and punched as shown in problem figures and four answer figure marked (a), (b), (c), (d) are given. Select the answer figure which indicates how the paper will appear when open (unfolded).*

6.

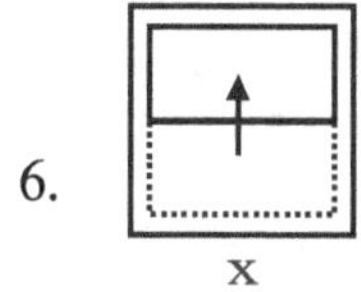

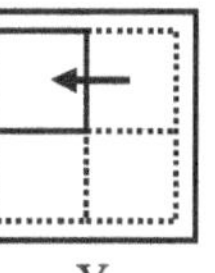

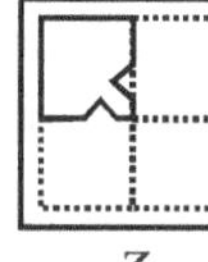

x y z

(a)

(b)

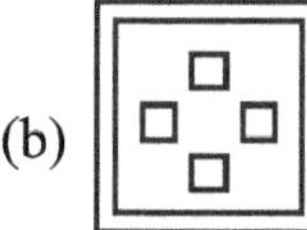

(c)

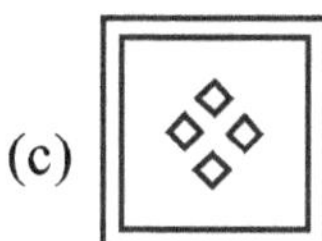

(d)

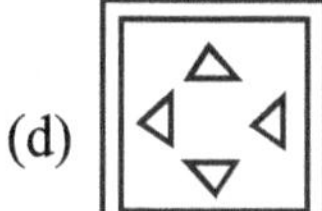

7.

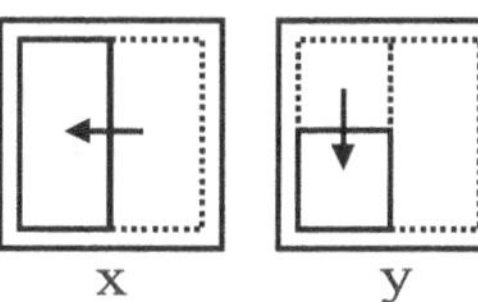

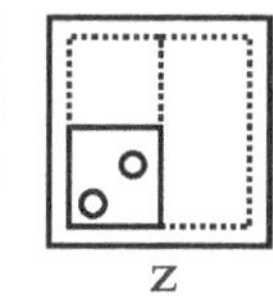

x y z

(a)

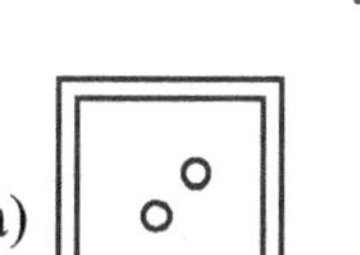

(b)

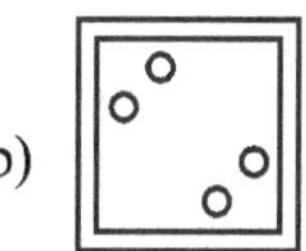

(c)

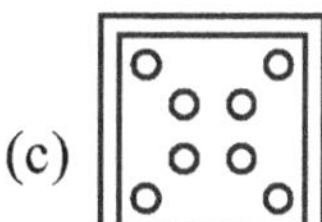

(d)

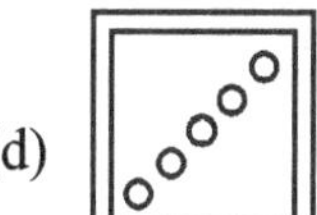

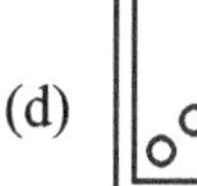

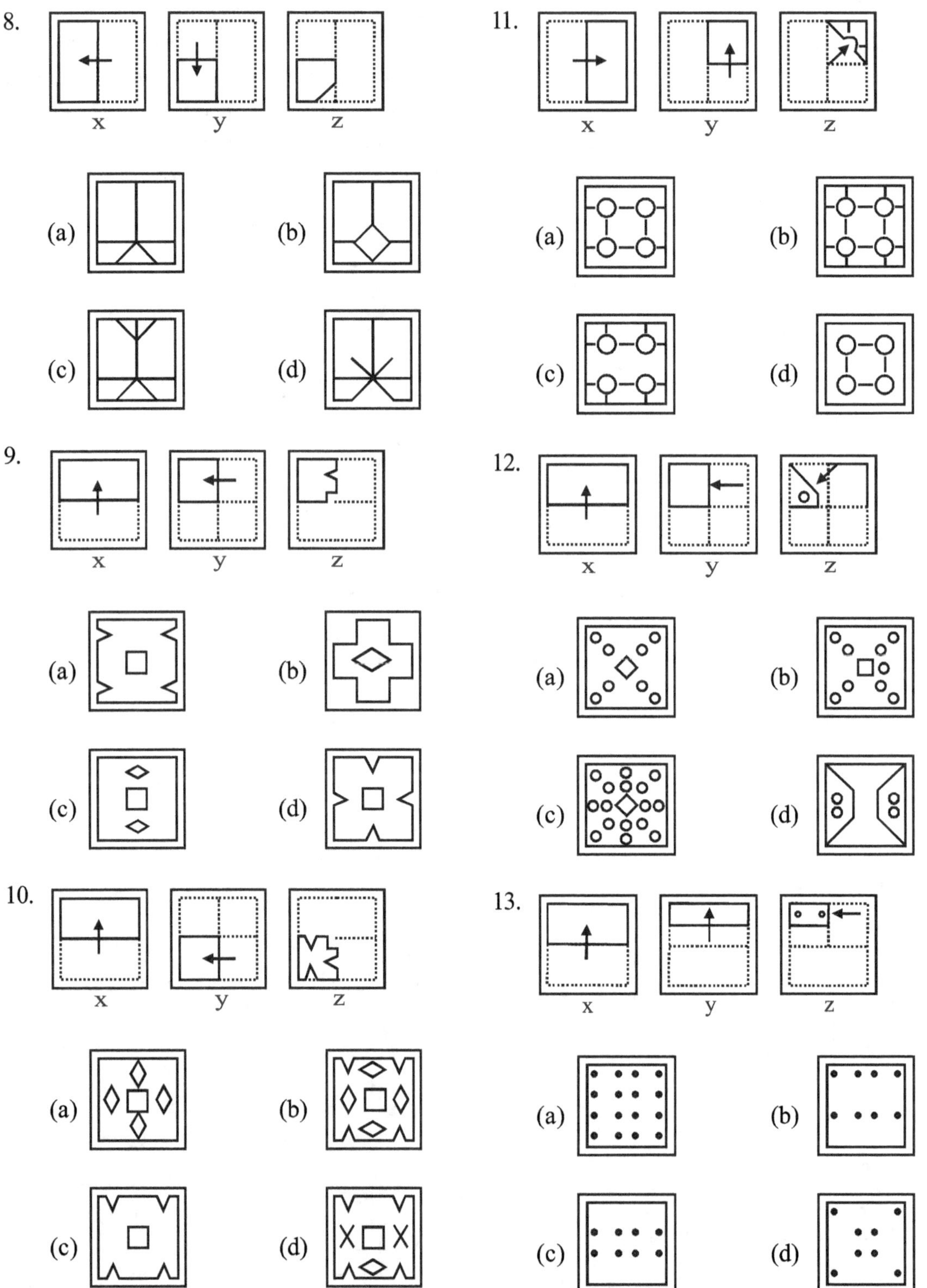
8.
x
y
z
(a)
(b)
(c)
(d)
11.
x
y
z
(a)
(b)
(c)
(d)
9.
x
y
z
(a)
(b)
(c)
(d)
12.
x
y
z
(a)
(b)
(c)
(d)
10.
x
y
z
(a)
(b)
(c)
(d)
13.
x
y
z
(a)
(b)
(c)
(d)

14.

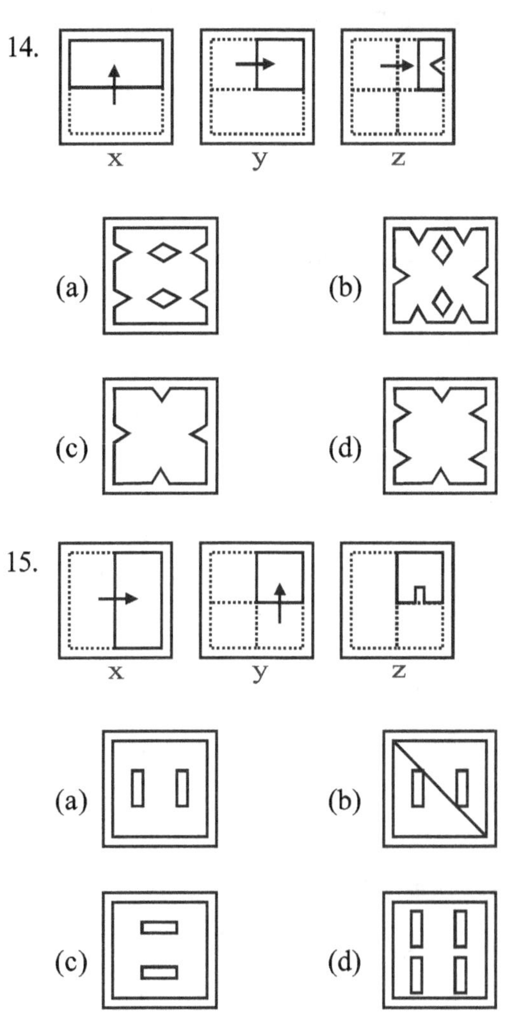

15.

DIRECTIONS (Qs. 16-20): *Consist a set of three figures showing a sequence of folding a piece of paper third question figures shows to manner in which the folded paper has been punched. These three figures are followed by four answer figures from which you have to choose a figure which would most closely resemble the unfolded form of third figure of question.*

16. **Question Figure**

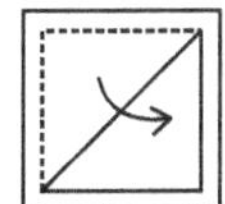  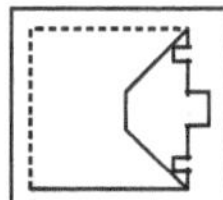

Answer Figures

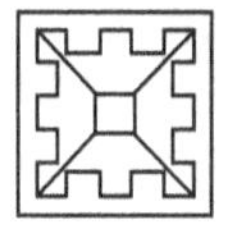   

(a) (b) (c) (d)

17. **Question Figure**

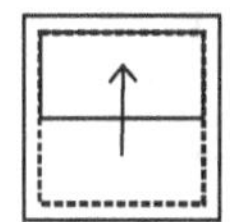 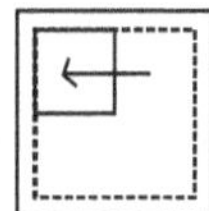 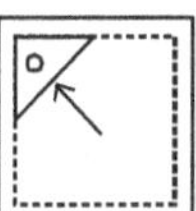

Answer Figures

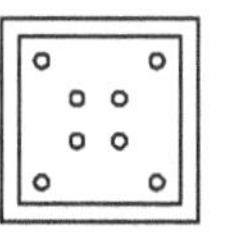 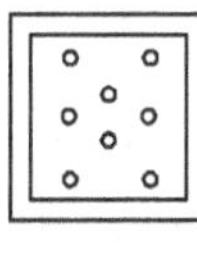 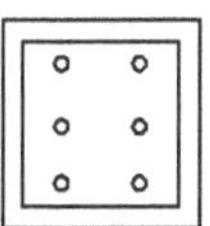 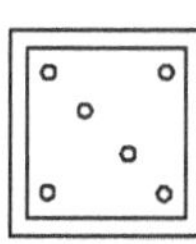

(a) (b) (c) (d)

18. **Question Figure**

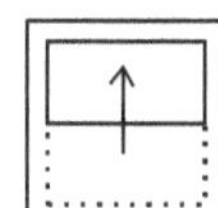 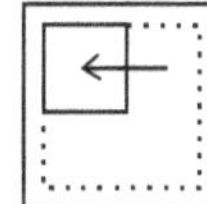 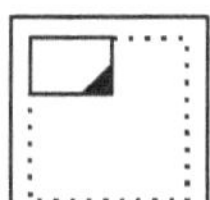

Answer Figures

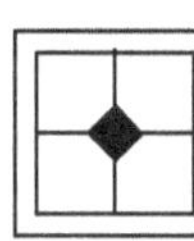 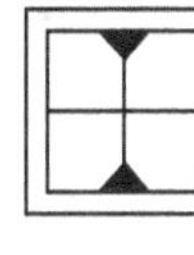 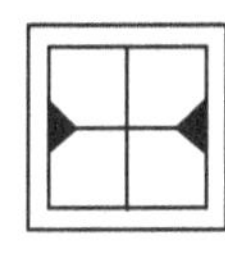 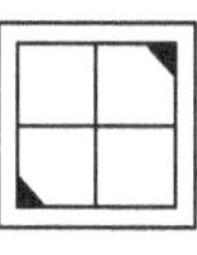

(a) (b) (c) (d)

19. **Question Figure**

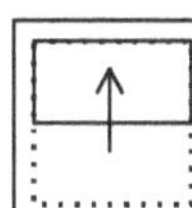 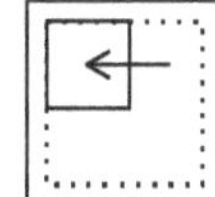 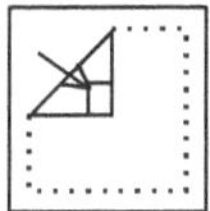

Answer Figures

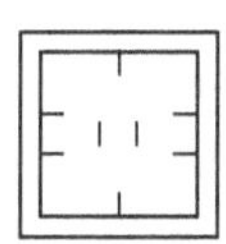 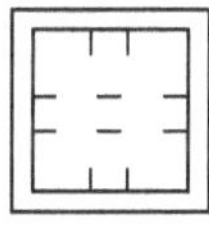 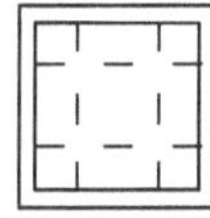 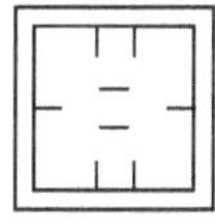

(a) (b) (c) (d)

20. **Question Figure**

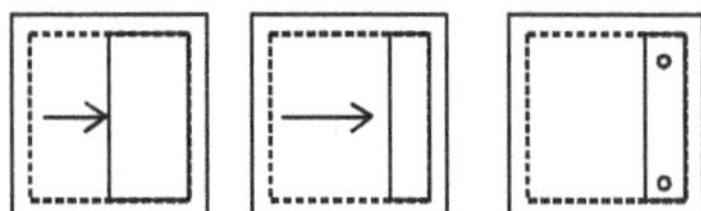

Answer Figures

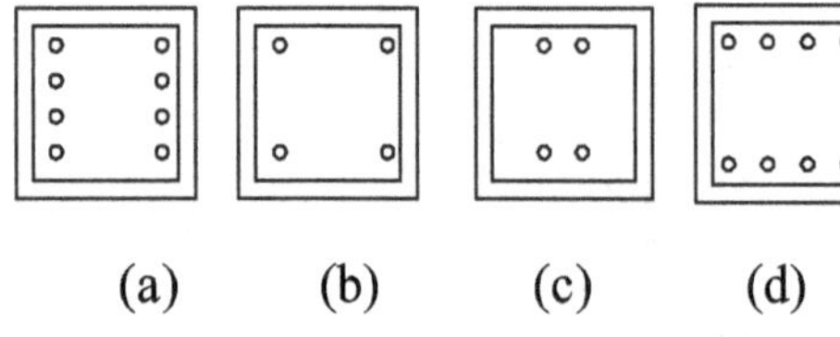

(a) (b) (c) (d)

DIRECTIONS (Qs. 21-25) : *These questions Consist of a set of three figures showing a sequence of folding a piece of paper third question figures shows to manner in which the folded paper has been punched. These three figures are followed by four answer figures from which you have to choose a figure which would most closely resemble the unfolded form of third figure of question.*

21. **Question Figures**

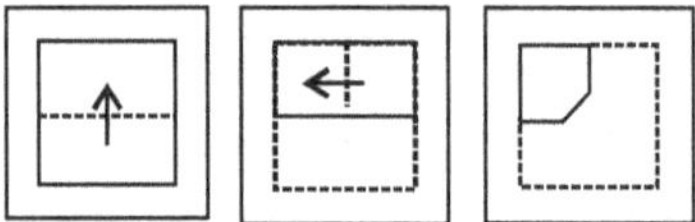

Answer Figures

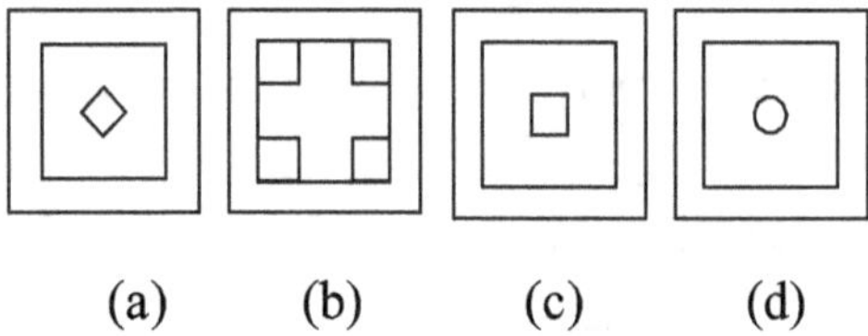

(a) (b) (c) (d)

22. **Question Figures**

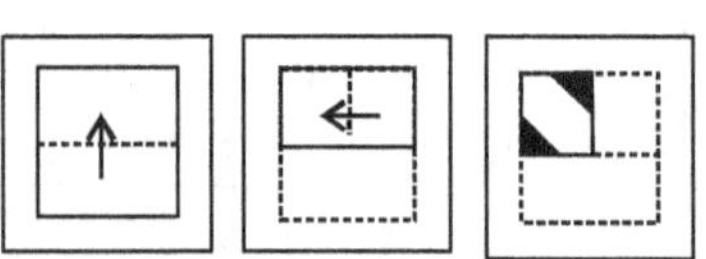

Answer Figures

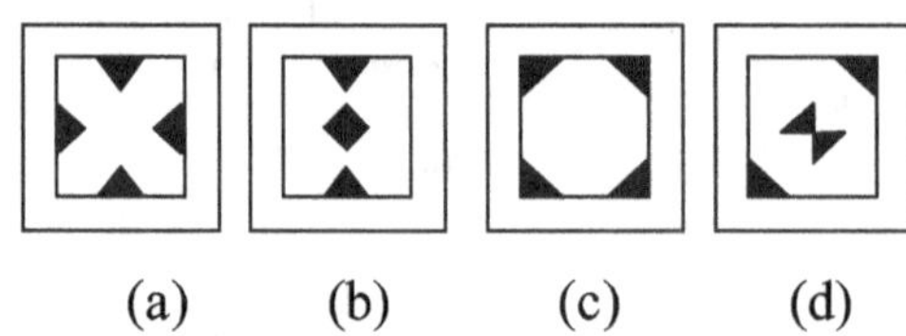

(a) (b) (c) (d)

23. **Question Figures**

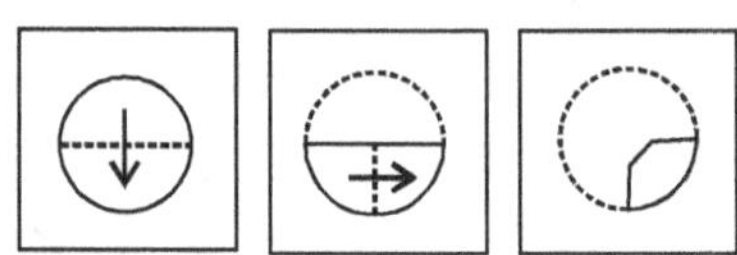

Answer Figures

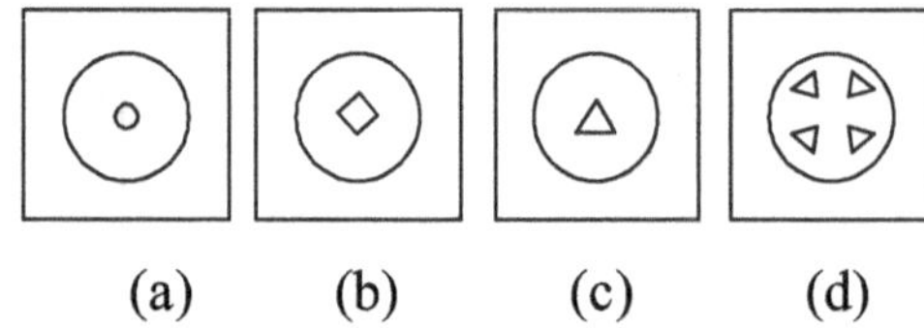

(a) (b) (c) (d)

24. **Question Figures**

Answer Figures

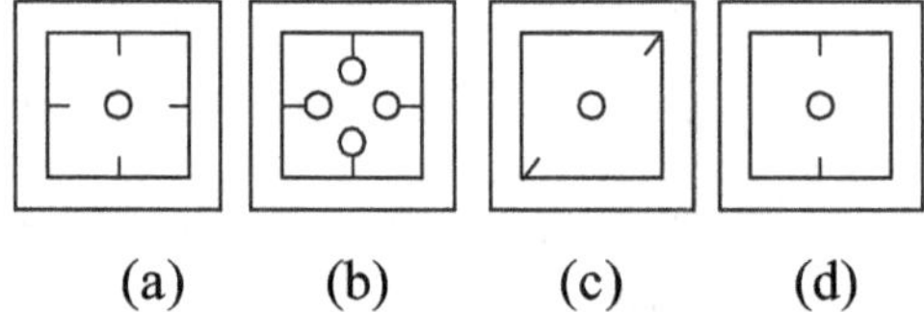

(a) (b) (c) (d)

25. **Question Figures**

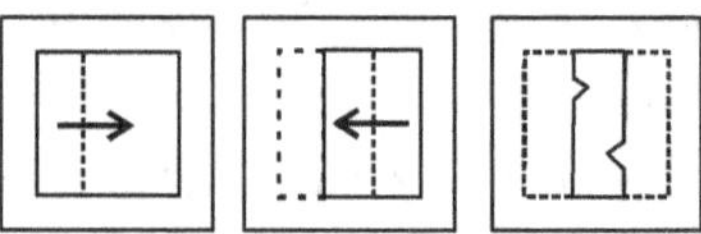

Answer Figures

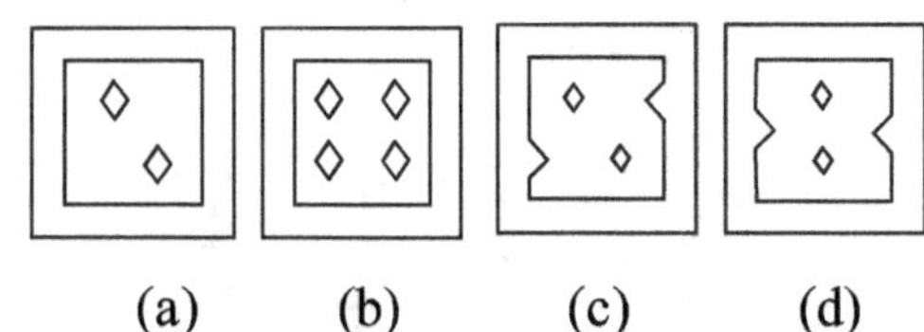

(a) (b) (c) (d)

DIRECTIONS: *In Question Nos. 26 to 29 a piece of paper is folded and punched as shown in question figures and four answer figures marked (a), (b), (c) and (d) are given. Select the answer figure which indicates how the paper will appear when opened (unfolded).*

26. **Question Figures**

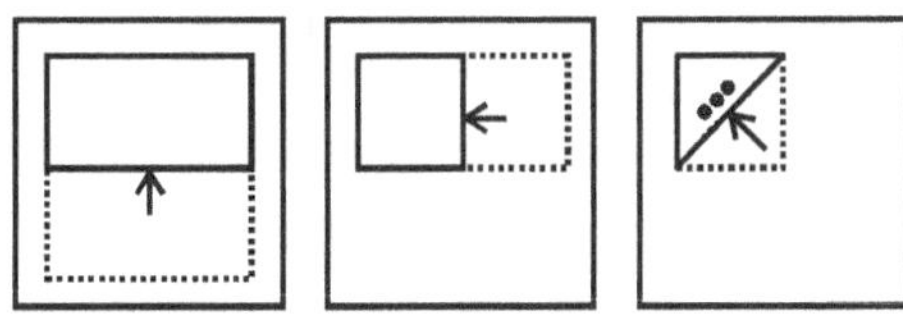

Answer Figures

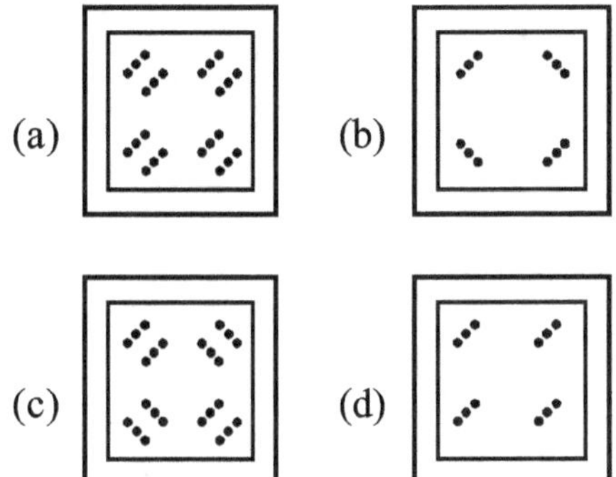

27. **Question Figures**

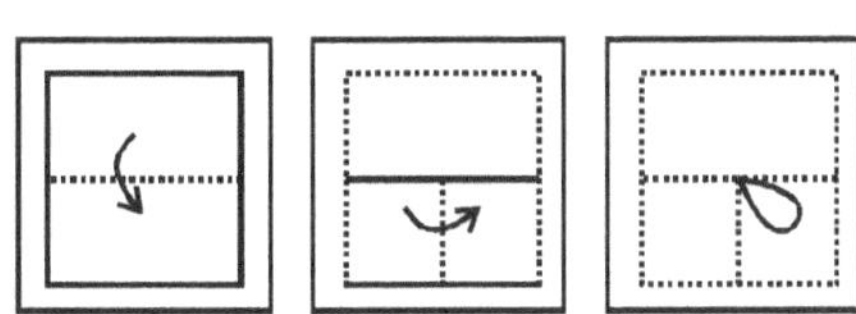

Answer Figures

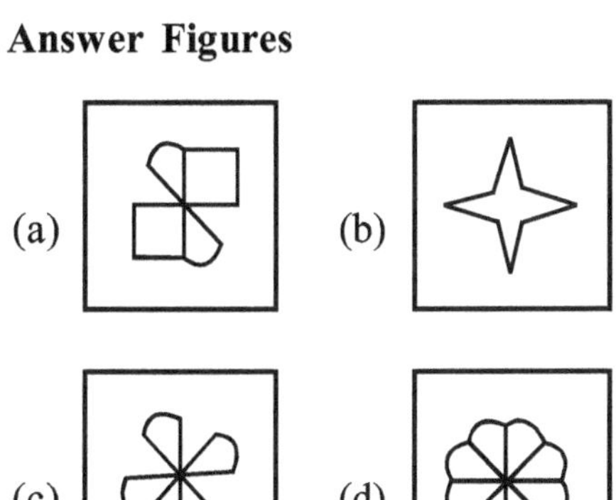

28. **Question Figures**

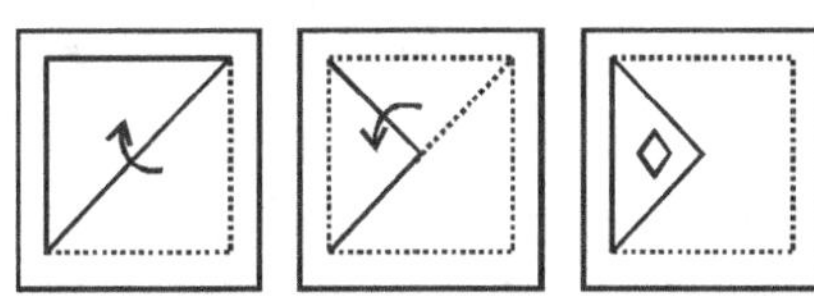

Answer Figures

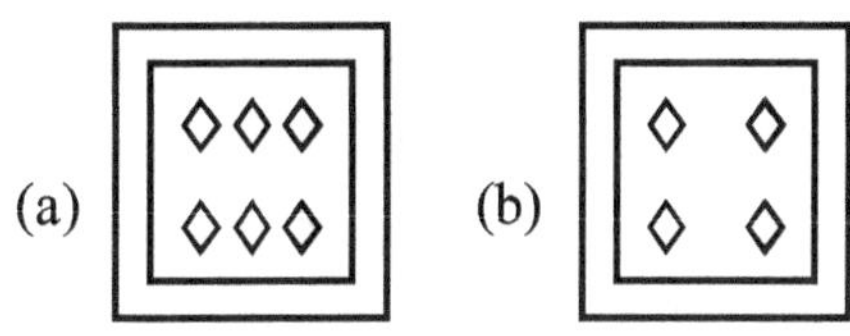

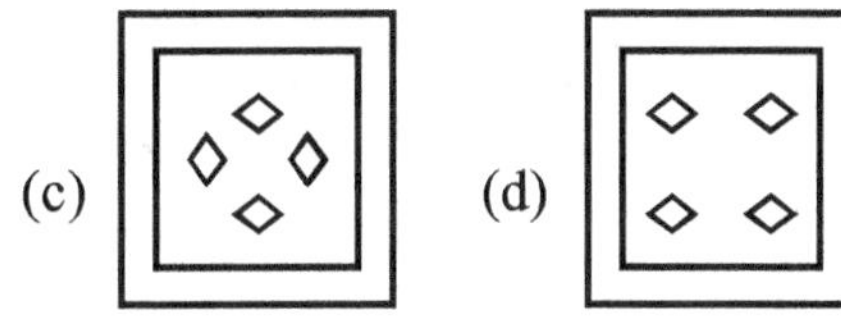

29. **Question Figures**

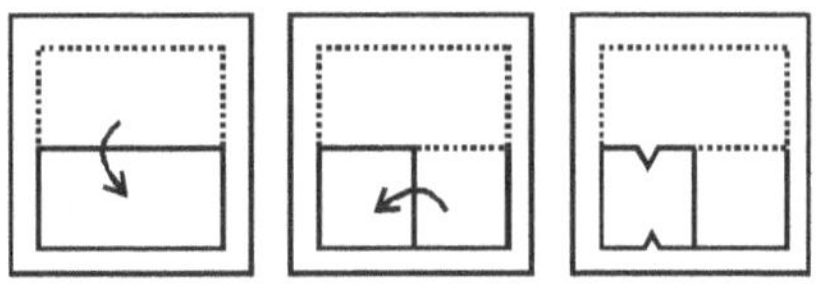

Answer Figures

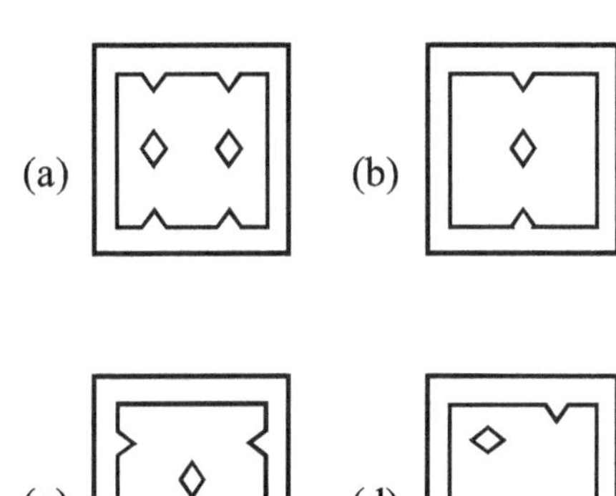

DIRECTIONS : *In Question Nos.* ***30*** *to* ***33****, a piece of paper is folded and punched as shown in the quesiton figures and four answer figures marked (a), (b), (c) and (d) are given. Select the answer figure which indicates how the paper will appear when opened (unfolded).*

30. **Question Figures**

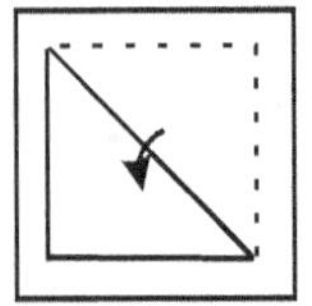 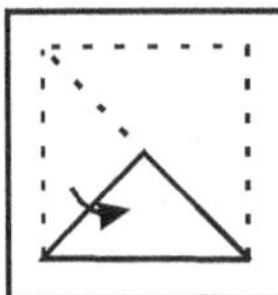 

Answer Figures

(a) 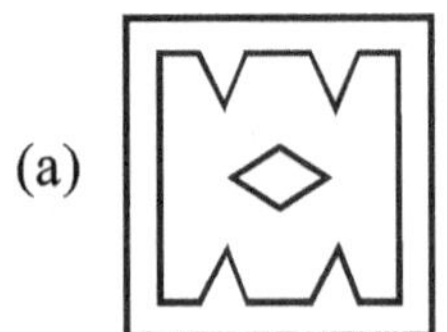 (b) 

(c) 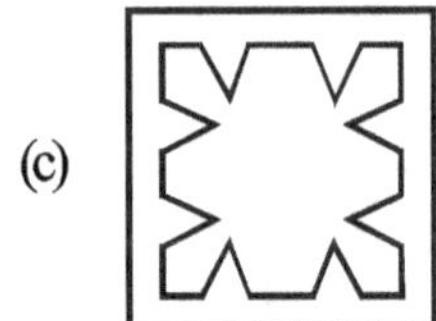 (d) 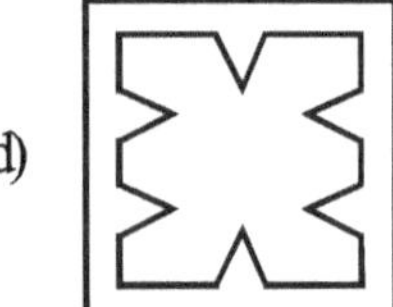

31. **Question Figures**

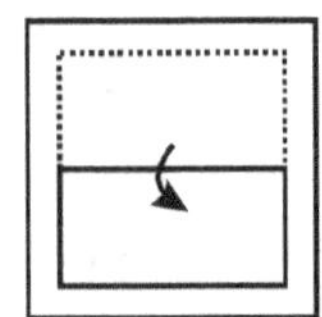 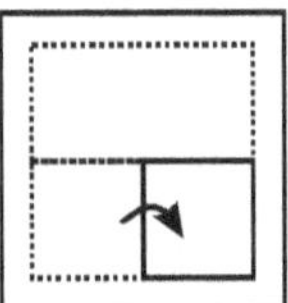 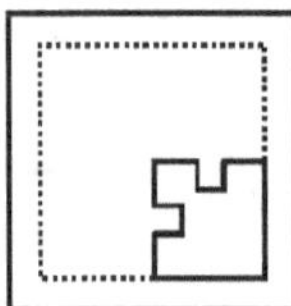

Answer Figures

(a) 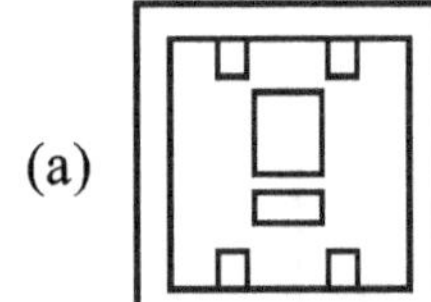 (b) 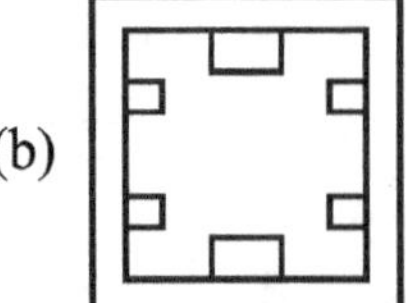

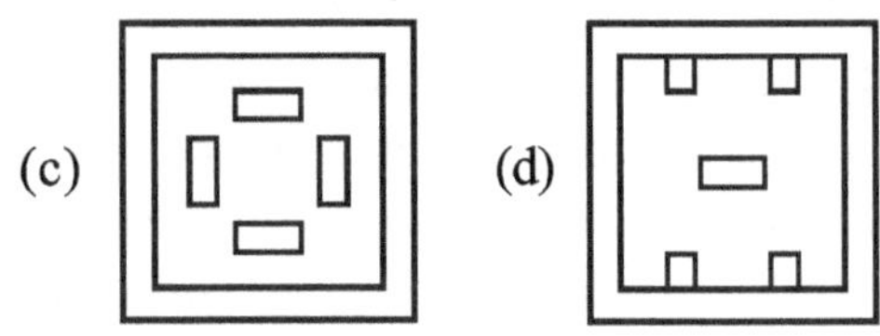

32. **Question Figures**

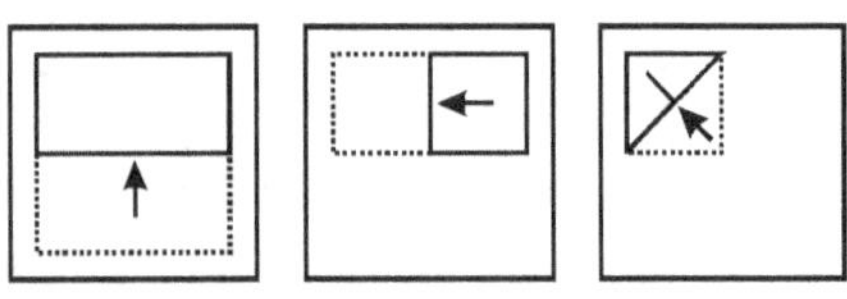

Answer Figures

(a) 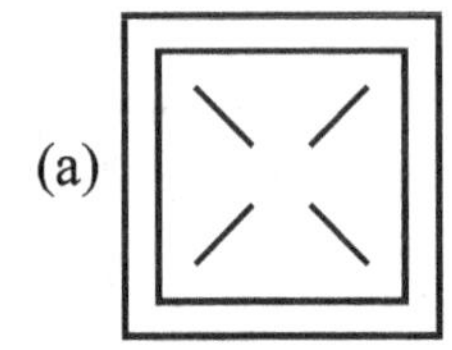 (b) 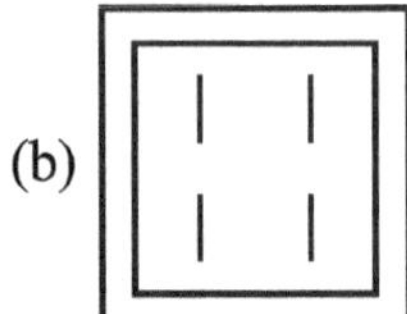

(c) 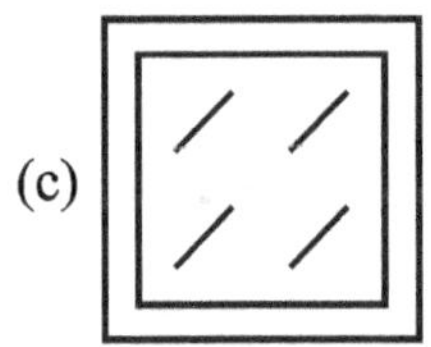 (d) 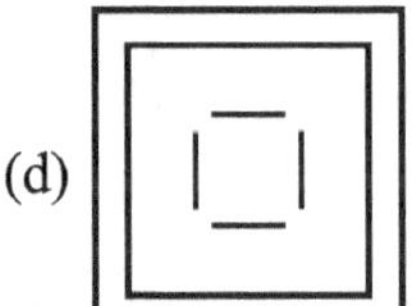

33. **Question Figure**

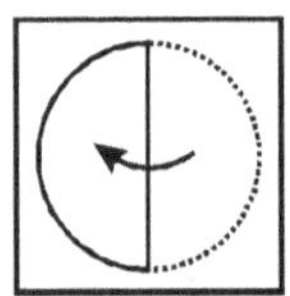 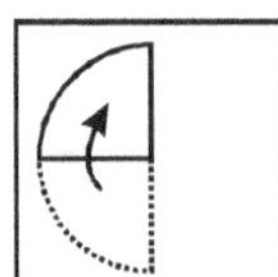 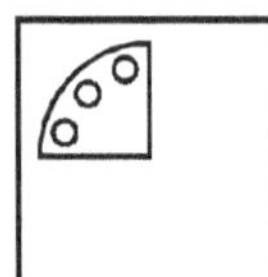

Answer Figures

(a) 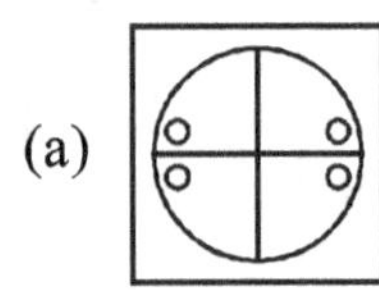 (b) 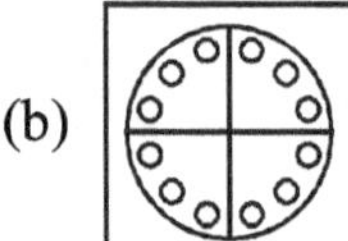

(c) 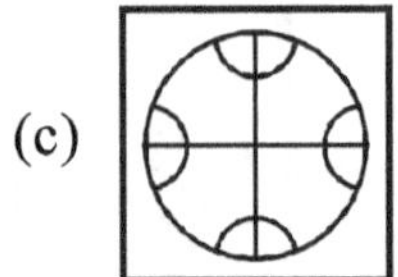 (d) 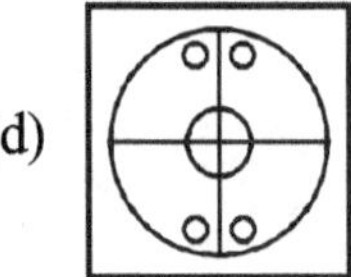

34. The given question consists of a set of three figures X, Y and Z showing a sequence of folding of a piece of paper. Fig. (Z) shows the manner in which the folded paper has been cut. Select a figure from the options which would most closely resemble the unfolded form of Fig. (Z). **[2019]**

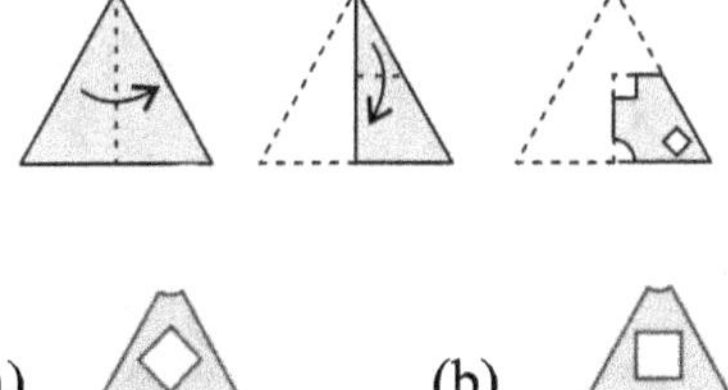

(a) (b) (c) (d)

35. The given question consists of a set of three figures X, Y and Z showing a sequence of folding of a piece of paper. Fig. (Z) shows the manner in which the folded paper has been cut. Select a figure from the options which would most closely resemble the unfolded form of Fig. (Z). **[2019]**

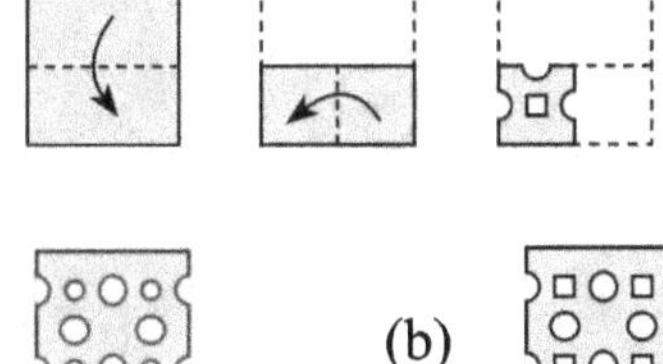

(a) (b)

(c) (d)

36. The given question consists of a set of three figures X, Y and Z which shows the folding of a piece of paper. Fig. (Z) shows the manner in which the folded paper has been cut. Select a figure from the options which shows the unfolded form of Fig. (Z). **[2021]**

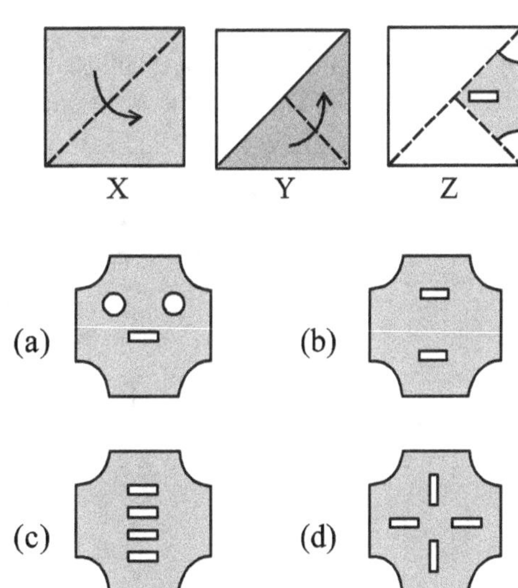

37. The given question consists of a set of three figures X, Y and Z which shows a sequence of folding of a piece of paper. Fig. Z shows the manner in which the folded paper has been cut. Select a figure from the options which would most closely resemble the unfolded form of Fig. Z. **[2022]**

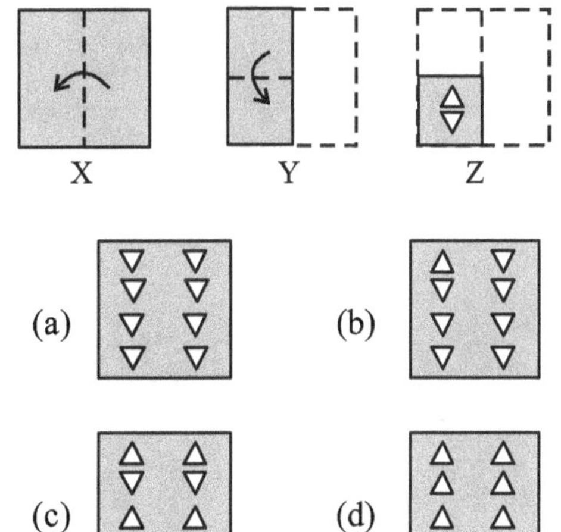

LEVEL 2

DIRECTIONS (Qs.1-5) : Consider the three figures, marked X, Y, and Z showing one fold in X, another in Y and the cut in Z. From amongst the four alternative figures 1, 2, 3 and 4, select the one showing the unfolded position of Z.

1.

X Y Z

(a) (b)

(c) (d)

2.

X Y Z

(a) (b)

(c) (d)

3.

4.

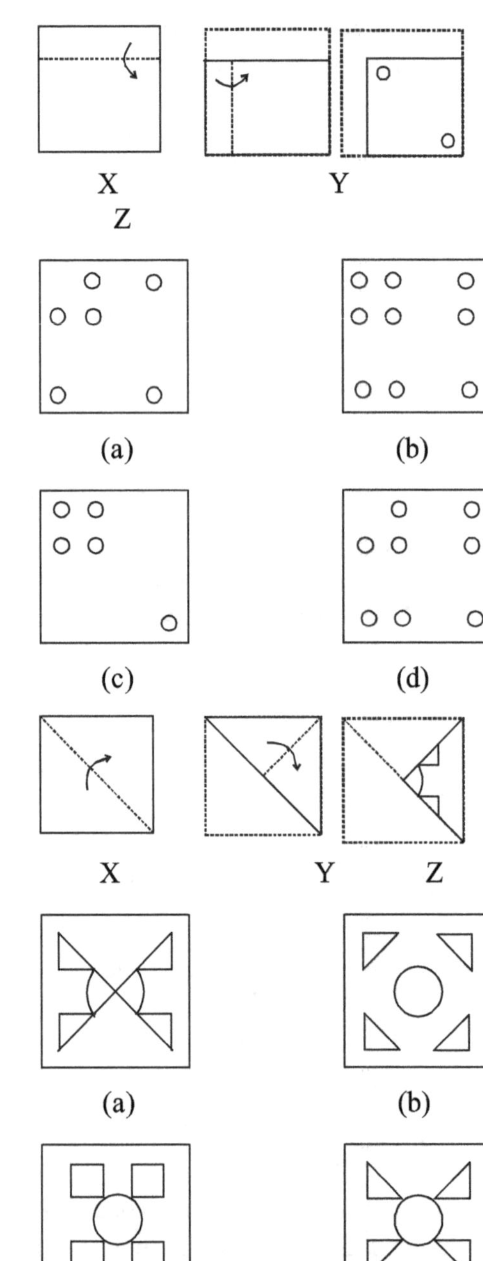

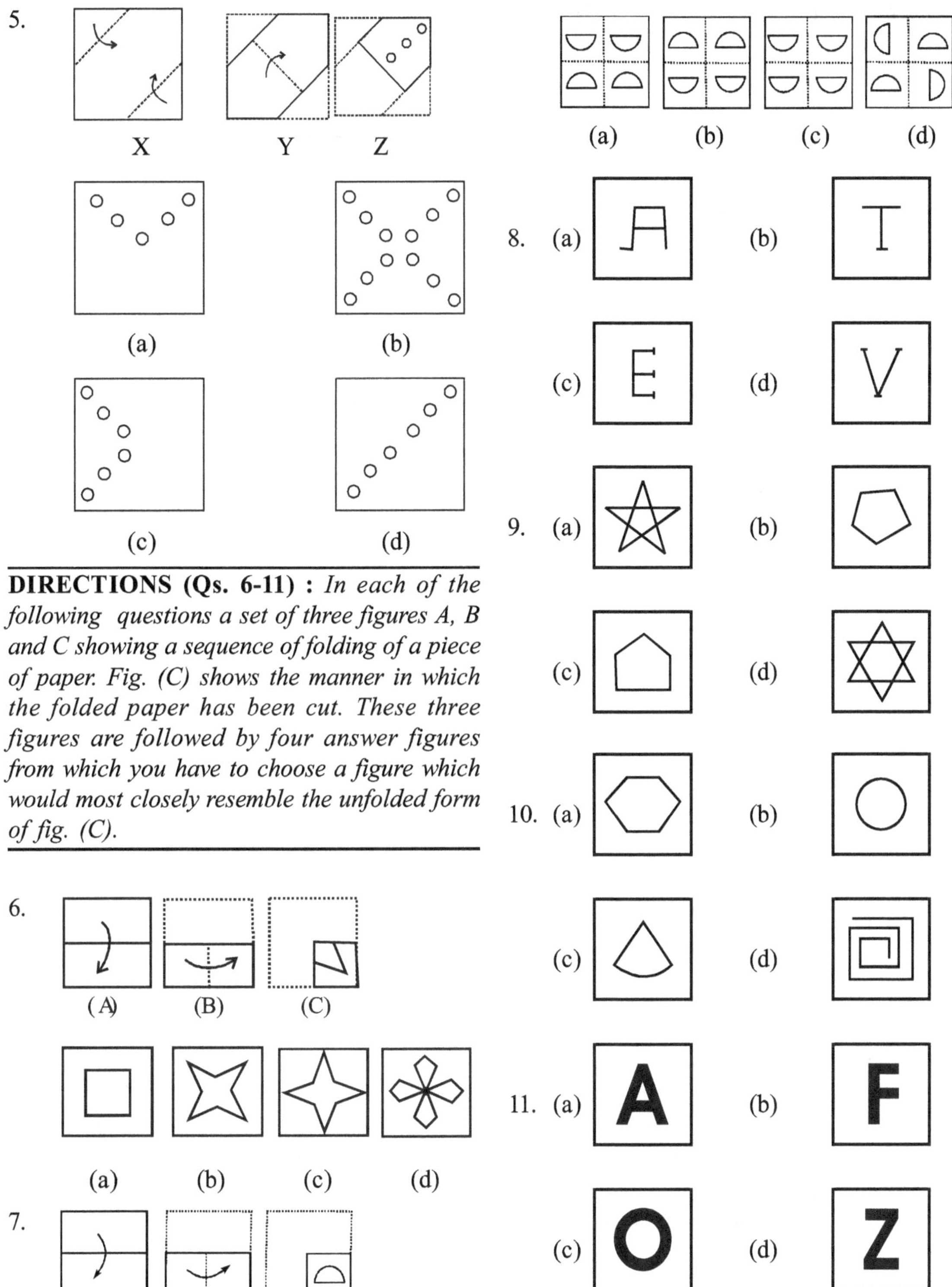

DIRECTIONS (Qs. 6-11) : *In each of the following questions a set of three figures A, B and C showing a sequence of folding of a piece of paper. Fig. (C) shows the manner in which the folded paper has been cut. These three figures are followed by four answer figures from which you have to choose a figure which would most closely resemble the unfolded form of fig. (C).*

12. The given question consists of a set of three figures X, Y and Z showing a sequence of folding of a piece of paper. Fig. (Z) shows the manner in which the folded paper has been cut. Select a figure from the options which would most closely resemble the unfolded form of Fig. (Z). **[2019]**

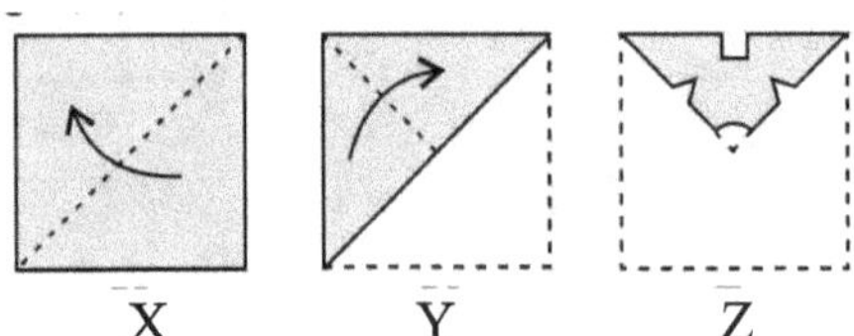

(a) 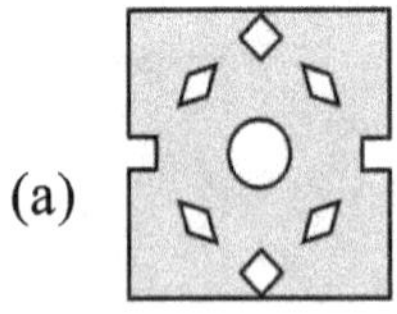

(b) 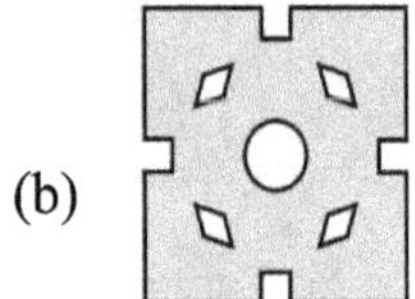

(c) 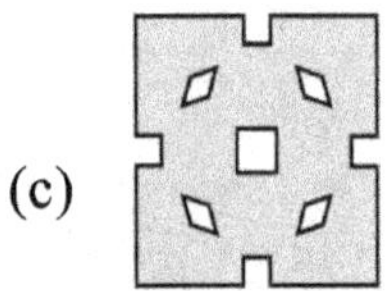

(d) 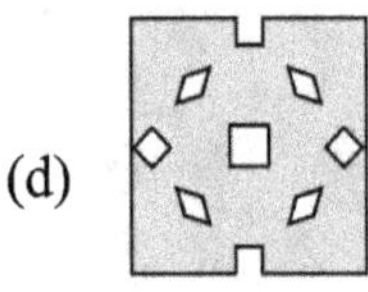

13. A square transparent sheet with a pattern and a dotted line on it is given. Find a figure from the options as to how the pattern would appear when the sheet is folded along the dotted line. **[2020]**

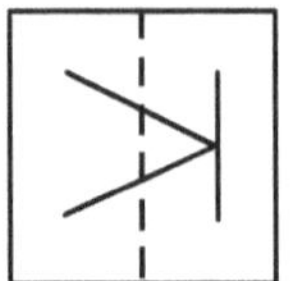

(a) 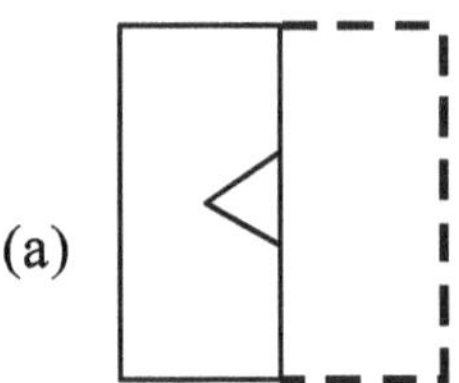

(b) 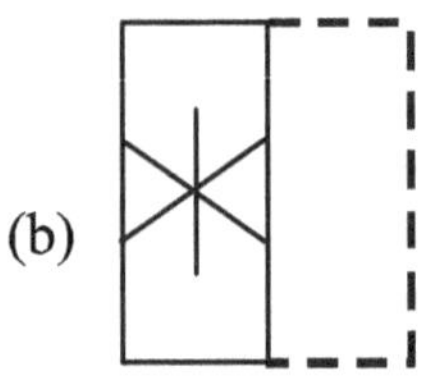

(c) 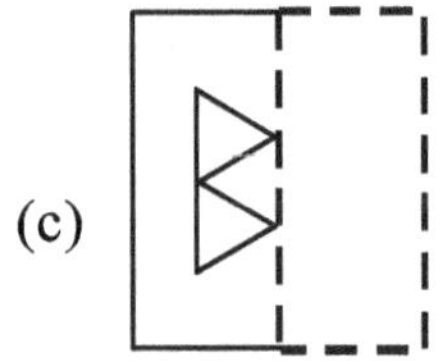

(d) 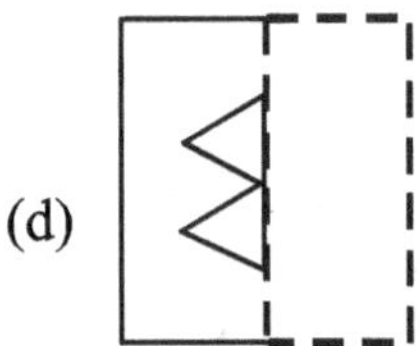

14. A square transparent Sheet (X) with a pattern and a dotted line on it is given. Select a figure from the options as to how the pattern would appear when the transparent sheet is folded along the dotted line. **[2021]**

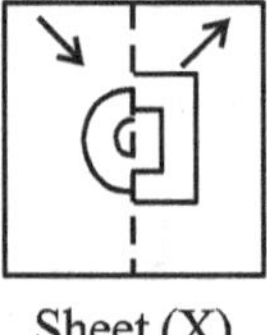

Sheet (X)

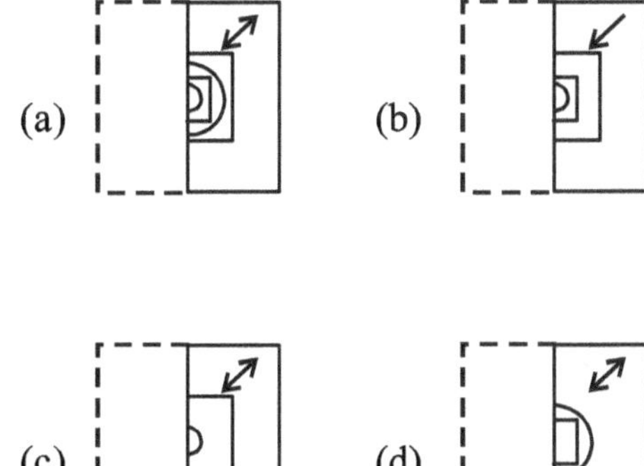

15. A set of three figures X, Y and Z showing a sequence of folding of a piece of paper is given. Fig. (Z) shows the manner in which the folded paper has been cut. **[2021]**
Select a figure from the options which shows the unfolded form of fig. (Z).

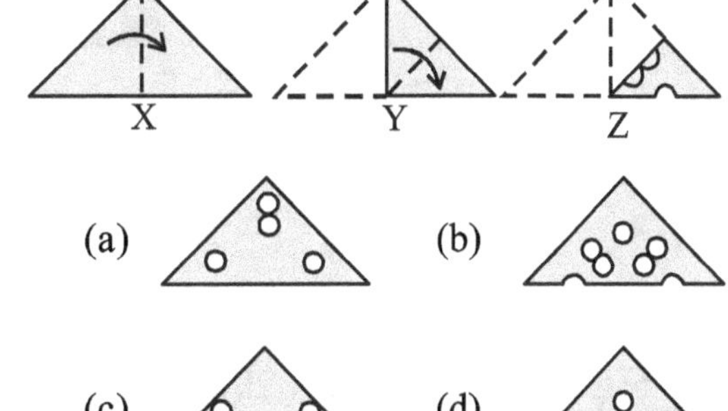

ANSWER KEY

LEVEL-1																			
1	(d)	**5**	(c)	**9**	(c)	**13**	(a)	**17**	(a)	**21**	(a)	**25**	(c)	**29**	(a)	**33**	(b)	**37**	(c)
2	(a)	**6**	(c)	**10**	(b)	**14**	(a)	**18**	(a)	**22**	(a)	**26**	(c)	**30**	(c)	**34**	(b)		
3	(b)	**7**	(c)	**11**	(b)	**15**	(a)	**19**	(c)	**23**	(b)	**27**	(c)	**31**	(c)	**35**	(b)		
4	(c)	**8**	(c)	**12**	(b)	**16**	(a)	**20**	(d)	**24**	(a)	**28**	(c)	**32**	(a)	**36**	(d)		
LEVEL-2																			
1	(c)	**3**	(c)	**5**	(d)	**7**	(a)	**9**	(d)	**11**	(c)	**13**	(c)	**15**	(b)				
2	(c)	**4**	(c)	**6**	(b)	**8**	(a)	**10**	(d)	**12**	(b)	**14**	(a)						

CHAPTER

Embedded Figures, Figure Completion

A figure (X) is said to be embedded in a figure Y, if figure Y contains figure (X) as its part. Thus problems on embedded figures contain a figure (X) followed by four complex figures in such a way that fig (X) is embedded in one of these. The figure containing the figure (X) is your answer.

DIRECTIONS (ILLUSTRATIONS 1 & 2) : In each of the following examples, fig (X) is embedded in any one of the four alternative figures (a), (b), (c) or (d). Find the alternative which contains fig. (X) as its part.

ILLUSTRATION 1 :

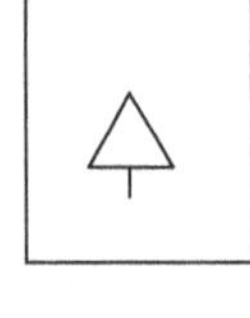

(X)

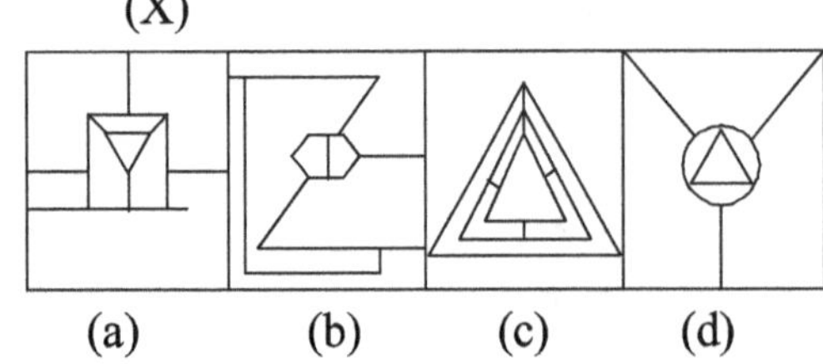

(a) (b) (c) (d)

***Sol.* (c)** On close observation, we find that fig. (X) is embedded in fig. (c) as shown below :

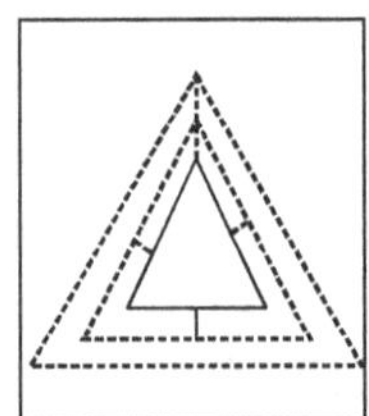

Hence, the answer is (c)

ILLUSTRATION 2 :

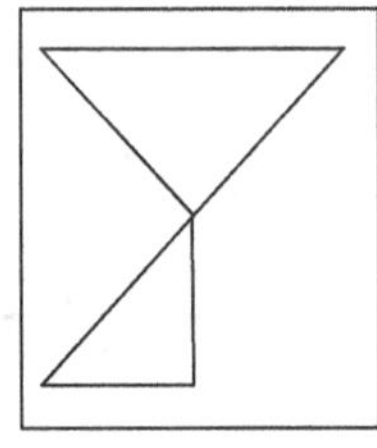

(X)

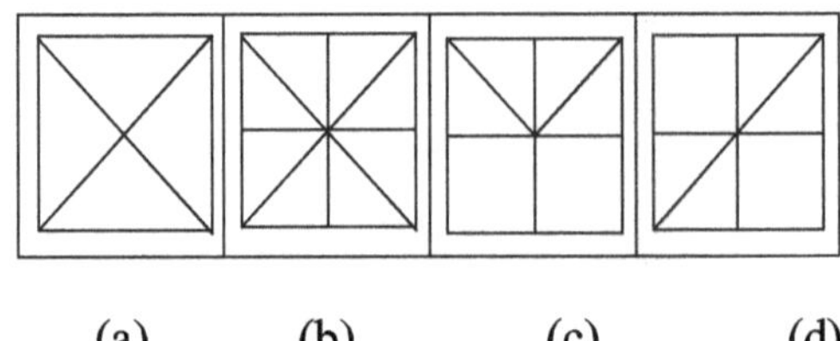

(a) (b) (c) (d)

***Sol.* (b)** Clearly, fig. (X) is embedded fig. (b) as shown below :

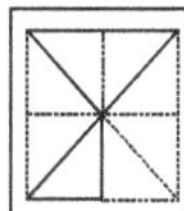

Hence, the answer is (b)

ILLUSTRATION 3 :

Find amongst the four alternatives (a), (b), (c) and (d), the figure which most nearly contains the figure (X).

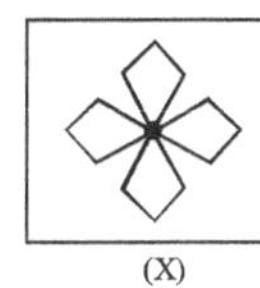

(X)

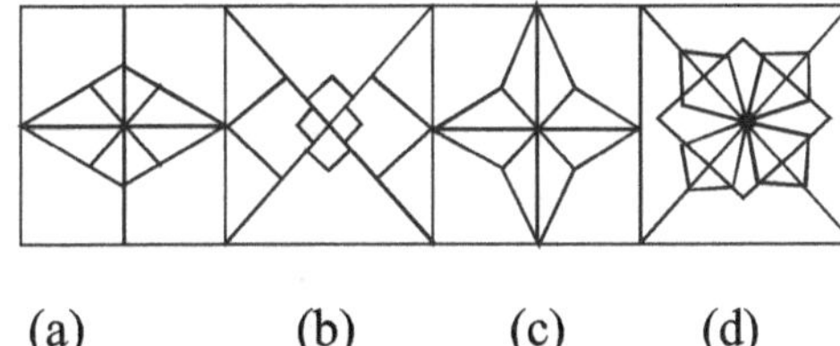

(a) (b) (c) (d)

Sol. (d) Figure (X) is not contained in (a), nor in (b) nor in (c) but in (d), (X) is embedded. Thus answer is (d).

COMPLETION OF INCOMPLETE PATTERN:

In such problems, a figure following a particular sequence or pattern is given, in which a part, usually one-fourth, is left blank. This problem figure is followed by four alternative figures. One is required to choose the one which best fits into the blank space of problem figure so as to complete the original pattern.

COMPLETION OF A SQUARE

Each problem in this topic contains five different parts numbered 1, 2, 3, 4 and 5. A square is to be constructed by selecting three parts out of five parts. The steps given below can help the candidate to do the needful:

(i) Select a piece which contains a right angle between two adjacent outer edges.

(ii) Try to fit another piece in its vacant spaces. If it does not fit, try another piece.

(iii) Repeat this system with different sets of such pieces till you are sure that the two pieces fit in each other.

(iv) Find the third piece out of the remaining three pieces to get the square complete.

ILLUSTRATION 4 :

Select a figure from the four alternatives, which when placed in the blank space of figure (X) would complete the pattern.

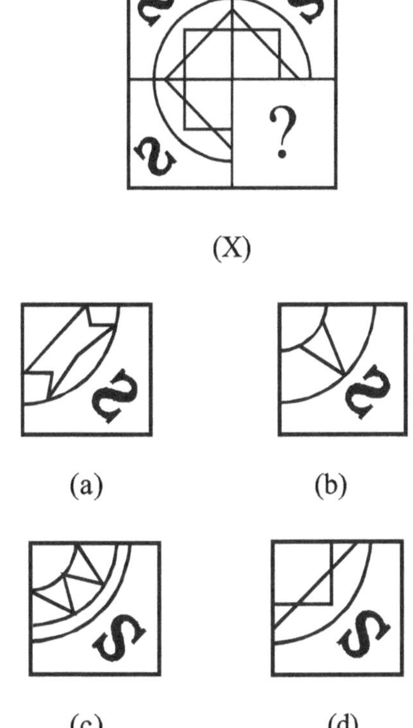

(X)

(a) (b)

(c) (d)

Sol. **(d)** Clearly, figure (d) will complete the pattern when placed in the blank space of figure (X) as shown below. Hence, the answer is (d).

ILLUSTRATION 5 :

Find out which of the figures (a), (b), (c) and (d) can be formed from the pieces given in figure (X)

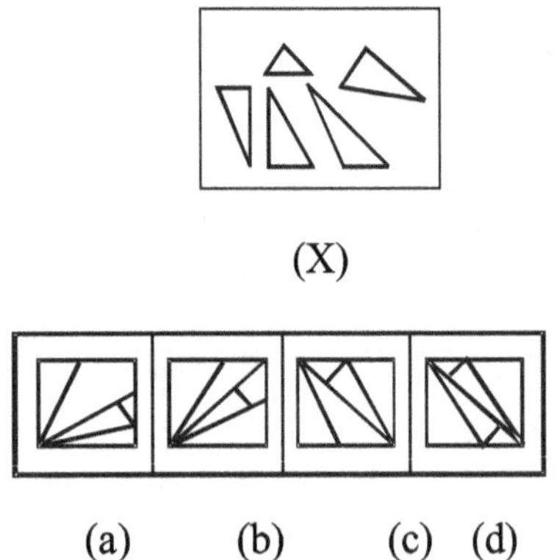

Sol. **(c)** Clearly the pieces in the figure (X) are in the figure (c).

The answer is therefore (c).

ILLUSTRATION 6 :

Find three figures out of the following five figures a, b, c, d and e which when fitted into each other would form a complete square.

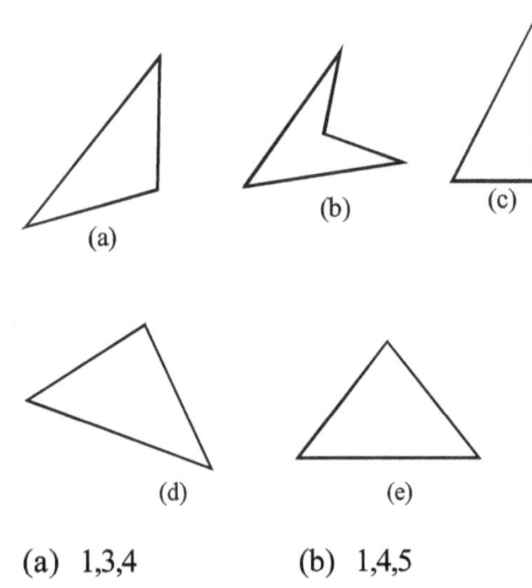

(a) 1,3,4 (b) 1,4,5

(c) 1,2,5 (d) 1,2,4

Sol. **(b)** We begin with choosing a figure having a right angle. Out of the five figures (b) seems to be having two equal sides including a right angle. Fitting along (d) with it, we have a figure as now. Looking into a vacant space, we find that out of the remaining three figures (a), (b) and (c) only fig. (a) will fit, hence the answer is (b).

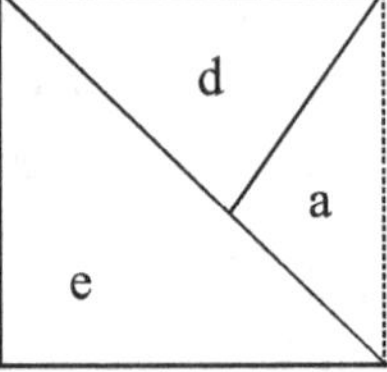

LEVEL 1

DIRECTIONS (Qs. 1-7) : *In each of the following questions, you are given a figure (X) followed by four alternative figures (a), (b), (c) and (d) such that fig. (X) is embeded in one of them. Trace out the alternative figure which contains fig. (X) as its part.*

1.

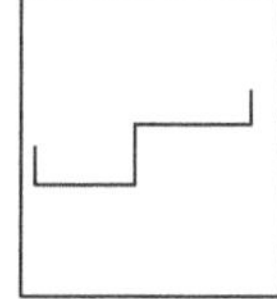

(X)

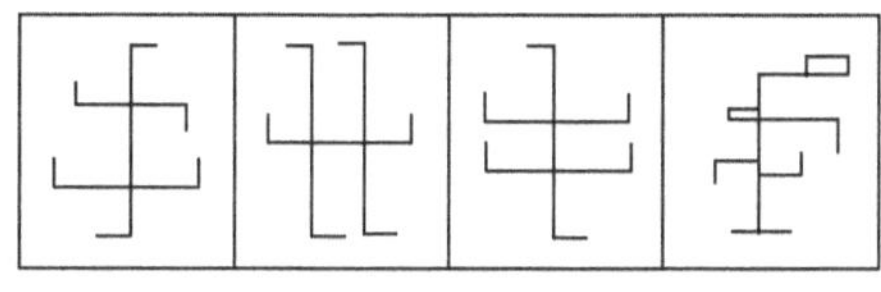

(a) (b) (c) (d)

2.

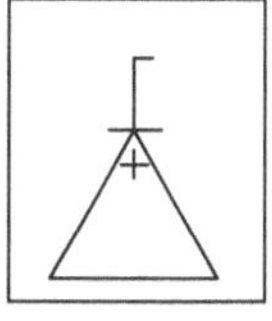

(X)

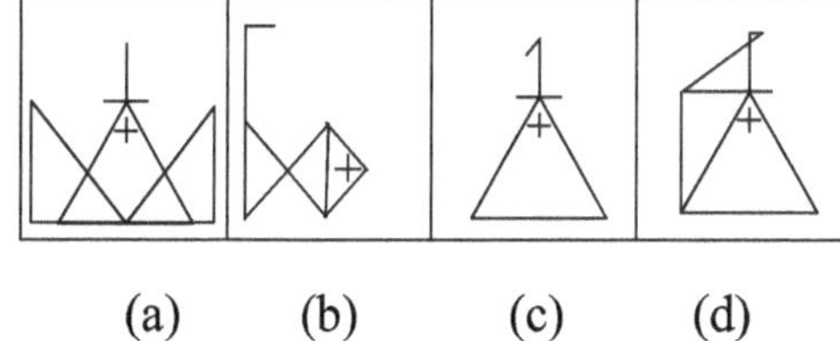

(a) (b) (c) (d)

3.

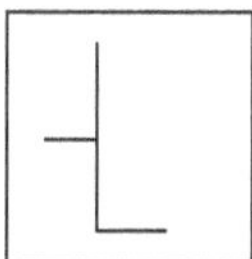

(X)

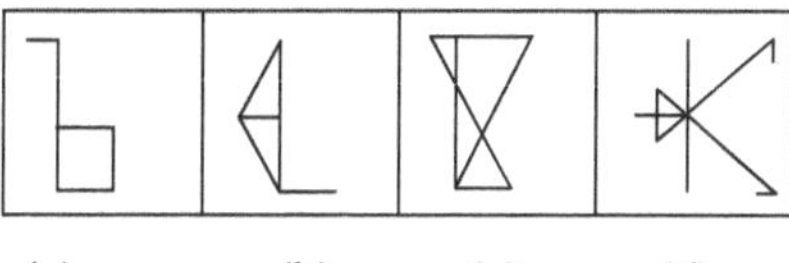

(a) (b) (c) (d)

4.

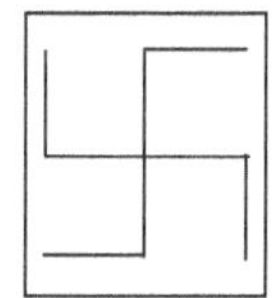

(X)

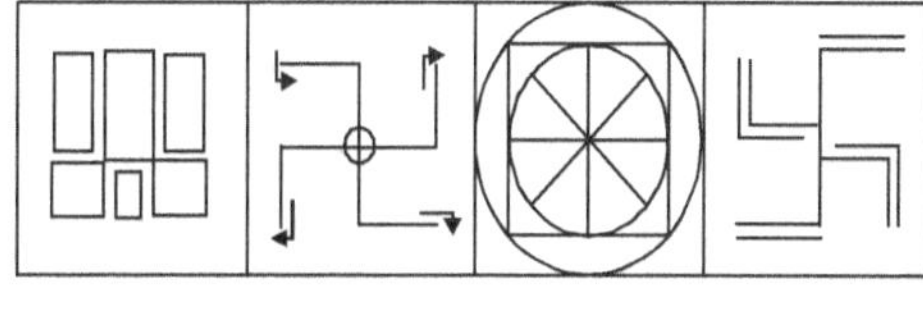

(a) (b) (c) (d)

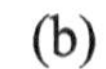

5.

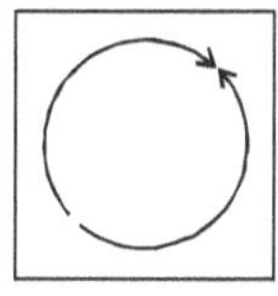

(X)

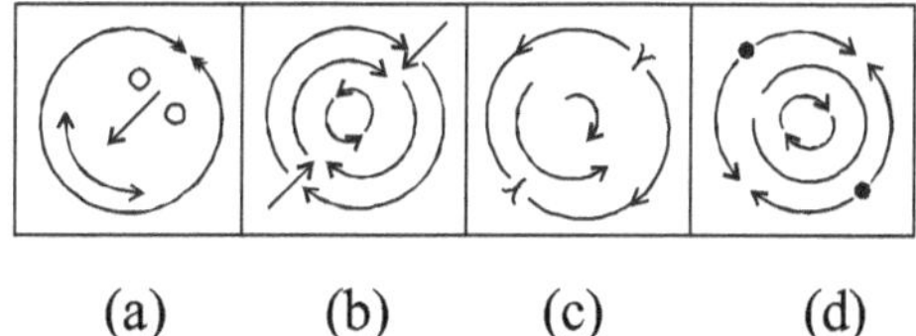

(a) (b) (c) (d)

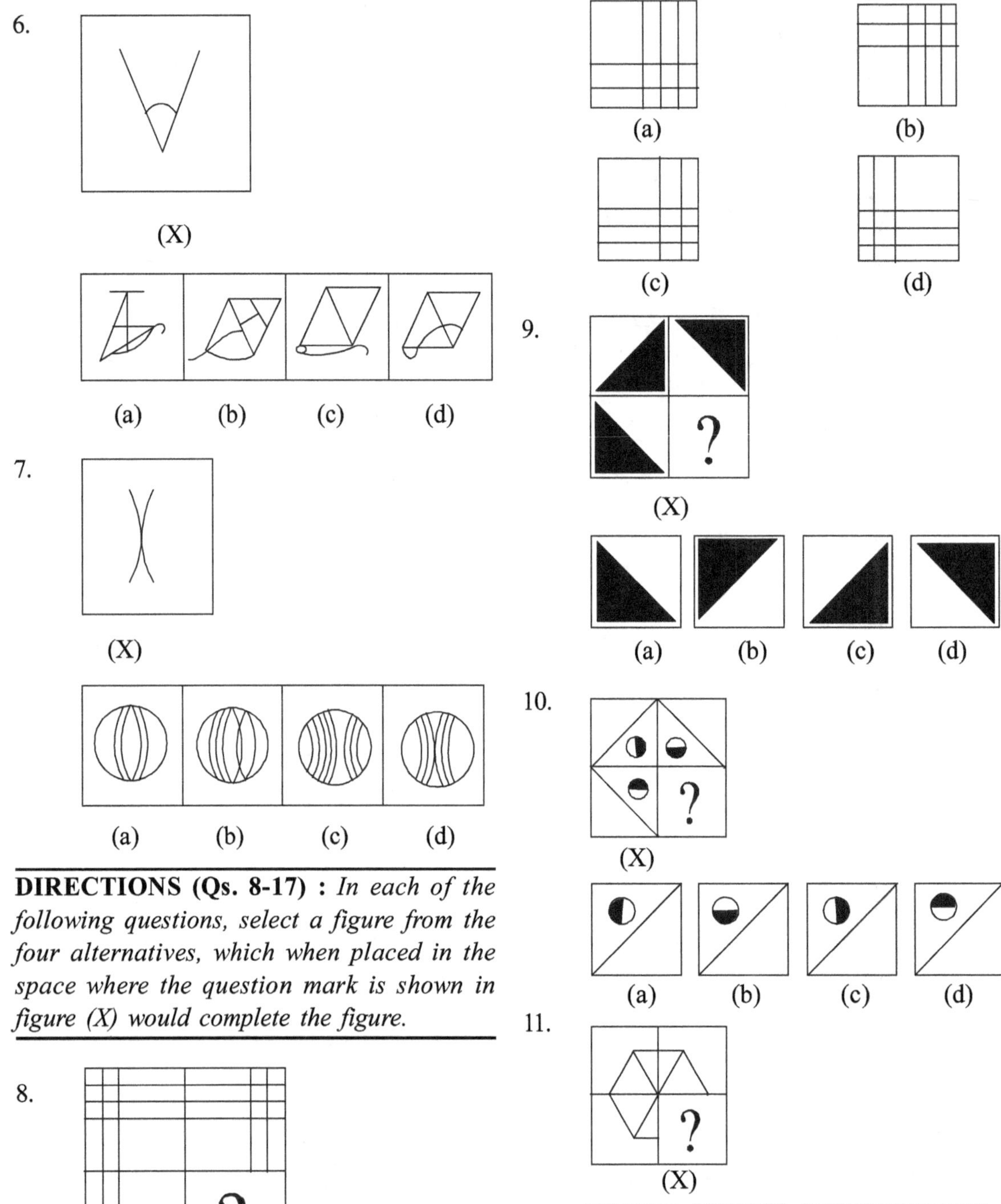

DIRECTIONS (Qs. 8-17) : *In each of the following questions, select a figure from the four alternatives, which when placed in the space where the question mark is shown in figure (X) would complete the figure.*

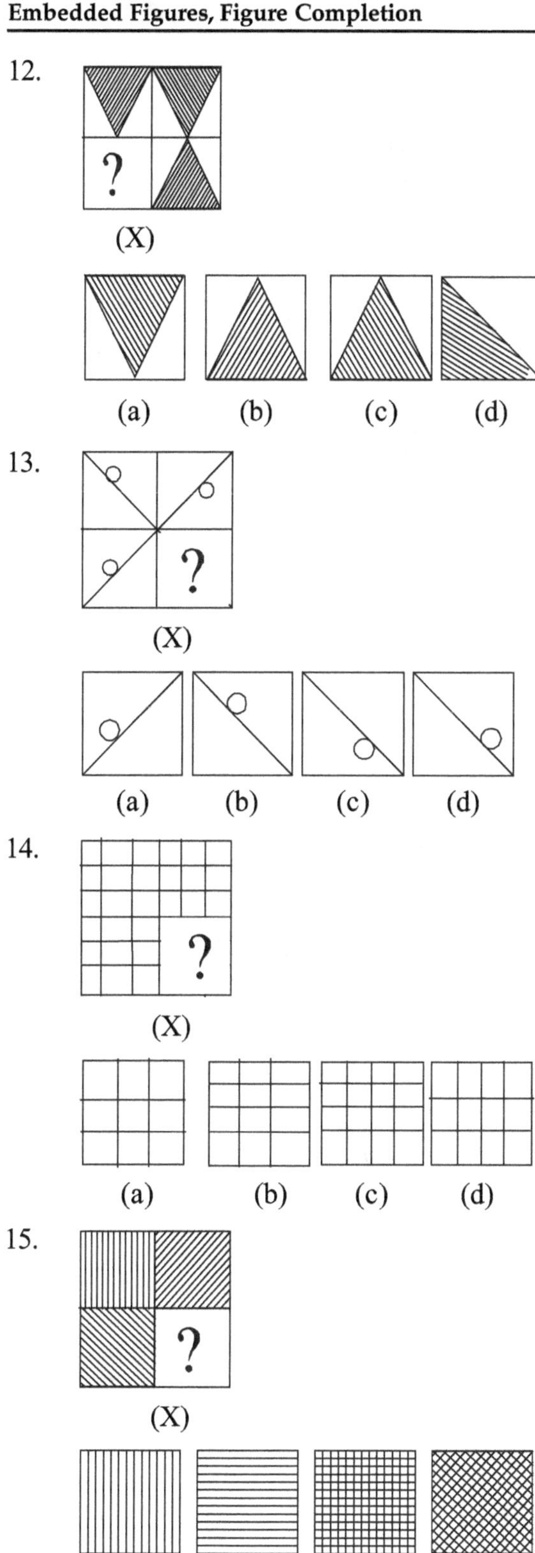

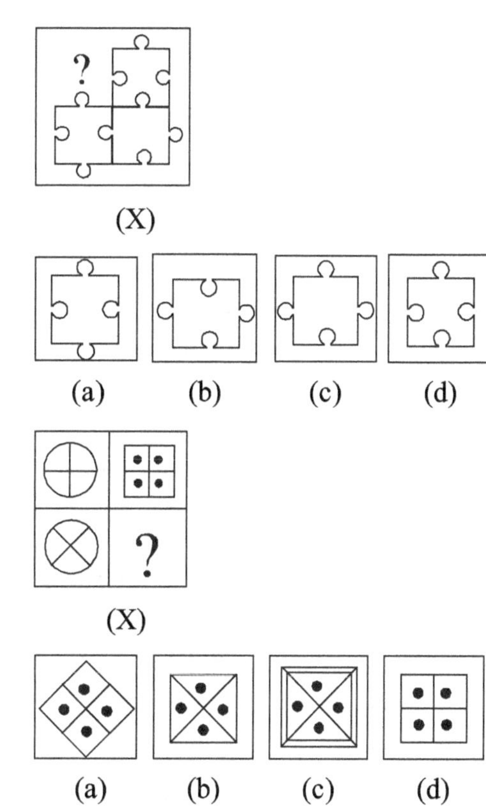

DIRECTIONS: *In questions 18 to 27 one part of a square or circle or triangle or rectangle is in the question figure and the other one is among the four answers (a), (b), (c), (d) are given. Find out the figure that completes the square or circle or triangle or rectangle.*

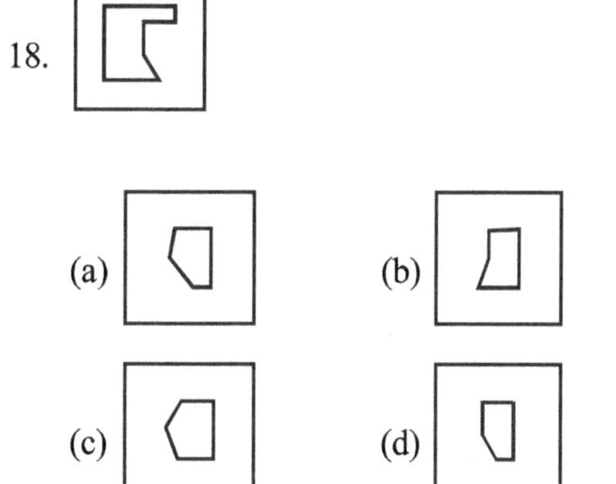

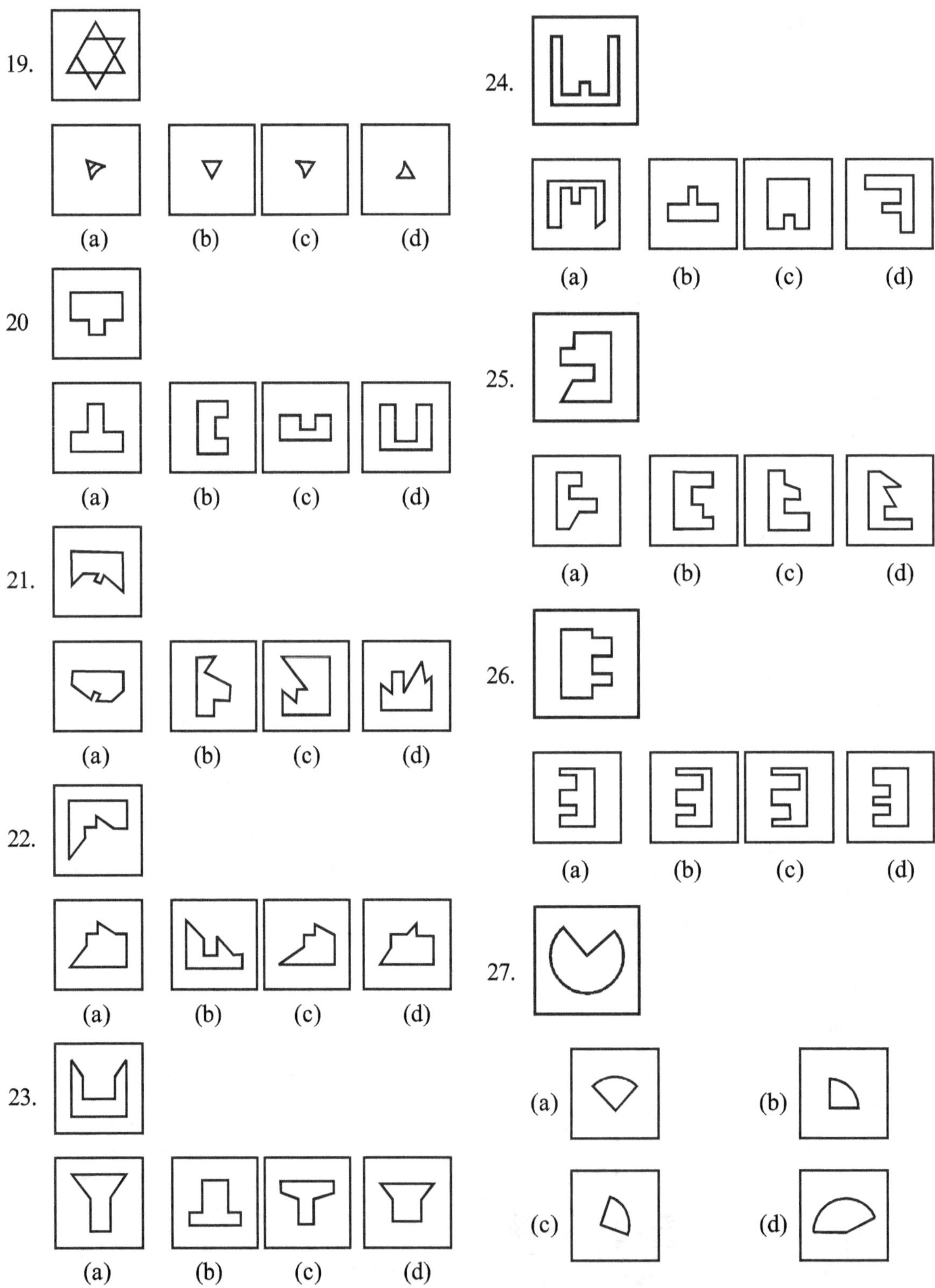
19.
(a)
(b)
(c)
(d)
20
(a)
(b)
(c)
(d)
21.
(a)
(b)
(c)
(d)
22.
(a)
(b)
(c)
(d)
23.
(a)
(b)
(c)
(d)
24.
(a)
(b)
(c)
(d)
25.
(a)
(b)
(c)
(d)
26.
(a)
(b)
(c)
(d)
27.
(a)
(b)
(c)
(d)

DIRECTIONS (Qs. 28-32): *There are four alternatives (a), (b), (c) and (d) given. Your have to select the alternatives which completes squares given in the question figure.*

28. **Question Figure**

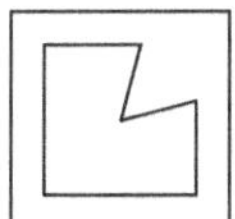

Answer Figures

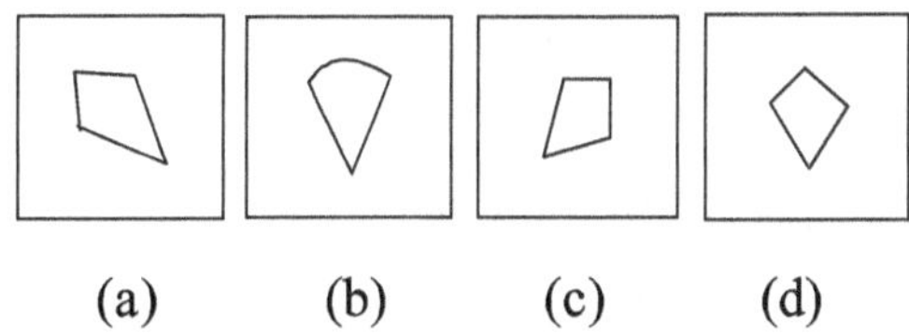

(a) (b) (c) (d)

29. **Question Figure**

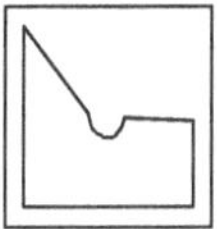

Answer Figures

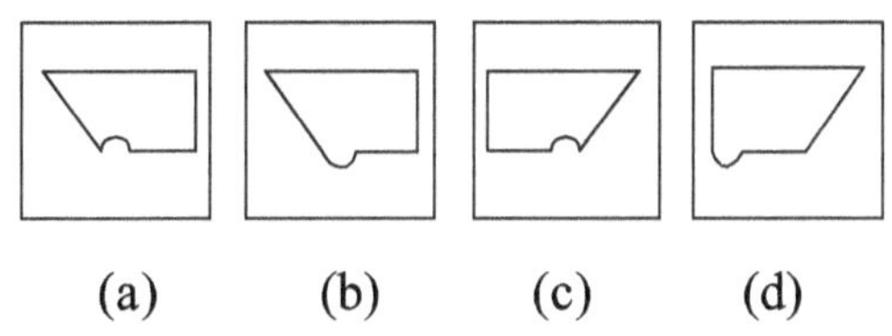

(a) (b) (c) (d)

30. **Question Figure**

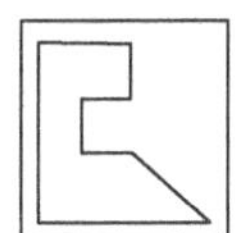

Answer Figures

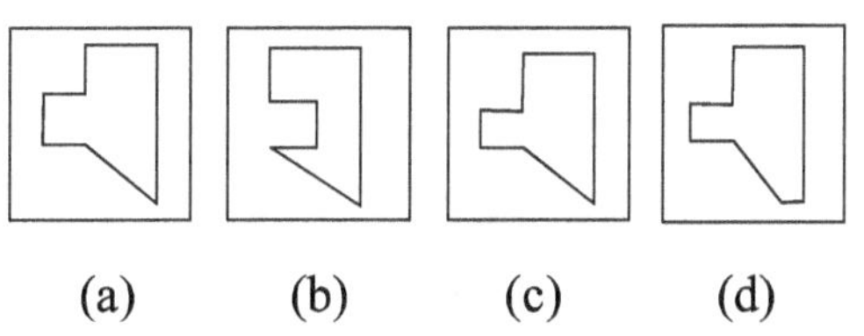

(a) (b) (c) (d)

31. **Question Figure**

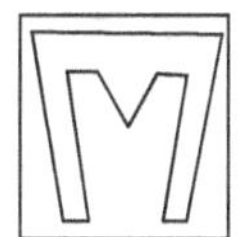

Answer Figures

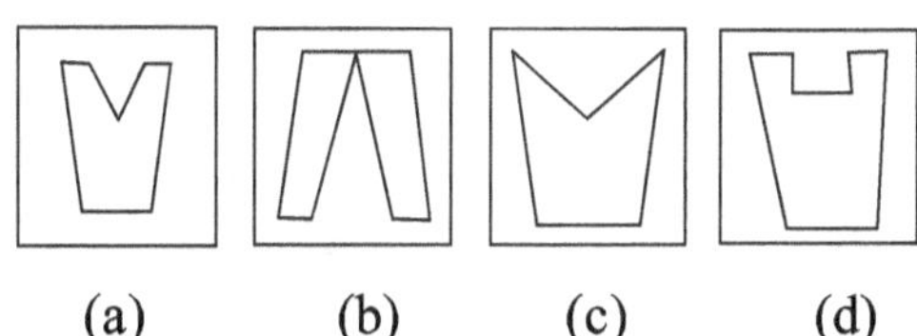

(a) (b) (c) (d)

32. **Question Figure**

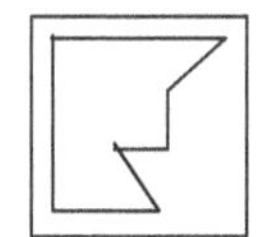

Answer Figures

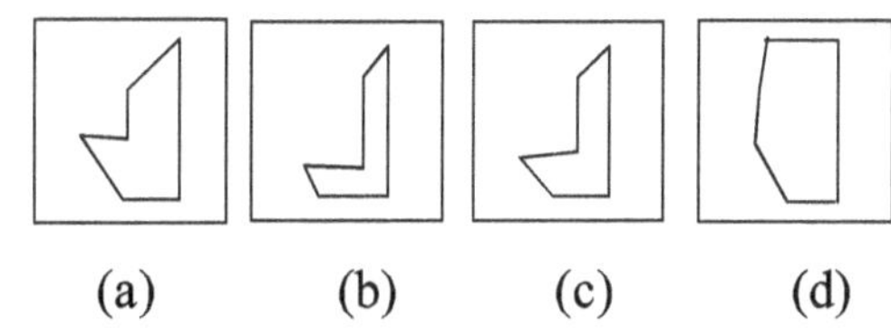

(a) (b) (c) (d)

DIRECTIONS (Qs. 33-37): *There are four alternatives (a), (b), (c) and (d) given. You have to select the alternatives which completes the geometrical figure given in the question figure.*

33. **Question Figure**

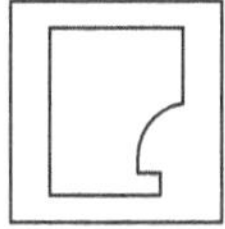

Answer Figures

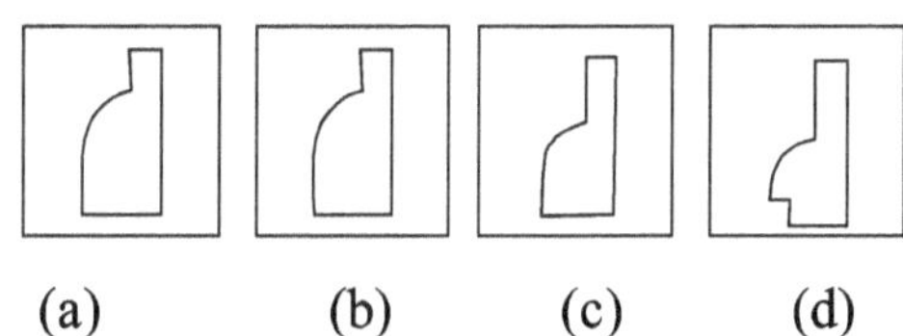

(a) (b) (c) (d)

34. **Question Figure**

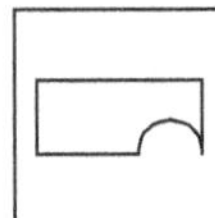

Answer Figures

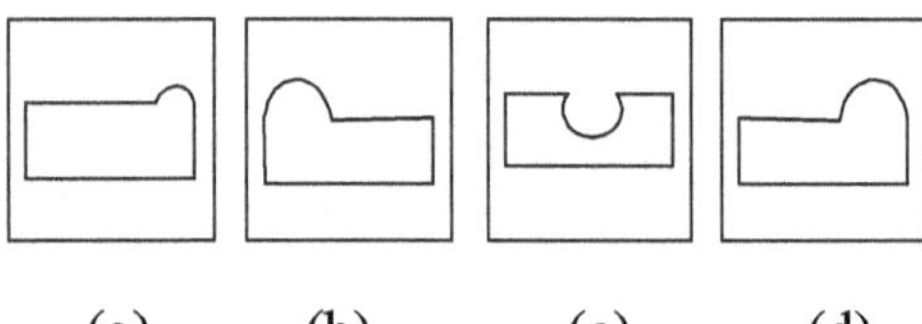

(a) (b) (c) (d)

35. **Question Figure**

Answer Figures

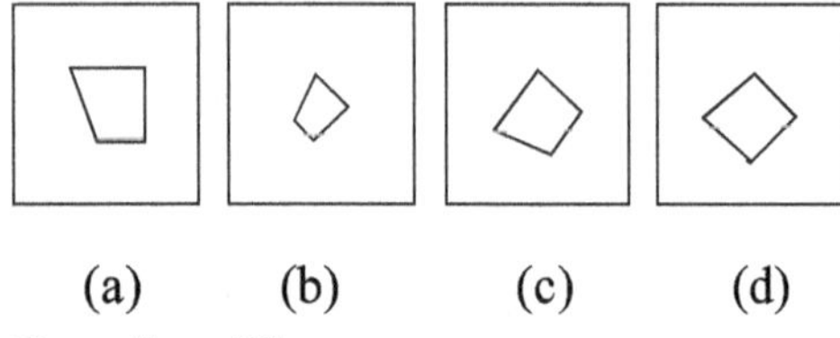

(a) (b) (c) (d)

36. **Question Figure**

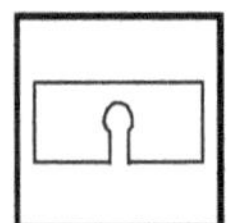

Answer Figures

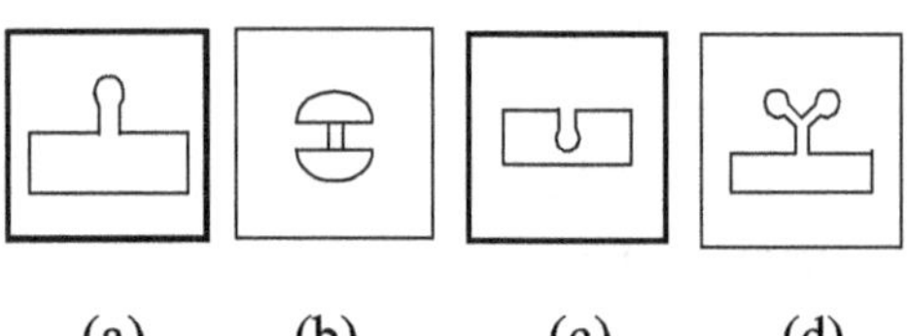

(a) (b) (c) (d)

37. **Question Figure**

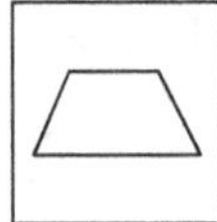

Answer Figures

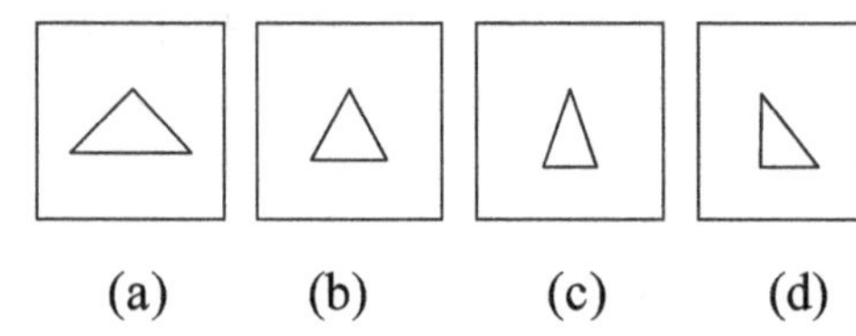

(a) (b) (c) (d)

DIRECTIONS: *In Question Nos. 38 to 41, one part of a geometrical figure (Triangle, Square, Circle) is as question figure and the other one is among the four answer figures (a), (b), (c) and (d). Find the figure on the right side that completes the geometrical figure.*

38. **Question Figure**

Answer Figures

(a) 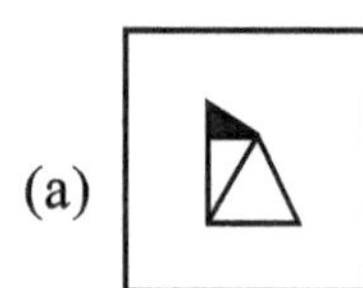

(b) 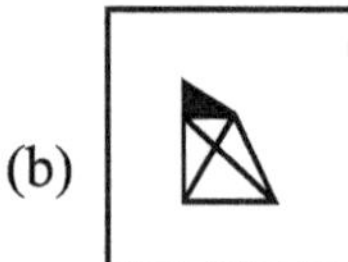

(c) 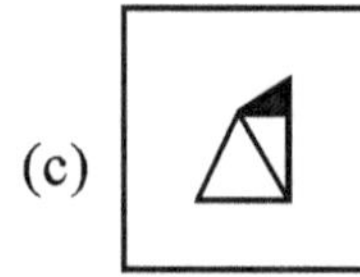

(d) 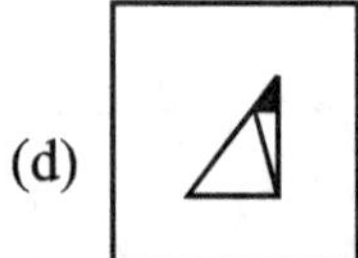

39. **Question Figure**

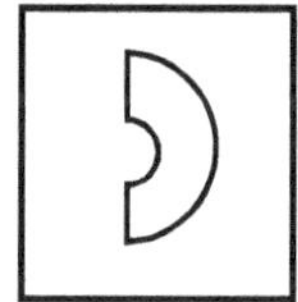

Answer Figures

(a) 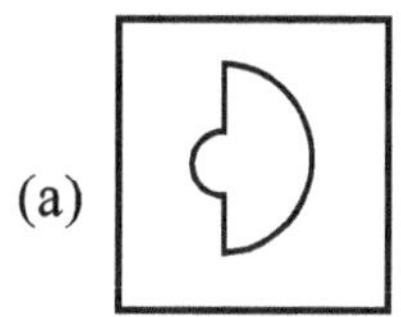 (b) 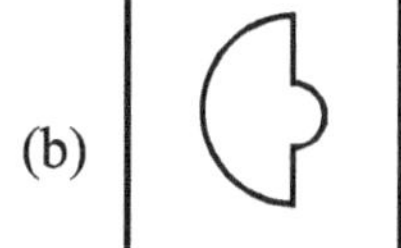

(c) 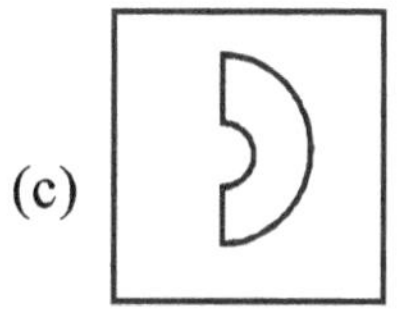 (d) 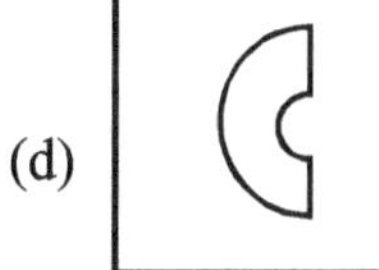

40. **Question Figure**

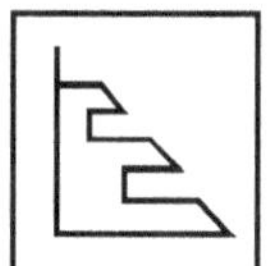

Answer Figures

(a) 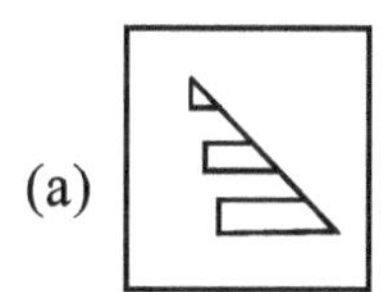 (b) 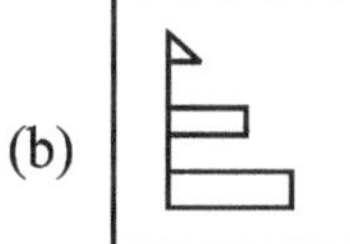

(c) 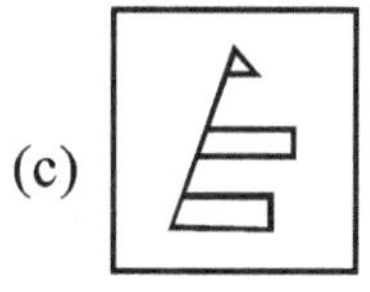 (d) 

41. **Question Figure**

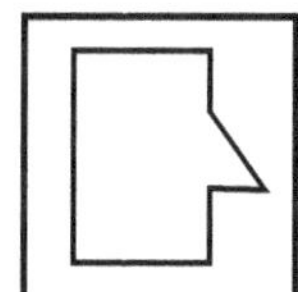

Answer Figures

(a) 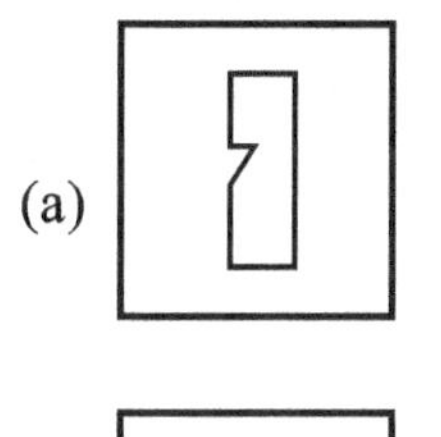 (b) 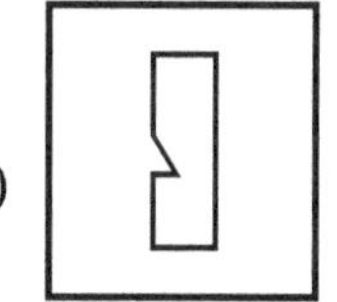

(c) 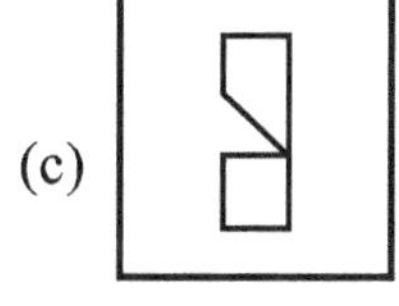 (d) 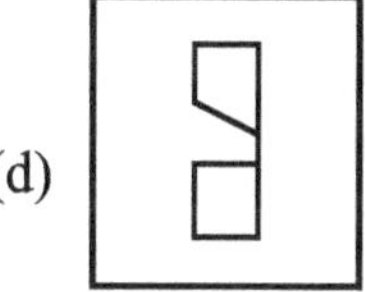

DIRECTIONS (Qs. 42 to 43) : *One part of a geometrical figure (Triangle, Square, Circle) is as question figure and the other one is among the four answer figures (a), (b), (c) and (d). Find the figure that completes the geometrical figure.*

42. **Question Figure**

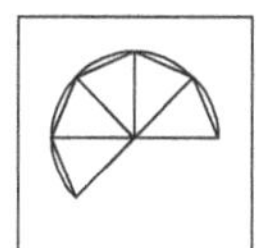

Answer Figures

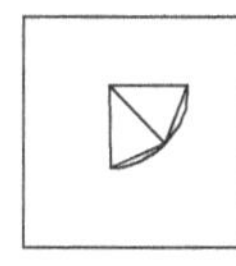 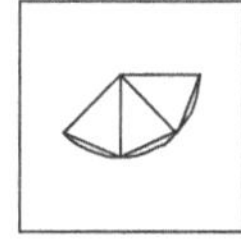 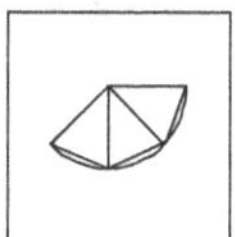 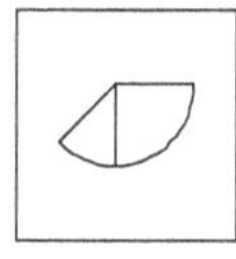

(a) (b) (c) (d)

43. **Question Figure**

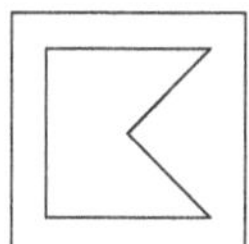

Answer Figures

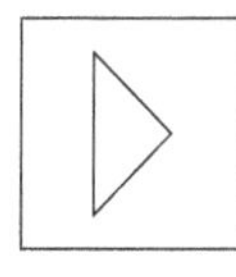 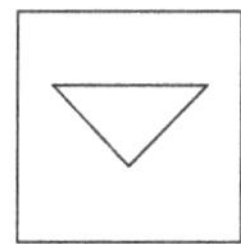 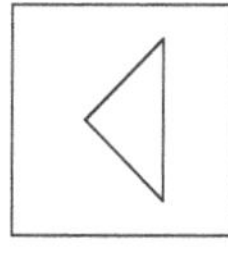 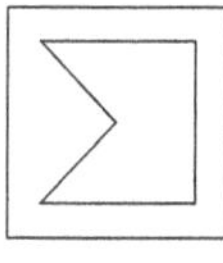

(a) (b) (c) (d)

DIRECTIONS (Qs. 44-47) : *One part of a geometrical figure (Triangle, Square, Circle) is as question figure and the other one is among the four answer figures (a), (b), (c) and (d). Find the figure that completes the geometrical figure.*

44. **Question Figures**

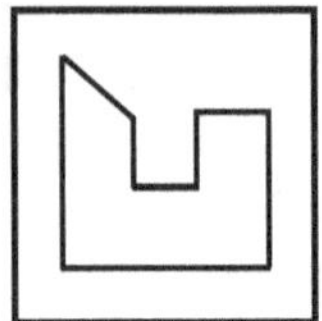

Answer Figures

(a) 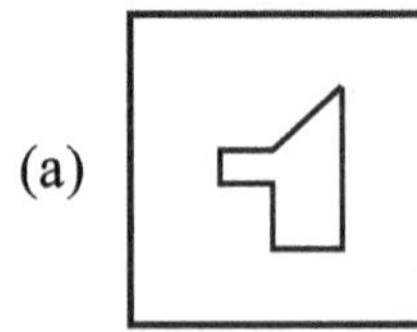

(b) 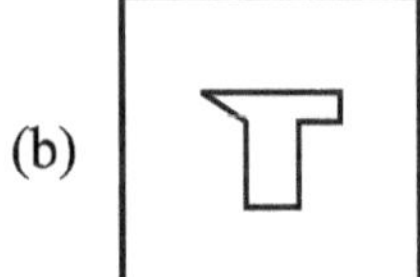

(c) 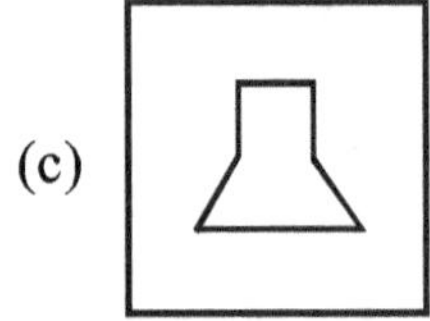

(d) 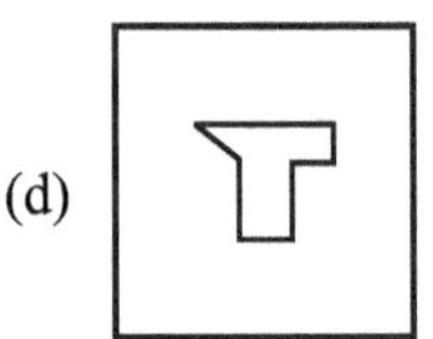

45. **Question Figures**

Answer Figures

(a) 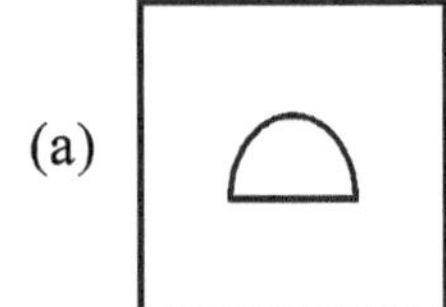

(b) 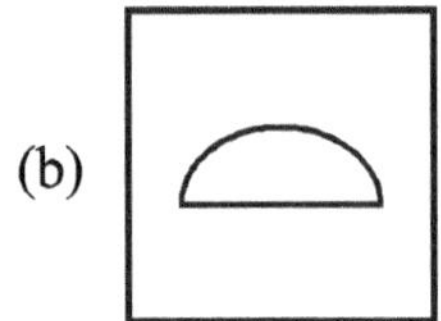

(c) 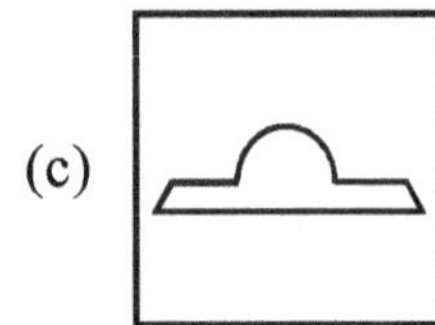

(d) 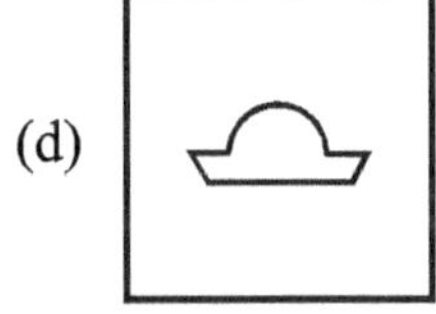

46. **Question Figures**

Answer Figures

(a) 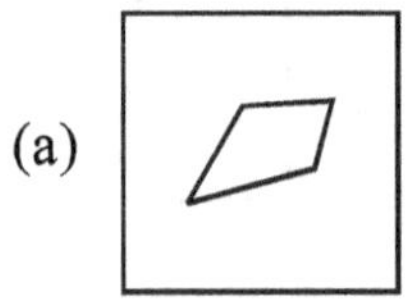

(b) 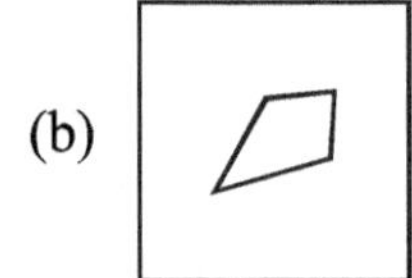

(c) 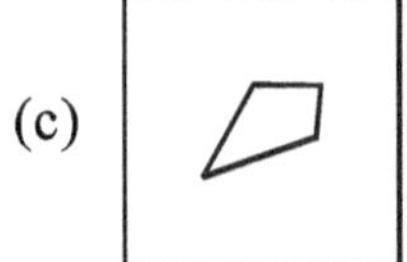

(d) 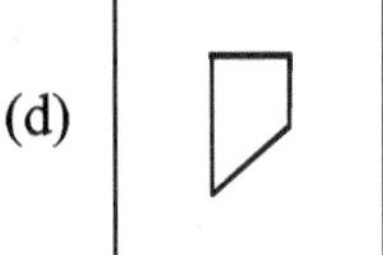

47. **Question Figures**

Answer Figures

(a) 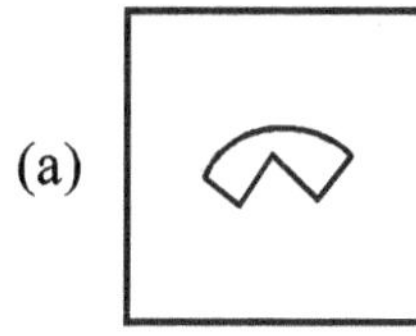

(b) 

(c) 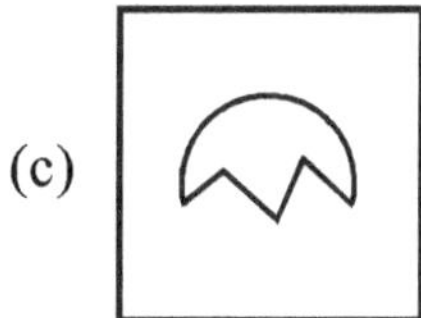

(d) 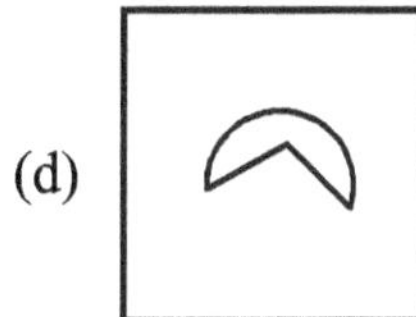

DIRECTIONS: *In questions 48 to 57 there is a problem figure, a part of which is missing. Observe the answer figures (a), (b), (c), (d) and find out the answer figure which without changing the direction, fits in the missing part of the problem figure in order to complete the pattern in the problem figure.*

48. 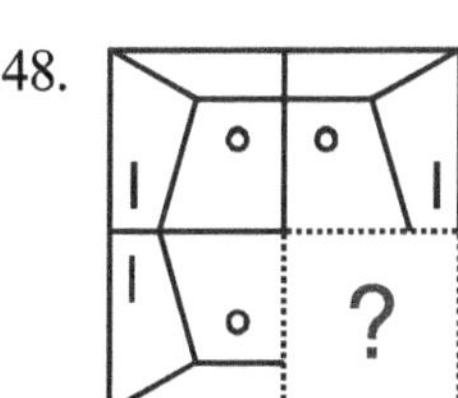

(a) 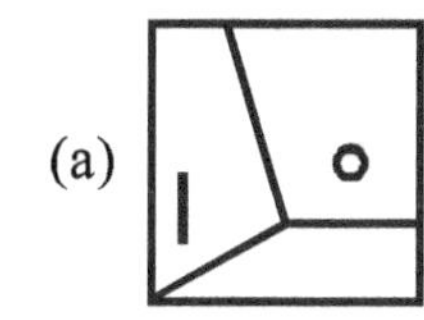

(b) 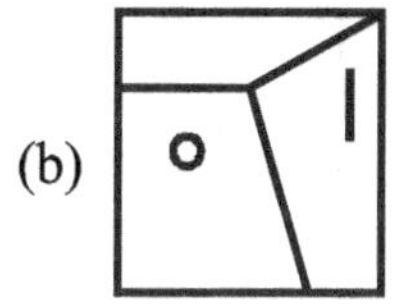

(c) 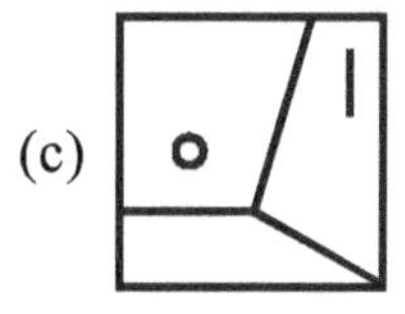

(d) 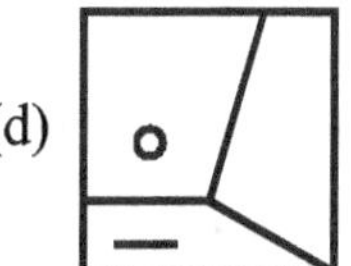

49. 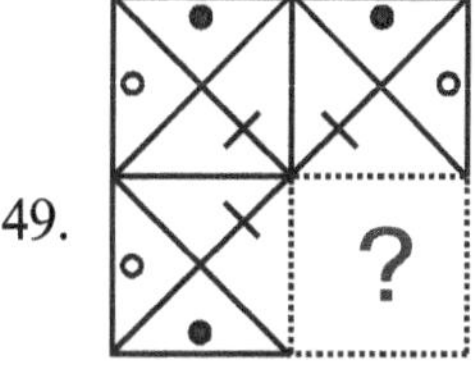

(a) 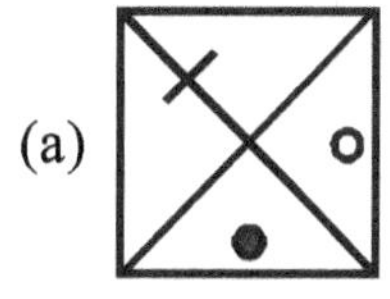

(b) 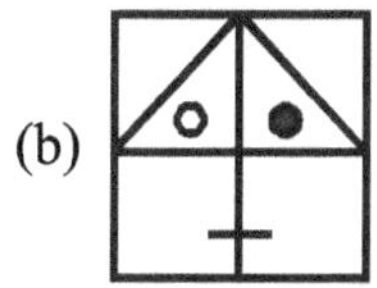

(c) 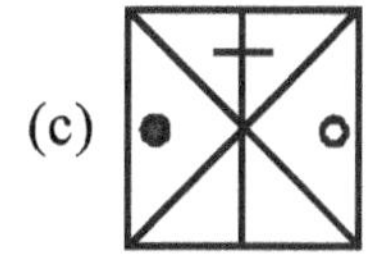

(d) 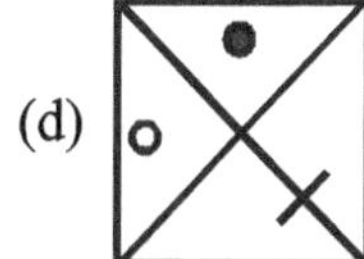

50. 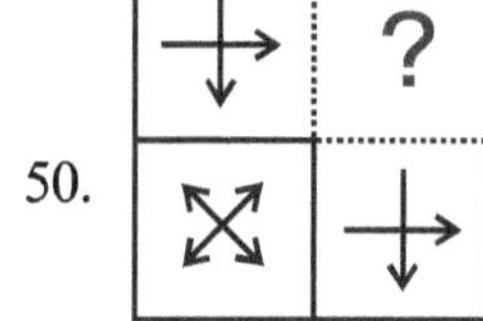

(a) 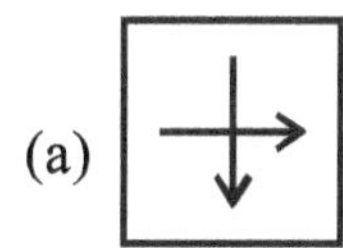

(b) 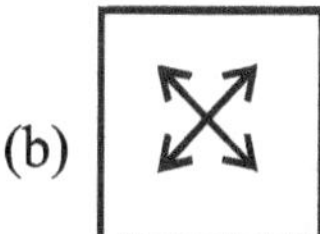

(c) 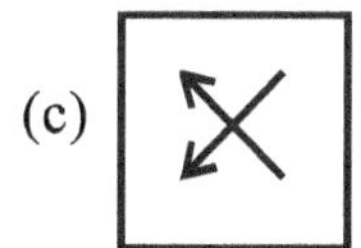

(d) 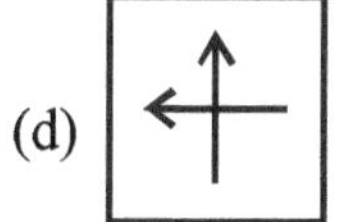

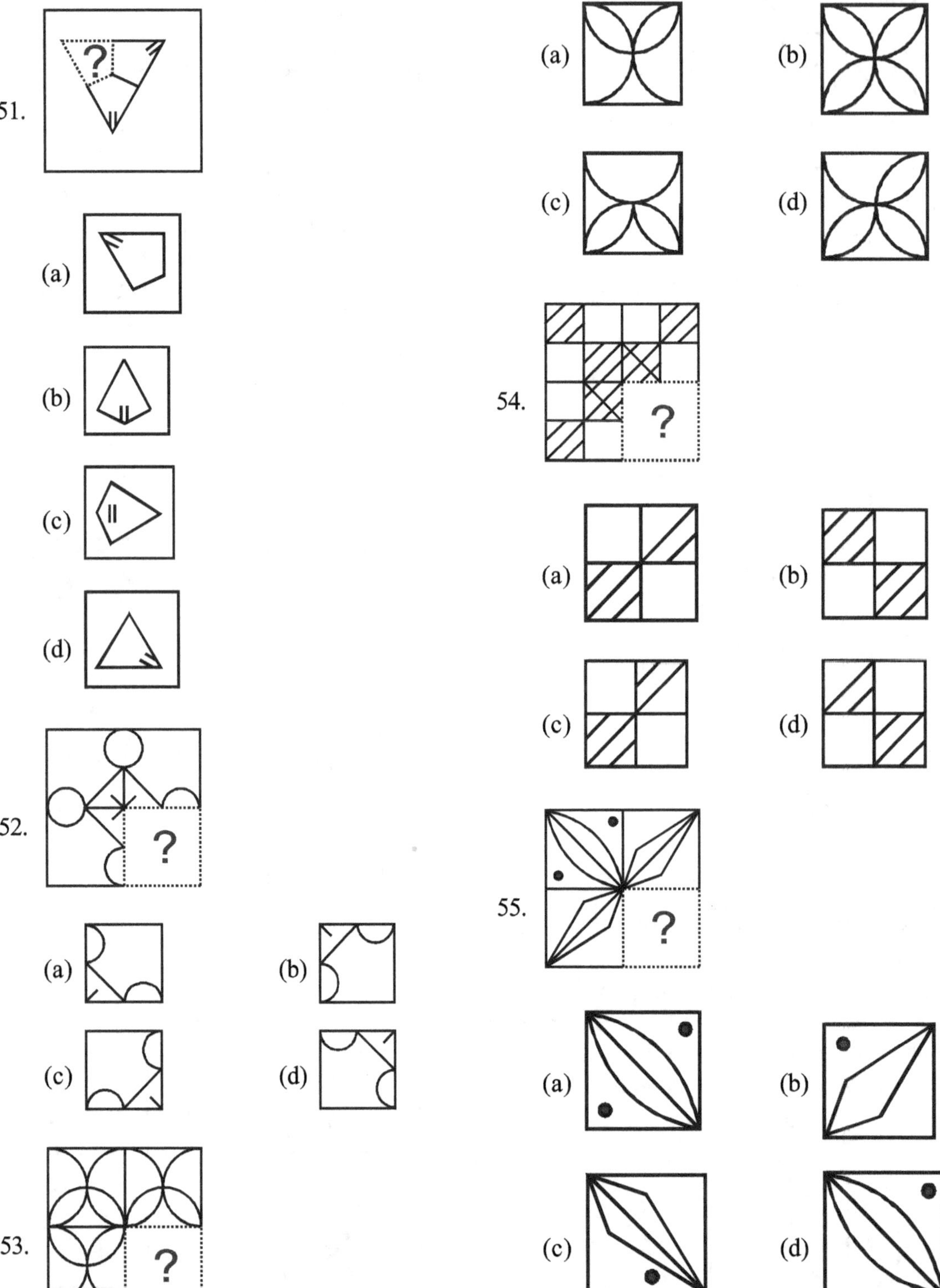
51.
?
(a)
(b)
(c)
(d)
52.
?
(a)
(b)
(c)
(d)
53.
?
(a)
(b)
(c)
(d)
54.
?
(a)
(b)
(c)
(d)
55.
?
(a)
(b)
(c)
(d)

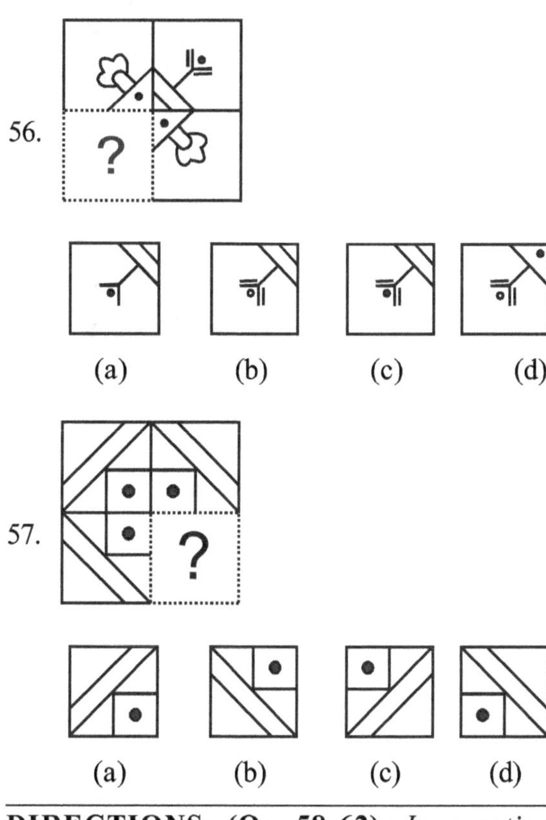

DIRECTIONS: (Qs. 58-62): *In question figure is given followed by four alternatives. Select a figure from the four alternatives, which when placed in the blank space of question figure would complete the pattern of question figure without alterting the direction of answer figure.*

58. **Question Figure**

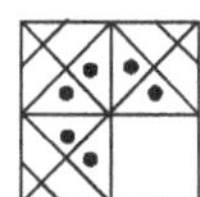

Answer Figures

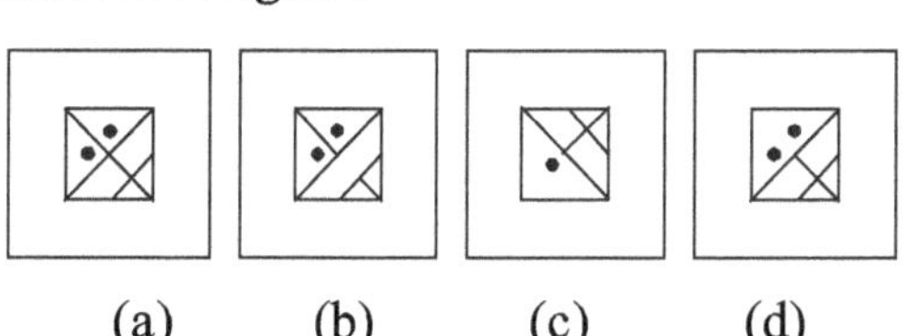

59. **Question Figure**

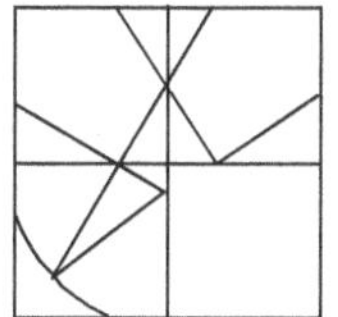

Answer Figures

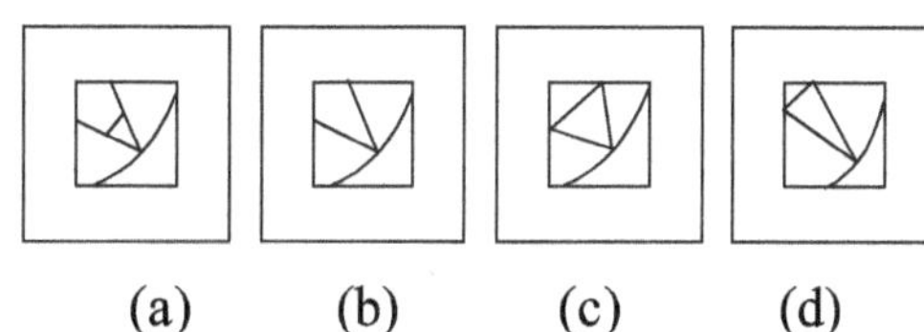

60. **Question Figure**

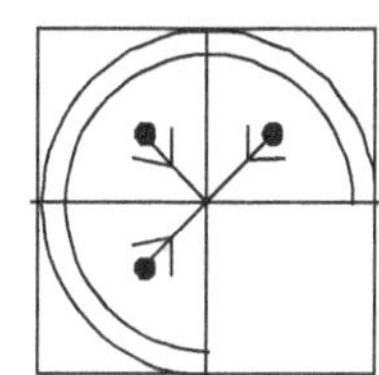

Answer Figures

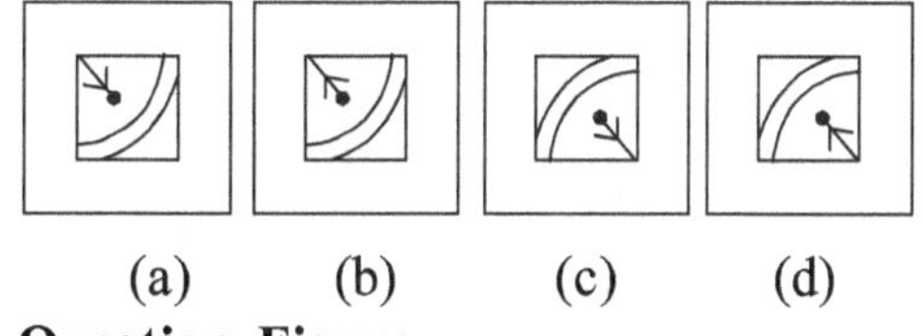

61. **Question Figure**

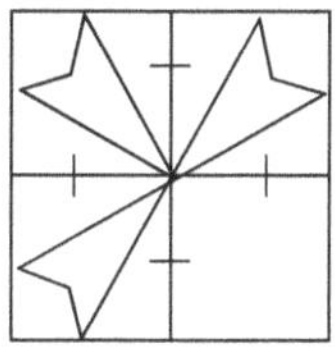

Answer Figures

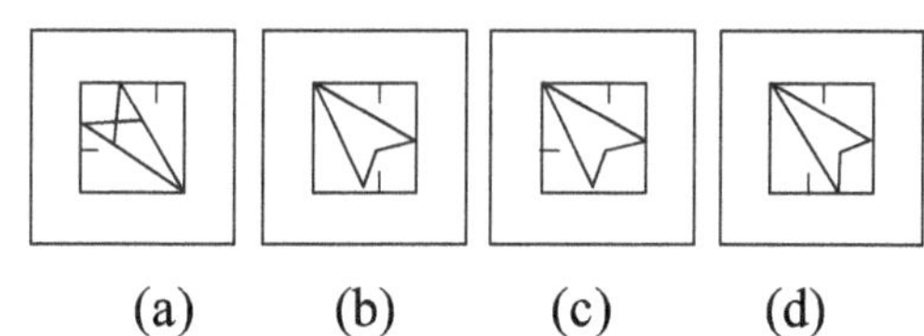

62. **Question Figure**

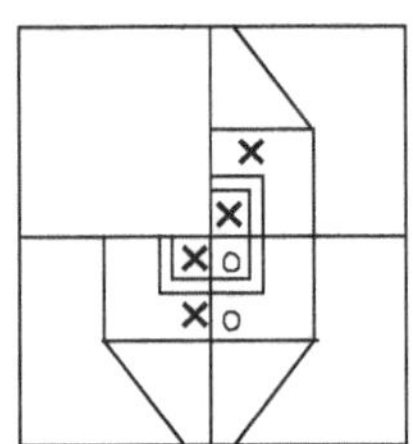

Answer Figures

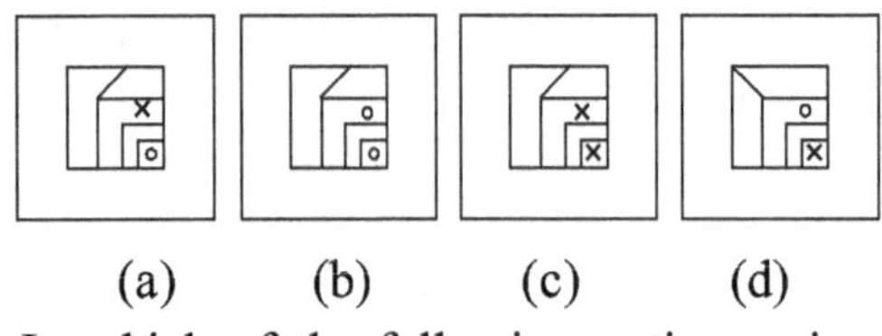

(a) (b) (c) (d)

63. In which of the following options, given figure is exactly embedded as one of its parts? **[2018]**

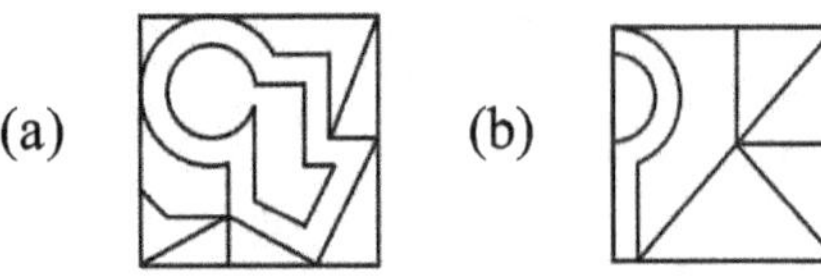

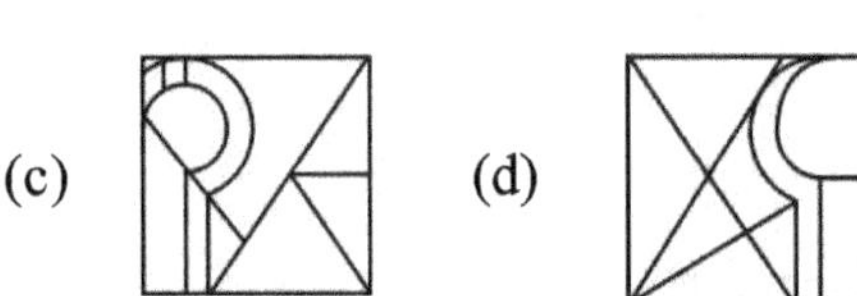

64. Select a figure from the options which will complete the pattern in the given figure. **[2018]**

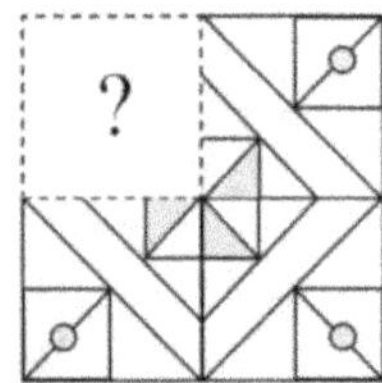

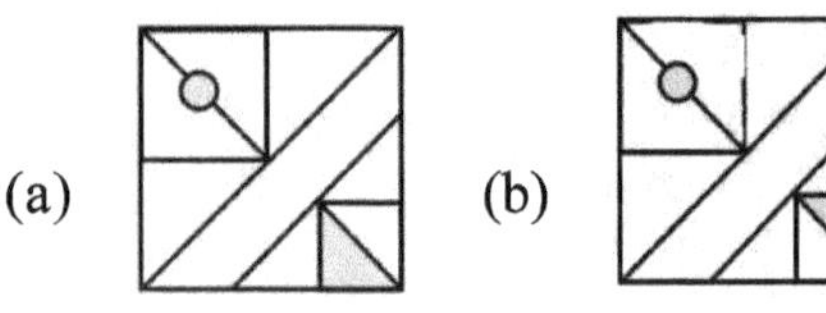

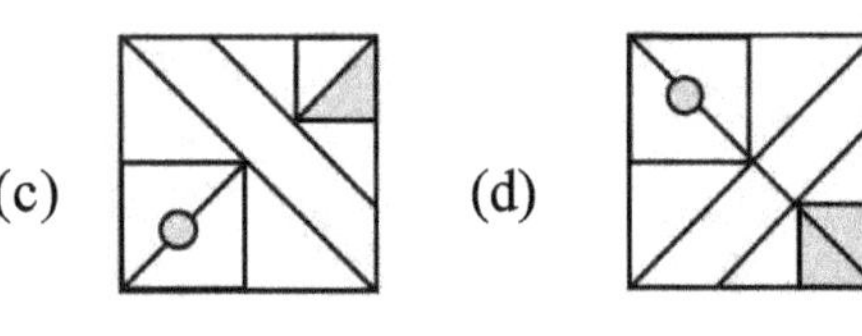

65. Select a figure from the options which when placed in the blank space of the given figure would complete the pattern. **[2019]**

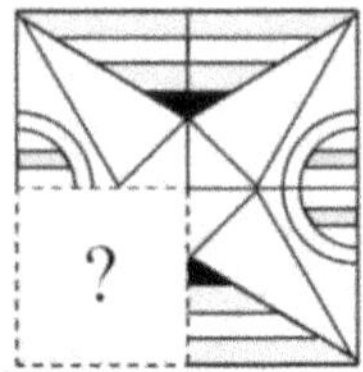

(a) 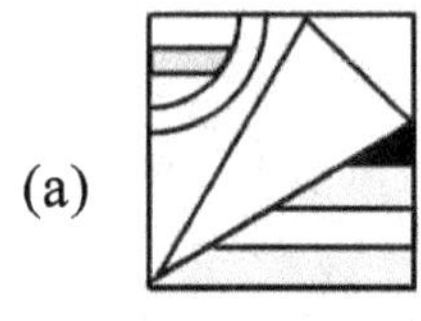

(b) 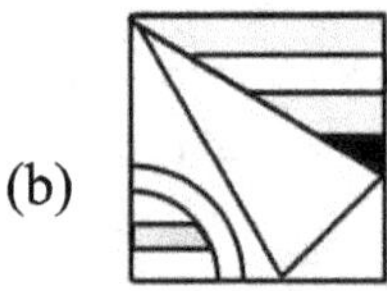

(c) 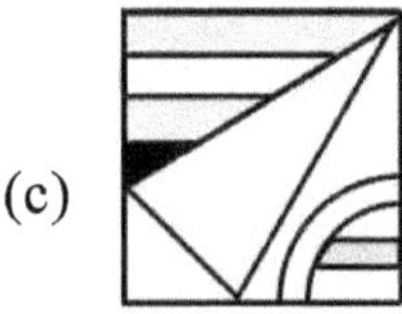

(d) 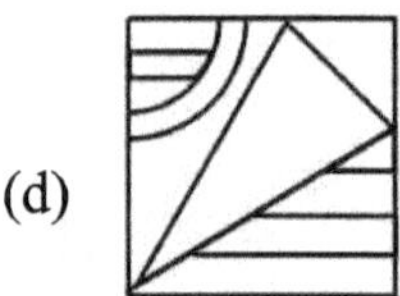

66. Select a figure from the options which is exactly embedded in the given figure as one of its parts. **[2019]**

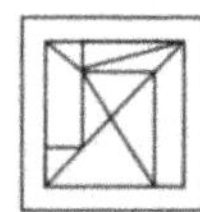

(a) 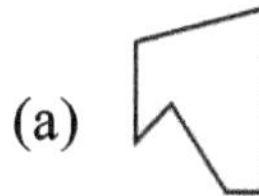 (b) 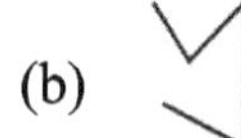

(c)  (d) 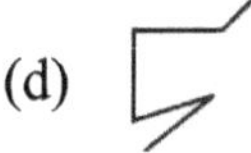

67. Which of the following figures will complete the pattern in the given figure? **[2020]**

(a)  (b) 

(c)  (d) 

68. Select a figure from the options in which the given figure is exactly embedded as one of its parts. **[2021]**

(a) 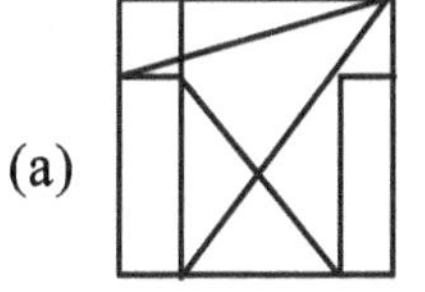 (b) 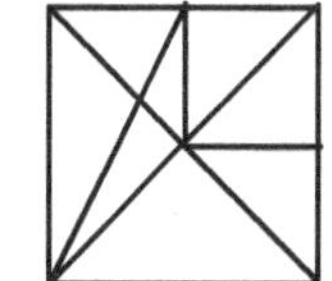

(c) 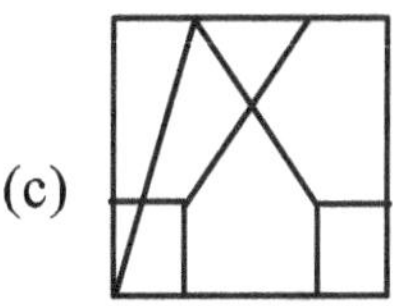 (d) 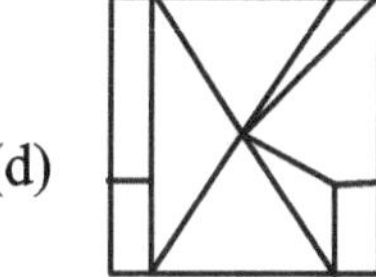

69. Select a figure from the options in which the given figure is exactly embedded as one of its parts. **[2021]**

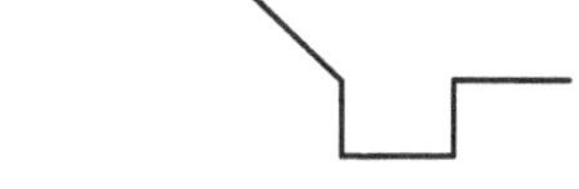

(a) 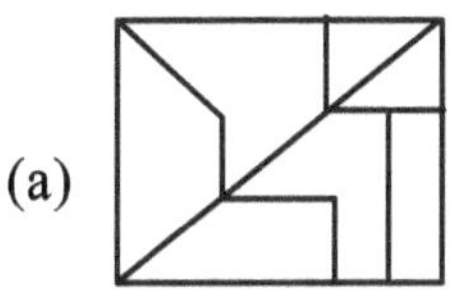 (b) 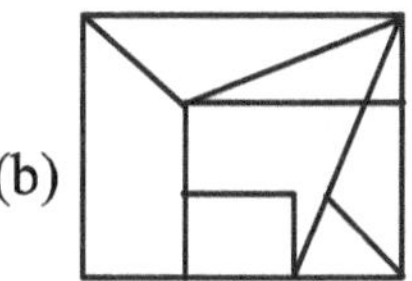

(c) 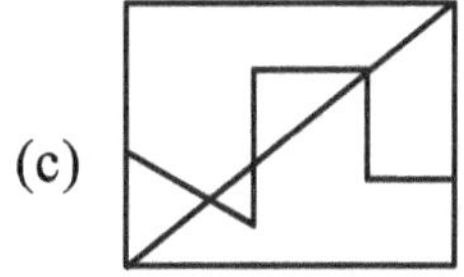 (d) 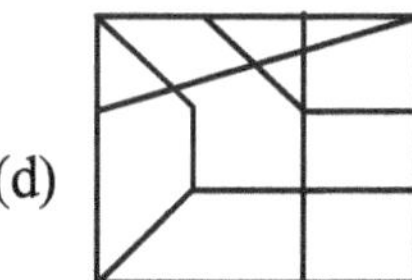

LEVEL 2

DIRECTIONS (Qs. 1-8) : *In each of the following questions, you are given a fig. (X) followed by four alternative figures (a), (b), (c) and (d) such that fig. (X) is embedded in one of them. Trace out the alternative figure which contains fig. (X) as its part.*

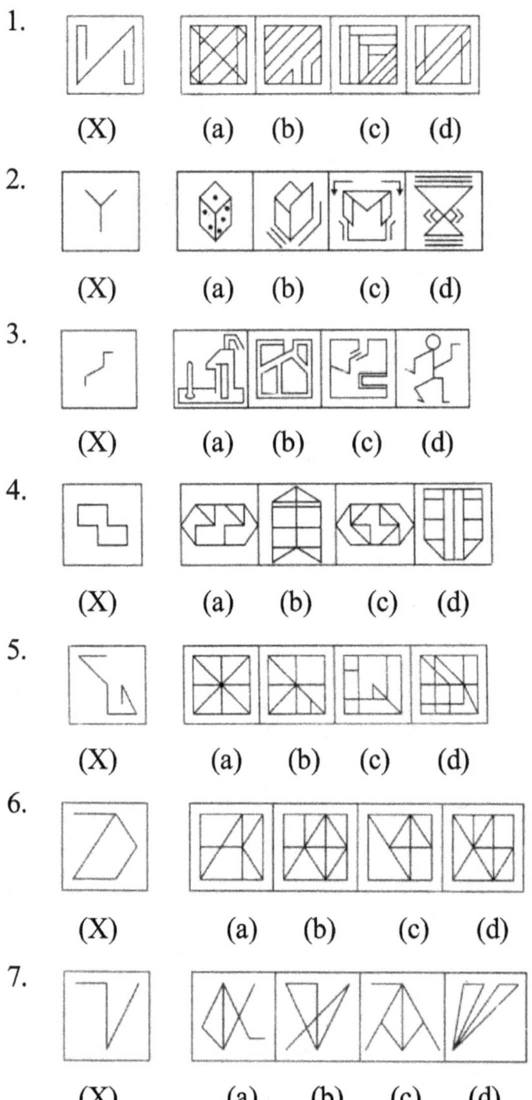

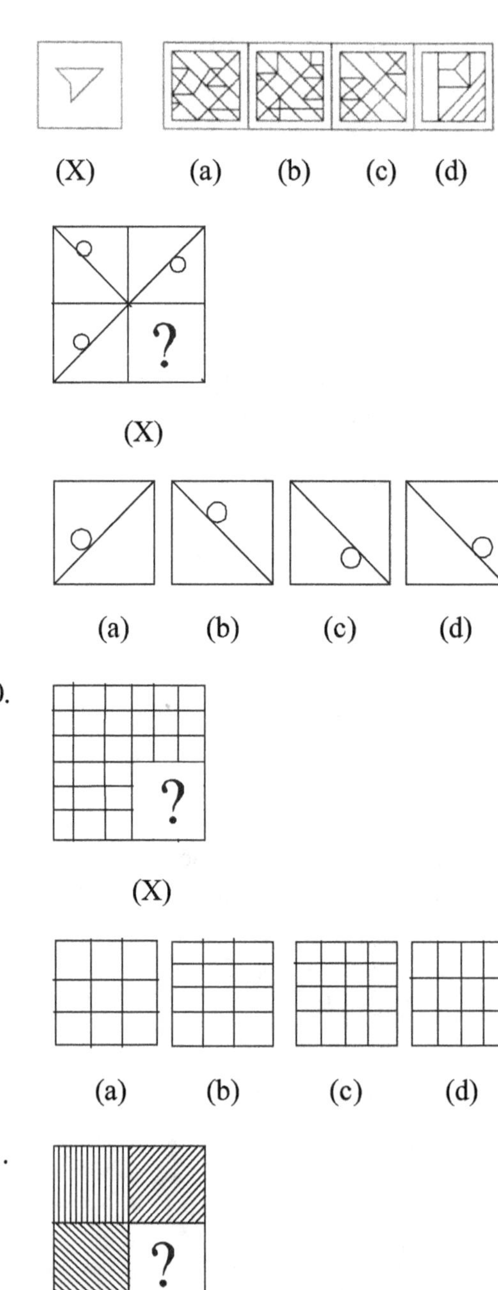

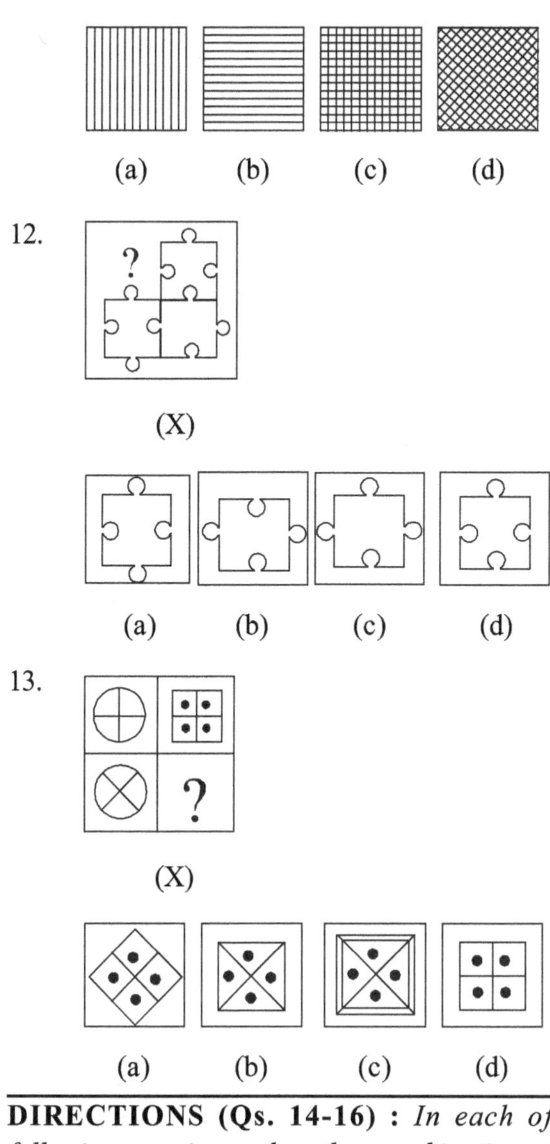

DIRECTIONS (Qs. 14-16) : *In each of following questions select that combination of parts (A), (B), (C), (D) and (E) which if fitted together will form an equilateral triangle.*

14.

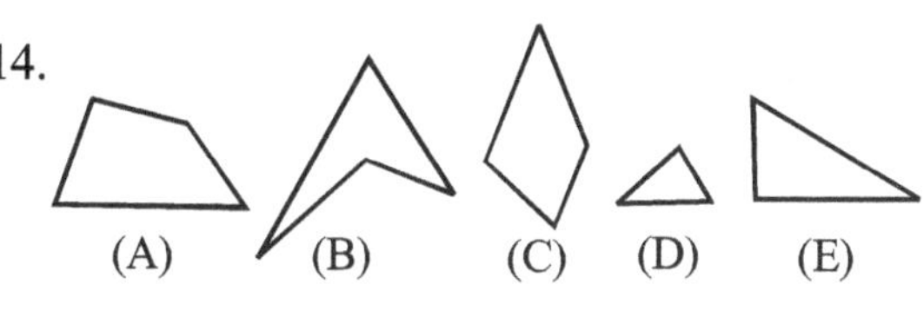

(a) ABC (b) BCD

(c) ABD (d) ABE

15.

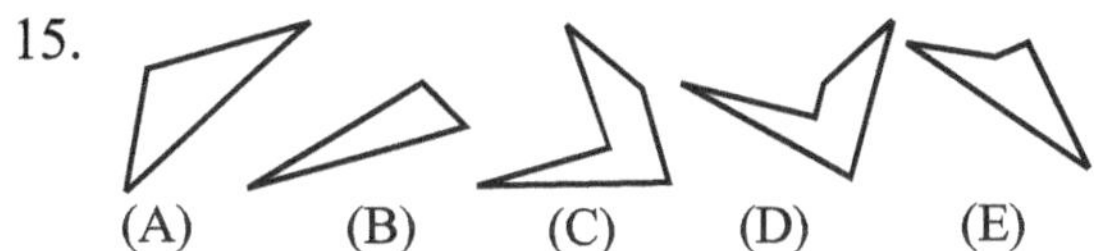

(a) ABC (b) ACE

(c) BCD (d) BDE

16.

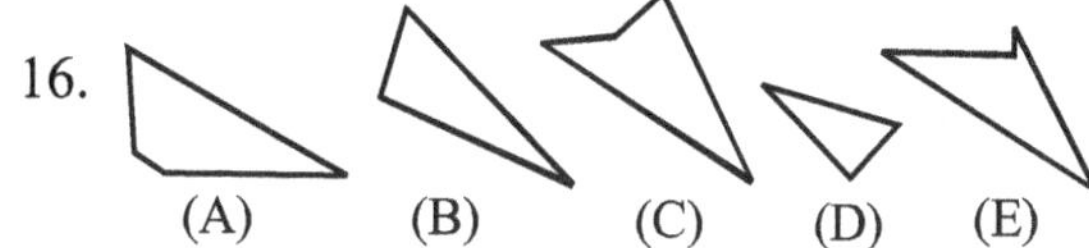

(a) ABE (b) BCE

(c) ADE (d) BDE

DIRECTIONS: *In questions 17 to 26 a problem figure is given and four answer figures, marked (a), (b), (c), (d) are given. Select the answer figure which the problem figure is hidded/embedded.*

17. 

(a) 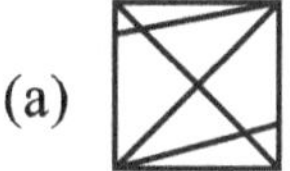 (b) 

(c)  (d) 

18. 

(a)  (b) 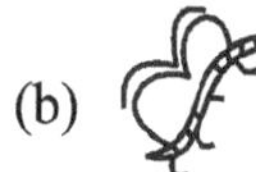

(c)  (d) 

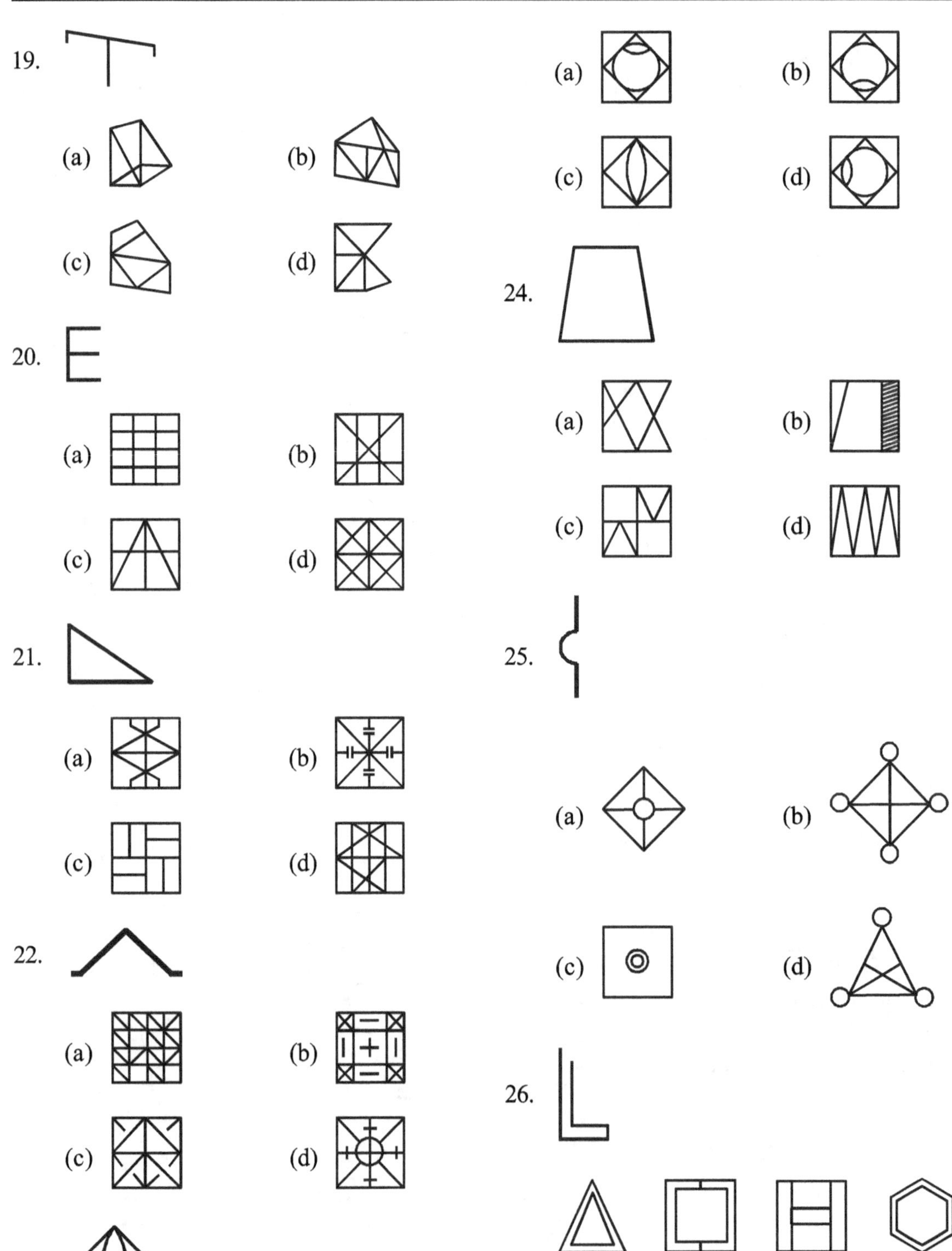
19.
(a)
(b)
(c)
(d)
20.
(a)
(b)
(c)
(d)
21.
(a)
(b)
(c)
(d)
22.
(a)
(b)
(c)
(d)
23.
(a)
(b)
(c)
(d)
24.
(a)
(b)
(c)
(d)
25.
(a)
(b)
(c)
(d)
26.
(a)
(b)
(c)
(d)

DIRECTIONS (Qs. 27-31): *Question figure is followed by four answer figures namely (a), (b), (c) and (d). Find out the correct answer figure from the given alternatives in which Question figure is hidden.*

27. **Question Figure**

Answer Figures

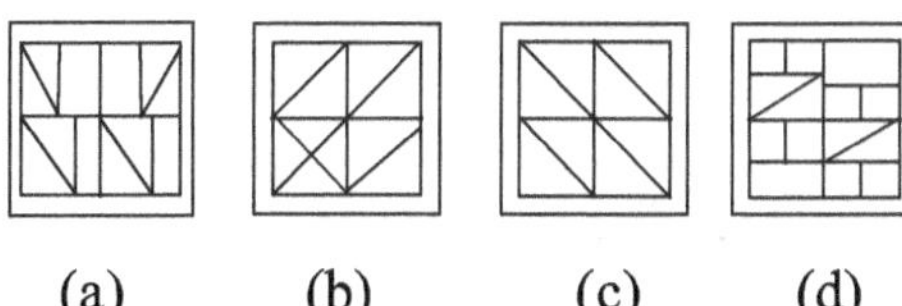

(a) (b) (c) (d)

28. **Question Figure**

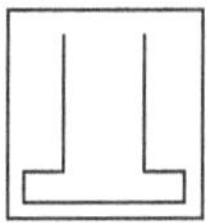

Answer Figures

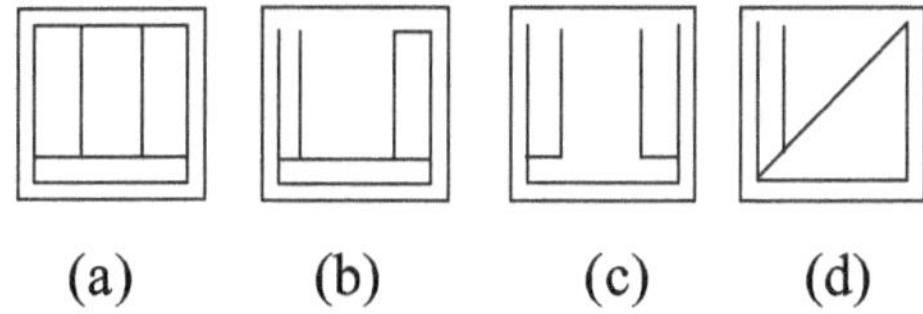

(a) (b) (c) (d)

29. **Question Figure**

Answer Figures

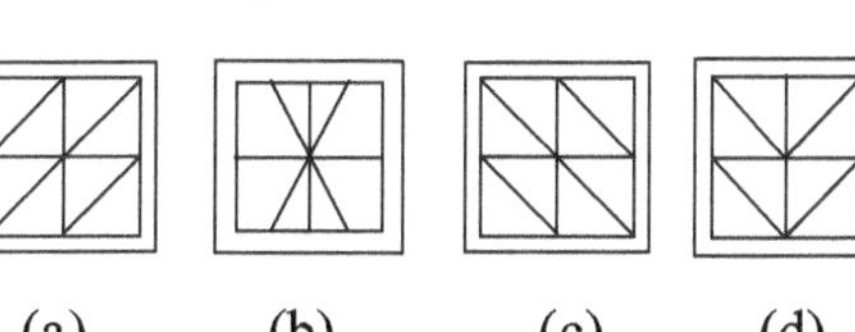

(a) (b) (c) (d)

30. **Question Figure**

Answer Figures

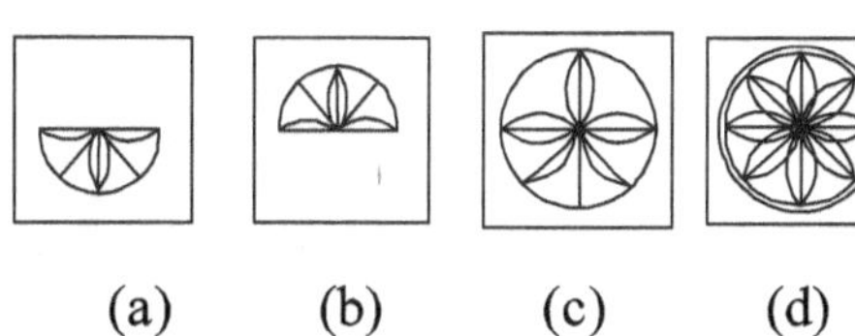

(a) (b) (c) (d)

31. **Question Figure**

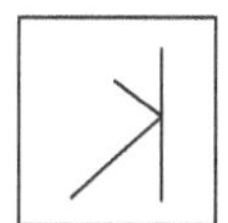

Answer Figures

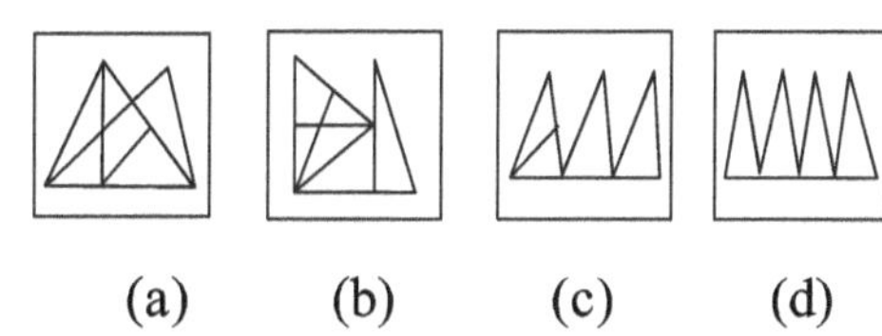

(a) (b) (c) (d)

DIRECTIONS (Qs 32-36): *Question figure is followed by four answer figures namely (a), (b), (c) and (d). Find out the correct Answer figure from the given alternatives in which question figure is hidden embedded.*

32. **Question Figure**

Answer Figures

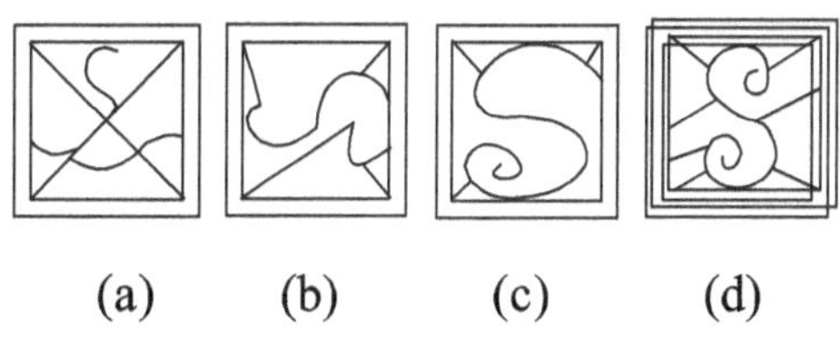

(a) (b) (c) (d)

33. **Question Figure**

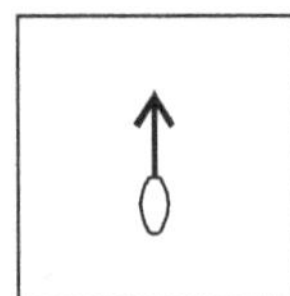

Answer Figures

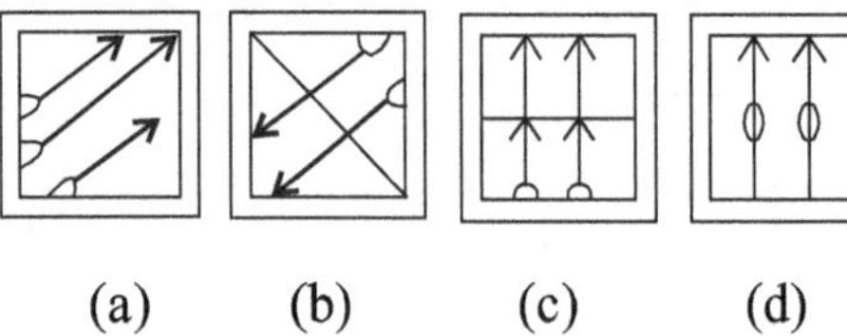

(a) (b) (c) (d)

34. **Question Figure**

Answer Figures

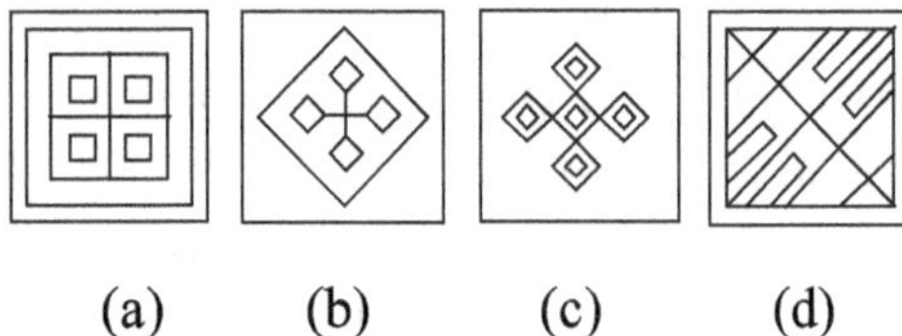

(a) (b) (c) (d)

35. **Question Figure**

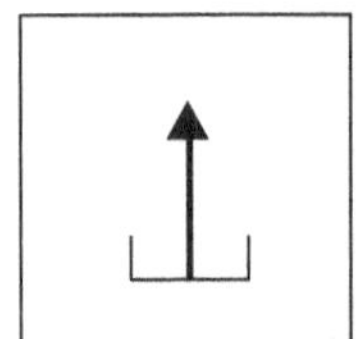

Answer Figures

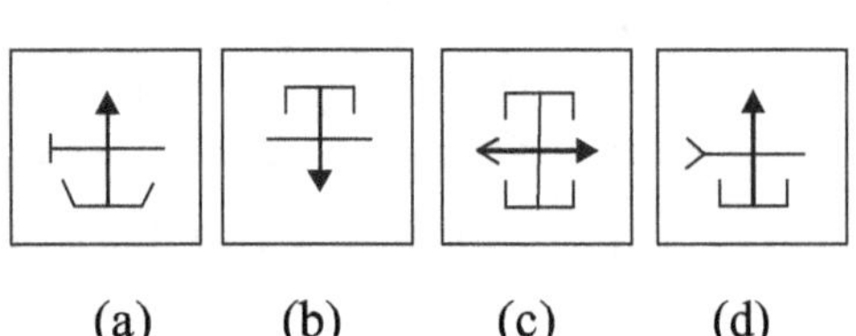

(a) (b) (c) (d)

36. **Question Figure**

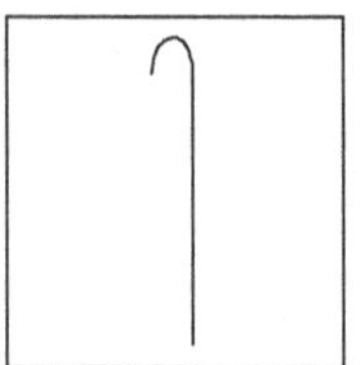

Answer Figures

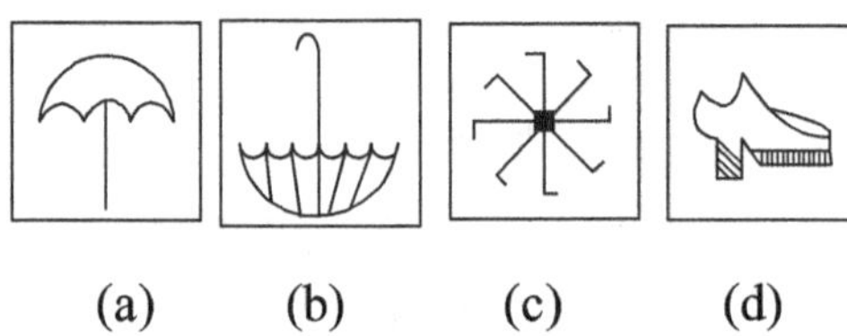

(a) (b) (c) (d)

DIRECTIONS: *In Question Nos. 37 to 40, a question figure and four answer figures, marked (a), (b), (c) and (d) are given. Select the answer figure in which the question figure is hidden/embedded.*

37. **Question Figure**

Answer Figures

(a)  (b) 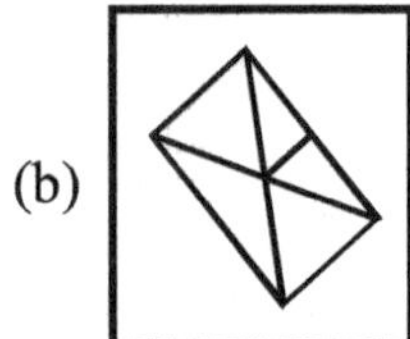

(c) 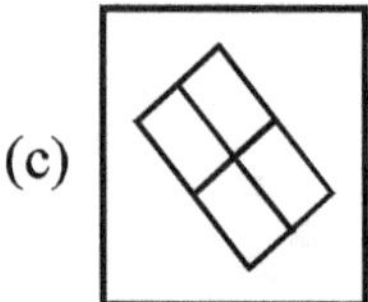 (d) 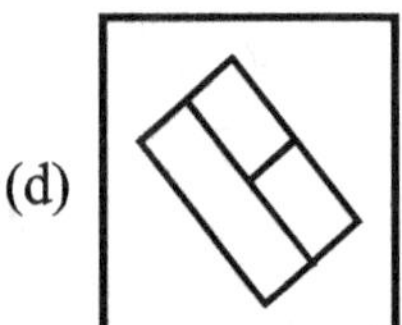

38. **Question Figure**

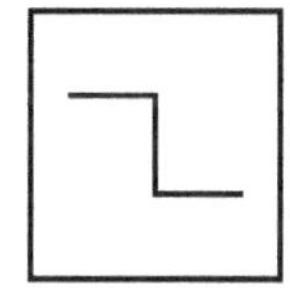

Answer Figures

(a) 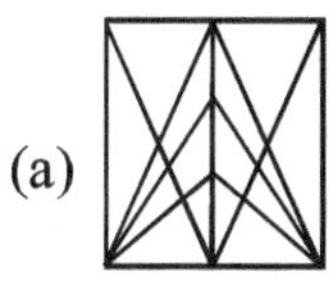 (b) 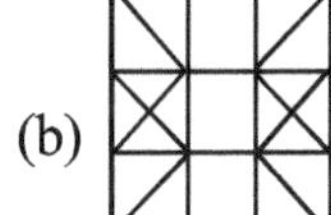

(c) 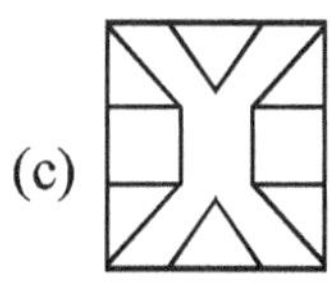 (d) 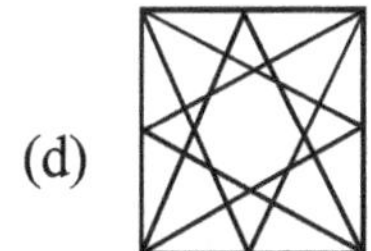

39. **Question Figure**

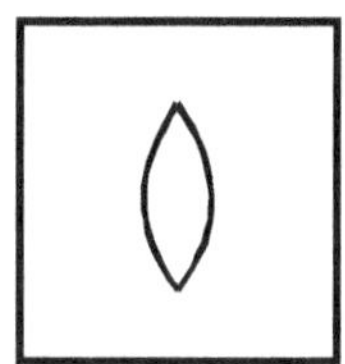

Answer Figures

(a) 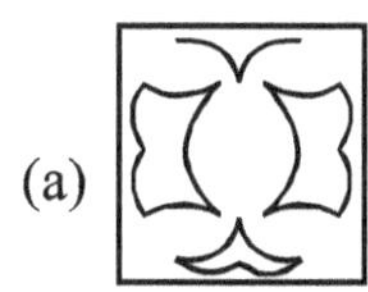 (b) 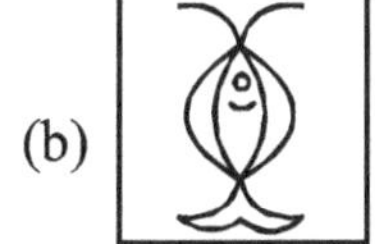

(c) 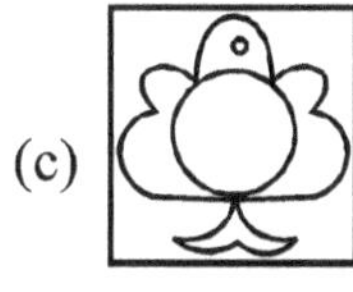 (d) 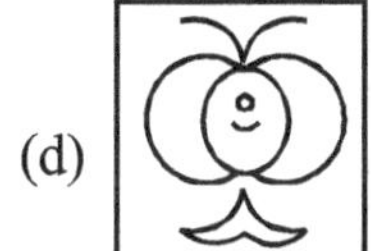

40. **Question Figure**

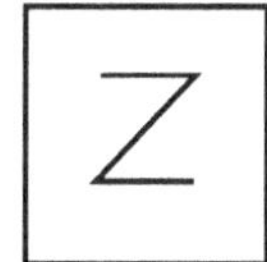

Answer Figures

(a) 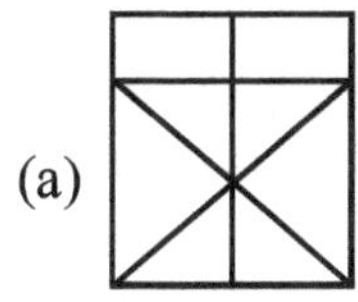 (b) 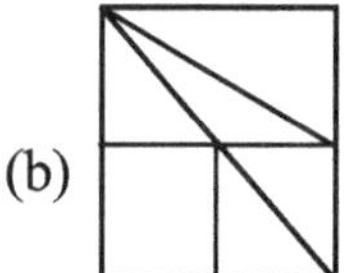

(c) 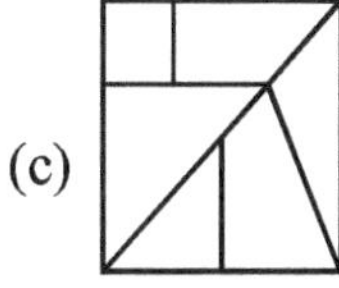 (d) 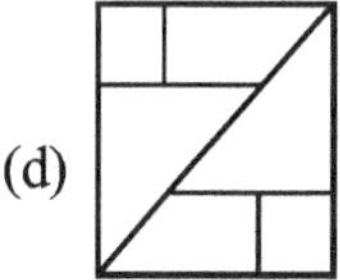

DIRECTIONS (Qs. 41 to 42) : *A question figure and four answer figures marked (a), (b), (c) and (d) are given. Select the answer figure in which the question figure is hidden/ embedded.*

41. **Question Figure**

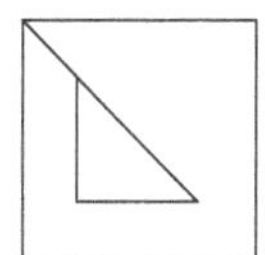

Answer Figures

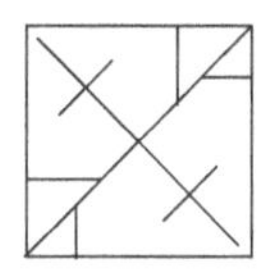 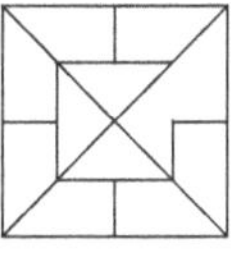 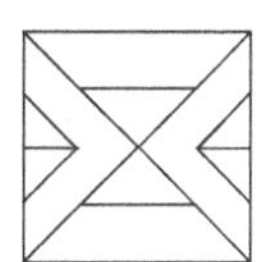 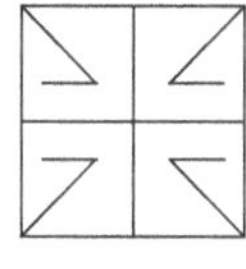

(a) (b) (c) (d)

42. **Question Figure**

Answer Figures

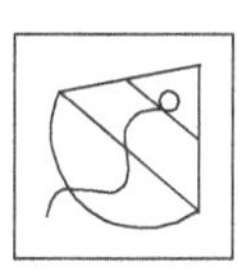 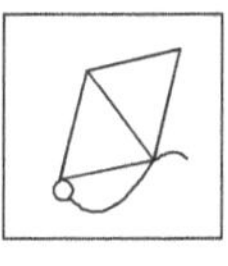 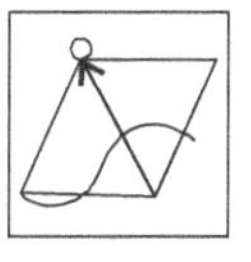 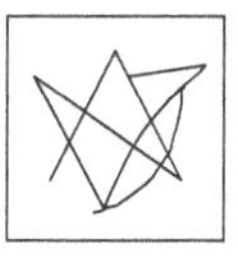

(a) (b) (c) (d)

DIRECTION : *In Question Nos. 43 to 46, a question figure along with four answer figures marked (a), (b), (c) and (d) are given. Select the answer figure in which the question figure is hidden/embedded.*

43. **Question Figure**

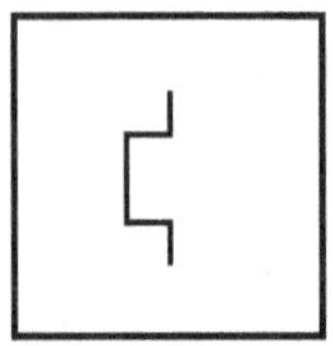

Answer Figures

(a) 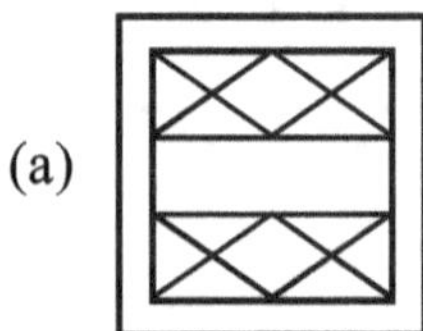

(b) 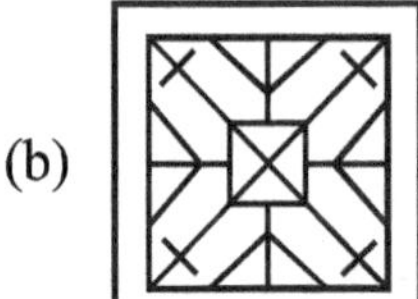

(c) 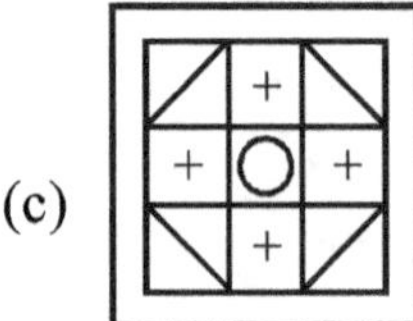

(d) 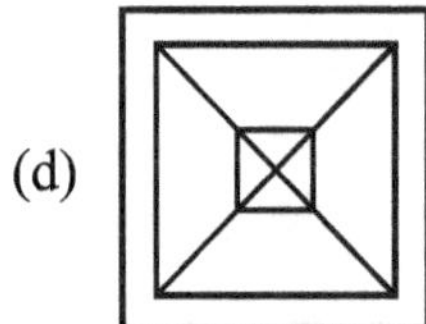

44. **Question Figures**

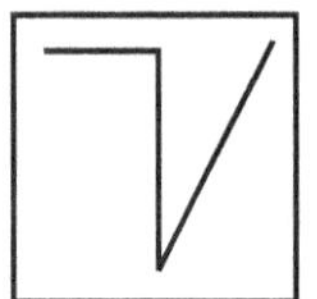

Answer Figures

(a) 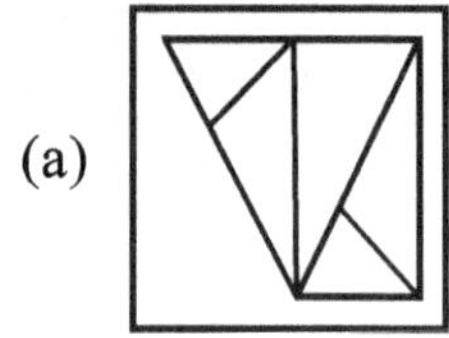

(b) 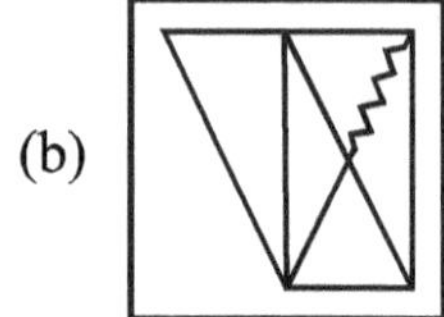

(c) 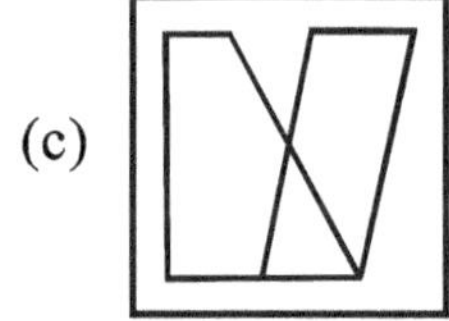

(d) 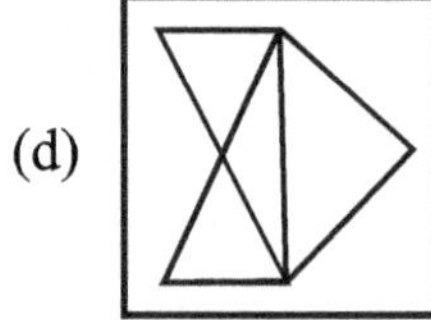

45. **Question Figure**

Answer Figures

(a) 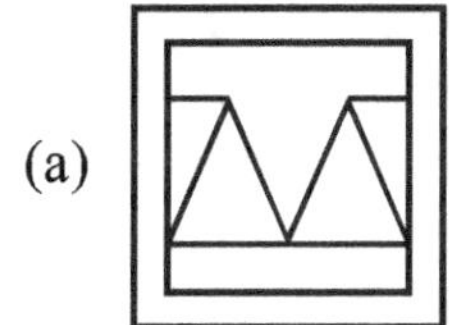

(b) 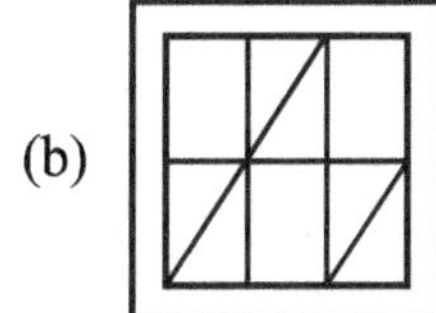

(c) 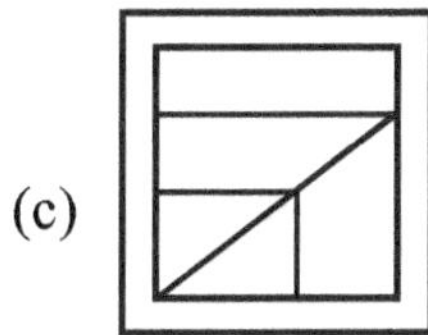

(d) 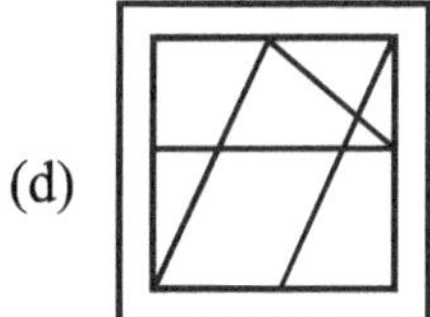

46. **Question Figure**

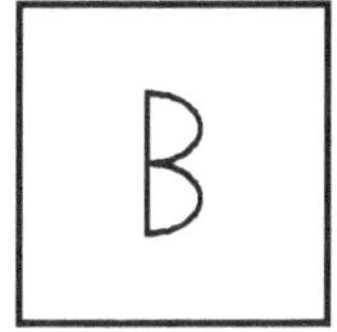

Answer Figures

(a) 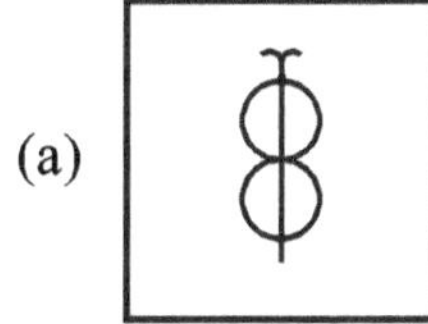

(b) 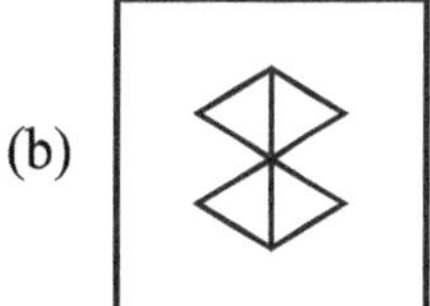

(c) 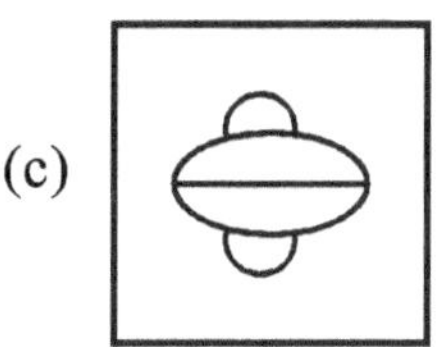

(d) 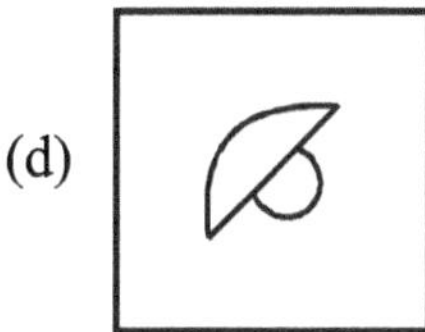

DIRECTIONS (Qs.47-50): *In each question, out of the four figures marked (a), (b), (c) and (d), three are similar in a certain manner. Howerer one figure is not like the other three. Choose the figure wchic is diffence from the rest.*

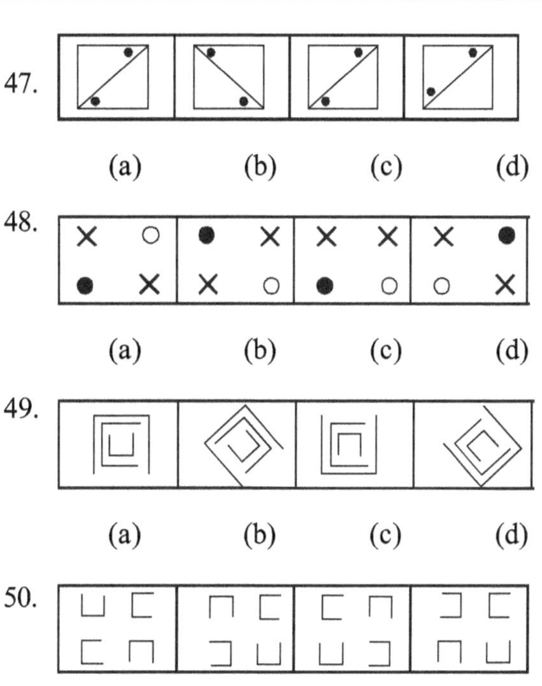

DIRECTIONS: *In questions 51 to 54, four figures (a), (b), (c), (d) have been given in each question. Of these four figures three figures are similar in some way and one figure is different. Select the figure which is different.*

51. (a) 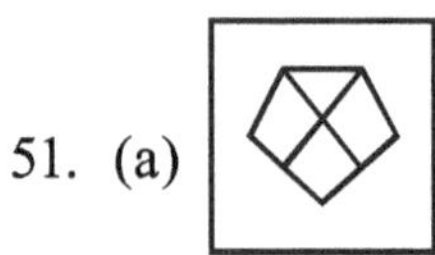

(b) 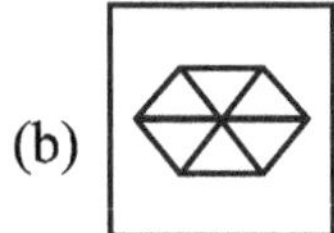

(c) 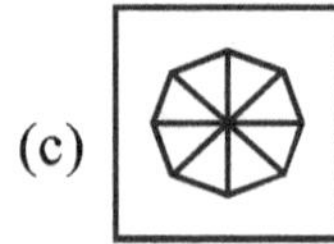

(d) 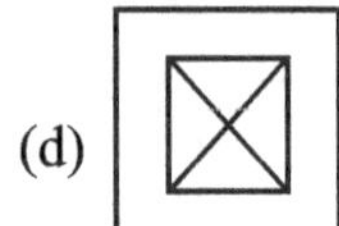

52. (a) 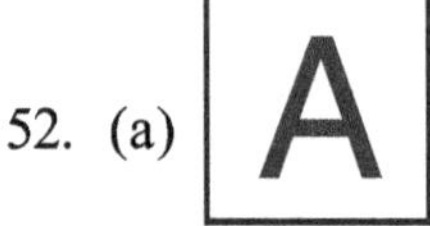

(b) 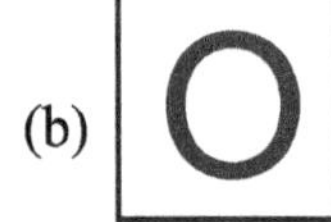

(c) 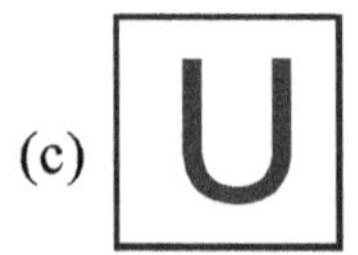

(d) 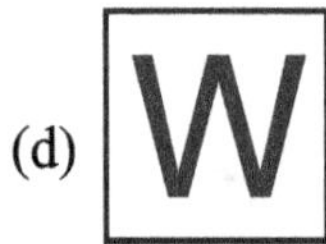

53. (a) 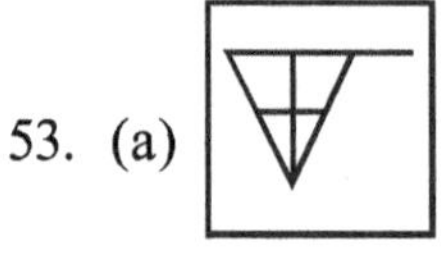

(b) 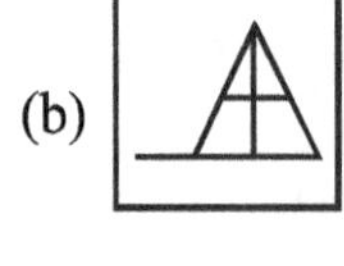

(c) 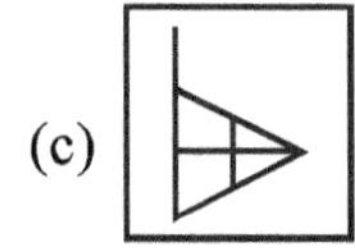

(d) 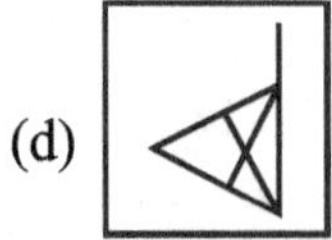

54. (a) 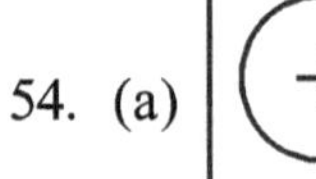 

(b) 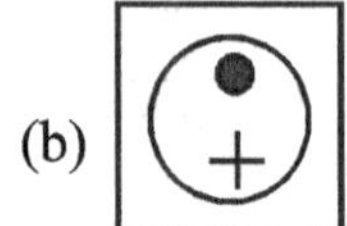

(c) 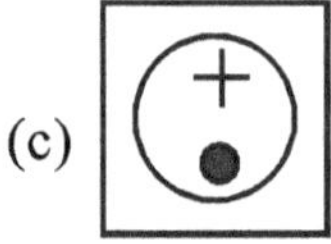

(d) 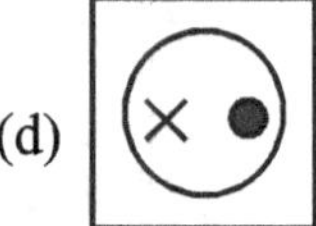

DIRECTIONS (Qs. 55-59): *Question figure is followed by four alternatives. Select a figure from the four alternatives, which when placed in the blank space of Question figure would complete the pattern of question figure without altering the direction of Answer figure.*

55. **Question Figure**

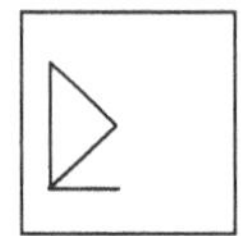

Answer Figures

 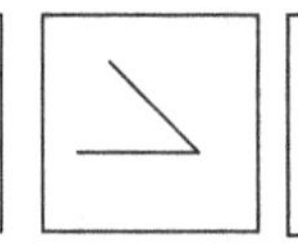 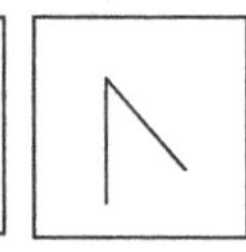

(a) (b) (c) (d)

56. **Question Figure**

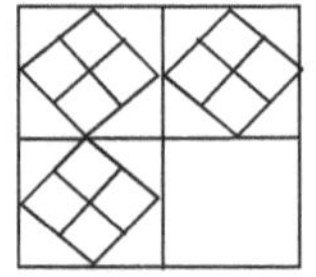

Answer Figures

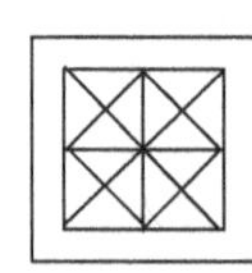 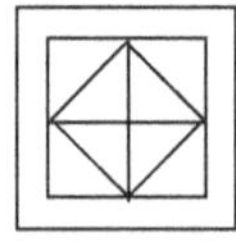 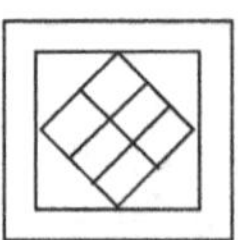 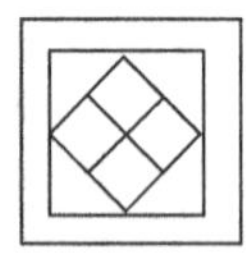

(a) (b) (c) (d)

57. **Question Figure**

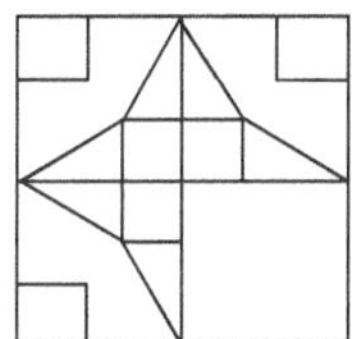

Answer Figures

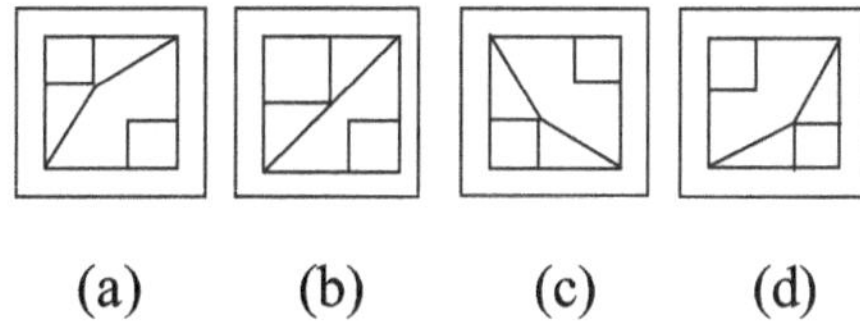

(a) (b) (c) (d)

58. **Question Figure**

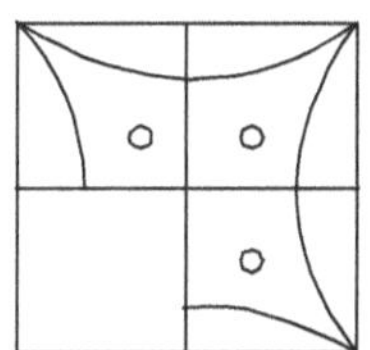

Answer Figures

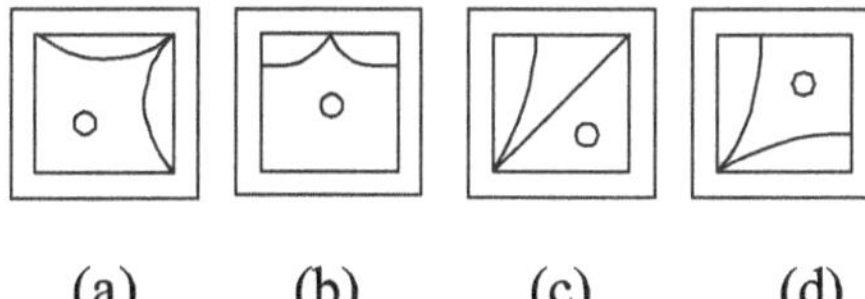

(a) (b) (c) (d)

59. **Question Figure**

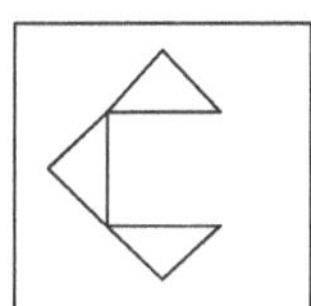

Answer Figures

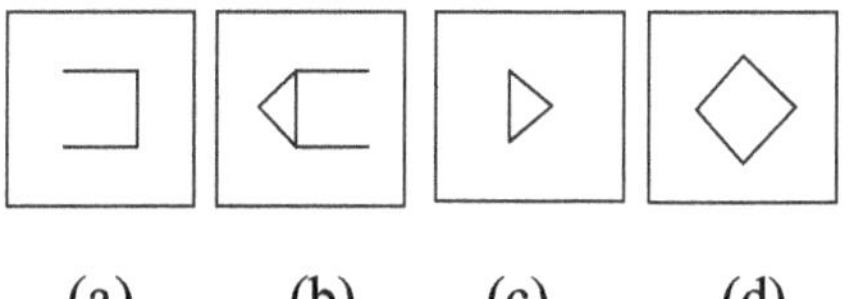

(a) (b) (c) (d)

DIRECTIONS: *In Question Nos. 60 to 63, there is a question figure, a part of which is missing. Observe the answer figures (a), (b), (c) and (d) and find out the answer figure which without changing the direction, fits in the missing part of the question figure in order to complete pattern in the question figure.*

60. **Question Figure**

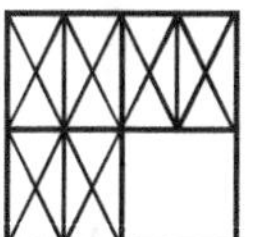

Answer Figures

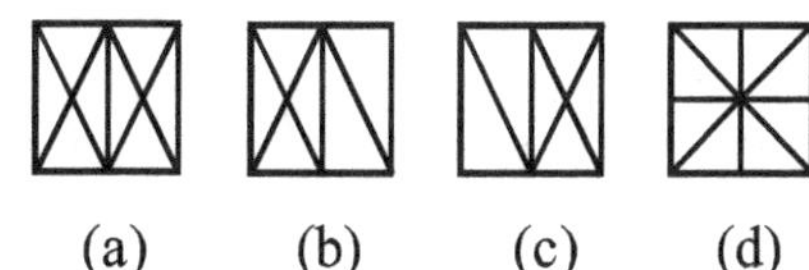

(a) (b) (c) (d)

61. **Question Figure**

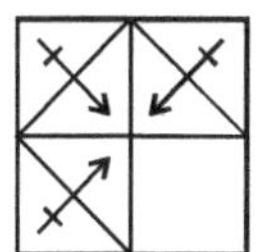

Answer Figures

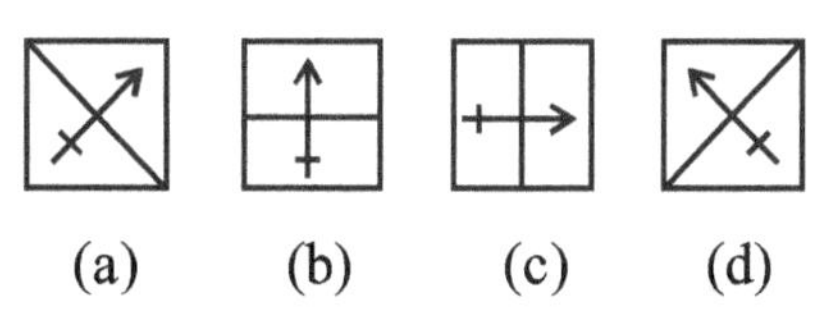

(a) (b) (c) (d)

62. **Question Figure**

Answer Figures

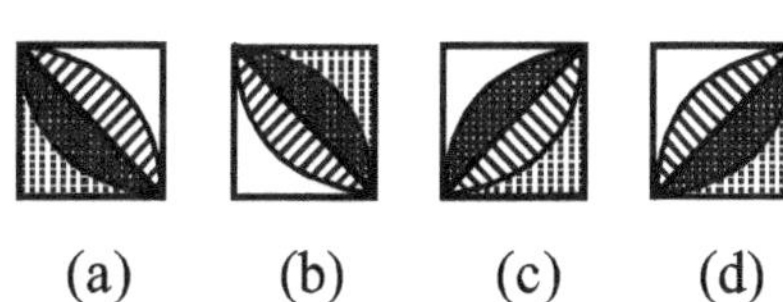

(a) (b) (c) (d)

63. **Question Figure**

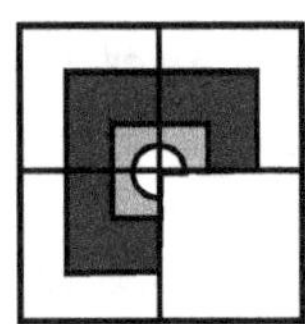

Answer Figures

 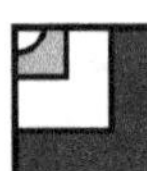 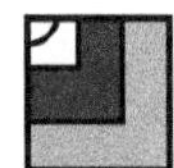 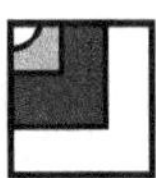

(a) (b) (c) (d)

DIRECTIONS (Qs. 64 to 65) : *There is a question figure, a part of which missing. Observe the answer figures (a), (b), (c) and (d) and find out the answer figure which, without changing the direction, fits in the missing part of the question figure in order to completer the pattern in the question figure.*

64. **Questions Figure**

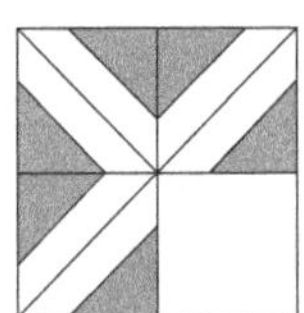

Answer Figures

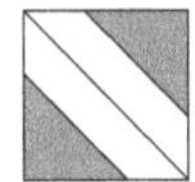 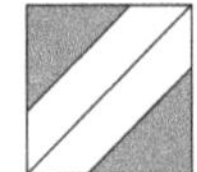 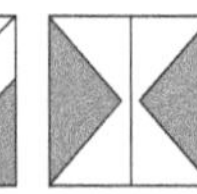 

(a) (b) (c) (d)

65. **Questions Figure**

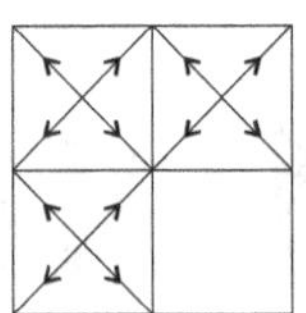

Answer Figures

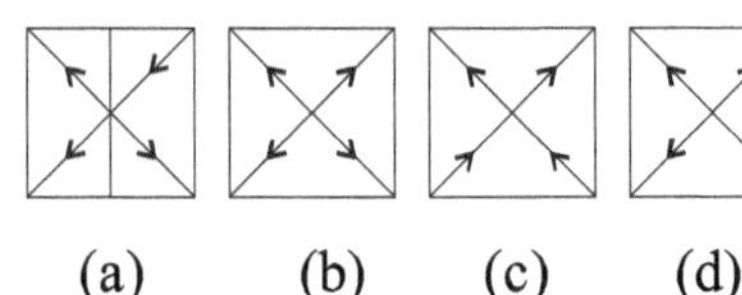

(a) (b) (c) (d)

DIRECTIONS (Qs. 66-69) : *There is a question figure, a part of which is missing. Observe the answer figures (a), (b), (c) and (d) and find out the answer figure which,* ***without changing the direction****, fits in the missing part of the question figure in order to complete the pattern in the question figure.*

66. **Question Figure**

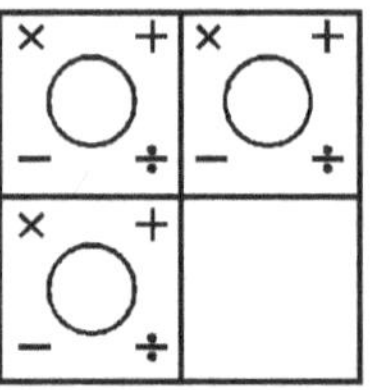

Answer Figures

(a) 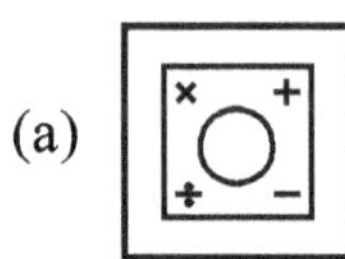

(b) 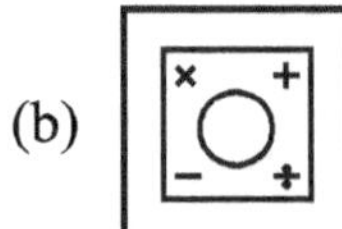

(c) 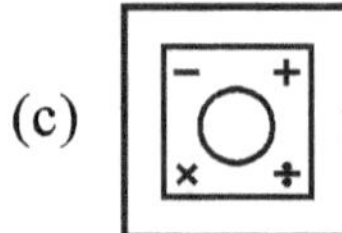

(d) 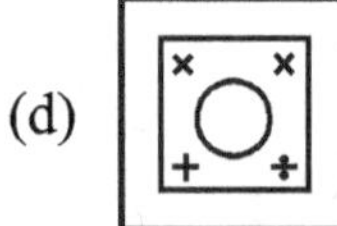

67. **Question Figure**

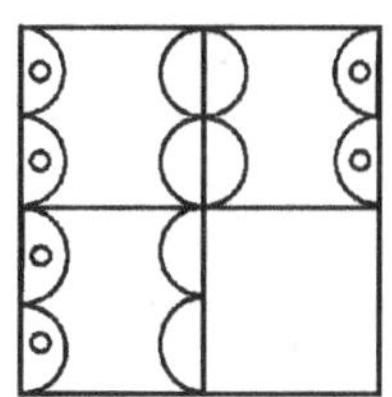

Answer Figures

(a) 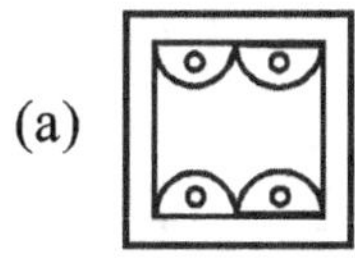

(b) 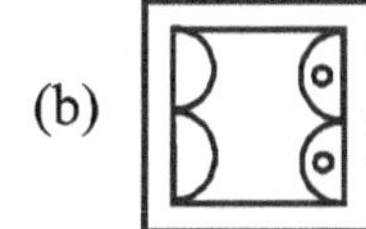

(c) 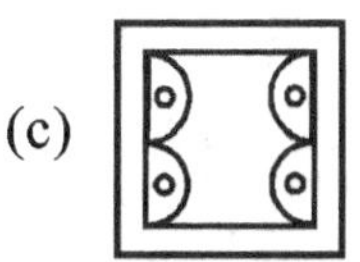

(d) 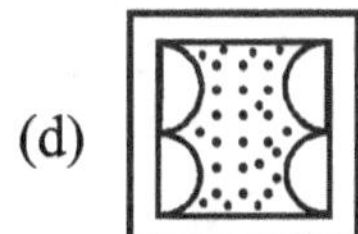

68. **Question Figure**

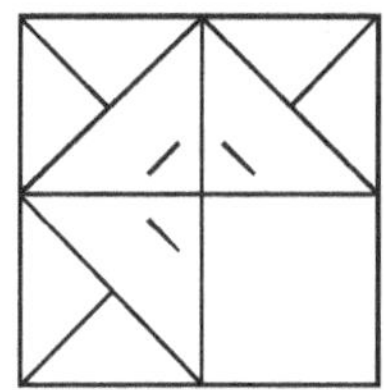

Answer Figures

(a) 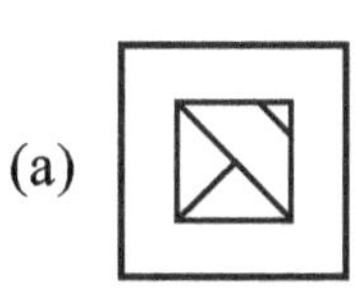

(b) 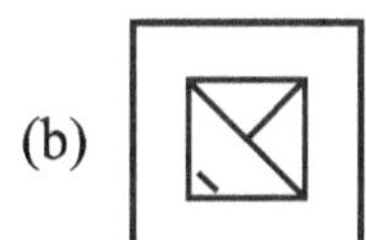

(c) 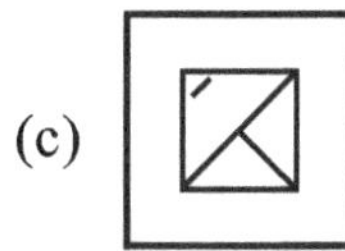

(d) 

69. **Question Figure**

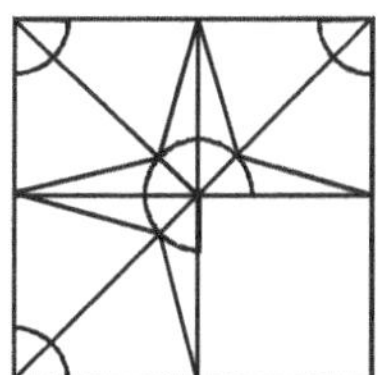

Answer Figures

(a) 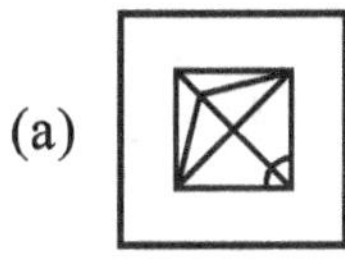

(b) 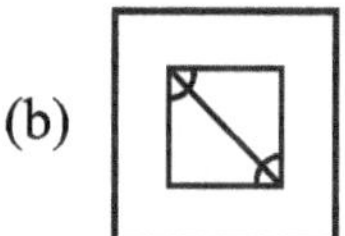

(c) 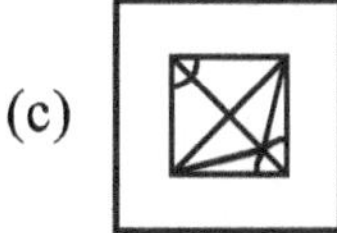

(d) 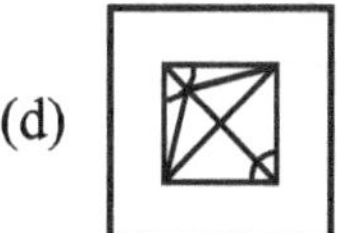

70. Select a figure from the options which is exactly embedded in the given figure as one of its parts.

[2019]

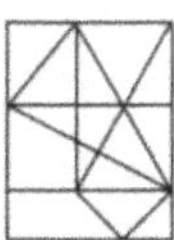

(a) 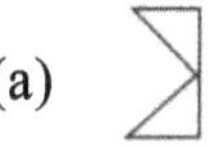

(b) 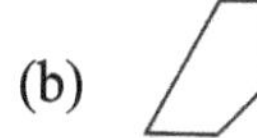

(c) 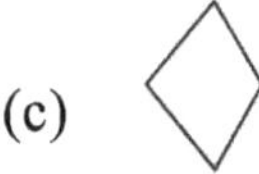

(d) 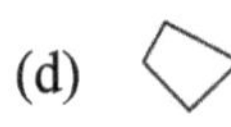

71. In which of the following figures, the given figure is exactly embedded as one of its parts? **[2020]**

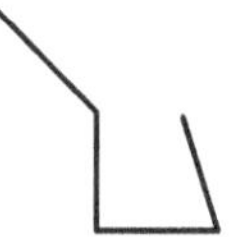

(a) 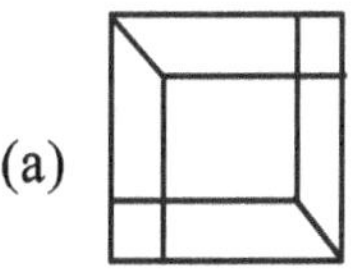

(b) 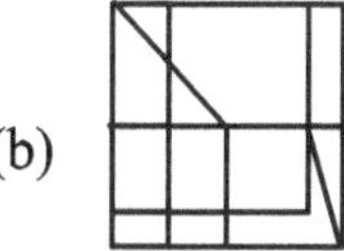

(c) 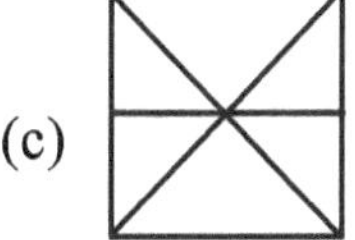

(d) 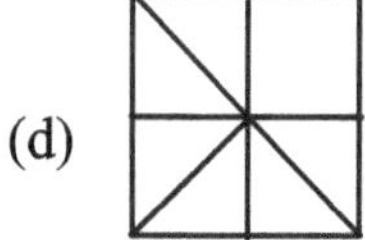

ANSWER KEY																			
LEVEL-1																			
1	(c)	**8**	(c)	**15**	(b)	**22**	(a)	**29**	(b)	**36**	(a)	**43**	(c)	**50**	(b)	**57**	(c)	**64**	(b)
2	(d)	**9**	(b)	**16**	(b)	**23**	(d)	**30**	(a)	**37**	(b)	**44**	(d)	**51**	(a)	**58**	(a)	**65**	(a)
3	(b)	**10**	(a)	**17**	(a)	**24**	(c)	**31**	(a)	**38**	(a)	**45**	(c)	**52**	(b)	**59**	(d)	**66**	(a)
4	(c)	**11**	(c)	**18**	(d)	**25**	(a)	**32**	(a)	**39**	(b)	**46**	(b)	**53**	(a)	**60**	(b)	**67**	(c)
5	(a)	**12**	(c)	**19**	(b)	**26**	(a)	**33**	(d)	**40**	(a)	**47**	(b)	**54**	(b)	**61**	(c)	**68**	(d)
6	(d)	**13**	(c)	**20**	(c)	**27**	(a)	**34**	(d)	**41**	(c)	**48**	(c)	**55**	(a)	**62**	(b)	**69**	(d)
7	(d)	**14**	(a)	**21**	(a)	**28**	(c)	**35**	(b)	**42**	(b)	**49**	(a)	**56**	(c)	**63**	(c)		
LEVEL-2																			
1	(d)	**9**	(c)	**17**	(a)	**25**	(a)	**33**	(d)	**41**	(b)	**49**	(a)	**57**	(a)	**65**	(b)		
2	(a)	**10**	(a)	**18**	(b)	**26**	(b)	**34**	(c)	**42**	(a)	**50**	(a)	**58**	(d)	**66**	(b)		
3	(d)	**11**	(b)	**19**	(b)	**27**	(b)	**35**	(b)	**43**	(b)	**51**	(a)	**59**	(c)	**67**	(b)		
4	(c)	**12**	(b)	**20**	(a)	**28**	(c)	**36**	(b)	**44**	(a)	**52**	(d)	**60**	(a)	**68**	(c)		
5	(d)	**13**	(b)	**21**	(d)	**29**	(b)	**37**	(c)	**45**	(a)	**53**	(d)	**61**	(d)	**69**	(d)		
6	(b)	**14**	(b)	**22**	(a)	**30**	(c)	**38**	(b)	**46**	(a)	**54**	(d)	**62**	(c)	**70**	(d)		
7	(b)	**15**	(d)	**23**	(c)	**31**	(b)	**39**	(b)	**47**	(d)	**55**	(b)	**63**	(d)	**71**	(b)		
8	(a)	**16**	(c)	**24**	(d)	**32**	(d)	**40**	(d)	**48**	(c)	**56**	(d)	**64**	(a)				

CHAPTER 14

Figure Matrix

In such type of problems, a 2×2 or 3×3 grid is given. Each cell of this grid has some design or symbols, on the basis of some specific rule. But a cell of the grid is left empty. A student is required to fill up the cell. For it one needs to analyse the grid and identify the rule along row-wise or column-wise in the grid.

EXAMPLE

Find out which figure in given option completes the figure matrix.

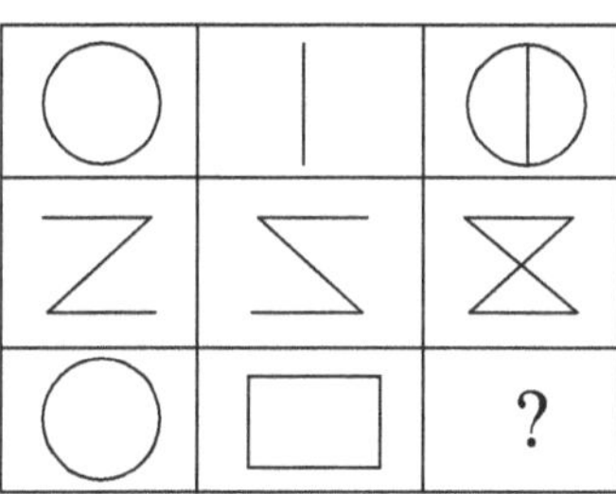

(a) 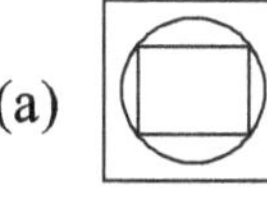 (b) 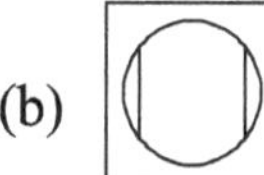

(c) 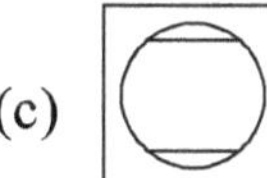 (d) 

Sol. **(a)** In each row, the third figure is the combination of the first and second figure.

LEVEL 1

1. Select a suitable figure from the four alternatives that would complete the figure matrix.

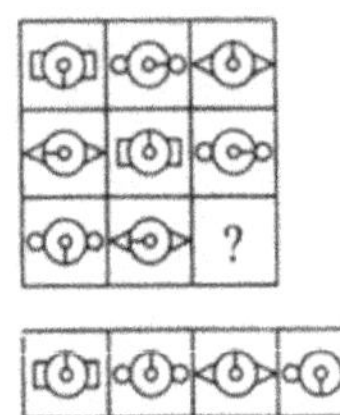

(a) (b) (c) (4)

(a) 1 (b) 2

(c) 3 (d) 4

2. Select a suitable figure from the four alternatives that would complete the figure matrix.

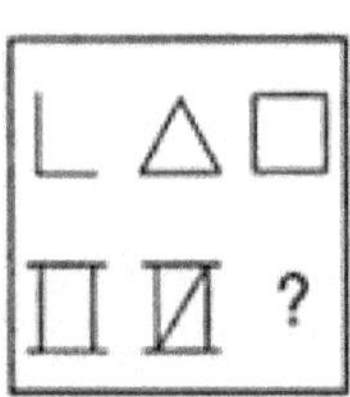

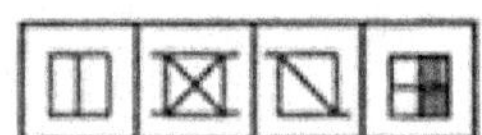

(a) (b) (c) (4)

(a) 1 (b) 4

(c) 3 (d) 2

3. Find out which of the answer figures (a), (b), (c), and (d) completes the figure matrix?

(a) (b) (c) (4)

(a) 1 (b) 2

(c) 3 (d) 4

4. Find out which of the answer figures (a), (b), (c), and (d) completes the figure matrix?

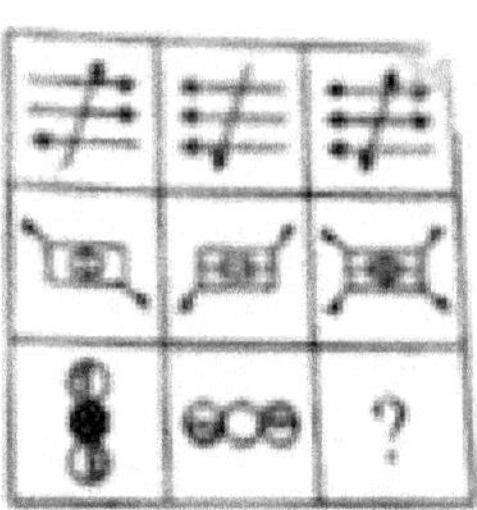

(a) (b) (c) (4)

(a) 1 (b) 2

(c) 3 (d) 4

5. In the following question, find out which of the answer figures (a), (b), (c) and (d) completes the figure matrix?

Problem Figures **Answer Figures**

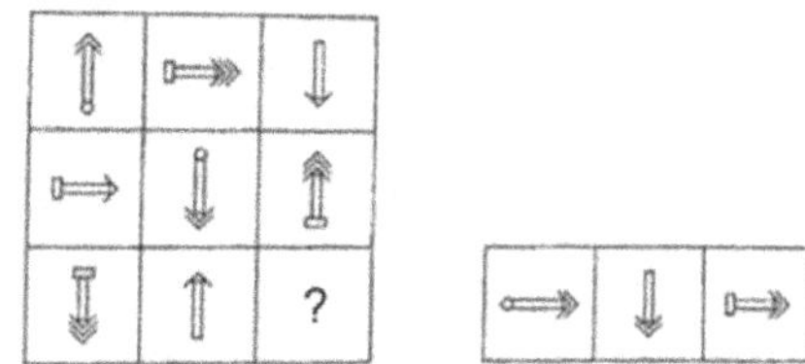

(a) (b) (c) (d)

(a) 2 (b) 1

(c) 4 (d) 3

6. In the following question, find out which of the answer figures (a), (b), (c), (d) and (e) completes the figure matrix?

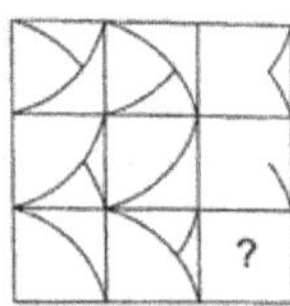

(a) (b) (c) (d) (e)

(a) 2 (b) 3

(c) 4 (d) 1

7. In the following questions, find out which of the answer figures (a), (b), (c), (d) and (e) completes the figure matrix?

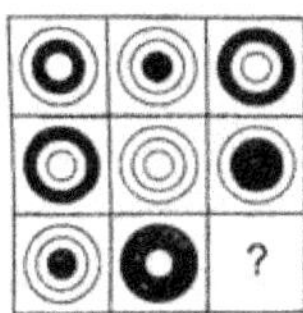

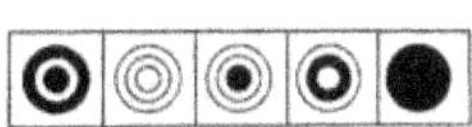

(a) (b) (c) (d) (e)

(a) 2 (b) 3

(c) 4 (d) 1

8. In the following question, find out which of the answer figures (a), (b), (c), and (d) completes the figure matrix?

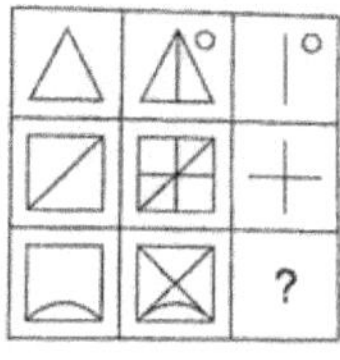

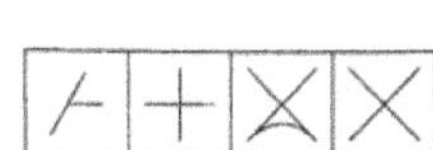

(a) (b) (c) (d)

(a) 2 (b) 3

(c) 1 (d) 4

9. Select a suitable figure from the four alternatives that would complete the figure matrix.

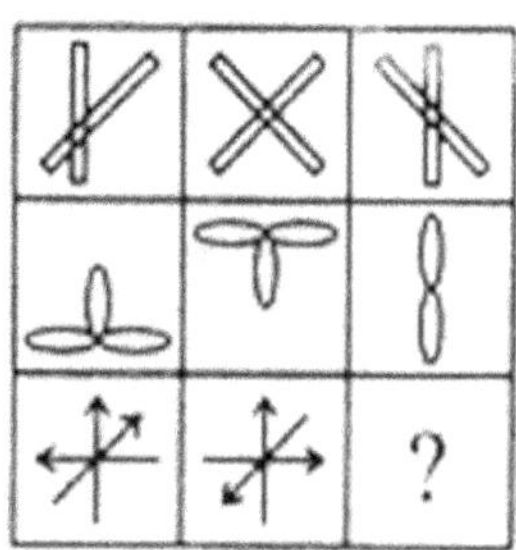

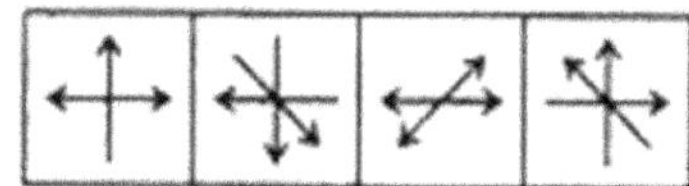

(a) (b) (c) (d)

(a) 1 (b) 2

(c) 3 (d) 4

10. Select a suitable figure from the four alternatives that would complete the figure matrix.

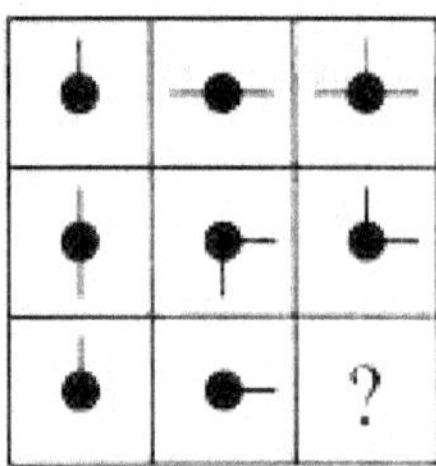

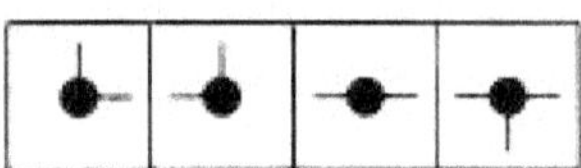

(a) (b) (c) (4)

(a) 1 (b) 2

(c) 3 (d) 4

11. Select the option in which all the components of the key figure (X) are available. **[2022]**

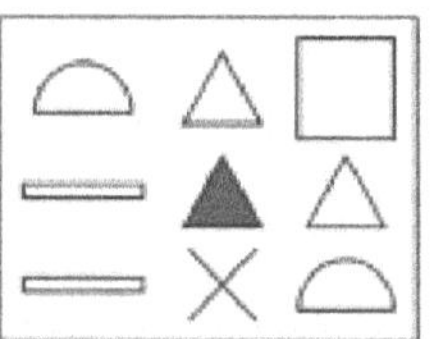

Figure (X)

(a) 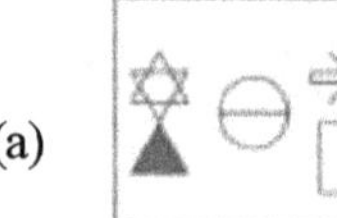 (b) 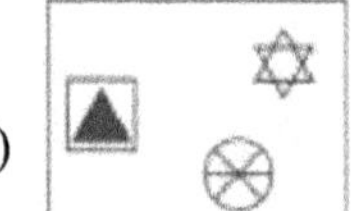

(c)  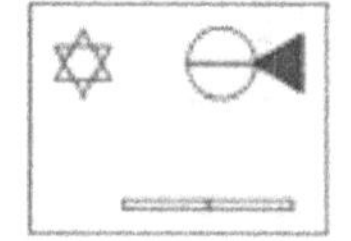 (d) 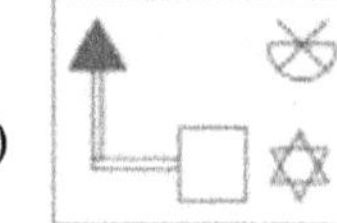

LEVEL 2

1. Select a suitable figure from the four alternatives that would complete the figure matrix.

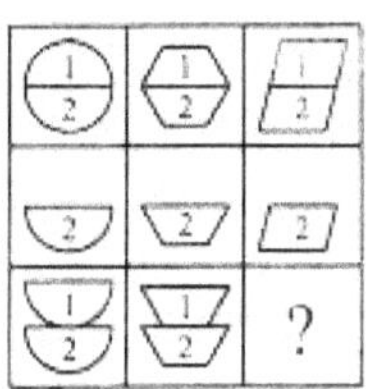

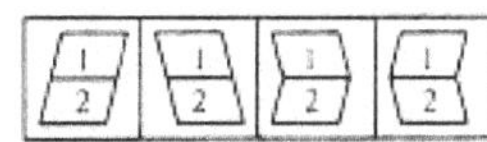

(a) (b) (c) (d)

(a) 1 (b) 2
(c) 3 (d) 4

2. Select a suitable figure from the four alternatives that would complete the figure matrix.

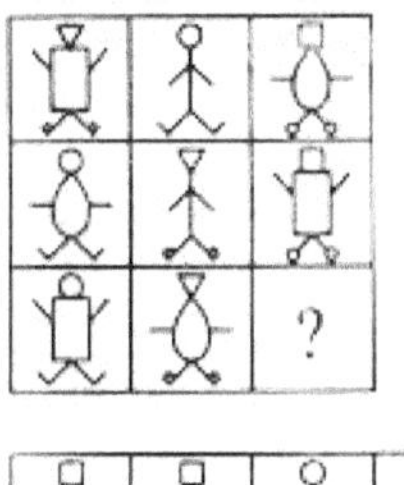

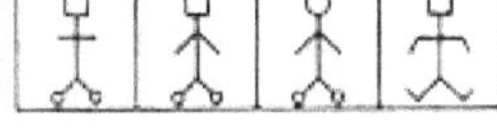

(a) (b) (c) (d)

(a) 1 (b) 2
(c) 3 (d) 4

3. Select a suitable figure from the four alternatives that would complete the figure matrix.

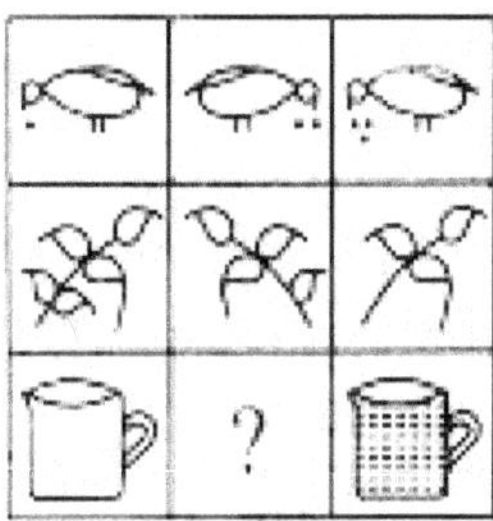

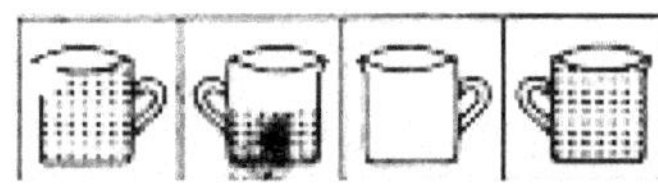

(a) (b) (c) (d)

(a) 1 (b) 2
(c) 3 (d) 4

4. Find out which of the answer figures (a), (b), (c) and (d) completes the figure matrix ?

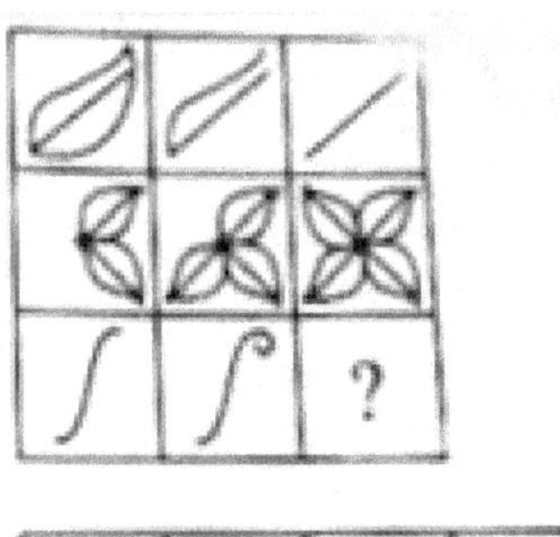

(a) (b) (c) (d)

(a) a (b) b
(c) c (d) d

5. Select a suitable figure from the four

alternatives that would complete the figure matrix.

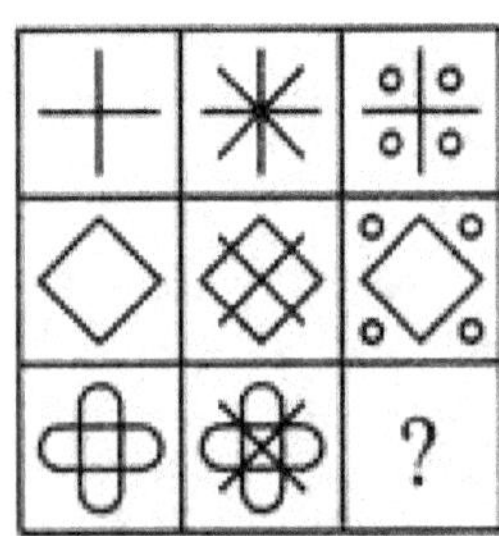

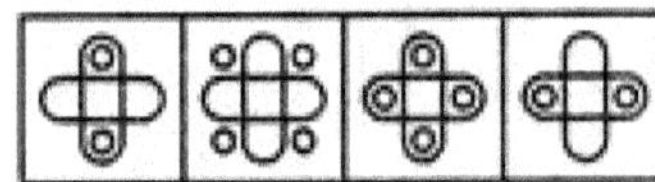

(a) (b) (c) (d)

(a) 2 (b) 4
(c) 3 (d) 1

6. Select a suitable figure from the four alternatives that would complete the figure matrix.

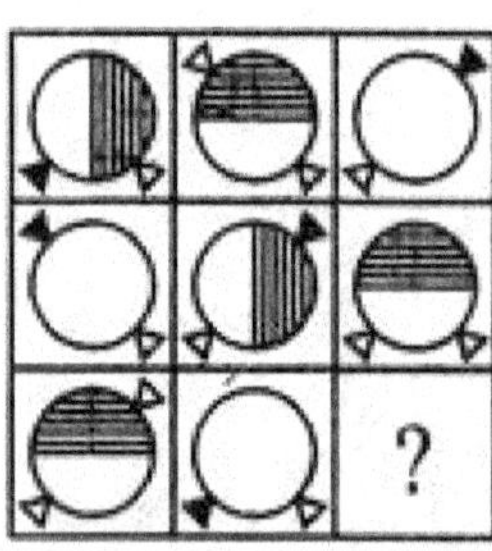

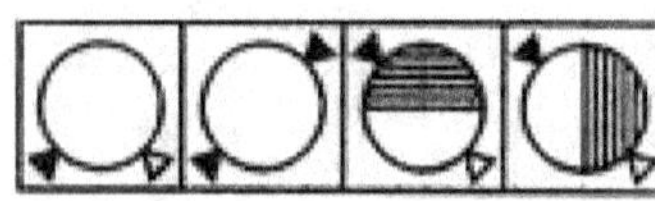

(a) (b) (c) (d)

(a) 1 (b) 2
(c) 3 (d) 4

7. Select a suitable figure from the four alternatives that would complete the figure matrix.

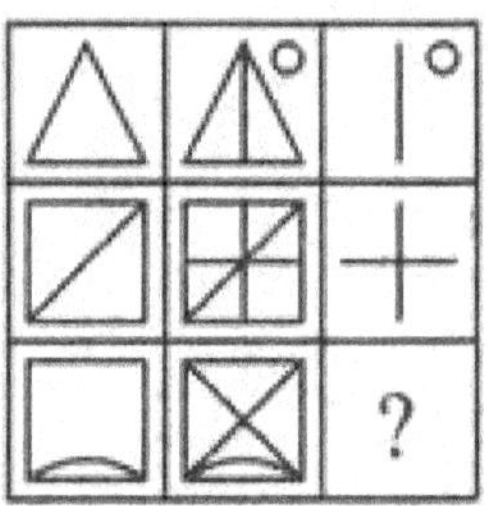

(a) (b) (c) (d)

(a) 1
(b) 2
(c) 3
(d) 4

8. Select one from the four alternative figures which one replace it?

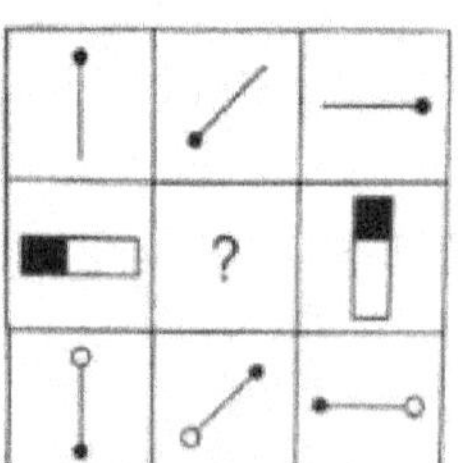

Answer Figures

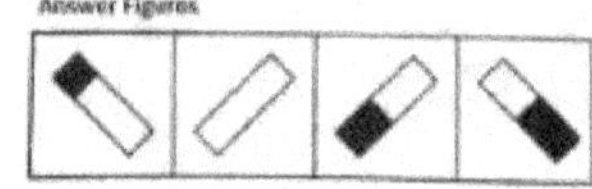

(a) (b) (c) (d)

(a) a
(b) b
(c) c
(d) d

9. Select a figure from the four alternatives that would complete the figure matrix.

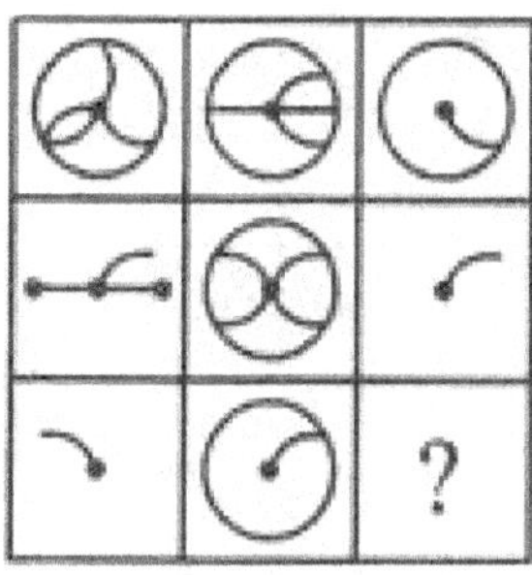

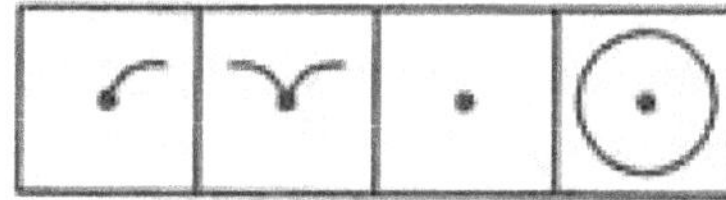

(a) (b) (c) (d)

(a) a (b) b

(c) c (d) d

10. Select a suitable figure from the four alternatives that would complete the figure matrix.

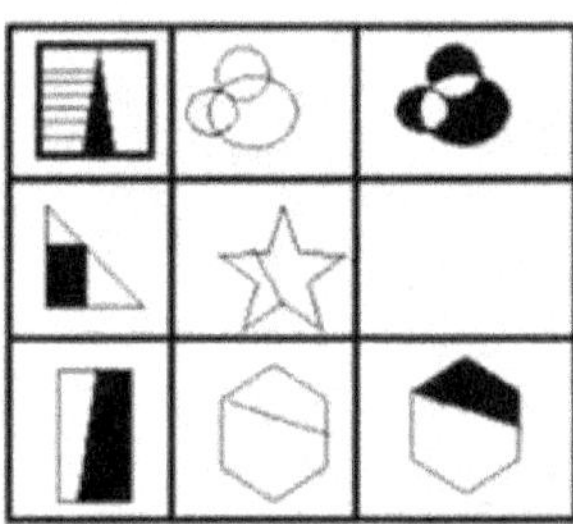

(A) (B) (C) (D)

(a) B (b) D

(c) A (d) C

11. Select a figure from the options which will complete the given figure matrix. **[2018]**

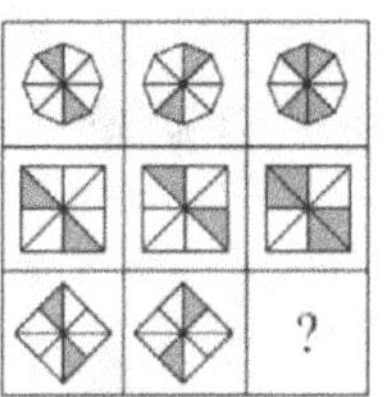

(a) 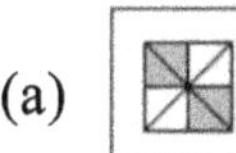 (b) 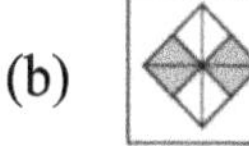

(c) 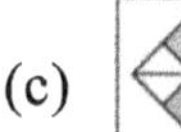 (d) 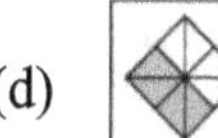

12. Group the given figures into three classes on the basis of their identical properties using each figure only once. **[2019]**

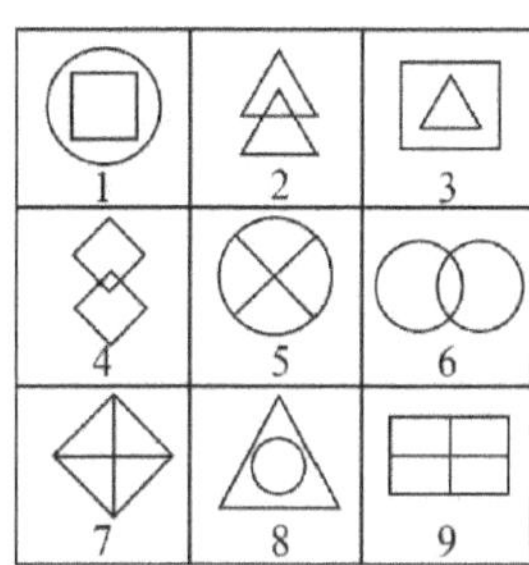

(a) 1, 2, 8; 3, 4, 5; 6, 7, 9

(b) 1, 3, 8; 2, 4, 6; 5, 7, 9

(c) 1, 3, 8; 2, 5, 7; 4, 6, 9

(d) 1, 3, 5; 2, 4, 8; 6, 7, 9

13. Select a figure from the options which will complete the given figure matrix. **[2019]**

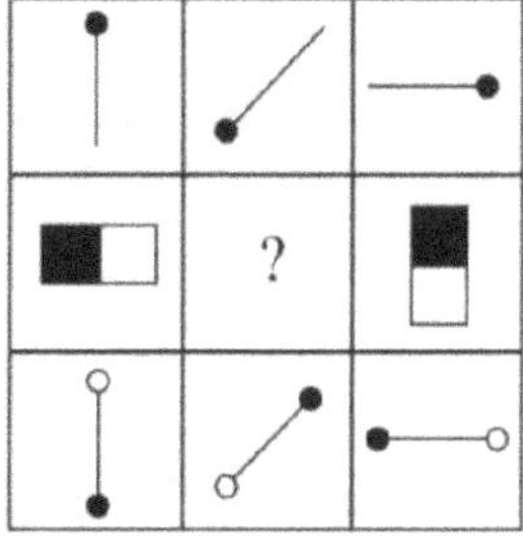

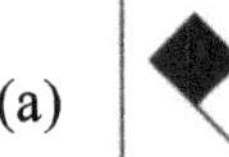

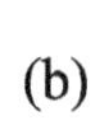 

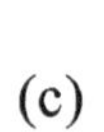 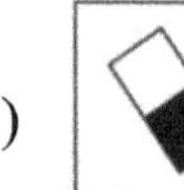

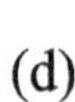 

14. Group the given figures into three classes on the basis of their identical properties using each figure only once. **[2020]**

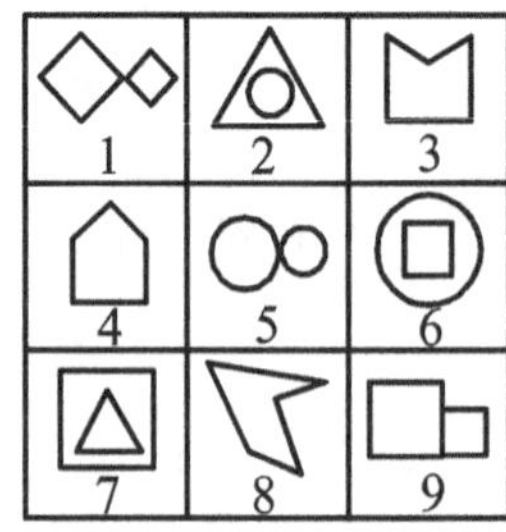

(a) 1, 5, 9 ; 2, 4, 8 ; 3, 6, 7
(b) 1, 4, 8 ; 2, 6, 7 ; 3, 5, 9
(c) 1, 6, 7 ; 2, 5, 9 ; 3, 4, 8
(d) 1, 5, 9 ; 2, 6, 7 ; 3, 4, 8

15. Select a figure from the options which will complete the given figure matrix. **[2021]**

(a) U (b) T
(c) I (d) J

16. Group the given figures into three classes on the basis of their identical properties using each figure only once. **[2021]**

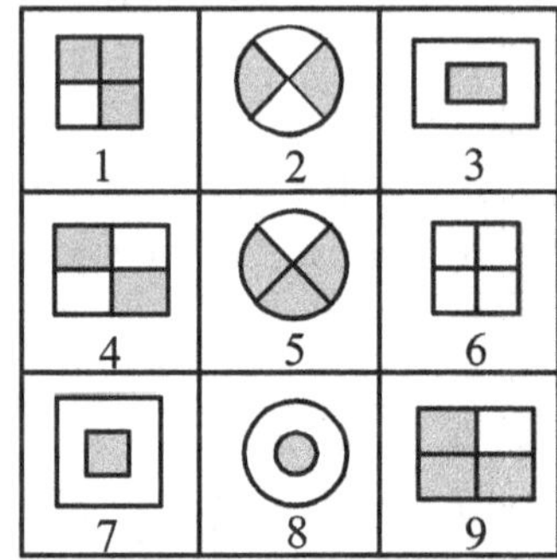

(a) 1, 4, 6; 2, 5, 9; 3, 7, 8
(b) 1, 7, 8; 2, 4, 6; 3, 5, 9
(c) 1, 6, 9; 2, 4, 5; 3, 7, 8
(d) 1, 5, 9; 2, 4, 6; 3, 7, 8

ANSWER KEY

LEVEL-1

1	(a)	**2**	(d)	**3**	(c)	**4**	(d)	**5**	(b)	**6**	(a)	**7**	(a)	**8**	(d)	**9**	(c)	**10**	(a)
11	(a)																		

LEVEL-2

1	(c)	**2**	(b)	**3**	(b)	**4**	(a)	**5**	(a)	**6**	(d)	**7**	(d)	**8**	(d)	**9**	(c)	**10**	(c)
11	(c)	**12**	(b)	**13**	(c)	**14**	(d)	**15**	(c)	**16**	(d)								

CHAPTER

15 Cube and Dice

Cube

A cube is a three dimensional figure, having 8 corners, 6 surfaces and 12 edges. If a cube is painted on all of its surfaces with any colour and further divided into various smaller cubes, we get the following results.

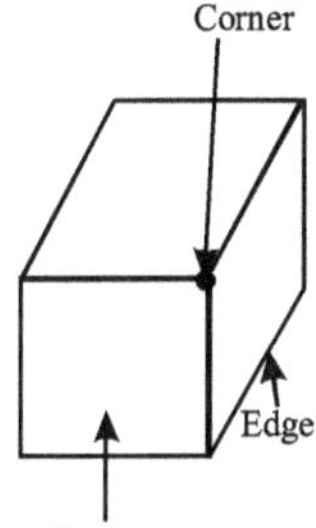

(a) Smaller cubes with three surfaces painted will be present on the corners of the big cube.

(b) Smaller cubes with two surface painted will be present on the edges of the big cube.

(c) Smaller cubes with one surface painted will be present on the outer surfaces of the big cube.

(d) Smaller cubes with no surface painted will be present inside the big cube.

If a cube is painted on all of its surfaces with a colour and then divided into smaller cubes of equal size, then after separation, number of smaller cubes so obtained will be calculated as under :

Number of smaller cubes with three surfaces painted = 8

Number of smaller cubes with two surfaces painted

$$= (n - 2) \times 12$$

Number of smaller cubes with one surface painted

$$= (n - 2)^2 \times 6$$

Number of smaller cubes with no surfaces painted = $(n - 2)^3$

Where n = No. of divisions on the surfaces of the bigger cube

$$= \frac{\text{length of edge of big cube}}{\text{length of edge of one smaller cube}}$$

TYPE-I : A cube is painted on all of its surfaces with a single colour and then divided into various smaller cubes of equal size.

DIRECTIONS : A cube of side 4 cm. is painted black on all of its surfaces and then divided into various smaller cubes of side 1 cm. each. The smaller cubes so obtained are separated.

$$\text{Total cubes obtained} = \frac{4\times4\times4}{1\times1\times1} = 64$$

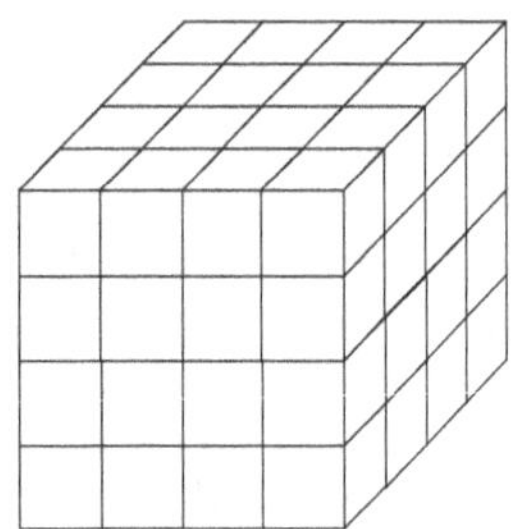

$$\text{Here,}\quad n = \frac{\text{side of big cube}}{\text{side of small cube}} = \frac{4}{1} = 4$$

1. Number of smaller cubes with three surfaces painted = 8
2. Number of smaller cubes with two surfaces painted

   $= (n-2) \times 12 = (4-2) \times 12 = 24$
3. Number of smaller cubes with one surface painted

   $= (n-2)^2 \times 6 = (4-2)^2 \times 6 = 24$
4. Number of smaller cubes with no surface painted

   $= (n-2)^3 = (4-2)^3 = (2)^3 = 8$

TYPE-II : A cube is painted on its surfaces with different colours and then divided into various smaller cubes of equal size.

DIRECTIONS : A cube of side 4 cm. is painted black on pair of opposite surfaces, blue on another pair of opposite surfaces and red on the remaining pair of opposite surfaces. The cube is divided into smaller cubes of equal side of 1 cm each.

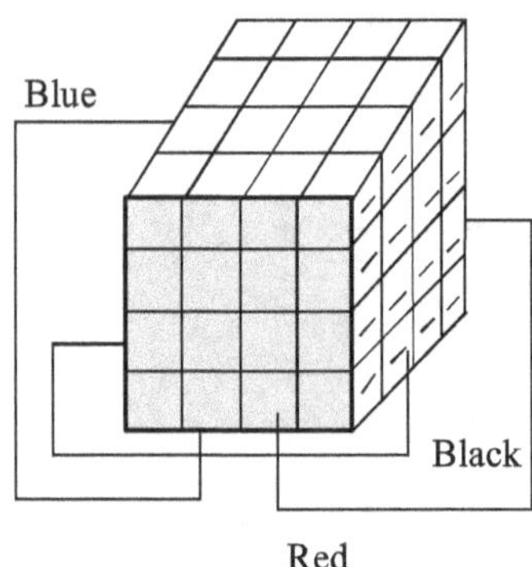

1. Number of smaller cubes with three surfaces painted = 8

   (These smaller cubes will have all three surfaces painted with different colours blue, black and red)
2. Number of smaller cubes with two surfaces painted = 24.

   And out of this

   (1) Number of cubes with two surfaces painted with black and blue colour = 8

   (2) Number of cubes with two surfaces painted with blue and red colour = 8

   (3) Number of cubes with two surfaces painted with black and red colour = 8
3. Number of smaller cubes with one surface painted = 24. And out of this

   (1) Number of cubes with one surface painted with black colour = 8

   (2) Number of cubes with one surface painted with blue colour = 8

   (3) Number of cubes with one surface painted with red colour = 8

TYPE-III : A cube is painted on its surfaces in such a way that one pair of opposite surfaces is left unpainted.

DIRECTIONS : A cube of side 4 cm. is painted red on one pair of opposite surfaces, green on another pair of opposite surfaces and one pair of opposite surfaces is left unpainted. Now the cube is divided into 64 smaller cubes of side 1cm. each.

1. Number of smaller cubes with three surfaces painted = 0 (Because each smaller cube at the corner is having a surface which is not painted)

2. Number of smaller cubes with two surfaces painted

   = Number of cubes present at the corners + Numbers of cubes present at the 4 edges = $8 + (n-2) \times 4 = 8 + 8 = 16$

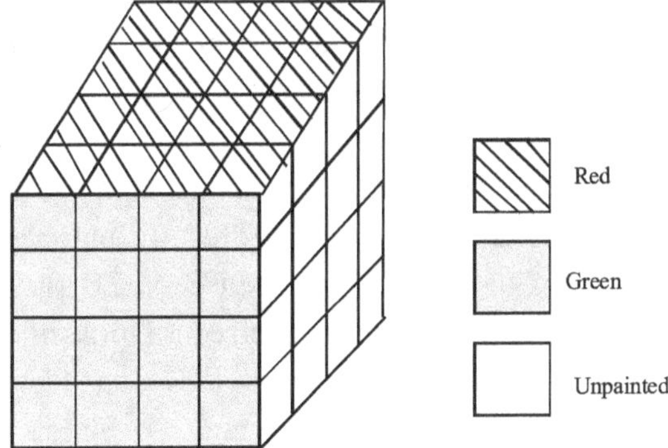

3. Number of smaller cubes with one surface painted.

   = Number of cubes present at 8 edges + number of cubes present at the four surfaces

   $= (n-2) \times 8 + (n-2)^2 \times 4 = 2 \times 8 + 4 \times 4 = 32$

4. Number of smaller cubes with no side painted.

   = Number of cubes on the two unpainted surfaces + number of cubes present inside the cube

   $= (n-2)^2 \times 2 + (n-2)^3 = 2 \times 4 + 8 = 16$

TYPE-IV : A cube is painted on its surfaces in such a way that one pair of adjacent surfaces is left unpainted.

DIRECTIONS : A cube of side 4 cm. is painted red on one pair of adjacent surfaces, green on the other pair of adjacent surfaces and two adjacent surfaces are left unpainted. Now the cube is divided into 64 smaller cubes of side 1 cm. each.

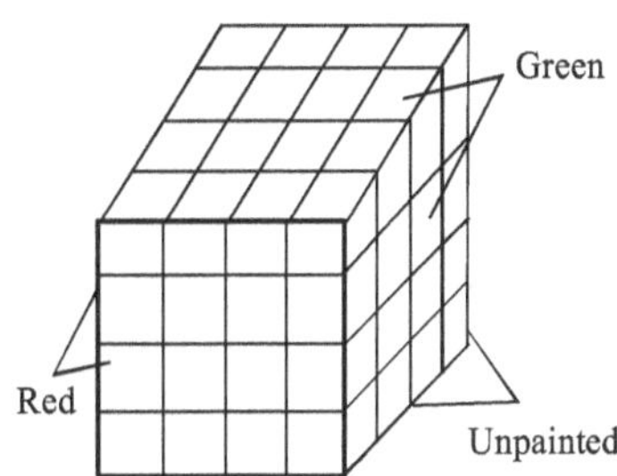

1. Number of smaller cubes with three surfaces painted = Number of smaller cubes at two corners = 2

2. Number of smaller cubes with two surface painted = Number of smaller cubes at four corners + Numbers of smaller cubes at 5 edges

   $= 4 + (n-2) \times 5 = 4 + 2 \times 5 = 4 + 10 = 14$

3. Number of smaller cubes with one surface painted

   = Number of smaller cubes at four surfaces

   + Number of cubes present at 6 edges

+ Number of smaller cubes at two corners

$= (n-2)^2 \times 4 + (n-2) \times 6 + 2$

$= 4 \times 4 + 2 \times 6 + 2 = 16 + 12 = 28 + 2 = 30$

4. Number of smaller cubes with no surfaces painted = Number of smaller cubes from inside the big cube +

Number of cubes at two surfaces + Number of cubes at one edge $= (n-2)^3 + (n-2)^3 \times 2 + (n-2)$

$= (2)^3 + (2)^2 + 2 = 8 + 8 + 2 = 18$

ILLUSTRATION 1 :

Count the number of cubes in the given figure.

(a) 6

(b) 8

(c) 10

(d) 12

***Sol.* (c)** Clearly, there is 1 column containing 3 cubes , 2 columns containing 2 cubes each and 3 columns containing 1 cube each.

ILLUSTRATION 2 :

Select from the alternatives the box that can be formed by folding the sheet shown in figure (X) :

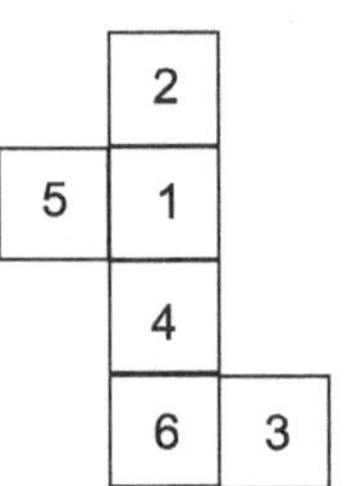

(X)

(a) 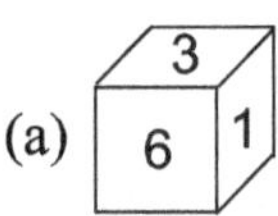

(b) 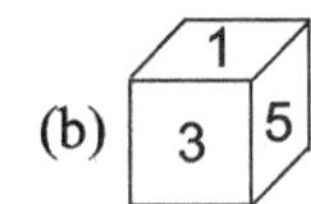

(c) 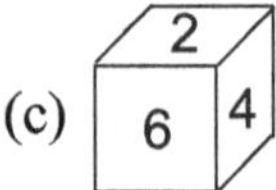

(d) 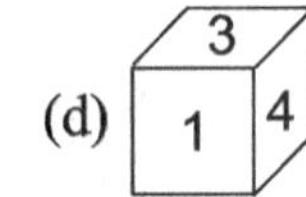

***Sol.* (d)** When the sheet in fig.(X) is folded to from a box (cube) then

The number 2 will lie opposite the number 4; the number 1 will lie opposite the number 6 and the number 5 will lie opposite the number 3. Fig. (a) has the numbers 1 and 6 on adjacent face, fig.(b) has number 3 and 5 on adjacent faces and the fig. (c) has the numbers 2 and 4 on the adjacent face. So, these three alternatives are not possible. Since, the numbers 1, 3 and 4 can appear on adjacent face, so fig.(d) is possible.

Hence, only the box shown in fig. (d) can be formed by folding fig. (X).

ILLUSTRATION 3 :

Count the number of cubes in the given figure.

(a) 68 (b) 69

(c) 70 (d) 71

***Sol.* (b)** In the figure, there are 11 columns containing 4 cubes each , 7 columns containing 3 cubes each and 2 columns containing 2 cubes each .

$\therefore$ Total number of cubes

$= (11 \times 4) + (7 \times 3) + (2 \times 2) = 44 + 21 + 4 = 69.$

ILLUSTRATION 4 :

The figures given below show the two different positions of a dice. Which number will appear opposite to number 2.

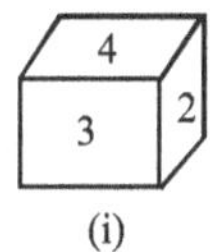

(i)

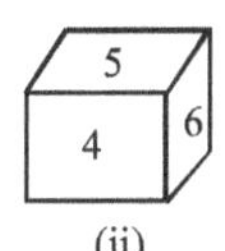

(ii)

(a) 3

(b) 4

(c) 5

(d) 6

***Sol.* (c)** The above question, where only two positions of a dice are given, can easily be solved with the following method.

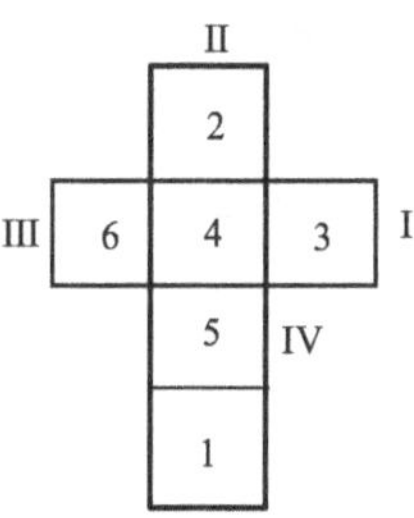

Step I : The dice, when unfolded, will appear as shown in the figure given on the right side.

Step II : Write the common number to both the dice in the middle block. Since common number is 4, hence number 4 will appear in the central block.

Step III : Consider the figure (i) and write the first number in the anti-clockwise direction of number 4, (common number) in block I and second number in block II. Therefore, numbers 3 and 2 being the first and second number to 4 in anticlockwise directions respectively, will appear in block I and II respectively.

Step IV : Consider figure (ii) and write first and second number in the anticlockwise direction to number 4, (common number) in block (III) and (IV). Hence numbers 6 and 5 will appear in the blocks III and IV respectively.

Step V : Write remaining number in the remaining block. Therefore, number 1 will come in the remaining block. Now, from the unfolded figure we find that number opposite to 6 is 3, number opposite to 2 is 5 and number opposite to 4 is 1. Therefore, option (c) is our answer.

LEVEL 1

1. Count the number of cubes in the given figure.

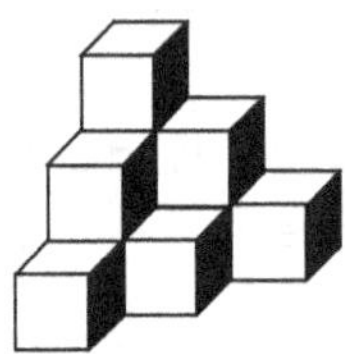

(a) 14 (b) 12
(c) 10 (d) 8

2. Select from the alternative, the box that can be formed by folding the sheet shown in figure (X)

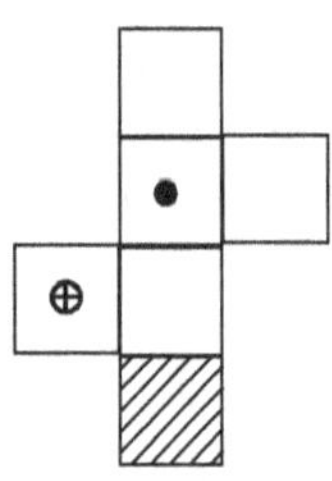

(X)

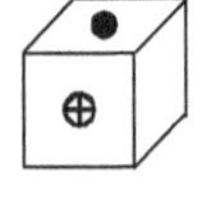
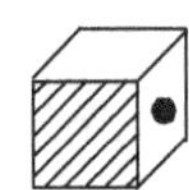
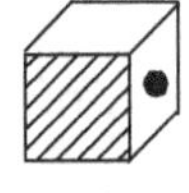
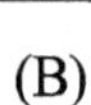
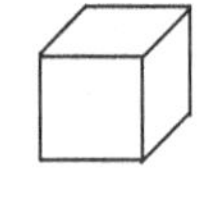
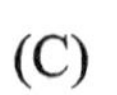

(A) (B) (C) (D)

(a) A only
(b) A and C only
(c) A , C and D only
(d) A, B, C and D

3. Select from the alternative, the box that can be formed by folding the sheet shown in figure (X) :

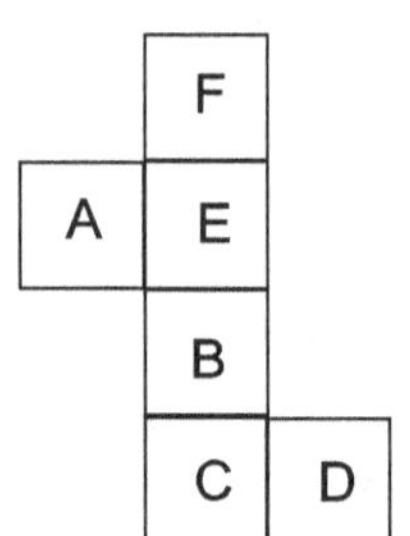

(X)

(A) 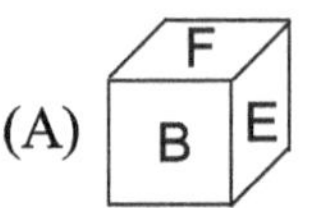

(B) 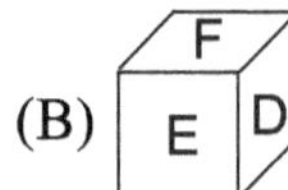

(C) 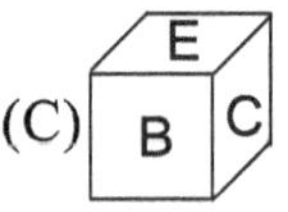

(D) 

(a) A only
(b) B only
(c) A and C only
(d) A, B, C & D

4. How many dots are their on the dice face opposite the one with three dots ?

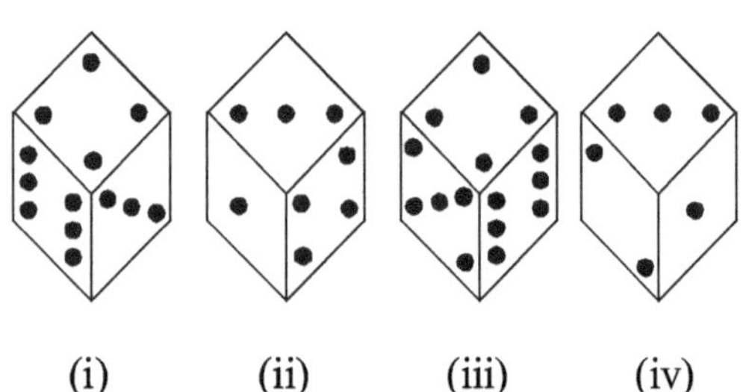

(i) (ii) (iii) (iv)

(a) 2
(b) 4
(c) 5
(d) 6

5. When the following figure is folded to form a cube, how many dots would lie opposite the face bearing five dots ?

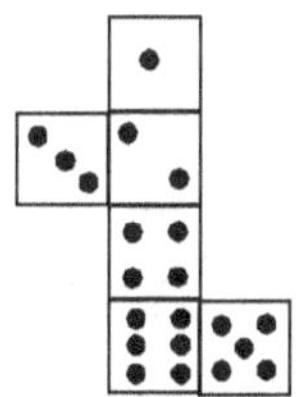

(a) 1 (b) 2
(c) 3 (d) 4

6. Which number lies opposite the face 4, if the four different positions of a dice are as shown in the figures given below.

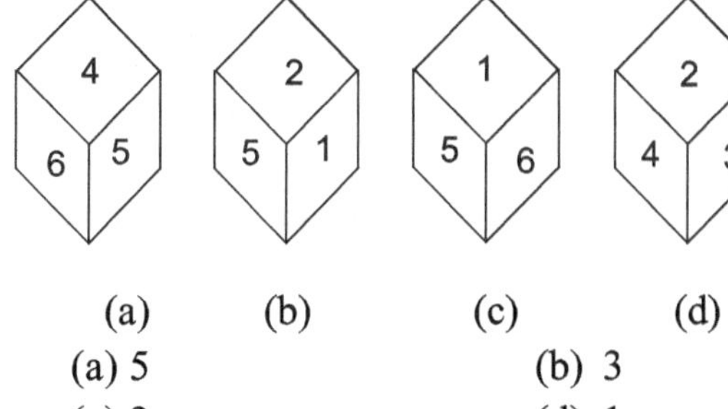

(a) 5 (b) 3
(c) 2 (d) 1

7. What should be the number opposite 3 ?

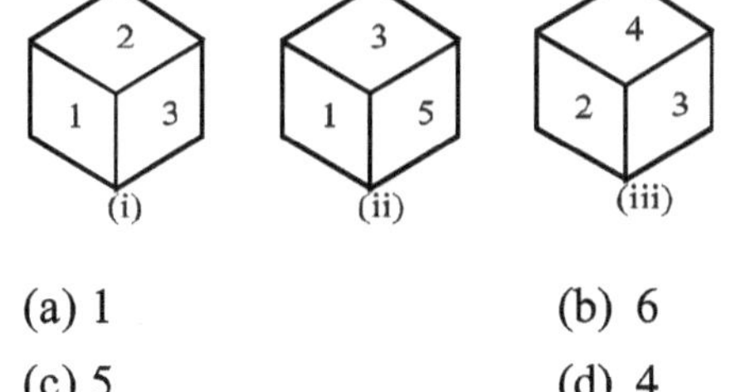

(a) 1 (b) 6
(c) 5 (d) 4

8. From the following positions of dice, find which number will come in place of "?"

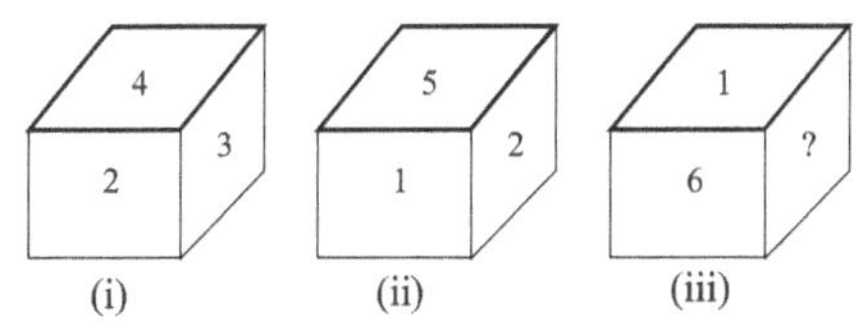

(a) 4 (b) 5
(c) 2 (d) 3

9. The following figure is converted into a cube. Its correct shape will be:–

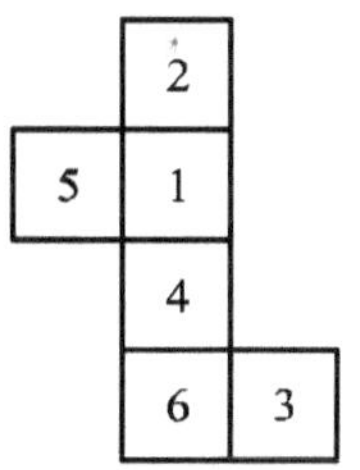

(a) 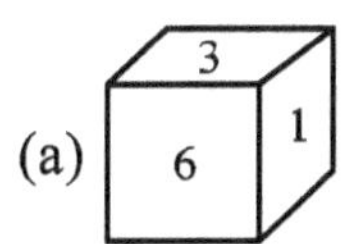

(b) 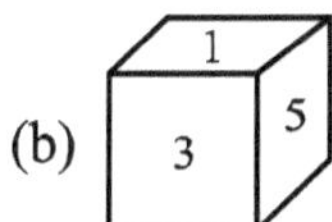

(c) 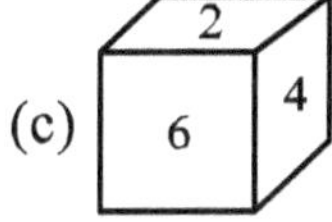

(d) 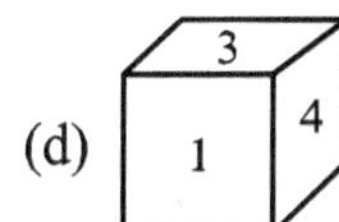

10. The following figure is converted into a cube. Its four positions (a), (b), (c), and (d) are shown. On the basis of these select correct alternative.

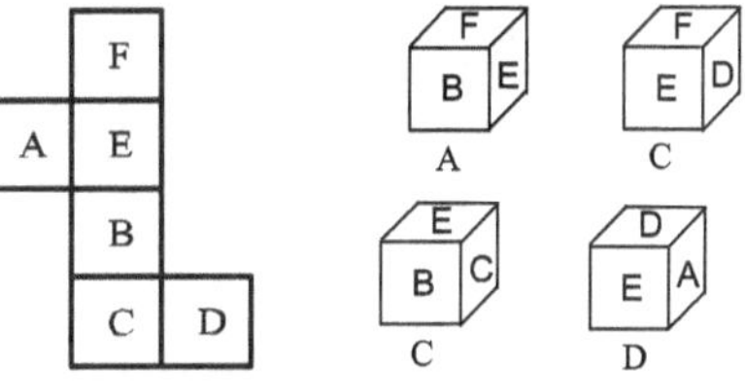

(a) A only (b) B only
(c) A and C only (d) A,B,C&D

11. Observe the dice given below and answer:

(a) 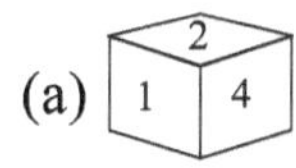

(b) 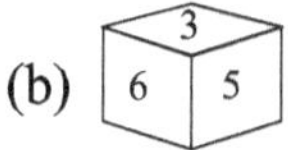

(c) 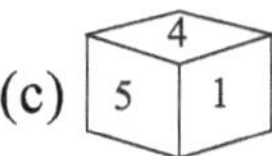

(d) 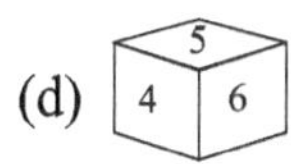

Which number is opposite 3 ?

(a) 1 (b) 2

(c) 4 (d) 6

12. If the total number of dots on opposite faces of a cubical block is always 7, find the figure which is correct?

(a) 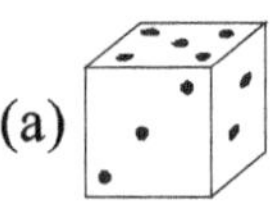 (b) 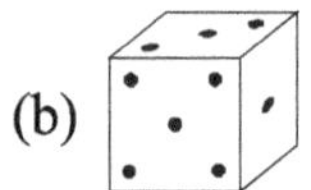

(c) 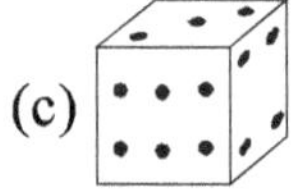 (d) 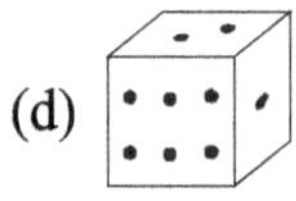

13. The following figure is converted into a cube. Its correct shape will be:

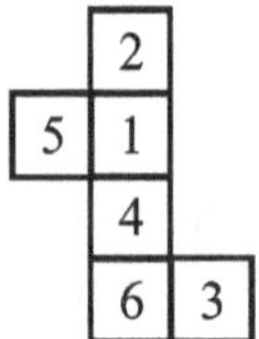

(a) 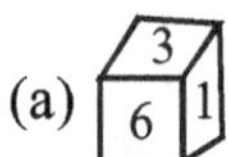

(b) 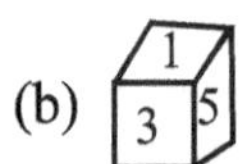

(c) 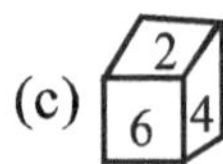

(d) 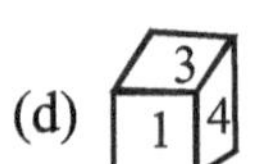

14. The following figure is converted into a cube. Its four positions (a), (b), (c) and (d) are shown. On the basis of these select correct alternative.

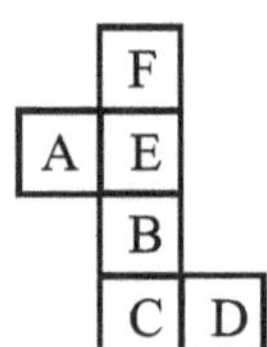

(i) F B E (ii) F E D

(iii) E B C (iv) D E A

(a) A only

(b) B only

(c) A and C only

(d) A, B, C and D

DIRECTIONS (Qs. 15–16) : In every question a dice has been shown in different faces on which numbers/symbol/colour have been written randomly. Carefully study the faces and answer the question based on it.

15. Which symbol is just opposite to symbol 'D'?

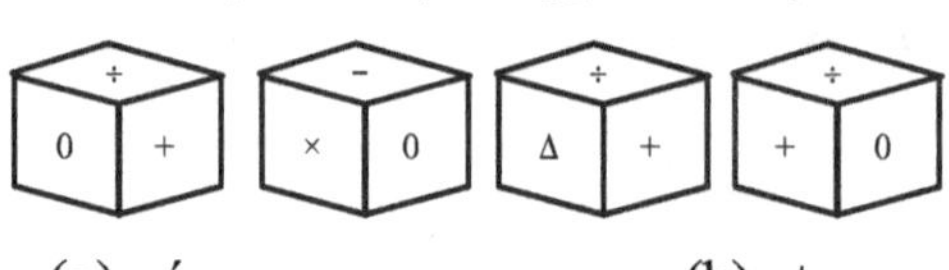

(a) ʹ (b) +

(c) 0 (d) ,

16. Which number will come at the bottom of last cube ?

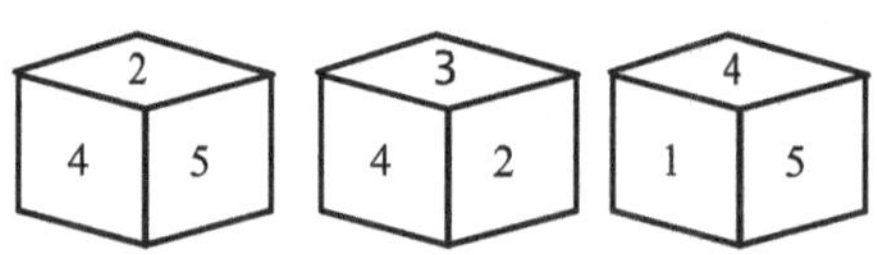

(a) 3

(b) 4

(c) 6

(d) 1

17. Four positions of a die are shown. Which symbol or number will be on the face opposite to the face with symbol ☆ (star)?

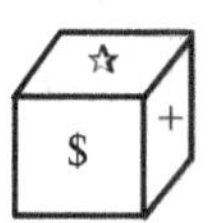

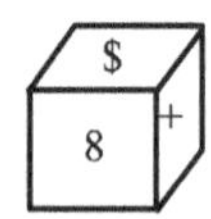

(a) @ (b) $

(c) 8 (d) +

18. The following figure is folded to form a cube.Observe the cube. Of the following cube figure find the most appropriate figure.

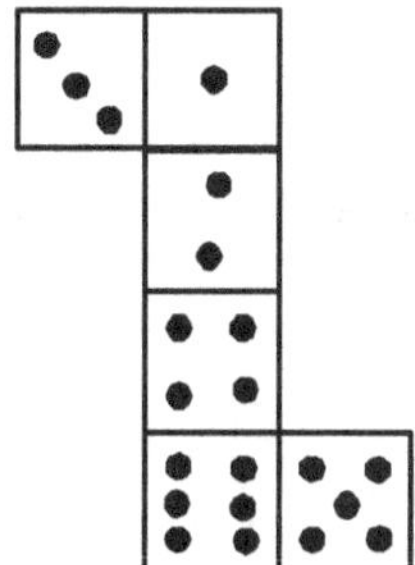

(a) 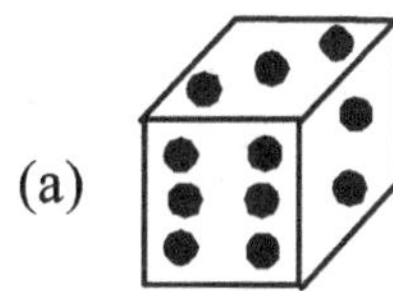

(b) 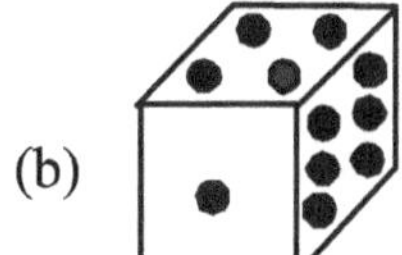

(c) 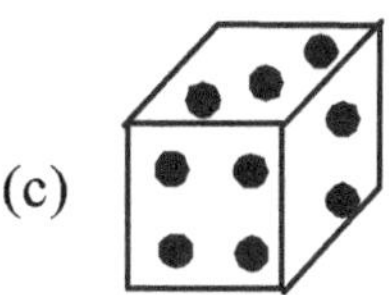

(d) 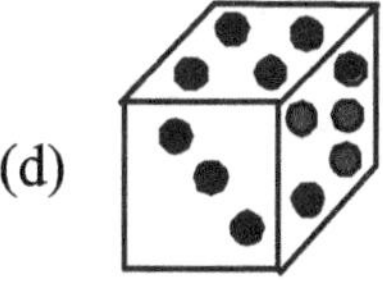

19. How many cubes are required to make the given figure? **[2019]**

(a) 13 (b) 14
(c) 10 (d) 11

LEVEL 2

1. A Dice Is Thrown Three Times And Its Three Different Positions Are Given Below. Find The Number On The Face Opposite The Face Showing 3. .

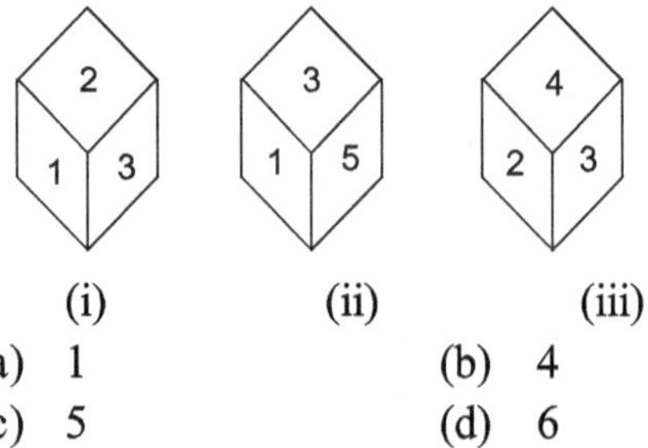

(i) (ii) (iii)

(a) 1 (b) 4
(c) 5 (d) 6

2. If the given figure is folded to form a box, which among the boxes below will be formed?

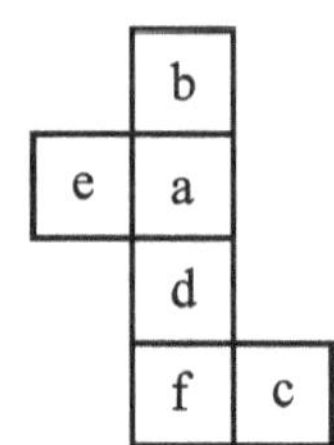

(a) 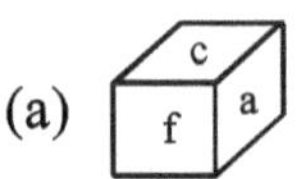

(b) 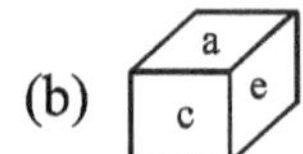

(c) 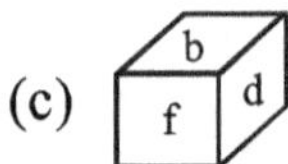

(d) 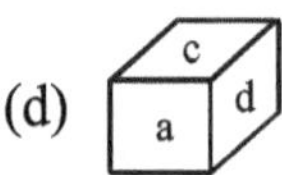

3 Three positions of a dice are shown below. If 6 is on the top, then which number will be at the bottom? **[2020]**

(a) 3 (b) 2
(c) 1 (d) 5

4. How many cubes are there in the given figure?

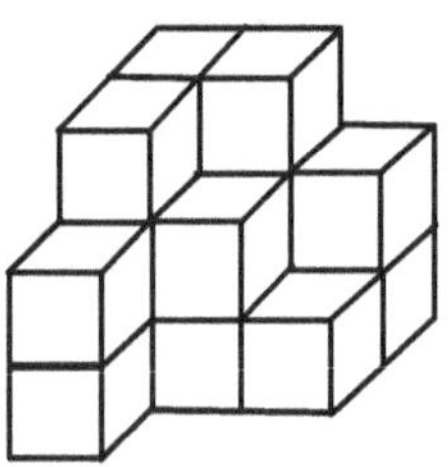

(a) 14 (b) 15 **[2021]**
(c) 16 (d) 18

5. Which of the following net can be used to form the given cube? **[2021]**

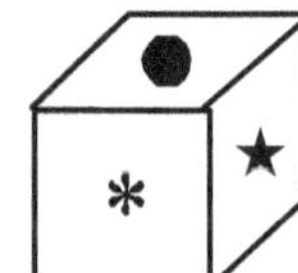

(a) 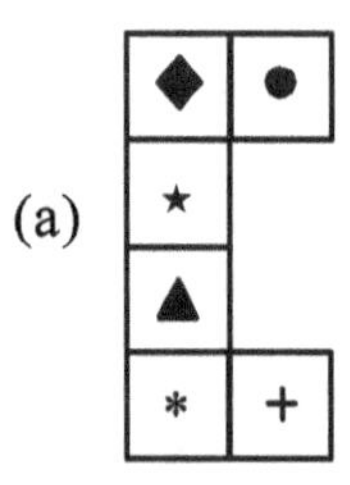

(b) 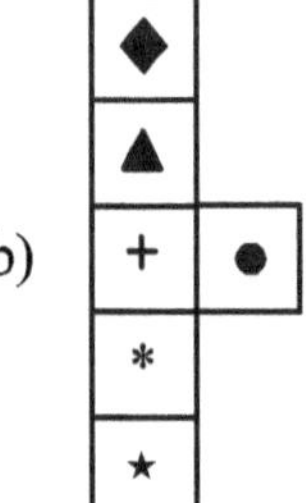

(c) 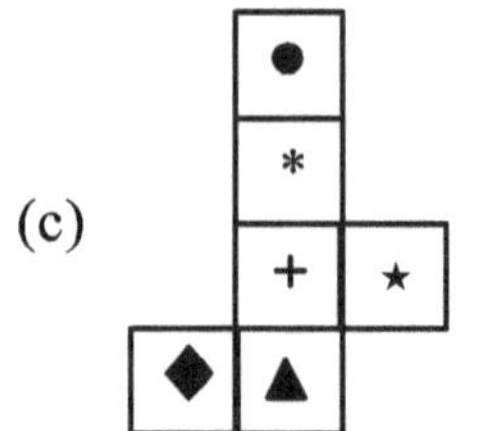

(d) 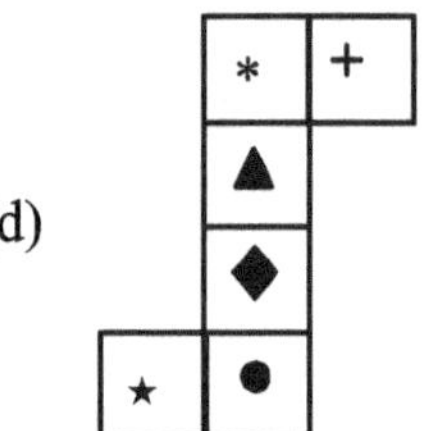

6. Which of the following net can be used to form the given cube? **[2021]**

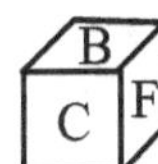

(a)
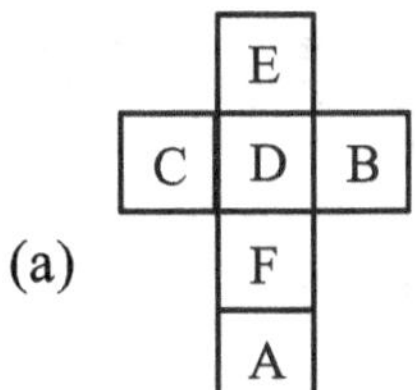

(b)
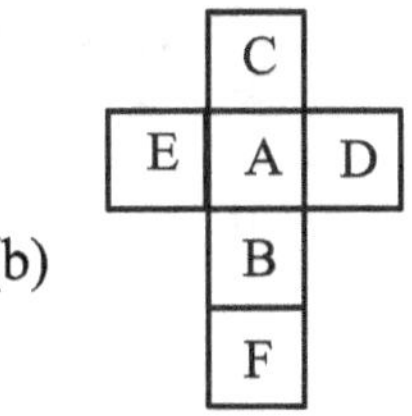

(c) (d)
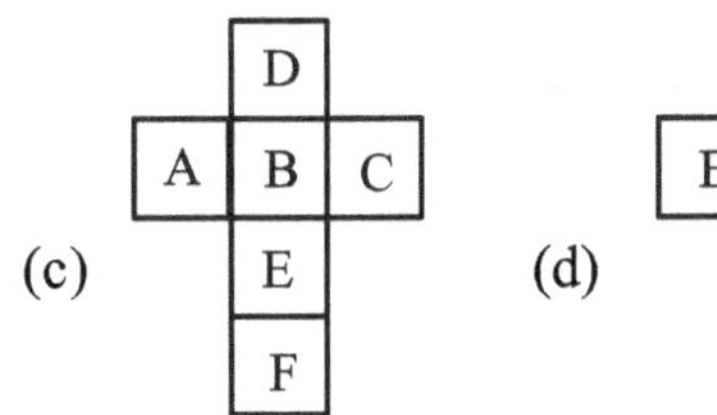

7. Two positions of a dice are shown below. If + is on the top, then what will be in the bottom? **[2021]**

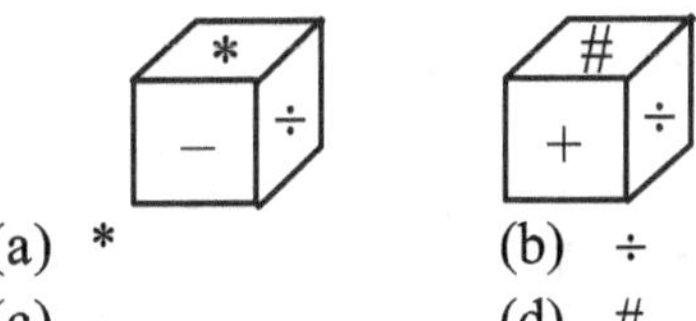

(a) * (b) ÷
(c) − (d) #

8. Select a box from the options that is similar to the box formed from the given sheet. **[2022]**

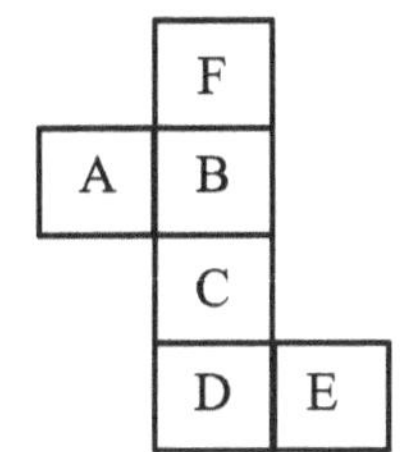

(a)
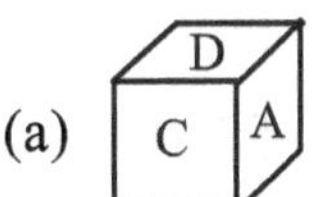

(b)
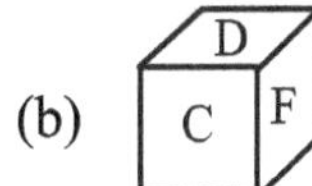

(c)
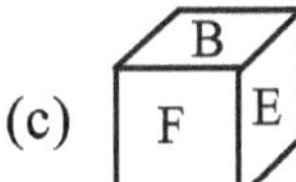

(d)

ANSWER KEY																			
LEVEL-1																			
1	(c)	**3**	(b)	**5**	(c)	**7**	(b)	**9**	(d)	**11**	(b)	**13**	(d)	**15**	(c)	**17**	(c)	**19**	(b)
2	(a)	**4**	(c)	**6**	(d)	**8**	(d)	**10**	(b)	**12**	(b)	**14**	(b)	**16**	(c)	**18**	(c)		
LEVEL-2																			
1	(d)	**2**	(d)	**3**	(a)	**4**	(c)	**5**	(c)	**6**	(d)	**7**	(c)	**8**	(a)				

CHAPTER 16 Dot Situation

DOT SITUATION :

The problems on dot situation involve the search of similar conditions in the alternative figures as indicated in the problem figure. The problem figure contains dots placed in the spaces enclosed between the combinations of square, triangle, rectangle and circle. Selecting one of these dots we observe the region in which this dot is enclosed i.e. to which of the four figures (circle, square, rectangle and triangle) is this region common. Then we look for such a region in the four alternatives. Once we have found it we repeat the procedure for other dots, if any. The alternative figure which contains all such regions is the answer.

DIRECTIONS (ILLUSTRATION 1-4) : *In each of the following examples, there is a diagram marked (X), with one or more dots placed in it. The diagram is followed by four other figures, marked (a), (b), (c) and (d) only one of which is such as to make possible the placement of the dot. Select this alternative as the answer.*

ILLUSTRATION 1 :

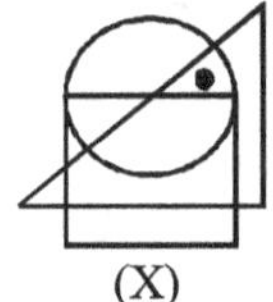

(X)

(a) 

(b) 

(c) 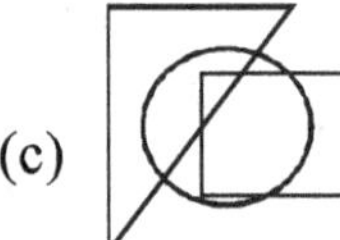

(d) 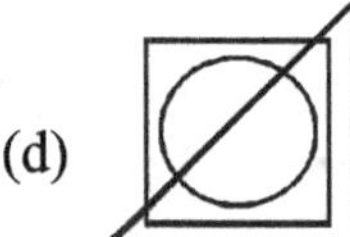

***Sol.* (c)** In figure (X), the dot lies in the region common to the circle and the triangle only. Such a region is present in figure (c) only.

ILLUSTRATION 2 :

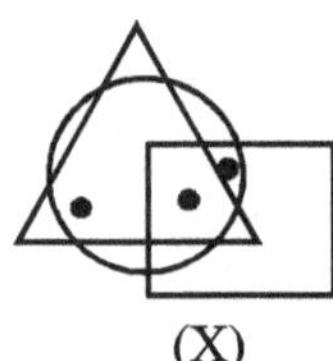

(X)

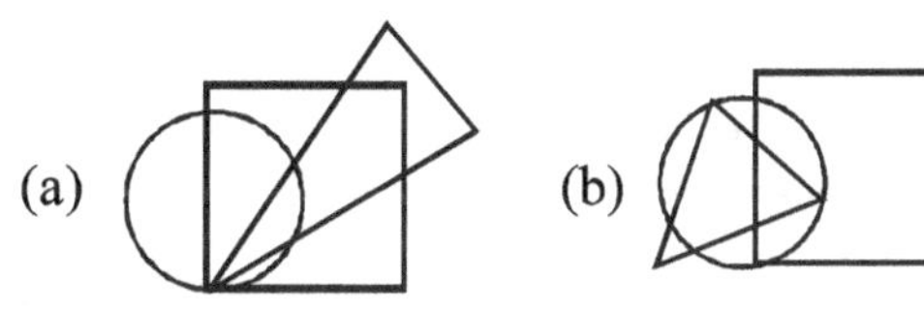

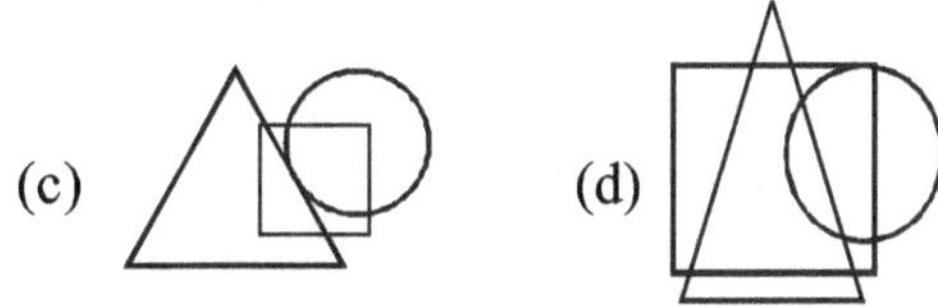

***Sol.* (b)** Figure (X) contains one dot in the region common to the circle and the triangle, another dot in the region common to all the three figures and the third dot in the region common to the square and the circle only. In figures (a) and (d), the region common to the circle and the triangle lies within the square. In figure (c), there is no region common to the circle and the triangle. Only figure (b) contains all the three types of regions.

ILLUSTRATION 3 :

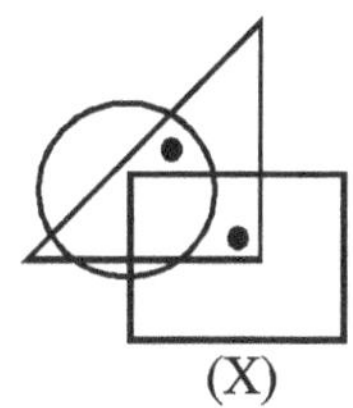

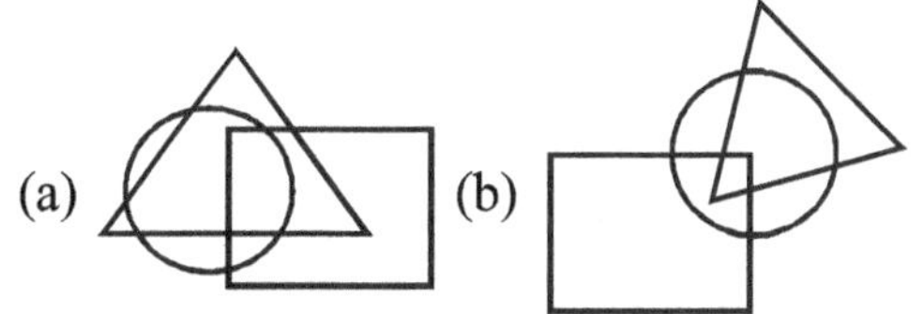

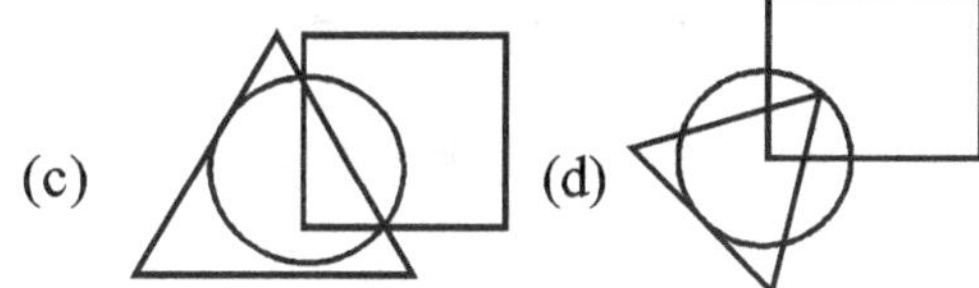

***Sol.* (1)** In figure (X), one of the dots is placed in the region common to the circle and the triangle and the other dot is placed in the region common to the triangle and the square. From amongst the figures (a), (b), (c) and (d), only figure (1) has both the regions, one common to circle and triangle and the other common to triangle and square.

ILLUSTRATION 4 :

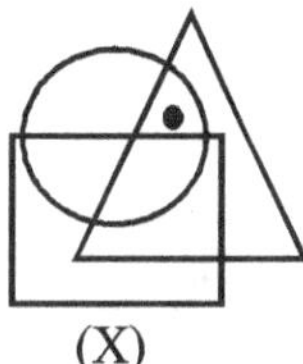

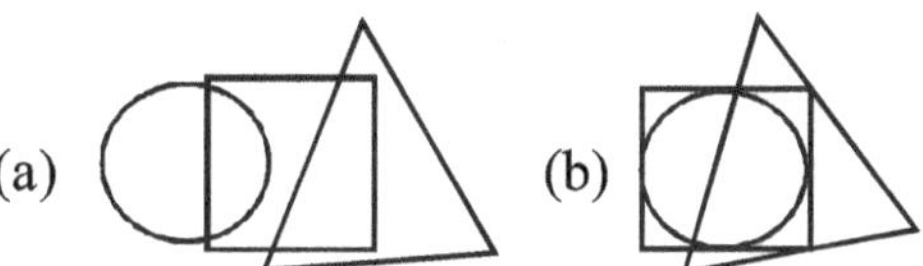

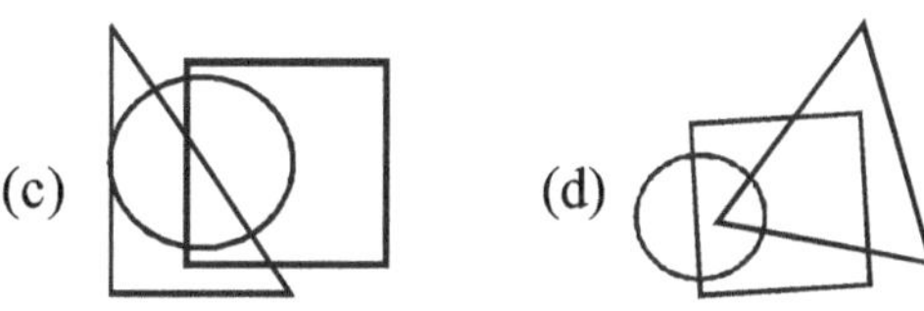

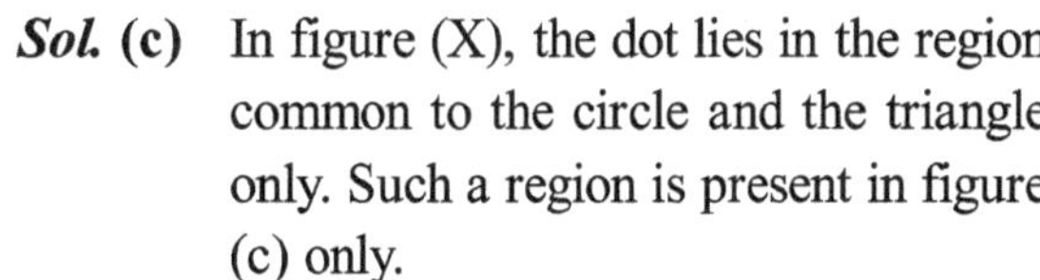

***Sol.* (c)** In figure (X), the dot lies in the region common to the circle and the triangle only. Such a region is present in figure (c) only.

ILLUSTRATION 5 :

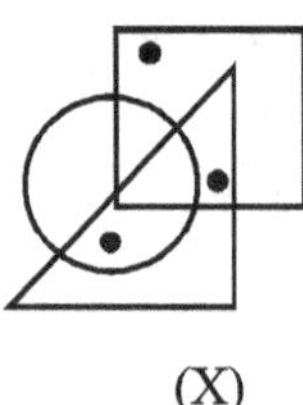

(X)

(a) 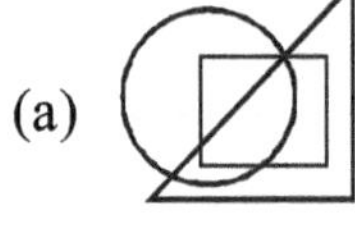

(b) 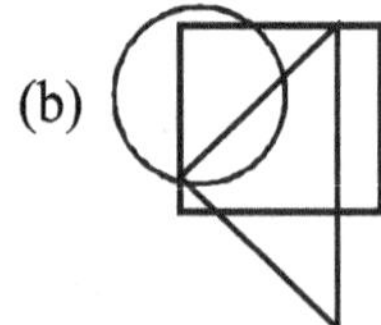

(c) 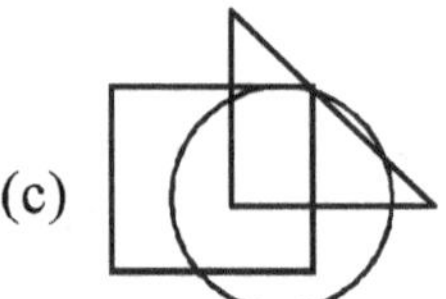

(d) 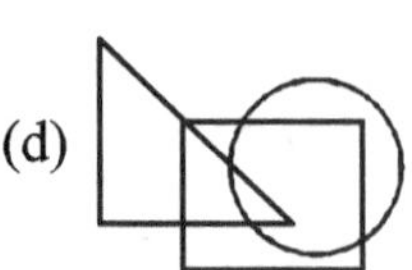

***Sol.* (c)** Figure (X), contains one dot in the square only, another dot in the region common to the square and the triangle only and the third dot in the region common to the circle and the triangle. Figure (a) does contain a region which lies in the square alone. Figures (b) & (d) do not contain any region common to the circle & the triangle. Only figure (c) contains all the three types of regions.

LEVEL 1

DIRECTION (Q. 1) : *In the following question, there is a diagram marked (X), with one or more dots placed in it. The diagram is followed by four other figures, marked (a)z, (b), (c) and (d) only one of which is such as to make possible the placement of the alternative in each these.*

1. 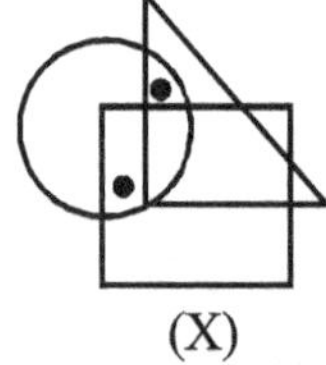

(X)

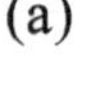

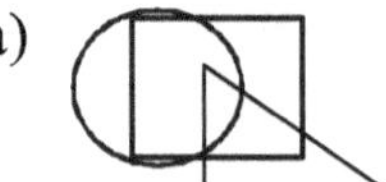

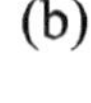

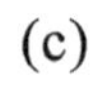

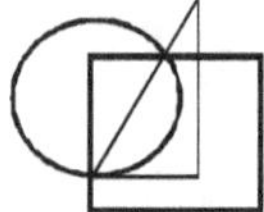

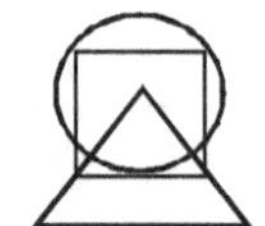

2. From amongst the figures marked (a), (b), (c) and (d), select the figure which satisfies the same conditions of placement of dots as in figure (X).

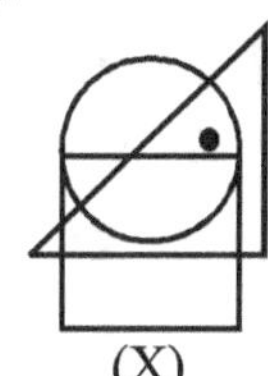

(X)

(a) 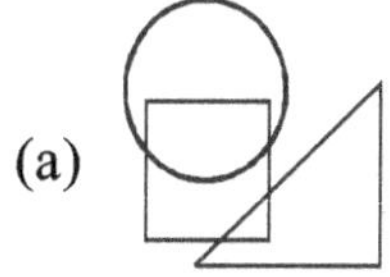

(b) 

(c) 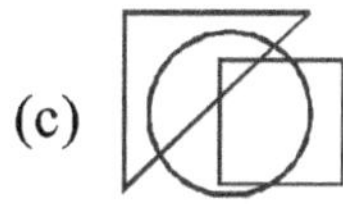

(d) 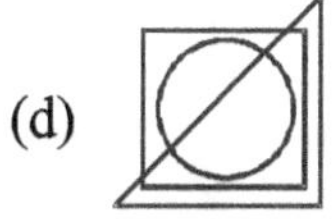

DIRECTIONS (Qs. 3-4) : *In each of the following questions there is a diagram (X) in which one or more dots have been placed in certain positions. Examine the placement of these dots carefully. From the four choices, select the one in which the placement of dots is similar to that in the diagram.*

3.

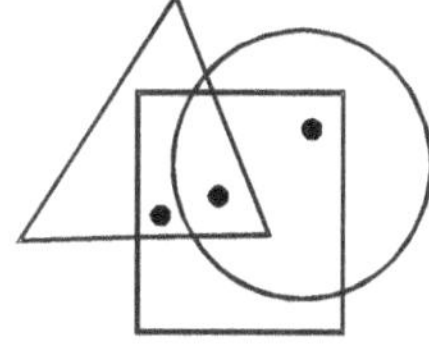

(X)

(a) 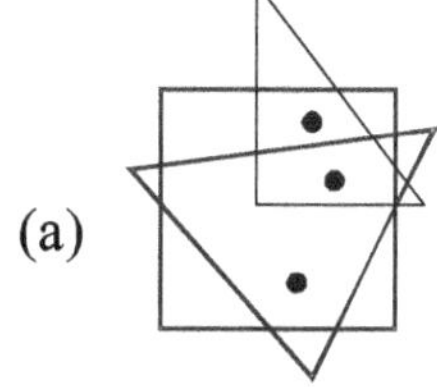

(b) 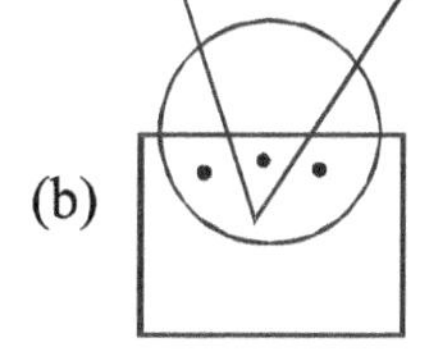

(c) 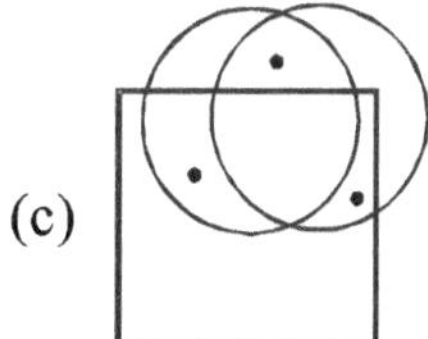

(d) 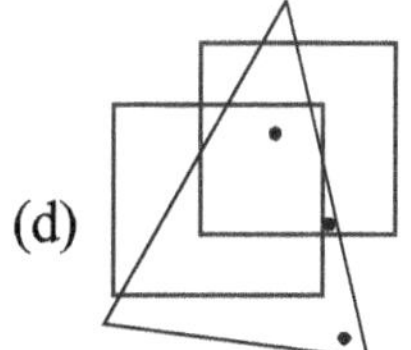

4.

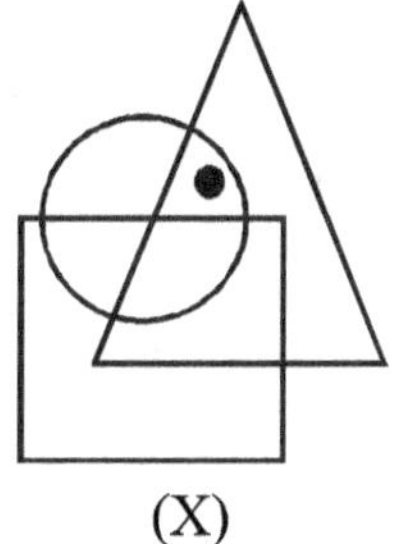

(X)

(a) 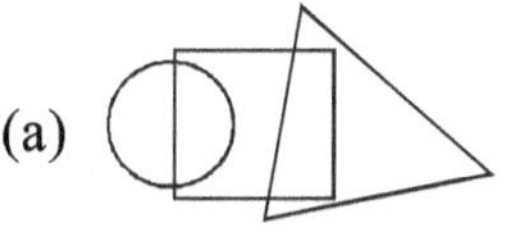

(b) 

(c) 

(d) 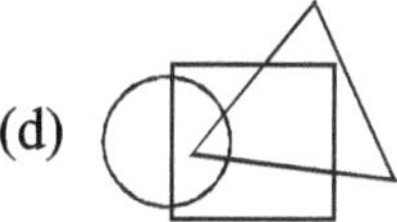

5. Select a figure from the options which satisfies the same conditions of placement of the dots as in the given figure. **[2019]**

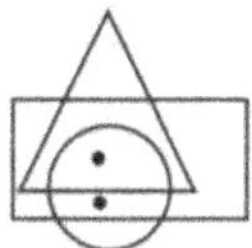

(a) 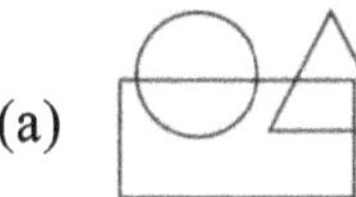

(b) 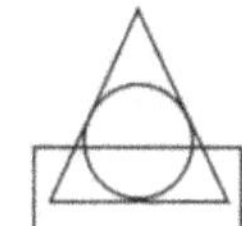

(c)  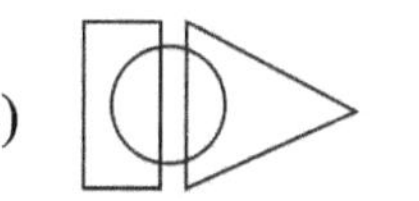

(d) 

6. Select a figure from the options which satisfies the same conditions of placement of the dots as in the given figure. **[2019]**

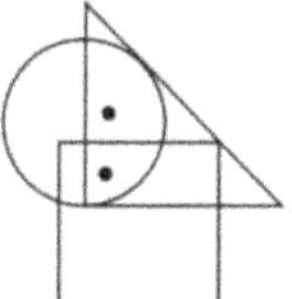

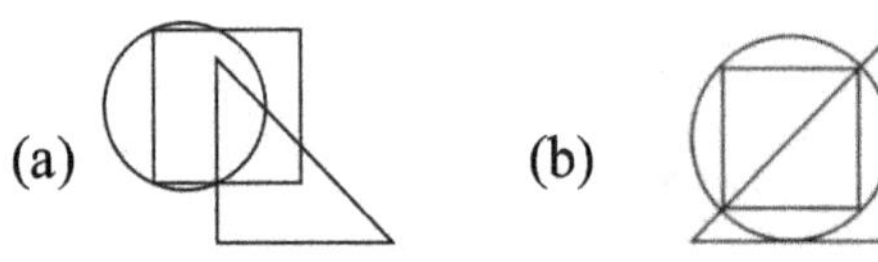

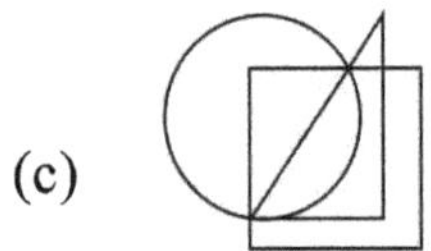

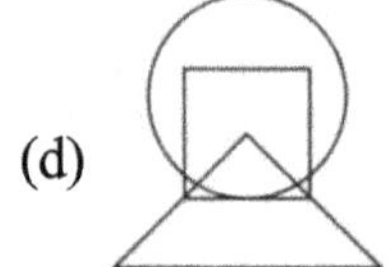

7. Select a figure from the options which satisfies the same conditions of placement of dots as in the given figure. **[2021]**

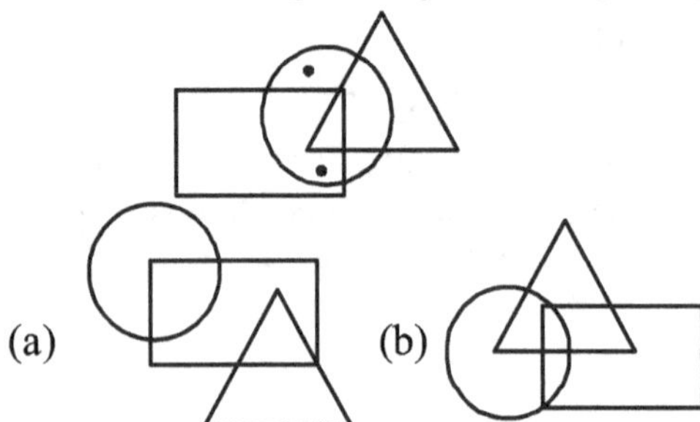

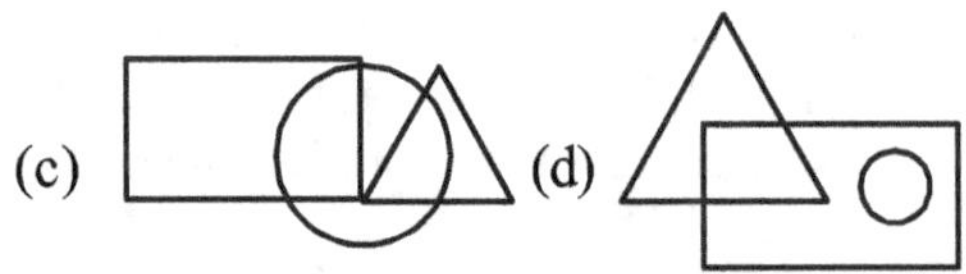

8. Select a figure from the options which satisfies the same conditions of placement of dots as in the given figure. **[2022]**

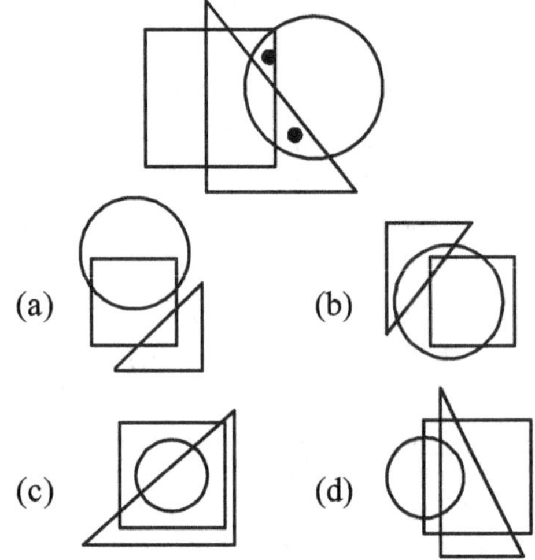

LEVEL 2

DIRECTIONS (Qs.1-6) : *In each of the following questions, from amongst the figures marked (a), (b), (c) and (d), select the one which satisfies the same conditions of placement of the dot as in fig. (X).*

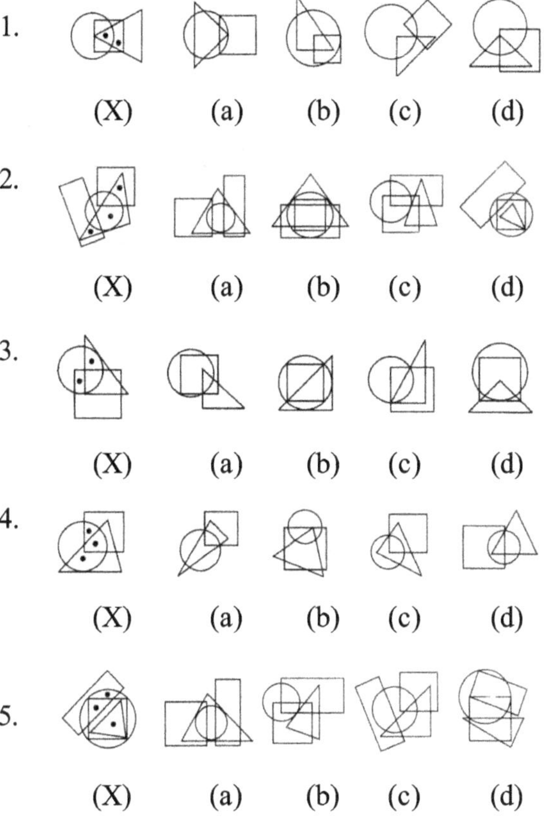

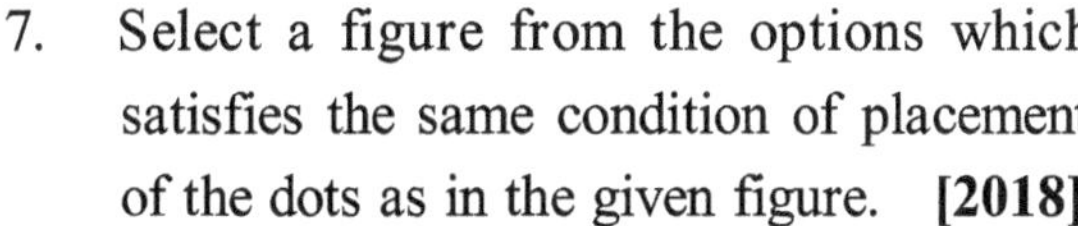

7. Select a figure from the options which satisfies the same condition of placement of the dots as in the given figure. **[2018]**

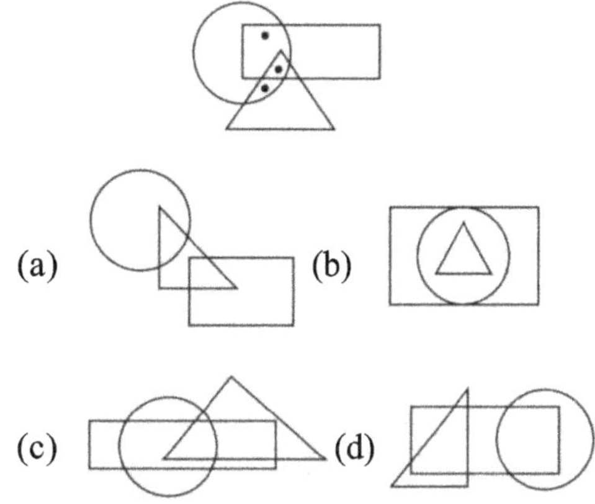

8. Select a figure from the options which satisfies the same conditions of placement of the dots as in the given figure. **[2019]**

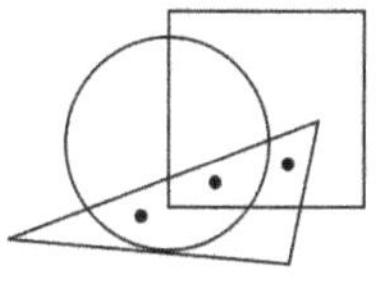

(a) 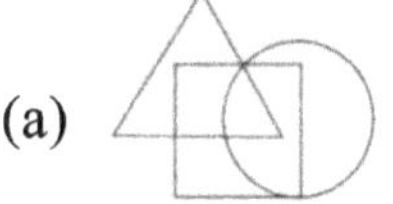

(b) 

(c) 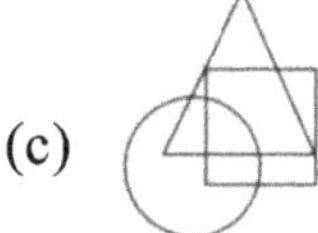

(d) 

9. Select a figure from the options which satisfies the same conditions of placement of dots as in the given figure. **[2021]**

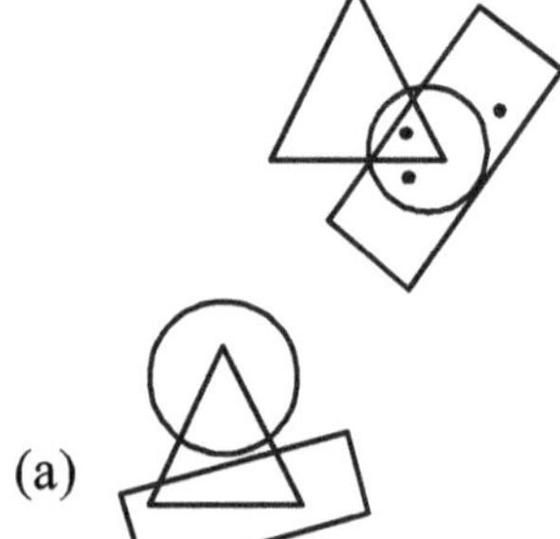

(a)

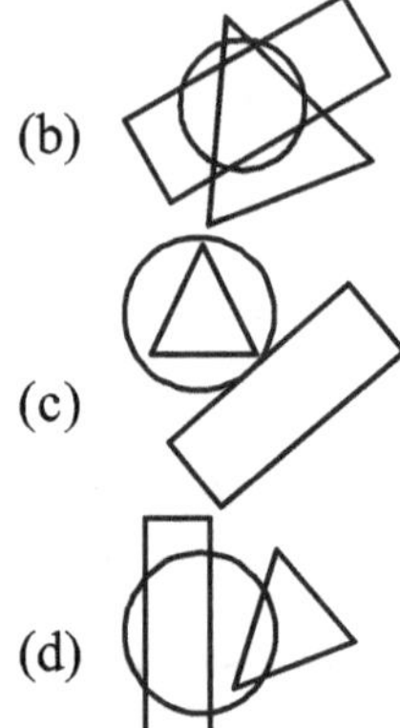

(b)

(c)

(d)

ANSWER KEY																			
LEVEL-1																			
1	(b)	**2**	(c)	**3**	(a)	**4**	(c)	**5**	(d)	**6**	(b)	**7**	(b)	**8**	(b)				
LEVEL-2																			
1	(d)	**2**	(a)	**3**	(b)	**4**	(d)	**5**	(d)	**6**	(b)	**7**	(c)	**8**	(c)	**9**	(b)		

HINTS & EXPLANATIONS

CHAPTER-1

LEVEL 1

1. **(a)** The rule is +11, +22, +44, +88, +176. The next number is 178 + 176 = 354.
2. **(c)** First letter : +2, +3, +4, +5 etc. Second letter : –2, –3, –4, –5 etc.
3. **(c)** +1, +2, +3, +4 in letters; +3, +5, +7, +9 in numbers.
4. **(d)** There are two alternate series .

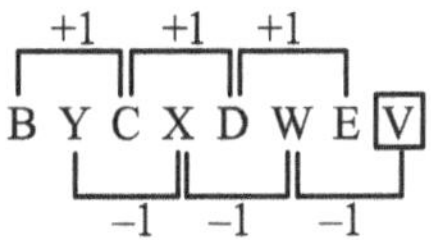

Series I : BCDE (natural order)

Series II : YXWV (reverse order)

5. **(b)** The difference between the letters increases at each step after beginning with two.

B D G K [P] V

+2 +3 +4 +5 +6

6. **(d)** The actual letters which are moving one step forward in the series are packed between B and D.

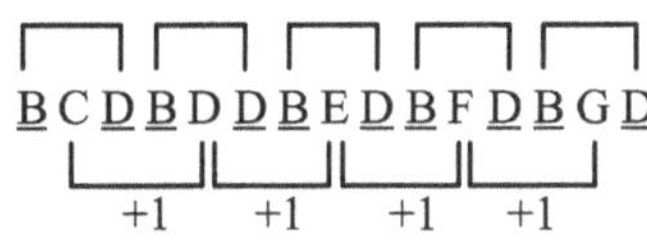

7. **(a)** The series is formed by moving the letters three and one steps forward alternately.

A D E H I L M P Q T U X Y

+3 +1 +3 +1 +3 +1 +3 +1 +3 +1 +3 +1

8. **(b)** The first number 3 is multiplied by 2 to get next number 6. The successive numbers are multiplied by 3, 4, 5, 6 etc. Hence the number next to 360 × 6 = 2160.
9. **(c)** B A A B/B A A B/B A AB/B A AB/ B A A B/B

   ∴ The proper series of missing letters are 'A B A B B A'
10. **(d)** The pattern is: 24 46 68 (90)

    +22 +22 +22
11. **(b)** Each difference is twice the previous difference.
12. **(b)** Triangular numbers, differences increase by 1.
13. **(a)** The series is +5, +9, +13, +17 .... The difference in successive nos. 9 – 5 = 13 – 9 = 17 – 13 = ... = 4. Hence, 35 is wrong. It should be 37.
14. **(c)** The series is + 5, + 7, + 9, + 11, ...
15. **(c)** The pattern of the series is as follows :

    63 58 51 40 27 [10]

    –5 –7 –11 –13 –17
16. **(a)** The number in the center of each figure is the cube of the number of sides of the figure
17. **(a)** Subtract the sum of the even numbers from the sum of the odd numbers.

    7 + 9 = 16   9 + 3 = 12

    2 + 4 = 6   4 + 6 = 10

    16 – 6 = 10   12 – 10 = 2
18. **(b)** The number at the centre is to be multiplied by 1, 2, 3, and 4, then subtract '1' from each to get the peripheral number.

19. **(c)** Moving clockwise,
We have : $594 \div 3 = 198 : 198 \div 3 = 66.$
So, missing number = $66 \div 3 = 22$

20. **(b)** In the first column, $6 \times 5 \times 4 = 120$.
In the second column, $6 \times 7 \times 3 = 126$
Let the missing number be x . Then in the third column, we have : $8 \times 5 \times x = 320$

$$\Rightarrow x = \frac{320}{40} = 8.$$

21. **(a)** Clearly, sum of numbers in each row is 17.
So, missing number = 17 – (4 +7) = 6.

22. **(b)** In the first row, $6\times\frac{3}{2}=9$, $6\times\frac{5}{2}=15$
In the second row,

$$8\times\frac{3}{2}=12,\ 8\times\frac{5}{2}=20.$$

$\therefore$ In the third row, missing number

$$= 4\times\frac{5}{2}=10$$

23. **(d)** In each step, one cross line disappears

24. **(d)** In each step, the center smaller element moves 90° ACW and topmost element gets shaded.

25. **(d)** In each step, the shaded portion and small dot move 90° CW and inside dots take new place alternately.

26. **(c)** $H \xrightarrow{+4} L \xrightarrow{+4} P \xrightarrow{+4} T$
$F \xrightarrow{+4} J \xrightarrow{+4} N \xrightarrow{+4} R$
$C \xrightarrow{+4} G \xrightarrow{+4} K \xrightarrow{+4} O$

27. **(d)** The figures gets laterally inverted in each step. Clearly, fig. (d) is obtained by the lateral inversion of fig. (c) Hence, fig (d) is the answer.

28. **(a)** Three, four, five .... line segments are added to the figure sequentailly at the lower end of the figure. Clearly, there should be nine line segments in fig. (d) Hence, fig. (a) is the answer.

29. **(c)** In each step, each one of the arrow rotates 90° CW.

30. **(d)** The circle moves to the opposite corner (of the square boundary) in each step. The arrow rotates 90°CW and 90°ACW alternately and moves along a diagonal (from lower-left to upper-right corner) sequentially.

31. **(c)** In each step, the outer larger element disappears; the inner smaller element enlarges to become the outer element and a new small element appears inside it.

32. **(c)** The 'S' shaped figure reverses its direction and gets rotated through 45°CW in each step.

33. **(c)** In every step, shaded region moves 90° clockwise.

34. **(a)** In each step, fish is rotating 90° clockwise.

35. **(a)** In each step, one line is added at every corner, in clockwise direction.

36. **(c)** One small circle is added on the outer side of the semicircle in every step.

37. **(a)** All the elements moves clockwise to the adjacent corner in each step.

38. **(b)** L and ↗ moves 90° clockwise in each step.

39. **(b)** Shaded circle moves half step clockwise.

40. **(a)** One line and one circle is added in each step.

41. (c) All symbols moves 1 step in anti-clockwise direction while the line segment changes to its mirror images.

42. (b) The slanting lines changes to the vertical lines in each alternate step and the region containing lines moves 1 step clockwise.

43. (b) In each next step number of leaves are increased by one on alternate side.

44. (d) Number of sides in each next figure is increased by 2.

45. (b) Number of petals in each next flower is decreased by 1.

46. (a) Each next figure is half of the previous figure.

47. (c) One circle is added in each next figure.

48. (d) One circle is added on each side of square in each step. So, answer (d) is correct.

49. (d)

50. (b) Triangle at the corner moves one step anti-clockwise and elements comes inside and outside the triangles alternately.

51. (a) Vertical line becomes horizontal and a new line is inserted in upper most part alternately.

52. (d) Figure is rotating 90° anti-clockwise in each step.

53. (b) Original figure is rotated by 90° in clockwise direction in every next step.

54. (a) In every next figure, a part of flower pattern added in clockwise direction.

55. (c)

56. (d) Original figure is rotated by 90° in anti-clockwise direction in every next figure.

57. (b) Here we get the pattern the arrow rotate ahead first anticlockwise and then anticlockwise direction again and so on.

58. (b) Here all the shapes with in the figure rotate one step ahead in clockwise direction as we can start from arrow.

59. (b) The figure is rotating 90° anti-clockwise in every next step.

60. (b) 61. (b)

62. (c) The figure is rotating 90° anti-clockwise in every next step.

63. (a)

$(1)^3$ $(2)^3$ $(3)^3$ $(4)^3$ $(5)^3$

$(6)^3$ $(7)^3$ $(8)^3$ $(9)^3$ $(10)^3$

Numbers in circle are cubes of consecutive natural numbers.
So in place of ? = $(6)^3 = 216$.

64. (b)

Rotation of figure at 90° in anticlockwise direction is followed in alternate figure.

65. (b)

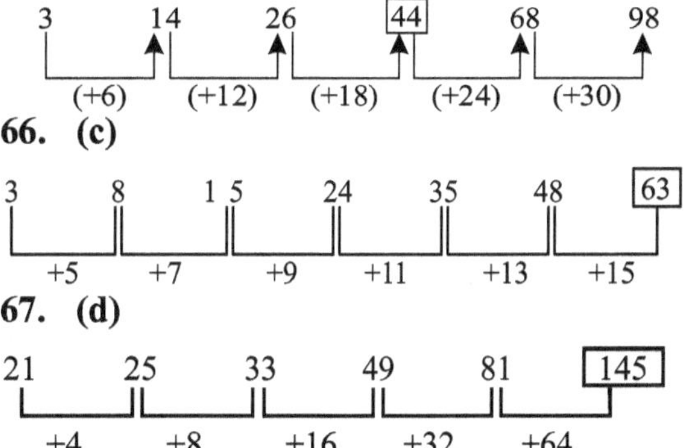

68. (c)

LEVEL 2

1. **(a)** Alphabets are grouped in rows of 4(ABCD, EFGH, IJKL.....) and an initial and final letter of the row in horizontal position is taken.
2. **(a)** Alternate terms are cubes of even and odd numbers respectively.
3. **(b)** Differences of the first set of differences are increasing by 1 viz.

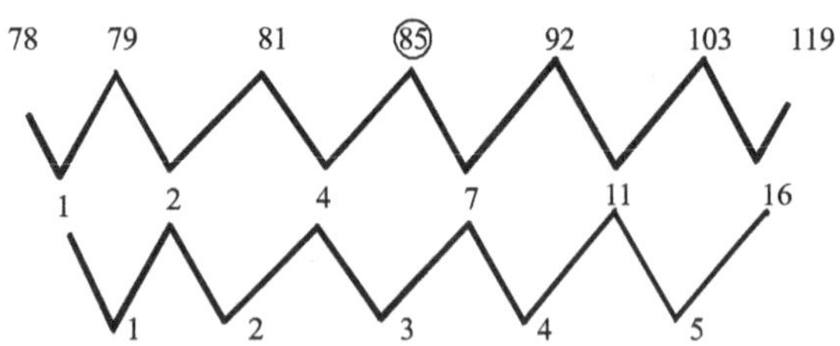

4. **(a)** b– a – bab – ab – a

   Option (a) i.e, abab provides the pattern baa bba / baa bb a
5. **(d)** a – baa – baa – ba

   Option (d) i.e, bbb provides the pattern in which first six terms are laterally inverted as below. abbaab/ baabba
6. **(d)** –baa –bbb–ab–

   Option (d) i.e, bbab provides the pattern bbaa bb / bbaabb
7. **(c)** The series is mno/nopq/opqrs/pqrst
8. **(a)** Add '1' and '0' to the alternate number to a series of odd-numbers in ascending order, viz.

   2 + 1, 3 + 3, 6 + 1, 7 + 3, 10 + 1, 11 + 3, 14 + 1, etc. to get 2, 3, 6, 7, 10, 11, etc.
9. **(b)** Subtract '1' from the alternate terms of the series

   1, 3, 5, 7, ... etc. Like, 1 – 1, 3, 5 – 1, 7, 9 – 1, 11, etc.
10. **(c)** The sequence of the series consists of the product of 2 even numbers in natural order i. e. ,

0	8	24	48	80	120
↓	↓	↓	↓	↓	↓
(0×2)	(2×4)	(4×6)	(6×8)	(8×10)	(10×12)

11. **(c)**

A	4	X
+3 ↓	↓ +5	↓ –3
D	9	U
+3 ↓	↓ +7	↓ –3
G	16	R
+3 ↓	↓ +9	↓ –3
J	25	O

    ∴ Option (c) is correct.
12. (c)

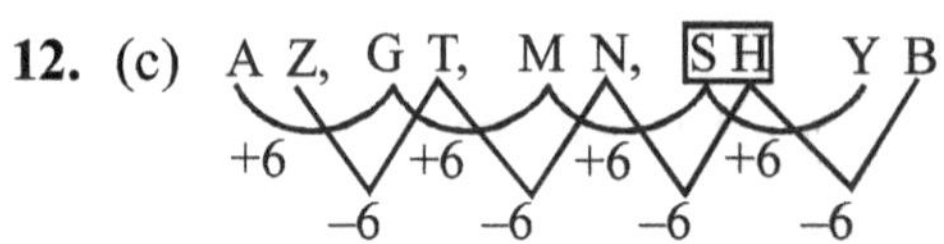

13. **(a)**

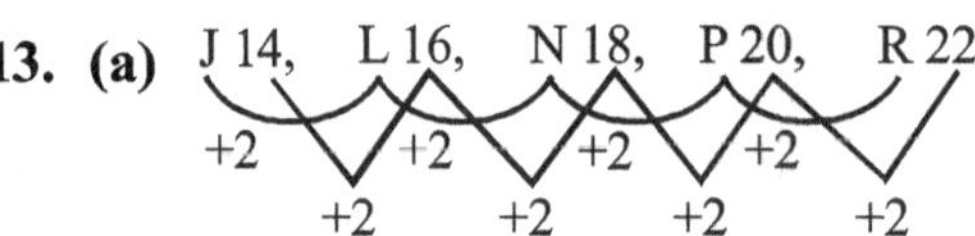

14. **(d)** The arrow moves one, two, three, four,..........spaces CW sequentially.
15. **(d)** In each step, the figure gets laterally inverted and a new line segment is added to the figure at the end opposite to the one having a dot.
16. **(b)** In each step, all the existing arrow get laterally inverted; the line segment is replaced by a new arrow pointing toward the left and a new line segment appears at the lowermost position.
17. **(b)** Similar figure repeats in every second step. Each time a particular figure reappears, it gets vertically inverted.
18. **(c)** In one step, the figure gets laterally inverted and a new circle is introduced inside the existing figure on the RHS and in the next step, the figure gets laterally inverted.

19. (b) Option (b) will be the next figure.

20. (d) Option (d) will be the next figure.

21. (d) option (d) is mathematical symbol.

22. (c) all outer elements having the replica of its present inside of that, except option (c)

23. (d) all inner figures are enclosed one except (d)

24. (c) the shaded region is present on the left bottom region, where as rest all has on top right region.

25. (a)

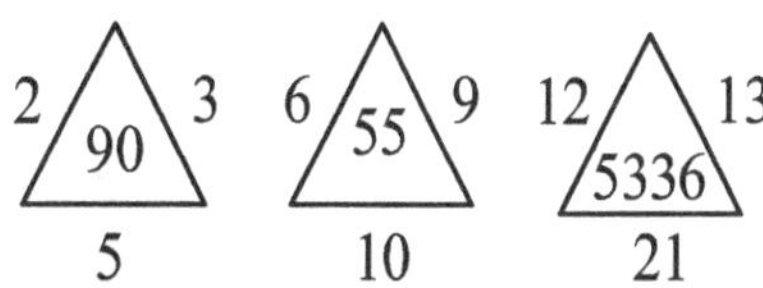

Cube of bigger number – [sum of cube of other two no]

i.e. $(5)^3 - [(2)^3 + (3)^3]$

$= 125 - [8 + 27]$

$= 90$

Similarly

$(10)^3 - [(6)^3 + (9)^3]$

$= 1000 - [216 + 729]$

$= 1000 - 945$

$= 55$

So, $(21)^3 - [(12)^3 + (13)^3]$

$\Rightarrow 9261 - [1728 + 2197]$

$\Rightarrow 5,336$

26. (b) In each subsequent figure no. of lines are increased by "4",

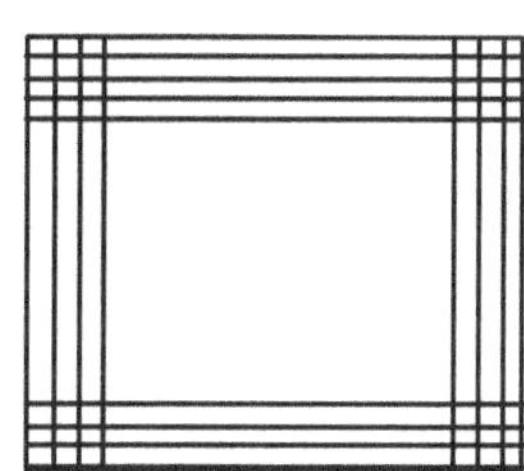

27. (d)

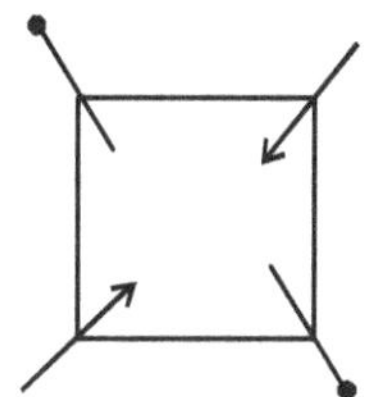

Repetition of figures after the 4th figure in sequence.

28. (c)

3	5	4
	7	

7	3	8
	53	

4	5	5
	?	

In fig.1,

$4 \times 3 = 12 = 7 + 5$

Similarly, In fig.2

$7 \times 8 = 56 = 53 + 3$

So, $4 \times 5 = 20 = 5 + \boxed{15}$

$\therefore$? = 15

29. (c)

108, 135, 9, 144, 171   132, 192, 12, 156, 168   323, 357, 17, 272, ?

$\Rightarrow (108 + 135 + 144 + 171) \div 9 = 558 \div 9 = 62$

$\Rightarrow (132 + 192 + 156 + 168) \div 12 = 648 \div 12 = 54$

Similarly $(323 + 357 + 272 + \boxed{374}) \div 17$

$= 1326 \div 17 = 78$

So, ? = 374.

30. (b) $\frac{6+4}{2} = \frac{10}{2} = 5$ ——— E

$\frac{11+3}{2} = \frac{14}{2} = 7$ ——— G

Similarly

$\frac{9+13}{2} = \frac{22}{2} =$ ——— $\boxed{\text{K}}$

31. (d)

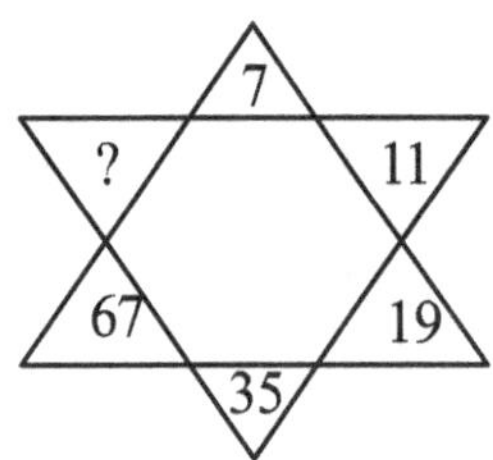

Starting from 7 ; $7 + 4 \rightarrow 11$

$7 + 8 \rightarrow 19$

$19 + 16 \rightarrow 35$

$35 + 32 \rightarrow 67$

$67 + 64 \rightarrow 131$

$\therefore ? = 131.$

32. (a)

B	G	N
D	J	R
H	P	Z

→

2	7	14
4	10	18
8	16	26

In column 1.

$2 + 2 \xrightarrow{} 4 + 4 \xrightarrow{} 8$ (×2)

$7 + 3 \xrightarrow{} 10 + 6 \xrightarrow{} 16$ (×2)

$14 + 4 \xrightarrow{} 18 + 8 \xrightarrow{} 26$ (×2)

$\therefore$? = 26 and 26 represent Z in alphabetical series.

33. (c)

42	28	38
28	35	23
39	14	37

Difference between Column 1 and Column 3 will be equal to the Quotients when column 2 is divided by 7.

i.e $42 - 38 = 4$; $28 \% 7 = 4$

$28 - 23 = 5$; $35 \% 7 = 5$

Similarly

$39 - 37 = 2$; $\boxed{} \% 7 = 2$ i.e 14.

34. (d) Symbols C,N, + and ↑ are moving one step clockwise than shifts diagonally and so on.

Option (d) will continue the series.

35. (a)

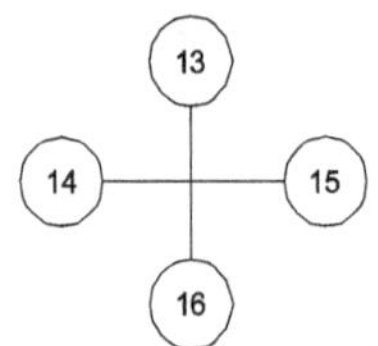

$13 + 16 = 14 + 15$

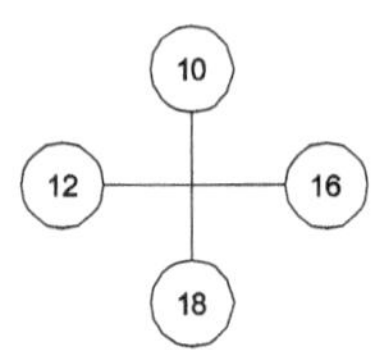

$10 + 18 = 12 + 16$

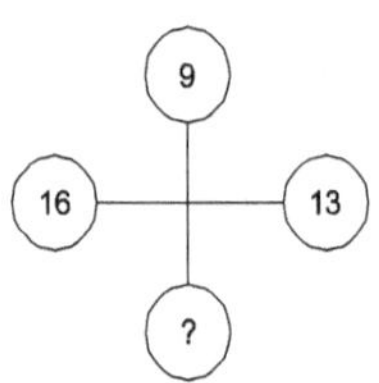

$9 + ? = 16 + 13$

$? = 29 - 9$

$29 = 29$

$28 = 28$ $\boxed{? = 20}$

36. (a)

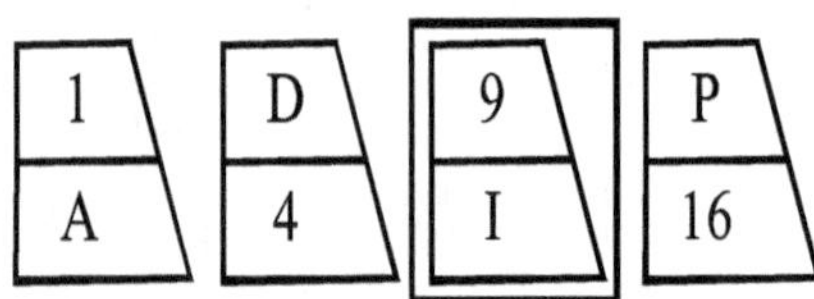

$\Rightarrow (1)^2, (2)^2, (3)^2, (40)^2$

$\Rightarrow$ 1, 4, 9, 16, in english alphabets.

$\Rightarrow$ A, D, I, P

37. (a)

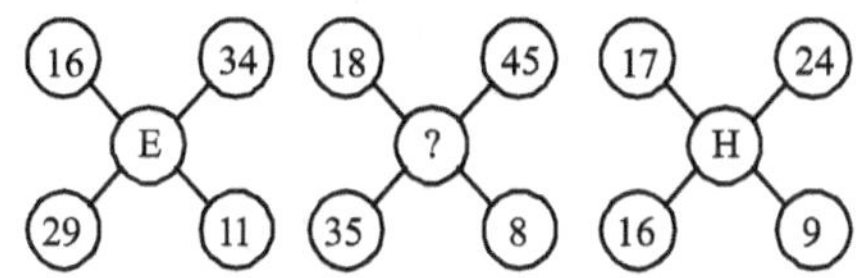

In middle circle, the alphabets which is at the place value of the difference between two diagonal no. is inserted.

Eg- $\left.\begin{array}{l}16-15=5\\34-29=4\end{array}\right\}\rightarrow$ is at place value of 5.

Similarly $\left.\begin{array}{l}17-9=8\\24-16=8\end{array}\right\}\rightarrow$ H is the place value of 8.

$\left.\begin{array}{l}18-8=10\\45-35=10\end{array}\right\}\rightarrow$ J is the place value of 10.

So ? = J

38. (b) $(3 \times 5) \times 2 = 30$
$(4 \times 6) \times 2 = 48$
$(5 \times 7) \times 2 = 70$

39. (b)

40. (c)

41. (c)

42. (a)

43. (c)

CHAPTER-2

LEVEL 1

1. **(c)** All except Earth denote Roman or Greek Gods and Goddesses.
2. **(c)** All except Acre are units of measuring distance, while acre is a unit of area.
3. **(c)** All except Baroda are famous for coal fields.
4. **(d)** All except Beethoven were scientists, while Beethoven was a musician.
5. **(d)** In all other pairs, first is used to hold the second.
6. **(d)** In all other pairs, second is a part of the first.
7. **(b)** In all other pairs, second is the result of the first.
8. **(b)** The words in all other pairs are synonyms.
9. **(b)** The total no. of digits is seven, others are six.
10. **(c)** It is the set of all prime numbers, other are not.
11. **(d)** The sum is not divisible, like other sets.
12. **(b)** The sum of all numbers in each set is 100 except $(2) \neq 100$.
13. **(c)** $(9-7)^2 = 4$, $(13-7)^2 = 36$, $(11-7)^2 = 16$, but $(9-5)^2 \neq 25$.
14. **(c)** Except (b), all others are used for writing.
15. **(d)** Whake is mammal.
16. **(d)** Brook is a natural stream of fresh water where as others may be artificially formed.
17. **(a)** Club is a heavy stick usually thicker at one end than the other. All others are used for writting or drawing.
18. **(b)** All others are different kinds of ornaments.
19. **(d)** Chandigarh is a union territory whereas others are states.

20. (a) April is the even month of the year whereas the other given months are odd.
21. (d) All others are professions.
22. (c) It is the female animal.
23. (b) Star is seen in the sky while all others are seen on earth itself.
24. (a) Others have sea-coast.
25. (d) All other groups contain two consecutive letters of the alphabets.
26. (c) Except (3), All others are pair of opposite letter.
27. (b) Other letters are consecutive.
28. (c) All other groups contain alternate letters of the alphabet in- order.
29. (d) In other groups, first two letters are consecutive and between second and third there is a gap of one letter.
30. (d) In other groups, the last two letters are consecutive in reverse order and between first and second letter there is a gap of 2 letters.
31. (b) This is the only group containing two vowels.
32. (a) All other groups begin with a vowel.
33. (a) In all other groups, the first three letters are in a reverse alphabetical order.
34. (b) First and second letters are alternate: fourth and third letters are alternate.
35. (d) $12 = 3^2 + 3$, $30 = 5^2 + 5$:
$20 = 4^2 + 4$: $? = 6^2 + 6$
36. (d) $3 = 2^2 - 1$, $10 = 3^2 + 1$
$8 = 3^2 - 1$, $? = 4^2 + 1$
$? = 17$
37. (b) 13 and 19 are primes with 17 left out in between.
$? = 290$
38. (d) $48 = 7^2 - 1$, $122 = 11^2 + 1$:
$168 = 13^2 - 1$, $? = 17^2 + 1$
39. (b) The letters are consecutive and written in reverse order.
40. (a) ABCD OPQR
EFGH STUV
41. (c) CEG is formed by skipping the letters in between them, the second set EGC is formed by simply putting the first letter of CEG at last to form EGC, and so on.
42. (b) The 5th letter from A correspond to 5th from Z and therefore 9th letter 'I' from A would correspond 9th letter 'R' from Z.
43. (a) The three letters moved 5, 4, and 3 and steps forward respectively.
44. (b) As Wine is made up by grapes, similarly Vodka is made up by rye or wheat or potatoes .
45. (a) As,

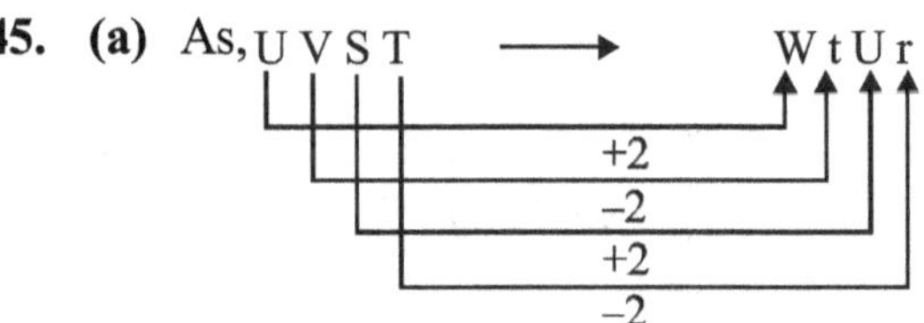

In the same way,

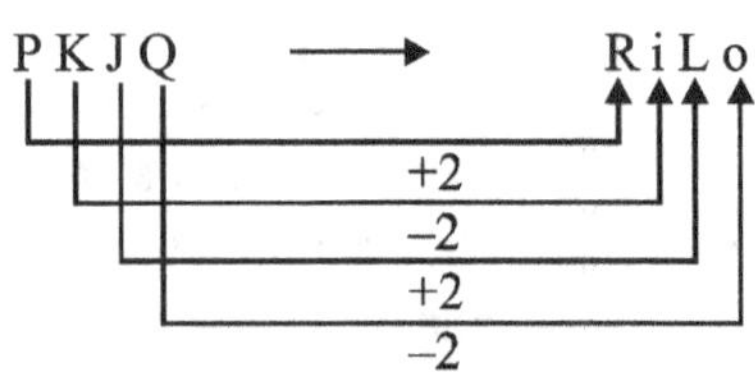

$\therefore$? = P K J Q
46. (c) Race causes fatigue and fast causes hunger.
47. (b) Moon is a satellite and Earth is a planet.
48. (b) First consists of the second.
49. (c) Bank is the land beside a river and coast is the land beside a sea.
50. (d) Both knife and chopper are used for the same purpose i.e. cutting. Similarly,

both quilt and blanket are used for protection from cold.

51. (d) Second is more intense form of the first. Convulsion and spasm means any violent contraction of muscles.

52. (c) A hungry person requires food and a weary person requires rest.

53. (b) All are natural sources.

54. (c) All are computer languages.

55. (a) As a man covers some distance after walking, in the same way, a fish covers some distance after swimming. Hence the correct answer is (1).

56. (a) As medicine cures sickness, in the same way, books remove ignorance.

57. (d) As supervisor supervises the worker, in the same way, officer supervises the clerk.

58. (d) First two letters of the first term are in reverse order in the second term and so are the next two letters.

59. (a) The largest ocean is Pacific Ocean. Similarly, the largest island is Greenland.

60. (b) Tie is worn in the neck and belt is worn on the waist.

61. (b) A, C, F, J are 1st, 3rd, 6th and 10th letters from the start of alphabets whereas Z, X, U, Q are the 1st, 3rd, 6th and 10th letters from the end. In the same way, EGJN are related to VTQM.

62. (b) As 'Chapter' is a part of a 'Book', in the same way, 'brick' is a part of a 'Building'.

63. (b) Second is the working place of the first.

64. (a) Second is a bigger unit than the first and both are used to measure the same quantity.

65. (c) S is the 3rd letter after P and W is the 3rd letter after T. Similarly, D & H are the 3rd letters after A and E respectively.

66. (a)

67. (d) In all other figures, the two double sided arrows intersect each other at right angles.

68. (c) In all other figures, the two line segments are parallel to each other.

69. (a) All other are vowels.

70. (b) Each one of the figures except fig. (2), consists of five arrowheads.

71. (a) All other figures can be rotated into each other. (In each figure except fig. (1) the middle element is obtained by rotating the outer element through 90°CW and the inner element is obtained by rotating the middle element through 90°CW).

72. (b) Each one of the figures except fig. (2), contains – one complete square, one cup-shaped element having side, one 'L'-shaped element having two sides and one straight line.

73. (c) In all other figures, the square has two line segments inside and one line segment outside.

74. (c) Fig. (c), is formed by a combination of A-shaped elements while all other figures are formed by a combination of V- shaped elements.

75. (c) All other figures can be rotated into each other.

76. (d) In all other figures, the dot appears in the same corner of the square as the line outside it.

77. (d) In all other figures, the handle of the umbrella is turned towards the side which has a larger number of lines in the upper part.

78. (c) In each one of the figures except fig. (3), the angle indicated between the two arrows is acute.

79. (c) In each one of the figures, the arrow in the same direction as the smaller row, occurs adjacent to the small arrow.

80. (b) In all the rest problem figures moving from white point first come left turn but in alternative (b) first comes right turn.

81. (a) Only Fig.(a), consists of an odd number of line segments

82. (d) In all the others, the triangle is in the largest rectangle, the shield is in the smallest rectangle (the square), and the other figure is in the second largest rectangle.

83. (c)

84. (a)

85. (b) Except option (b), in all other 'T' and '●'are opposite to each other.

86. (d). From fig. (b) to fig.(a), the straight lines are converted to curved lines (or arcs).

87. (c) The two lower arcs of the right hand side design of problem figure (A) turns over vertically, then the whole design of right hand side reverses horizontally and shifts to left hand side in the problem figure (B). The uppermost arc of left hand side design of problem figure (A) reverses vertically and shifts to the right hand side in the Problem Figure (B). Applying the same rule with Problem Figure (C), the answer figure (c) is obtained.

88. (a) From problem figure first to second whole design reverses vertically. Applying the same rule with the problem figure (C), the answer figure (a) is obtained.

89. (d) Clearly fig.(A) rotate through 135^0 CW to from fig. (B) Similar relationship will give fig. (d) from fig. (C).

Hence, fig. (4) is the answer.

90. (d) The two partially shaded circles rotate through 180°.

91. (d) The curved pin rotates 90°ACW and moves to the adjacent side (of the square boundary) in a CW direction. The curved arrow rotates 90°ACW and moves to the adjacent side in a CW direction

92. (d) The contents of the outer main figure rotate through 45°CW.

93. (b) The upper part of the figure gets separated along the line and is lost.

94. (c) The upper-left and the lower-right elements rotate 90°CW while the upper-right and the lower-left elements rotate 90°ACW.

95. (d) The inner element gets enlarged, rotates 45°CW and becomes the outer element. The outer element reduces in size, gets vertically inverted and becomes the inner element.

96. (a) The two elements approach each other and get overlapped.

97. (e) The figure gets laterally inverted.

98. (d) Except option (d), all the figures can be obtained by rotating each other.

99. (d) In option (d), the two elements drawn inside the circle are different from other figures.

100. (d) Except option (d), all others has one headed arrow with curve attached to other end.

101. (d) In option (d), curved line is more inside the circle than in others.

102. (d) In option (d), the outer line area is not pointed than the other figures.

103. (a) Except option (a), arrow is drawn from mid point of one side triangle.

104. (c) Except option (c), all others can be abtained by rotating each other.

105. (b) In option (b) position of dots are different.

106. (b) In option (b), the direction of arrows is not alternate.

107. (b) Figure in option (b) is different amongst the all figures.

108. (b) Only four symbols (+, ×, =, O) are used in (a), (c) and (d).

109. (b) The arrow head and square are in opposite direction in (a), (c) and (d).

110. (d) Inner and outer figures are same in (a), (b) and (c).

111. (b) Dots are on same side of line in (a), (c) and (d).

112. (b) Number of sides are reduced by one of the innermost figure in (a), (c) and (d).

113. (a) Except option (a), in all others, inner most figure (part) and outer most figure (part) are similar.

114. (c) Except option (c), all other options can be obtained by rotating each other.

115. (c) Except option (c), all others form a right angle.

116. (c) Except option (c), in all other options, line is dividing the figure into two equal parts

117. (c) In option (c), eyes of face are in opposite direction.

118. (b) Number of circles is equal to the number of sides in the geometric figure enclosed by the circle. In option (b) a quadrilateral have four sides, so four circles should be there but it is only three circles.

119. (c) Letter 'R', 'N' and 'U' are present in option (a), (b) and (d). But in option (c) letter N, K and U are present.

120. (d) In figure (d) three are some common spaces formed by three circle.

121. (b) Figure (a), (c) and (d) are common and get be obtained by rotating any of the figure. But figure (b) is different.

122. (b) Except option (b) other triangles are right angle triangle.

123. (d) Except option (d) all have same alphabet K, I and T.

124. (c) In all the three figures, symbols are in even numbers, except figure (c).

125. (a) In all the three figures P, Q, R and S are in anti-clokwise order except figure (a).

126. (d) In all the three figures, vertex of triangle is towards inside except figure (d).

127. (c) In all the three figures, letters C, I and T are common except figure (c).

128. (a) A successful finish of 'Education' equips one with 'Diploma'. Similary, a successful finish in 'Sports' equips one with 'Trophy'.

129. (c) Jewellery consists of Necklace ie 'Necklace' is a kind of 'Jewellery'. Similarly, 'Shirt' is a kind of 'Apparel'.

130. (b) Here, the first is the working place of the second.

131. (b) Uncle and Aunt are opposite words, similarly Cock is opposite to Hen.

132. (d) Table is made of wood, like that Coat is made of cloth.

133. (b) (Boy - Girl) are opposite pair word like that (Nephew - Neice) are opposite Pair word.

134. (d) Physicist deals with the subject Physics and biologist with subject anatomy.

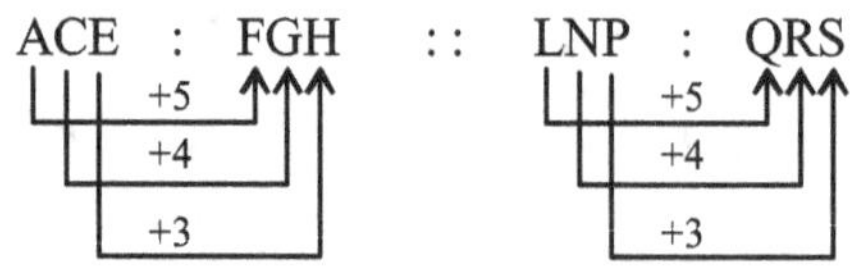

135. (c) The related words are near in meaning.

136. (a) The three letters are moved 5, 4 and 3 steps forward respectively.

137. (d) The word is divided into two sections and the letters are written backwards.

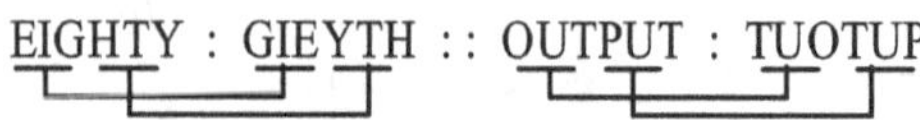

138. (b) The missing number is

$(13)^2 = 169$

$(17)^2 = 289$

139. (c)

140. (c) According to the question,

12 : 168 :: 16 : ?

As, $12 \times 14 = 168$

So, $16 \times 14 = 224$

141. (a) Except (a) in all others, the outer and inner figures are the same.

142. (a) Except (a) in all others, the first two outer figures are same.

143. (d)

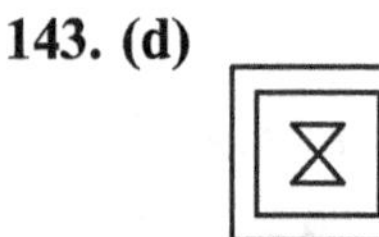

144. (a) The element at the bottom is moved to the diagonal corner, the element in the top is enlarged and moved to the centre and element in the middle is reduced and moved to the bottom right corner.

145. (d) Second image is the mirror image of (vertically placed mirror along y-axis) first image.

146. (b)

147. (c)

148. (a)

149. (a)

150. (d)

151. (d) Except option (d) all other figures have base.

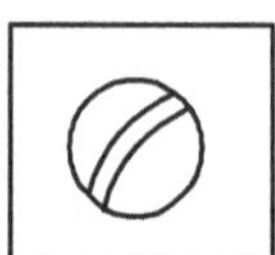

152. (a) Sign X, – and + are moving diagonally

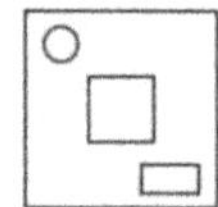

So, option (a) will be the correct figure.

153. (d) No. of sides in Outer figures is one more than the no. of sides in inside figure.

But in option "D" outer figure consistes of no. of sides less than the no. of sides than inside figure

154. (d) Except option (d), all other options are divisible by 5

155. (c) 14 : 72

$14 \times 5 + 2 = 72$

? : 82

$? \times 5 + 2 = 82$

$? = 80/5$

$? = 16$

156. (c)

R		T		W
(18)	+2	(20)	+3	(23)
K		M		P
(11)	+2	(13)	+3	(16)
A		C		E
(1)	+2	(3)	+2	(5)
Q		S		V
(17)	+2	(19)	+3	

157. (c) $\frac{3 \times 4 \times 6}{9} = \frac{72}{9} = 8$

Similarly

$\frac{5 \times 9 \times 2}{9} = \frac{90}{9} = 10$

158. (c)

−1

+1

L N Q : M O P

+1

Similarly

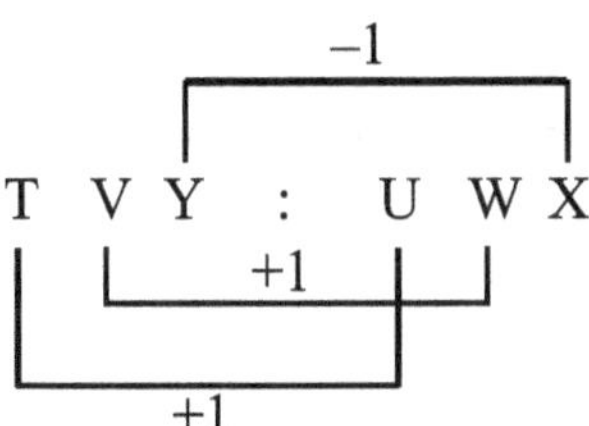

LEVEL 2

1. **(a)** Second is the function of the first.
2. **(b)** Second comes out of the first.
3. **(c)** Second grows on the first. "Pelt" is the skin of an animal with the fur or hair still on it.
4. **(a)** Ring is related to telephone in the same way knock is related to door.
5. **(a)** The words in each pair are antonyms.
6. **(d)**
7. **(b)** Figure become smaller in size and shaded.
8. **(b)** Horizontal line rotates 45° in anti-clockwise direction and vertical line rotates 135° in clockwise direction.
9. **(b)** Second figure is obtained by rotating the first figure 90° clockwise.
10. **(c)** Elements move 180° in clockwise direction and the vertical line becomes horizontal.
11. **(c)**
12. **(a)** Inner and outer figures interchange their positions and the position of lines remains same.
13. **(d)**
14. **(a)** Inner and outer figures interchange their positions.
15. **(c)** Second figure is obtained by rotating the first figure 180° in clockwise direction.
16. **(b)** Line segments are removed from the bottom right corner.
17. **(b)** Inner and outer shapes are interchanged and the inner shape becomes unshaded.
18. **(d)** First figure in the first pair gets rotated in anticlockwise direction and is joined by second half symmetric figure. Also the upper half part gets shaded and centre line gets removed.
19. **(b)** The second figure of first pair is the mirror image of first figure.
20. **(d)** Number of sides is increased by 1 from first figure to second figure.
21. **(b)** From first figure to second, figure rotates 90° clockwise.
22. **(c)** Inner figure becomes outer and outer figure becomes inner.

23. (b) Second figure is used to operate first figure.

24. (b) Second figure is the water image of first figure.

25. (b) Second figure is obtained by adding a vertical line to first figure.

26. (c) Order of the geometric figure reverse. Hence required figure will have triangle inner most, then square and circle in the outer most.

27. (b) Second figure is the mirror image of first figure like that fourth figure will be mirror image of third figure.

28. (d) Second figure is optained by rotating first figure by 90° in anti-clockwise direction. Similarly fourth figure of obtained by rotating third figure by 90° in anti-clockwise.

29. (b) Symbol inside the first figure touches the perimeter in second figure. So, required figure is given in option (b).

30. (c) By symmetry from the question figure we get option (c) replace the mark of interrogation.

31. (b) By symmetry from the question figure we get option (b) as the small geometric figure, is inside the big geometric figure here circle is smaller than square so circle will go inside the square as

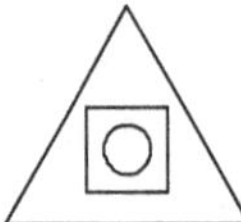

32. (c) In first question figure, design is in circle. So, in second question fiigure, there are 16 circles. In the same way, in third question figure, the design is in square. So, in answer figure, there should be 14 squares.

33. (b) Second question figure is the middle part of first question figure. Similarly, answer figure (b) is the middle part of third question figure.

34. (a) Second question figure is the mirror image of first question figure. Similarly, answer figure (a) is the mirror image of third question figure.

35. (c) The figure is rotating 180°.

36. (a) M is only consonant, rest are vowel.

37. (c) only U is vowel

38. (d) rest all are horizontal element except (d) which is vertical

39. (c) rest all has three petals.

40. (d) number of turning increases with a sequence.

41. (b) the line segment along with the circle are eight except option (b)

42. (d) all rotates in anti clock wise direction except option (d)

43. (d) one arrow is facing towards the centre.

44. (d) Draw the water imge of the centre figure. Small figures are changing their places diagonally draw mirror image of '↜' and rotate '↵' 90° anticlockwise.

45. (a) Second figure is diagonally rotation of first figure.

Similarly

Fourth figure is diagonally rotation of third figure.

46. (d)

47. (b)

CHAPTER-3

LEVEL 1

1. **(b)** Type – Direct substitution (Direct fashion)

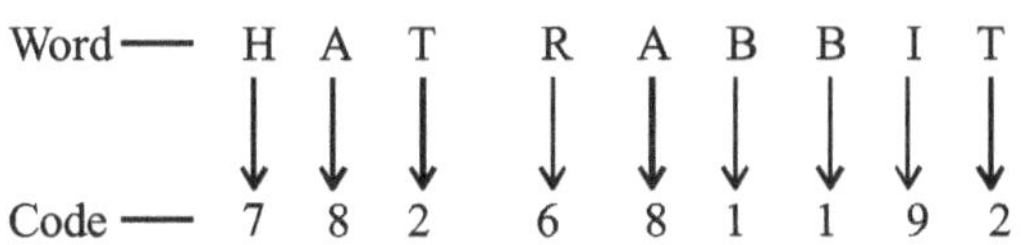

Thus the code for the given word

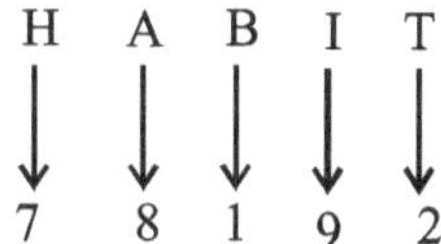

Thus option (2) is the correct answer.

2. **(b)** Alphanumeric coding type.

Word	Code value (alphabet series)	Final code
CAT	$C = 3, A = 1, T = 20$ $3 + 1 + 20 = 24$	$24 \times 2 = 48$
Z	26	$26 \times 2 = 52$
TEA	$T = 20, E = 5, A = 1$ $20 + 5 + 1 = 26$	$26 \times 2 = 52$

3. **(d)** Type – Pattern substitution (+1)

Word — H E L M E T (each +1)

Code — I F M N F U

∴ C H O C O L A T E (each +1) → D I P D P M B U F

4. **(b)** Type – Pattern substitution (moving forward in ascending order).

Word — F A I R (+3, +4, +5, +6) T A P E (+3, +4, +5, +6)

Code — I E N X W E U K

5. **(d)** Type – Direct substitution (direct fashion)

So, code for CALICUT – 8251896.

6. **(a)** Type – Direct coding (Direct fashion)

$5 \rightarrow P, 4 \rightarrow O, 6 \rightarrow E, 1 \rightarrow A, 3 \rightarrow R.$

Therefore, 54613 is coded as POEAR.

7. **(a)** Type – Simple arrangement (SWAP CODING)

Interchange F and D, R and N and I and E.

Similarly, DESERT is coded as TRESED.

8. **(b)** Type – Simple Arrangement (Swap coding).

In the word AFFAIR, the positions of first A & first F are interchanged second A & second F are interchanged and I and R are interchanged.

Similarly, FERRARIS is coded as EFRRRASI.

9. **(a)** Simple arrangement (Swap Coding)

10. **(b)** P O P U L A R (each +1)

Q P Q V M B S

F A M O U S

↑ −1 ↑ −1 ↑ −1 ↑ −1 ↑ −1 ↑ −1

G B N P V T

Thus, FAMOUS is the answer.

11. (b) PATTERN SUBSTITUTION (+ 1)

Sol. (12 - 13)

Direct substitution in jumbled – fashion.

S. No.	Code	SENTENCE
1	782	— Flowers are beautiful.
2	692	— Roses are red.
3	628	— Roses are beautiful.

The digit '2' in the code is common in all three codes, similarly on the sentence side, 'are' is the word common in all the three sentences. Therefore, the digit '2' is the representation for 'are'.

Similarly, on the code side '8' is the digit common in 1st & 3rd codes, therefore, '8' stands for 'beautiful'.

Thus '7' is the representation for 'flowers'.

Also, the digit '6' is common in 2nd & 3rd codes and so is the word 'roses'. Therefore, '6' stands for '7' 'roses'. Thus '9' stands for 'red'.

12. (b)

13. (c) Red.

Sol. (14 -15)

$M \rightarrow 9$ $I \rightarrow 7$

$S \rightarrow 6$ $T \rightarrow 5$

$A \rightarrow 4$ $K \rightarrow 1$

$E \rightarrow 2$ $N \rightarrow 8$

$D \rightarrow 8$

14. (a) $D \rightarrow 3, I \rightarrow 7, S \rightarrow 6, T \rightarrow 5,$
$A \rightarrow 4, N \rightarrow 8, T \rightarrow 5$

15. (d) $S \rightarrow 6, T \rightarrow 5, A \rightarrow 4, I \rightarrow 7, N \rightarrow 8$

16. (c) No. of alphabets in REASON
$= 6 - 1 = 5$
No. of alphabets in BELIEVED
$= 8 - 1 = 7$
$\therefore$ GOVERNMENT $= 10 - 1 = 9$.

17. (d)

M	U	M	B	A	I
(13)	(21)	(13)	(2)	(1)	(9)
+1	+2	+3	+4	+5	+6
N	W	P	F	F	O
(14)	(23)	(16)	(6)	(6)	(15)

Similarly

C	A	R	P	E	T
(3)	(1)	(18)	(16)	(5)	(20)
+1	+2	+3	+4	+5	+6
D	C	U	T	J	Z
(4)	(3)	(21)	(20)	(10)	(26)

18. (d)

P	R	O	T	E	I	N
(16)	(18)	(15)	(20)	(5)	(9)	(14)
−1	+2	−1	+2	−1	+2	−1
O	T	N	V	D	K	M
(15)	(20)	(14)	(22)	(4)	(11)	(13)

Similarly

M	I	N	E	R	A	L
(13)	(9)	(14)	(5)	(18)	(1)	(12)
–1	+2	–1	+2	–1	+2	–1
L	K	M	G	Q	C	K
(12)	(11)	(13)	(7)	(17)	(3)	(11)

19. **(c)**

N	O	I	S	E
(14)	(15)	(9)	(19)	(5)
+2	+2	+2	+2	+2
P	Q	K	U	G
(16)	(17)	(11)	(21)	(7)

Similarly,

P	E	A	C	E
(16)	(5)	(1)	(3)	(5)
+2	+2	+2	+2	+2
R	G	C	E	G
(18)	(7)	(3)	(5)	(7)

20. **(c)**

LEVEL 2

1. **(a)** B E A U T I F U L
↓ ↓ ↓ ↓ ↓ ↓ ↓ ↓ ↓
Z X O A B T Y A M

2. **(a)** F L A I R
↓ ↓ ↓ ↓ ↓
Y M O T W

3. **(b)** B U I L T
↓ ↓ ↓ ↓ ↓
Z A T M B

4. **(c)** V A L I D
↓ ↓ ↓ ↓ ↓
C O M T I

5. **(d)** A F R A I D
↓ ↓ ↓ ↓ ↓ ↓
O Y W O T I

6. **(b)** B U L L E T
↓ ↓ ↓ ↓ ↓ ↓
Z A M M X I

7. **(a)** It is clear that ***pie*** means ***light***. So there can be only b correct options (a) or (b).

But ***mie*** means ***blue*** for sure so (b) is wrong.

8. **(a)**

	18	5	1	19	15	14
	R	E	A	S	O	N
As,	–2 ↓	+2 ↓	–2 ↓	+2 ↓	–2 ↓	+2 ↓
	16	7	25	21	13	16
	P	G	Y	U	M	P

Similarly,

4	9	18	5	3	20
D	I	R	E	C	T
–2↓	+2↓	–2↓	+2↓	–2↓	+2↓
B	K	P	G	A	V
2	11	16	7	1	22

So, DIRECT will be coded as BKPGAV.

9. **(b)**

(16)	(8)	(15)	(14)	(5)
P	H	O	N	E
(–1)↓	(–1)↓	(–1)↓	(–1)↓	(–1)↓
O	G	N	M	D
(15)	(7)	(14)	(13)	(4)

"1" is subtracted from the place value of alphabets in alphabetical series to get the results.

Similarly

(14)	(1)	(20)	(9)	(15)	(14)	(1)	(12)
N	A	T	I	O	N	A	L
↓(−1)	↓(−1)	↓(−1)	↓(−1)	↓(−1)	↓(−1)	↓(−1)	↓(−1)
M	Z	S	H	N	M	Z	K
(13)	(26)	(19)	(8)	(14)	(13)	(26)	(11)

10. (c)

(1)	(5)	(9)	(15)	(21)
A	E	I	O	U
(+2)↓	(+2)↓	(+2)↓	(+2)↓	(+2)↓
C	G	K	Q	W
(3)	(7)	(11)	(17)	(23)

"2" is added in each alphabet in their alphabetical order to get the results.

Similarly

(9)	(11)	(18)	(17)	(16)
I	K	R	Q	P
(+2)↓	(+2)↓	(+2)↓	(+2)↓	(+2)↓
K	M	T	S	R
(11)	(13)	(20)	(19)	(18)

11. (a) Nice big home → emoh gib ecin.
Nice small family → glimab llams ecin.
In coded form, words as well as alphabets in these words are written in reverse order.
So, "all the best" can be coded as "tseb eht lla".

12. (d)

$	*	×	+	r	#	&
O	L	Y	M	P	U	S

So word in "OLYMPUS"

13. (c)

B	R	I	G	H	T
(2)	(18)	(9)	(7)	(8)	(20)
−2	+2	−2	+2	−2	+2
Z	T	G	I	F	V
(26)	(20)	(7)	(9)	(6)	(22)

Similarly

A	R	O	U	N	D
(1)	(18)	(15)	(21)	(14)	(4)
−2	+2	−2	+2	−2	+2
Y	T	M	W	L	F
(25)	(20)	(13)	(23)	(12)	(6)

14. (c)

G Y P S U M → G M P S U Y
(7) (25) (16) (19) (21) (13) → (7) (13) (16) (19) (21) (25)

Alphabets are arranged in increasing alphabetical order.

Similarly

G A R D E N → A D E G N R
(7) (1) (18) (4) (5) (14) → (1) (4) (5) (7) (14) (18)

15. (b)

M I R A C L E → A C E I L M R
↓ ↓ ↓ ↓ ↓ ↓ ↓ ↓ ↓ ↓ ↓ ↓ ↓ ↓
13 9 18 1 3 12 5 1 3 5 9 12 13 18

Alphabets are arranged in increasing order in alphabetical,
Series,
Similarly

B U I L D E R → B D E I L R U

↓ ↓ ↓ ↓ ↓ ↓ ↓ ↓ ↓ ↓ ↓ ↓ ↓ ↓

2 21 9 12 4 5 18 2 4 5 9 12 8 21

16. (c)

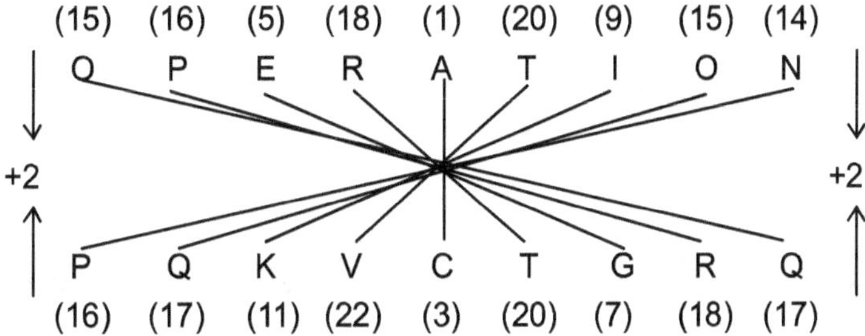

Similarly

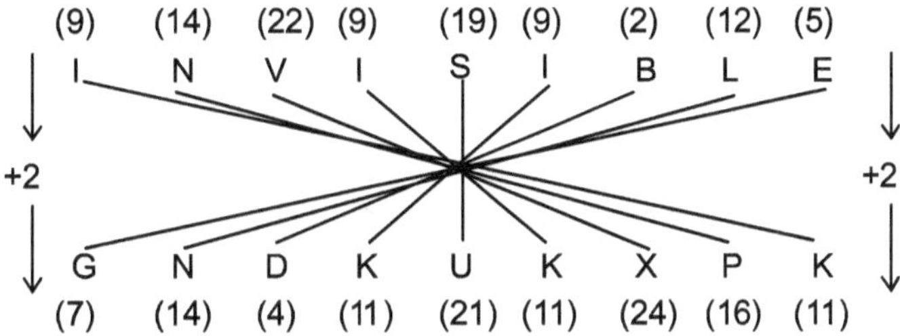

17. (a) C R E A T E ⟶ A C E E R T
(3) (8) (5) (1) (20) (5) (1) (3) (5) (5) (18) (20)

Alphabets are arranged in increasing alphabetical order.
Similarly

B R I G H T ⟶ B G H I R T
(0) (18) (9) (7) (8) (20) (2) (7) (8) (9) (18) (20)

18. (d)

P L A Y E R
(16) (12) (1) (25) (5) (18)
+3 +3 +3 +3 +3 +3
S O D B H U
(19) (15) (4) (2) (8) (21)

Similarly

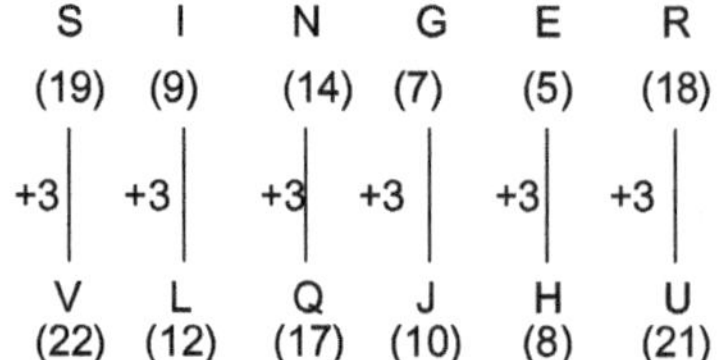

19. (d)

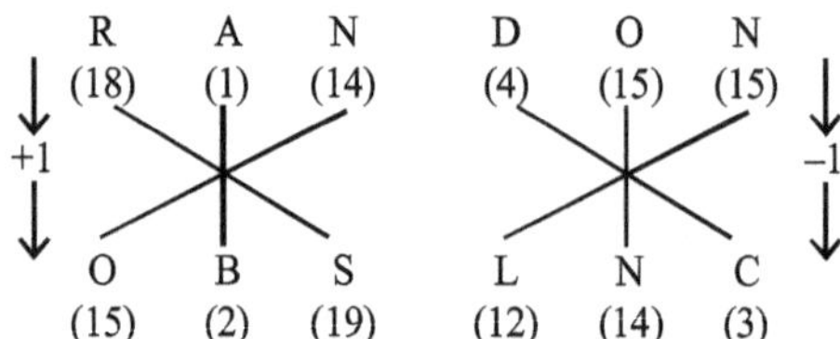

Similarly

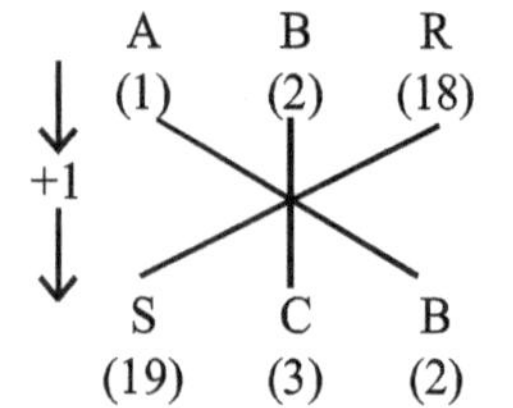

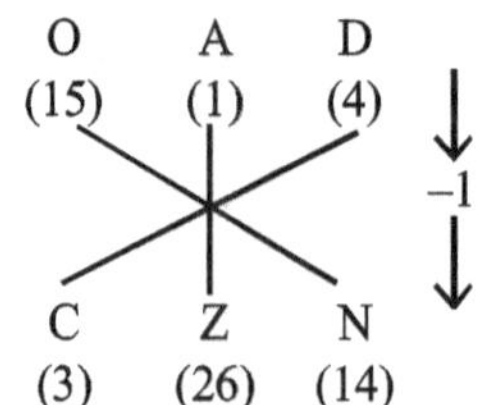

20. (a)

21. (b)

CHAPTER-4

LEVEL 1

1. **(a)** D is the brother of E and E is the daughter of B. This means that D is the son of B. Also, A is the mother of B. So, A is the grandmother of D.

2. **(b)** Father's Wife — Mother; Mother's daughter — Sister Deepak's sister's younger brother— Deepak's brother.

3. **(d)** Studying the statements carefully, was find that B is the brother of A and A's son is the brother of D, so D is the daughter of A. Since C and D are sister, so C is also the daughter of A. The B is the uncle of C. The answer is (d)

4. **(d)** The relationship chart, based on the given problem can be worked out as given below.

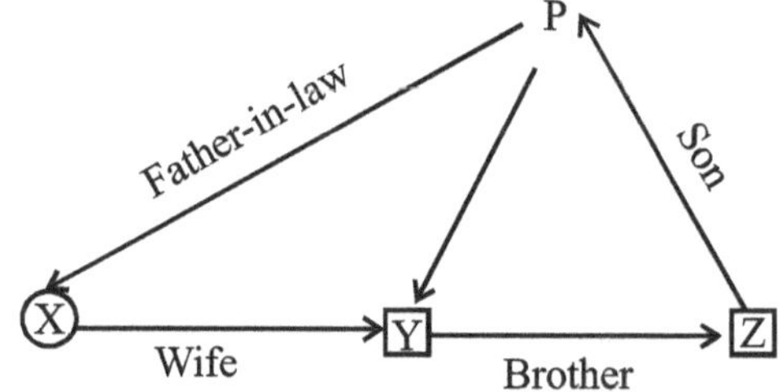

'Y' is the brother of 'Z' who is son of "P' So. Z' is also the son of 'P' When 'P' is the father of 'Y' and X' is the wife of 'Y' then 'P is the father-in-law of 'X'

5. **(d)**

1\.

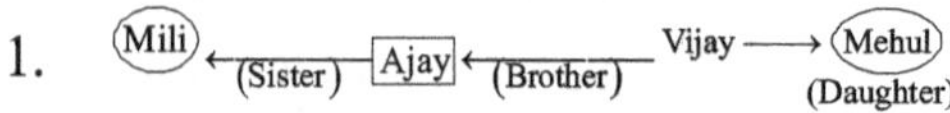

2\. Sanjay (brother) → Rahul

There are two sets of relationship information given is incomplete and no relation can be established between the two sets.

6. (c) Clearly, the lady is the grandmother of man's sister's son i.e, the mother of the mother of man's sister's son i.e, the mother of man's sister.

7. (b) B is the daughter of C and C is the daughter in law of P. So P is the grandfather of B. Also, A is uncle of B i.e, A is the brother of B's father. Thus, A is the son of P.

8. (d) C is B's daughter and D is B's son. So, D is the brother of C.E is a male married to C so, E is the husband of C, whose brother is D. Thus, D is the brother in-law of E.

9. (b) It is clear that C is the Brother of B but how B is related to C depends on the sex of B.

10. (c) Only son of Archana's grandfather means Archana's father & his son is Archana's brother.

11. (a) $P+Q \Rightarrow$ P is daughter of Q.

$Q-R \Rightarrow$ Q is husband of R.

Represents this in diagrammatic form. We get,

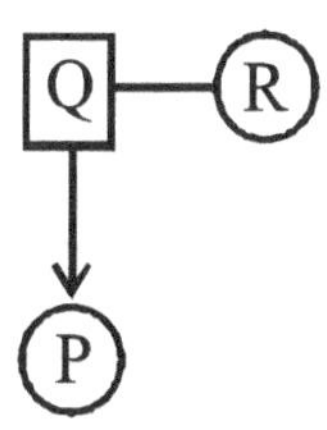

Then, R is mother of P.

Sol. (12-15)

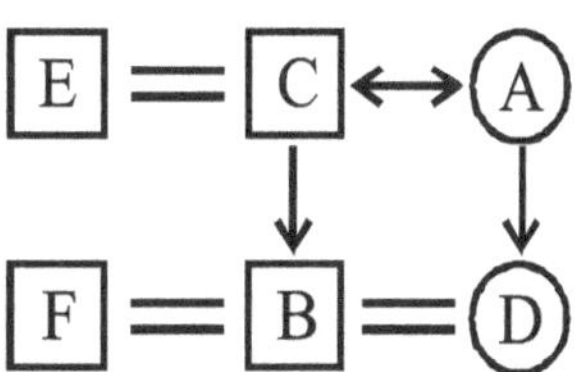

where, □ ⇒ Male; ○ ⇒ Female;

= ⇒ Sibling relationship; ↔ ⇒ spouse relationship.

12. (d) There are 4 male members are there in the family.

13. (d) A is mother of B

14. (c) A have three children

15. (d) AD is a pair of females.

16. (d) The blood relation diagram is as shown below:

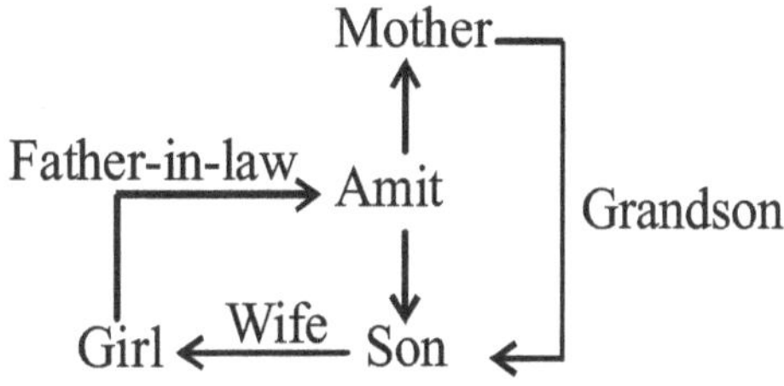

So, Amit is father-in-law to the girl.

17. (d)

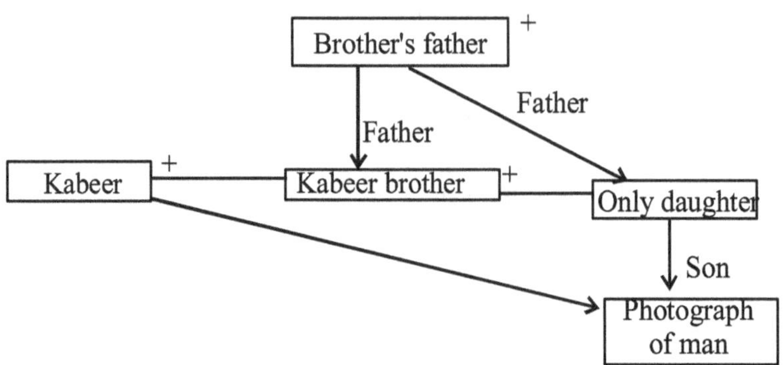

Kabeer is maternal uncle of the man in the photograph.

18. (c)

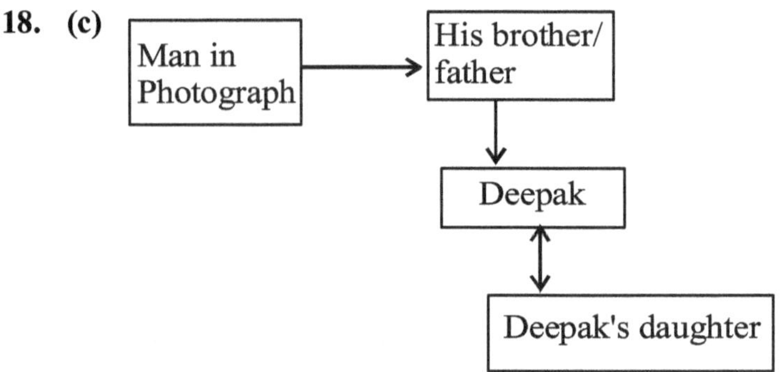

Man is photograph is uncle of Deepak.

19. (a)

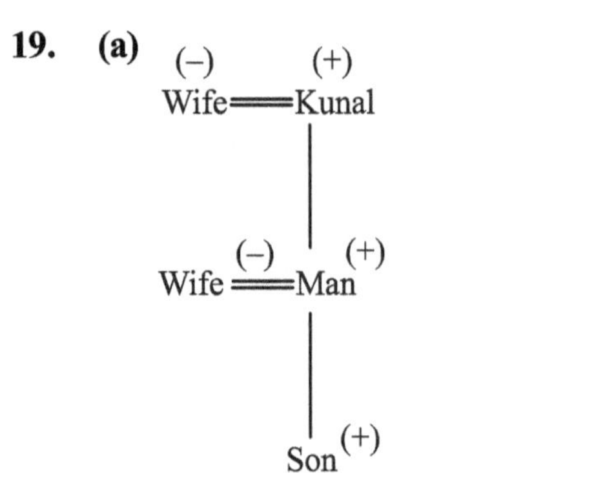

Man is the Son of Kunal's wife.

20. (d)

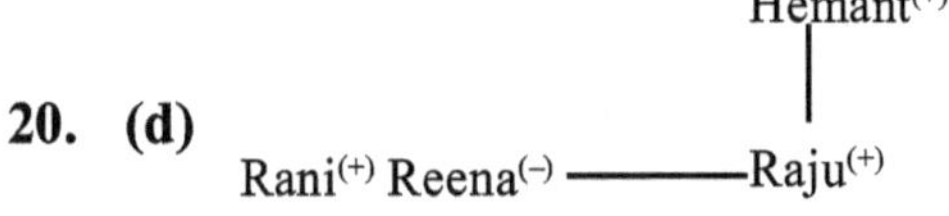

Ram is the son-in-law of Hemant.

LEVEL 2

1. (b) P is the daughter of V, who is spouse of T. T is the daughter of S. So, T is the mother and V is the father of P. Therefore, S is the grandfather of P.

2. **(a)** R and S are brother and Q is the child of R and T is the child of S. So, cousin of Q is T.

3. **(b)** A is the sister of B and B is the son/daughter of C. So, A is the daughter of C. So, D is grandfather of A.

4. **(b)**

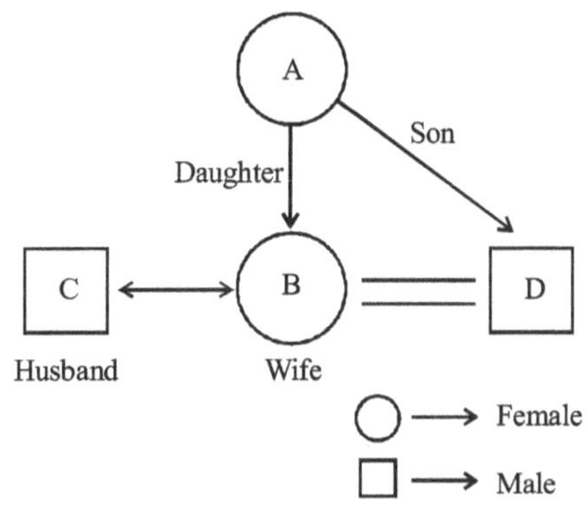

'D' is brother of B

5. **(d)**

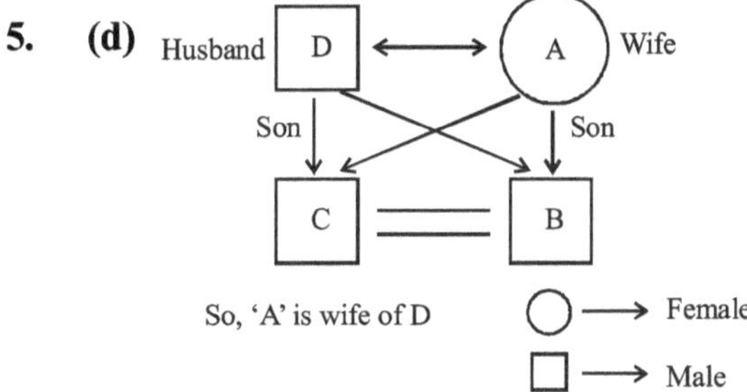

6. **(c)** Male members in family
:- Father → 2
Married son → 4
Unmarried son → 2
Two married son have 2 sons each = 4.
Two married son have 1 son and 1 daughter each = 2.
Total male members = 2 + 4 + 2 + 4 + 2 = 14

7. **(c)**

(–) Women

Shivam (+) —— Brother (+) // Wife (–)

niece (–)

The woman is mother-in-law of Shivani's brother.

8. **(b)** Person (+) ——— Brother (+)

Arjun (+)

Daughter (–)

The person is the uncle of Arjun.

9. **(c)**

D⁻ — F⁻, E⁺ — G⁺ — G⁻

∵ "I" represents son/daughter relation
"=" represents husband/wife relation
∵ O^{+} represents male
O^{-} represents female
"–" represents brother/sister relation.
H is grandfather of D.

10. (c)

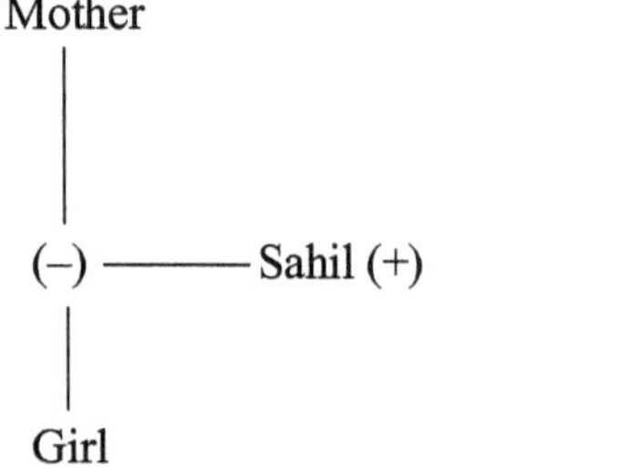

Sahil is the maternal uncle of the girl.

11. (a)

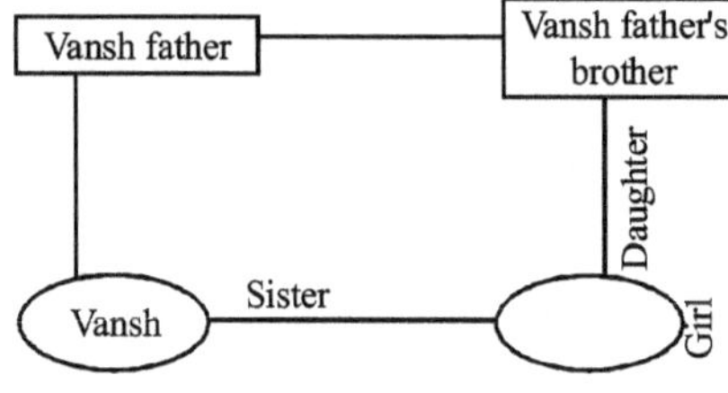

Girl is vansh sister.

12. (c) (–) (+)

SP

Q(–) R(–)

S is the wife of P.

13. (b)

14. (c)

CHAPTER-5

LEVEL 1

1. **(d)** Clearly comparing the direction of A w.r.t C in the second diagram with that in the first diagram, A will be south-west of C.

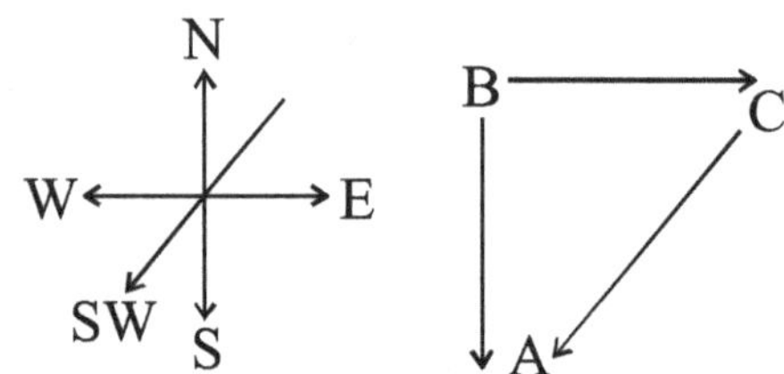

2. **(c)**

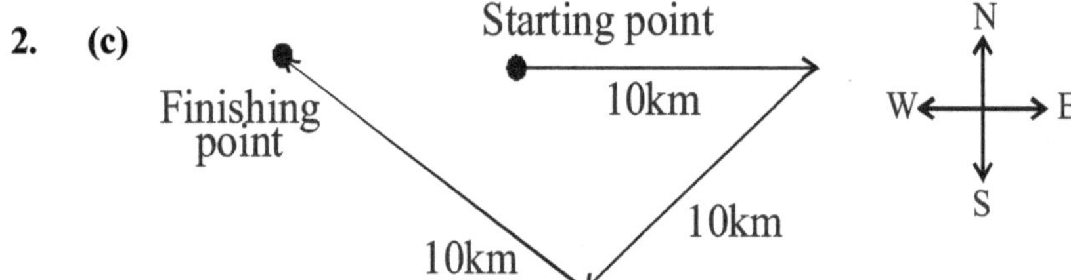

3. (d)

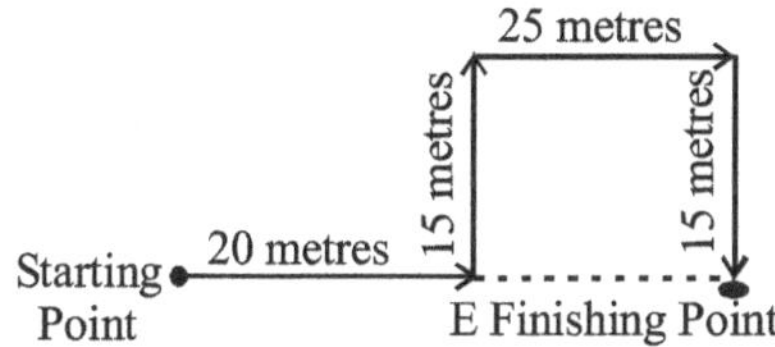

4. (c) (12 km + 5 km = 17 km)

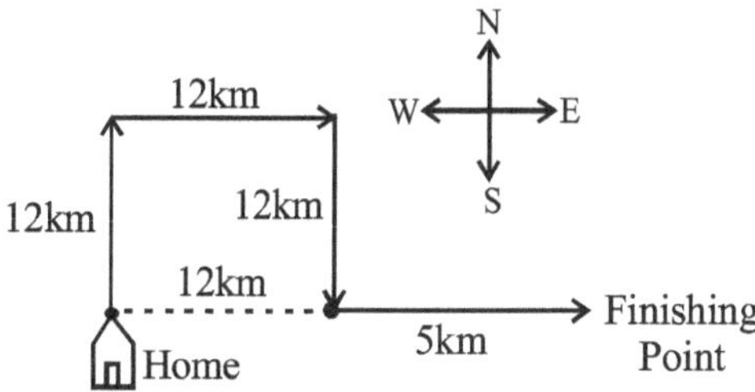

5. (d) The movements of Ramakant are as shown in fig.

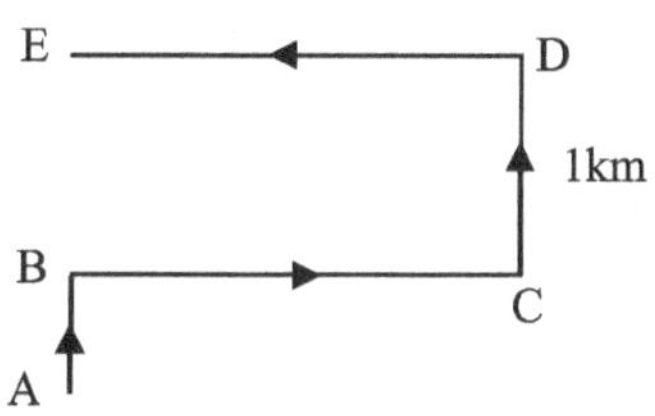

Clearly he is finally walking in the direction DE i.e, west

6. (d) Clearly, the seating arrangement is as shown in the adjoining figure. So, S is at the south-west position.

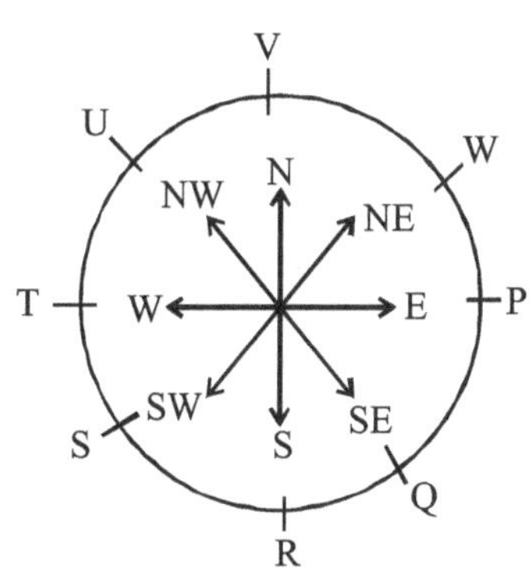

7. (a) Original directions

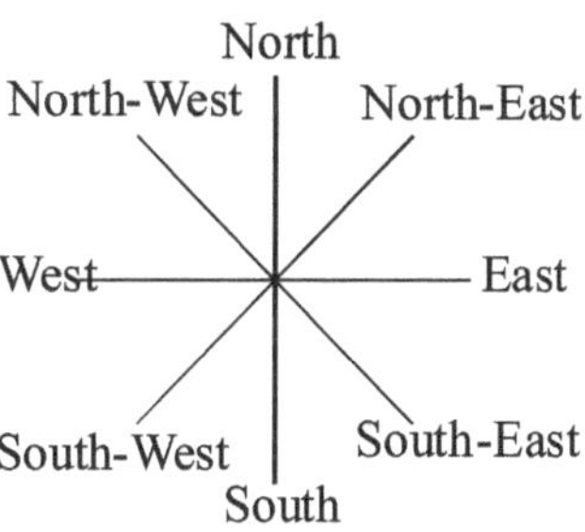

Changed directions

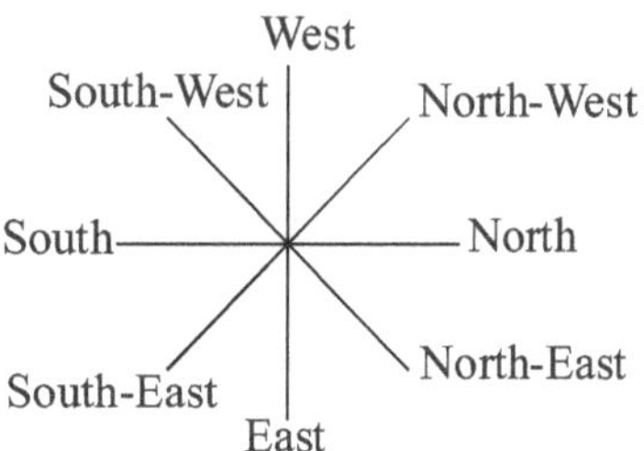

8. (c) The directions to be followed will be :

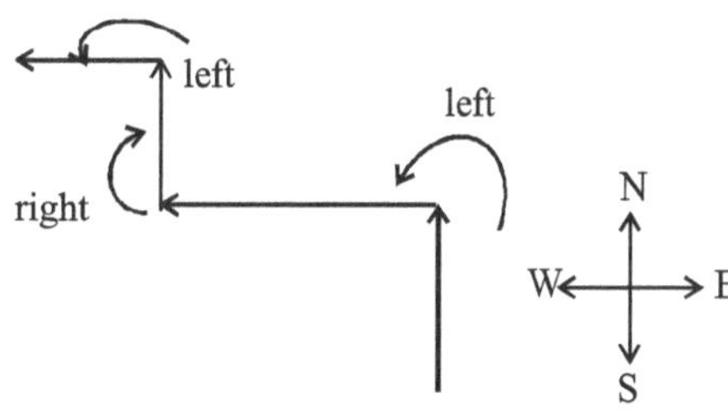

9. (c) The movements of Lokesh are as shown in figure. (A to B, B to C, C to D to E). Clearly, his final position is E which is to the North of his house A.

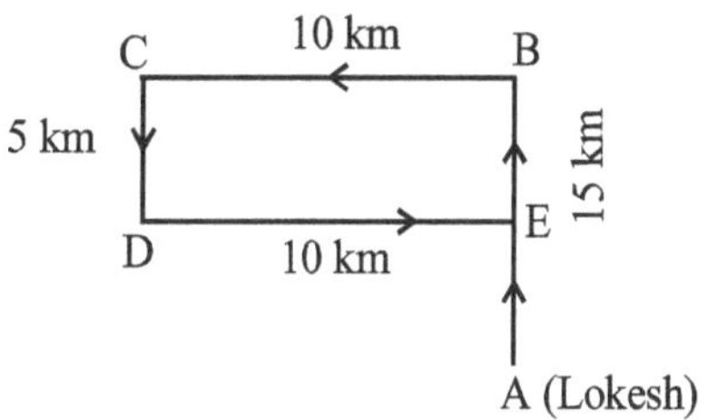

10. (d) Deepa started from A, moved 75 m upto B turned left and walked 25 m upto C. She then Turning to the right at an angle of 45°, she was finally moving in the direction DE i.e., south west.

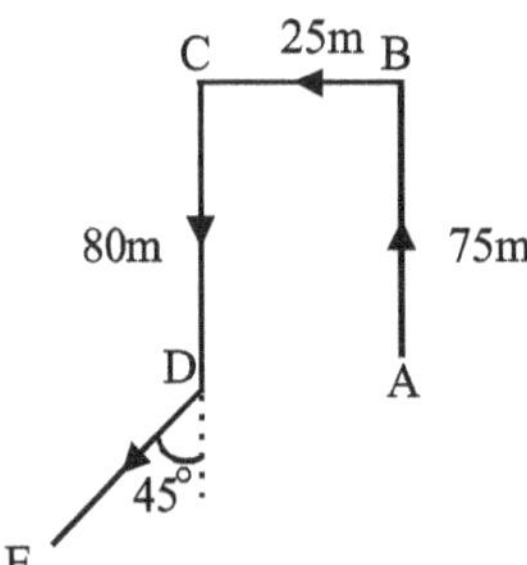

11. (a) Clearly, Johnson drove 15 km from A to B north wards and then 10 km from B to C towards west. He then moves 5 km southwards from C to D and 8 km eastwards upto E. Finally, he turned right and moved 10 km upto F.

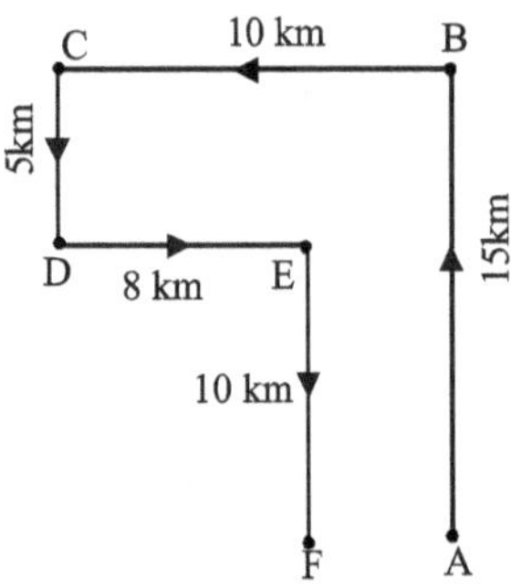

∴ A and F lie in the same straight line and F lies to the west of A.

So, Johnson's distance from the starting point

A = AF = (BC – DE) = (10 – 8) km = 2 km.

12. (c) The movements indicated are as shown in fig. (A to B, B to C. C to D and D to E). Clearly, E lies to the east of A.

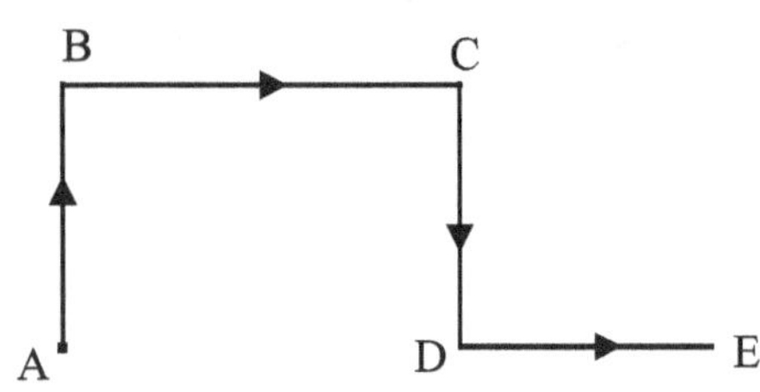

13. (d)

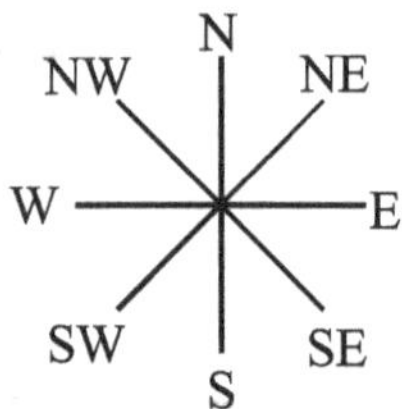

N NW NE W E SW S SE

A is to south west of C.

14. (c) The direction diagram of a farmer is as follows:

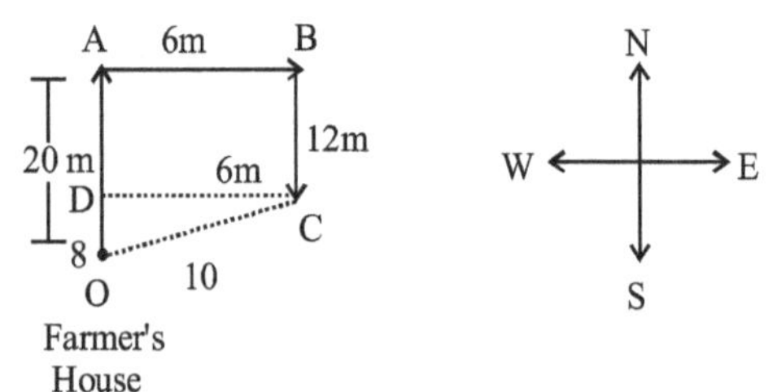

Here, In ΔODC,

$$\angle D = 90°$$

$$\therefore\ OC = \sqrt{8^2 + 6^2} = \sqrt{100} = 10.$$

So, he is 10 m from his original position.

15. (c) According to the question, if the first person face is towards north then the right hand of second person will be in west direction.

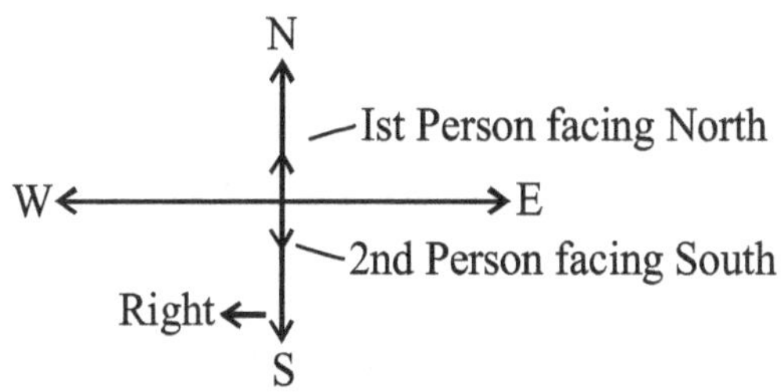

16. (b)

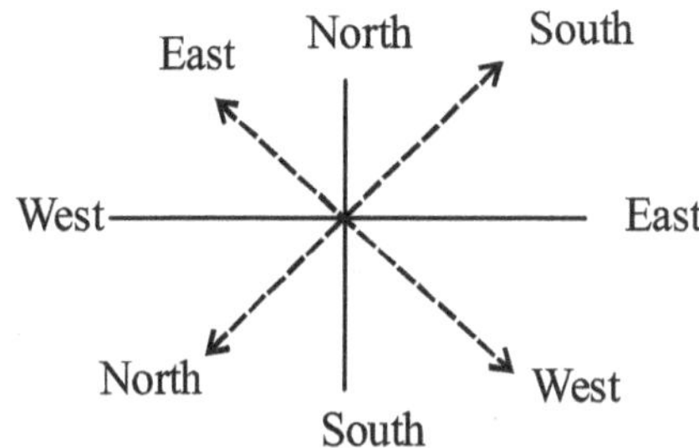

West will become North East.

17. (c)

3 m 3 m

5 m

She is 5m for now from her starting point

LEVEL 2

1. (d) The movements of the person are from A to F, as shown in fig.

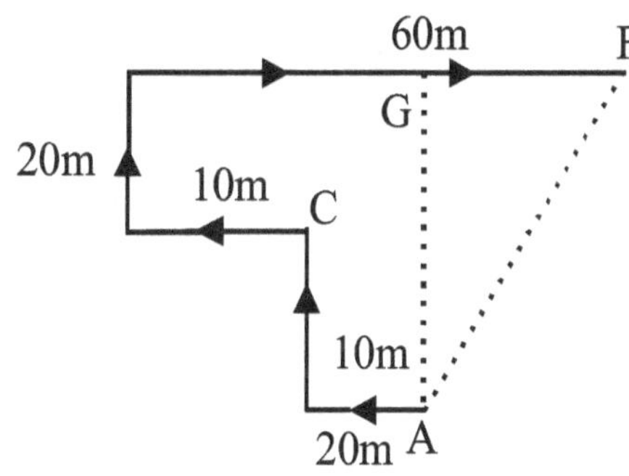

Clearly, the final position is F which is to the north east of the starting point A.

2. (a) The movements of Radhika are as shown in fig (A to B,B to C, C to D and D to A)

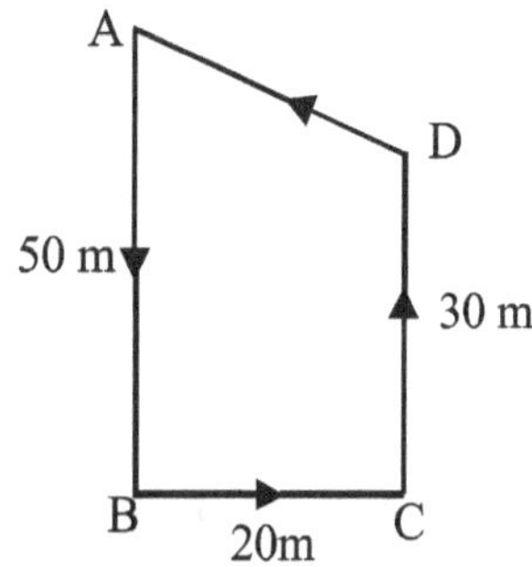

Clearly she is finally moving in the direction DA i.e, north west.

3. (b) Here, Ravi starts from home at A, moves 10 km southwards up to B, turns right and moves 10 km up to C, turns right again and moves 10 km up to D and finally turns left and moves 10 km up to E.

Thus, his distance from initial position A = AE

= AD + DE

= BC + DE = (5 + 10) km = 15 km.

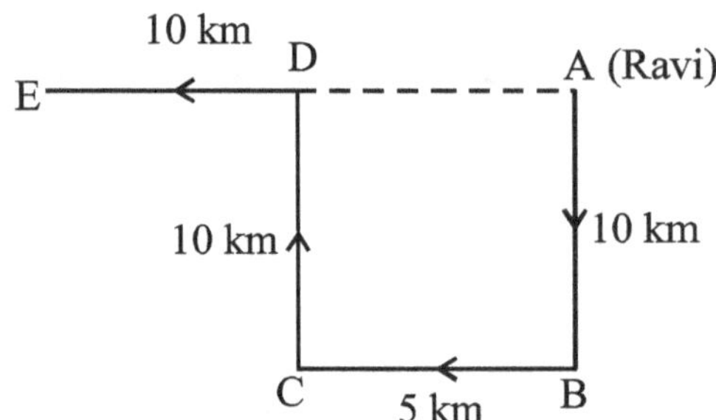

4. **(d)** The direction diagram is as shown below :

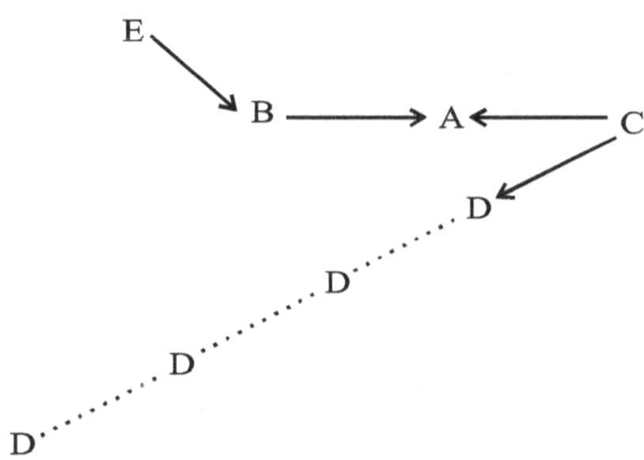

In the above figure when seen from west to east, then all given sequence are possible.

5. **(b)** The direction diagram is as shown below :

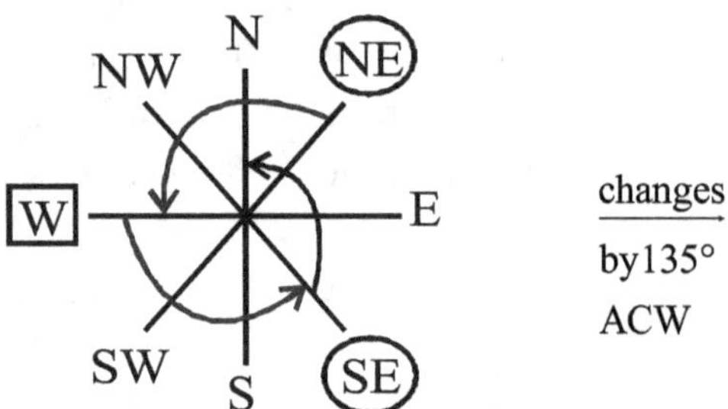

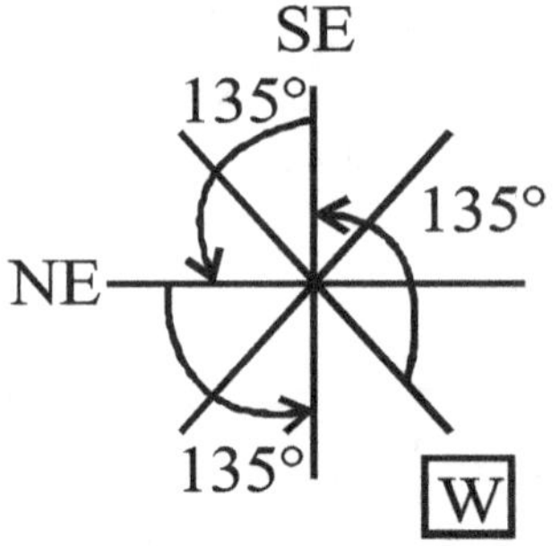

So, it is clear from the above diagram that west becomes south - east.

6. **(b)**

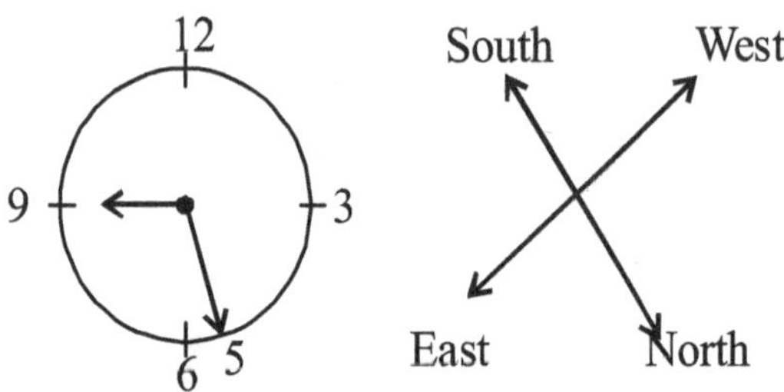

Hour hand will be in South East direction.

7. **(a)**

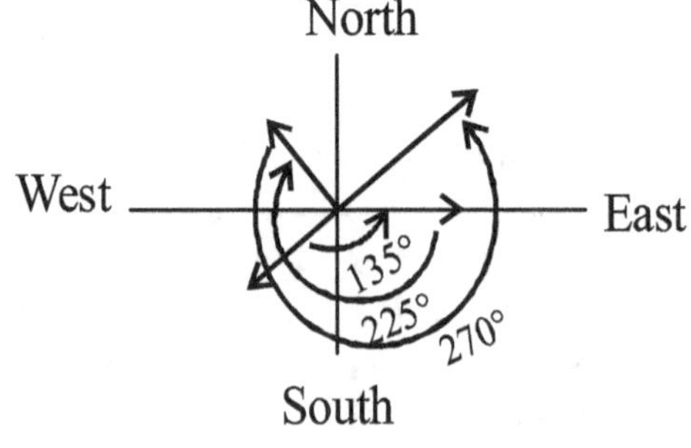

He is facing North-East.

8. (c)

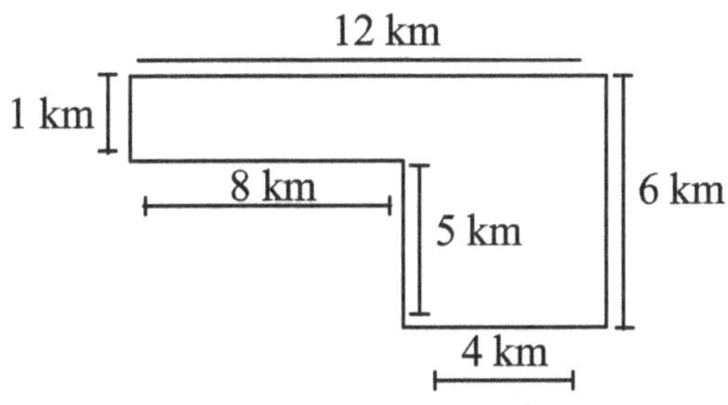

Shanaya is 4 Km west from her starting position.

9. (c)

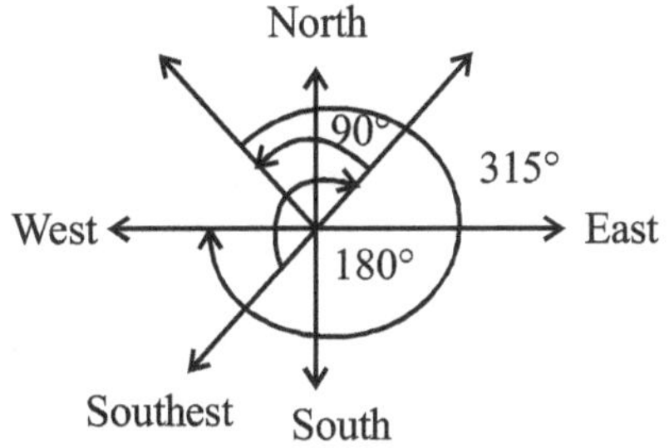

Ashwini is facing west.

10. (a)

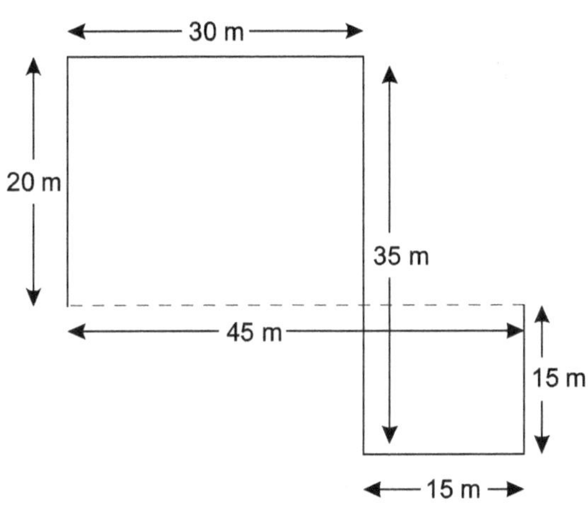

She is 45m, East with respect to her starting point.

11. (c)

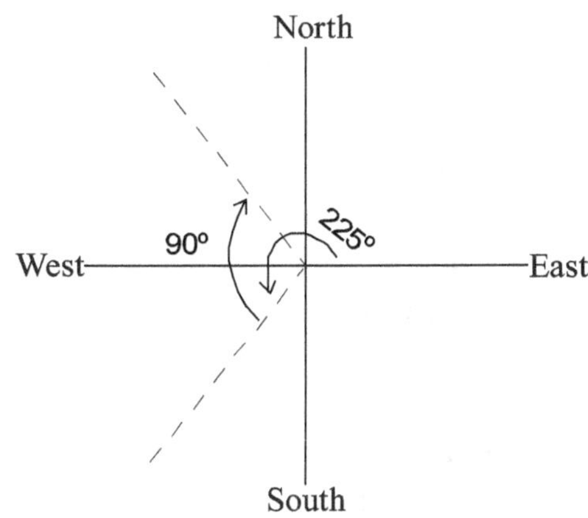

12. (c)

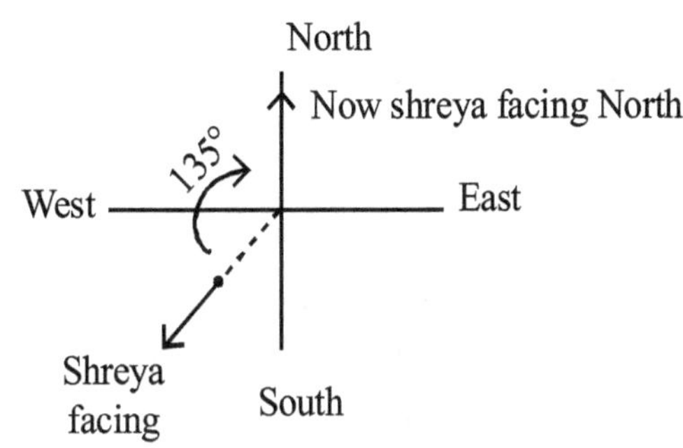

After turning 135° clockwise, now Shreya is facing North direction.

13. (a)

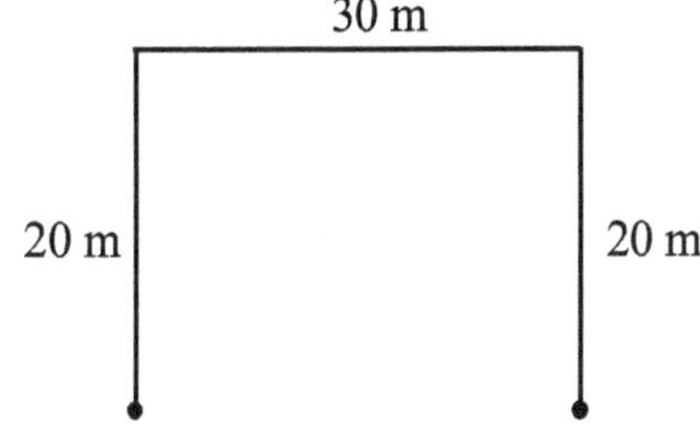

Ali is 30 m, East from the starting Point.

14. (b)

15. (d)

CHAPTER-6

LEVEL 1

1. **(a)** From the relationship given in the question, we observe that each of the objects carries something in common to one another. A Tennis fan can be a cricket player as well as student. Hence Diagram (1) represents this relationship.

2. **(b)** Bidi smokers is a subset of smokers cancer patient may be a smoker, bidi smoker and non- smoker. Hence third object shares a common relationship with first and second object as well.

3. **(b)**

Some **educated** are **citizens.**

Some **citizens** are **educated.**

But, both **educated** and **citizens are men.**

4. **(a)**

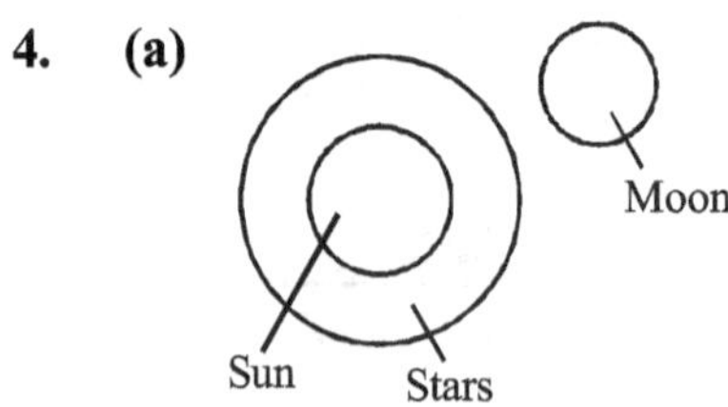

Sun is a **Star**. But, **Moon** is entirely different.

5. **(e)**

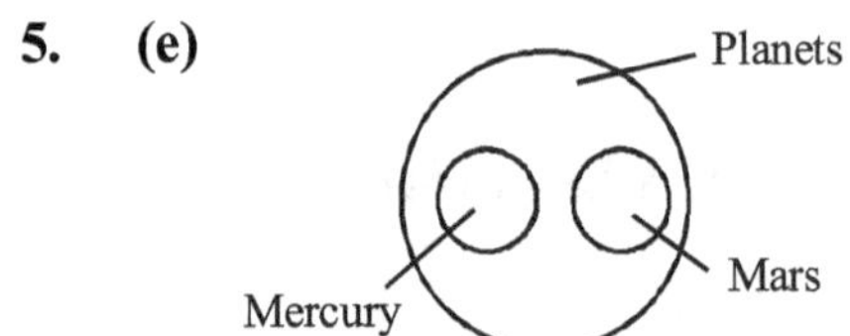

Mercury and **Mars** are entirely different. But, both are **planets.**

6. **(d)**

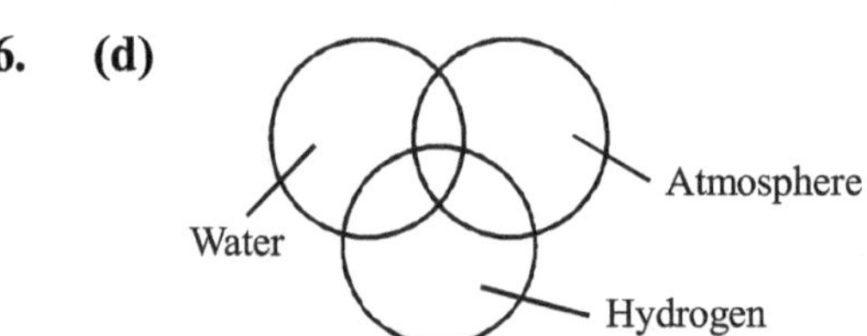

Hydrogen is a **constituent** of both **water** and **atmosphere. Water** is present in **atmosphere.**

7. **(e)**

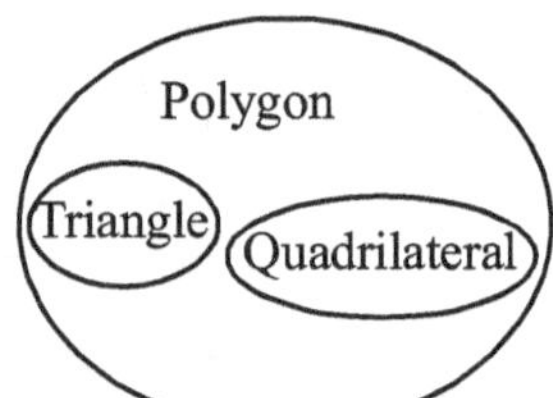

Doctors and **Lawyers** are entirely different. But, both are **professionals**

8. **(a)** Only Science = b
9. **(c)** $M \cap H$ only = e
10. **(b)** $M \cap H \cap S = g$
11. **(d)** Only $S \cap H = d$
12. **(b)**
13. **(d)**
14. **(a)**

Polygon

(Triangle) (Quadrilateral)

15. **(c)**

16. **(d)**

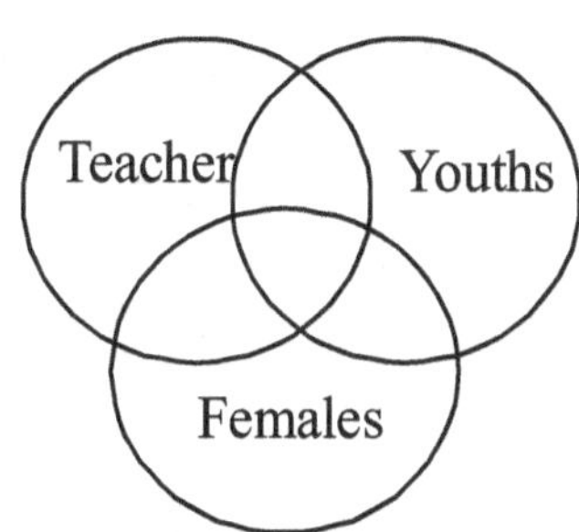

17. **(d)**

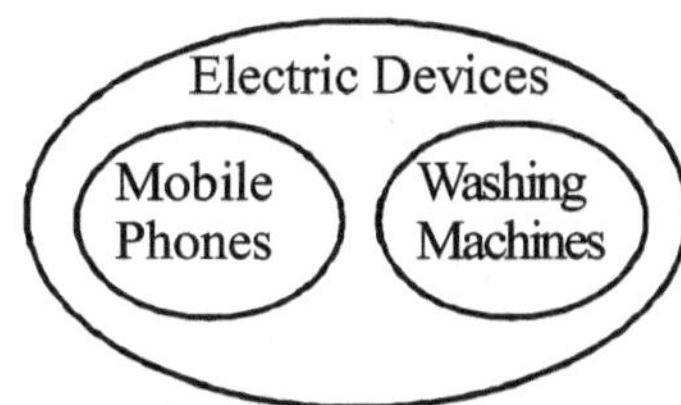

18. **(a)**

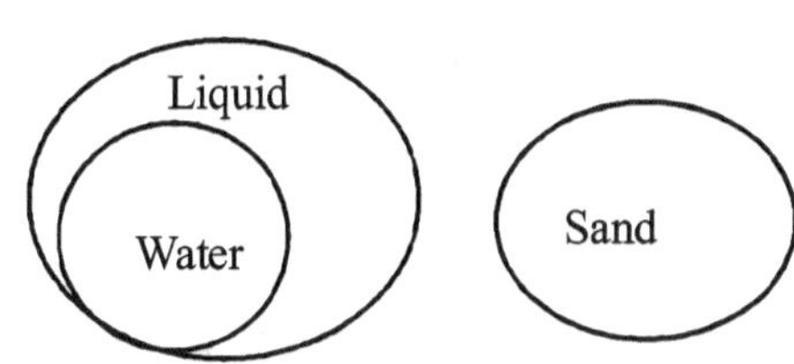

LEVEL 2

1. **(c)** 24 + 16 + 10 + 4 = 54
   54 tourists have visited at least two states.
2. **(b)** 24 + 16 + 10 = 50
   50 tourists have visited only two states.
3. **(b)** The best relation among men, fathers and teachers is as shown below :

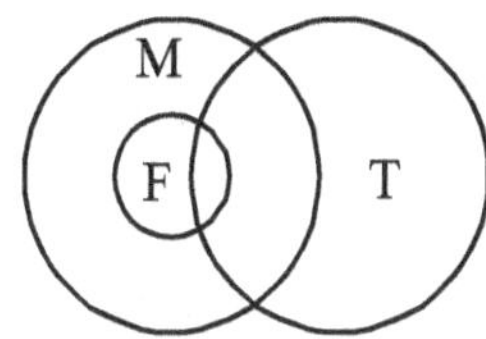

Here, all fathers are men and some fathers can be teachers. So, option (b) is correct answer.

4. **(b)**

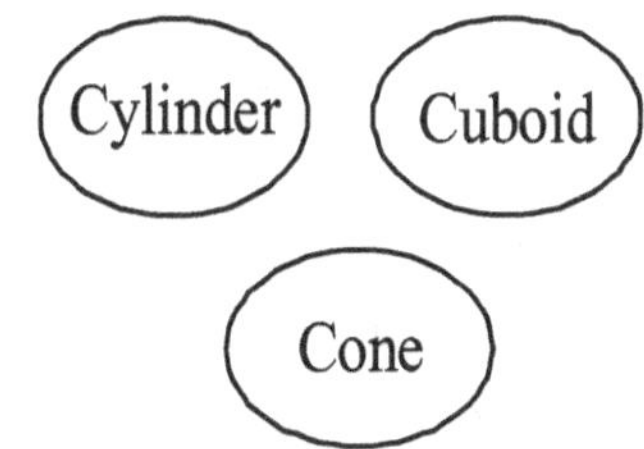

5. **(a)** 'b' represents the youths who are educated but are not pilots.
6. **(c)** Square represents people who like to play Badminton i.e 5, 4, 7. Circle represents people who like to ply Cricket i.e 1, 2, 5. Triangle represents people who like to watch movies i.e 2, 5, 4, 3.
   "2" represents people who like to play Cricket as well as watch movies but do not like to play Badminton.
7. **(d)**

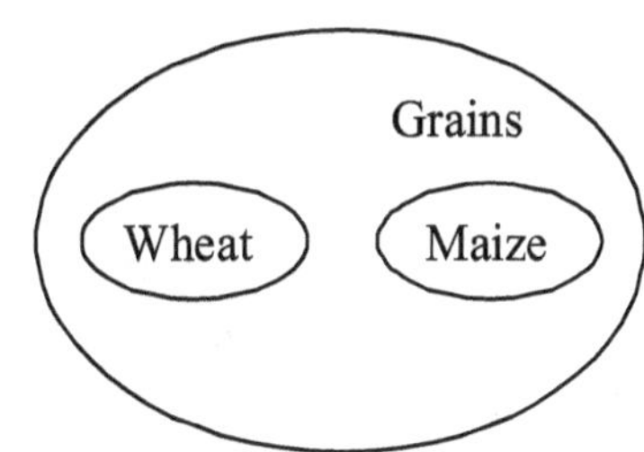

8. **(d)**

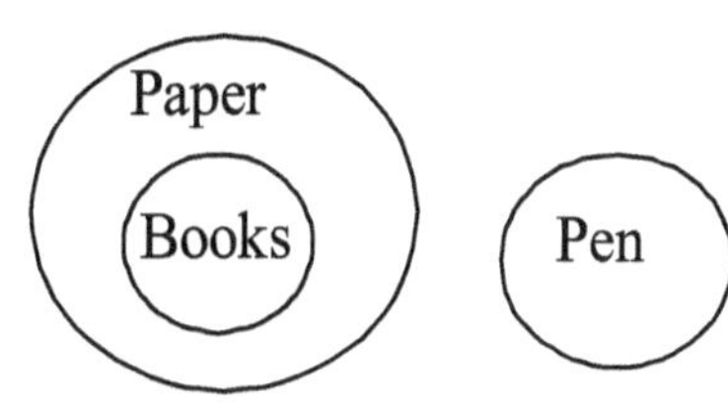

CHAPTER-7

LEVEL 1

1. **(a)** Arranging the words in alphabetical order, we have
Random, Restrict, Robber, Rocket.
So the word in the 2nd position is Restrict and the correct answer is (a)
2. **(c)**
3. **(a)**
4. **(d)**
5. **(d)**
6. **(b)**
7. **(c)**
8. **(a)**
9. **(a)** The given alphabet series is
x c w m v c x [w m w] m x c wm x m
So, only 1 time m is succeeded by w and preceded by w.
10. **(b)** The sequence is :
M L K J I H G F E D C B A Z Y X W V [U] T S R Q P O N
12th letter from left 7th letter right of B.
So, U is 7th to the right of the 12th letter from the left side.
11. **(c)** There are only two no. i.e 3 and 5 which are following multiple of 2 which are 3, 2 and 5, 4.
12. **(c)** Original series
A C B E D G F I H K J M L O N Q P S R U T W V Y X Z
According to question, when every alternate letter starting from C is deleted from the series, then new series.
A B D F H J L N P R T V X
Eight letter from the left end will be "N".
13. **(b)** 24 days are working in that month.
14. **(c)** E T H C O N O L Y G
'N' would be the fifth letter from the right end.
15. **(b)** 122 523 134 947 519
947 523 519 134 122
Middle digit of the second number is
$\Rightarrow$ 5 [2] 3
16. **(b)** There are 3 odd numbers each of which is not immediately followed by a multiple of 2.
(3, 1), (1, 5), (1, 3)
17. **(d)** 486 441 634 932 873
–2 –2 –2 –2 –2
484 439 632 930 871
highest no. $\rightarrow$ 930
2nd highest no. $\rightarrow$ 871
Required sum of 2nd digit of both these two no.$\rightarrow$ 3 + 7 = 10.
18. (d) Five consonants are there in the series which is immediately procceded by a vowel
ET, ES, AW, IP, OT
19. **(b)**
3- Book
2- Chapter
5- Paragraph
4- Sentence
1- Word
20. **(b)** $40 + 1 - 11 = 30^{th}$

LEVEL 2

1. **(b)** Cancelling every second letter after reversing the alphabet the series becomes.
Z X V T R P N L J H F D B
The middle letter is N.

2. **(c)** Counting from the right end i.e. from Z, the 16th letter is K. Counting from K towards the left, the 8th letter is C.
3. **(a)** There are ten letters between H and S and as such there is no letter which lies in the middle.
4. **(d)** J is the tenth letter in the first half. The tenth letter in the later half is W.
5. **(d)** 22nd letter from the left is V and 21st letter from the right is F. The letter midway F and V is N.
6. **(b)** The new alphabet series is
M L K J I H G F E D C B A
N O P Q R S T U V W X Y Z
The 9th letter from right is R and the ninth letter to the left of R is E.
7. **(c)** The new alphabet series is B A D C F E H G J I L K N
M P O R Q T S V U X W Z Y
The seventeenth letter from the right is I.
8. **(a)** C E
9. **(d)** R U T H L E S S
By arranging alphabetically we get,
E H L R S S T U
∴ Last Letter = U
10. **(a)** Required letter = 12 + 4 = 16th from left end starting from z = k
11. **(a)** Reverse order of alphabets is
Y Z W X U V S T Q R O P M N K L I J G H E F C D A B
Fourteenth letter from left and = N.
Sixth letter to the right of N is "H".
12. **(d)** 3. i.e 4, 5, 5; 4, 5, 6 ; 4, 5, 2
13. **(b)**

E	X	P	L	O	R	A	T	I	O	N
↓	↓	↓	↓	↓	↓	↓	↓	↓	↓	↓
1	2	3	4	5	6	7	8	9	10	11

Taken Alphabets
E, L, A, N
Meaningful words = LANE, LEAN,
"Y" as more than one word is formed.
14. **(d)** There are eight symbols each of which is immediately followed by an even digit.
%6, #2, @4, ?2, %8, *6, $8, @2
15. **(b)**

5	6	3	1	2	4
|	|	|	|	|	|
R	H	Y	T	H	M

16. **(b)** There are two 7 which is immediately preceded by 3 and immediately followed by 8.
17. **(d)**

CHAPTER-8

LEVEL 1

1. **(a)** On interchanging + and ÷, and 2 and 3, we get the equations as $(2 + 4) \div 3 = 2$ or $6 \div 3 = 2$ or $2 = 2$, which is true.
2. **(c)** Given expression
$= (10 \times 4) + (4 \times 4) - 6 = 50$
3. **(b)** Using correct symbols, we have
Given expression $= 18 \times 12 \div 4 + 5 - 6$
$= 18 \times 3 + 5 - 6 = 54 + 5 - 6 = 53$
4. **(c)** Using the proper signs, we get:
$36 - 8 \div 4 + 6 \div 2 \times 3$
$= 36 - 2 + 3 \times 3 = 36 - 2 + 9 = 45 - 2$
$= 43$

5. (d) Using the correct symbols, we have:

Given expression $= 8 + 36 \div 6 - 6 \div 2 \times 3 = 8 + 6 - 3 \times 3 = 5$

6. (a) Using the proper signs in the given expression , we get

$175 \div 25 + 5 + 20 - 3 \times 10$

$\Rightarrow 7 + 5 + 20 - 30 \Rightarrow 2$

7. (d) Using the correct symbols, we have

Given expression $= 24 \times 12 + 18 \div 9$

$= 288 + 2 = 290.$

8. (b) Using the correct symbols, we have

Given expression

$= (3 \times 15 + 19) \div 8 - 6$

$= 64 \div 8 - 6 = 8 - 6 = 2.$

9. (d) Using the correct symbols, we have

Given expression $= 12 - 12 \times 28 \div 7 + 15$

$= 12 - 12 \times 4 + 15 = 12 - 48 + 15$

$= 27 - 48 = -21.$

10. (d) The rule is the digits are jumbled in an order.

11. (a) By making the interchanges given in (a), we get the equation as $2 - 5 + 3 = 0$ or $0 = 0$ which is true.

By making the interchanges given in (b), we get the equation as

$3 - 2 + 5 = 0$ or $6 = 0$, which is false.

By making the interchanges given in (c), we get the equation as

$5 - 3 + 2 = 0$ or $4 = 0$ which is not true.

So, the answer is (a).

12. (d)

13. (d)

14. (d) $15 - 2 \div 900 + 90 \times 100 = ?$

$\Rightarrow 15 \times 2 + 900 \div 90 - 100 = 15 \times 2 + 10 - 100$

$\Rightarrow 30 + 10 - 100 = 40 - 100 = -60$

15. (b) $52 < 4 \wedge 5 > 8 \vee 2$

$52 - 4 \times 5 + 8 \div 2$

$52 - 4 \times 5 + 4$

$56 - 20 = 36$

16. (a) $175 \div 25 + 5 \times 30$

$\Rightarrow 7 + 5 \times 30$

$\Rightarrow 7 + 150$

$= 157$

17. (b) 2 Q 40 P 10 R 6 S 8

$\Rightarrow 2 \times 40 \div 10 + 6 - 8$

$\Rightarrow 8 + 6 - 8$

$\Rightarrow 6$

18. (b) 25 M 5 L 10 P 2 J 15

$25 \div 5 - 10 \times 2 + 15$

$5 - 20 + 15$

$= 0$

19. (c) $34 \times 2 + 14 \div 7 - 8$

$= 34 \times 2 - 8$

$= 68 + 2 - 8 = 62$

LEVEL 2

1. (c) Given that,

$33 \times 11 \div 9 \times 28 + 4 - 5$

after changing the sign $\div$ $33 \times 11 \div 9 \times 28 + 4 - 5$

$= -33 + 11 - 9 + 28 \div 4 \times 5$

$= -33 + 11 - 9 + 7 \times 5 = -42 + 46 = 4$

So, option (3) is correct answer.

2. (a)

3. (b) $Q \rightarrow (+), J \rightarrow (\times), T \rightarrow (-), K \rightarrow (\div)$

3 0 k 2 Q 3 J 6 T 5

$30 \div 2 + 3 \times 6 - 5$

$15 + 18 - 5$

$33 - 5 = 28$

4. (a) $(16 + 64 \div 8 - 4 \times 2) \div (2 \times 15 + 15 \div 3 - 8)$

$= (16 + 8 - 8) \div (30 + 5 - 8)$

$= 16 \div 27$ i.e $\frac{16}{27}$

5. (c) 30 © 6 @ 5 $ 4 & 2

$\Rightarrow 30 \div 6 \times 5 + 4 - 2$

$\Rightarrow 5 \times 5 + 4 - 2$

$\Rightarrow 25 + 4 - 2$

$\Rightarrow 27$

6. (c) $120 \div 8 + 14 \times 4 - 16$

$= 15 + 56 - 16$

$= 55$

7. (b) $5 + 14 - 2 \times 3$

$\Rightarrow 5 \times 14 \div 2 - 3$

$\Rightarrow 5 \times 7 - 3$

$\Rightarrow 32$

CHAPTER-9

LEVEL 1

1. (a) 1st Row ⇒ D

2nd Row ⇒ E

3rd Row ⇒ C

4th Row ⇒ A

5th Row ⇒ B

2. (b) M N O P Q

Bus O is in the middle of the five.

3. (a)

Left — M R P L O — Right

Hence, P coach is in the middle of the five coaches.

4. (b)

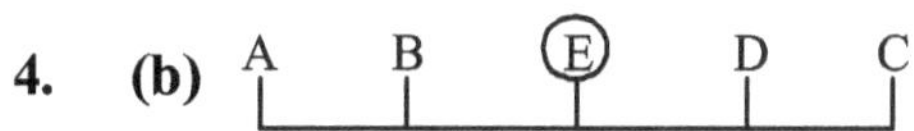

5. (d) Standing arrangement : (facing south)

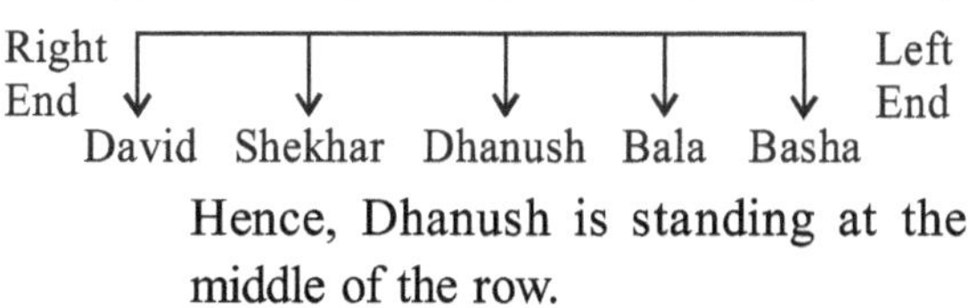

Hence, Dhanush is standing at the middle of the row.

6. (d) Standing Arrangement:

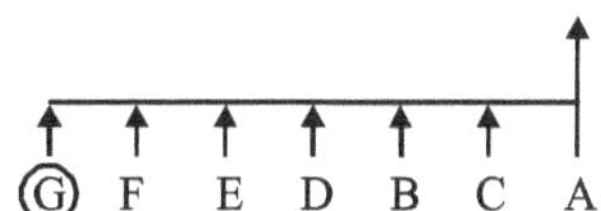

G is standing on the extreme left.

7. (a) C > D > A > E > B

So, A is in the middle.

8. (c) East

T B V M S H Y

So, vehicle B is second to the left of the M.

9. (a)

E F G A C B D H

E is sitting at the other corner.

LEVEL 2

1. (c) H is a person who is neither hard working nor ambitious.

2. (b) G is a person who is ambitious but he is neither honest nor hard working.

3. (d) From the statements given, the correct order is A, C, D, B, E Clearly, D is sitting in the centre.

It is given that A, B, C, D and E are sitting facing you. So your right and left will be considered as left and right respectively.

Sol. (4-6)

The given information can be analyzed as under :

	Hockey	**Volleyball**	**Baseball**	**Cricket**	**Football**
Ravi	√	√	√		
Kunal	√	√		√	
Sachin	√		√		√
Gaurav		√	√	√	√
Michael			√		√

4. **(b)** Kunal is good in Hockey, Cricket and Volleyball.
5. **(c)** Gaurav is good in Baseball, Cricket, Volleyball and Football.
6. **(c)** Ravi is good in Baseball, Volleyball and Hockey.

Sol. (7-9) The arrangement is as following :

1	Sanskrit	Science	Hindi	English	Mathematics
Dinesh	✓	✓	✓		
Ganesh			✓	✓	✓
Umesh		✓	✓	✓	
Nita	✓	✓	✓		
Gita	✓		✓	✓	

7. **(c)** Hindi subject opted by the most students.
8. **(b)** Mathematics opted by the least students
9. **(d)** Three students opted sanskrit subject.

Sol. (10-12)

The sitting arrangement is as following :

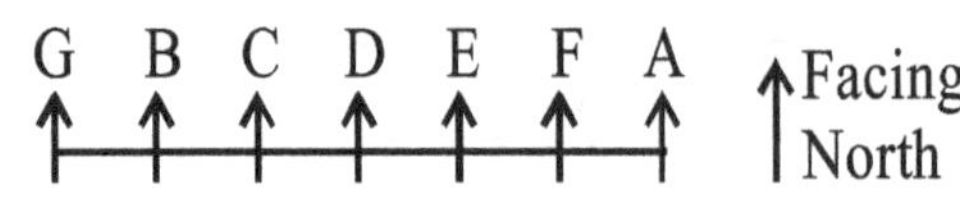

10. **(c)** G and B are to the left of C.
11. **(b)** C and G are the neighbours of B.
12. **(a)** E is to the immediate left of D is not true.
13. **(b)**

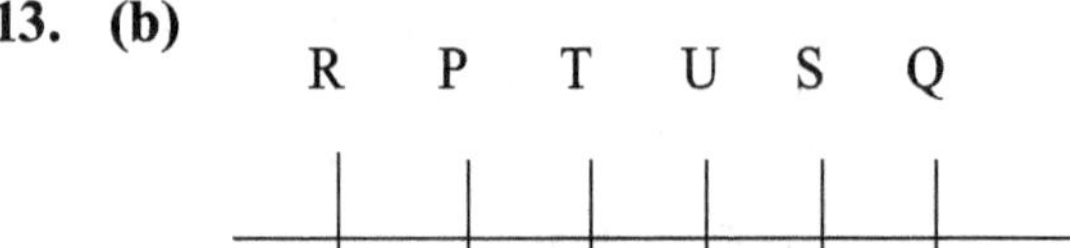

'P' is to the immediate right of 'R'

Sol. (14-17)

We may prepare a table as follows:

	Nehru House	Gandhi House	Tall	Short	Glasses	No glasses
A	✓			✓	✓	
B	✓			✓		✓
C		✓		✓	✓	
D		✓	✓		✓	
E		✓		✓		✓
F		✓	✓			✓

14. (c) B and E are short and not wearing glasses.
15. (b) E belongs to Gandhi House, is short and does not wear glasses.
16. (d) F belongs to Gandhi House, is tall and is not wearing glasses.
17. (b)

Subject→ / ↓Name	Hindi	Sanskrit	Science	Maths	English
Riya	✓	✓	✓		
Kiara	✓	✓		✓	
Seema	✓		✓		✓
Garima		✓	✓	✓	✓
Meena			✓		✓

Kiara is good in Hindi, Maths, Sanskrit.

18. (a) ↑ ↑ ↑ ↑ ↑ ↑

P Q R S T U

R is second to the left of T.

19. (a)

R →			S →
→			Q →
P →		Or	P →
Q →			→
S →			R →

S cannot be seat at 2nd place in either case because it is given in question that R and S cannot be together.

20. (d)

CHAPTER-10

LEVEL 1

1. (c) We can label the figure as shown.

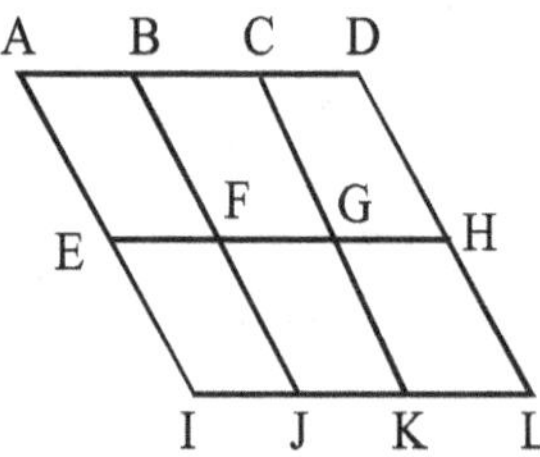

The simplest parallelogram are ABFE, BCGF, CDHG, EFJI, FGKJ and GHLK. These are 6 in number.

The parallelograms composed of two components each, are ACGE, BDHF, EGKI, FHLJ, ABJI, BCKJ and CDLK. Thus, there are 7 such parallelograms. The parallelogram composed of four components each are ACKI and BDLJ i.e. 2 in number. There is only one parallelogram composed of six components, namely, ADLI. Thus, there are 6 + 7 + 2 + 1 = 16 parallelograms in the figure.

2. (b) Let us count the number of triangles vertex wise.

From vertex 1, we can count 4 triangles.

From vertices 2 and 3, we can count 3 triangles each.

From vertices 4, 5, 6, we have 2 triangles each.

Finally, from vertices, 7, 8, 9, 10, we have 1 triangle each.

We thus have $4 \times 1 + 3 \times 2 + 2 \times 3 + 1 \times 4$

= 40 triangles.

These are however, upright triangles only.

From vertices 12, 13, 14 we have 1 + 2+ 1 = 4 triangles in inverted shape.

From 8, 9, we have 1 triangle each and from 5, we have 1 triangle. Thus, total no. of inverted triangles = 7

Hence, total no. 20 + 7 = 27

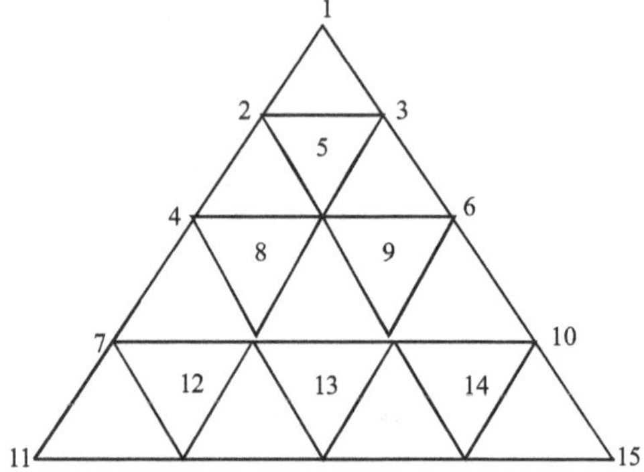

Extending this pattern of counting, let us count the triangles in fig.

Upright triangles

$= 5 \times 1 + 4 \times 2 + 3 \times 3 + 2 \times 4 + 1 \times 5$

$= 35$

Inverted triangles

$= (1 + 2 + 2 + 1) + (1 + 2 + 1) + (1 + 1) + 1 = 13$

Hence total number = 48

3. (d) Each small square is bisected by its diagonals to give 4 triangles of half the size of the square and 4 triangles of 1/4th the size of the square.

Thus there are 8 × 4 = 32 triangles in the four squares.

Then there are six triangles as shown

in the adjoining figure. Total no. of triangles
$= 32 + 6 = 38$

4. **(d)** Consider the longest vertical strip.
It has six rectangles (excluding squares).
In the second vertical strip there are 3 rectangles. In the second vertical strip there are 3 rectangles.
This pattern is repeated with the largest horizontal strip and the second horizontal strip.

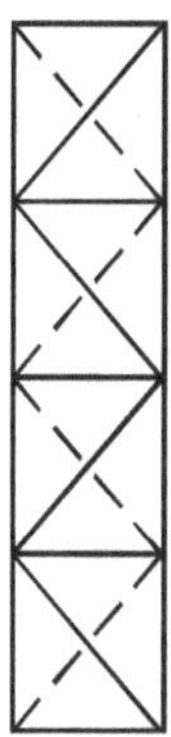

Next consider the third vertical and horizontal strips. Each has one rectangle.
Again, consider two vertical and horizontal strips together . Each has one rectangle.
Hence total no. of rectangles
$= 2\,(6 + 3 + 1 + 1) = 22$

5. **(a)** Minimum 3 colours are required.
6. **(b)** 16 rectangular are present in the figure.
7. **(d)** Minimum 14 straight lines required to draw the given figure8

LEVEL 2

1. **(d)** The figure may be labelled as shown :

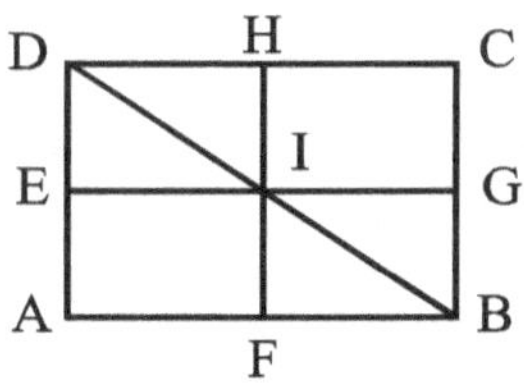

The simplest triangles are – DHI, DEI, IFB, IGB, i.e. 4 in number.

The triangles composed of three components each are – DAB, DCB i.e. 2 in number.

So, total triangles are = (4 + 2) = 6

The simple quadrilaterals are – DEHI, HIGC, EIFA, FIGB i.e. 4 in number.

The quadrilaterals composed of two components each are – DHFA, HFBC, DECG, EABG, i.e. 4 in number.

The quadrilateral composed of your components is – ABCD. So quadrilaterals are = (4 + 4 + 1) = 9

2. **(c)** The figure may be labelled as shown :

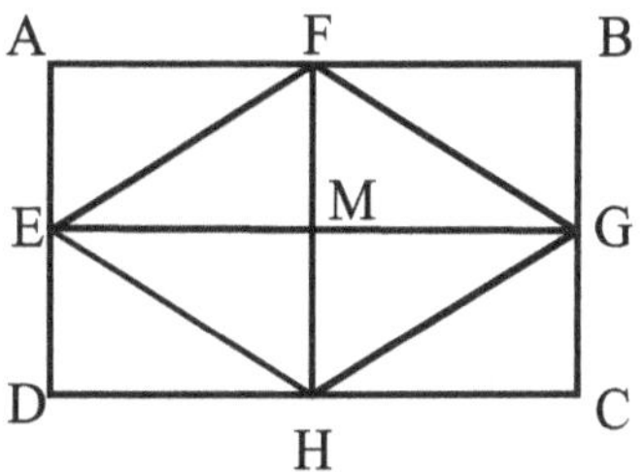

The quadrilaterals composed of two components each are –
AFME, FMGB, EMHD, MGCH i.e. 4 in number.

The quadrilaterals composed of four components each are –

AEGB, AFHD, FBCH, EDCG, EFGH i.e. 5 in number

The quadrilateral composed of eight components is –

ABCD i.e. in number

So, quadrilaterals are = (4 + 5 + 1) = 10

3. **(a)**

4. **(a)** The figure may be labelled as shown.

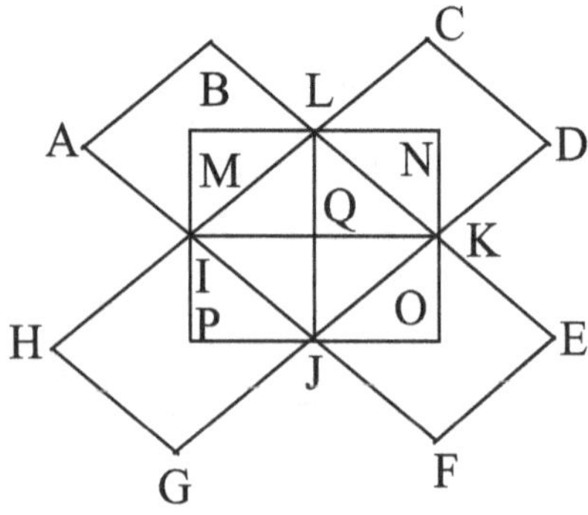

The simplest squares/rectangles are - ABCI, LCDK, HIJG, JKEF, MLQI, LNK, QKOJ and QJPIQ i.e 8.

The squares/rectangles composed of two components each are ABKJ, ILEF, HLKG, IJCD, MLQJP, LNOJ, MNKI and IKOP i.e 8

The squares/rectangles composed of three/four components each are - ABEF, HGDC, ILKJ and MNOPL i.e 4.

Total no. of squares/rectangles in the figure = 8 + 8 + 4 = 20.

5. **(c)** The figure may be labelled as shown.

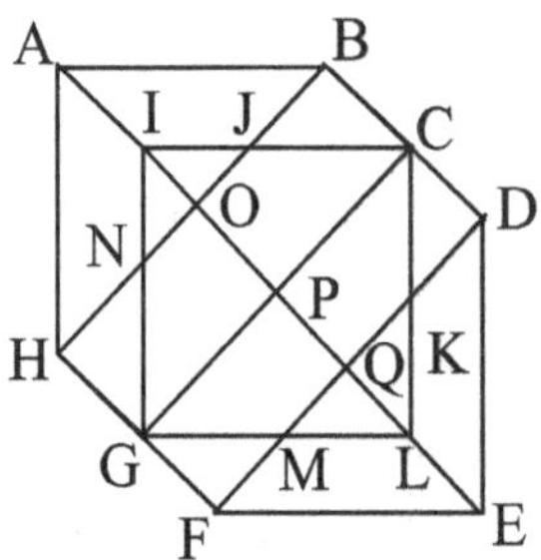

The simplest triangles are IJO, BCJ, CDK, KQL, MLQ, GFM, GHN and NIO i.e. 8 in number.

The triangles composed of two components each are ABO, AHO, NIJ, IGP, ICP, DEQ, FEQ, KLM, LCP and LGP i.e. 10 in number

The triangles composed of four components each are HAB, DEF, LGI, GIC, ICL and GLC i.e. 6 in number.

Total number of triangles in the figure = 8 + 10 + 6 = 24.

6. **(b)** 14 is the minimum no. of straight lines required to form figure.

7. **(a)** 30 triangles are there in the given figure.

8. **(c)** 15 no. of straight lines are required.

9. **(d)** There are 32 triangles in the given figure.

10. **(a)** There are 15 straight lines required to draw the given figure.

11. **(d)** There are 24 triangles in the given figure.

12. **(c)** 12 square are there in the Figure.

13. **(a)** Option (a) is the correct answer

CHAPTER-11

LEVEL 1

1. **(c)** Mirror image for the letters 'D' is 'ᗡ', 'R' is 'Я', 'E' is 'Ǝ', 'A' is 'A' and 'M' is 'M' . Since the word ends with M, i.e., where the mirror is placed, therefore the mirror image will start from the mirror image of M, i.e., M. Thus the mirror image for water is MAƎЯᗡ.

2. **(a)** Mirror image for the letters 'N' is 'И', 'E' is 'Ǝ', 'W' is 'W' and 'S' is 'Ƨ'.

3. **(d)** Mirror image for the letters 'j' is ꞁ, 'e' is 'ɘ', 'a' is 'ɒ', 'I' is I, 'O' is 'O', 'u' is 'u' and 'S' is 'Ƨ'

4. **(d)** Mirror image of numbers — '3' is 'Ɛ', '1' is '⌉', '2' is 'Ƨ', '5' is 'ट', '6' is 'ə' and '8' is '8'.

5. **(b)** If we rotate the mirror image, i.e., '8' 90° clockwise, then it will be 'ꟺ'.

6. **(c)** If we rotate the mirror image, i.e., 'Ƨ٦' to 90° anticlockwise, then it will be '⅃ᔕ'.

7. **(d)** If we rotate the mirror image, i.e., '•⟶' to 90° clockwise, then it will be '↓'

8. **(a)** 10 : 30 | 1 : 30 —90° CW rotation→ 4 : 45

Hence, option (a) is the answer.

9. **(c)**

TIME | ƎMIT —90°CW rotation→

Hence, option (c) is the correct answer.

10. **(a)** The mirror image of circle remains a circle and the arrow facing west will face towards east and arrow facing east will face towards west. Thus, time will be 2 : 45.

11. **(b)**

Hence option (b) is the answer.

12. **(a)** If we rotate the mirror image, i.e., 'ϛ' to 90° anti-clockwise, then it will be ᓚ. Thus, option (a) is the answer.

13. **(b)** If we rotate the mirror iamge i.e., 'TИA' to 90° anti-clockwise, then it will be 'TИA'. Thus, option (b) is the answer.

14. **(b)** The mirror image of circle ramins a circle. The arrow facing south will also remains the same. But the arrow facing north-west will face north-east.

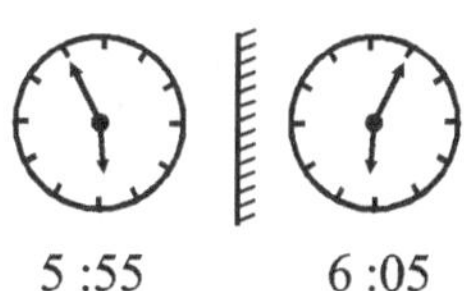

5 :55 6 :05

15. (d) Mirror images for the numbers '8' is '8', '9'is 'ɐ', '3' is 'ɛ' and '4' is '৮'.

16. (b)

17. (b)

18. (d)

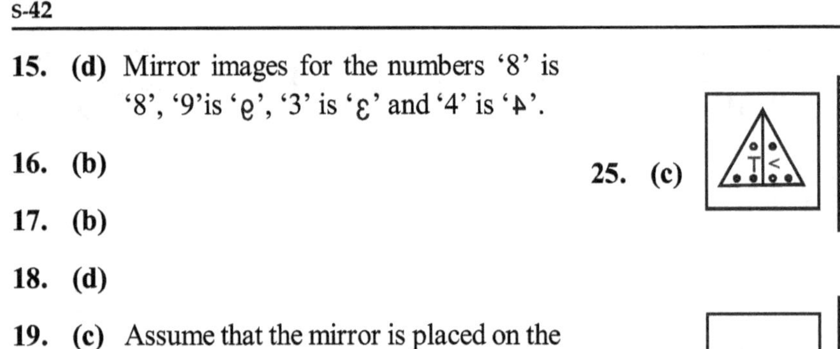

25. (c)

19. (c) Assume that the mirror is placed on the right hand side of the given object, unless mentioned or drawn near the object.

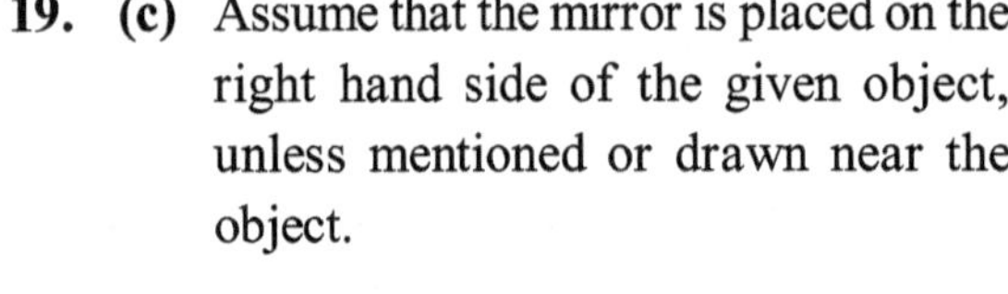

26. (b)

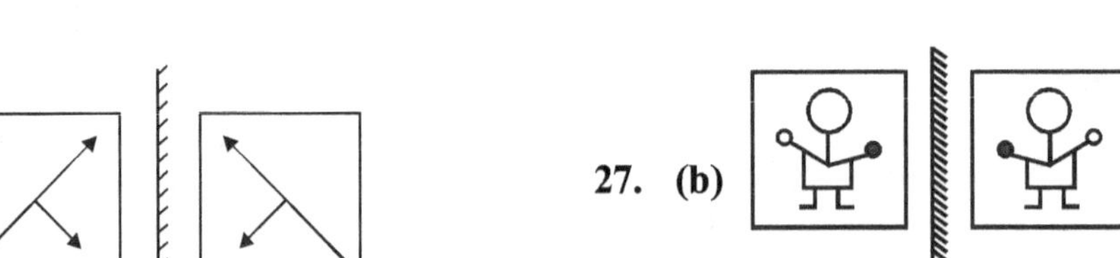

27. (b)

20. (c)

21. (c)

28. (b)

22. (c)

29. (c)

23. (c)

30. (c)

24. (c)

31. (c)

32. **(b)** 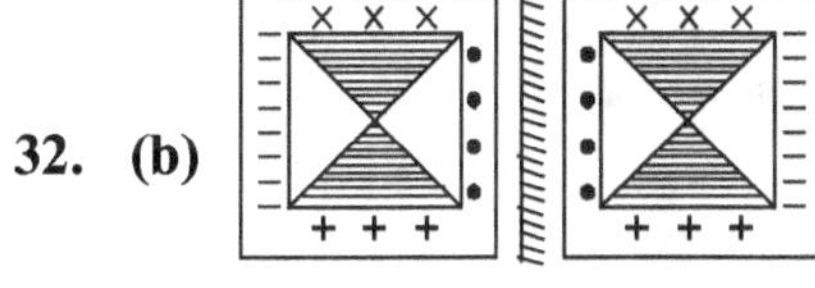

33. **(c)** 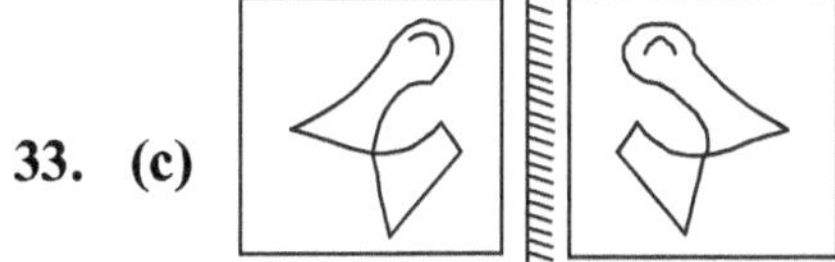

34. **(a)** 

35. **(b)** 

36. **(d)** 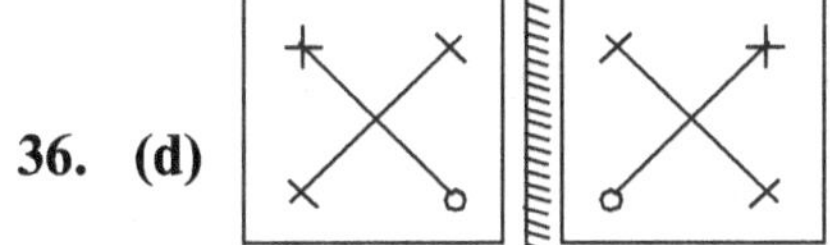

37. **(b)** 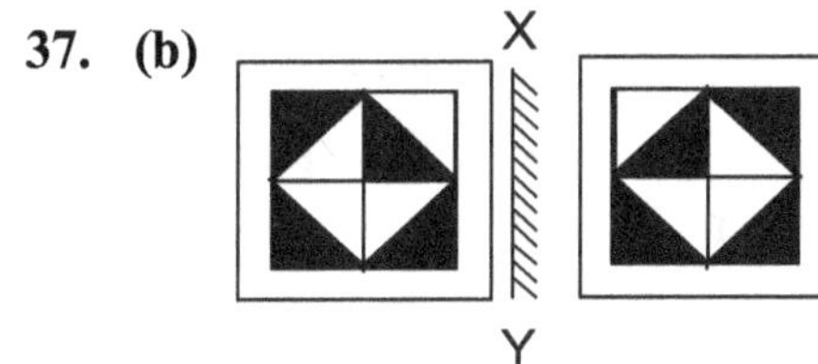

38. **(d)** 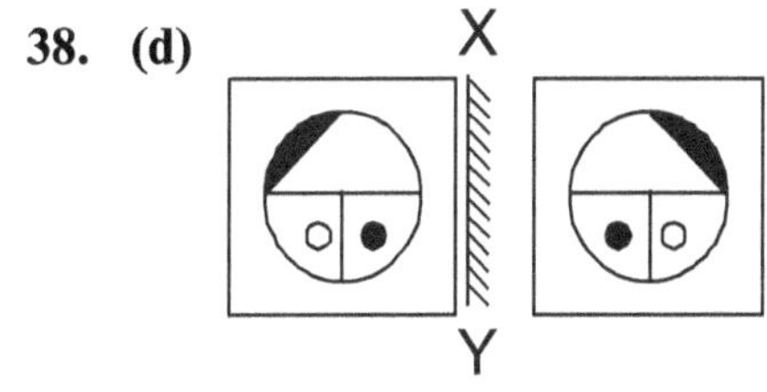

39. **(a)** 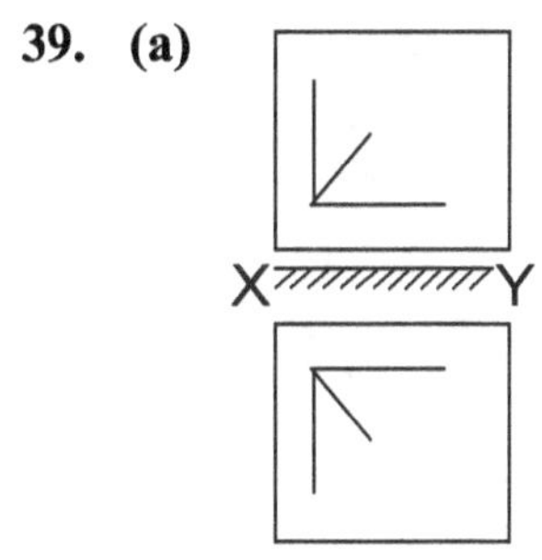

40. **(d)** 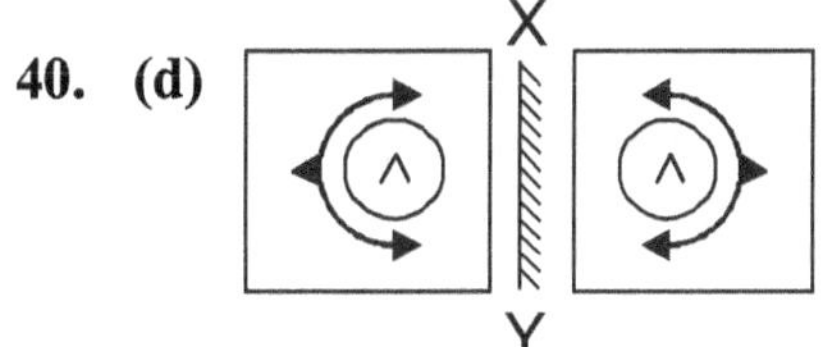

41. **(b)** 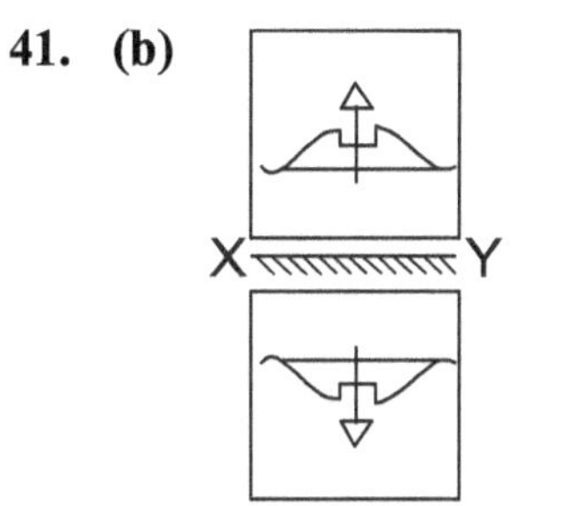

42. **(b)** Mirror imge of 'FAN' is given in option (b)

43. **(c)** Mirror imge of question figure is given in option (c)

44. **(c)** Mirror imge of question figure is given in option (c)

45. **(a)** Mirror imge of question figure is given in option (a)

46. **(a)** A vertical mirror is placed, so the object on the left will appear right in reverse position and vice-versa. So, option (a) is the correct option.

47. (c) A vertical mirror is placed, so the object on the left will appear right in reverse position and vice-versa. Option (a) and (d) will be eliminated as signs in the same direction and in option (b) position of (–) and (÷) is not correct. So, the correct option is (c).

48. (a)

49. (d)

50. (a)

51. (c)

52. (b) SWIMMING

ƧWIMMIИG

53. (d)

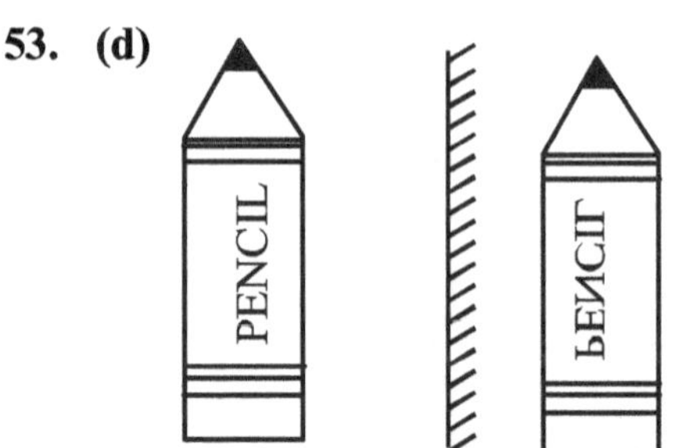

54. (a) INDIANAIRFORCE

IИDIAИAIRFORCE

55. (b)

56. (a)

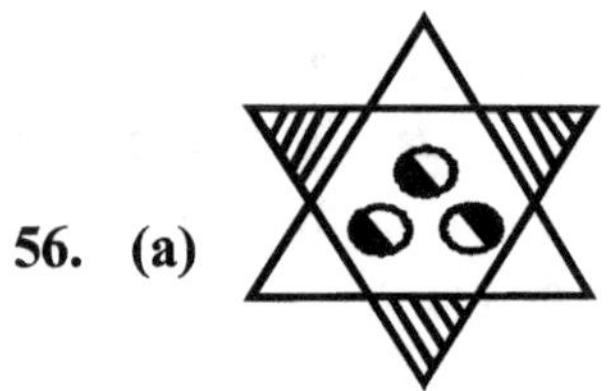

57. (a)

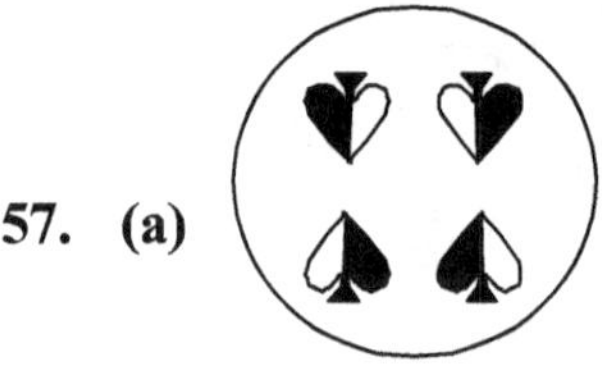

58. (a) PLAY | PL AY

59. (b) HINDI | I DNIH

LEVEL 2

1. **(c)** The water image of 'P' is 'ᑲ', 'L' is 'Γ', 'E' is 'E', 'D' is 'D', 'G' is 'G' and 'E' is 'E'.

2. **(b)** The water image of 'h' is 'µ', 'e' is 'ɘ', L is 'Γ' and 'P' is 'ᑲ'.

3. **(b)** The water image of 'D' is 'D', 'O' is 'O', 'L' is 'Γ' 'A' is '∀' and 'R' is 'ʁ'.

4. **(a)** The water image of 'a' is 'ɐ', 'b' is 'p', 'S' is 'Ƨ', 'e' is 'ɘ', 'n' is 'u', 'c' is 'c' and 'e' is 'ɘ'.

5. **(d)** The water image of number — '9' is '6', '1' is '1', '8' is '8', '4' is '4', '2' is 'Ƨ' and '3' is '3'

6. **(b)** The water image of '?' is '¿'.

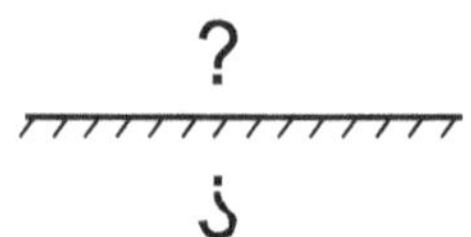

7. **(c)** The water image of 'g' is 'ɓ', 'L' is 'Γ', 'a' is 'ɐ' and 'd' is 'q'.

8. **(a)** The water image of 'S' is 'ƨ', 'N' is 'И', 'O' is 'O' and 'W' is 'M'

9. **(b)** The water image of 'd' is 'q', 'r' is 'ɹ', 'a' is 'ɐ', 'i' is 'r' and 'n' is 'u'

10. **(c)** The water image of 'Z' is 'Z', 'E' is 'E', 'B' is B, 'R' is 'ᴚ' and 'A' is '∀'

11. **(b)** The water image of '6' is '9', '7' is '⅃' and '1' is ⇂.

12. **(c)** The water image of '9' is '6', '2' is 'ƨ', '8' is '8' and '3' is '3'.

13. **(a)** Since, in case of water images, usually the image drawn is just under the actual object. So the shaded and dotted portion will come up on their respective sides, because the portion of the object near water surface will remain near the water surface in case of the image as well.

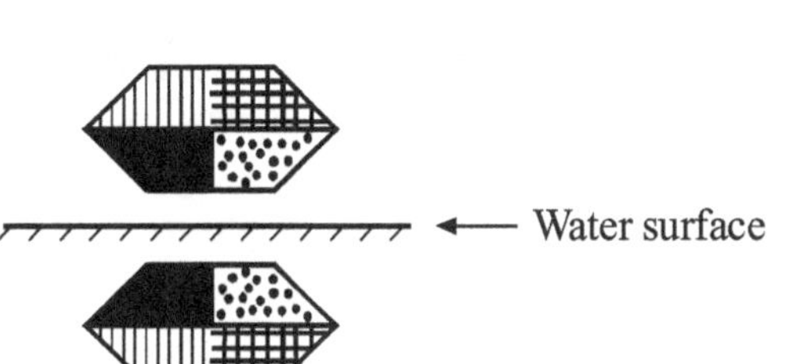

14. **(d)**

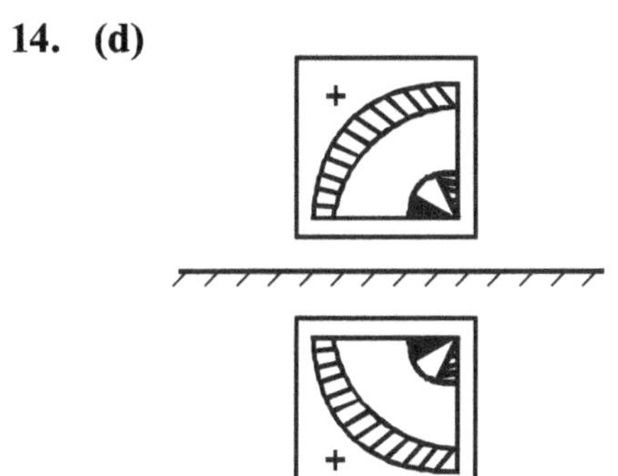

15. **(d)**

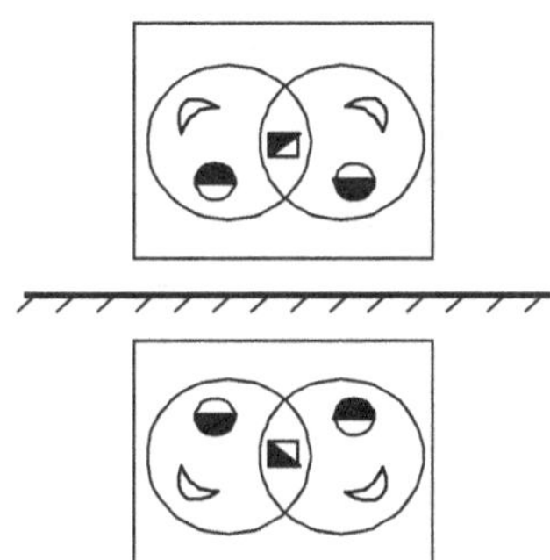

16. **(b)**

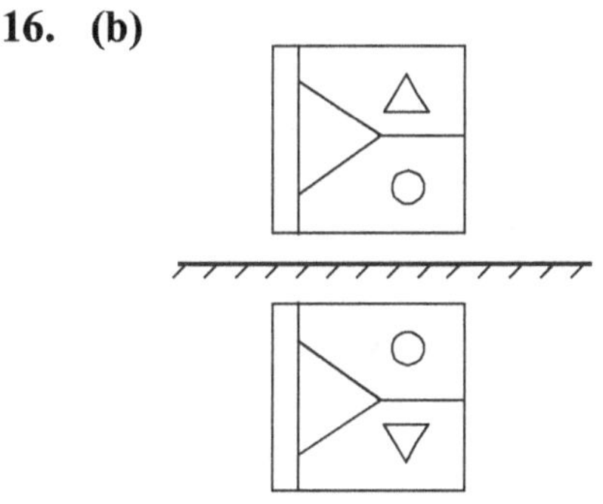

17. **(c)**

18. **(a)**

19. **(d)**

20. **(b)**

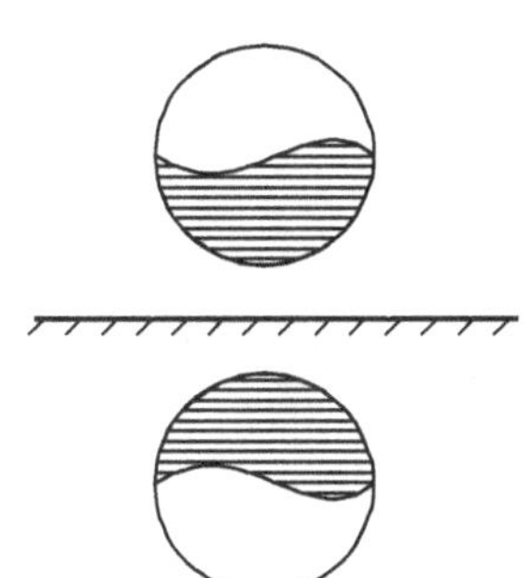

21. (b)

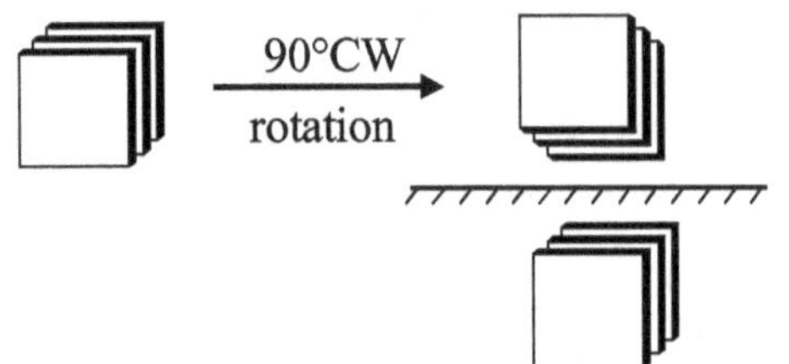

This is the final image

Thus option (b) is the correct answer.

22. (b)

23. (d) In all others head of "T" faces the vertex of the triangle.

24. (d) Figure in options (a), (b) and (c) have shaded fraction equal to $\frac{1}{2}$.

25. (a) Options (b) and (c), (d) have line of symmetry.

26. (d) Options (a), (b) and (c) have same outer most and inner most element.

27. (b)

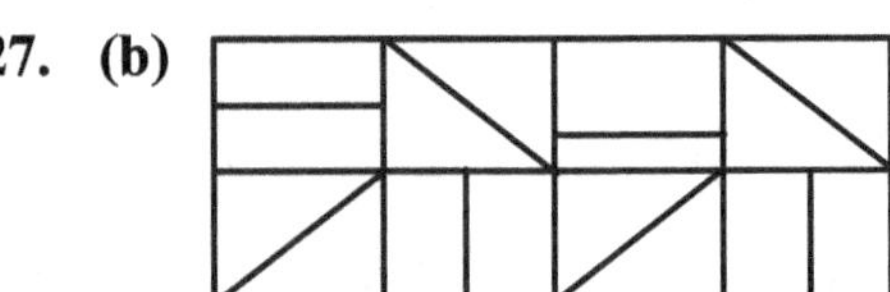

28. (a)

29. (a)

30. (c)

CHAPTER-12

LEVEL 1

1. (d)
2. (a)
3. (b)
4. (c)
5. (c)
6. (c)
7. (c)

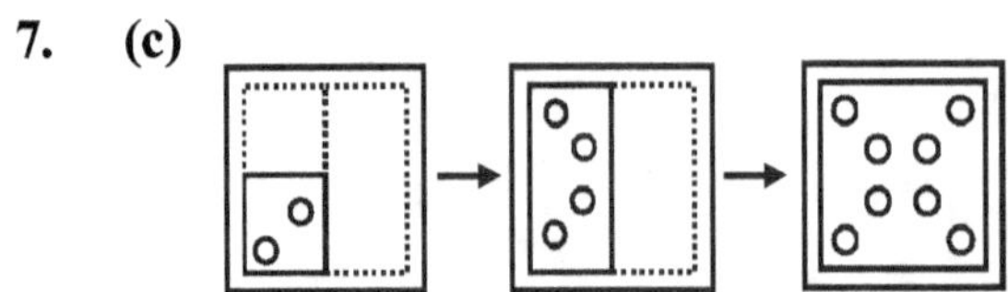

8. (c)
9. (c)
10. (b)
11. (b)

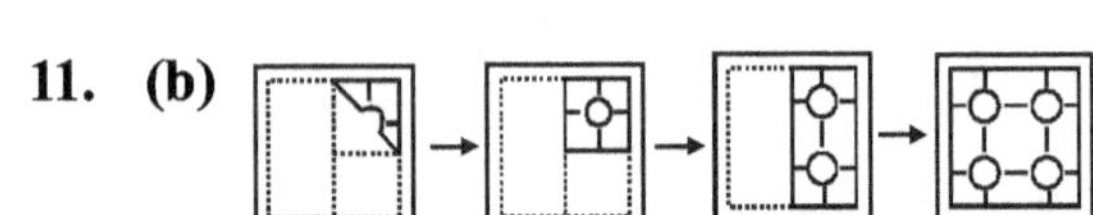

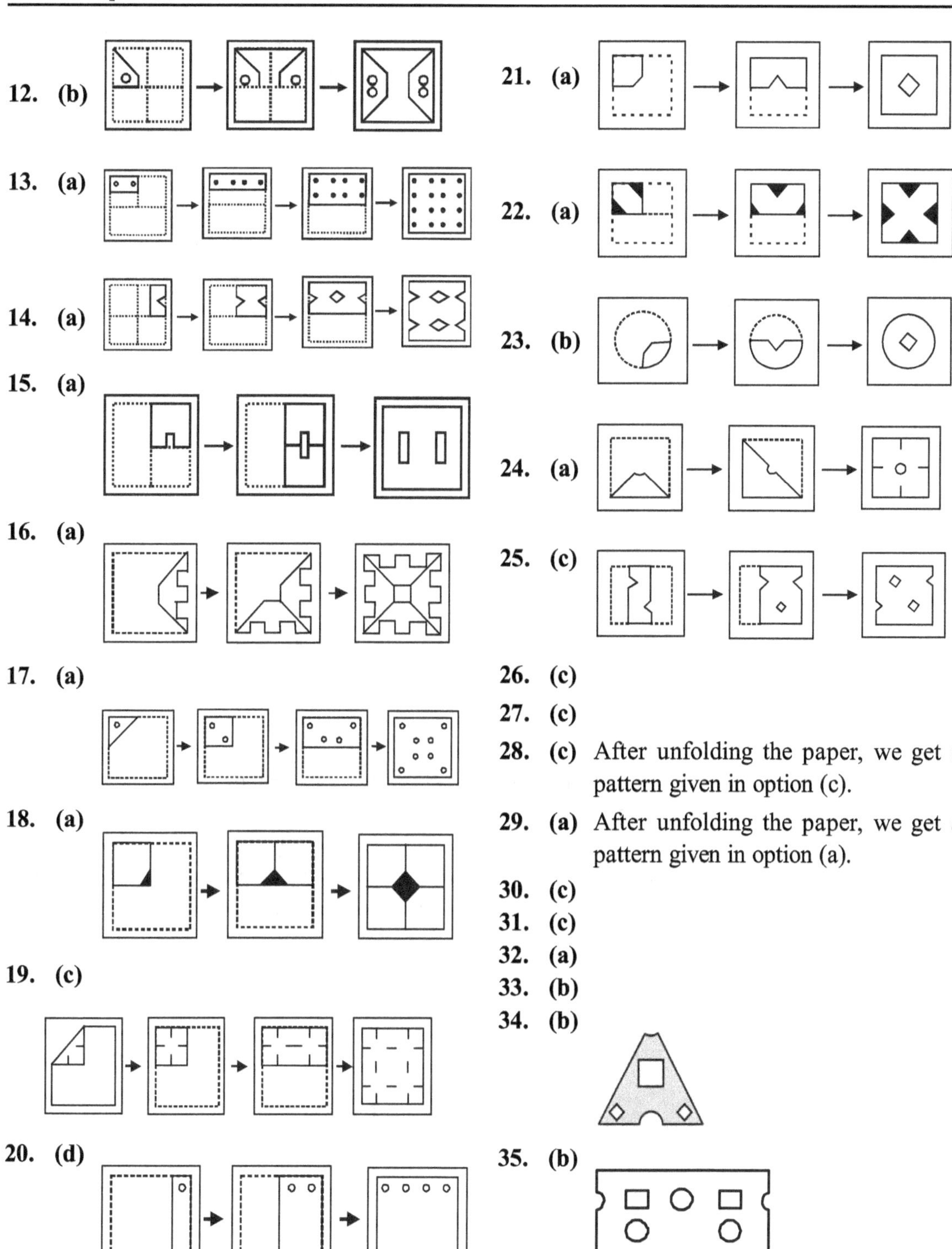

12. (b)

13. (a)

14. (a)

15. (a)

16. (a)

17. (a)

18. (a)

19. (c)

20. (d)

21. (a)

22. (a)

23. (b)

24. (a)

25. (c)

26. (c)

27. (c)

28. (c) After unfolding the paper, we get a pattern given in option (c).

29. (a) After unfolding the paper, we get a pattern given in option (a).

30. (c)

31. (c)

32. (a)

33. (b)

34. (b)

35. (b)

36. **(d)** 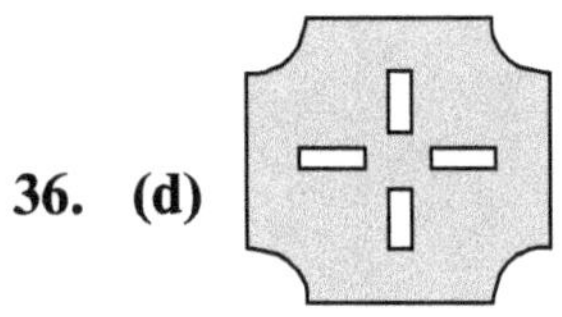

37. **(c)** 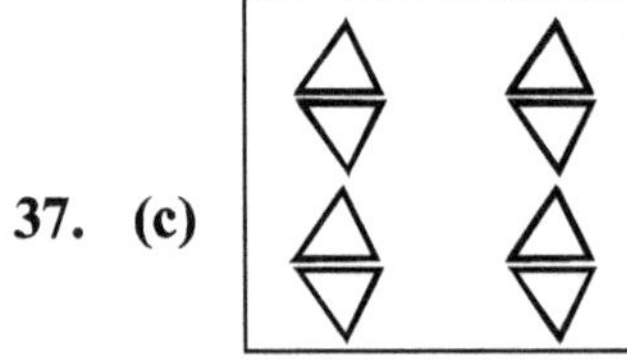

LEVEL 2

1. **(c)**
2. **(c)**
3. **(c)**
4. **(c)**
5. **(d)**
6. **(b)**
7. **(a)**
8. **(a)** Each element except in option (a) have exactly one line of symmetry.
9. **(d)** Elements in options (a), (b) and (c) are formed from 5 straight lines.
10. **(d)** (a), (b) and (c) are closed figures.
11. **(c)** Elements in options (a), (b) and (d) are made with straight line only.
12. **(b)** 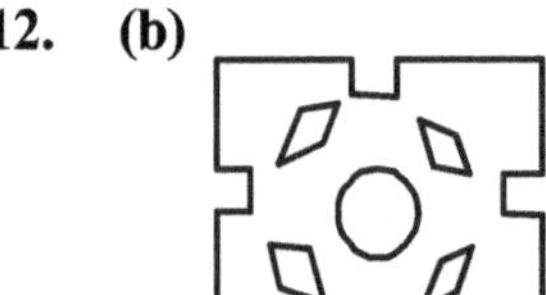
13. **(c)** 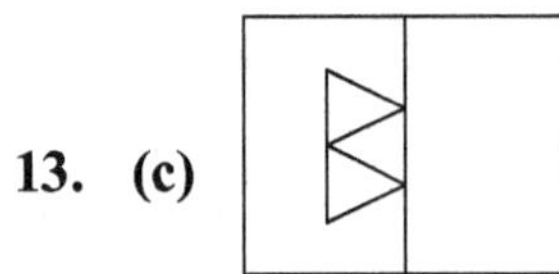
14. **(a)** 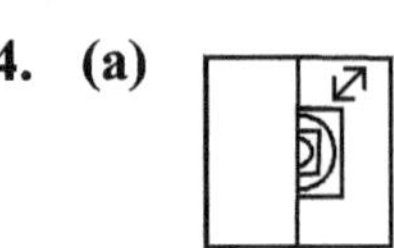
15. **(b)** 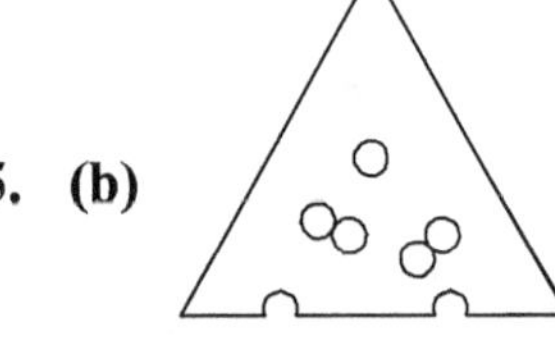

Option (b) shows the unfolded form of fig. (z)

CHAPTER-13

LEVEL 1

1. **(c)** 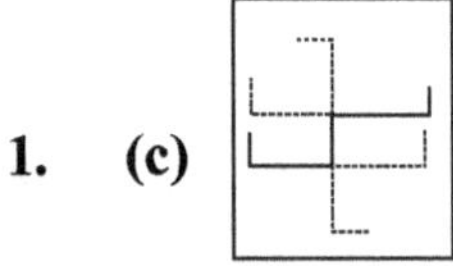
2. **(d)** 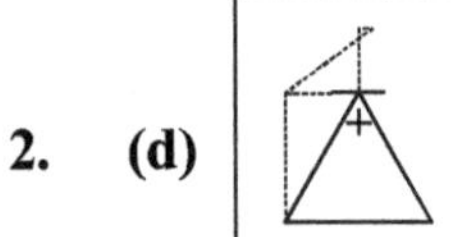
3. **(b)** 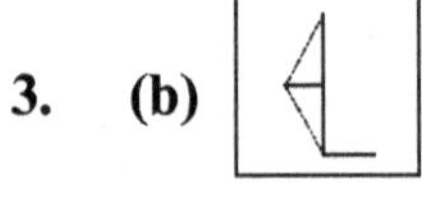
4. **(c)** 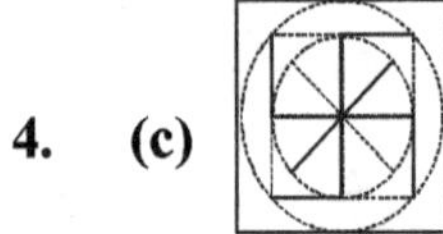
5. **(a)** 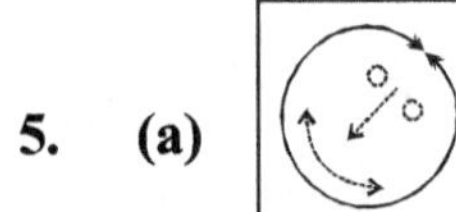

6. (d)

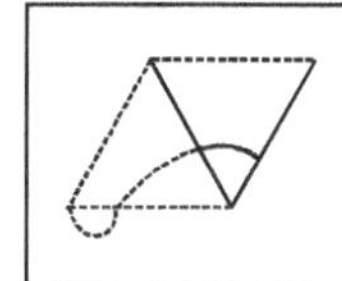

7. (d)

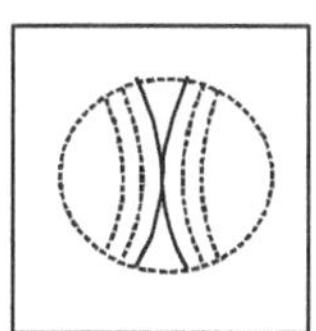

8. (c)

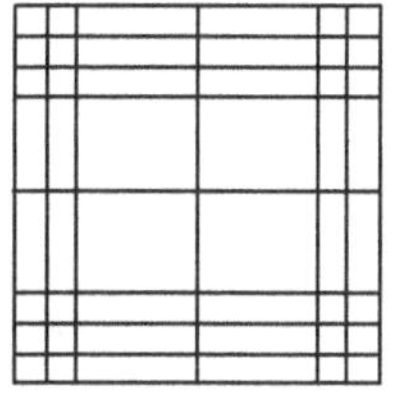

9. (b)

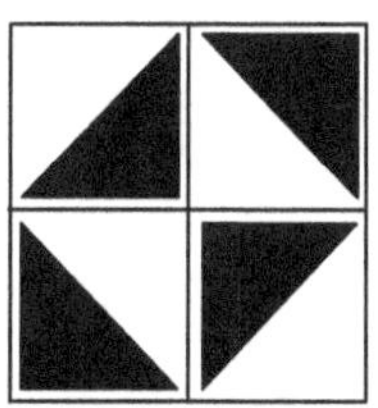

10. (a)

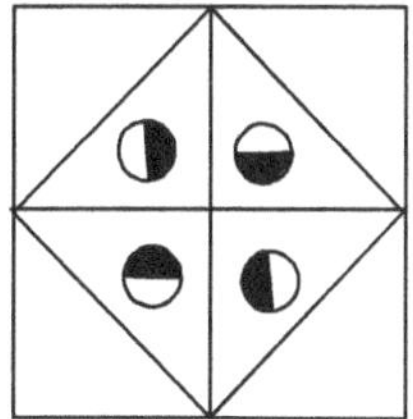

11. (c)

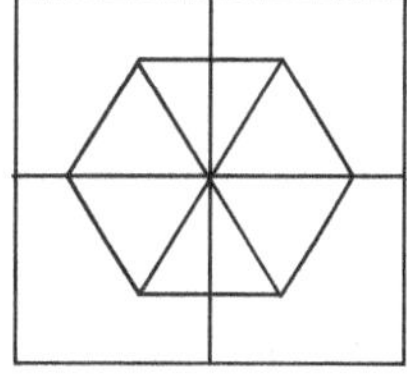

12. (c)

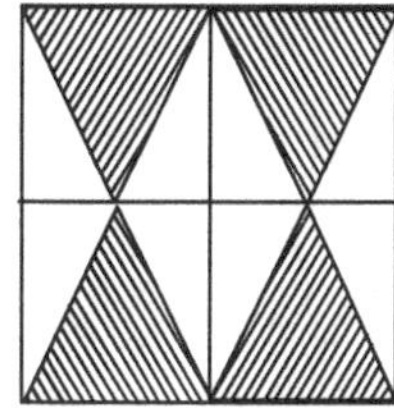

13. (c)

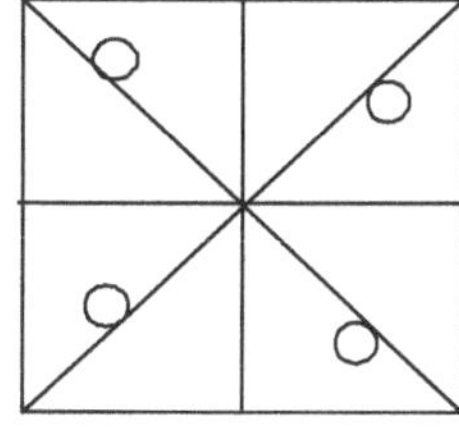

14. (a)

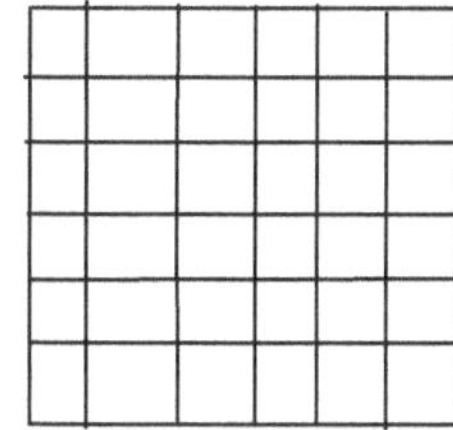

15. (b)

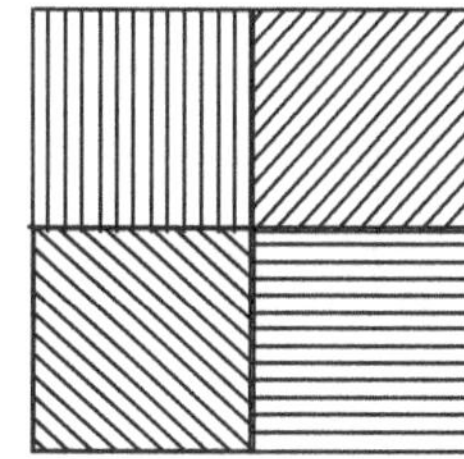

16. (b)

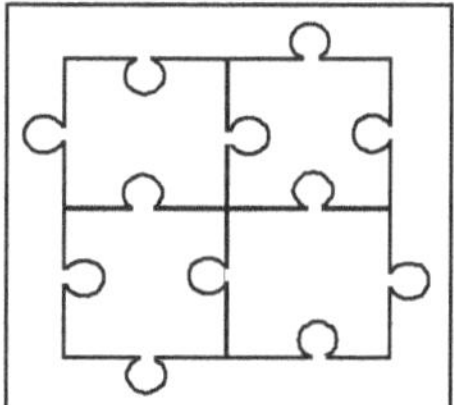

17. (a)

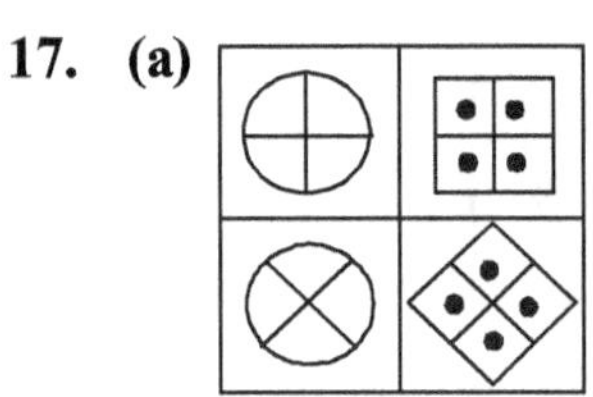

18. (d)

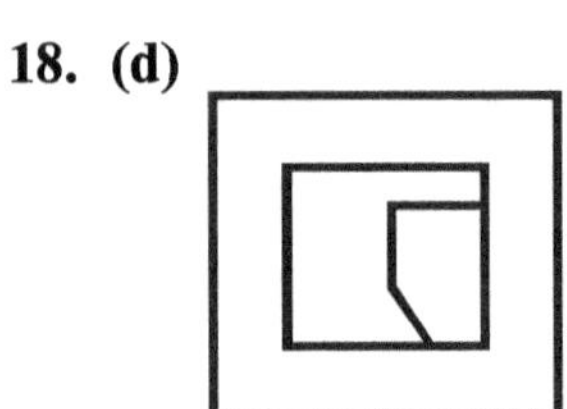

19. (b)

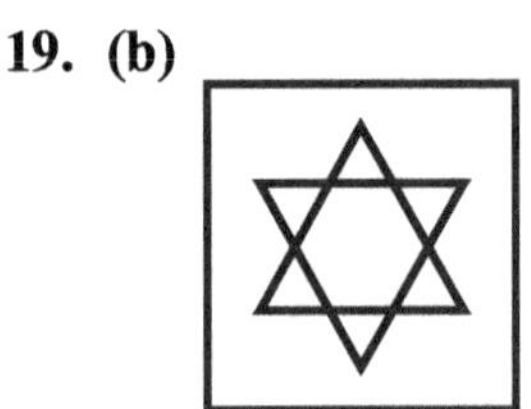

20. (c)

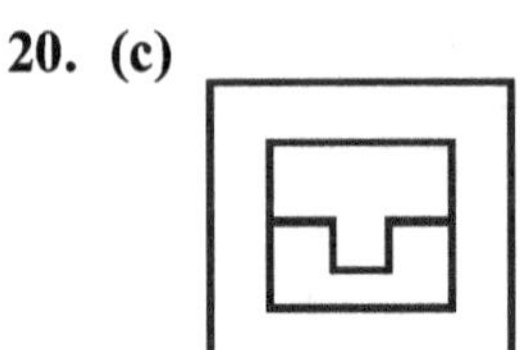

21. (a)

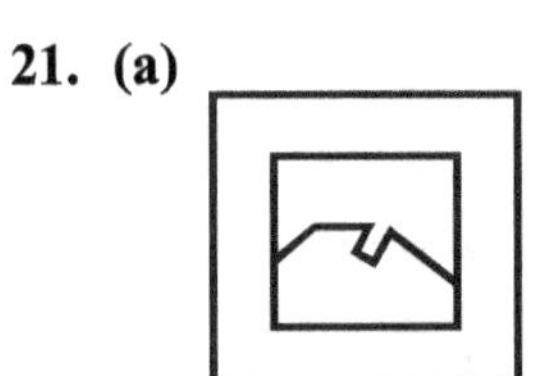

22. (a)

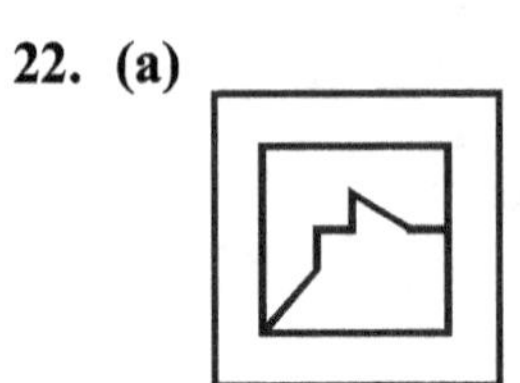

23. (d)

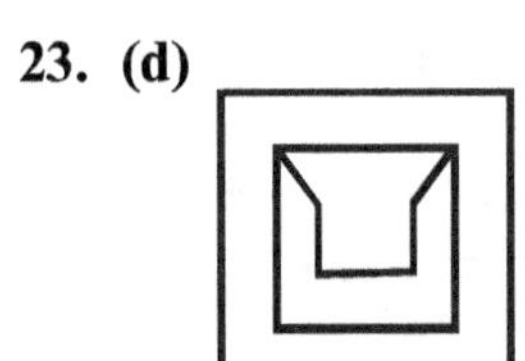

24. (c)

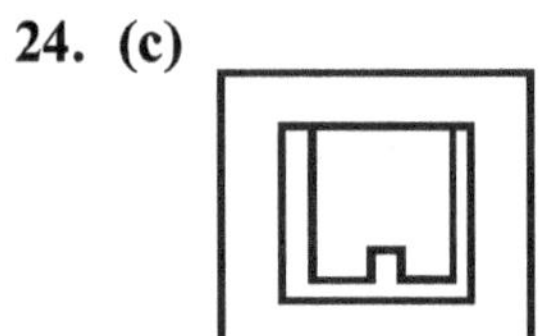

25. (a)

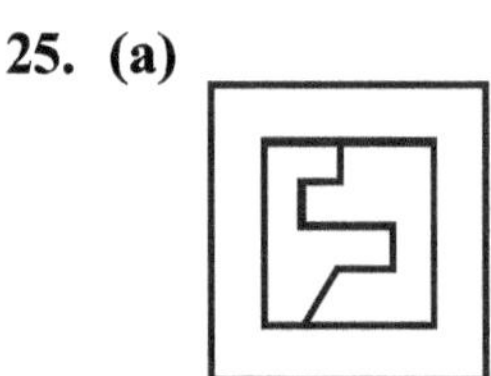

26. (a)

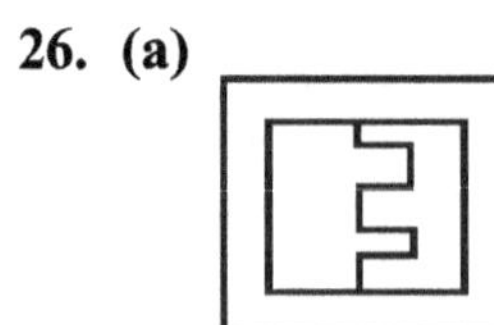

27. (a)

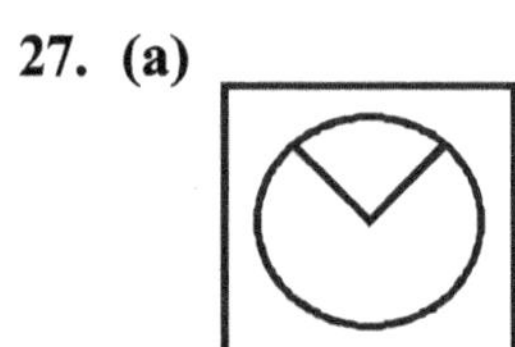

28. (c)

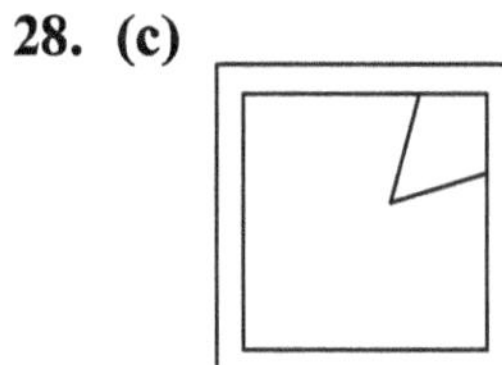

29. (b)

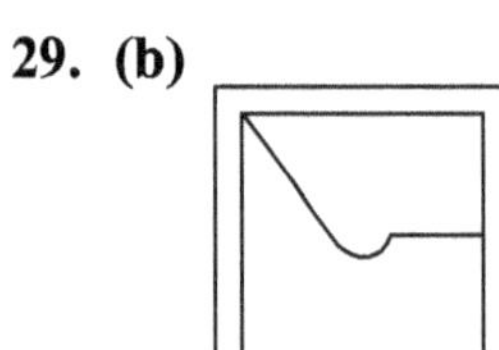

30. (a)

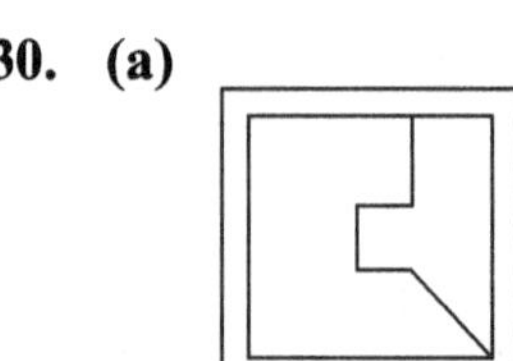

31. (a) The question is incorrect since it does not form a complete square.

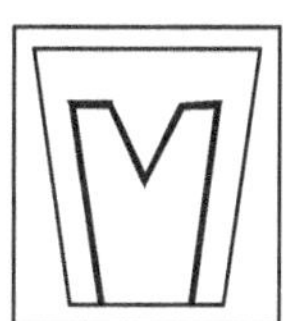

32. **(a)**

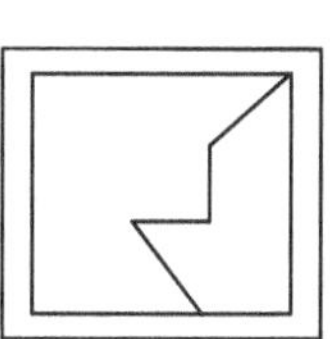

33. **(d)**

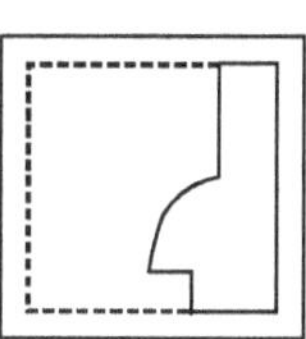

34. **(d)**

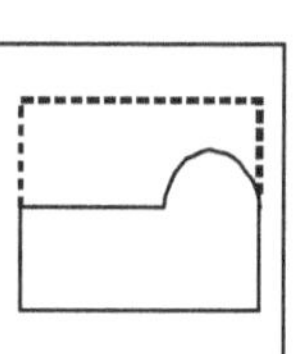

35. **(b)**

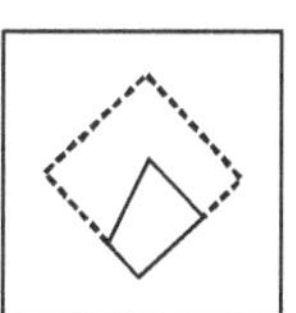

36. **(a)**

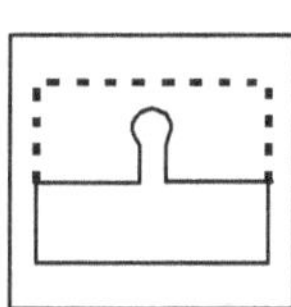

37. **(b)**

38. **(a)**

39. **(b)**

40. **(a)**

41. **(c)**

42. **(b)** Option (b) completes the geometrical figure.

43. **(c)** Option (c) completes the geometrical figure as

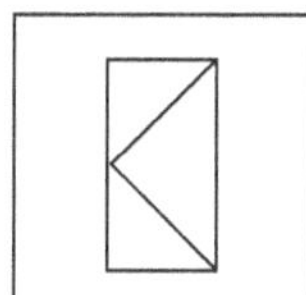

44. **(d)**

45. **(c)**

46. **(b)**

47. **(b)**

48. **(c)**

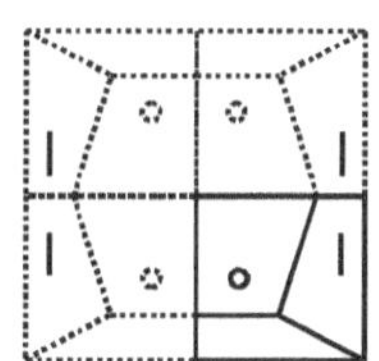

49. **(a)**

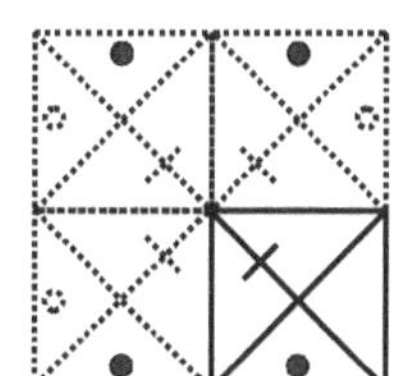

50. **(b)**

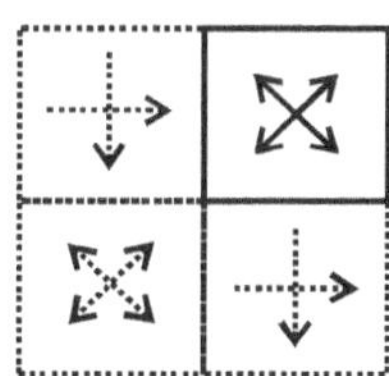

51. **(a)**

52. (b)

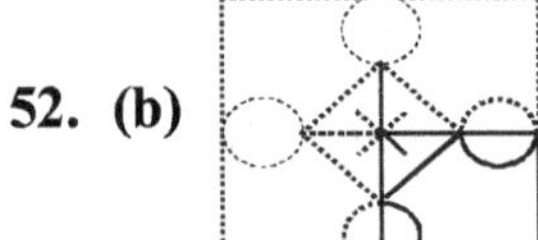

53. (a)

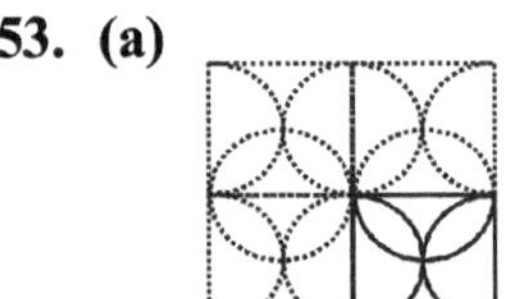

54. (b)

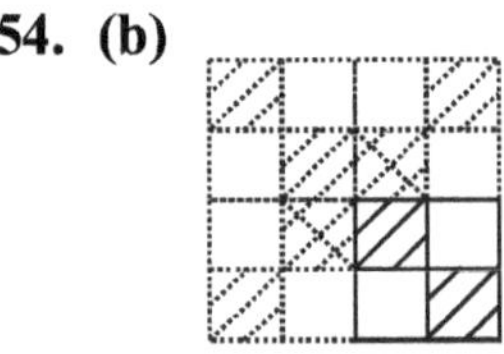

55. (a)

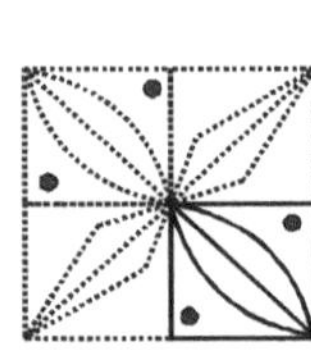

56. (c)

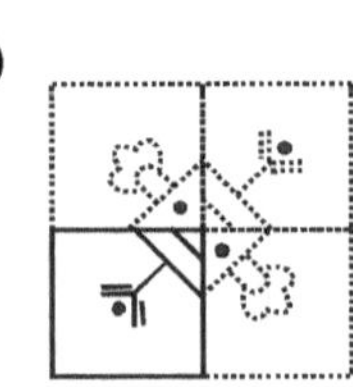

57. (c)

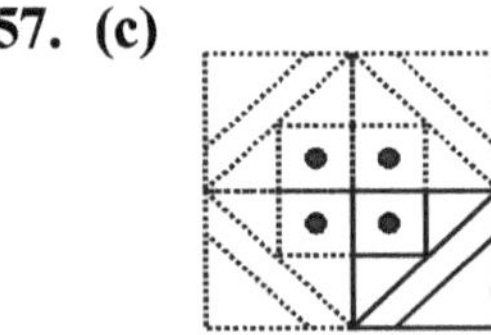

58. (a)

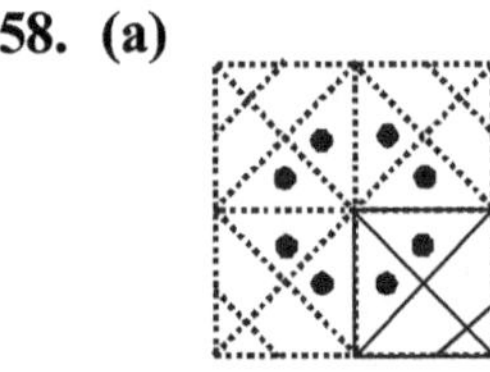

59. (d)

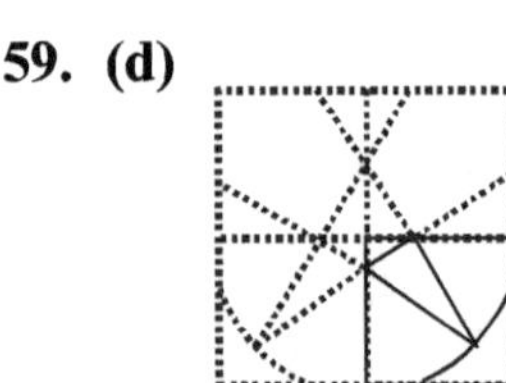

60. (b)

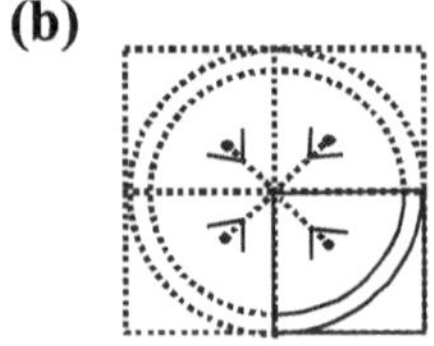

61. (c)

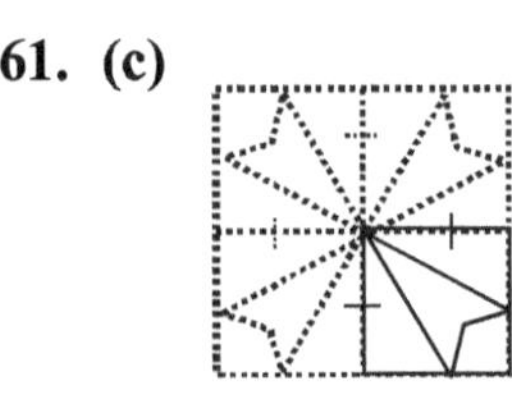

62. (b)

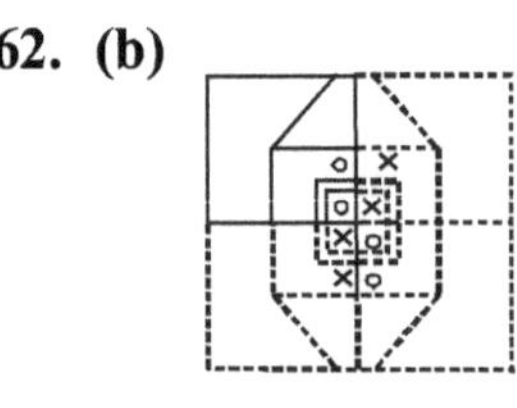

63. (c)

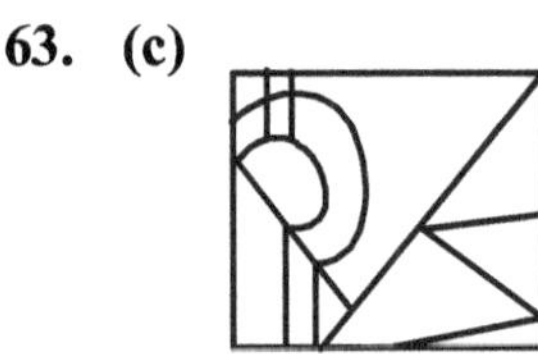

64. (b)

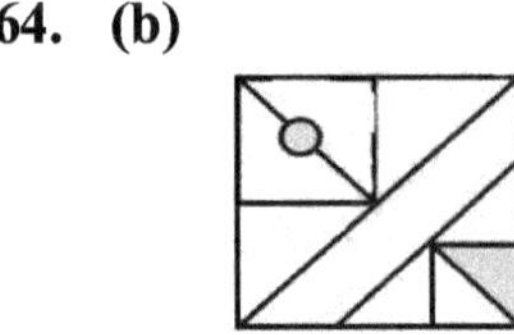

65. (a)

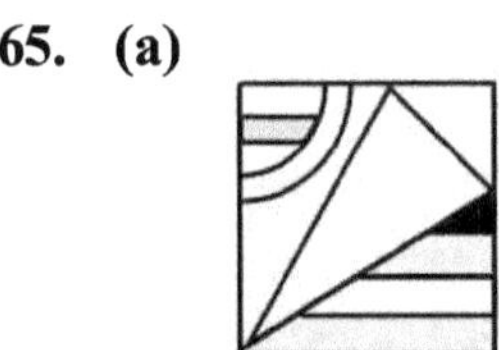

Option (a) will comptele the figure.

66. (a)

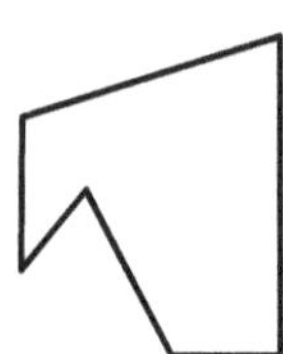

67. (c)

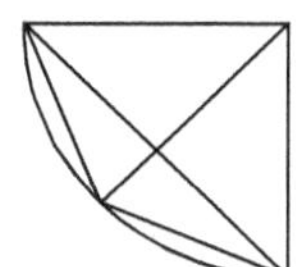

68. (d)

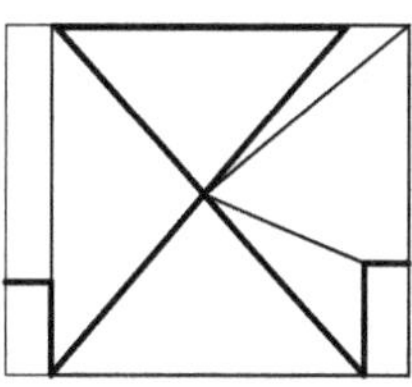

69. (d)

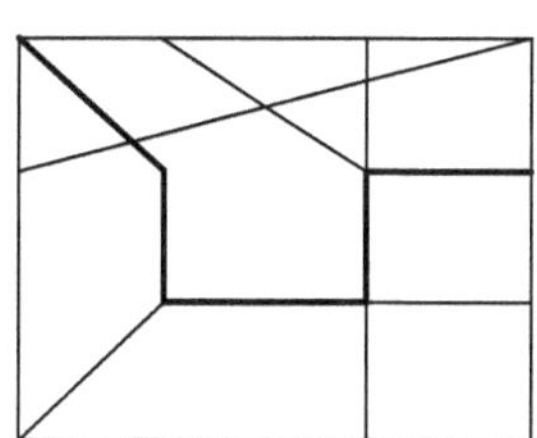

LEVEL 2

1. (d)

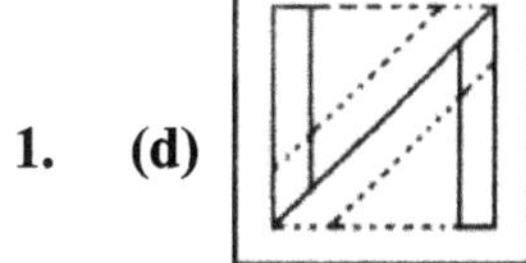

2. (a)

3. (d)

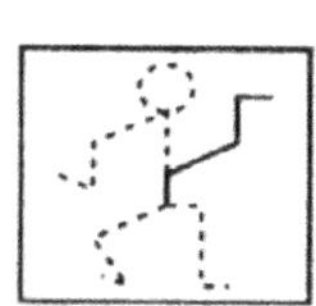

4. (c)

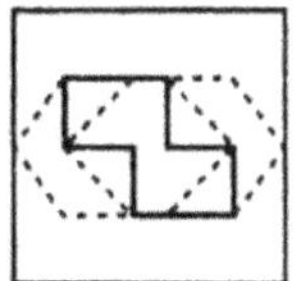

5. (d)

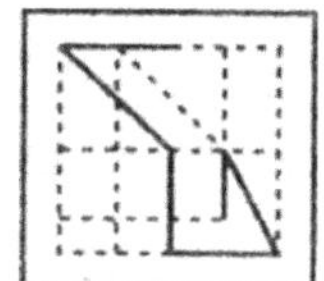

6. (b)

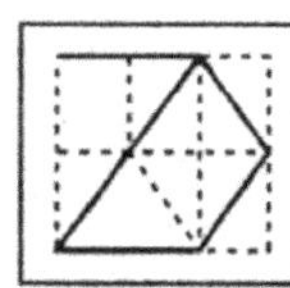

7. (b)

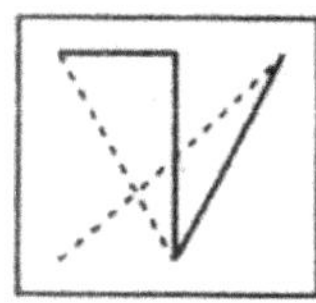

8. (a)

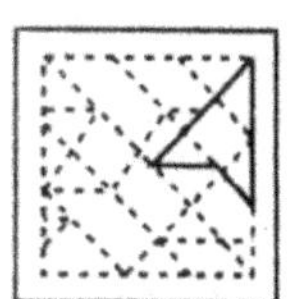

9. (c)

10. (a)

11. (b)

12. (b)

13. (b)

14. (b)

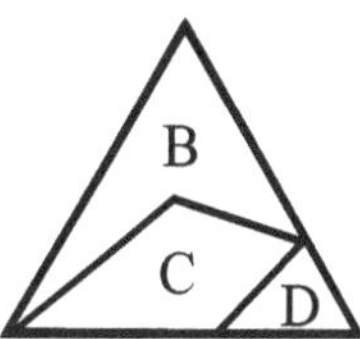

15. (d)

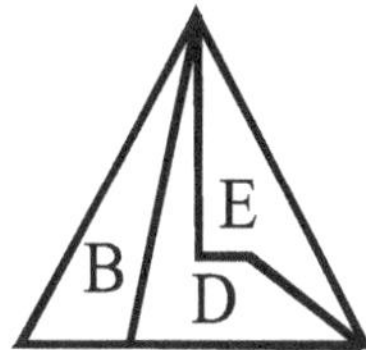

16. (c)

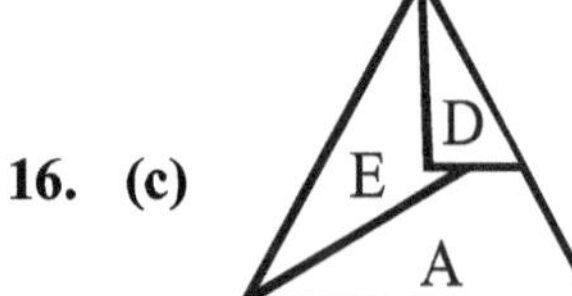

17. (a)

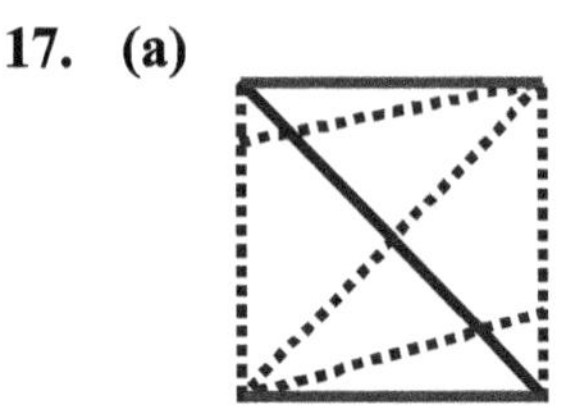

18. (b)

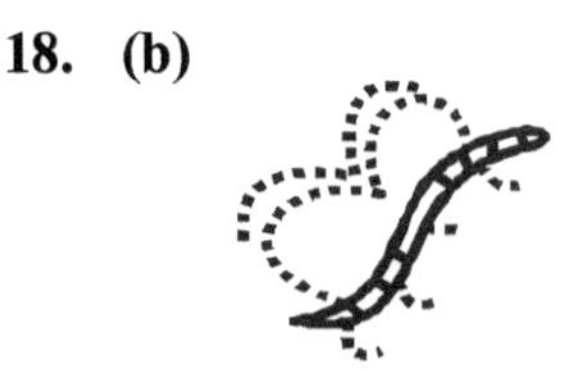

19. (b)

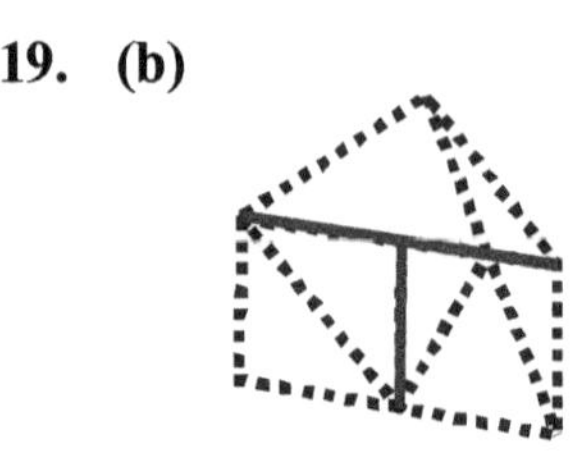

20. (a)

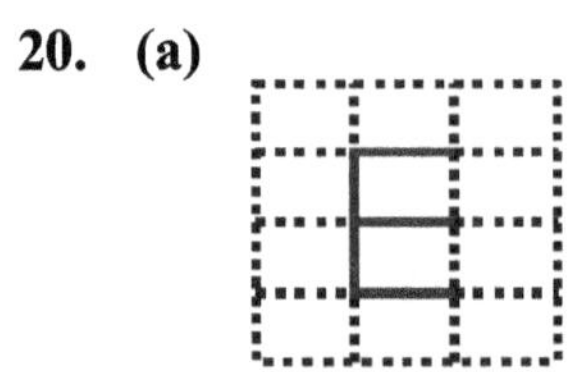

21. (d)

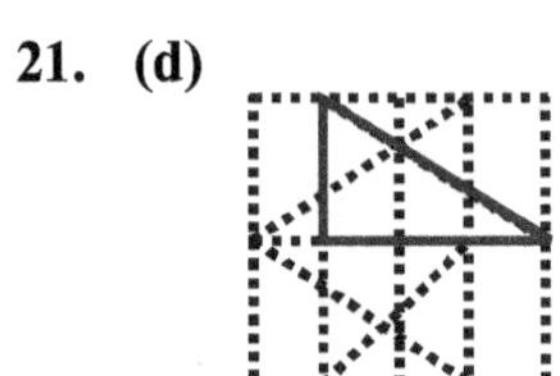

22. (a)

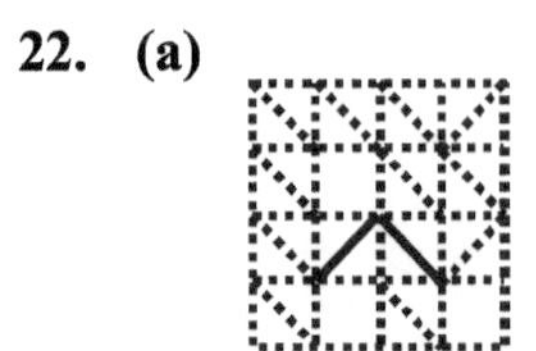

23. (c)

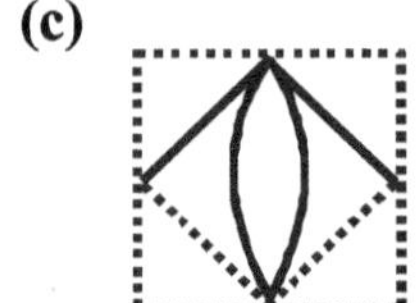

24. (d)

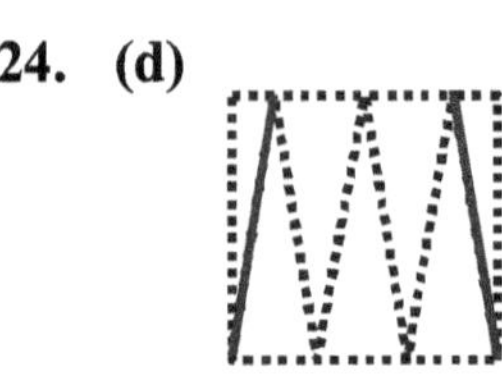

25. (a)

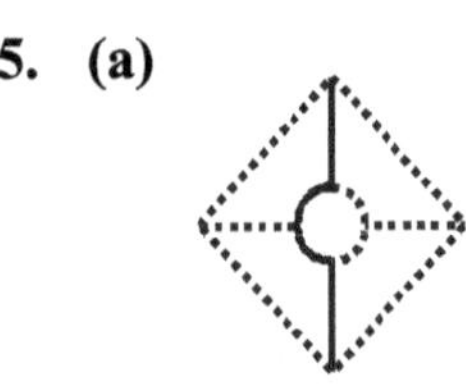

26. (b)

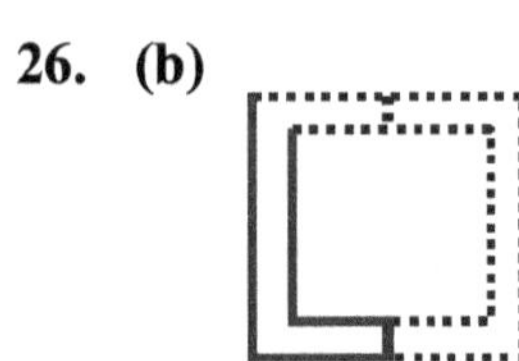

27. (b)

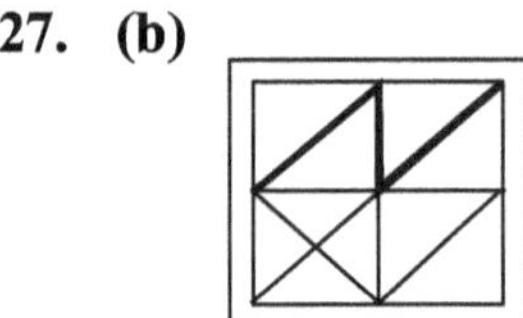

28. (c)

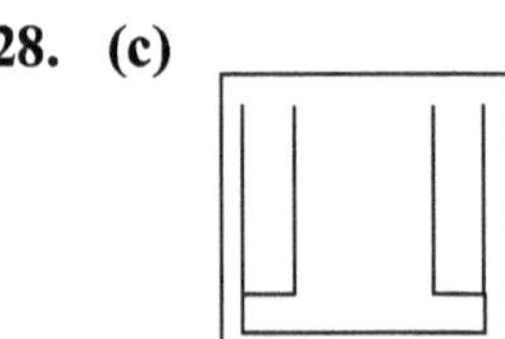

29. (b)

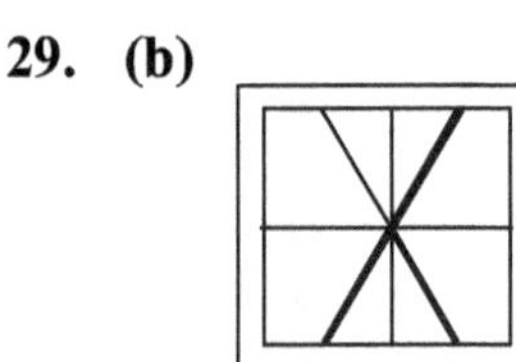

30. (c)

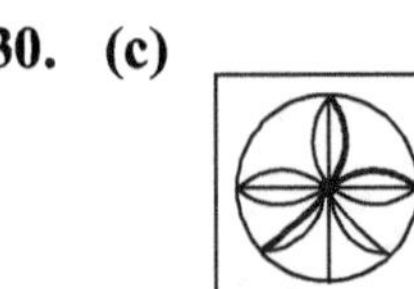

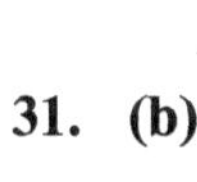

31. (b) 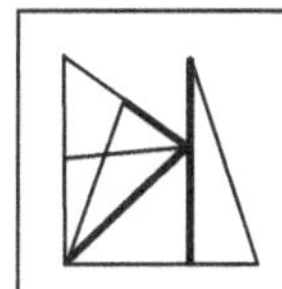

32. (d) 

33. (d) 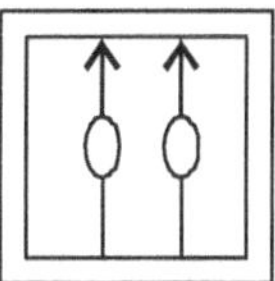

34. (c) 

35. (b) 

36. (b) 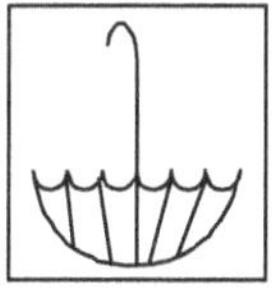

37. (c) Question figure is hidden in answer figure (c).

38. (b) Question figure is hidden in answer figure (b).

39. (b) Question figure is hidden in answer figure (b).

40. (d) Question figure is hidden in answer figure (d).

41. (b) 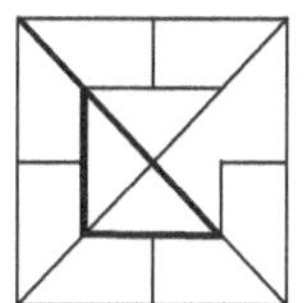

In the above figure represented by dark line is hidden in the question figure.

42. (a) 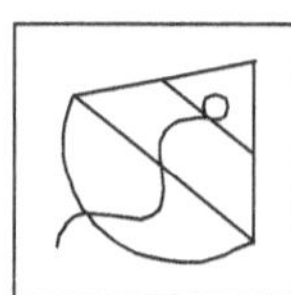

In the above figure represented by dark line is hidden in the question figure.

43. (b) 

44. (a) 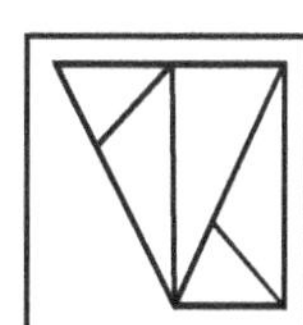

45. (a) 

46. (a) 

47. (d) all except (d) dots are on either side of the line.

48. (c) Except (c) rest elements of figures are diagonally opposite direction.

49. (a) all other figure can be rotated into each other. The middle element is obtained by rotating the outer element through 90 degree clock wise and the inner element is obtained by rotating the middle element through 90 degree clock wise.

50. (a) only in figure (a) two of the four elements are oriented in the same direction.

51. (a) Elements in option (b), (c) and (d) have diagonals.

52. (d) Letters in options (a), (b) and (c) are vowels.

53. (d) Except option (d), all the figures can be obtained by rotating each other.

54. (d) In option (d), the two elements drawn inside the circle are different from other figures.

55. (b)

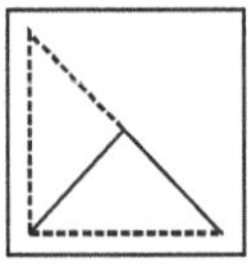

56. (d)

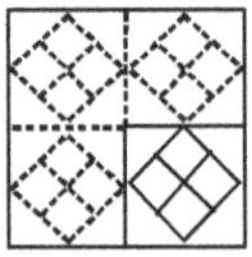

57. (a)

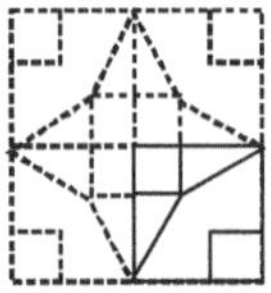

58. (d)

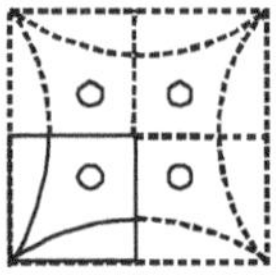

59. (c)

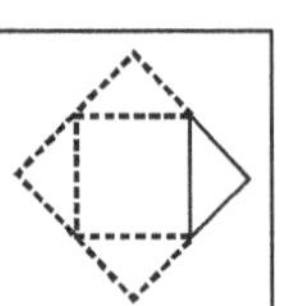

60. (a) Figure given in option (a) will complete the question figure.

61. (d) Figure (d) is based on the pattern and will complete the question figure.

62. (c)

63. (d)

64. (a) 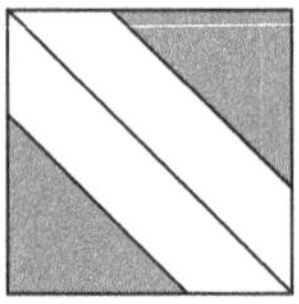 option (a) is the missing part.

65. (b)

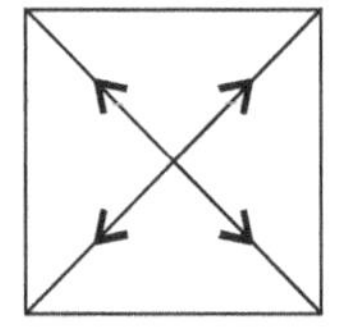

option (b) is the missing part.

66. (b)

67. (b)

68. (c)

69. (d)

70. (d)

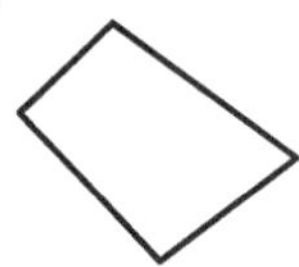

71. (b)

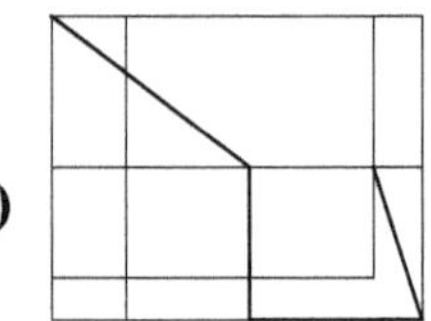

CHAPTER-14

LEVEL 1

1. **(a)** In each row, the central part of the first figure rotates either 90o CW or 90o ACW to form the central part of the second figure and the central part of the first figure rotates through 180 degrees to form the central part of the third figure. Also, in each row, there are 3 types of side elements - rectangles, circles, and triangles.
2. **(d)** One line is increasing in each subsequent figure.
3. **(c)** There are 3 types of shadings in the triangles, 3 types of legs, 3 positions of circles, each of which is used only once in a single row. The circle is shaded in alternate figures.
4. **(d)** In each row, the third figure is a combination of the first and second figures.
5. **(b)** There are types of arrows - a single-headed arrow, a double-headed arrow, and a triple-headed arrow. There are three positions of arrows-Upwards, downwards, and towards the right. The arrows have 3 types of base-plane, rectangular and circular. Each of these features is used once in each row.
6. **(a)** The contents of the third figure in each row (and column) are determined by the contents of the first two figures. Lines are carried forward from the first two figures to the third one, except where two lines appear in the same position, in which they are cancelled out.
7. **(a)** In each row (and column), the superimposition of all the three figures results in a darkened circle.
8. **(d)** The third figure in each row comprises parts that are not common to the first two figures.
9. **(c)** The third figure in each row comprises of parts which are not common to the first two figures.
10. **(a)** In each row, the third figure comprises of a black circle and only those line segments which are not common to the first and the second figures.
11. **(a)**

LEVEL 2

1. **(c)** In each column, the second figure (middle figure) is obtained by removing the upper part of the first figure (uppermost figure) and the third figure (lowermost figure) is obtained by vertically inverting the upper part of the first figure.
2. **(b)** There are 3 types of faces, 3 types of bodies, 3 types of hands and 3 types of legs, each of which is used only once in a single row. So, the features which have not been used in the first two figures of the third row would combine to produce the missing figure.
3. **(b)** In each row, the figures are getting laterally inverted in each step. The number of components or the quantities are either increasing or decreasing from left to right sequentially.

4. **(a)** The number of components in each row either increases or decreases from left to right . In the third row, it increases.

5. **(a)** In each row, the second figure is obtained from the first figure by adding two mutually perpendicular line segments at the centre and the third figure is obtained from the first figure by adding four circles outside the main figure.

6. **(d)**

7. **(d)**

8. **(d)**

9. **(c)**

10. **(c)**

11. **(c)**

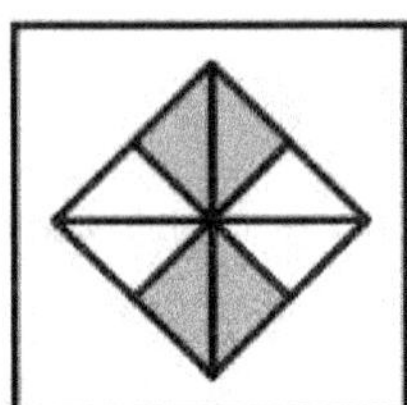

Column 1 and Column 2 is added to get column 3.

12. **(b)** Group (1, 3, 8) has different Small figures in the big figures.

Group (2, 4, 6) has two figures inter connected.

Group (5, 7, 9) has the figures divided in four equal parts.

13. **(c)** Rotate the figure 135° anticlockwise.

Option (c) will complete the figure.

14. **(d)** Group (1, 5, 9) has one big and one small same figures.

Group (2, 6, 7) has different small figure inside the big figure.

Group (3, 4, 8) has five sides figure.

Option (d) is the correct Answer.

15. **(c)**

A (1)	C (3)	D (4)
F (6)	I (9)	O (15)
H (8)	Q (17)	Y (25)

Addition of place value of alphabets in alphabetical series of first two column results in 3rd column.

i.e., $1 + 3 \rightarrow 4$

$8 + 17 \rightarrow 17$

Similarly

$6 + \square \rightarrow 15$

$\square \rightarrow 15 - 6$

$\square \rightarrow$ a i.e. I

16. **(d)** Property used in grouping is number of figures which are shaded and manner in which shaded,

So, 1, 5, 9 (3 figure are shaded continuously)

2, 4, 6, (2 figures are shaded, which are opposite to each other)

3, 7, 8 (1 figure is shaded)

CHAPTER-15

LEVEL 1

1. **(c)** Clearly, in the figure there are --1 column containing

   3 cubes, 2 columns containing 2 cubes each and 3 columns containing 1 cube each.

   Number of cubes in columns of 3 cubes $= 1 \times 3 = 3;$

   Number of cubes in columns of 2 cubes $= 2 \times 2 = 4;$

   Number of cubes in columns of 1 cubes $= 3 \times 1 = 3;$

   Therefore, total number of cubes $= 3 + 4 + 3 = 10.$

2. **(a)** When the sheet shown in fig. (X) is folded to from a cube, then the face bearing the dot lies opposite to the shaded face, the face bearing a circle (With '+' sign inside it) lies opposite to a blank face and the remaining two blank faces lie opposite to each other. Clearly, the cubes shown in figures (B) and (D) cannot be formed since they have the shaded face adjacent to the face bearing a dot and the cube shown in fig. (C) cannot be formed since it shown all the three blank face adjacent to each other. Hence, only the cube shown in fig.(A) can be formed.

3. **(b)** When the sheet in fig. (X) is folded to form a cube , then 'F' appears opposite 'C' and 'A' appears opposite 'D'. Therefore, the cube in fig. (A) which shows 'F' adjacent to 'B', the cube in fig.(C) which shows 'E' adjacent to 'C' and the cube in fig. (D) which shows 'A' adjacent to 'D' cannot be formed.

4. **(c)** From figure (i) (ii) and (iv), we conclude that 6, 4, 1 and 2 dots appear adjacent to 3 dots. Clearly, there will be 5 dots on the face opposite the face with 3 dots.

5. **(c)** When this figure is folded to form a cube then the face bearing three dots will lie opposite the face bearing five dots.

6. **(d)** From figures (i) and (iv) we conclude that 6, 5, 2 and 3 lie adjacent to 4. It follows that 1 lies opposite 4.

7. **(b)** From the three given figures, it is clear that the 1,2,5 and 4 appear adjacent to 3, so none of these can appear opposite 3. Therefore, 6 appears opposite 3.

8. **(d)**

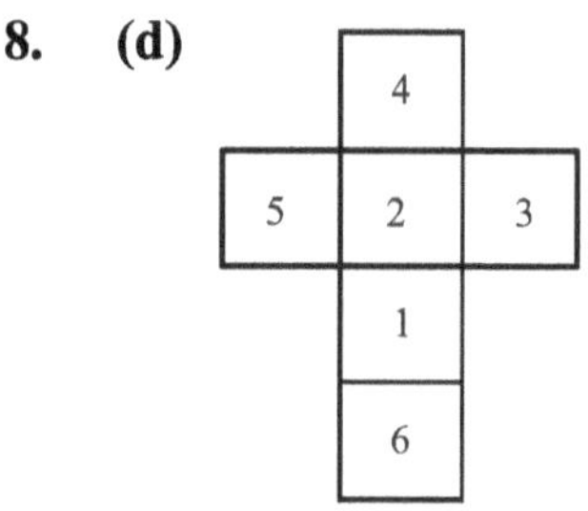

   Hence, the numbers that are adjacent to 1 are 5, 2, 6 and 3.

9. **(d)** The opposite pairs are – (2, 4), (1, 6) and (3, 5)

   Therefore, option (d) is correct choice.

10. **(b)** The opposite pairs are – (F, B), (A, D) and (E, C). Hence option (b) is the correct choice.

11. **(b)**

Number opposite to 3 is 4.

12. **(b)** 1 is wrong as 2 dots can't be opposite 5 dots; 3 is wrong as 3 dots can't be opposite 4 dots; 4 is wrong as 6 can't be opposite 1 dot.

13. **(d)** Opposite pair are (2, 4), (1, 6) and (3, 5)

i.e. from option only (4) is in correct shape.

14. **(b)** Opposite pair are (B, F), (C, E) and (A, D)

i.e. from option only (2) is in correct shape.

15. **(c)**

16. **(c)**

17. **(c)**

	–	
$	*	@
	+	
	8	

18. **(c)** Option (c) is correct answer.

19. **(b)** 14 cubes are required to make the given figure.

LEVEL 2

1. **(d)** The number 3 occurs most often in the given three figures. From these three figures it is clear that 1, 2, 5 and 4 lie adjacent to 3. Clearly, 6 lies opposite the face showing 3.

2. **(d)** The cube formed will be

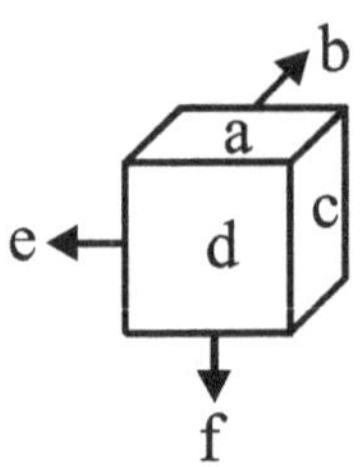

(a) is wrong as with c on top f and a are opposite to each other.

(b) is wrong as with a on top c and e

(c) is wrong as with b is opposite to d

(d) is correct

3. **(a)** Number '4' is common in first and second dice.

write from '4' clockwise.

4	2	6
4	5	3

Number '3' will be at the bottom.

4. **(c)** 16

5. **(c)** In the given figure '★' is at the right side.

In option (d), '★' will come at the left side.

In option (c), '★' will come at the right side.

So, option (c) is the correct answer.

6. **(d)**

	A	
E	B	F
	C	
	D	

7. **(c)** Sign (÷) is common in both the dice
Write from (÷) Clockwise:-

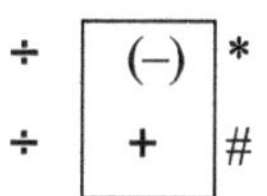

Sign (–) will be in the bottom

8. **(a)** In the figure:- D is below C and A at the left side and E at the Right side.
In option (a)- C is below D, So, A at the right side
Option (a) is the correct answer

CHAPTER-16

LEVEL 1

1. **(b)** In figure (X), one of the dots lies in the region common to the circle and the triangle only and the other dot lies in the region common to the circle and the square only. In figures (a), (c) and (d), the region common to the circle and the triangle lies within the square. Only figure (b) contains a region common to the circle and the triangle only and also a region common to the circle and the square.
2. **(c)** In figure (X) the dot lies in the region common to the circle and the triangle only.
Such a region is present in fig. (c).
3. **(a)** One point lies in all three figures. Two points lie in between two figures.
4. **(c)** In fig. (X), the dot is placed in the region common to the circle and the triangle. Amongst the four alternatives only in figure (c), we have a region common to circle and triangle only. Hence figure, (c) is the answer.

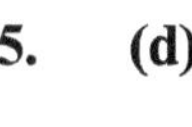

5. **(d)**

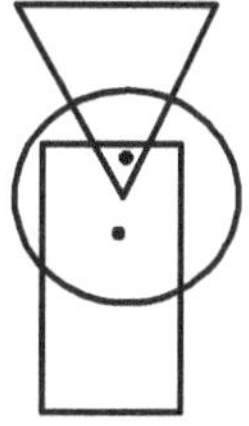

6. **(b)**

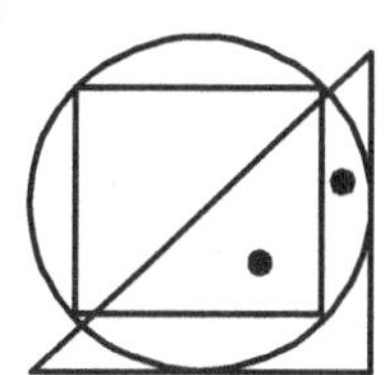

7. **(b)**

8. **(b)**

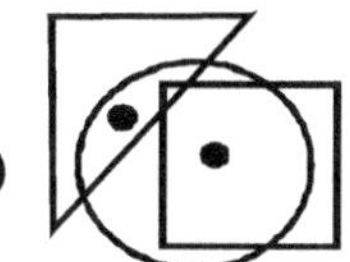

LEVEL 2

1. **(d)** In fig. (X), one of the dots lies in the region common to the square and the triangle only and the other dot lies in the region common to all the three figures—the circle, the square and the triangle. In each of the alternatives (a) and (b), there is no region common to the square and the triangle only. In alternative (c), there is no region common to all the three figures. Only, alternative (d) consists of both the types of regions.

2. **(a)** In fig. (X), one of the dots lies in the region common to the square and the triangle only, another dot lies in the region common to the circle and the triangle only and the third dot lies in the region common to the triangle and the rectangle only. In fig. (b), there is no region common to the square and the triangle only. In fig. (c), there is no region common to the circle and the triangle only. In fig. (d) there is no region common to the triangle and the rectangle only. Only fig. (a) consists of all the three types of regions.

3. **(b)** In fig. (X), one of the dots lies in the region common to the circle and the triangle only and the other dot lies in the region common to the circle and the square only. In each of the figures (a), (c) and (d), there is no region common to the circle and the triangle only. Only fig. (b) consists of both the types of regions.

4. **(d)** In fig. (X), one of the dots lies in the region common to the circle and the triangle only, another dot lies in the region common to all the three figures– the circle, the square and the triangle and the third dot lies in the region common to the circle and the square only. In each of the figures (a) and (c), there is no region common to the circle and the square only and in fig. (b), there is no region common to the circle and the triangle only. Only fig. (d) consists of all the three types of regions.

5. **(d)** In fig. (X), one of the dots lies in the region common to the circle and the rectangle only, another dot lies in the region common to the circle, the square and the rectangle only and the third dot lies in the region common to the circle, the square and the triangle only. In each of the figures (a) and (c) there is no region common to the circle, the square and the rectangle only and in fig. (b), there is no region common to the circle, the square and the triangle only. Only fig. (d) consists of all the three types of regions.

6. **(b)** In fig. (X), one of the dots lies in the region common to the circle and the triangle only, another dot lies in the region common to the circle, the square and the triangle only and the third dot lies in the region common to the circle, the square and the rectangle only. In each of the figures (a) and (c) there is no region common to the circle and the triangle only. In fig. (d) there is no region common to the circle, the square and the rectangle only. Only fig. (b) consists of all the three types of regions.

7. **(c)**

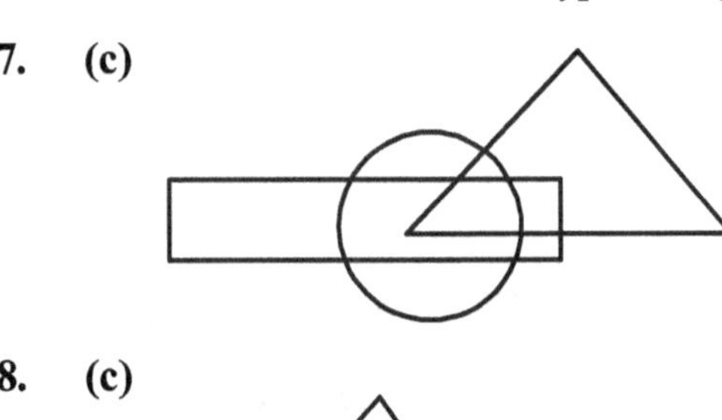

8. **(c)**

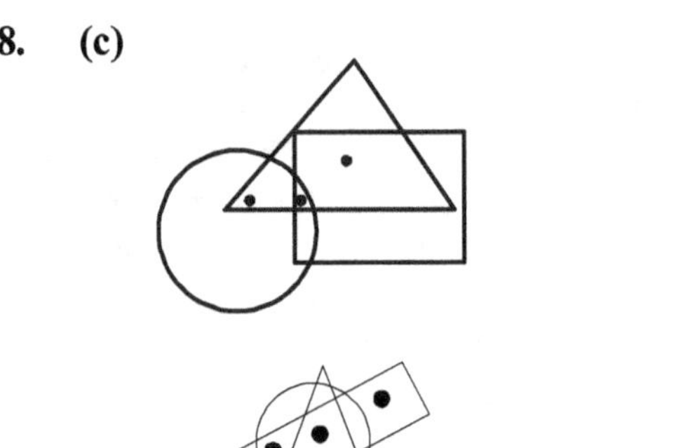

9. **(b)**

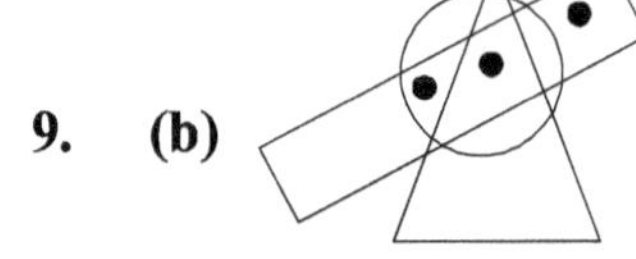

www.ingramcontent.com/pod-product-compliance
Lightning Source LLC
LaVergne TN
LVHW080104160726
843469LV00047B/1896